The Nationalities Question in the Post-Soviet States

# The Nationalities Question in the Post-Soviet States

edited by
GRAHAM SMITH

LONGMAN
London and New York

Longman Group Limited,

Longman House, Burnt Mill, Harlow,
Essex CM20 2JE, England
*and Associated Companies throughout the world.*

*Published in the United States of America
by Longman Publishing, New York*

First edition © Longman Group UK Limited 1990
This edition © Longman Group Limited 1996

*First published 1990*
*2nd Edition published 1996*

ISBN 0 582 21808X CSD
ISBN 0 582 218098 PPR

**British Library Cataloguing-in-Publication Data**

A catalogue record for this book is
available from the British Library.

**Library of Congress Cataloguing-in-Publication Data**

A catalog record for this book is
available from the Library of Congress.

Set by 5 in 11/12pt Garamond
Produced by Longman Singapore Publishers (Pte) Ltd.
Printed in Singapore

In memory of Andrus and Vito

# Contents

CONTENTS

# PART IV: THE SOUTH-WESTERN BORDERLANDS

# PART V: TRANSCAUCASIA

# PART VI: MUSLIM CENTRAL ASIA

# PART VII: THE DIASPORA NATIONALITIES

# Preface

This book is not so much a second edition of *The Nationalities Question in the Soviet Union* as a new volume on nationality and ethnic relations in the post-Soviet states: it could hardly be otherwise. Who, after all, would have imagined in 1989, when the typescript of the first edition of *The Nationalities Question* was completed, that its very topic of enquiry would have contributed within such a short space of time not only to the end of the twentieth century's last multiethnic empire but also to reshaping the geopolitical map of the former Soviet Union? What the first edition did, however, was to help bring to the fore a hitherto neglected theme in Soviet Studies: the nationalities question. In the process, it signalled not only that nationalism was far from the spent force it had long been regarded as by Moscow, but also the immeasurable difficulties that Gorbachev's reform programme was facing and would continue to face in managing stability in the ethno-republics. As the conclusion to chapter one put it, 'History may prove Lenin right in viewing the Soviet federation as a transitional form but not in the way he envisaged'.

As the face of Northern Eurasia has been redrawn, we need, perhaps more crucially than ever, to get inside the identities of the peoples that now form the core nations of the post-Soviet states as well as the minorities whose statuses have been redefined as a consequence of statehood. In order to take on board the nature of these changes, chapters have been rewritten and updated and new chapters added. The plan of the book has also been reorganised and is now divided into seven parts. Part I provides two overviews of nationalities policy, the first in relation to the Soviet period, the second since the establishment of the post-Soviet states. Chapters three to twenty are divided into five parts, covering the nationalities of the Russian Federation, the Baltic States, the South-Western Borderlands, Transcaucasia and Muslim Central Asia, while Part VII examines the diaspora nationalities. In again bringing together a large group of contributors with expertise on particular nationalities, it is hoped that this book will illustrate to the

ix

reader the often strikingly different ways in which national and ethnic groups have been affected by and have responded to the transition from one multiethnic federation to fifteen multiethnic states.

In order to ensure continuity and the book's overall coherence, each contributor has followed a similar format. Chapters begin by briefly locating each nation within a historical, geopolitical and cultural context. Next, each nation is dealt with as part of the Soviet Union, paying particular attention to socio-economic and political developments during the Soviet period, and to relations with Moscow. Each chapter then focuses on analysing developments during the Gorbachev period (1985–91), with particular attention to such common themes as the impact of the reforms on national cultures and local economies, the role of native leaders in relation to such changes, issues pertinent to fuelling ethnic and territorial demands, and the emergence and consolidation of new national organisations and other forms of ethno-cultural resistance. The final section explores the reshaping of national and ethnic identities since 1991 and how in the process relations between the national and ethnic groups are reconstituting themselves.

The major acknowledgement an editor of a volume such as this needs to make is to the contributors. All of them responded with enthusiasm to the project, and I am particularly grateful for their willingness to follow editorial guidelines, which, we hope, provide the coherence in approach and balance in coverage that was intended. I should also like to thank Chris Harrison at Longman for his enthusiasm for commissioning a second edition and his steady guidance throughout, and Ian Agnew for patiently redrawing the maps and putting up with constant requests to incorporate my thumbnail sketches of new boundaries and place-name changes. The book is dedicated to the memory of two colleagues, Andrus Park and V. Stanley Vardys both of whom died in 1994 and were to have contributed to this edition.

Graham Smith
Cambridge
January 1995.

# List of Maps

# List of Contributors

*Aadne Aasland*, Institute of Russian and East European Studies, University of Glasgow.

*Shirin Akiner*, School of Oriental and African Studies, University of London.

*Annette Bohr*, Sidney Sussex College, Cambridge.

*Marie Broxup*, Society for Central Asian Studies, London.

*Ralph Clem*, Department of International Relations, Florida International University.

*Simon Crisp*, St. Catherine's College, Oxford.

*Simon Dixon*, Department of Modern History, University of Glasgow.

*Tamara Dragadze*, School of Slavonic and East European Studies, University of London.

*Peter Duncan*, School of Slavonic and East European Studies, University of London.

*Jonathan Eyal*, Institute for Defence Studies, London

*Yoram Gorlizki*, Department of Government, University of Manchester.

*Edmund Herzig*, Department of Middle Eastern Studies, University of Manchester.

*Caroline Humphrey*, King's College and the Department of Social Anthropology, University of Cambridge.

*Anthony Hyman*, Central Asian Survey, London.

*Stephen Jones*, Mount Holyoke College, Massachusetts.

*Riina Kionka*, Research Section, Radio Free Europe, Munich.

*Edward Lazzerini*, Department of History, University of New Orleans

LIST OF CONTRIBUTORS

*Robert Parsons*, BBC Russian World Service, Moscow.

*John Payne*, Department of Linguistics, University of Manchester.

*Alfred Senn*, Department of History, University of Wisconsin, Madison.

*Graham Smith*, Sidney Sussex College and the Department of Geography, University of Cambridge.

*Ingvar Svanberg*, Centre for Multi-Ethnic Research, Uppsala University.

*Raivo Vetik*, Department of Political Science, Tartu University, Tartu.

*Piers Vitebsky*, Scott Polar Research Institute, University of Cambridge.

*Andrew Wilson*, Sidney Sussex College, Cambridge.

Figure 1 : **THE POST - SOVIET STATES**

RUSSIA

KAZAKHSTAN

KYRGYZSTAN

TAJIKISTAN

UZBEKISTAN

TURKMENISTAN

Almaty

Bishek

Dushanbe

Tashkent

Ashgabat
(Ashkabad)

Moscow

ESTONIA

LATVIA

LITHUANIA

KALININGRAD

BELARUS

MOLDOVA

UKRAINE

GEORGIA

ARMENIA

AZERBAIJAN

Riga

Tallinn

Vilnius

Minsk

Kiev

Chisinau

Tbilisi

Yerevan

Baku

0   kilometres   1000

# PART I

# Nationalities Policy: From the Soviet Union to the Post-Soviet States

CHAPTER ONE

# The Soviet State and Nationalities Policy

Graham Smith

Alex de Tocqueville's remark that the most dangerous time for a bad government is when it starts to reform itself has a particular applicability to the last few years of the Soviet Union's existence. Following Mikhail Gorbachev's election to First Party Secretary in March 1985, the Soviet Union underwent major social, political and economic upheavals activated by a reform-minded leadership willing to engage in the country's systemic transformation. This 'revolution from above' also inadvertently fuelled a scale of ethnic unrest unparalleled in Soviet history as the nationalities within the world's largest multiethnic society seized the opportunities opened up by *glasnost'* (openness) and democratisation to put forward demands for greater national self-determination. It was not only the traditionally assertive nationalities such as the Georgians, Estonians and Latvians that were drawn into the arena of ethnic politics, but also nationalities such as the Belarusians, Moldovans and Armenians which up to the mid-1980s had been considered the most loyal. Nationalisms emerged to take various janus-like forms, resurrecting long-held national beliefs and prejudices rooted in the collective imagination and projected on to the reality of past and current inequalities. Indeed, the growing disjuncture between nationality demands, as reflected in the scale and level of violence, demonstrations and strikes, and the centre's inability to convince the nationalities of the validity of its policies, became so great that the nationalities question came to pose the greatest challenge not only to Gorbachev's reforms but ultimately to the very existence of the Soviet state.[1]

This chapter examines the nature of the nationalities question during the Soviet period by focusing on the evolution of nationalities policy from Lenin to Gorbachev. In particular it attempts to tease out the fact that throughout the seventy years of the Soviet Union's existence, although nationalities policy was not immune to change, it remained grounded within a Marxist-Leninist tradition. What ultimately proved the Soviet Union's undoing was the inability of its reform-minded leadership to recognise until it was too late that the political institutions that had enabled the Soviet Union to function as a near-perfect system of control – notably the federal system – had finally outlived their legitimacy.

## LENIN AND NATIONAL SELF-DETERMINATION

Classical Marxism had little to say about the national question and offered no advice on the issue of national self-determination. It did, however, bequeath a vision of historical progress and a methodology from which a theoretical and practical position on the nation was developed.[2] That both Marx and Engels should treat the national question as peripheral and ethnic divisions as purely contingent to social and economic development was in part due to their interpretation of capitalism as leading to the eventual dissolution of national differences. While the growth of nations – considered as essentially bourgeois phenomena – was viewed as inseparable from the rise of modern capitalism, for the politically important working class, nationality differences were seen to be gradually losing their meaning and would not outlive capitalism. Concerned with the universal and necessary properties of all capitalist societies, cultural differences between societies tended to be treated as 'complicating factors' that were both methodological and programmatic distractions from ensuring the establishment of socialism. Consequently, nations tended to be treated as either reactionary or progressive, depending on their social location within the world economic order. From their writings also sprang a bias in favour of large state formations, for as Engels insisted, one lesson to be drawn from capitalism's development was the favourable conditions that large territorial organisations could provide for social and economic development. This, it was held, was in contradistinction to federalism which, in perpetuating regional division and isolation, preserved traditional values and economic backwardness.[3] It would seem, however, that neither Marx nor Engels envisaged either linguistic universalism or a world in which there would be no role for nations.

The right of nations to national self-determination was adopted and incorporated into the Programme of the Second International at its 1896 London Congress, but it was not until a few years later, at the 1903 Congress of the Russian Social Democratic Workers' Party (RSDWP), that the Leninist notion of national self-determination began to take shape. Particularly influential in formulating Leninist policy was the counter-reformist position adopted by the Austro-Marxists, Otto Bauer and Karl Renner.[4] For them, as for many socialists in the turn of the century empires of Eastern–Central Europe, the multiethnic character and growing political salience of ethnic divisions made the role of nations in the establishment of socialism and their future position in a socialist society a far more problematic affair than in the established nation-states of Western Europe. If the economic logic of both capitalism and socialism led to large state formations, then in Eastern–Central Europe this implied that the boundaries of existing polities would constitute the basis for further integration. Moreover, there was also the problem of those nationality groupings living outside their national territories. For Bauer and Renner territory was not to be a prerequisite feature of the nation; rather, the nation was deemed to be a product of a common history, as 'an aggregate of people bound up into a community of fate' and as 'a cultural community no longer tied to the soil'.[5] Consequently, nations should be granted cultural autonomy without regard to the compactness of their geographical settlement. In offering each nation the right to educational and cultural autonomy within the overall framework of a multiethnic federal state, a practical vision was presented where support of the nationality groupings was essential to the building of socialism. Inspired by such proposals, representatives of the Jewish Bund, who had founded their own working-class organisation in 1879, and whose appeal to a diaspora nationality employed Yiddish as the language of the *shtetl*, called on the Congress to acknowledge ethnic interests in structuring a nationalities policy and in the right of nations to set up and run their own party organisations.

It was precisely this formulation of national self-determination that was interpreted by Lenin as politically retrogressive and divisive. Lenin saw a centralised party as essential to securing socialism, and later was to extend the centralised principle to the state. In an attempt to rebut the Austro-Marxist proposals polemically, Lenin requested Stalin to formulate a position on the national question, which was to set the basic guidelines for subsequent generations of Soviet policy-makers and thinkers.

In his *Marxism and the National and Colonial Questions*, Stalin provided a restrictive conception of nationhood that was still suffi-ciently vague to allow for political manoeuvrability. He took the nation to be 'an historically constituted, stable community of people, formed on the basis of a common language, territory, economic life, and psychological make-up, manifested in a common culture'.[6] For Lenin, however, what actually constituted a nation was trivial compared with securing within the boundaries of the Russian empire the mobilisation and unity of the emerging industrial working class against tsarist autocracy, for above all else the nationality problem was viewed as a problem of securing political power. It was therefore precisely due to such a concern with providing the optimal conditions for mobilisation against capitalism and other retrogressive forces that his interpretation of national self-determination was developed. In forwarding the right of nations to self-determination, which he saw as linked exclusively with the right to political secession, Lenin was adopting a political strategy for resolving Russia's national question. By granting Russia's minority nations the right to statehood he was in effect acknowledging national sensibilities for, according to this logic, if nations were not given this right, then, among peoples whose national consciousness was emerging as a political force, it would encourage a combative nationalism which would run counter to the establishment of socialism in Russia.[7] But endorsing the right of nations to secession, for Lenin, did not mean that *any* separatist movement should be supported. In an oft-quoted analogy, Lenin noted that 'the right of divorce is not an invitation for all wives to leave their husbands'.[8] Such a viewpoint was therefore wholly consistent with the resolution passed at the April 1917 conference of the Russian Communist Party, which reasserted the right of 'all nations forming part of Russia' to 'free separation and the creation of an independent state'.[9] Moreover, Lenin believed that even if small nations did seize the opportunity to declare themselves states, they would soon realise the benefits of being part of a larger territorial unit and would opt for reincorporation. For Lenin the ethnic constitution of such a polity included proposals to divide the country into 'autonomous and self-governing territorial units according – among other things – to nationality; freedom and equality of languages, and the protection of the cultural and educational rights of minorities'.[10] With socialism's establishment, such a programme also envisaged the *sblizhenie* ('coming together') and eventual *sliyanie* ('merger') of the proletariat of different nations.

## THE SOVIET FEDERATION

After 1917, Lenin's position on federation underwent a complete change: from regarding 'the right to federation' as 'meaningless'[11] to an acceptance of it as the most suitable form of organisation for a multiethnic state. In the 1918 constitution, the Party had decided on a federal form of state organisation and in 1919 was proposing 'a federated union of states, organised in a soviet manner', 'as one of the transitional forms on the road to complete unity'.[12] The extent to which such a federation could be realised following the Bolshevik Revolution of October 1917 and the freeing of 'the prison of the peoples', from the shackles of a territorially disintegrating empire was, however, another matter. Between 1918 and 1920, Bolshevik support outside the ethnically Russian heartland was restricted to large urban centres, while in most parts of the ethnic periphery anti-Soviet forces predominated. The 1918 Treaty of Brest-Litovsk had praved the way for independence for Finland, Poland, Estonia, Latvia and

Lithuania, which meant that primarily for geostrategic reasons, these borderland states were beyond possible Bolshevik control. In Ukraine, Central Asia and Transcaucasia, however, Bolshevik interests remained alive, even although sovereign statehood had also been proclaimed throughout these regions in 1918. Different positions were being publicly formulated among leading Bolsheviks in both Moscow and the provinces as to the exact form that relations between these states should take. Rakovsky and the Georgian Bolsheviks, Mdivani and Makharadze, favoured a loose political arrangement by treaty, in which socialist states would remain sovereign entities, thus rejecting the founding of an integral Soviet federation. At the other end of the spectrum, Stalin had put forward the notion of 'autonomisation', which in effect meant withdrawing state sovereignty from the independent socialist republics and providing them with only limited autonomous status. His conception of the right of nations to self-determination had also undergone refinement, for now the right to its exercise was restricted to the working population. Lenin was clearly uneasy about the blanket way in which Stalin employed the notion of 'proletarian self-determination', and at the 8th All-Russia Congress in March 1919 pointed out that such a formulation often exaggerated existing intra-national class differences and unity, pointing out that the right to national self-determination must also apply to socially less-developed peoples, like the Bashkirs.[13] By 1922, Stalin, along with Kamenev and Manuilsky, was arguing for a unitary form of territorial organisation in which the non-Russian nationalities would become autonomous republics within a Russian-dominated Soviet federation.[14] This, however, was rejected by Lenin on the grounds that it would provide a privileged status to Russians and would fuel Russian chauvinism.

A middle road was adopted by Lenin in what is euphemistically referred to as the federal compromise, but it was a combination of the outcome of the Civil War and Stalin's notion of 'proletarian self-determination' that sealed the nature of this 'compromise'. In the case of Georgia, independent statehood, under a successfully led Menshevik government (1918–20), was overthrown by the Red Army, a decision made by Lenin apparently as a result of Stalin and Ordzhonikidze purposely misinforming the General Secretary of local political circumstances.[15] The right of secession was in effect replaced by the right to unite, for it was in the interests of the workers to remain part of a larger proletarian state in which secession that was contrary to the interests of the workers could not occur. Constitutionally (as spelt out in the Union Treaty of December 1922),[16] the larger non-Russian nationality groupings were offered equality of union republic status within a Soviet federation which would honour their right to secession and would grant their major nationalities considerable cultural and administrative autonomy. In return for these guarantees, the nationalities would given up their present form of state sovereignty and become part of a socialist federation of states.

With incorporation into the Soviet federation, the national oppression of the nationalities was deemed to have been automatically eliminated; they were now acknowledged as free to develop towards fulfilment of their national aspirations. The policy of promoting the equality of nations, however, was bound up with a conception of nationhood in which the status of territorial homeland was fundamental, for it was on this basis that the more important national groups were given the most meaningful administrative, constitutional and legal expressions of nationhood in the form of union republic status. It was these indigenous peoples in particular that benefited from the new policy of *Korinezatsiya* ('nativisation'), introduced in 1923 and designed to promote the training and development of native personnel, rather than Russian or Russified elements. Other policies were designed to promote the local language, education and culture, and generally to de-Russify the non-Russian cities. As part of Party policy, the Russian language was officially discriminated against in Ukraine and Belarusia, while in the Central Asian republics, with their non-literary languages, encouragement was given to develop titular alphabets and linguistic structures.[17] Moscow also began purposely to link the economic development of the less-developed regions, which by and large were the non-Russian borderlands, with nationalities policy, and considerable strides were made, particularly in the most backward region of Central Asia, in providing the beginnings of a modern urban-industrial economy and in improving the economic well-being and education of its indigenous peoples. As elsewhere, the migration of Russian specialists and workers into the non-Russian republics was also encouraged.

Never far from the surface of this attempt to incorporate a cultural pluralism into Soviet state-building was what Lenin had referred to as his fear of 'Great Russian chauvinism'.[18] The support and cooperation of the non-Russians in the building of socialiam could proceed only, he argued, through suppressing Russian nationalism. Yet for Stalin, no doubt concerned about the level of indigenisation that was occurring in the non-Russian republics, which he probably interpreted as contrary to the effective implementation of his far-reaching economic policies, it was minority nationalisms that posed the greater threat. Nationalism was considered a reason for opposition to collectivisation in Ukraine, and the purging of Ukrainian personnel was presented as necessary in stamping out centrifugal tendencies. In referring to the non-Russian nationalities, he noted in a 1934 speech that 'survivals of capitalism in the minds of men are much more long-lived in the realm of the national question than in any other area'.[19] The Russification of the non-Russian republics began, which included the Russification of the native languages. By the late 1930s the Russian language was being vigorously promoted in schools, and the number of Russian schools in the provinces was being increased. During the Second World War the promotion of Russian and the Russian people as 'the elder brother' reached new heights, with Russian patriotic symbolism permeating Soviet propagandistic and ideological statements. For Stalin, it therefore did not seem inappropriate, as part of the 1945 victory celebrations, to propose 'a toast to our Soviet people, and in particular to the health of the Russian people ... the leading nation of all nations belonging to the Soviet Union', because the Russian people had 'earned in this war general recognition as the guiding force of the Soviet Union among all the peoples of our country'.[20]

## KHRUSHCHEV AND THE 1961 PARTY CONGRESS

In 1956, at the historic 20th Party Congress, the new General Secretary, Nikita Khrushchev, publicly rebuked Stalin and Stalinist practices. He exposed and denounced the forced mass resettlement of some of the nationalities – the Balkars, Chechens, Ingush, Karachai and Kalmyks – that had been moved during the Second World War from their homelands for geostrategic reasons, and fully rehabilitated and restored their nationality rights. (Putting right previous wrongs did not, however, extend to the other deported nationalities – the Crimean Tatars, Meskhetians and Volga Germans.)[21] Accusations that Stalin was deviating from Lenin's nationality policy were followed by a clear endorsement by the Congress of committing the Party to the flourishing (*ratsvet*) of nations. Other policies also seemed to bode well for nationality development, particularly economic policy. Nationalities policy was linked to improving the socio-economic development of the non-Russian republics, with a commitment to bringing the least developed up to the level of the most advanced. In 1957, in an attempt to improve economic management, a degree of autonomy was granted to the regions through the setting up of regional economic councils (*sovnarkhozy*), resulting in the granting of substantial powers to various regions within the larger republics and to the smaller nationality republics.

Yet while Khrushchev continued in subsequent major speeches to reiterate the Party's commitment to the flourishing of nations, it was increasingly evident that this was to occur concomitantly with a policy of encouraging their 'coming together' (*sblizhenie*). Within the arena of nationality education in particular, there was widespread concern in the non-Russian republics that the 1958–59 educational reforms would further promote the Russian language, to the detriment of the native tongues. The reforms favoured Russian as a medium of instruction in native schools while exempting Russians from learning local languages.

This paved the way for the promotion of Russian language teaching, with particularly negative effects for the languages of the more minor, non-union republic-based nationalities.[22] Whereas almost half of the non-Russian population claimed a knowledge of Russian by the 1979 census, only 3.5 per cent of Russians could claim a similar knowledge of another Soviet language,[23] in spite of the high proportion (a fifth of all Russians) living outside Russia.[24] That Khrushchev should choose increasingly to emphasise and step up assimilative aspects of nationality development probably had much to do with the emergence during the late 1950s of what Moscow labelled 'localism' (*mestnichestvo*) and 'national narrow-mindedness', for the opportunities opened up by the newly founded economic autonomy of the nationality republics had resulted in the promotion of local interests. In the republics deemed to have gone too far, local leaders were purged.

However, at the 22nd Party Congress in 1961 Khrushchev spoke of his commitment to the dialectics of nationality development, so providing the basis for an official policy that was to remain largely unchallenged for the next twenty-five years. Separate national cultures were to 'flourish' alongside their 'drawing together' until their final 'merger' (*sliyanie*) was realised.[25] Despite Khrushchev's optimism about achieving full communism in the foreseeable future, he did not envisage that reaching this end-stage of historical development was concomitent with *sliyanie*. Paraphrasing Lenin, he noted that 'state and national differences will exist long after the victory of socialism in all countries'.[26] So, while supporting the notion of *sliyanie*, he considered it to be a long way off, preferring in the short term the more politically pragmatic commitment to achieving the unity (*edinstvo*) of nations. His usage of this term should not be interpreted as interchangeable with *sliyanie*, but rather, as Rutland rightly notes, as a purely political notion meaning no more than the 'brotherly alliance' of Soviet nations ensured by the efforts of the Communist Party of the Soviet Union (CPSU). Furthermore, 'it does not imply any social policies that threaten their nationhood; on the contrary, "unity" logically entails the continued existence of nations, rather than their abolition'.[27] Yet when Khrushchev insensitively referred to the administrative divisions that formally described the national territorial homelands as 'losing their former significance',[28] he was being consistent not only with Lenin's vision of the federation's transitional nature, but probably also with the viewpoint current at the time that the logic of planning for modern economic conditions was counter to the continuation of nationality-based administrative divisions.[29] It is unlikely, however, that Khrushchev envisaged the current state of *rapprochement* was sufficiently developed to abolish the federation.

# THE SOVIET PEOPLE AND 'DEVELOPED SOCIALISM'

The whole tenor of the Brezhnev administration differed from that of its predecessor. In contrast to Khrushchev, who had attempted to enact far-reaching economic and administrative reforms, and who had committed the regime to achieving rapid economic growth, the Brezhnev leadership pursued an increasingly cautious and conservative approach, more pragmatic and less idealistic in character. The return to centralised ministerial control over the economy by the mid-1960s ended further experimentation with the sort of institutional reforms that had previously threatened to undermine central authority. Western analysts interpreted the abandonment of such reforms and Brezhnev's emphasis on 'harmonious development'[30] as the price the regime was willing to pay for ensuring social stability.[31] Relations between Moscow and the nationality republics began to take on an increasingly corporatist character.[32]

In return for maintaining ethno-territorial stability and meeting more realistically set production targets, Moscow was prepared to allow republic political élites both greater flexibility in native appointments to local positions and some *de facto* administrative leeway. Brezhnev's policy of putting greater trust in native and local cadres certainly made party and state life in the republics less turbulent and more comfortable. The Brezhnev regime also made clear its continuing commitment to ethno-regional equalisation, to full employment (often at considerable economic cost), and to improving standards of living, all of which contributed to a general rise in the material well-being of the regions during the 1960s and 1970s. While occasions did arise when republic leaders were deemed by Moscow to have gone too far in putting republic interests first, such outbursts were the exception. Those who expressed nationalist views exceeding the bounds permitted by Moscow were subject to dismissal and repression.

The more cautious and socially pragmatic thrust to the Brezhnev administration was reflected in official policy towards the national question. The central tenets of the 1961 Congress, however, although subject to refinement and to the notable dropping from major policy speeches of the commitment to *sliyanie*, remained essentially intact. While it was never included in the Party programme, at that Congress Khrushchev had referred to the emergence of a new historical community, that of the Soviet people (*Sovetskii narod*). At the 1971 Party Congress, Brezhnev expanded on and made great play of the emergence of this 'new human community sharing a common territory, state, economic system, culture, the goal of building communism and a common language'.[33] Within the arena of nationality relations, the concept of *Sovetskii narod* in effect emerged as a synonym for the newly self-designated era of 'developed socialism', of how far the party and state had progressed in the flourishing and coming together of the nationalities, but also as a shorthand reminder of the progress that society had still to make along the road of *sblizhenie*. As Brezhnev made evident on his fiftieth anniversary speech marking the foundation of the Soviet state: 'nationality relations, even in a society of developed socialism, are a reality which is constantly developing and putting forth new problems and tasks'.[34] He also made it clear that the further 'coming together' of nations was an objective process, and that the Party was against forcing integration.

Official policy throughout the 1970s and early 1980s continued to accept tacitly the existence of a multiethnic society of culturally distinct yet integrated nationalities.[35] This was extended to include statehood, an issue that was resurrected during the years leading up to the formulation of the 1977 Soviet constitution. Those favouring the abolition of nationality-based administrative divisions contended that the *rapprochement* between nations had proceeded sufficiently far to make the notion of federation obsolete.[36] Brezhnev, however, made it clear that he was against any proposals advocating either the federation's abolition or curtailment of the constitutional right (as included in the 1924 and 1936 constitutions) of union republics to territorial secession. 'We should,' he noted, 'be taking a dangerous course if we were artificially to accelerate this objective process of *rapprochement* between nations'.[37]

At his last Party Congress in 1981, Brezhnev reiterated the success of *Sovetskii narod* and of a multiethnic state more united than ever. Again he noted with concern the tendencies designed to artificially speed up *sblizhenie* and obliterate national identities. But although the Soviet people were united more than ever, for the General Secretary this did not imply 'that all the problems of the relations between the nationalities have been resolved. The dynamics of the development of a large multi-ethnic state like ours gives rise to many problems requiring the party's tactful attention.'[38] However, he singled out the socio-economic development and the further contribution of the republics to 'developed socialism' for particular comment. While declaring that 'there are no backward ethnic outskirts today', he did make it clear that one of the Party's objectives was 'to increase the material and cultural potential of each republic', which would, at the same time 'make the maximum use of this potential for the balanced development of the country as a whole'. Their 'coming together in every field', he went on to argue, would be speeded up through the intensive social and economic development of each republic. Like his predecessors, he also reminded his audience of the role played by the 'disinterested assistance of the Russian people' in the socio-economic development of the republics.[39]

Certainly by the early 1980s the increasing stagnation of the Soviet economy was beginning to be widely felt throughout the republics, with the gap in living standards growing between the more advanced, such as Russia proper and the Baltic, and the less developed.[40] The corporatist character of centre–union republic relations was being further undermined by new challenges from Moscow to the regions. By the late 1970s, the Brezhnev regime was calling for the promotion of the Russian language in the non-Russian republics through increasing the teaching of Russian, from kindergartens to universities.[41] And at the 1981 Party Congress, spurred on by growing concern in Moscow as to the scale of indigenisation of cadre appointments at the republic level, Brezhnev raised the delicate issue of non-Russian representation in the non-Russian republics. 'In recent years,' he noted, 'there has been a considerable growth in some republics in the number of citizens from the non-indigenous nationalities. These have their own specific ends in terms of language, culture and everyday life. The central committees of the Communist Parties of the republics and the territorial and regional committees should go deeper into these matters and opportunely suggest ways of meeting these needs.'[42] In a speech the following year, Candidate Politburo Member Boris Ponomarev hinted that affirmative action policies might have gone too far, reminding his audience that every republic should 'serve the interests of all labouring peoples regardless of whether they belong to the titular nationality'.[43] The problem of encouraging particularly the movement of specialist labour into areas of growing shortages was becoming a major issue. The demographers Litvinova and Urlanis cited affirmative action policies and the rootedness to place they encouraged as contributing to this problem: 'this policy [of preferential treatment] was justified during the initial post-war revolutionary years, but it should be changed in the light of current conditions.'[44]

Yuri Andropov, who succeeded Brezhnev in 1982, reiterated concern about cadre policy and that past nativisation policies had gone too far. Although supporting the need for fairer representation of all nationalities within the union republics, he rejected the notion of formal quotas, for 'an arithmetic approach to the solutions of such problems is inappropriate'.[45] However, he appeared to take a more integrationist approach by stating that the goal of nationalities policy was 'not only the *sblizhenie* of nations, but also their *sliyanie*'.[46] But as Olcott rightly argues, the reintroduction of *sliyanie* after a decade of omission from major policy speeches should not be interpreted as indicative of an active commitment to the fusion of nations; the firm line adopted had more to do with Andropov reasserting the role of the General Secretary as a leading authority on the nationalities question,[47] for in other respects he adopted a more conciliatory line. He reiterated his commitment to federalism, to 'the free development of each republic and each nationality within the boundary of the fraternal union'. He also made it clear that national differences would exist for a long time, 'much longer than class differences'.[48]

## GORBACHEV AND THE NATIONAL QUESTION

Despite Gorbachev's willingness to set the pace, to tackle systemically the problems of the ailing Soviet economy and to overhaul the state-censored society he inherited in March 1985, the new leadership continued to treat the nationalities question as relatively insignificant. In contrast to the other major social and economic problems the administration inherited, it was only when the reform programme triggered off growing ethnic discontent that the leadership was prepared to take the nationalities question on board the reformist agenda. In his honeymoon first year as General Secretary, on the few occasions that he spoke on the nationalities question, Gorbachev merely restated Brezhnev's policy. In the summer of 1985, on the occasion of the celebrations commemorating the fortieth anniversary of the Soviet victory in the Second World War, he referred to the continuing flourishing and *rapprochment* of nations, which continued to manifest itself in the deeply felt sense of belonging to 'a single family – the Soviet people'.[49] He also emphasised the role played by the Russian people in the final victory over fascism, as well as Stalin's contribution, but the general tenor of his speech 'was presented in class and anti-imperialist rather than nationalist terms'.[50] His insensitivity to the multiethnic nature of Soviet society was particularly evident on a visit to Kiev on 25 June 1985, in which on two occasions he referred to the Soviet Union as Russia.[51]

Although Gorbachev was the first Soviet leader since Lenin without any career background in a non-Russian republic, he was not without experience of the national question. A Russian by nationality, he was born and brought up in Stavropol *krai*, an area of the North Caucasus within the Russian republic (RSFSR). After a spell at Moscow State University during the early 1950s, he returned to his homeland, where he spent all his early career before returning to the capital city in 1978 to take up a promotion. In late 1943, when Gorbachev was twelve years old, Stalin had ordered the wholesale forced deportation of two national minorities of Stavropol *krai*, the Karachai and Cherkess. Gorbachev was probably too young to comprehend what had happened, but by the late 1950s, when Khrushchev had allowed these peoples to return to their native homelands, he was already First Secretary of the Stavropol town *Komsomol*, and a member of the *Kraikom Komsomol Bureau*. He must therefore have carried some responsibility both for overseeing the reinstatement of the Karachai-Cherkess Autonomous *Oblast* and for finding employment and housing for these peoples.[52] Later in his career, Gorbachev made a number of statements on the national question before becoming General Secretary, but as Motyl points out, such pronouncements 'are notable only for their dullness, clichés and naïve optimism'.[53]

It was not until the 27th Party Congress, in February 1986, that

Goroachev made his clearest statement, although it was brief, on the national question. In most respects, there was little departure from the Brezhnevite line: no reference was made to *sliyanie* of nations while much was again made of a united Soviet people, *Sovetskii narod*, 'cemented by the same economic interests, ideology and political goals'.[54] However, he noted that such achievements 'must not create the impression that there are no problems in the national processes. Contradictions are inherent in any kind of development, and are unavoidable in this sphere as well.'[55] He went on to acknowledge that these contradictory tendencies, which included 'national isolationism, localism and parasitism' were a problem, and to speak of 'attempts to isolate oneself from the objective process by which national cultures interact and come closer together (*sblizhenie*)'.[56] But while he acknowledged a problematic side to ethnic relations, no proposals other than vague references to *sblizhenie* were forthcoming. Indeed, as in earlier speeches, when he had stressed the importance of prioritising those aspects of the economy that promised the greatest and most immediate return,[57] at the 27th Party Congress the onus was on prioritising investment in those sectors and regions of the economy commensurate with economic modernisation and intensive development. Expensive, large-scale projects, particularly important to the development of peripheral regions, were to be either abandoned or given lower priority. In playing down the more balanced development among different regions of the USSR that his predecessors had been careful to stress and had identified as an important aspect of nationalities policy,[58] Gorbachev chose to emphasise the importance of the republics' contribution to 'the development of an integrated national economic complex' which 'should match their [republic] grown economic and spiritual potential'.[59] Although he also advocated greater power for republic and local interests, like his programme for economic modernisation and socio-economic accleration (*uskorenie*), no attempt was made to link such policy shifts to the nationalities question.

As the scale of nationalist unrest increased, the Gorbachev regime began to revise its attitude towards the nationalities. The Kazakh riots of mid-December 1986 in Alma Ata were the first major blow from the ethnic periphery to the reform programme. The riots were triggered off by the replacement of a Kazakh First Party Secretary with a Russian, which broke with the previously universal practice of appointing a native to such a post. Bringing in an outsider in order to reassert control over a republic economically cripped by élite corruption and mismanagement may have made sense, but for many Kazakhs, numerically outnumbered and feeling socially vulnerable and economically deprived in their own homeland, it showed the new regime as being totally insensitive to national sensibilities. From that point onwards, as incidences of ethnic unrest on a scale previously unknown to Soviet society quickly unfolded across the country, the illusion of a society having secured cultural coexistence and moving steadily towards *rapprochement* was shattered. Following ethnic demonstrations throughout 1987, by the Crimean Tatars, Baltic peoples and Ukrainians, in February 1988 the epicentre of ethnic unrest switched unexpectedly to Transcaucasia. The ethnically Armenian-dominated enclave of Nagorno-Karabakh, administered as part of Azerbaijan, passed a resolution calling for its territory's transfer to Armenia. The demonstrations, riots and bloodshed that followed prompted Gorbachev to declare publicly that the nationalities question was now a vital political issue on the Kremlin's agenda.[60]

After the Kazakh riots, Moscow was willing to concede that past mistakes had been made in nationalities policy, and a Central Committee Plenum, meeting in January 1987, acknowledged that the root causes of ethnic unrest were not unique to Kazakhstan.[61] Social scientists were singled out for creating too rosy a picture of national relations and were accused of creating a growing gap between their scientific research and reality. As the nationalities expert, Bagramov, admitted, 'in practice, the sphere of national relations had been treated as if everything were harmonious ... and that which did not fit into this harmony was simply dismissed and stigmatised as a manifestation of bourgeois nationalism'.[62] Gorbachev's response to the events in Alma Ata was to call for 'greater internationalist education', particularly among the young, but he also gave the stern warning that 'those who would like to play on nationalist or chauvinist prejudices should entertain no illusion and expect no loosening up'.[63] In a speech in Tallinn, the capital of Estonia, in February 1987, Gorbachev adopted a more conciliatory tone but without departing from Brezhnevite thinking: 'The flourishing of nations and nationalities has been ensured by Leninist nationalities policy. Of course there were shortcomings and mistakes in that Great Course, as well as aggravations [of the situation], and we are aware of them and do not overlook or forget them.'[64]

Rather than formulating a coherent nationalities policy, Gorbachev's approach to the nationalities question was to respond to each new ethnic crisis as it arose, in which there was a tendency to treat each as a distraction from the central tasks of economic restructuring, *glasnost'* and democratisation, by which ethnic unrest could be largely resolved. In its crisis management, Moscow tended to favour short-term, piecemeal measures – in particular, instances linked to some economic and cultural programme – as a means of appeasing some of the more problematic ethnic demands, as in the case of the Kazakhs, Crimean Tatars and the peoples of Nagorno-Karabakh. Indeed, the regime was slow to acknowledge officially that such measures were not sufficient to resolve ethnic conflict.[65] At the special 19th Party Conference in June 1988 it was announced that a Special Party Plenum would be held to re-examine nationalities policy.

Little comfort, however, was offered by Gorbachev at the Conference to nationalities with either extra-territorial claims or aspirations to elevate the administrative status of their homelands, for he made plain his commitment to 'the existing state structures of our union'.[66] The Special Conference did, however, go some way to incorporating the demands of the nationalities represented on the federal map into the overall reformist schema of greater economic decentralisation and democratisation. Yet there was no consistent policy response when demands from or events in the nationality republics seemed to be getting out of Moscow's control. The November 1988 constitutional crisis in Estonia, for example, precipitated by proposed changes to the Soviet constitution, which were seen in the republic as a challenge to their constitutionally guaranteed sovereignty, resulted in Moscow going some way to accommodating Estonian demands. In Georgia in April 1989, however, ethnic tensions between Georgians and Abkhazians resulted in the use of force to normalise the situation.

While muddling through in its handling of a multiplicity of complex and very different nationality problems, Moscow had reluctantly come round to recognising that the success of the whole reform programme now depended on a resolution to the nationalities question. As Gorbachev had noted in a 1989 summer address to the country, 'inter-ethnic conflict threatens to determine, not only the fate of *perestroika*, but also the integrity of the Soviet state'.[67] However, despite its belated willingness to take on board the nationalities question, Moscow remained resolutely opposed to any proposals emanating from the nationality republics that either challenged the Soviet Union's territorial integrity or questioned the legitimacy of Soviet socialism. It was prepared to go only as far as undertaking a radical renewal of nationalities policy,[68] based on Lenin's works and on his general conception of a multiethnic society based on equality and friendship between nations. The reform communists, in seeking ideological justification for their position on the nationalities question, were willing to reconsider nationalities policy only against the background of Lenin's 1922 conception of federalism as set down in the original Soviet constitution. To do otherwise would have undermined the legitimacy of seventy years of Soviet socialism. Thus a 1989 article in *Kommunist* referred to Lenin's notion of national self-determination as a declaration still to be implemented: 'the command-administrative system' was held to be responsible for the demise of national self-determination and for nationality unrest.[69] The Stalinist and post-Stalinist period and the failure of successive regimes to implement a proper nationalities policy was represented as a futile diversion from the path laid down by Lenin. As Gorbachev noted in a July 1989 speech, the sources underlying current ethnic tensions emanate from a variety of distortions and acts of lawlessness in the past, whose result was 'indifference towards ethnic interests, the failure to resolve many socio-economic problems of the republics and autonomous territories, deformations in the development of the languages and cultures of the country's people, the deteriorating of the demographic situation, and many other negative consequences'.[70]

Reformation of nationalities policy was therefore to occur within the framework of Lenin's conception of a Soviet federation, in effect to 'restore . . . the original Leninist principles of a Soviet federation, a union of republics possessing real sovereignty in all spheres of state life'.[71] As Gorbachev reminded the Soviet people in his July 1989 speech, *perestroika* meant 'fully implementing in practice the principles on which Lenin based the union of Soviet republics'.[72] The proposals put forward by the CPSU Platform on Nationalities, which were eventually endorsed by the Special Plenum on the Nationalities in September 1989, reflected the views of Gorbachev as enunciated in his speech of July 1989.[73] However, the Plenum's proposals, which followed the proposals recommended by the Platform, did not go far enough. Despite plans to devolve more economic and political autonomy to the republics, including the right to establish relations with foreign states and international organisations, and to recognise the right of the autonomous republics, if they so wished, to adopt the language of the nationality of the namesake republic as the state language, which would be recognised by the union,[74] the federation was to remained centralised. In particular, the centralised role of the Party was to continue; thus reform was not to include the federalisation of what for seventy years had functioned as the main arm of centralised territorial control.

It was a vision of a multiethnic society increasingly at odds with the union republics, particularly the radically minded Baltic republics, Georgia, Moldova and Azerbaijan. In a unilateral decision in December 1989, the Lithuaian Communist Party took the watershed decision to declare its independence from the CPSU. Four months later, on 11 March 1990, the Lithuanian parliament became the first republic to declare its independence from Moscow. Although the other fourteen union republics did not go so far, the Lithuanian decision paved the way for sovereignty declarations by them throughout 1990.

## RETHINKING THE FEDERATION: THE NEW FEDERAL TREATY

The 'revolution from above' had by 1990 become 'a revolution from below' in which the nationality republics now set the pace in putting onto what was left of the reform agenda not only the nationalities question but also the question of whether the Soviet Union was to continue as a territorial entity. This challenge from the union republics to the federal status quo was bound up with a variety of powerful resources linked to their federal status. Firstly, the union republics were already 'statelets in embryo', with complete institutions of government, national symbols, traditions of cultural production in their own literary vernaculars, a legitimate standing in Soviet law and even the (theoretical) right to secession written into the federal constitution. Thus, through federalism, the union republics were in effect furnished with the institutions, organisations, and access to resources to forward their national interests and to mobilise their constituents behind securing a greater measure of national self-determination. Secondly, the union republics had amassed a series of grievances against the centre that were translatable into national grievances. The politicisation of such grievances, which ranged from issues of differential development, Russian immigration and environmental degradation to limited native career opportunities and the circumstances surrounding incorporation into the Soviet federation, was greatly facilitated by *glasnost'*. For the first time in Soviet history, the nationality republics were in effect able to publicly re-examine in entirety their relationship with Moscow. Thirdly, most of the union republics now possessed not only a local leadership willing to challenge the centre but also leaders capable of mobilising their national constituents behind the cause of greater home rule, if not independent statehood. Within the arena of federal politics, a number of republics had seen by 1990 federal leaders either replacing those who had supported the federal status quo or changing their preferences in taking an increasingly radical stance on national autonomy. At the forefront were the Baltic republics which, having been permitted to set up grassroots-based social movements in support of *perestroika* in 1988, had quickly become autonomist in their demands, these movements eventually replacing the old-guard local communist party leadership as the focus of local political power.[75] However, a change in leadership in the largest and most politically influential republic, Russia, was to prove crucial. With the election of Boris Yeltsin in 1990 to the post of Chairman of the Russian Supreme Soviet, Russia not only embarked on a course of securing its own national sovereignty but also sided openly against Gorbachev with the other nationality republics in their aim of securing more control over local affairs.

The New Federal Treaty was Gorbachev's last attempt to keep the Soviet Union together. Although its earlier drafts imposed strict limits on what was permissible, its final formulation was to involve the participation of those republics willing to enter into a voluntary federal arrangement, offering considerable scope for providing a basis for a more decentralised federation.[76] In a radical departure from previous policy, it envisaged a federal system in which the republics would be able to choose voluntarily what powers to delegate to the centre, and to decide what republic laws were to have priority over federal laws and vice versa. Membership of the federation could only be entered into voluntarily: this in effect recognised what had been consitutionally enshrined in the original, centrally-imposed federal treaty of Lenin, but had remained nothing but a theoretical possibility. Thus in striking a new federal compromise between Yeltsin's Russia and the political leadership of the other eight pro-union republics, Gorbachev had in effect rejected imposing through force a federal arrangement from above. The so-called 9 plus 1 federal Treaty agreement, also known as the *Novo-Ogarevo* Accord, was approved on 15 August 1991 and was due to be ratified five days later. It signalled not only Gorbachev's recognition of the sovereignty of the union republics, but also the right of republics that so wished to leave the federal union. The right-wing Moscow coup of 19 August, rather than leading to a re-centralised federation as its supporters wanted or, when the coup failed, to ratification of a more decentralised Soviet federation along the lines proposed by the New Federal Treaty, instead issued the Soviet Union's final death warrant. Ethno-nationalism had triumphed over federation.

Ultimately a more decentralised federation, which still clung to its legitimation based on seventy years of Soviet socialism, could no longer be justified for a number of reasons. Firstly, the official ideology that underpinned Gorbachev's conception of federation was bankrupt. As Gellner put it, 'The ... secular ideology was strong enough to suppress ... nationalism, as long as it retained faith in itself and the determination to use all means to retain control'.[77] Having renounced repression, in part in order to retain Western goodwill, Gorbachev resisted using coercion in order to keep the federation together, other than in selected and usually provoked incidents. This was to help ensure that, compared to the disintegration of Yugoslavia, the end of the Soviet federation was remarkably peaceful. Secondly, the idea of federation as a powerful weapon for uniting peoples against a common enemy, as Lenin had so skilfully done in the early 1920s, had outlived its usefulness. With the end of the Cold War, what justification that could be made for a federation grounded in the need for common regional security had gone. For the nationalistically-minded republics, new geopolitical fault lines were opening up that exploded the myth of a federal society based on multiethnic coexistence. Finally, the idea that federal unity was crucial to national economic well-being also foundered. Gorbachev had made a great play about 'a common economic space' and stated that because of republics' economic interdependency, fragmentation would spell economic disaster for even the richer republics.[78] It was an argument that had only limited appeal, not least because of the failure of the federation's reformers to revitalise the national economy and to reverse falling living standards. In the world of the 1990s, economic sovereignty was no longer conceived by many of the republics as a condition for nation-statehood; indeed the secessionist-minded republics played up the idea that their future well-being lay in going simultaneously local and global, of attaining their political independence but securing their material prosperity through membership of new regional markets and trading blocs. History was therefore to prove Lenin right in viewing the Soviet federation as a transitional form, but not in the way he had envisaged.

## NOTES

1. For accounts of the Gorbachev leadership's attempts to reformulate nationalities policy see, for example G. Lapidus, V. Zaslavsky and P. Goldman (eds) *From Union to Commonwealth, Nationalism and Separatism in the Soviet Republics* (Cambridge, Cambridge University Press 1992); A. Motyl 'The sobering of Gorbachev: nationality, re-structuring and the West, in S. Bialer (ed.) *Inside Gorbachev's Russia: Politics, Society and Nationality* (Boulder, CO, Westview Press 1989), pp. 149–73; G. E. Smith 'Gorbachev's greatest challenge: perestroika and the national question' *Political Geography Quaterly*, vol. 8, no. 1 (1989), pp. 7–20.
2. For one of the most comprehensive analyses of the development and practice of nationalities policy in socialist societies, see W. Connor *The National Question in Marxist-Leninist Theory and Strategy* (Princeton, NJ, Princeton University Press 1984).
3. F. Engels 'The movements of 1847' in K. Marx and F. Engels *Collected Works* vol. 6 (Moscow, Progress Publishers 1979).
4. H. B. Davis (ed.) *The National Question: Selected Writings* (New York, Monthly Review Press).
5. Quoted by E. H. Carr *The Bolshevik Revolution, 1917–1923* vol. 1 (London, Macmillan), p. 421.
6. J. V. Stalin 'Marxism and the National Question' in *Collected Works* vol. 2 (Moscow 1952–55), p. 307.
7. Carr, op. cit. pp. 260–62.
8. V.I. Lenin *Sochineniya* 4th edn, vol. 23 (Moscow, Institute Marksizm-Leninizm 1941–57), pp. 61–2.
9. As quoted in Carr, op. cit. p. 262.
10. Lenin, op. cit. vol. 20, p. 432.
11. Ibid., p. 411.
12. J. Peters 'Stalin's nationality policy: an interpretation' (Unpublished Ph.D. thesis, University of Pennsylvania 1964), p. 146.
13. Lenin, op. cit. vol. 29, pp. 150–51.
14. R. Szporluk 'Nationalities and the Russian problem in the USSR: an historical outline' *Journal of International Affairs* vol. 27, no. 1 (1973), pp. 22–40.
15. Peters, op. cit. pp. 168–69.
16. For a discussion of the 1922 Treaty and 1924 Constitution, see S. Bloem-bergen 'The union republics: how much autonomy?' *Problems of communism* vol. 16, no. 5 (1967), pp. 27–35.

17. I. Kreindler (ed.) *Sociolinguistic Perspectives on Soviet National Languages* (Berlin, Mouton de Gruyter 1985).
18. Lenin, op. cit. vol. 23, p. 335.
19. Peters, op. cit. p. 288.
20. Quoted by F. Barghoorn *Soviet Russian Nationalism* (New York, Oxford University Press 1956), p. 27.
21. I. Kreindler 'The Soviet deported nationalities: a summary and an update' *Soviet Studies* vol. 38, no. 3 (1986), pp. 387–405.
22. B. Silver, 'The status of national minority language in Soviet education: an assessment of recent changes' *Soviet Studies* vol. 26, no. 1 (1974), pp. 28–40.
23. Calculated from *Vestnik Statistiki* no. 7 (1980), p. 43; no. 8 (1980), pp. 64–70; no. 9 (1980), pp. 61–70; no. 10 (1980), pp. 67–73; and no. 11 (1980), pp. 60–4.
24. Yu Arutunyan, V. *et al. Sotsial' no-kul 'turnyi oblik Sovetskikh Natsii (po materialam etnosotsiologischeskogo issledovaniya)* (Moscow, Nauka, 1986), p. 32.
25. *XXII s"ezd kommunisticheskoi Partii Sovetskogo Soyuza. Stenograficheskii otchet* (Moscow 1961).
26. Ibid., p. 216.
27. P. Rutland 'The "nationality problem" and the Soviet state' in N. Harding (ed.) *The State in Socialist Society* (London, Macmillan 1984), pp. 150–78.
28. See Note 25.
29. See, for example, the article by Alampiev and Kistanov in *Literaturnaya gazeta*, 28 May 1961.
30. *Pravda* 7 Nov. 1964.
31. See, for example, S. Bialer *The Soviet Paradox: External Expansion, Internal Decline* (London, I.B. Tauris 1986); V. Zaslavsky *The Neo-Stalinist State* (Brighton, Harvester Press 1982).
32. G. Smith 'The Soviet federation: from corporatist to crisis politics' in M. Chisholm and D. Smith (eds) *Shared Space: Divided Space: Essays on Conflict and Territorial Organisation* (London, Unwin Hyman 1990) pp. 84–105.
33. *Materialy XXIV se"zda KPSS* (Moscow, Izadel'stvo Politicheskoi Literatury 1971), p. 76.
34. *Pravda* 22 Dec. 1972, p. 3.
35. Olcott, op. cit. p. 105.
36. For example, S. E. Ebzeeva 'Sovetskaya federatsiya na etape zrelogo sotsializma' *Sovetskoe Gosudarstvo i Pravo* 7 (1982), pp. 10–14.
37. *Pravda* 5 Oct. 1977.
38. *Pravda* 24 Feb. 1981.
39. *XXVI s"ezd kommunisticheskoi partii Sovetskogo Soyuza. Stenograficheskii otchet* (Moscow 1981), Part I, pp. 70–5.
40. See, for example, E. Jones and F. Grupp 'Modernisation and ethnic equalisation in the USSR' *Soviet Studies* vol. 36, pp. 159–84.
41. R. Solchanyk 'Russian language and Soviet politics' *Soviet Studies*, vol. 34 (1982), pp. 23–42.
42. See Note 39.
43. Quoted by G. Lapidus 'Ethnonationalism and political stability: the Soviet case' *World Politics*, vol. 36, no. 4 (July 1984), pp. 568–69.

44. Litvinova and Urlanis 'Demograficheskaya politika v SSSR' *Sovetskoe Gosudarstvo i Pravo* 3, pp. 38–46.
45. Yu Andropov 'Shest' desyat let SSR', *Kommunist* no. 1 (1983), p. 8.
46. Ibid., p. 5.
47. Olcott, op. cit. p. 103.
48. Andropov, op. cit. p. 6.
49. M. Gorbachev *Ibrannye rechi i stat'i* (Moscow Izdatel'stvo Politicheskoi Literatury 1985), p. 52.
50. P. Duncan 'The Party and Russian nationalism in the USSR: from Brezhnev to Gorbachev' in P. Potichenyi (ed.) *The Soviet Union: Party and Society* (Cambridge University Press 1988), p. 240.
51. Y. Bilinsky 'Nationality policy and Gorbachev's first year', *Orbis* (Summer 1986), p. 341.
52. Z. Medvedev *Gorbachev* (Oxford, Basil Blackwell 1988), pp. 31–2.
53. Motyl, op. cit. p. 156.
54. M. Gorbachev, *Politicheskii doklad tsentral'nogo komiteta KPSS XXVII Sëzdu Kommunisticheskoi Partii Sovetskogo Soyuza* (Moscow, Izdatel'stvo Politicheskoi Literatury 1986), p. 101.
55. Ibid., p. 101.
56. Loc. cit.
57. *Pravda* 12 June 1985.
58. See, for example, D. Bahry *Outside Moscow: Power, Politics and Budgetary Policy in the Soviet Republics* (New York, Columbia University Press 1987), pp. 30–1.
59. Gorbachev (1986), op. cit. p. 101.
60. *Pravda* 18 Feb. 1988.
61. *Pravda* 28 Jan. 1987.
62. *Pravda* 14 Aug. 1987.
63. *Pravda* 28 Jan. 1987.
64. *Tass* 21 Feb. 1987.
65. Gorbachev clearly acknowledged this in his speech of 1 July 1989 (*Soviet News* 5 July 1989).
66. *Pravda* 29 June 1988.
67. Soviet News 5 July 1989.
68. *Pravda* 17 Aug. 1989.
69. *Kommunist* no. 9 (1989).
70. Gorbachev's television speech, the text of which is reproduced in *Soviet News* 5 July 1989, p. 218.
71. *Tass* 14 March 1989.
72. See Note 70.
73. Ibid.
74. *Pravda* 17 Aug. 1989.
75. G. Smith 'The emergence of nationalism', in G. Smith (ed.) *The Baltic States. The National Self-Determination of Estonia, Latvia and Lithuania* (London, Macmillan 1994), pp. 121–43.
76. See *Pravda* 24 November 1990, p. 1, *Izvestiya* 22 February 1991.
77. E. Gellner, 'Nationalism and politics in Eastern Europe' *New Left Review*, No. 189, (1991), p. 132.
78. Gorbachev's speech to the CPSU Central Committee on 19 September 1989, *Pravda*, 21 Sept. 1989.

# CHAPTER TWO

# The Post-Soviet States and the Nationalities Question

Andrew Wilson

Despite the formal declarations of independence by all fifteen Union republics in the wake of the failed August 1991 coup attempt,[1] it was still far from clear what status the fifteen would claim or what kind of relations might develop between them. Several options continued to be discussed.[2] The three Baltic republics made or renewed their claims to be independent nation-states, and were quickly recognised by the international community as such, followed by Moldova, Georgia and Armenia, albeit with less immediate diplomatic success. On the other hand, although the *Novo-Ogarevo* '9 plus 1' formula (see chapter one) was clearly dead, Russia, Belarus, Azerbaijan, and the Central Asian states (Kazakhstan in particular), still expressed interest in some form of loose confederation. In the middle was Ukraine, which began a referendum campaign to confirm its declaration of independence in August, but which nevertheless remained nervous about the reaction of its large Russian minority to independence and concerned about the lessons to be drawn from Yugoslavia on the dangers of over-hasty dissolution of the Union. The most important change, however, was that Gorbachev's political eclipse and the rise of Yeltsin meant that 'the centre' was now Russia itself rather than the institutions of the USSR, and Yeltsin's new government was increasingly inclined towards a go-it-alone strategy of building liberal capitalism in one country. Formally, however, the USSR continued to exist, its status unclear and its prospects uncertain.

Therefore the failure of the August 1991 coup attempt did nothing in itself to resolve the nationality question and indeed introduced several new complicating elements into the equation. The former republics still faced potential conflicts among themselves and with minority groups on their territory, now suddenly reclassified as ethnic minorities, potential *irredentas* or stranded diasporas. Moreover, although the rush to independence now seemed unstoppable and pro-Union sentiments were for the moment unfashionable, countervailing forces still existed and soon began to resurface in a variety of guises.

This chapter therefore outlines how the nationalities question developed after August 1991. First, it briefly reviews the history of the Commonwealth of Independent States that emerged in December 1991 as a partial successor to the USSR and outlines possible models for its future development. Second, it presents an overview of the different ways in which the nationalities question has unfolded in the successor states. Lastly, it analyses possible models for nationality conflict and management in the future.

## THE ESTABLISHMENT OF THE CIS

Negotiations on some kind of loose constitutional framework to maintain at least the semblance of a Union continued from September to November 1991.[3] Gorbachev's last throw of the dice was the agreement announced on 14 November 1991 that envisaged an extremely decentralised 'union of sovereign states', albeit with some central institutions such as a directly elected president and bicameral legislature. Russia, Belarus and the Central Asian five indicated their support for the plan, but Ukraine, as throughout 1990–1, remained in two minds, despite attending the negotiations. Three key factors doomed the accord, however (the initialing ceremony planned for 25 November never took place). First, Yeltsin identified Gorbachev's desire to retain some central institutions with his personal attempt to hang on to power. Yeltsin now simply wanted Gorbachev out of the way and was prepared to abolish the office along with the man. Second, Yeltsin's newly-appointed Russian government under Gennadii Burbulis and Yegor Gaidar was preparing to go it alone economically and was convinced that Russia's economic salvation depended on cutting the other republics loose. Third, although the most important non-Russian actor, Ukraine, participated in Gorbachev's negotiations, all major political forces in the republic had temporarily united behind the campaign for independence (the nationalists were joined by the majority of former communists, who regarded independence as the best means of insulating themselves from the anti-communist crusade emanating from Yeltsin's Russia). As a result, Ukrainian independence was endorsed by a massive 90.3 per cent vote in the referendum on 1 December 1991, and the USSR received its final death-blow.

The leading role played by Russia and Ukraine in the destruction of the Union was demonstrated on 7–8 December when the leaders of Russia, Ukraine and Belarus, Boris Yeltsin, Leonid Kravchuk and Stanislau Shushkevich, met in a dacha at Belovezhkaya Pushcha near Minsk to engineer the USSR's downfall.[4] Proceeding from the fact that Russia, Ukraine and Belarus were the three original signatories to the Union Treaty that formally established the USSR in 1922, they declared their right to dissolve that which they had themselves first created and asserted that 'the USSR as a subject of international law and as a geopolitical reality has ceased to exist'.[5] Within three weeks of the agreement the USSR was indeed no more. Its institutions, in particular the Supreme Soviet, were dissolved, and Gorbachev himself finally resigned on 25 December 1991.

According to the Belovezhkaya Pushcha agreement, however, the USSR was to be replaced by a 'Commonwealth of Independent States' (CIS). The USSR was to leave more historical traces than Yugoslavia had done. Nevertheless, although the signatories promised to 'abide by international agreements signed by the former USSR', it was unclear how the powers, authorities and obligations of the former Union were to be divided between the CIS, its three member states, and the other former republics which were not members. From the very beginning, therefore, the agreement was subject to a variety of different interpretations.

For the Ukrainians, the 'CIS was not a state formation'. Sovereignty, both over internal affairs and in international law, had passed to the newly independent states, which could themselves decide what powers to delegate or not to delegate to the CIS. The CIS was merely 'a civilised means [to ensure] the collapse of the old Union', an infinitely preferable alternative to Yugoslavia's over-precipitate dissolution into independent nation-states.[6] The CIS would also function as a necessary clearing-house for post-Soviet problems such as debt management and the control of nuclear weapons.

Russia's motives were mixed. Yeltsin's main priority was probably the removal of Gorbachev; other Russians envisaged the CIS becoming an Eastern Slav Union of the kind first proposed by Alexander Solzhenitsyn back in 1990;[7] while a third group accepted the replacement of the Soviet Union by the CIS but thought that Russia itself rather than the CIS and/or its constituent parts should inherit the sovereign rights and responsibilities of the USSR (many Russians bitterly opposed the agreement, but the political tide was not running in their favour). Belarus, despite hosting the December meeting, was in reality only a bit-player, although it hoped to gain some benefits from its proposal to house the central institutions of the CIS in Minsk rather than in Moscow.

Whatever the signatories' original vision, matters were soon complicated by the nuclear and military questions and by the expansion of the CIS from three members to eleven. In order to win international acceptance for the creation of the CIS and for its own declaration of independence, Ukraine agreed to 'preserve and maintain under united command a common military-strategic space, including control over nuclear weapons'.[8] This Ukrainian concession, however, implied that the CIS would to some degree become a supra-state structure, while at the same time leaving a huge area of mutual relations ill-defined, creating the seedbed for inevitable future arguments over what should come under the definition of 'strategic' forces (especially as Ukraine simultaneously claimed control over all ex-Soviet armed forces on its territory).

The Central Asian states, Armenia and Aberbaijan reacted angrily to their exclusion from the 8 December agreement, fearing that it would leave them marginalised politically, economically and militarily. Their protests were orchestrated by the Kazakhstan President, Nursultan Nazarbayev, who hinted that Russia would be faced with a united 'Turkestan' drifting into the Islamic orbit if the CIS were to remain a wholly Slav affair. Consequently at the Alma-Ata summit on 21 December, the CIS was expanded to include all the states of the former USSR except Georgia and the Baltic republics, although Moldova's parliament failed to ratify accession. Moreover, all the CIS's now eleven members were to be regarded as equal founders of the Commonwealth. As the possibility of an Eastern Slav Union faded into the background, however, the CIS became much less homogeneous and many of the conflict lines of the old USSR were effectively restored.

Moreover, the Alma-Ata summit further complicated matters by accepting the principle that Russia alone should succeed to the USSR's seat on the United Nations' Security Council. At the same time Russia was unilaterally taking control of former all-Union ministries and Soviet embassies abroad. Two lines of succession from the former USSR were therefore established, and it was far from clear which rights and responsibilities passed to the CIS, and which to Russia alone.

## THE DEVELOPMENT OF THE CIS

In its first year of existence the CIS was wracked by debilitating arguments, and centrifugal tendencies appeared to predominate.[9] Its very survival seemed to be in doubt. However, in 1993–4 its prospects revived as Russia recovered strength and ambition and economic and political difficulties forced several states to contemplate recentralising strategies.

In 1992 the CIS was unable to find solutions to several key problems. First and foremost was the failure to address the consequences of Russia's unilateral decision to begin radical economic reforms in January 1992, which quickly undermined the commitment in the original CIS agreement to 'defend a single economic space', 'a single currency' and to 'refrain from any economic actions which would harm other member states'. Most of the non-Russian states were more or less forced to copy Russia's price liberalisation to some degree, but at the same time sought to insulate themselves from its effect by subsidisation or by raising trade barriers of various sorts. Alongside the growing tendency towards economic particularism and nationalism, however, certain all-Union practices survived. In particular the retention of the rouble as a common currency led to monetary and fiscal chaos. As each new state now had its own central bank, all were able to print money but none were responsible for the consequences. By July 1993 Russia concluded that the collective economic indiscipline of the CIS was damaging its own drive for economic reform and effectively demanded that other states submit to Russian financial discipline or create their own currencies (Ukraine had already been forced out of the rouble zone in November 1992). Meanwhile the CIS proved itself powerless to prevent beggar-my-neighbour economic policies which fuelled the spiralling decline in intra-CIS trade and national levels of production.

The second main area of argument was the division of Soviet armed forces. In particular, Russia and Ukraine locked horns over the question of ownership of the Black Sea fleet. Proposals for joint CIS control over conventional as well as 'strategic' forces and the creation of joint CIS peacekeeping forces continued to be made throughout 1992 and 1993, but were undermined by the suspicions of the non-Russian states that they were only a cover for the restoration of a unified quasi-imperial military force under *de facto* Russian control. Unilateral Russian military action in Moldova, Georgia and Tajikistan did nothing to dispel this impression. In June 1993 the dissolution of the CIS Joint Command signalled an end to the attempt to create a genuine CIS military force.[10] The Black Sea fleet problem, however, rumbled on.

The CIS was also undermined by horizontal disputes between its members, notably Armenia and Azerbaijan (the latter formally quit the CIS in mid-1992, only to rejoin in late 1993), and by individual states seeking to develop their relations with outside third parties (the Central Asian states and Azerbaijan with Turkey, Iran and/or the Gulf states; Moldova with Romania; Ukraine with the Visegrad states). Moreover, the most important bilateral relationship, between Ukraine and Russia, grew increasingly strained through 1992. Ukraine, as the only serious potential rival to Russia, accused Russia of undermining the CIS by usurping the functions of the USSR that should have passed to the individual states and/or the CIS. As well as the USSR's seat on the UN Security Council, the former Union's debts and assets devolved to Russia, which also continued to receive the lion's share of the world's diplomatic attention, much to Ukraine's chagrin. Ukraine's nationalist lobby was demanding departure from the CIS as early as January 1992, although an equally strong opposing lobby developed in Russian-speaking areas of eastern and southern Ukraine in late 1992 and 1993 in support of closer integration with the other Slav states. As a result, the CIS's most important non-Russian member often participated only formally in CIS affairs, unable to act effectively in either direction.

Although by late 1992 the CIS appeared to be collapsing into eleven component nation-states, strong countervailing forces were also at work. While Ukraine, Moldova and Turkmenistan (the last has a relatively small Russian minority, and substantial oil and gas reserves) remained reluctant members, the hard-core states of Russia, Belarus, the rest of Central Asia and on occasion Armenia were increasingly prepared to resurrect the idea of loose confederation they had last toyed with in November 1991. Many had been reluctant to become independent states in the first place, others became increasingly aware of the rising economic and social costs that resulted from the dissolution of the USSR.

As early as May 1992 a collective security agreement was signed in Tashkent by Russia, Armenia, Kazakhstan, Kyrgyzstan, Tajikistan and Uzbekistan. The pact was stillborn, however. Armenia was in search of specific assistance in its war with Azerbaijan which was never likely to be forthcoming, while the Central Asian states, having enemies but no armed forces of their own, were simply seeking to come under Russia's security umbrella (to date, however, only Turkmenistan has signed a substantive bilateral military accord with Russia, largely as a means to avoid becoming ensnared in multilateral commitments). As the non-Russian signatories to the pact were unable to contribute much materially to collective security arrangements, the Tashkent agreement amounted to little more than an early legitimation of Russia's continued military role beyond its new borders.

In Autumn 1992 Russia took the first steps towards establishing a CIS 'Interparliamentary Assembly', ostensibly in order to coordinate the plethora of new laws emerging from the successor states, but also to float the idea of reviving a supra-national legislature. Again, however, attendance at the first session in St Petersburg was confined to the core group – Russia, the Central Asian states and Belarus. A small Ukrainian delegation was present only as 'observers'.

In January 1993 seven states (Russia, Kazakhstan, Uzbekistan, Kyrgyzstan, Tajikistan, Belarus and Armenia) signed a CIS 'Charter' which aimed to widen and deepen relations at the same time as placing them on a more definite footing. The possibility of signing some sort of Charter had first been raised at the Moscow summit in July 1992, but proposals for it to include collective security provisions, an economic court to settle trade disputes between member states and a human rights commission to cover minority affairs all came to naught. Moreover, despite intense internal argument in Ukraine, President Kravchuk refused to join up immediately. Consequently Ukraine, along with Moldova and Turkmenistan, was given a year's grace before deciding whether or not to sign (Azerbaijan only sent observers to the summit, and Georgia was not represented at all).

However, the long discussions concerning the Charter finally resulted in the initialling of an ambitious plan for 'Economic Union' in September 1993. The pact envisaged open borders between member states, the free circulation of goods, services and capital, the co-ordination of economic legislation and monetary and fiscal policies, and an eventual currency union. No arrangements were actually made for the implementation of the plan, however, which remained on the drawing board. Ukraine, as always, signed only as a potential 'associate member'.

Lastly, Russia even floated the idea of the CIS being granted some form of special status at the UN. In other words the CIS would itself become an international organisation in its own right, something more than a mere 'commonwealth' and just short of an actual state.[11]

By 1993, however, the economic strains caused by the break-up of the USSR were beginning to spread recentralising sentiments beyond the predictable core states. Only the three Baltic states were coping reasonably well with the economic consequences of independence. Other states (having already suffered severe output falls in 1989–91) registered falls in national income ranging from –11 per cent (Belarus) to –42.6 per cent (Armenia) in 1992, and –4.2 per cent (Uzbekistan) to –28.5 per cent (Armenia again) in 1993.[12] Inflation also ravaged their economies after most were compelled to follow Russia's experiment with price liberalisation in January 1992. Rates ranged from 599 per cent in Uzbekistan in 1992 to 1,110 per cent in Russia. In 1993 Ukraine topped the scale with inflation at 2,431 per cent.

In 1991–2 nationalists in every state (including Russia) had tended to argue that their own particular state was uniquely exploited by the centre and would be economically better off with independence. By 1993–4, however, most were forced to accept that the hyper-centralised nature of the old USSR economy meant that no individual successor state was likely to achieve economic self-sufficiency in the short or medium term. Each state's new-found freedom to exploit its comparative economic advantage was vastly outweighed by the near-complete breakdown in inter-republican trade, which had accounted for more than 70 per cent of GDP for more or less all republics in the Soviet era. Moreover, new European markets failed to materialise. In 1993–4, therefore, calls to put back together that which had been rent asunder became increasingly popular, although few stopped to consider whether the process would actually work in reverse.

The CIS's overarching structures also appeared to offer to the states with increasingly bitter internal ethnic disputes the possibility of the calming influence of a disinterested third party in the case of purely internal disputes (such as Georgians versus Abkhazians or Azerbaijanis versus Lezgins), or of closer connections with the motherland in the case of aggrieved diasporas (such as Russians in Ukraine or Uzbeks in Tajikistan). In some cases (Georgia) the very survival of the state seemed to be threatened by such conflicts; in others it was deemed preferable to settle disputes through some sort of multinational forum, rather than allowing minorities to appeal directly to their patron states.

Throughout the former Union public opinion began to swing back towards the idea of renewing ties with other former republics, Russia in particular. In some regions the main impetus towards this 'backlash effect' was ethnic and political; in others economic pragmatism predominated. Lithuania, ironically given its prominent role in the events leading up to the dissolution of the Union (see chapter nine), set the trend. The victory of the renamed and revamped Communist Party in legislative elections in Autumn 1992 was quickly followed by former party leader Algirdas Brazauskas' triumph in presidential elections in February 1993 (replacing Vytautas Landsbergis, the hero of January 1991). In Transcaucasia, two stalwarts of the 1980s USSR Politburo returned to power. Eduard Shevardnadze returned as Georgian leader in March 1992 and a military coup in Azerbaijan in June 1993 replaced the Popular Front leader Abulfaz Elchibei with Geidar Aliev, bringing both countries closer into the Russian orbit.

In Moldova the Agrarian Democrats and Socialists swept back to power in the February 1994 parliamentary elections, while in both Ukraine and Belarus presidential elections in July 1994 were won by Russophile candidates. In Ukraine the more nationalist incumbent, Leonid Kravchuk, was narrowly defeated by Leonid Kuchma, his former Prime Minister, in an ethnically and regionally polarised election. In Belarus, on the other hand, a populist deputy and anti-corruption campaigner, Alexander Lukashenko, won a landslide victory on an unambiguously pro-Russian platform.

Events in Russia were of crucial importance, however. Since 1989–90 Russian politics has revolved around the split between 'nation builders' who wish to disentangle Russia from the legacy of the USSR and build a nation-state in the boundaries of the Russian Federation, and 'empire savers' who would seek to resurrect the USSR in some form or other.[13] Although the former group gained the ascendancy in late 1991 and early 1992 with the collapse of the Union and the banning of the Communist Party, the revival of neo-imperial sentiment right across the Russian political spectrum from late 1992 onwards was dramatic. Growing economic difficulties and a marked decline in Russia's Great Power status increased nostalgia for the USSR, while concern for the status of Russians in the 'near abroad' and a straightforward reluctance to accept the legitimacy of many of the successor states (particularly Ukraine, Belarus and Kazakhstan) led to a growing consensus in favour of Russia exercising a stronger role in the rest of the former Union. The depth and breadth of this consensus was demonstrated by the failure of the October 1993 events and December 1993 elections to alter political sentiment in the Russian parliament, other than by shifting it further to the right. The departure of Yegor Gaidar, the foremost representative of the 'nation builders', and his supporters from government in early 1994 merely capped the process.

Whereas in 1992 the CIS seemed more likely to lose than to gain members, in 1993 the reverse was true. Ukraine remained in the fold, and in late 1993 Georgia reluctantly signed up for membership, Azerbaijan rejoined and the Moldovan parliament failed by only four votes to ratify full membership in the Commonwealth. In early 1994, therefore, the CIS embraced all of the former USSR except the three Baltic states.

Voices calling for recentralisation undoubtedly grew stronger throughout the former USSR in 1993–4, although the trend was uneven. However, practical implementation of plans for economic and especially political recentralisation proved extremely difficult. The future prospects of the CIS therefore remain profoundly uncertain.


## THE FUTURE GEOPOLITICS OF THE CIS

The following models are all possible, though the list is by no means exhaustive. First, the nation-state may triumph and the CIS wither on the vine. Second, recentralisation and possible refederation may restore some facisimile of the USSR, or certain parts thereof. Third, recentralisation may stop short of political (re)union and create a 'common economic space' instead. In both the second and third cases, however, growing reintegration may lead to the CIS becoming a Trojan Horse for restored Russian hegemony in the Eurasian region. Lastly, perhaps in reaction to growing Russian predominance, the CIS may splinter into regional blocks, with attempts at economic and/or political reintegration being made at a local level.

A necessary condition for the fulfilment of the first scenario is that the former republics possess or develop the key material, ideological and institutional resources to sustain their existence as independent nation-states.[14] The Baltic states, never members of the CIS, seem best placed to succeed on all three counts. On the other hand, several smaller states with an equally strong sense of national identity, such as Georgia and Armenia, are devastated by war and economic collapse, while larger states with potentially a more substantial economic base, such as Ukraine and Kazakhstan, have suffered more than proportionately from the collapse of the old all-Union economy. Both are also essentially deeply divided bi-ethnic states. Belarus and Tajikistan do not possess a strong enough national identity to underpin the attempt to go it alone, while the majority of Central Asian states are inhibited by imbalanced economic development and a lack of military self-sufficiency (although Turkmenistan, Kazakhstan and to a lesser extent Uzbekistan have considerable potential to exploit their mineral and energy resources). The ouster of Stanislau Shushkevich as chairman of the Belarusian parliament in January 1994 effectively signalled Belarus's abandonment of a separate path of development. In Moldova voices calling for a reunion with Romania have been stilled by the rebellion of the country's large Slav minority, concentrated on the left bank of the river Dniester.

Russia itself, however, may be the most problematical would-be nation-state. Before and indeed after 1991 many Russians failed to distinguish between ethnic and imperial Russia (between *Rus* and *Rossiia*). For many Russians, 'Russia' and the USSR were one and the same. Both Romanov Russia and then the USSR were created by contiguous land settlement, and therefore to many Russians neither seemed like an empire. The shrunken borders of the post-1991 Russian Federation, which west of the Urals more or less represent a return to the boundaries of Russia before Peter the Great, are alien and incomprehensible to many Russians. Moreover, the presence of over 25 million Russians in the new states, often in neighbouring territories such as Narva in north-east Estonia, the Donbas in eastern Ukraine and northern Kazakhstan,[15] plus the fact that many Russians cannot conceive of Belarus and Ukraine as 'real' states with separate histories and identities to those of Russia proper, means that many Russians are neither reconciled to their own status as the Russian Federation nor able to accept the legitimacy of key states such as Kazakhstan or Ukraine, at least in their present borders.

A key barrier to political and/or economic reintegration is therefore distrust of the reviving predominance of Russia. A new Union would not necessarily be a union of equals. Other factors working against political reintegration include international pressure (although after the experience of Yugoslavia it is doubtful how far the West would actually intervene to curtail Russian ambition), and the difficulties of constructing *democratic* refederation strategies. A new federation would have to have greater democratic legitimacy than its constituent parts, but the growing diversity of interests in the former USSR makes it impossible to imagine how either efficient representation or effective government could emerge from new trans-national elections (the 1989 all-Union elections largely came before the arrival of true mass politics). Authoritarian refederation strategies would also find it difficult to meld widely divergent interests and produce the economic recovery or revival of international prestige on which the legitimacy of such a regime would undoubtedly depend. Moreover, the largely ex-communist élites that have inherited the leadership of the new non-Russian states have growing incentives to maintain their own political backyard, with all the associated benefits connected with maintaining separate institutions, local resource control, and international recognition.[16] The communist successor parties restored to power in Lithuania and Moldova, for example, are now strongly committed to national independence, although the same could not be said of the Communist Party of Ukraine.

Economic reintegration is also fraught with difficulty. Proposals to restore a common currency in 1993–4, if only in Belarus and Central Asia, foundered on Russia's fears of the inflationary consequences of such a move. Proposals for a CIS 'Economic Union', much discussed in 1993, have yet to produce any substantial result, as converting widespread nostalgia for the integrated command economy of the Soviet era into mutually beneficial economic exchange in an era when market relations are rapidly replacing the administrative transfer of goods and services is likely to prove exceptionally difficult.[17] Moreover, the Russian leadership itself was split over whether economics (domestic fiscal and monetary stability) should take priority over politics (the restoration of links with the rest of the CIS).

A restored 'common economic space' would be more likely to succeed if it were based on genuine market exchange. Otherwise, it is likely to be bedevilled by accusations that it will mean the restoration of directed exchange between the new states and the return of political control from Moscow, and that the non-Russian states will be locked into patterns of economic dependency on Russia. Many non-Russian nationalists see plans for economic reintegration as a simple cover for restored Russian imperial ambition, and would prefer to develop alternative ties among themselves and/or with neighbouring states, although such efforts have brought little success to date.

The fourth possibility, growing Russian dominance within the CIS, has already been discussed. Bilateral relations are likely to become more asymmetric, with Russia increasingly able to impose its political and economic priorities on the other successor states, but full-scale reintegration is unlikely. However, the sheer weight of Russian economic and political preponderance, Russian control of raw materials and energy supply, and the legacy of Moscow-based hypercentralisation from the days of the USSR make the last possibility, the formation of alternative regional groupings, also unlikely. For nearly all the successor states bilateral relations with Russia remain more important than multilateral ties or horizontal links with one another. For all, save perhaps the Baltic states, Russian trade and favour is the key to economic revival or plain survival.

Nevertheless, plans for closer links between the Central Asian states to help ease the region away from the Russian orbit were discussed in June 1990, April 1992 and January 1993, but produced little result until Kazakhstan, Uzbekistan and Kyrgyzstan agreed to form a 'common economic space' in January 1994.[18] The three Baltic states formed a 'Baltic Council' as early as 1992 and have discussed plans for deepening economic and military cooperation. Ukrainian radicals have floated the idea of an anti-Russian 'Baltic–Black Sea Alliance', encompassing the

Baltic states, Belarus, Ukraine, Moldova and possibly Transcaucasian and neighbouring Central European states. Cooperation between the states surrounding the Black Sea is well advanced, and has already led to the formation of a Black Sea Assembly and regional development bank. However, all such schemes are at an early stage. None has sufficient countervailing attraction to justify quitting the CIS.

## POSSIBILITIES FOR FUTURE DEVELOPMENTS IN THE SUCCESSOR STATES

After 1991, the fifteen 'titular nationalities' of the former republics of the USSR achieved nominal independence. As well as working out relations among themselves, however, the fifteen now have to put into practice models for their own political and social development and for relations with their ethnic minorities. Several paths of development are possible.[19]

The first is for the fifteen to follow the model of the classical nation-state, consolidated around an ethnic core, including all the trappings of a national bureaucracy, economy and armed forces, an education system in the language of the titular nationality, and so on. However, the successor states, like the USSR before them, are far from homogeneous ethnically. Moreover, the development of loyalties to the new successor states is likely to be undermined by the fact that 'the Soviet regime institutionalised both territorial–political and personal–ethno-cultural models of nationhood as well as the tensions between them.[20] In other words, titular nationalities were collectively enshrined in their own geographically-defined union-republics or autonomous republics, but at the same time 'the nationality of persons did not depend on place of residence'.[21] Individuals were allocated a 'passport nationality' according to immutable cultural or ethnicist principles. Moreover, children nearly always received the passport nationality of their father.

Ethnic or national loyalties are therefore of a dual nature, both to territorial communities and to trans-national (or sub-national) ethnic groups. The two rarely coincide. Therefore the potential for conflict both within and across new state borders is enormous, as the new territorial polities clash with cross-cutting ethnic loyalties.

Most of the successor states have problems with substantial ethnic minorities (Gagauz in Moldova, Lezgins in Azerbaijan, Poles in Lithuania). Many minorities are also diasporas and/or potential *irredentas*. The 25.3 million Russians who live outside the Russian Federation (but in the former USSR) have received most attention, but there are also 6.8 million Ukrainians living outside Ukraine and 2.6 million Uzbeks outside of Uzbekistan. In many cases territorial contiguity leads to demands for reunion with the ethnic core, as with Russians in northern Kazakhstan, South Ossetians in Georgia seeking unity with North Ossetia in Russia, or even (implausibly) ethnic Ukrainians in the Kuban region of the north Caucasus.

Moreover, in many parts of the former USSR the mismatch between political and ethnographic boundaries was increased by Stalin's policies of ethnic gerrymandering and mass deportations. Crimea was never really an integral historical part of Ukraine until its transfer (by Khrushchev) from the Russian republic to the Ukrainian SSR in 1954. On the other hand, the left bank of the Dniester in what is now Moldova was an integral part of the (Slav) Ukrainian SSR until 1940. Nagorno-Karabakh was first a part of Armenia before being transfered to Azerbaijan in 1924, when both were part of the Transcaucasian federation. The return of deported peoples to their historical homelands also creates problems. Even if every one of an estimated 400,000 to 500,000 Crimean Tatars returned to Crimea they would still form only 20 per cent of the local population, too small a number to enforce their demands for sovereignty over the whole peninsula, but too many to be effectively assimilated. The Ingush people deported in 1944 began returning home to the north Caucasus after 1957 to find that their homes had been settled by Ossetians and the borders of their republic arbitrarily changed. Two million Soviet Germans are still denied any form of territorial or other representation as a result of their deportation during the Second World War.

According to some accounts, therefore, the successor states are likely to be plagued by continuing unrest at the sub-national level; a phenomenon described as 'matrioshka nationalism'.[22] According to others, such protests may remain muted because non-titular nationalities lack the institutional resources to underpin their protests.[23] Moreover, in comparison to the titular nationalities whose languages and cultures were to an extent protected by the institutions of the federal system (national parliaments, academies of sciences, at least some native language schooling), the new national minorities tend to have lower levels of national consciousness and to be Russified to a much greater degree, although this makes it easier for them to make common cause with Russia now that it once again seems to be asserting its neo-imperial ambitions.

Other factors likely to influence the level of ethnic conflict in the successor states include the very process of democratisation itself (elections can exacerbate ethnic conflicts as well as help to contain them),[24] the institutional forms chosen for the regulation and management of conflict (parliamentary or presidential government, the type of electoral law chosen, the amount of power ceded to sub-national units),[25] the extent of freedom of action granted to opposition groups, and the socio-economic situation (each state's absolute performance, its position in comparison to neighbouring states, and the relative economic performance of given ethnic groups). When patterns of uneven development are overlaid by a strong sense of cultural difference, economic grievances may help to fuel ethno-nationalism, conceivably among relatively advanced groups who feel other groups are holding them back (such as Estonians with respect to their Russian minority), among relatively backward groups who feel exploited by other groups (such as Central Asians in their attitude to Russia), or among relatively equal groups in competition for limited resources (as with Meshketians in Uzbekistan or, potentially, Russians and Ukrainians in Ukraine).[26] Moreover, the relative weakness of religious and class cleavages in many of the states of the former USSR (Armenia and Azerbaijan notwithstanding) is also likely to increase the salience of ethnic divisions.[27]

As few if any of the successor states are likely to proceed swiftly and smoothly towards the building of effective nation-states, it is useful to follow one taxonomy of eight possible forms for the development of relations between titular nationalities and minorities, namely:

1   genocide

2   forced mass population transfers

3   partition and/or secession (self-determination)

4   integration and/or assimilation

5   hegemonic control

6   arbitration (third-party intervention)

7   cantonisation and/or federalisation

8   consociationalism or power-sharing.

The first four are methods for eliminating differences between ethnic groups, in the first two cases violently, in the next two possibly by agreement (although population transfers can also occur voluntarily). The last four, on the other hand, are means of managing or learning to live with ethnic differences. Only (5) and possibly (6) are likely to involve coercion.[28]

To date, ethnic antagonisms in the former USSR have not yet erupted in full-scale genocide, in the sense of the attempted wholesale destruction of one ethnic group by another, if only because of lack of opportunity in particular instances. However, on a smaller scale pogroms against ethnic groups have been widespread, such as the massacre of ethnic Armenians in Sumgait in 1988 and the large-scale slaughter in Osh between Kyrgyzs and Uzbeks in 1990. Forced population transfers, such as the departure of Georgians from Abkhazia in 1993, have also been common, as have relatively voluntary preemptive departures, including the large numbers of Russians who have left Kyrgyzstan and Tajikistan in the early 1990s.

Partition and/or secession struggles have also multiplied since 1991. In several areas, such as the breakaway would-be 'Dniester Republic' in Moldova, or Abkhazia and South Ossetia in Georgia, full-scale civil war has resulted. By 1993 Armenian force of arms had effectively cut off Nagorno-Karabakh from the rest of Azerbaijan. In other cases, such as north-east Estonia or the Ukrainian Donbas, conflict for the moment remains confined to a political level, although the election of the avowed separatist Yurii Meshkov as Crimean President in January 1994 seemed likely to result in the creation of yet another regional hot-spot.

Integration and/or assimilation can be either voluntary or enforced. In the latter case it is unlikely to be successful with groups that have already reached a sufficient degree of collective self-consciousness (in the USSR the groups most vulnerable to assimilation were the smaller Siberian nationalities in the Russian SFSR). Voluntary assimilation, on the other hand, may be the key to the survival of many of the new states. The economic performance and international prestige of the new states is likely to be a crucial factor in encouraging or discouraging assimilation. Immigrants to Catalonia, even those from Castile, have been prepared to learn the Catalan language and accommodate themselves to Catalan culture, as this is perceived as a necessary means to self-advancement. Russians in Ukraine or Kazakhs in Uzbekistan are much more likely to learn the local language and participate in local politics if they similarly feel that it is in their material interest to do so.[29] Poor economic performance in most of the successor states, however, has so far reduced incentives for minorities to assimilate.

Unfortunately, hegemonic control, or the simple denial by one ethnic group of political and social rights to others, is also a common form of ethnic conflict regulation. The Baltic states, Estonia and Latvia in particular, have been accused by Russia of attempting to turn themselves into 'ethnic democracies' or even '*Herrenvolk* democracies' by denying citizenship, and therefore political rights, to their substantial Russian minorities. (An 'ethnic democracy', such as (arguably) Israel, formally guarantees certain key civil and political rights to all regardless of ethnic origin, but is nevertheless marked by the 'institutional dominance over the state of one of [its] ethnic groups'; a '*Herrenvolk* democracy' on the other hand, such as South Africa under apartheid, simply denies any democratic rights at all to the subordinate group.)[30] Latvia has adopted a highly restrictive citizenship law, *de facto* based on narrowly ethnic criteria, although the Estonian law is more liberal. Both states insist that those who cannot prove descent from citizens of the inter-war republics (i.e. most Russians) must pass stringent residence and language proficiency requirements to gain citizenship, and Latvia sets a tight quota for annual admissions.[31]

It should be pointed out, however, that most of the successor states have to date maintained a territorial approach to questions of citizenship and civil and political rights (in other words citizenship is available to all inhabitants of a given state rather than just members of the titular nationality). Most new states are acutely conscious of the need to reconcile ethnic minorities to the new realities of independent statehood. Kazakhstan and Ukraine have adopted liberal citizenship laws embracing all those resident within the republic's borders at the time of independence. Turkmenistan has adopted a law allowing dual citizenship with Russia. Both Kazakhstan and Ukraine have also largely refrained from imposing their native languages in state institutions and the educational system, although Ukraine's nationalist minority continues to press for the adoption of 'Ukrainianisation' policies.

On the other hand, other analysts would argue that there will be a long-term tendency for titular nationality élites to seek to nativise 'their' new states, 'because of the institutionalised expectations of "ownership" that the successor states inherited from the Soviet nationality regime',[32] and as a means of protecting themselves from outsider competition. Titular nationality ruling élites may find the exploitation of narrowly ethnic myths and symbols and grievances the best, or the only, means of shoring up their political legitimacy. Paradoxically, poor economic performance may make this even more necessary. Instead of the paradigmatic extremes of a narrow ethnic nationalism (Latvia) or a generous and open territorial conception (Kazakhstan), many states may therefore end up closer to 'ethnic-led territorialism'.[33] In other words, ethnic minorities will be tolerated, and their language and culture allowed free expression, but only on the understanding that the state and its institutions are the preserve of the dominant titular nationality. Lithuania with respect to its Poles, and Moldova in its relations with its Slav minority, could initially be considered examples of such states.

Arbitration or third-party intervention in ethnic conflicts has also been increasingly common, especially if one bears in mind that the arbiter can easily be self-appointed. European and/or global security agencies, their fingers burned in the former Yugoslavia, have largely steered clear of involvement in the former USSR. Therefore, after a period of introspection in 1992–3 in the immediate aftermath of the break-up of the USSR, the stage has been clear for Russia to become increasingly self-assertive, intervening in a variety of ethnic conflicts on its periphery. Russian troops policed the 1992 Moldovan–Dniestran cease-fire, and were instrumental in settling the Georgian–Abkhazian conflict in 1993. Few other real potential third parties, or regional hegemonic powers, exist. Ukraine may aspire to leadership in the former Soviet west, and Kazakhstan and Uzbekistan vie for supremacy in Central Asia (many Uzbek nationalists argue that the whole of Central Asia south of Kazakhstan, in other words the region of 'Turkestan' under the Romanovs, is their natural patrimony), but in practice such ambitions have taken second place to the developing *Pax Russica*.[34] Ukraine has been unable or unwilling to intervene in Moldova, despite the left bank of the Dniester being contiguous to Ukraine rather than to Russia. Uzbekistan, despite the presence of some 1.2 million of its co-nationals in war-torn Tajikistan, has also had to cede the role of regional peacekeeper to Russia.

Cantonisation and/or federalisation is a possible option to help forestall or contain the development of separatist movements. Dagestan has devised an elaborate scheme for sharing power between its various ethnic groups, none of which are close to a numerical majority. By 1993 Georgia was forced to concede considerable autonomy to both Abkhazia and South Ossetia. In Ukraine various groups, from Russians in the Donbas to Ruthenians in Transcarpathia, have demanded some form of local autonomy. Russia itself, however, is the best example of an ethnic federation among the successor states. The new Russian constitution approved by referendum in December 1993 in some respects resembled that of the old USSR, with Tatarstan, Bashkortostan and the other ethno-regions now playing the role of the former Union Republics. However, the new system was complex and asymmetrical. Ordinary Russian oblasts, or even Moscow and St Petersburg, did not enjoy the same rights as the ethnic republics. Moreover, the exact division of powers between Moscow and the ethnic republics was in constant flux, with the ebb of power from the centre to the regions at least temporarily reversed after the October 1993 events.

Titular nationality élites throughout the former USSR have expressed the fear that federal systems are likely to encourage rather than contain separatism, and lead to the 'Bantustanisation' of their states and cross-border appeals to *irridentas*. Often, therefore, the successor states, mindful of how they themselves undermined the USSR in the late 1980s, have moved in the opposite direction. Lithuania abolished a measure of Polish self-rule in the wake of the 1991 coup attempt, accusing local Polish leaders of supporting the junta. Ukraine has consistently refused to deliver on promises of autonomy for Transcarpathia and the Donbas, although the pressure to create a federal state may grow after Leonid Kuchma's victory in the 1994 presidential elections.

The final, related, possibility is to develop some form of consociational system. Classical cases of consociationalism involve elaborate constitutional schemes for sharing power in deeply divided societies, such as community autonomy, mutual vetoes, grand coalition governments of national accord, and a proportional division of government and bureaucratic posts (and often state expenditure) between groups. Consociational arrangements in individual Soviet successor states need not necessarily follow such formulae exactly, but several have designed arrangements in keeping with a consociational spirit. After the 1992 war the Moldovan authorities and the rebels on the left bank of the Dniester began to edge towards a *de facto* consociational accord according to the formula 'two societies in one state', especially after the 1994 Moldovan elections resulted in victory for the relatively moderate Agrarian Party. In Tajikistan a short-lived government of national accord which embraced the Islamic opposition was formed in an unsuccessful attempt to avert civil war in 1992, while the 1992 Russian Federal Treaty granted considerable *de facto* autonomy to the Autonomous Republics.

Other states have adopted different strategies, short of outright consociationalism, to promote what might be termed 'ethnic accommodation'. The Crimean Tatars, who claim sovereignty over the whole Crimean peninsula, proposed a fully-fledged consociational scheme involving a dual presidency and bicameral parliament (with the Crimean Tatars controlling the vice-presidency and upper house), but in the end had to be satisfied with a special quota of 14 out of 98 seats in the Crimean Supreme Soviet elected in March–April 1994. In Tatarstan meanwhile, ethnic Tatars, despite making up only 48 per cent of the local population, were granted close to full autonomy over domestic affairs by Russia in 1994.

In Kazakhstan President Nazarbayev has tried to bargain for ethnic peace by promising the large Russian (and other Slav) minority a combination of cultural autonomy and equal citizenship and voting rights. In other words, unlike in an 'ethnic-led territorialism', members of the ethnic minority are allowed to participate in affairs of state, but, unlike in a formal consociational agreement, are not granted formal collective rights. Ukraine has followed a similar strategy. Since independence in 1991 (and arguably before), Ukrainian administrations have been delicate coalitions of Ukrainian-speaking nationalists from the west and centre of Ukraine with Russian-speakers from the industrial east and the south, although the balance is never explicitly codified. While the west and centre were dominant in 1992 and early 1993, the balance of power titled strongly back towards the east in 1993–4.

## CONCLUSIONS

No single formula or theoretical hypothesis can capture the full complexity of developments in nationality politics in the Soviet successor states. Although centrifugal trends amid the euphoria of the early post-independence period were clearly reversed by 1993–4, as the practical consequences of economic disruption sank in and Russia recovered its historical hegemonic role in the Eurasian region, it should not be assumed that there is now a simple unilinear trend towards reintegration. Each of the successor states will continue to have to grapple with its own peculiar conditions. The dissolution of apparent uniformity that began with the collapse of the USSR still has a long way to go.

## NOTES

1. Georgia and Lithuania regarded their independence as already established; Estonia, Latvia, Ukraine, Moldova, Azerbaijan, Belarus, Uzbekistan, Kyrgyzstan, Tajikistan and Armenia declared independence by the end of September 1991, followed by Turkmenistan on 27 October and finally Kazakhstan on 16 December. Only Russia made no formal declaration.
2. Mark R. Beissinger 'The Deconstruction of the USSR and the Search for a Post-Soviet Community' *Problems of Communism* vol. XL, no. 6 (November–December 1991), pp. 27–35.
3. On the transition period between August 1991 and the establishment of the CIS, see John B. Dunlop *The Rise of Russia and the Fall of the Soviet Empire* (Princeton: Princeton University Press 1993), chapter 6.
4. Ann Sheehy 'Commonwealth Emerges from a Disintegrating USSR' *RFE/RL Research Report* vol. 1, no. 1, 3 January 1992.
5. The text of the agreement can be found, *inter alia*, in *Holos Ukrainy* 10 December 1991.
6. *Za vilnu Ukrainu* 12 December 1991.
7. On Solzhenitsyn's proposals, see Alexander Solzhenitsyn, *Rebuilding Russia: Reflections and Tentative Proposals* (London: Harvill, 1991), and the commentary in *Report on the USSR* vol. 2, no. 40, 5 October 1990.
8. As note 5 above.
9. See the *RFE/RL Research Report* special edition on 'The CIS and the Republics' vol. 1, no. 7, 14 February 1992; Ann Sheehy, 'The CIS: A Progress Report', and 'The CIS: A Shaky Edifice' *RFE/RL Research Report* vol. 1, no. 38, 25 September 1992 and vol. 2, no. 1, 1 January 1993 respectively; and Andrei Zagorsky, 'The Commonwealth: One Year On' *International Affairs* (Moscow), no. 2, February 1993.
10. Stephen Foye 'End of CIS Command Heralds New Russian Foreign Policy?' *RFE/RL Research Report* vol. 2, no. 27, 2 July 1993.
11. Suzanne Crow 'Russia Promotes the CIS as an International Organisation' *RFE/RL Research Report* vol. 3, no. 11, 18 march 1994.
12. Eric Whitlock, 'The CIS Economies: Divergent and Troubled Paths' *RFE/RL Research Report* vol. 3, no. 1, 7 January 1994. The Turkmenistan economy actually grew 5% in 1993. See also Economist Intelligence Unit *Country Reports* and *Country Profiles, passim*.
13. Roman Szporluk 'Dilemmas of Russian Nationalism' *Problems of Communism* vol. 30, no. 4 (July–August 1989), pp. 15–35.
14. On economic resources, see Gertrude Schroeder, 'On the Economic Viability of New Nation-States' *Journal of International Affairs* vol. 45, no. 2 (1992), pp. 549–74.
15. It is often political pressure from 'colonists' rather than neo-imperial ambition at the (former) imperial centre that prevents the establishment of normal relations between states. See Ian Lustick, *State-Building Failures*

*in British Ireland and French Algeria* (Berkeley: Institute of International Studies, 1985), which makes similar points about colonists obstructing the integration of colonised regions into new would-be nation-states.

16. For the importance of such élites in winning and maintaining independence, see Valerii Tishkov, 'Inventions and Manifestations of Ethno-Nationalism in and after the Soviet Union' in Kumar Rupesinghe, Peter G. King and Olga Vorkunova (eds) *Ethnicity and Conflict in a Post-Communist World: The Soviet Union, Eastern Europe and China* (London: Macmillan, 1992), pp. 41–64; and Mark R. Beissinger, 'Elites and Ethnic Identities in Soviet and Post-Soviet Politics', in Alexander J. Motyl (ed.) *The Post-Soviet Nations: Perspectives on the Demise of the USSR* (New York: Columbia University Press, 1992), pp. 141–69.

17. Erik Whitlock, 'Obstacles to CIS Economic Integration', and 'The Return of the Ruble' *RFE/RL Research Report* vol. 2, nos 27 and 35, 2 July and 3 September 1993.

18. Bess Brown, 'Three Central Asian States Form Economic Union' *RFE/RL Research Report* vol. 3, no. 13, 1 April 1994. The accord envisaged the free circulation of goods, capital and labour, and common policies on credit, prices, taxes and foreign exchange. All border posts between the three states were reported dismantled in early 1994.

19. See the following general surveys of nationality politics after 1991: Alexander J. Motyl (ed.) *The Post-Soviet Nations: Perspectives on the Demise of the USSR* and *Thinking Theoretically About Soviet Nationalities* (both New York: Columbia University Press, 1992); Robert Levgold and Timothy Colton (eds) *After the Soviet Union: From Empire to Nations* (New York: W. W. Norton, 1992), especially chapter 3 by Roman Szporluk; Kumar Rupesinghe, Peter King and Olga Vorkunova (eds) *Ethnicity and Conflict in a Post-Communist World: The Soviet Union, Eastern Europe and China* (London: Macmillan, 1992); Richard L. Rudolph and David F. Good, (eds) *Nationalism and Empire: The Hapsburg Monarchy and the Soviet Union* (New York: St. Martin's Press, 1992); Teresa Rakowska-Harmstone, 'Chickens Coming Home To Roost: A Perspective on Soviet Ethnic Relations' *Journal of International Affairs* vol. 45, no. 2 (winter 1992), pp. 519–48; Ian Bremmer and Ray Taras (eds) *Nations and Politics in the Soviet Successor States* (Cambridge: Cambridge University Press, 1993); M. Rywkin, Moscow's Lost Empire, (Armonk, NY: M.E. Sharpe, 1994); Dominic Lieven and John McGarry 'Ethnic conflict in the Soviet Union and its successor states' in John McGarry and Brendan O'Leary (eds) *The Politics of Ethnic Conflict Regulation: Case Studies of Protracted Ethnic Conflicts* (London: Routledge, 1993). A special issue of *Nationality Papers* (vol. XX, no. 2, fall 1992) is devoted to 'The Ex-Soviet Nationalities Without Gorbachev'. Nadia Dink and Adrian Karatnycky *New Nations Rising: The Fall of the Soviet Empire and the Challenge of Independence* (New York: John Wiley and Sons, 1993) is a straightforward study. Ronald Grigor Sumy *The Revenge of the Past. Nationalism, Revolution and the Collapse of the Soviet Union* (Stanford: Stanford University Press, 1993) is largely historical. The best general survey to date is Karen Dawisha and Bruce Parrott *Russia and the New States of Eurasia: The Politics of Upheaval* (Cambridge: Cambridge University Press, 1994).

20. Rogers Brubaker 'Nationhood and the national question in the Soviet

Union and post-Soviet Eurasia: An institutionalist account' *Theory and Society* vol. 23, no. 1, 1994, pp. 47–78, at p. 65.

21. Ibid., p. 55.
22. Ian Bremmer, 'Reassessing Soviet Nationalities Theory' in Bremmer and Taras (1993, op. cit.), pp. 3–28, especially p. 22.
23. Brubaker (1994, op. cit.), p. 62.
24. Renée de Nevers, 'Democratization and Ethnic Conflict' *Survival* vol. 35, no. 2 (summer 1993), pp. 31–48.
25. On the impact of electoral systems, see James McGregor, 'How Electoral Laws Shape Eastern Europe's Parliaments' *RFE/RL Research Report* vol. 2, no. 4, 22 January 1993. On the impact of the institutional architecture (such as the difference between presidential and parliamentary systems) in the new states on ethnic politics, see Thomas F. Remington's Introduction and Conclusion in Remington (ed.) *Parliaments in Transition: The New Legislative Politics in the Former USSR and Eastern Europe* (Boulder: Westview Press, 1994), pp. 1–28 and 217–32.
26. Timothy M. Frye 'Ethnicity, Sovereignty and Transitions from Non-Democratic Rule' *Journal of International Affairs* vol. 45, no. 2 (winter 1992), pp. 599–623, at pp. 611–2.
27. Ibid., pp. 603–6.
28. John McGarry and Brendan O'Leary, 'Introduction: the macro-political regulation of ethnic conflict' in McGarry and O'Leary (1993, op. cit.), pp. 1–40, at p. 4.
29. David D. Laitin, Roger Peterson and John W. Slocum, 'Language and the State: Russia and the Soviet Union in Comparative Perspective' in Alexander J. Motyl (ed.) *Thinking Theoretically About Soviet Nationalities* (1992, op. cit.), pp. 129–68; and David D. Laitin, 'The National Uprisings in the Soviet Union' *World Politics* vol. 44 (October 1991), pp. 139–77.
30. Sammy Smooha, 'Minority status in an ethnic democracy: The status of the Arab minority in Israel' *Ethnic and Racial Studies* vol. 13, no. 3 (July 1990), pp. 389–413, at p. 391 and p. 411. See also S. Smooha and T. Hanf 'The Diverse Modes of Conflict Regulation in Deeply Divided Societies' in Anthony D. Smith *Ethnicity and Nationalism* (Leiden: E.J. Brill, 1992), pp. 26–47.
31. See Graham Smith, Aadne Aasland and Richard Mole 'Statehood, Ethnic Relations and Citizenship' in Graham Smith (ed.) *The Baltic States. The National Self-Determination of Estonia, Latvia and Lithuania* (London: Macmillan, 1994), pp. 181–205, especially pp. 188–92; Rogers Brubaker 'Citizenship Struggles in Soviet Successor States' *International Migration Review* vol. 26, no. 2 (1992), pp. 269–290; and Dzintra Bungs, Saulius Girnius and Riine Kionke, 'Citizenship Legislation in the Baltic States' *RFE/RL Research Report* vol. 1, no. 50. 18 December 1992.
32. Brubaker (1994, op. cit.), p. 66.
33. Anthony Smith, *Nationalist Movements* (London: Macmillan, 1976), p. 5.
34. Mark Smith, *Pax Russica: Russia's Monroe Doctrine* (London: Royal United Services Institute for Defence Studies, 1993); Suzanne Crow, 'Russia Seeks Leadership in Regional Peacekeeping' *RFE/RL Research Report* vol. 2, no. 15, 9 April 1993.

# PART II

# The Russian Federation

While the creation of the Russian state in 1991 signalled a victory for state-building over empire-saving, for many Russians it did not fully resolve their relationship to where or what is Russia (see Fig. 2). Having occupied a special place within both the Russian Empire and the Soviet Union, the Russian sense of 'national self' has had difficulty in coming to terms with the loss of empire or with living within a polity based on a multiethnic federation of nations, in which most of the new state's one fifth non-Russians have been granted substantial political, economic and cultural autonomy. As chapter three shows, it is this complexity of post-coloniality and the extent to which Russians can come to terms with their new position and status that is central to understanding post-Soviet Russia.

Although non-Russians make-up a substantial minority, only four of the thirty-three federally-recognised nations number more than one million (Tatars, Chuvash, Bashkirs and Mordovians), with the Tatars being by far the largest (5.5 million). In many of these administrative homelands, the proportion of Russians is significant, making them an overall ethnic majority in the Adygeya, Buryat, Giornyi-Atai, Karelian, Khakassian, Mari, Mordovian, Udmurt and Sakha (Yakut) Autonomous Republics, as well as in some of the more minor Autonomous Territories. Although many non-Russian ethno-regional groups played a part in nationalist politics during the last few years of Soviet rule, it is only since the establishment of the Russian state that nationalism has emerged to become a powerful political force. This has been the case in the Muslim republics of Tartastan, Bashkortostan and the North Caucasus. The lengths to which Moscow is prepared to go in order to prevent the country's fragmentation was demonstrated in December 1994 when Chechnya, the only remaining republic not to sign a federal treaty with Moscow, was forcibly brought back into the federal union. Such secessionist nationalism contrasts with Sakha (Yakutia) and Buryatia whose peoples, although beginning to engage in a nation-building process designed to reverse decades of cultural Russification and economic neglect, have confined their state-building to an acceptance of membership of the Russian Federation.

Figure 2 : **THE RUSSIAN FEDERATION**

Chukchi
Koryak
kamchatka
Magadan
KHABAROVSK
Sakhalin
PRIMORSKY
Jewish Autonomous Oblast
Amur
SAKHA (YAKUTIA)
Chita
Agay Buryatia
BURYATIA
Irkutsk
Ust Orda Buryatia
TUVA
ALTAI
Taymyr
Evenk
KRASNOYARSK
Khakassia
Kemerovo
ALTAI
Novosibirsk
Tomsk
Yamal Nenets
Khanty-Mansi
Omsk
Tyumen
Kurgan
Nenets
Sverdlovsk
Chelyabinsk
KOMI
Komi-Permyak
Perm
Murmansk
Arkhangelsk
KARELIA
St. Petersburg
Pskov
Vologda
Kirov
UDMURT
MARI-EL
CHUVASH
TATARSTAN
BASHKORTOSTAN
Orenburg
Novgorod
Tver
Yaroslavl
Ivanovo
Kostroma
Nizhni Novgorod
Smolensk
Mos-cow
Kaluga
Vladimir
Ryazan
Penza
Ulyanovsk
Samara
Bryansk
Orel
Tula
Kursk
Tambov
Saratov
Belgorod
Voronezh
Volgograd
Rostov
Astrakhan
KALMYKIA
DAGESTAN
KRASNODAR
ADYGEYA
STAVROPOL
Kaliningrad

ETHNIC REPUBLICS
1 - KARACHAI-CHERKESS
2 - KABARDINO-BALKAR
3 - NORTH OSSETIA
4 - CHECHNYA and INGUSHETIA
     (boundary not defined)

| | |
|---|---|
| **BURYATIA** | - **ETHNIC REPUBLIC** |
| *ALTAI* | - *KRAI* |
| Tomsk | - Oblast |
| *Evenk* | - *Autonomous Oblast (as indicated)* |
| | - Autonomous Okrug |
| Moscow | - Federal cities enjoying status |
| St. Petersburg | equivalent to an Oblast |

0    km    1000

46

# CHAPTER THREE

# The Russians and the Russian Question

Simon Dixon

'What exactly is Russia? . . . Who, today, considers himself part of the future Russia? And where do Russians themselves see the boundaries of their land?'[1] When Solzhenitsyn first posed these questions in 1990, uncertainty was understandable: the Soviet Union had yet to crumble, and many still thought its residual strengths sufficient to ensure its survival. In the aftermath of the USSR's dissolution on 31 December 1991, the need to persist with his inquiries might seem redundant, since the restoration of sovereign Russian statehood would appear to have resolved them. Yet as Solzhenitsyn himself has stressed since returning to Russia in 1994, the creation of the Russian Federation, far from dispelling anxiety about Russian national identity, has merely served to deepen it, and the 'Russian question', rather than being definitively answered by the collapse of the Soviet Union, has instead been given a new lease of life.[2]

The kernel of the 'Russian question' is revealed in the opening line of the new constitution, approved by 52 per cent of votes cast (28 per cent of eligible voters) in a referendum on 12 December 1993: 'We, the multi-national people of the Russian Federation . . .'.[3] Although, according to the 1989 census, some 25 million Russians were left outside the Russian Federation – leading critical Russians to speak of 'a dismembered nation'[4] – only 82 per cent of the population within its borders is ethnically Russian. Since the remainder – some 27 million people – comprises more than 180 different nationalities, the linguistic composition of the Federation is as complex as the ethnic one.[5] While this state of affairs has produced pleas for tolerant language planning to avert the danger of 'linguistic nihilism'[6] on the part of the dominant nationality, it has also aroused misgivings among Russians who fear that the new state barely qualifies as Russian at all since its non-Russian republics 'profit from immeasurably greater rights than the Russian areas'.[7] To indicate their unease, Russians employ a distinction that is easier to express in their own language than in English, for Russian uses the adjective *russkii* – derived from medieval *Rus'* – to signify someone or something ethnically Russian, and *rossiiskii* – derived from *Rossiia* – in relation to the multinational Russian state's territory and people. This chapter will show not only that Russian nationalists are split between advocates of a *russkii* and of a *rossiiskii* solution to the Russian question, but also that those who urge their government to support the *russkii* option do so more in hope than expectation.[8] The Russian Federation is no more likely to satisfy them than were tsarist and Soviet regimes in the past.

If, at one level, the nature of the Russians' identity crisis is explicitly territorial, it is also, at a deeper level, profoundly psychological. Within a matter of months, Russians have been exposed, without the protection of a recognised legal framework, to free elections and the free market, to consumerism, inflation and unemployment (an offence until 1991), to pornography and organised crime. They have also heard their former state, so recently proclaimed by Marxism-Leninism as an inevitable product of historical progress, disowned and discredited by many of its former leaders. Gennadii Ziuganov, leader of the rump Russian Communist Party, declared in an election broadcast in November 1993 that 'privatisation is essential'.[9] Exemplifying the well-attested capacity of the Russian mind to embrace one extreme ideology after another with equal fervour, former *apparatchik* Boris Yeltsin has made his own distinctive contribution to this topsy-turvy new world by joining the capitalist leaders' G7 group in spring 1994. Moreover, he has done so on the West's own terms since Russia's superpower status came to an end with the Cold War. There could surely be no more poignant image of the new world order than the sight of Russian soldiers who once guaranteed a seemingly indissoluble Warsaw Pact joining mourners at the funeral of NATO's Secretary General in August 1994 (unless it be the opening, in the same week, of a top-secret Russian submarine from the Brezhnev era as a tourist attraction on the River Thames).

If it has scarcely been easy for bewildered Russians to come to terms with any of these transformations, the search for a new international role has been the most traumatic of all. Now that Russians no longer have imperial pride to compensate them for poor living standards, they are doubly uncertain of their future.[10] Their sense of insecurity can be estimated from a study conducted by scholars at the Academy of Sciences' Institute of Ethnology and Anthropology led by Iu. V. Arutiunian. The original version, submitted to the press just before the collapse of the USSR, reached the following immodest conclusion.

It would be no exaggeration to say that the most populous nation in Europe with its highly distinctive social character – the Russians – in many respects influences the fate of the planet. All world processes – war and peace, revolutionary upheavals and profound social reforms of the state and society as a whole – wherever they may take place, are to some degree linked, directly or indirectly, to the Russians, and therefore study of them [the Russians] is meaningful not only in relation to contemporary social development, but in many respects to the future of humanity as a whole.[11]

When Arutiunian rephrased this claim in an essay published early in 1994, it had undergone a significant modification: the Russians' ubiquitous influence, far from determining the future of humanity, was now said to be a thing of the past. Small wonder that the abandonment of pretensions on such a scale has resulted in what Arutiunian calls 'colossal changes in the Russians' socio-political consciousness'.[12]

It is not surprising, therefore, that while Russians who found Soviet society repressive greeted its demise as the dawn of a 'new era',[13] many patriots regarded the emergence of the Russian Federation with a scepticism bordering on despair. Economic deprivation and national humiliation were bitter pills to swallow for intellectuals accustomed to proselytising the messianic virtues of their native culture.[14] Solzhenitsyn, in characteristically apocalyptic mood, declared 'the Great Russian Catastrophe of the 1990s' a tragedy on the scale of the Time of Troubles (1605–13) and 1917.[15] As this analogy suggests, any initial temptation on the part of the nationalist intelligentsia merely to extinguish the memory of an inglorious recent past was rapidly overtaken by their preoccupation with patterns in history. Since the Russians' obsession with the past extends far beyond the confines of the historical profession and has traditionally been expressed not only in factual but also in literary form – and, most interestingly, in 'intergeneric' works such as Tolstoy's *War and Peace* and Solzhenitsyn's own *The Red Wheel*[16] – discussions of their current predicament, and especially their attempts to escape from it, are almost always set in a historical context.

Viktor Aksiuchits's religious philosophy may not be universally shared, even by fellow Russian nationalists, but he expressed a widespread belief when claiming that:

Everything that has taken place in Russian history is also manifest in our present. The past is not there to be forgotten or contemplated in the abstract, but for us to choose the true future.[17]

For instance, at the opposite end of the political spectrum from Aksiuchits, the largest and most vigorous party of economic and democratic reform – led by Yegor Gaidar and significantly named 'Russia's Choice' – proclaimed its commitment to Westernisation by picking as its emblem in 1993 a silhouette of Falconet's statue of Peter the Great, unveiled in St Petersburg in 1782 and immortalised by Pushkin as *The Bronze Horseman* in 1833.[18] Whatever 'usable past' the various Russian political parties may seek to resurrect, the gravity of the historic 'choice' they face scarcely needs to be emphasised. As the editors of *Voprosy filosofii* warned in May 1994 – having suggested that Russia's destiny might lie anywhere on a continuum 'from liberal democracy to national socialism disguised as false *sobornost'* or pseudo-Eurasianism' – the decision about Russia's way forward constitutes 'a risk in the strongest and most real sense of the word. In essence, it might become a choice between life and death'.[19]

## THE RUSSIANS AND THEIR EMPIRE, 1721–1917

Like contemporary Russian nationalists, we turn first to the pre-revolutionary period.[20] In one reading, its history marks the triumph of inexorable Russian expansion. Partly by exploiting their position as tribute-collectors to the Mongol khans, the princes of Moscow brought several rival principalities under their own hegemony between 1304 and 1462. Having consolidated their rule in central Russia, the Muscovites advanced eastwards into Siberia under Ivan IV (the Terrible) in the mid-sixteenth century.[21] By doing so, they had already begun to disturb the ethnic balance of a population whose self-identity owed much to its religion, Russian Orthodoxy.[22] But the greatest challenge was yet to come as the Russian state moved further into territory with heterodox, non-Slavic populations. In 1654, the annexation of the Ukraine brought a pronounced Latin and Catholic influence; in the Great Northern War against Sweden (1700–21), Peter I (the Great) conquered the predominantly Protestant Baltic lands; successive victories against the Muslim Ottoman Turks culminated in 1783 with the annexation of the Crimea; and three partitions of Poland under Catherine II (the Great) – in 1772, 1793 and 1795 – not only brought more Catholics into the empire, but also effectively created Russia's Jewish question. Georgia and Finland were acquired in 1801 and 1809 respectively, and further expansion into Central Asia and the Far East in the second half of the nineteenth century incorporated still more non-Russian territory and people.[23] Here, apparently, is ample evidence to support Kliuchevskii's famous argument, advanced in *The Course of Russian History* (1904–11), that colonisation in a boundless plain is the fundamental fact of Russian history.[24]

At first sight, it may seem perverse to argue that pre-revolutionary Russian nationalism was fragile. Yet three fundamental flaws deserve emphasis, suggesting that tsarist expansion offers no straightforward lessons to nationalists who seek to learn from its example in the 1990s.

If we accept Gellner's definition of nationalism as the 'imposition of a high culture' on 'an anonymous, impersonal society . . . held together above all by a shared culture of this kind',[25] it is hard to exaggerate the restraint imposed on the development of its nineteenth-century Russian variant by the persistence of a rigidly hierarchical social structure. In the eighteenth century, there was nothing particularly anachronistic about the fact that many Russian nobles 'did not identify themselves with the nation as a whole but were convinced that they *were* the nation': the same might equally have been said of other European élites.[26] In the following hundred years, however, while the social barriers of Western *anciens régimes* were dissolving into the kind of amorphous society Gellner takes as the pre-condition of modern nationalism, the Russian estate system – which divided the population at birth into inflexible (though not immutable) juridical categories, peasantry, nobility, merchantry and so on – was, by contrast, being deliberately extended and reinforced.[27] In such a carefully calibrated corporate society, in which privilege was legally enshrined, no shared 'national' culture could readily develop. To quote Heinz-Dietrich Löwe, 'Russian nationalism remained weak, because the gulf between the privileged few and the masses could not be narrowed quickly enough'.[28]

Dostoevsky thought much the same, but in his view the educated classes had been prised apart from the peasantry not so much by force of law as by their devotion to Western values.[29] Thus, if the first significant weakness in pre-revolutionary Russian nationalism was fundamentally social, the second was the cultural fault-line dividing the Muscovite era from the Petersburg period which followed it. The scale of the rupture is, in fact, easily exaggerated. But in imperial Russia (1721–1917), to idealise Orthodox, peasant Muscovy as the golden age of authentic national consciousness was implicitly to undermine the legitimacy of the Westernised, secular state symbolised by the new capital Peter the Great founded in 1703. One way of getting round the difficulty was to explain it away – as has one of the most subtle of contemporary Russian patriots, Academician D. S. Likhachev – by stressing Russian culture's distinctive capacity for assimilation: 'Petersburg is Russian and *therefore* extraordinarily receptive to anything foreign or to a creative reworking of what is basically foreign'.[30] But it was more common for nineteenth-century nationalists to contrast Peter's personal virility, marking him out as a model of Russian manhood, with his betrayal of national tradition by the systematic imposition of a rational bureaucracy.[31]

So long as such qualms remained confined to the intelligentsia, their political impact was limited. However, when the last two tsars sought to reassert Muscovite values in contradistinction to the Westernised bureaucracy and court ceremonial that both mistrusted, they themselves inadvertently became 'a force for disorder' by 'pursuing goals at variance with those of [their] ruling elite'.[32] Neither tsar sought to disguise his distaste for St Petersburg and everything it represented. When Alexander III built the Church of the Saviour on the Blood on the site of his father's assassination, he deliberately thrust incongruous cupolas, modelled on Moscow's St Basil's Cathedral, above St Petersburg's baroque and neo-classical skyline.[33] Nicholas II christened his only son Aleksei in memory of Peter the Great's father,

Aleksei Mikhailovich (1645–76), celebrated the Westernised capital's bicentenary with a ball in Muscovite costume, and trusted Rasputin as the voice of peasant Russia rather than listening to his ministers or the constitutionalists in the Duma.[34] At the end of the old regime, therefore, the reassertion of Russianness served not, as was intended, to reinforce the regime, but rather to betray 'the autocrat's own ambivalence about the heritage, nature and goals of the state'.[35] Even in the 1990s, the same ambivalence still frustrates attempts to restore an authentic Russia, though now it is the government that emphasises the benefits of Westernisation, and the nationalist opposition that preaches Muscovite virtue.

However, the tsarist period's most significant bequest to the twentieth century – and the third flaw in pre-revolutionary Russian nationalism – was a paradox resulting from the political and demographic realities of a multiethnic empire: the Russians could be strengthened only at the expense of a large number of non-Russians whose passive quiescence (and preferably active collaboration) was a prerequisite of state security. Looking back, Nicholas II's former minister S. Iu. Witte complained that successive tsarist governments had failed to appreciate that the motto of a multinational Russian empire (*Rossiiskaia imperiia*) simply could not be 'to convert everyone into true Russians (*istinno-russkie*)'.[36] Yet, to give them their due, Russia's rulers in the eighteenth and early nineteenth centuries had made no such attempt. While national consciousness remained less significant than rational uniformity in affairs of state, successive tsars down to Alexander I (1801–25) granted privileges to local élites in newly-acquired territories in order to ensure their smooth assimilation into a centrally administered empire. By this means Russia benefited, in particular, from the talents of the Ukrainian and Baltic German nobilities, both of which became influential not only in their own lands but also at court in St Petersburg.[37] Until 1825, indeed, tsarist nationality policy was emphatically *rossiiskii* rather than *russkii*.[38]

That such a policy caused relatively little resentment among educated Russians at the time owes much to the fact that eighteenth-century nationalists, rather than lay claim to some innate superiority, were anxious to demonstrate that Russian culture deserved to rank alongside other Western civilisations with common roots in the classical past.[39] It was only under Nicholas I (1825–55) – when subtle Slavophile writings on the distinctiveness of Russian culture, inspired by the spiritual heritage of Orthodox Muscovy, were corrupted into more aggressive messianic creeds – that Russians were no longer content merely with administrative assimilation and started to demand cultural penetration as well.[40] The state began in the 1830s by reversing its previous emphasis: now the thrust of its policies was increasingly *russkii* rather than *rossiiskii*. For example, Ukrainian Uniates were forcibly 'reunited' with Orthodoxy in 1839, many Baltic peasants were converted *en masse* in the 1840s, and a renewed attempt to baptise the Muslim Tatars was coordinated by the ecclesiastical academy founded expressly for the purpose at Kazan' in 1842. Yet the regime's enthusiasm for such assertive action faded when it provoked civil unrest. Despite the formulation of a doctrine of 'official nationality'[41] in the 1830s, effective cultural penetration was never achieved. Even in 1917, 'much of Russia–Rossiia remained foreign to Rus', and unassimilated'.[42] In Benedict Anderson's neat formulation, it proved in practice impossible to stretch 'the short, tight skin of the nation over the gigantic body of the empire'.[43]

The futility of aggressive Russification was appreciated by one of the most intelligent, and most conservative, of Alexander II's ministers. When the nationalist journalist Mikhail Katkov demanded tougher measures against the Poles in the wake of the Polish Revolt of 1863, P. A. Valuev, the Minister of Internal Affairs, sent him maps of European Russia showing the division of the population by nationality, religion and social estate, and begged him to consider 'what measures would be necessary, with such a centre and such a periphery, to ensure the development of centripetal rather than centrifugal tendencies'.[44] The same question still tantalises Yeltsin in the 1990s. Gorbachev learned the answer the hard way, as he saw the Soviet Union pulled apart by the centrifugal force of non-Russian nationalism.[45] Intransigent Russians, however, have never been willing to accept that their own ethnic interests must be subordinate to the overall demands of the multinational state. No less a person than the tsarevich regarded Valuev's sensitivity to the problems of a dynastic empire as mere pandering to the Poles: the minister had simply failed to understand the needs of his native Russia.[46] When he succeeded to the throne in 1881, therefore, Alexander III determined on a straightforward policy of 'Russia for the Russians' (*Rossiia dlia russkikh*). Though the new tsar was rumoured to have ordered Russians to attack Jews, his regime would surely have regarded the disorder that accompanied the pogroms of 1881 as too high a price to pay for an anti-Semitic crusade.[47] Instead it was the peoples of the Baltic lands who bore the brunt of a more carefully considered attempt to impose the Russian language and religion later in the 1880s.[48] The fact that even this ruthless campaign ultimately proved abortive demonstrated that the conundrum outlined by Valuev was not susceptible to resolution by force.

Long before 1917, the seeds were sown of a bitter and lasting conviction among Russians that theirs was the only great empire in which the needs of the 'imperial' nation were subservient to those of the peoples it colonised. Thus, for Geoffrey Hosking, 'the most important fact about Russian history' is not, as Kliuchevskii had it, colonisation itself, but the fact that in Russia 'the empire has always oppressed the nation. State-building has impeded nation-building.'[49]

# RUSSIANS IN THE SOVIET UNION BEFORE GORBACHEV

The fate of the Russians between 1917 and 1985 serves to illustrate Hosking's point.[50] Having seen their nation weakened in the First World War, nationalists feared its extinction in the aftermath of the Bolshevik revolution: 'Our Russia has perished, they have destroyed Russia, no longer is there any Russia', lamented the poet Aleksei Remizov.[51] If this is a characteristic instance of the Russians' tendency to exaggerate their own vulnerability, it cannot be denied that the prospects for Russian nationalism were grim in 1917. As social divisions once again assumed greater significance than national ones, it seemed that any surviving *russkii* element of the Russian nation might be absorbed once and for all into an amorphous international proletariat.

Considerations of raw power were as important as ideology in shaping the Bolsheviks' anti-Russian strategy. Lenin realised, as the last two tsars had not, that what he pejoratively dubbed 'Great Russian chauvinism' stimulated separatist non-Russian nationalism: that was why the 12th Party Congress in April 1923 explicitly set its face against it.[52] Thus, in the mid-1920s, while attitudes to the Russian past within emergent Soviet cultural circles were characterised by 'a strange amalgam of reverence and hostility',[53] it was the *émigré* intelligentsia that, having reluctantly abandoned the fatherland in order to escape communist persecution, [54] became self-appointed preservers and defenders of the Russian 'tradition'.

The version they canonised was understandably shaped by the circumstances of the time. Exiled historians inspired by the spiritual and mystical revival of Russian culture's Silver Age concentrated on their medieval heritage, especially on its religious iconography, while literary critics revered Pushkin rather than Dostoevsky lest the West be tempted to exploit the latter's fascination with the morbid Russian soul to rationalise Russian acquiescence to Soviet rule. Of course, the emigration also had writers of its own, and when, in 1933, Ivan Bunin became the first Russian to receive the Nobel Prize for literature, it seemed that twentieth-century Russian identity might ironically be defined by 'Russia abroad'.[55]

It was at that point, however, as Stalin's government responded to the twin challenges of Western fascism and domestic dislocation brought about by forced industrialisation, that a rival conception of Russian nationality was about to be resuscitated within the USSR. Like another non-Russian – the Pole Feliks Dzierzynski at the head of the Cheka – Stalin, as Commissar for the Nationalities, had proved to be more Russian than the Russians in Lenin's government. Stalin wanted the Soviet constitution to reflect Russia's pre-eminence in the revolutionary movement, and he got his way: the Constitution of 1924 was, in Hosking's pithy phrase, 'Leninist in form, but Stalinist in content'.[56] The same Georgian that rescued Russian domination of the new socialist state in the 1920s presided, from 1934, not only over a predominantly Russian élite, but also over a revival of Russian imagery. The reputations of heroic Russian leaders, and especially of Peter the Great, were favourably reassessed. Though elements of the negative view of Petrine society propagated in the 1920s by M. N. Pokrovskii survived, and the tsar's interest in the West continued to be played down, positive evaluations of Peter's energy, especially in diplomatic and military affairs, now reappeared in the history books.[57]

In 1941, the entry of the Soviet Union into the 'Great Patriotic War' – in which, in contrast to Russia's experience in 1914–18, it was to gain territory larger than Spain and Portugal and another 23 million non-Russians – heralded the mobilisation of nationalist historical imagery on a still more ambitious scale. 'May you be inspired in this war', Stalin exhorted the Russians, 'by the indomitable image of our great ancestors Alexander Nevskii, Dmitrii Donskoi, Kuzma Minin, Dmitrii Pozharskii, Alexander Suvorov, Mikhail Kutuzov!'[58] Film director Sergei Eisenstein was awarded a Stalin prize for the first part of his *Ivan the Terrible*, released in 1945.[59] The war allowed even the Orthodox Church, split by schism in the 1920s, some respite from persecution. In return for supporting the war effort, presenting Stalin in Christ-like terms, and portraying the Russians as God's chosen people, the church was granted a council in 1943. Three years later, in a repetition of the events of 1839, the Uniate Church in recaptured Western Ukraine was 'reunited' (forcibly reincorporated) with Orthodoxy.[60] Pleased with the results of his Russian rehabilitation, Stalin pronounced the Russian people the 'leading' Soviet nation in a toast to Red Army commanders in May 1945, and proclaimed that the Russians' conduct in the war had earned them 'general recognition as the guiding force of the Soviet Union'.[61]

The immediate post-war years thus saw the zenith of the crudest possible state-inspired Russian chauvinism, predicated on the existence of supposedly 'cosmopolitan' (the code-word for Jewish) and masonic conspiracies against the USSR. Ironically, however, the dubious prod-ucts of late-Stalinist culture merely served to reinforce among the more sophisticated Russian *intelligenty* an exaggerated respect for the West.[62] This was true even of writers as dedicated to the Russian tradition as Pasternak and Akhmatova, notoriously denounced by Zhdanov as 'half nun, half whore', who recognised that the strident Russian element in Stalin's cultural policy was in fact subordinate to an overall reassertion of Marxist-Leninist orthodoxy. It was not so much the Russians' literary and spiritual heritage that was lauded in the late-Stalinist years as their muscular contribution to the building of Soviet socialism.[63] So, although the church maintained a precarious peace with the state until it was assaulted by Khrushchev's militantly anti-religious campaign in the late 1950s,[64] the early years of the Cold War were relatively bleak for the more sensitive Russian nationalists.

Paradoxically, it was Khrushchev himself, a sworn enemy of nation-alist causes, whose policies were largely responsible for their revival. Not only did his denunciation of Stalin in 1956 implicitly challenge the infallibility of Marxist-Leninist dogma, but the search for alternatives was further encouraged by the 'thaw' in censorship policy that allowed the publication of overtly critical writings. It was in this period, for example, that a number of authors who later contributed to the nationalist journal *Nash sovremennik* made their name in *Novyi mir*, the periodical notable under the editorship of the poet Tvardovskii for its 'tradition of truthful investigation of the life of ordinary people, especially peasants, throughout the upheavals of Soviet history'.[65] Characteristically, the principal appeal to Tvardovskii of Solzhenitsyn's *A Day in the Life of Ivan Denisovich*, first published in *Novyi Mir* in November 1962, appears to have lain in its portrait of a true Russian peasant (*muzhik*).[66] In addition to these literary developments, the demolition of many churches under Khrushchev allowed nationalist sympathies to be channelled through conservationist outlets. Indeed, the conservationist movement remained until the late 1980s an important strand of Russian nationalist activity, notably in the guise of the All-Russian Society for the Protection of Historical and Cultural Monuments (*VOOPIK*), founded in 1965.

Conservationism was not, however, the only element of lasting significance in the Russian revival of the 1960s. The spectrum identified by Dunlop[67] ranged from moderate 'Russian patriots', many of them Orthodox believers, who had no truck with crude chauvinism but sought to defend Russian (*russkii*) culture, through a central group, who took a more alarmist view of the future – characterised by Vladimir Osipov's warning in his short-lived dissident journal *Rumour* (*Veche*, 1972) that the Russian nation could disappear[68] – to so-called National Bolsheviks, most of them militantly anti-religious, whose support for Russian (*rossiiskii*) state power lay in the armed forces and among party hardliners. These various strands of Russian nationalism all survived into the 1980s, when they were to move further than ever apart. Their differences were one important reason why the latent challenge to Soviet rule that some claimed they posed never in fact materialised.[69] While in retrospect the 1970s can be seen as a period of consolidation and development among Russian nationalists, their political impact at the time was limited.[70] Indeed, so great was the apparent success of Brezhnev's pragmatic nationalities policy that even his arch-critic Alexander Zinoviev declared that 'any expectation that conflicts between nationalities will cause the ruin of the Soviet Empire derives from a total misconception of the real situation in the country'.[71] This was in *The Reality of Communism*, first published in Paris in 1981, a book that devotes a mere half page to the nationalities problem. It was probably the only half page with which Gorbachev would have agreed.

# THE RUSSIANS UNDER *GLASNOST'* AND *PERESTROIKA*

Though Gorbachev himself exemplified the type of 'Soviet patriot' whose sole use for Russian nationalism was as a kind of Soviet social cement, it was not immediately obvious that his relations with the Russians would end in irreconcilable conflict. There were, in fact, several issues on which their interests coalesced. For example, both he and the nationalists believed that the environmental price paid for decades of Soviet economic development had been far too high. Thus, in 1986, nationalists were able to play an important part in forcing the abandonment of an irrigation project that would have diverted several Russian rivers south into Ukraine, Moldavia and especially Kazakhstan and Central Asia.[72] Since ecological destruction serves as a metaphor for moral decay in the 'village prose' of nationalist writers associated with *Nash sovremennik*,[73] one can see why they were also attracted by Gorbachev's anti-corruption and anti-alcohol campaigns. Yet it was Gorbachev's more daring attempt to exploit the political and social benefits to be gained from allowing the churches greater flexibility of action – the most significant way in which his cultural reform programme departed from Khrushchev's 'thaw' – that offered the most welcome olive-branch to Russian nationalists (with the important exception of atheist National Bolsheviks, whom it merely offended). Symbolic gestures like the high-profile celebrations of the Orthodox millennium in June 1988 – notable for their Great Russian, anti-Ukrainian bias – were matched by tangible changes in the provision of worship. Three new Orthodox parishes were registered in 1985, ten in 1986, sixteen in 1987, 809 in 1988 and 2,185 in 1989.[74] By 1992, there were over seventy working parishes in St Petersburg alone, the great majority of which had already assumed full control of their churches under the 1990 Law on Property which granted the church full rights of ownership.[75] Here is evidence of a remarkable religious revival: at its height, in October 1991, 64 per cent of those who responded to a Russia-wide survey thought that the wider diffusion of religious beliefs would benefit society, while only 6 per cent believed that it would be harmful.[76]

Unfortunately for him, having emancipated Soviet intellectuals in the hope of limiting their role to approval for his reforms, Gorbachev was unable to squeeze the genie back into the bottle. The case of the historians shows how grave were the consequences of his failure to control the intelligentsia. Professional scholars, long confined by the canons of Marxism-Leninism, were initially slow to react to the opportunities offered by *glasnost'*. Even by the latter years of *perestroika*, they had made no more than modest progress towards revising their approach to other countries' history.[77] Yet the impact of revisionist work about their own past – designed as much to assuage professional guilt as to 'purify'[78] the historical record – was ultimately traumatic. Alec Nove captured the essence of early attempts to fill in some notorious Soviet 'blank spots' in a witty chapter title: 'The Rehabilitation of History – or the History of Rehabilitation'.[79] But it proved impossible to halt the de-mythologisation of Stalin at the rehabilitation of Bukharin. As a sophisticated nationalist, Vadim Kozhinov, implied in his review of *Deti Arbata*, Anatolii Rybakov's fictional exposé of early Stalinism, the tragedy of those years was ultimately attributable not to one man but to the Bolshevik revolution and the Communist Party itself.[80] So profoundly was the historical legitimacy of the Soviet state thrown into question by revelations about its past that school history examinations had temporarily to be abandoned. *Glasnost'*, begun in an attempt to regenerate communism, ended by undermining it. As the preface to a pioneering new political history declared in 1991: 'The time has passed when we had only one Leader, one Party, one Ideology, and one Textbook'.[81]

In one sense the new pluralism offered a welcome opportunity to Russian nationalists. As émigré writings flowed freely into the USSR for the first time – a bibliography of *émigré* literature and associated criticism issued by Soviet publishers between 1986 and 1990 lists some 5,272 items[82] – a severed cultural world was recovered and the schism dividing the native intelligentsia from 'Russia abroad' began to heal. Yet there were even stronger reasons why glasnost' was regarded with intense suspicion in nationalist circles. That it appeared to tolerate homosexuality and prostitution appalled them;[83] that it offered the prospect of unrestricted proselytism to Orthodoxy's rivals was even worse. Most damaging of all, from the nationalist perspective, was that Gorbachev appeared to extend a historical pattern in which Russia herself was dissipated by the dilution of strong, centralised rule. While *perestroika* was compared in some quarters to past 'reforms from above' by Peter the Great and Stolypin,[84] nationalist critics who thought it lacked the requisite degree of ruthlessness instead harked back to a different era, as *Moskva* pointedly serialised the work of N. M. Karamazin (1766–1826), a champion of Muscovite autocracy, and of S. M. Solov'ev, the founder of the so-called 'state school' of nineteenth-century historiography.[85]

Ultimately, the frustrations experienced by Russian nationalists under *perestroika* allowed their cause to be appropriated by Gorbachev's rivals on the radical 'left' and hardline 'right' of the party, both of which recognised the political capital to be gained from 'putting Russia first'.[86] So impotent was Gorbachev in the face of growing pro-Russian public opinion – demonstrated, ironically, by opinion polls pioneered by his reformist ally Tat'iana Zaslavskaia – that in June 1990 he was forced to concede the formation of a Russian Communist Party and was powerless to prevent Russia's own declaration of sovereignty (a defiant response to the Baltic republics' campaign for independence and a clear challenge to the Soviet constitution). Meanwhile, nationalists themselves, not content merely to be manipulated, had followed a widespread trend by forming unofficial associations like *Fatherland* (*Otechestvo*) in defence of their own interests.[87] For example, November 1988 saw the appearance in Moscow of the *Tovarishchestvo russkikh khudozhnikov* (Association of Russian Artists) coordinated by writers associated with *Nash sovremennik* to combat separatist minority nationalist tendencies by proselytising Russian culture.[88] As the first issue of its newssheet, *Russkoe tovarishchestvo*, declared:

When we are asked on whose side we stand, with which party or group, or in the name of what ideals we live, then we reply soberly and quietly that our ideals are historic: the Faith, the People, and the Fatherland. Our party is Russia.[89]

By contrast, the proclamations of the most notorious nationalist organisation, *Pamiat'* (Memory), were neither quiet nor sober. *Pamiat'* owed its immediate origins to a literary–historical society at the Aviation Ministry in Moscow in the early 1980s.[90] However, as the journalist Vitalii Korotich observed – having been dubbed by a *Pamiat'* heckler 'the foreman of the scum of restructuring' – this was no 'organisation of nice kindly folks whose sole wish is to preserve historical monuments'.[91] Instead, by resurrecting Zionist conspiracy theories, *Pamiat'* provided a release-mechanism for some of the most distasteful anti-Semitic tendencies latent in Russian nationalism; and in its association with violence, repeatedly denied by the leadership, it inaugurated a means of political argument that was to become familiar in the coming years.[92] Perhaps the most surprising thing about such an organisation was that it should have attracted the support of subtle writers, including Valentin Rasputin, whose association with *Pamiat'* did much to discredit them. 'Village prose', however, is not to blame for *Pamiat'*,[93] and anti-Semitism is not synonymous with Russian nationalism. More mainstream nationalist sentiments were reflected among the self-help associations formed in response to economic crisis. In theory, these might have formed a seed-bed for the sort of small-scale cooperative aid (*pomoch'*) revered by nationalists as the heritage of the pre-revolutionary peasant commune. But it was not to be. In practice, Russia's burgeoning charitable organisations all too often 'found themselves distributing Western food parcels'.[94]

One response to such a humiliation was to reject the state responsible for inflicting it. Seeing precious Russian resources once again diverted to subdue restive nationalities on the periphery, where Russians feared a violent backlash, Valentin Rasputin used the first Congress of People's Deputies in 1989 to campaign for Russian secession from the USSR.[95] As Solzhenitsyn argued from exile, the time had come to make 'an uncompromising choice between an empire of which we ourselves are the primary victims, and the spiritual and physical salvation of our own people'.[96] Once Gennadii Yanaev's coup failed in August

1991, and Yeltsin outmanoeuvred a failing Gorbachev by publicly declaring the rebirth of Russia, the USSR's days were numbered. When Yeltsin's vice-president, Alexander Rutskoi, condemned the projected inter-republican agreement of October 1991 for treating Russia like a 'milch-cow', it was clear that they had come to an end.[97]

Yet although there had been advocates of Russian separation earlier in the 1970s and 1980s – the émigré Petr Boldyrev was one[98] – such an option had never attracted widespread support. By contrast, from the hardline communist Nina Andreeva, who explicitly denounced Russian nationalists but implicitly assumed Russian hegemony in the Soviet Union, to the members of Russia's incipient democratic movements, most of whom 'wanted to democratise the USSR, not to destroy it',[99] a wide spectrum of Russian opinion feared that a Soviet collapse might herald the dismemberment of Russia itself. Indeed, it was disagreement over the impact of disintegration that precipitated the first major split in 'Democratic Russia' in November 1991. The Democratic Party of Russia, led by Nikolai Travkin, the Constitutional Democratic Party, under Mikhail Astaf'ev, and the Russian Christian Democratic Movement, inspired by Aksiuchits, all abandoned the coalition in the belief that the dismantling of the Soviet Union was detrimental to Russia.[100] Since there were as many 'empire savers' as there were 'nation builders' among Russian nationalists,[101] the restoration of Russian sovereignty in the form of the Russian Federation would plainly offer no ready-made panacea for Russian ills.


## THE FIRST YEARS OF THE RUSSIAN FEDERATION

The problems facing the new federation were multiplied because nationalists initially overestimated the Russian president's commitment to their cause. Even before he became chairman of the Russian parliament in May 1990, Yeltsin, sensing the power of populism in Russian clothing, exploited temporary food shortages and panic buying in Moscow to play on the economic insecurity of the majority of Russians. A year later, in his campaign for the presidency, he could legitimately claim that Russian prestige had been enhanced since his return to power.[102] Yet, as Dunlop stresses, the nationalist card Yeltsin played in June 1991 'was "Russian" in the sense of rossiiskii, not russkii. In all his public pronouncements, Yeltsin leaned over backwards to avoid any hint of ethnic Russian particularism.'[103] The fact that this same multinational emphasis remained one of the few consistent features of his early years in power explains the disdain shown by the russkii faction on the nationalist spectrum for Yeltsin and his government.[104] But the contempt of the rossiiskii faction was also guaranteed by the identification of 'federal' periods in the

Russian past with national weakness (by contrast with the periods of strong, autocratic rule that most nationalists find more congenial), and the related fact that a weak Russian state is vulnerable to Western influence.

It is natural to begin with the problem of borders, and the sense that Russian identity suffers from the persistent failure of the country's physical territory to correspond with her 'spiritual geography'.[105] In common with many Russians, Academician Likhachev emphasises the 'kinship' between the three Slavic cultures – Russian, Ukrainian, and Belarusian – and finds it hard to imagine a Russian state that excludes Kiev, the cultural and political centre of medieval Kievan *Rus'*. 'Breadth', he wrote in 1988, 'was peculiar not only to the area populated by *Rus'* but also to the nature of the Russian person and Russian culture.'[106] For National Bolsheviks, however, Likhachev's Slavic vision is too narrow: not surprisingly, senior military men have been prominent among those calling for a restoration of the old Soviet borders.[107] Yet their solution, in turn, alarms those who believe that 'to speak of the USSR as Russia, as our "imperial" patriots do, is to work towards ... perhaps the most dangerous myth propagated by the Bolsheviks' – the notion that Soviet and Russian identities are indistinguishable.[108] Anxious to avoid this trap, Vladimir Zhirinovskii advocates a return to the tsarist frontiers of 1915. As indicated by moderate opponents in the centre – never a comfortable position in Russian politics – Russia, should Zhirinovskii's dream be realised, would once again swallow up Poland and Finland and reach Port Arthur in the Far East.[109] Since Solzhenitsyn has expressed a widespread view by declaring that there could be no 'worse caricature of Russian patriotism' than Zhirinovskii – he thinks it 'impossible to suggest a more direct way to drown Russia in blood' than by following his neo-fascist policies[110] – it is worth stressing that, however bizarre a figure the Liberal Democrat leader may be, his view of the territorial problem is shared by less eccentric politicians. In October 1992, for example, Arkadii Volskii, leader of Civic Union and representative of the Soviet industrial élite, dismissed 'the current flight to separate national components' as a 'temporary fluctuation of history and geography', argued the need for 'an inspiring national idea, which Russia now lacks', and proclaimed his own preference for a Russian state in its 'pre-revolutionary form, not the currently truncated version'.[111]

In the light of this ubiquitous dissatisfaction with their country's straitened circumstances, it is paradoxical that so many of the Russians who wish to see her borders expand should be unwilling to face the consequences of living in a multinational state. Instead, they have been dismayed to see recreated – even in the 'truncated' Russian Federation – what from their point of view were the worst features of the USSR. In particular, the government has been forced to placate secessionist Tatars and Chechens, both of whom declared their own sovereignty in 1992 in an attempt to exploit Russian weakness after the coup of August 1991.[112] 'In Russia', complains Sergei Fomin, 'it is simply not done to speak of Russian national interests' because the government wants to 'arouse in the Russian people not so much *russkii* as *rossiiskii* state patriotism', a policy that must inevitably 'lead to the disorientation of Russian national consciousness'. Typical is the authorities' disapproval of the words *russkii* and *russkii narod*, and their preference for the antiquated term *Rossiianin*, already passé by 1917. Decades of communist rule have prevented the Russians from thinking of themselves as a nation. Now, declares Fomin, the Russian nation must 'fight' to restore Russian statehood: Russia must be Russia and not the Russian Federation.[113] The fight will be all the harder since the more paranoid nationalists detect a russophobic conspiracy on the part of the government to 'degrade' the Russian nation by permitting rampant crime and by conducting a 'total struggle against Orthodoxy'.[114]

Much as Yeltsin may dislike his nationalist opponents, such a conspiracy is, of course, imaginary. That it can seem even remotely credible offers some indication of the prevalent degree of discontent with the new federal structure. It must be acknowledged that historical precedent is unpromising. Federalism's few advocates in imperial Russia were regarded as unhinged. When the liberal diplomat Prince N. A. Orlov privately suggested in 1865 that Russia's 'whole future' lay in a 'federal state' in which all inhabitants' needs could receive 'legal satisfaction' in 'local parliaments', his idea was dismissed as 'childish babble'.[115] Twentieth-century nationalists have been no more charitable. General A. I. Denikin, who thought that Russia's 'state link' with her borderlands was 'preordained by history', rightly said that his fellow White officers in the Russian Civil War (1918–21) would not have fought for a 'Federated Republic'.[116] Having identified four periods of 'federal' weakness – the Kievan period (1000–1240), the years spent under the Tatar yoke (1240–1480), the Time of Troubles (1605–13) and the Provisional Government of 1917 – the *émigré* writer I. A. Il'in (1883–1954), widely quoted by nationalists in the 1990s, remarked in a mid-century essay that

One would have to be totally shortsighted and politically naive to imagine that . . . the Russian nation's thousand-year incapacity to form a federation could now change . . . into the ability to create small states, pay loyal respect to the laws, observe everlasting treaties and surmount political differences of opinion in the name of the general good. In fact, there is every reason to predict the opposite.[117]

These ominous words sound a loud contemporary echo. In particular, the image of liberal impotence in the Provisional Government has become a powerful component of nationalist charges against democrats in the 1990s who are said to prefer talk to action. By contrast, nationalists claim, all the most important reforms in Russian history have been conducted by a strong centralised power, notably a ruthless individual.[118]

While it is true that the fractious politics of the Russian Federation's first years have been chaotic – Russia was dubbed 'Weimar on the Volga' by *The Economist* at the height of confusion in December 1993 – there is little profit in seeking to apportion blame.[119] Though Yeltsin's populism has certainly hindered the formation of political parties, only a zealot like Ruslan Khasbulatov could label the early reform faction Democratic Russia unfit to provide 'the basis of a stable parliament' on the grounds that its 'entire purpose' lay 'in uncompromising struggle'.[120] Such accusations bear more than a passing resemblance to old-style Soviet charges of sabotage. A more plausible explanation of recent Russian political instability lies elsewhere. A period of confusion may be expected when an entrenched oligarchy breaks down in circumstances in which popular politicisation is incipient but necessarily limited. In Western Europe, as Norman Stone has written, the 1880s were just such a time as 'politics ceased to be a matter for a few local big men' and a multiplicity of parties began instead 'to organize seriously and to appeal for the votes of the masses that were too large to be controlled in the old way'.[121] This vocabulary, describing the confused transition between the age of Liberalism and the age of mass politics in the West, needs little transposition to make it applicable to Russia after the collapse of the communist monopoly.

One remedy for political chaos is the restoration of economic stability. From a nationalist perspective, however, it is unfortunate that Russia's principal source of support in the short term should be the materialist West. While some Russian scholars believe that only Western aid on the scale of the Marshall plan can rescue their ailing economy,[122] nationalists regard the influence of 'Chicago-school' economics as a form of insidious cultural imperialism in which privatisation and Protestantism form a diabolic conspiracy designed to subvert Russian values.[123] A second remedy for political chaos is a stable constitution, guaranteed by law. Yet Western-style legalism is no less suspect in nationalist eyes than capitalism. In the USSR, where the law was derided as bourgeois, 'advocacy was alien to the state'.[124] But it was only because pre-revolutionary legal norms had been so weak that the Bolsheviks were able so insouciantly to ignore them after 1917. Despite attempts to develop a legal consciousness in late-imperial Russia,[125] the predominant conception of the law remained that of an edict requiring unquestioning submission rather than a codified source of authority open to interpretation by professionally trained minds. Even in the nineteenth century, therefore, 'those who looked primarily to what they regarded as the real, historical Russian tradition, the Russian way of life – of whom Dostoevsky is typical – rather despised law as a mark of an inferior society'.[126] It would be a fine irony if Yeltsin were to redeem himself in nationalist eyes by showing his own respect for Western legalism to be merely transitory. It is not, however, an impossible outcome to imagine. Confronted by the Russian Constitutional Court in September 1993, the president found that the most convenient solution was to dismiss its chairman, Valerii Zorkin; confronted by the Russian Parliament, he shelled it into submission.

The period between the crisis of September–October 1993 and the constitutional referendum and elections of 12 December marks the high point of Russian political instability down to the summer of 1994. When a random sample of 1,655 Russians was asked to 'assess the political situation today' on 3 December 1993, 7 per cent feared the establishment of dictatorship, 14 per cent claimed to identify the development of democracy, 17 per cent thought the old order was being preserved under a new name, 20 per cent found it hard to say, and a massive 42 per cent predicted the loss of order and increasing anarchy.[127] In the event, not only was order preserved in early 1994 but, for a variety of reasons, a degree of stability was restored. First, the constitution itself helped to cement presidential power; second, the prime minister, Viktor Chernomyrdin, managed to control inflation more successfully than his reputation had led commentators to anticipate; third, Zhirinovskii's unexpected electoral success forced a reorientation of government policy which, despite augmenting the parliamentary opposition with disappointed reformists from Russia's Choice, took more explicit account of nationalist opinion; fourth, most Russians relapsed into apathy, suggesting that their support for Zhirinovskii derived as much from disillusion with the 'democrats' in power as it did from any firm commitment to his extremist policies. It remains to be seen whether the semblance of stability bestowed by this curious conjunction of circumstances amounts, in the long term, to anything more productive than paralysis.

# PROSPECTS

Shortly after arriving in St Petersburg in 1914, the French ambassador Maurice Paléologue wrote in his diary:

The Russian nation is so heterogenous in its ethnical and moral composition, it is formed of elements so incongruous and anachronistic, it has always developed in such defiance of logic, through such a maze of clashes, shocks and inconsistencies, that its historic evolution utterly defies prophecy.[128]

Looking back on what the Russians have undergone in the intervening eighty years, their fate is scarcely more predictable in 1994.

To those who regard the nation-state as the natural political entity and see 'the chances of transcending the nation and superseding nationalism' as 'slim',[129] it is inconceivable that Russia can long survive as a multinational state comprising no fewer than eighty-nine administrative units, some of which are openly agitating for secession. For those people, the ultimate submission of the Russian Federation to centrifugal force is no less inevitable than the dissolution of the Soviet Union.[130] But this is surely too reductionist. A more convincing argument must take into account not only the demographic domination of the Russians, but also the international context. If the West played a crucial part in the dismantling of Soviet power, it will be no less vital to the preservation of Russia. It is simply not in Western interests to see Russia infinitely weakened. As Yeltsin and his foreign minister, Andrei Kozyrev, have come to appreciate, this fact, far from condemning them to slavish obedience to Western commands, may give them sufficient flexibility to disarm nationalist opposition by flattering 'Russia first' sensibilities.

Foreign policy, however, is perhaps the only sphere in which nationalists will be able to translate such sensibilities into clear policy goals (however impracticable some may be). Although advocates of the predominantly metaphysical 'Russian idea' recognise that they must also inject into it some positive plans for internal regeneration, most, like Solzhenitsyn, have been unable to move beyond earnest exhortations to live a moral, Christian life.[131] This is shaky ground: the religious revival of the 1980s has not only passed its peak, but it can also be seen in retrospect to have involved many non-believers for whom the sole value of religion was as a symbol of national identity. Crucially, religious commitment has had no more than a marginal impact on Russian believers' voting habits.[132] Yet, in other respects, the nationalists are even less well prepared to implement a positive programme. Above all, the very intensity of their rejection of the government's 'religion of economics' has precluded any serious consideration of an alternative economic strategy of their own. Asked, during a round table of opposition leaders convened by *Nash sovremennik* in mid-1993, whether the nationalists had a long-term policy for national reconstruction, Il'ia Konstantinov, representing Russian Unity (*Rossiiskoe edinstvo*), admitted that they did not; only Sergei Baburin, coordinator of Russia (*Rossiia*), could advance beyond vacuous generalities.[133]

Some potential implications of the contemporary 'Russian idea' nevertheless emerge from a term devised by the philologist G. A. Gachev to characterise the Russian *mentalité* – *kosmopsikhologos*.[134] Though his terminology seems to derive from Berdiaev,[135] Gachev follows a tradition stretching from Montesquieu to Solzhenitsyn in emphasising the impact of Russia's size on the form of her government. The spatial element of his composite – *kosmos* – signifies the huge

Russian land. Because feminine 'mother Russia' is so attractive to foreigners that they want to attack her, she needs the masculine protection not only of her sons and husbands – the Russian people – but of a second masculine force, the state. As the source of economic as much as military discipline, a strong state must be the country's 'principal boss'. Nationalisation is inevitable in the Siberian wastes: 'Privatise the tundra if you can!' In turn, the Russian psyche ought to complement the country's vastness rather than defy it. Yet past regimes have opted to 'torture and persecute both people and country' by attempting too much too quickly. Peter the Great, Lenin and Stalin, and Gorbachev himself all preached *uskorenie* (economic acceleration), and all of them came to grief. By contrast, a truly Russian policy – conceptualised in the *logos* of Gachev's composite – would be reconciled to slower development.

The pace of change had already begun to slow in 1994: Gaidar's economic shock tactics have given way to a less intellectually consistent but politically more stable regime under Chernomyrdin. That may offer some small comfort to many Russians. But it is not in their nature to be optimistic. Whatever solution may be found to the Russian question, it is hard to imagine that Russian nationalism will lose its traditionally defensive and 'sacrificial' tone.[136] For as Igor Shafarevich – then a dissident mathematician, now a prominent nationalist spokesman – wrote in 1972: 'however great the misfortunes that Russia has brought on other peoples, she has always brought even greater ones on her own'.[137]

# ACKNOWLEDGEMENTS

I am grateful to Dr Evan Mawdsley for reading this chapter in draft and suggesting a number of improvements. I alone am responsible for any remaining errors of fact or interpretation.

# NOTES

1.  A. Solzhenitsyn, *Rebuilding Russia: Reflections and Tentative Proposals*, trans. A. Klimoff (London, Harvill Press 1991), p. 11.
2.  Id., 'Russkii vopros k kontsu XX veka', *Novyi mir*, (1994), no. 7, pp. 135–76.
3.  *Konstitutsiia Rossiiskoi Federatsii* (Moscow, 1993), p. 1.
4.  A. S. Barsenkov, A. I. Vdovin and V. A. Koretskii, *Russkii vopros v natsional'noi politike XX vek* (Moscow, Moskovskii rabochii 1993), pp. 126–38. The Russian diaspora is treated separately in chapter twenty-five.
5.  See Appendix 2.

6. V. P. Neroznak, 'Sovremennaia etnoiazykovaia situatsiia v Rossii', *Izvestiia Akademii nauk, seriia Literatury i iazyka*, vol. 53, no. 2 (1994), pp. 18, 27.

7. S. Fomin, 'O russkikh natsional'nykh interesakh', *Molodaia gvardiia*, (1993), no. 2, p. 15.

8. For the sake of simplicity, I have employed the masculine singular form throughout.

9. *The Economist*, vol. 329, no. 7839, 27 Nov. 1993, p. 48.

10. J. Dunlop, 'Russia: confronting a loss of empire', in I. Bremmer and R. Taras (eds), *Nation and politics in the Soviet successor states* (Cambridge, Cambridge University Press 1993), p. 46.

11. Iu. V. Arutiunian *et al.*, *Russkie: Etnosotsiologicheskie ocherki* (Moscow, Nauka 1992), p. 426.

12. Iu. V. Arutiunian, 'Simptomy istoricheskoi transformatsii sotsial'no-politicheskogo soznaniia russkikh', *Otechestvennaia istoriia*, (1994) no. 3, p. 126.

13. See, for example, A. Posadskaya (ed.), *Women in Russia: A New Era in Russian Feminism* (London, Verso 1994).

14. C. Emerson, 'The Shape of Russian Cultural Criticism in the Post-communist Period', *Canadian Slavonic Papers*, vol. 34, no. 4 (1992), p. 362 and *passim*.

15. Solzhenitsyn, 'Russkii vopros', p. 174.

16. See R. F. Christian, *Tolstoy's War and Peace: A Study* (Oxford, Oxford University Press 1962), chapter 2, and especially A. B. Wachtel, *An Obsession with History: Russian Writers Confront their Past* (Stanford, CA, Stanford University Press 1994).

17. V. Aksiuchits, 'Orden russkoi intelligentsii', *Moskva*, (1994), no. 4, p. 92.

18. *The Economist*, vol. 329, no. 7834, 23 Oct. 1993, p. 49.

19. 'Risk istoricheskogo vybora v Rossii (materialy "kruglogo stola")', *Voprosy filosofii*, (1994) no. 5, p. 3. The pejorative language illustrates lack of sympathy for extreme nationalism.

20. The early years of the Russian Federation have seen the widespread reprinting of books published in late-imperial Russia, and demonstrated a popular demand for salacious material about her rulers, especially Catherine II, Nicholas II and Rasputin. The pre-revolutionary white, blue and red tricolour has replaced the hammer and sickle as the national flag.

21. See R. O. Crummey, *The Formation of Muscovy 1304–1613* (London, Longman 1987).

22. M. Cherniavsky 'Russia', in O. Ranum (ed.), *National Consciousness, History & Political Culture in Early-Modern Europe* (Baltimore, MD, Johns Hopkins University Press 1975), pp. 118–43.

23. A. Kappeler, *Russland als Vielvölkerreich: Entstehung, Geschichte, Zerfall* (Munich, 1992), is the best modern work on the empire in any language.

24. See e.g. P. Dukes, 'Klyuchevsky and The Course of Russian History' in P. Dukes (ed.), *Russia and Europe* (London, Collins and Brown 1991), pp. 108–15.

25. E. Gellner, *Nations and Nationalism* (Oxford, Blackwell 1983), p. 57 and *passim*.

26. I. Serman, 'Russian National Consciousness and its Development in the Eighteenth Century', in R. Bartlett and J. M. Hartley (eds), *Russia in the Age of the Enlightenment* (London, Macmillan 1990), p. 43. Cf. L. Greenfeld, *Nationalism: Five Roads to Modernity* (Cambridge, MA, Harvard University Press 1992), pp. 238–42, on the less exclusive formulations of non-noble writers in the mid-eighteenth century.

27. G. L. Freeze, 'The *Soslovie* (Estate), Paradigm and Russian Social History', *American Historical Review*, vol. 91, no. 1 (1986), pp. 11–36.

28. H.-D. Löwe, 'Russian Nationalism and Tsarist Nationalities Policy in Semi-Constitutionalist Russia, 1905–1914', in R. B. McKean (ed.), *New Perspectives in Modern Russian History* (London, Macmillan 1992), p. 252.

29. See e.g. the January 1881 issue of his 'Diary of a Writer', written just before his death: F. M. Dostoevskii, *Polnoe sobranie sochinenii*, 30 vols (Leningrad, Nauka 1970–1990), vol. 27, pp. 5–26.

30. D. S. Likhachev, *Reflections on Russia*, ed. N. Petro, trans. C. Sever (Boulder, CO, Westview 1991), p. 166, emphasis added. Cf. Dostoevskii, *op. cit.*, p. 15: 'Petersburg is absolutely not [synonymous with] Russia. For the great majority of Russians, the only significance of St Petersburg is that the tsar lives there.'

31. See e.g. L. A. Tikhomirov, *Monarkhicheskaia gosudarstvennost'* (St Petersburg, Rossiiskii imperskii soiuz-orden 1992), pp. 289–96, 334–40. This volume, by a famous revolutionary turned monarchist, was reprinted from the original 1905 edition by contemporaries 'fighting for the restoration of Holy Orthodox Russia, the Russian Orthodox Tsardom' (p. 6).

32. R. Wortman, 'Moscow and St Petersburg: The Problem of Political Center in Tsarist Russia, 1881–1914', in S. Wilentz (ed.), *Rites of Power: Symbolism, Ritual and Politics since the Middle Ages* (Philadelphia, PA, 1985), pp. 244–74, quoted at p. 268.

33. M. S. Flier, 'The Church of the Savior on the Blood: Projection, Rejection, Resurrection', in R. P. Hughes and I. Paperno (eds), *Christianity and the Eastern Slavs, vol II: Russian Culture in Modern Times, California Slavic Studies*, vol. 17 (Berkeley, CA, University of California Press 1994), pp. 27–30, 42–3.

34. R. Wortman, 'Nikolai II i obraz samoderzhaviia', *Istoriia SSSR*, (1991) no. 2, pp. 120–1; B. Otmetev and J. Stuart, *St. Petersburg: Portrait of an Imperial City* (London, Cassell 1990), pp. 116–7; D. Lieven, *Nicholas II: Emperor of All the Russias* (London, John Murray 1993), chap. 7.

35. Wortman, 'Moscow and St Petersburg', p. 268.

36. S. Iu. Vitte, *Vospominaniia*, ed. A. L. Sidorov, 3 vols (Moscow, Nauka 1960), vol. 3, p. 274.

37. See, e.g., D. Saunders, *The Ukrainian Impact on Russian Culture 1750–1850* (Edmonton, Canadian Institute of Ukrainian Studies 1985), pp. 65–111.

38. N. I. Tsimbaev, 'Rossiia i russkie: Natsional'nyi vopros v Rossiiskoi imperii', in Iu. S. Kukushkin *et al.*, *Russkii narod: istoricheskaia sud'ba v XX v.* (Moscow, ANKO 1993), p. 46.

39. H. Rogger, *National Consciousness in Eighteenth-Century Russia* (Cambridge, MA, Harvard University Press 1960), *passim*.

40. Compare A. Gleason, *European and Muscovite: Ivan Kireevsky and the*

*Origins of Slavophilism* (Cambridge, MA, Harvard University Press 1972) with the thinkers discussed by E. C. Thaden, *Conservative Nationalism in Nineteenth-Century Russia* (Seattle, WA, University of Washington Press 1964).

41. See N. V. Riasanovksy, *Nicholas I and Official Nationality, 1825–1855* (Berkeley, CA, University of California Press 1969).

42. S. Hackel, *The Poet and the Revolution: Aleksandr Blok's 'The Twelve'* (Oxford, Clarendon Press 1975), p. 41, and *passim* for reflections on the 'different, and possibly irreconcilable, connotations' of *Rossiia* and *Rus'*.

43. B. Anderson, *Imagined Communities*, revised edn (London, Verso 1991), p. 86.

44. *Russkaia starina*, vol. 116 (1916), quoted at p. 356, undated confidential letter, summer 1864.

45. For the argument that the USSR was held together by a balance of centripetal and centrifugal tensions, see A. Besançon, 'Nationalism and Bolshevism in the USSR', in R. Conquest (ed.), *The Last Empire: Nationality and the Soviet Future* (Stanford, CA, Hoover Institution Press, 1986), pp. 1–13.

46. I. Vinogradoff (ed.), 'Some Russian Imperial Letters to Prince V. P. Meshchersky (1839–1914)', *Oxford Slavonic Papers*, vol. 10 (1962), pp. 111–2, letters of June–July 1867.

47. M. Aronson, *Troubled Waters: The Origins of the 1881 Anti-Jewish Pogroms in Russia* (Pittsburgh, PA, University of Pittsburgh Press 1990), pp. 228–31 and *passim*.

48. E. C. Thaden, (ed.), *Russification in the Baltic Provinces and Finland, 1855–1914* (Princeton, NJ, Princeton University Press 1981), esp. pp. 54–75.

49. G. Hosking, 'The Russian Myth: Empire and People', in P. J. S. Duncan and M. Rady (eds), *Towards a New Community: Culture and Politics in Post-Totalitarian Europe* (Hamburg and Münster, LIT Verlag), p. 37.

50. See G. A. Hosking, *A History of the Soviet Union* (London, Collins 1985), chaps 4, 9, 14; J. B. Dunlop, *The Faces of Contemporary Russian Nationalism* (Princeton, NJ, Princeton University Press 1983); and B. Nahaylo and V. Swoboda, *Soviet Disunion: A History of the Nationalities Problem in the USSR* (London, Hamish Hamilton 1990). The first two are sympathetic to the Russians; the last is not.

51. A. Remizov, 'Ognevitsa', quoted in Hackel, *The Poet and the Revolution*, p. 175. Remizov used '*Rossiia*' rather than '*Rus*''.

52. G. Simon, *Nationalism and Policy towards the Nationalities in the Soviet Union: From Totalitarian Dictatorship to Post-Stalinist Society*, trans. K. and O. Forster (Boulder, CO, Westview 1991), pp. 73, 77.

53. For quirky essays on this theme, see B. Thomson, *Lot's Wife and the Venus of Milo: Conflicting attitudes to the cultural heritage in modern Russia* (Cambridge, Cambridge University Press 1978), quoted at p. 139.

54. For an account of Bolshevik cultural policy placing the shift towards intolerance in spring 1922, see R. Pipes, *Russia under the Bolshevik Regime, 1919–1924* (London, Harvill 1994), chap. 6.

55. M. Raeff, *Russia Abroad: A Cultural History of The Russian Emigration* (New York, Oxford University Press 1990), pp. 96–8, 100; V. Pachmuss, trans. and ed., *A Russian Cultural Revival: A Critical Anthology of*

*Emigré Literature before 1939* (Knoxville, TN, University of Tennessee Press 1981).

56. Hosking, *Soviet Union*, p. 118.
57. N.V. Riasanovsky, *The Image of Peter the Great in Russian History and Thought* (Oxford, Oxford University Press 1985), pp. 255–90; J. Barber, *Soviet Historians in Crisis, 1928–1932* (London, Macmillan 1981), *passim*.
58. Quoted by I. Golomstock, *Totalitarian Art in the Soviet Union, The Third Reich, Fascist Italy and the People's Republic of China*, trans. R. Chandler (London, Collins Harvill 1990), p. 244.
59. M. Perrie, *The Image of Ivan the Terrible in Russian Folklore* (Cambridge, Cambridge University Press 1987), pp. 15–27.
60. P. Duncan, 'Orthodoxy and Russian Nationalism in the USSR, 1917–1988', in G. A. Hosking (ed.), *Church, Nation and State in Russia and Ukraine* (London, Macmillan 1991), pp. 314–8.
61. Quoted in J. Barber and M. Harrison, *The Soviet Home Front 1941–1945: A social and economic history of the USSR in World War II* (London, Longman 1991), pp. 115–6.
62. I. Berlin, *Personal Impressions* (London, Hogarth Press 1980), pp. 161, 177, 197.
63. See e.g. A. M. Pankratova, *Velikii russkii narod* (Moscow, 1952).
64. A penetrating contextual study is O. Chadwick, *The Christian Church in the Cold War* (London, Allen Lane 1992).
65. G. A. Hosking, *The Awakening of the Soviet Union* (London, Heinemann 1990), p. 107.
66. E. R. Frankel, *Novy Mir* (Cambridge, Cambridge University Press 1981), p. 150. For the subsequent furore, see Zh. A. Medvedev, *Desiat' let posle 'Odnogo dnia Ivana Denisovicha'* (London, Macmillan 1973).
67. Dunlop, *Contemporary Russian Nationalism*, chap. 10; idem, *The New Russian Nationalism* (New York, Praeger 1985).
68. P. Duncan, 'The Fate of Russian Nationalism: The *Samizdat* Journal *Veche* Revisited', *Religion in Communist Lands*, vol. 16, no. 1 (1988), pp. 36–53.
69. See especially A. Yanov, *The Russian Challenge and the Year 2000*, trans. I. J. Rosenthal (Oxford, Blackwell 1987).
70. L. Drobizheva, 'Perestroika and the ethnic consciousness of Russians', in G. W. Lapidus *et al.* (eds), *From union to commonwealth: Nationalism and separatism in the Soviet republics* (Cambridge, Cambridge University Press 1992), pp. 100–1. See also P. J. S. Duncan, 'The party and Russian nationalism in the USSR: from Brezhnev to Gorbachev', in P. J. Potichnyi (ed.), *The Soviet Union: Party and Society* (Cambridge, Cambridge University Press 1987), pp. 229–44.
71. A. Zinoviev, *The Reality of Communism*, trans. C. Janson (London, Paladin 1985), p. 241. In a sense, of course, he was right: national conflicts were as much a symptom as the cause of the Soviet collapse.
72. Their opposition centred on the potential for damage to fish habitats in the Ob-Irtysh basin: see P. Sinnot, 'Water diversion politics', *Radio Liberty Research Bulletin*, 374/88; A. Sheehy and S. Voronitsyn, 'Ecological protest in the USSR 1986–8, ibid., 191/88; C. E. Ziegler, *Environmental Policy in the USSR* (London, Pinter 1987), *passim*.
73. See G. A. Hosking, *Beyond Socialist Realism: Soviet Fiction since*

*Ivan Denisovich* (London, Granada 1980), chap. 3, and K. F. Parthé, *Russian Village Prose: The Radiant Past* (Princeton, NJ, Princeton University Press), chap. 5.

74. P. Valliere, 'The Social and Political Role of the Orthodox Church in Post-Communist Russia', *Nationalities Papers*, vol. 20, no. 1 (1992), p. 3, n. 4.
75. V. E. Volkov, L. I. Krynitsa, I. B. Turkevich, *Novyi Peterburg: Spravochnik* (St Petersburg, 1992), pp. 83–94.
76. S. White, I. McAllister, O. Kryshtanovskaya, 'Religion and Politics in Postcommunist Russia', *Religion, State and Society*, vol. 22, no. 1 (1994), p. 75.
77. For comment by a mildly bewildered American scholar, see M. Rediker, 'The Old Guard, the New Guard, and the People at the Gates: New Approaches to the Study of American History in the U.S.S.R.', *William and Mary Quarterly*, vol. 48, no. 4 (1991), pp. 580–97. I owe this reference to Professor A. A. M. Duncan.
78. 'Purification' is the revealing title of O. Volobuev and S. Kuleshov, *Ochishchenie: istoriia i perestroika* (Moscow, Novosti 1989).
79. Y. Afanasyev, 'Filling in the Blank Spots in Soviet History', trans. V. Voronin and A. Shulman, in Dukes (ed.), *Russia and Europe*, pp. 124–35; A. Nove, *Glasnost' in Action: Cultural Renaissance in Russia* (Boston, Unwin Hyman 1989), chap. 3. See also R. W. Davies, *Soviet History in the Gorbachev Revolution* (London, Macmillan 1989).
80. V. Kozhinov, 'Pravda i istina', *Nash sovremennik*, 4/1988, pp. 160–75; Hosking, *Awakening*, pp. 108–9.
81. S. V. Kuleshov, *et al.*, *Nashe otechestvo: opyt politicheskoi istorii*, 2 vols (Moscow, Terra 1991), I: 7. The unabashed emphasis on politics, rather than on society and economics, in itself marks a significant departure from Marxist-Leninist practice.
82. *Literatura russkogo zarubezh'ia vozvroshchaetsia na rodinu*, 2 parts (Moscow, Rudomino 1993). Among *émigré* writings on Russian national identity, see especially N. O. Losskii, *Kharakter russkogo naroda* (Frankfurt am Main, Posev 1957).
83. See e.g. A. P. Lanshchikov, *Natsional'nyi vopros v Rossii* (Moscow, Sovremennik 1991), p. 4.
84. E. V. Anisimov, *Vremia petrovskikh reform* (Leningrad, Lenizdat 1989); V. Seliunin, 'Istoki', *Novyi mir*, (1988) no. 5, pp. 185–6; V. G. Sirotkin, 'Stolypin i Gorbachev: popytki dvukh reform "sverkhu"', in idem, *Vekhi otechestvennoi istorii* (Moscow, Mezhdunarodnye otnoshenie 1991), pp. 31–42.
85. For an important nationalist essay, see V. Kozhinov, 'Samaia bol'shaia opasnost', *Nash sovremennik*, (1989), no. 1, pp. 141–75.
86. These manoeuvrings are analysed in detail by J. B. Dunlop, *The Rise of Russia and the Fall of the Soviet Empire* (Princeton, NJ, Princeton University Press 1993), chap. 1.
87. See G. A. Hosking, J. Aves and P. J. S. Duncan, *The Road to Post-Communism: Independent Political Movements in the Soviet Union 1985–1991* (London, Pinter 1992), esp. pp. 83–4.
88. Dunlop, *Rise of Russia*, pp. 130–2.
89. Quoted by V. Pudozhev, '"Putem samosoznaniia:" obozrenie novykh russkikh gazet', *Nash sovremennik*, (1991), no. 1, p. 165.

90.  J. Wishnevsky, 'The origins of Pamiat'', *Survey*, vol. 30, no. 3 (1988) pp. 79–91.
91.  *BBC Summary of World Broadcasts*, SU/0366 B/3, 24 Jan. 1989; M. Mihajlov, 'A Talk with *Ogonek*'s Chief Editor, Vitalii Korotich', Radio Liberty *Report on the USSR*, 3 March 1989, pp. 32–4.
92.  For a revealing collection of documents, see M. Deich and L. Zhuravlev, *"Pamiat"*: *Kak ona est'* (Moscow, Tsunami 1991).
93.  Parthé, *Russian Village Prose*, pp. 92–8.
94.  A. White, 'Charity, Self-help and Politics in Russia, 1985–91', *Europe–Asia Studies*, vol. 45, no. 5 (1993), p. 806.
95.  *Izvestiia*, 8 June 1989, p. 6.
96.  Solzhenitsyn, *Rebuilding Russia*, p. 15.
97.  *The Economist*, vol. 321, no. 7729, 19 Oct. 1991, p. 66.
98.  P. Boldyrev, *Uroki Rossii: Dnevnik rossiiskogo separatista* (Tenafly NJ, Ermitazh 1993).
99.  N. Andreeva, *Nepodarennye printsipy, ili kratkii kurs istorii perestroiki: izbrannye stat'i, vystupleniia* (Leningrad, 1992), *passim*; P. Duncan, 'The rebirth of politics in Russia', in Hosking, Aves and Duncan, *The Road to Post-Communism*, p. 77.
100. By the end of 1992, all were firmly identified with the opposition to Yeltsin, either as part of the relatively moderate Civic Union or in alliance with the more extreme National Salvation Front. V. Tolz, 'The Burden of the Imperial Legacy', *RFE/RL Research Report*, vol. 2, no. 20, 14 May 1993, pp. 41–3.
101. These terms are Dunlop's.
102. See S. White, I. McAllister, and O. Kryshtanovskaya, 'El'tsin and his Voters: Popular Support in the 1991 Russian Presidential Elections and After', *Europe–Asia Studies*, vol. 46, no. 2 (1994), pp. 285–303.
103. Dunlop, *Rise of Russia*, p. 55.
104. For example, while Yeltsin twice refused to support a new version of the law on freedom of conscience designed to favour the Orthodox Church at the expense of its Protestant rivals, Rutskoi signalled his willingness to sign the new law without delay on 25 September 1993. V. Sirotkin, 'Pravoslavie: uroki istorii', *Nezavisimaia gazeta*, 30 September 1993, p. 5. In the circumstances, it is hardly surprising that Patriarch Aleksii's attempts to 'mediate' between Parliament and the president in talks at the Danilov monastery led to accusations that the Orthodox hierarchy were agents of political reaction.
105. Iu. S. Kukushkin, 'Sud'ba naroda – sud'ba strany', in Kukushkin *et al.*, *Russkii narod*.
106. Likhachev, *Reflections on Russia*, p. 169.
107. Since February 1992, their views have been articulated by the Russian Officers' Union: S. Foye, 'The Defense Ministry and the New Military "Opposition"', *RFE/RL Research Report*, vol. 2, no. 20, 14 May 1993, p. 70.
108. G. Podleskikh (ed.), 'Prosveshchennyi patriotizm P. A. Stolypina – Novaia politicheskaia real'nost' v Rossii', *Moskva*, (1991) no. 5, p. 6.
109. V. Berezovskii, 'Vladimir Zhirinovksii kak fenomen rossiiskoi politiki', *Svobodnaia mysl'*, (1994) no. 4, p. 106.
110. Solzhenitsyn, '"Russkii vopros"', p. 171.

111. Quoted by E. Lohr, 'Arkadii Volsky's Political Base', *Europe–Asia Studies*, vol. 45, no. 5 (1993), p. 815.
112. A. Sheehy, 'Russia's Republics: A Threat to its Territorial Integrity?', *RFE/RL Research Report*, vol. 2, no. 20, 14 May 1993, pp. 34–40.
113. Fomin, 'O russkikh natsional'nykh interesakh', pp. 7–8, 11, 16–17. It is worth emphasising, *pace* Fomin, that Russia has never been a nation-state.
114. E. Volodin, 'Rusofobiia kak gosudarstvennaia politika', *Molodaia gvardiia*, (1994), no. 2, p. 16.
115. By his correspondent, the influential censor E. M. Feoktistov, *Vospominaniia za kulisami politiki i literatury* (reprinted Newtonville, MA, Oriental Research Partners 1975), pp. 58–9.
116. Quoted in E. Mawdsley, *The Russian Civil War* (Boston, MA, Allen & Unwin 1987), pp. 281, 283.
117. I. A. Il'in, *Nashi zadachi: stat'i 1948–1954gg.*, 2 vols (Paris, Russkii Obshche-Voinskii Soiuz 1956), vol. 1, p. 190.
118. D. Il'in, '"Russkaia ideia" na poligone "Demokratii"', *Nash sovremennik*, (1991) no. 2, pp. 26–7.
119. *The Economist*, vol. 329, no. 7842, p. 37. For a valiant attempt to impose order on chaos, see R. Sakwa, *Russian Politics and Society* (London, Routledge 1993); a useful biographical dictionary is A. S. Barsenkov, V. A. Koretskii, and A. I. Ostapenko, *Politicheskaia Rossiia segodnia*, 2 vols (Moscow, Moskovskii rabochii 1993). I am grateful to Dr Ostapenko for presenting me with a copy.
120. Y. M. Brudnyi, 'The Dynamics of "Democratic Russia", 1990–1993', *Post-Soviet Affairs*, vol. 9, no. 2 (1993), pp. 168–9; R. Khasbulatov, *The Struggle for Russia: Power and change in the democratic revolution*, ed. R. Sakwa (London, Routledge 1993), p. 240.
121. N. Stone, *Europe Transformed 1878–1919* (London, Fontana 1983), p. 42.
122. S. A. Karganov *et al.*, 'Zapadnaia pomoshch' Rossii: v chem ee oshibki?', *Znamia*, (1994) no. 4, pp. 157–83.
123. Father A. Moroz, 'Ostorozhno-Protestanty', *Moskva*, (1993), no. 10, pp. 197–8.
124. D. Kaminskaya, *Final Judgement: My Life as a Soviet Defence Lawyer*, trans. M. Glenny (London, Harvill 1983), p. 14; Hosking, *Awakening*, p. 127.
125. R. S. Wortman, *The Development of a Russian Legal Consciousness* (Chicago, IL, Chicago University Press 1976).
126. L. Schapiro, 'The Importance of Law in the Study of Politics and History', in idem, *Russian Studies* (London, Collins Harvill 1986), p. 41.
127. *The Economist*, vol. 329, no. 7841, p. 29, quoting a poll conducted by the All-Russian Centre for Public Opinion.
128. M. Paléologue, *An Ambassador's Memoirs*, trans. F. A. Holt, 3 vols (London, Hutchinson 1923), vol. 1, p. 77.
129. A. D. Smith, *National Identity* (Harmondsworth, Penguin 1991), p. 175.
130. See e.g. J. E. Stern, 'Moscow Meltdown: Can Russia Survive?', *International Security*, vol. 18, no. 4 (1994), pp.40–65.
131. Solzhenitsyn, '"Russkii vopros"', p. 176.

132. White *et al.*, 'Religion and Politics in Postcommunist Russia', *passim*. See also my essay: 'What Price an Orthodox Revival? The Dilemmas of the Russian Church' in Duncan and Rady (eds), *Towards a New Community*, pp. 81–92.
133. 'Oppozitsiia i russkii vopros', *Nash sovremennik*, (1993) no. 6, pp. 98–104, quoted at p. 101.
134. 'Rossiiskaia mental'nost' (materialy "kruglogo stola")', *Voprosy filosofii*, (1994) no. 1, pp. 25–8.
135. See e.g. N. Berdiaev, *Sud'ba Rossii: Opyty po psikhologii voiny i natsional'nosti* (1918, reprinted Moscow, MGU 1990).
136. L. N. Vdovina, 'Chto est' "my" (Russkoe natsional'noe samosoznanie v kontekste istorii ot Srednevekov'ia k Novomu vremeni)', in Kukushkin *et al.*, *Russkii narod*, p. 18.
137. I. Shafarevich, 'Does Russia Have a Future?', in A. Solzhenitsyn *et al.*, *From Under the Rubble*, trans. M. Scammell *et al.* (London, Collins Harvill 1975), p. 293.

# CHAPTER FOUR

# Tatarstan and the Tatars

Marie Bennigsen Broxup

Although they possessed an administrative homeland in the Tatar ASSR, according to the 1989 census only approximately 26 per cent of the USSR's 6,648,760 Tatars lived there, the majority constituting large diaspora communities elsewhere in the Middle Volga and Urals, in Central Asia and Azerbaijan, the Donetsk region and Ukraine, and in smaller pockets stretching from the western borders of the USSR to the Pacific Ocean (notably in small rural colonies in the original homelands of other historical Tatar groups, such as Astrakhan, Kalmykia, West Siberia and the Baltic republics). According to the same census data, they accounted for 48.5 per cent (47.6 per cent in 1979) of the republic's total population of 3,642,000 in 1989. Latest figures available for the Republic of Tatarstan in the second half of 1992 give the total population of the republic as 3,695,900 with 1,700,110 Tatars. The data, however, may be inaccurate because unofficial estimates put the Tatar population of the republic at 52 per cent. The Tatars are Sunni Muslims of the Hanafi school and the most Westernised and Russified of the Muslims of the Former Soviet Union.

## BACKGROUND

In August 1989, the Muslim Religious Board for European Russia and Siberia celebrated the anniversary of eleven centuries since the official adoption of Islam by the kingdom of the Bulgars. The celebrations were heralded by the Kazan Tatar intelligentsia and political élite as 'the first true national festival' since the khanate of Kazan, heir to the Bulgar kingdom and the Golden Horde, was conquered and destroyed by the army of Ivan the Terrible in 1552.

Islam was already widely spread on the shores of the Volga and Kama river when Ibn Fadlan, the envoy of Caliph Jafar Al-Muktadir, reached the kingdom in 922, the year that marks the conversion of the Bulgars to Islam. As the Russian historian S. M. Solov'ev wrote:

For a long time Asia, Muslim Asia built here a home; a home not for nomadic hordes but for its civilisation; for a long time, a commercial industrial people, the Bulgars had been established here. When the Bulgar was already listening to the Quran on the shores of the Volga and the Kama, the Russian Slav had not yet started to build Christian churches . . . and had not yet conquered these places in the name of European civilisation.[1]

The Volga Tatars offer a unique example in the history of Dar ul-Islam, that of a Muslim nation which has survived over four centuries of foreign domination. Since the fall of Kazan the Russians have persistently tried to eradicate Islam, considered as an alien and hostile element. This they tried to achieve through several methods, most notably through colonisation and conversion to Christianity.

Military conquest was followed by a systematic policy of colonisation. The ruling classes were ruined, Muslims were expelled from Kazan, their richest lands were confiscated and distributed among the Russian nobility, the Orthodox monasteries and, later, the peasants. Fortresses were built across the region with merchants and artisans brought from Russian cities. Thus by the end of the sixteenth century the former territory of the khanate of Kazan was already ethnically mixed and by the end of the eighteenth century the present territory of the Tatar ASSR had a majority Russian population.[2]

After an initial period of religious tolerance under Ivan the Terrible, Tsar Feodor launched into an energetic missionary activity. As a result, a relatively large group of natives became Christian Orthodox but maintained the use of Tatar as a spoken and liturgic language. (They have survived until today as a separate community, the Staro-Kryashens.) From the Times of Trouble and the reign of the first Romanovs to that of Catherine II various measures were taken to eradicate Islam: mosques were destroyed, *waqf* property confiscated, special schools were opened for the children of Tatar converts, Muslims were expelled from villages where groups of converts had been formed and deported to remote districts, while Muslim proselytism was punishable by death. Peter the Great gave renewed vigour to the Christian campaign. His reign, and particularly that of Anna (1738–55), can be compared in terms of persecutions to the worst period of Stalin's purges: between 1740 and 1743 alone, 418 out of 536 mosques of the Kazan *guberniya* were destroyed.[3] These policies resulted in a massive exodus of the Tatars throughout the centuries towards Turkestan, the Kazakh Steppes and Siberia, in frequent armed uprisings at first led by the feudal aristocracy, and later in an active participation in the great popular uprisings of Stepan Razin and Pugachev. However, Catherine II did correct the dramatic errors of her predecessors. She halted the anti-Muslim campaign and established a Central Muslim Spiritual Board in Orenburg in 1783 and for a century afterwards the Tatar merchant class cooperated loyally with the Russian government.

The conquest of Central Asia put an end to this rewarding partnership, and new economic and religious pressures were once again brought to bear by the Russian government. In 1863 Nikolai Il'minsky of the Religious Academy of Kazan devised a policy, not unlike that of the early bishops of Kazan, aimed at creating a new Tatar intelligentsia converted to Orthodoxy but speaking and writing Tatar. This policy achieved some spectacular successes.[4] More than economic harassment (a decree of 1886 forbade the Tatars to own property and companies in Central Asia), the policy of religious assimilation was viewed as a deadly danger by the community and gained the Russians the undying resentment of the Tatar élites. However, the Tatar élites were quick to react. They understood perfectly well that in order to survive they had to regain intellectual, cultural and economic equality with the Russians, preserve Islam as the basis of Tatar society, keep the unity of the Muslim *umma* and reject all social conflicts within the community. This awareness resulted in the first and most widely spread modern reformist movement of the Muslim world – Jadidism. The *jadid* movement began as a religious reform (initiated by Shihabeddin Marjani between 1818 and 1889) seeking to break away from conservative traditionalism in order to allow Islam to survive in a modern world. It encompassed all aspects of social life: religion, education, literature, women's liberation and so on.

The movement flourished thanks to an extraordinary unity of purpose between the Tatar *ulema* and the bourgeoisie. At the end of the nineteenth century the cultural level of the Tatars was extremely high: the percentage of literacy was higher among the Tatars than among the Russians in the Kazan *guberniya*.[5] Kazan, Ufa and Orenburg became prestigious intellectual centres rivalling Istanbul, Cairo and Beirut. Spreading from the Volga, Jadidism, strongly imbued with Pan-Islamic and Pan-Turkic ideals, influenced all the Muslim intellectual élites of the Russian empire.

On the eve of the 1905 Revolution, the Tatars were a 'developed' nation with a sophisticated capitalist and even industrial experience. After the defeat of the Russian army in Manchuria in 1905, the *jadid* movement became politicised. Three Muslim congresses were held in quick succession in 1905 and 1906, and a Muslim Union (*Ittifaq al-Muslimin*) was founded under the aegis of the Tatars Abrurrashid Ibragimov, Yusuf Akchura and Sadri Maksudi. The aims of *Ittifaq* were moderate: equal civic rights for the Muslims, freedom of religion, education and press. Despite this, hopes of achieving liberal reforms and national equality were frustrated when in 1908 the monarchy adopted an intransigent attitude towards nationalist demands. As a result the leadership of the national movement became more radical and revolutionary. Confrontation was inevitable and at the time of the October Revolution the Tatar struggle against Russian centrism was at its height. Two factions could be distinguished: firstly, a Pan-Islamic and Pan-Turkic faction, advocating national and cultural extra-territorial autonomy for all Muslim nations within a unified, but decentralised and democratic, state; and secondly, a more narrowly nationalistic faction represented by the socialist and 'leftist' groups which favoured a federal solution and national territorial autonomy.

Revolution and Civil War were fought in all the Muslim territories. Because of the blunders and tactical errors of the White generals, the Bolsheviks were seen by most of the native leaders as a lesser threat to their aspirations. Lenin and Stalin's clever political manoeuvring (the Appeal to the Muslim Workers of Russia and the Soviet East of the Soviet People's Commissar of 20 November 1917), and the concessions they gave to the Muslims while the outcome of the Civil War was uncertain gained the unstinting support of the Tatar nationalists to the Soviet state until 1921.

On 23 March 1918 a decree of the NARKOMNATS (People's Commissariat of Nationalities) proclaimed the creation of the 'Tatar-Bashkir Soviet Republic of the Russian Soviet Federation on the territory of Southern Ural and Middle Volga', but the outbreak of the Civil War in May 1918, with the Tatar-Bashkir territory at the heart of the confrontation, rendered the decree meaningless. The hopes of the nationalists for a large Turkic state on the Volga were crushed with the creation on 23 March 1919 of the Bashkir Autonomous Soviet Socialist Republic, followed by the Tatar Autonomous Soviet Socialist Republic on 27 May 1920. The borders of the republics were drawn arbitrarily – they left 75 per cent of the Tatar population outside the boundaries of their nominal republic while in the Bashkir ASSR Tatars represented the majority ethnic group.

From 1921 Tatar national political life and dissent were channelled through the Party. Muslim National Communism soon became a deviation from the Party line, and from 1923 to 1928 became an active opposition movement. The greatest exponent of Muslim National Communism was the Tatar, Mir Said Sultan Galiev. The highest ranking Muslim in the Communist Party, he was the son of a Tatar schoolteacher. He joined the Russian Communist Party in November 1917. His rise through the Party hierarchy was meteoric. He became simultaneously a member of the Central Muslim Commissariat (MUSKOM), chairman of the Muslim Military Collegium, a member of the little Collegium of the NARKOMNATS, editor of Zhizn' Natsional'nostei, and a member of the Central Executive Committee of the Tatar republic. The basis of Sultan Galiev's thinking was the idea of 'proletarian nations'. He argued that all the classes of Muslim colonised peoples had the right to be called 'proletarian' because of the oppression imposed by colonisers. Priority had to be given to national liberation, the class struggle postponed indefinitely, and the cohesion of the Muslim society preserved at all costs. He left no doubts as to the identity of the colonisers: the Russians including the Bolsheviks, whom he considered totally incapable of solving the national problem. Sultan Galiev wanted to give Marxism a 'Muslim' national face. He campaigned for the establishment of an independent Muslim Communist Party with its own elected Central Committee and for the creation of a Muslim Red Army with Muslim commanders and officers. He hoped to form a Colonial International independent from the Komintern, and a large Muslim-Turkic state, the 'Republic of Turan', which would have stretched from Kazan to the Pamirs. He dreamed of channelling the energies unleashed by the Revolution in the direction of Asia, rather than the industrial West where 'the fire of revolution no longer burned'. Sultan Galiev was arrested, on the personal initiative of Stalin,[6] in May 1923 'for counter-revolutionary nationalist conspiracy against the power of the Soviets'. Freed in 1924, he was arrested again in 1928, tried as a 'traitor' in 1929, and condemned to ten years' hard labour in the Solovki camp. He was executed in December 1939.[7]

## VOLGA TATARS UNDER SOVIET RULE

Between 1924 and 1939 the political battle within the Communist Party of the Volga Tatar ASSR (or Tatarstan) was fought by the 'right' – Tatar partisans of Sultan Galiev – and the 'left' – almost exclusively Russian Communists. The tragic outcome was the liquidation of all the Tatar political and intellectual élite. The conflict between the 'right' and 'left' broke out at the 9th Regional Conference of the Communist Party organisation of Tatarstan in May 1924. For the first time, the Tatar 'right' was directly attacked by the Russian Communists. The Tatars were reminded that 'one should not confuse the objectives of World Revolution with the aspirations of the Tatars. Without denying the importance of the rise of oppressed nationalities, one must not forget that the future of the Revolution depends on the West alone'.[8] Furthermore, it was stated that Russian chauvinism did not exist among Russian Communists and that it was merely an invention of the Tatar nationalists aimed at disguising their own subversive activity. Soviet historians recognise today that the brutal politics of collectivisation, confiscation of *kulaks'* lands and the introduction of the class struggle in Tatar society between 1923 and 1928 was clumsy and gave rise to a violent outburst of Muslim nationalism within the Tatar Communist Party and the *Komsomol*. Indeed, after April 1926, Tatar Communists, previously divided into 'right' and 'left' factions, united in one national front against their Russian comrades, and for two years attempted to block the policy of the Party and of the Russian Communists whom they accused of leading 'an imperialist policy contrary to the national interests of Tatarstan'.[9]

The condemnation of Sultan Galiev was followed by systematic purges. The first victims were Sultan Galiev's companions and the right wing of the Tatar Communists: Keshaf Muhtarov, president of the executive Central Committee of Tatarstan, Kasym Mansurov, head of the propaganda section, Rauf Sabirov, First Secretary of the *obkom*, Gayaz Maksudov, Mikdad Burundukov and many others. All were accused of having created an illegal 'counter-revolutionary, anti-Soviet, anti-Communist and anti-Russian party' under the leadership of Sultan Galiev, with the aim of installing a bourgeois, capitalist regime. Furthermore, they were accused of having contacts with the Basmachi rebels of Turkestan, Milli Firqa (the Crimean Tatar national party), White *émigrés* and British imperialists.

In quick succession, the Party's offensive was then directed against the university, the literary circles, and in 1931 the Communist Party of Bashkiria, which still sheltered many partisans of Sultan Galiev. By 1933 organised opposition had ceased, but the purges continued until 1939 among the Tatar and Bashkir intelligentsia and affected all those – former partisans or opponents of Sultan Galiev – who defended the political or cultural autonomy of native Muslims. (Even linguists opposing the introduction of the Latin alphabet became a target.)

In 1940 the campaign against nationalism slowed down, which allowed the Tatar Mufti of Ufa, Abdurahman Rasulaev, one of the few *jadid* clerics to have survived the religious and political persecutions, to approach Stalin with the proposal of normalising relations between the Soviet government and Islam. Stalin accepted Rasulaev's proposal. A concordat was signed granting Islam legal status and an official Islamic administration.

In the post-war period, Tatarstan underwent an intensive industrialisation and urbanisation programme together with a heavy Russian immigration. This resulted in a dangerous polarisation of society in Tatarstan where the Tatars represented mainly the rural, peasant communities and the Russians the urban industrial workers and technical cadres. Although urban migration began later among the Tatars than among the Russians, it remained fairly steady between 1930 and 1950, the gap between the two communities beginning to widen in the late 1950s. As an example, the percentage difference between the Tatar and Russian urban population in the republic was 13 per cent in 1926, increasing to 28.4 per cent in 1959 and 30.5 per cent in 1979.[10] Altogether, according to the All-Union census of 1979, the Tatars represented only 38 per cent of the urban population of the republic. It is likely that their proportion of the urban population of Tatarstan is continuing to diminish today as imports of Russian and other 'European' labour remains uncontrolled, while Tatars from other areas of the former USSR wishing to return to their homeland are discriminated against and find difficulty in settling in the cities. As a result of this, imbalance of qualification of Tatar workers is becoming lower than that of the other national groups of the republic, and the proportion of national cadres in key sectors of the economy is unequal to other nationalities. In recent years, inter-ethnic tension has grown, especially in areas with a high influx of immigrants.

## TATARS SINCE *PERESTROIKA*

In the post-Stalin era, Tatar nationalism, more sophisticated and less outspoken than nationalism in Central Asia and the Caucasus, could mainly be discerned in the efforts of the intelligentsia to rehabilitate their political history and literature. Of particular importance in this revival was the founding of the Tatar Public Centre (*Tatarskii Obshchestvennyi Tsentr*) or TOTs, which held its founding congress in February 1989 and came to play, until the end of 1993, the role of a national and popular front not unlike that of the Baltic states. TOTs' original manifesto clearly defined the concerns of the Tatar élites at the time.[11] Some of the problems it addressed were common to all the Soviet nationalities, others were specific to the Tatars. Some issues must be singled out because they remain relevant, although in different form, despite the signature of a treaty between Tatarstan and the Russian Federation in February 1994. The main topic concerned federalism and sovereignty. Dissatisfaction with the 'second rate' status of the Tatar republic had been endemic since the days of Sultan Galiev. It surfaced in 1936 when a new constitution of the USSR was being adopted, again in the 1960s and 1970s resulting in purges of the national élites, and again in 1986 when an active campaign was unleashed demanding that the republic be upgraded from 'autonomous' to 'union republic' status. TOTs' manifesto stated in its introductory lines the need for a genuine federal system that could guarantee the sovereignty of all the republics and nations of the USSR. Without this fundamental prerequisite there could be no *perestroika*:

In the course of the establishment of the Soviet state various kinds of national–state structures were formed. Some peoples received the status of 'union', others of 'autonomous' national–state structures. Originally the distinction did not presuppose any limitation in the right of the autonomous republics, and did not hold back the development of their peoples. Later, however, nations in our country turned out to have unequal rights and opportunities.

Or as put more succinctly by Rafael Hakimov, in an article in *Komsomolets Tatarii*:[12]

It is essential to equalise the rights of federal and autonomous republics as sovereign governments. If a republic exists it must be sovereign otherwise it amounts to no more than an oblast. The notion of an autonomous republic as a government without sovereignty is a juridical and political nonsense.

Another issue concerned the economy. Unlike other Soviet Muslim republics, Tatarstan was saturated with heavy industries, in particular the military-industrial complex. It had a qualified native personnel and a highly productive agricultural sector. It provided a substantial portion of Russia's oil requirements. Intensive industrialisation in the past had served as an excuse for demographic 'manipulation' through massive Russian immigration to the industrial urban centres in order to reduce the proportion of Tatars in their republic. TOTs demanded public consultation before any further industrialisation of the region and a reassessment of the republic's contribution to the all-Union budget, estimated at the time at 98 per cent of the republican output.

Finally, questions relating to the large Tatar diaspora, its extra-territorial national, cultural and political autonomy – a recurrent concern of the Tatar intelligentsia since the days of the *jadids* – featured high on TOTs' agenda.

## The Road to Independence

Despite initial opposition from the authorities, TOTs rapidly established itself as the voice of national interests, coopting most of the national political élites, including those within the Communist Party. As events began to precipitate, on 30 August 1990 the Supreme Soviet of Tatarstan proclaimed sovereignty, the first autonomous republic to do so. Its example was soon followed by other autonomous republics. Importantly, the Declaration of Sovereignty made no mention of Tatarstan being part of the RSFSR.

On 17 March 1991, while the Soviet Union held a referendum to decide on the future of the Union, Tatarstan refused to take part in the vote, held simultaneously in the RSFSR, on the instigation of a popularly elected president. Preparations for the presidential elections of the RSFSR were met in Kazan by massive demonstrations and a hunger strike led by deputy Fauzia Bayramova, the leader of the radical nationalist party Ittifaq. As a result, on 27 May 1991 when the Soviet leaders met in the Kremlin to sign the Union Treaty, Mintimer Shaymiyev, then leader of Tatarstan's Supreme Soviet, declared that Tatarstan intended to sign the treaty only as a subject of the USSR and not as a vassal of Russia. The next day Tatarstan's Supreme Soviet declared that the republic would elect its own president and forbade republican civil servants to take part in the forthcoming RSFSR elections.

On 12 June 1994, the day of the Russian elections, Mintimer Shaymiyev, the only candidate, was elected president of Tatarstan.

Only 36 per cent of the Tatarstan electorate took part in the federal elections, of which 14 per cent voted for Yeltsin. 60 per cent voted in the Tatar elections, with two-thirds of the votes supporting Shaymiyev. These figures showed that the Russian population of Tatarstan distanced itself from Moscow's politics.

The year that followed the Declaration of Sovereignty was particularly dramatic – demonstrations and political strikes spread throughout Tatarstan and, in solidarity with the republic, across Tatar regions as far afield as Kazakhstan and Siberia. Their intensity in many cases surprised the leaders of the national movement. During the August 1991 coup, Shaymiyev, usually a cautious man, hastily sided with the junta, unlike most other political leaders in the Muslim republics who cautiously avoided official pronouncements in the early hours of the coup, with the notable exceptions of Askar Akaev and Dzhokhar Dudaev who immediately gave their support to Yeltsin. But when in the autumn Yeltsin tried to remove Shaymiyev, Yeltsin received the support of the nationalists who considered him a lesser evil than the alternative of a Russian president in the person of Vasily Likhachev, the Vice-president. When the CIS was set up in December 1991, Tatarstan announced that it wanted to be admitted as a founding member, an intention equivalent to a demand to be recognised as an independent state.

On 21 February 1992, in response to nationalist pressure, the Parliament of Tatarstan took the decision to hold a referendum to determine once and for all the status of the republic. The referendum was planned for March 1992 when the other former autonomous republics of the RSFSR were due to sign the Federation Treaty. The question put to the voters was deliberately obscure so as not to alarm the Russian electorate: 'Do you consider that the Republic of Tatarstan is a sovereign state, a subject of international law, entitled to develop relations with the Russian Federation and other states on the basis of treaties between equal partners?' Paradoxically, Moscow first supported this initiative while TOTs hesitated, fearing an inconclusive response. However, it rapidly became evident that the majority, including Russians and other non-Tatars, would respond positively. At that stage Moscow turned, using all the might of its propaganda power, to influence the result of the voting: on 5 March the Russian Parliament appealed to Tatarstan, warning against the danger of civil war, and asked for a judgement of the Constitutional Court on the legality of the referendum. Ruslan Khasbulatov declared that Shaymiyev 'should be brought to Moscow in a iron cage'. On 13 March the Constitutional Court duly pronounced that the reference to 'equal partners' was unconstitutional, as well as the sections of the Declaration of Sovereignty that curtailed the Russian legislation on the territory of the republic. However, in his report to the Russian Parliament the president of the Constitutional Court, Valery Zorkin, while accusing the Tatar leadership of dishonesty noted that in the event of a positive response by the electorate of Tatarstan, the referendum could provide a legal base for secession. Tatarstan was inundated with political leaflets; over 3000 agitators were dispatched from Moscow. Russian directors of the military-industrial complex factories threatened their employees with dismissal if they took part in the referendum; the procurator general of Tatarstan, Antonov, 'forbade' the referendum. On the eve of the referendum Yeltsin himself appealed to the people of Tatarstan to vote 'no' in order not to endanger the Russian Federation. To back the argument, military manoeuvres took place in the neighbouring Volga republics. However, Moscow overplayed its hand. Many people who were still hesitating decided to vote in favour of independence after Yeltsin's last-minute interference. According to ITAR-TASS the results of the referendum were as follows: 82 per cent of the electorate took part with 61.4 per cent voting in favour and 37.2 per cent against.[13] In the rural areas with a predominantly Tatar population, 75.3 per cent voted 'yes', and in the towns with a greater ethnic mix 55.7 per cent. The exception was Kazan, a city with a majority Russian population, where 51.2 per cent voted 'no'. Thus out of all those eligible to vote, 50.3 per cent voted for independence and 30.5 per cent against. This showed that support for independence was not limited to the Tatars.

On 26 October 1992, the Parliament of Tatarstan met to vote on the adoption of a new constitution. Yury Yarov and Oleg Rumiantsev, respectively Deputy Chairman and Secretary of the Constitutional Commission of the Supreme Soviet of the Russian Federation, attended the session in an attempt to bolster the pro-Russian lobby of the Tatar parliament. Their presence was viewed by the nationalist 'Sovereignty' faction as interference in Tatarstan's internal affairs in an effort by Moscow to impede the proceedings and delay the adoption of the constitution.[14] The session lasted ten days and the constitution was finally adopted by a vote of 174 deputies out of 249 – just over the required two-thirds majority. Tatarstan became the first republic in Russia to adopt a new constitution.

On 6 November 1992, the Supreme Soviet of the Russian Federation urged the Parliament of Tatarstan to refrain from passing the law enforcing the constitution, and instead to submit a legislative initiative to the Russian Parliament for the change in the legal status of the republic. This was deemed unacceptable in Kazan, and on 30 November 1992 the Parliament of Tatarstan passed a bill 'On Implementing the Constitution of the Republic of Tatarstan'.

The short Section 5 of the Constitution was considered the most controversial, in particular Article 59 which stipulated the supremacy of Tatarstan's laws over those of the Russian Federation, and Article 61 which stated: 'The Republic of Tatarstan is a sovereign state, a subject of international law, associated with the Russian Federation on the basis of a [forthcoming] Treaty on mutual delegation of powers and spheres of authority'. The Russian federalists argued that Tatarstan was not entitled to adopt a constitution before the Russian Federation, and that independence and equality between the two states could not be envisaged because, according to the constitution still in force in the Russian Federation, Tatarstan constituted a part of the federation.[15] The pro-Russian lobby of the Tatarstan Parliament, 'Soglassiya' and 'Narodovlasti', interpreted the Constitution as Tatarstan's secession from the Russian Federation. A statement to this effect, co-signed by Alexander Rutskoy and Nicolay Travkin, was distributed at the session of the Parliament of Tatarstan on 30 November 1992. For their part, the Tatar nationalists also objected to Article 61. Their criticism of the clause on mutual delegation of powers was voiced most vividly by a leading academic, Abrar Karimullin, who compared such delegation of power to 'delegating one's marital rights to a neighbour'.[16]

Finally Tatarstan refused to approve the Russian Federation Constitution, which it described as 'a screen for a unitarian state',[17] by failing to respond to the nationwide referendum called on 12 December 1993 by Boris Yeltsin to endorse it – only 14 per cent of the electorate of Tatarstan voted in this referendum.[18]

## The February 1994 Treaty

Following the Tatarstan referendum (March 1992) and the adoption of the Tatarstan Constitution (November 1992), the popularity of President Shaymiyev grew. Many Tatar nationalists came to believe that their government acted in the best interests of the republic and the Tatar nation, while the Russian population of Tatarstan, less politicised than the Tatars, was satisfied with the political stability and the republic's relative economic prosperity. This was due mainly to a cautious path towards privatisation and the one-channel taxation in force since the collapse of the USSR. Although pressure on Tatarstan to sign the Federation Treaty increased after the dissolution of the Supreme Soviet in October 1993 in Moscow and the promulgation of the new federal constitution, political activity and opposition decreased, the nationalists being contented that each new round of negotiations brought further concessions from Moscow. A belief prevailed that the negotiation process and the legal and democratic measures taken by the republic – Declaration of Sovereignty, presidential elections, referendum and constitution – would bring fruit, and that recognition of the sovereign status of Tatarstan was only a question of time and a little patience.

The Treaty signed by Tatarstan's president, Mintimer Shaymiyev, on 15 February 1994, was a political victory for Russia. It negated the principle of sovereignty, cancelled the *de facto* economic independence gained in bilateral agreements since 1991, and fully delegated political power to Moscow. Even the republic's 'associated' status with the

Federation, as described in Tatarstan's constitution, was denied, to be replaced by the formula of Tatarstan being 'a state united with Russia, on the basis of the constitutions of the two states and the Treaty on the delimitation of Spheres of Authority and the Mutual Delegation of Powers'.[19] To all intents and purposes Tatarstan has been brought back into line with the other members of the Federation with the exception of Chechnya.

The Treaty took the Parliament of Tatarstan and the Tatar nationalists – radical opposition and moderates alike – completely by surprise. While Shaymiyev's principal adviser, Rafael Hakimov, was officially negotiating a draft treaty in Moscow, a second draft was secretly prepared overnight by Vice-president Likhachev, a close friend of Sergey Shakhray. At the last moment the three main negotiators – Hakimov, Tagirov and Safiullin – were excluded surreptitiously from the talks, and all posts of presidential advisers were abolished in order to get rid of Rafael Hakimov. It is believed that this was done on Shakhray's instruction as a pre-condition to signing the Treaty. Shaymiyev's explanation of the need for such a Treaty – the threat of an economic blockade – was unsatisfactory. Indeed, economic blockade has been threatened and applied on several occasions since 1991. Tatarstan, being a major communication centre, was able to retaliate by shutting pipelines, immobilising numerous factories in Russia. The cost to Russia was too great and the blockade was lifted within half an hour. The contention of the Tatar opposition was that Shaymiyev's government had mismanaged the economy to such an extent that it needed Russia to bail it out. A more cynical explanation was that the Tatar government played the nationalist card until privatisation was completed and ownership of the republican resources divided among its inner circle. Now that this had been achieved the government needed the support of Moscow to avoid accountability. Some Tatar government officials also implied in private that there was a threat of military intervention, although this was denied officially. Whatever the case, it can be assumed that intimidation was exerted. The radical nationalist leader, Fauzia Bayramova, noted a change in President Shaymiyev after the storming of the Moscow Parliament[20]. As opposed to the Western media's assessment of this event as a triumph for democracy, all national regions of the Russian Federation understood it as a clear message that dissent would no longer be tolerated. The February Treaty was applauded with indecent triumphalism in Moscow and among the Russian lobby in Kazan, where it was somewhat inelegantly interpreted as 'Shaymiyev wetting his pants when Moscow raised its voice'.

The mood in Kazan has remained gloomy. An open letter to Shaymiyev, heavily charged emotionally, was circulated on 17 February 1994 by the famous Tatar writer, Zulfat Hakim. It best exemplified the reaction to the Treaty.

President,

I write about the 'present' you have offered our trusting and forgiving nation in this holy month of Ramadan.

According to the Russian custom you have exchanged three kisses with Yeltsin. For your long-suffering people, living particularly difficult days, it is as if you had spat three times in their faces from the height of a Russian golden dome.

What will this treaty, signed in sinister and greedy Moscow, give to the people of Tatarstan?

In 1917 the Bolsheviks had already granted statehood to the Tatars in the form of autonomy. Will the treaty you signed allow improvement in the government structure of the republic? We are not all naïve. There are thinking people in Tatarstan, they will tell you that this treaty has destroyed the hope for freedom, that it proclaimed a final and arrogant 'No' to independence.

President, do not bother to explain and demonstrate that there was no other alternative. Simply you did not want to fight because you are indifferent to the interests of your nation . . . You do not love your nation. . .

You have chosen the easy way, the path of least resistance and personal profit. You have bowed to the Russian throne whose tsar can bombard a popularly elected parliament with impunity in full view of the nation which has elected it. You have deliberately accepted the rule of Russia – a land 'which intelligence alone cannot comprehend'. You have accepted the yoke of a monster, overfed with blood and flesh.

This treaty. . . will bring no blessings to the people of Tatarstan. On the contrary, tragically, it has confirmed the subjugation of Kazan to Moscow.

It is the first time in our history that a document, legalising the rule of Russia over Tatarstan, has been signed. It is a crime against our ancestors, a crime against the nation. To accept this yoke is a betrayal of our forefathers who fought to defend Kazan in 1552.

I am not a politician. . . I speak only in the name of my father, my mother, my relatives, who still dream of true independence. I speak in the name of grandfathers who have left this foul world without having breathed freedom. I speak in the name of my ancestors who have shed their blood for their faith, their fatherland, their freedom. In the memory of our nation, tormented by the thirst for freedom, you will be remembered along with Shah Ali[21] and other traitors.

Our nation, unfashionably naïve, has trusted you with its destiny, and you have behaved as a Muscovite. . .

You have done nothing for our people, and yet they have done everything for you, they have defended you when you were threatened, they have put you in the chair that you do not deserve. . .

However strange this may seem, the national spirit is still alive, but no thanks to you. It has survived in the prisons and the mines, and somehow, I hope, will survive your betrayal.

What right do you have who have given nothing to your people, to dispose of their destiny and delegate it to Moscow?

President, if you do not have the strength to fight, if you are too old for the struggle, you must go.

To walk in the bazaars and markets, to visit the sovkhoz, to issue primitive weekly interviews as you do, photographed on a background of carrots, cabbages and potatoes, does not require much brain or strength. . .

Our mass media, in its concern with the daily progress of potato growing and other agricultural issues balanced with pseudo folkloric themes and silly love stories. . . is geared at animals not humans. . . Yet Tatars deserve better than daily reports on the growth of vegetables.

'Simplicity is a worse sin than thieving' say the Russians whose power you like. There is a simplicity which comes from a noble heart . . . but there is also a simplicity born of mindlessness, primitive standards of living, low education . . . Such a simplicity is prevalent among us. It is this image we give today, and this is why we have not been recognised as a nation and a state.

Maybe this is why you decided to surrender to Moscow. Yet there are among us young people capable of working and fighting . . . but they are not allowed near the corridors of power by a bunch of ageing, incompetent, impotent, and ossified bureaucrats.

Probably my letter will serve no purpose. I will conclude: I, personally, did not elect you. In 1990 I saw you as a farmer, not a president. But after the failed coup of the August putchists whose initiative you supported, you were attacked from all sides. Then, together with the whole Tatar nation, I defended you. I did not defend you for your own sake but as the president of our nation. And you have betrayed this nation.

This I will not forgive you.

I know that my curse will be of no consequence to you as you have shown in what contempt you hold your nation. As a communist you probably do not fear our malediction. The sense of fear, as well as love, cannot be injected as a vaccine, it must come from within. Nevertheless, to carry the curse of one's nation must be frightening.

Following the Treaty, Russians have been nominated as 'number twos' and deputies in most key government posts. They boast that nothing can be decided without their approval as in the days of the Communist regime. Russian chauvinism, dormant in Tatarstan in the past two years, is on the rise again. Ominously, Tatars are now accused of being recent 'migrants' on the Volga. Such arguments have preceded ethnic cleansing in other troubled mixed ethnic regions. The new budget allows large increases to the *apparat*. The budget of the education and cultural sector – the core of the national movement – on the other hand has been drastically cut (from 25 per cent in 1993 to 1.4 per cent in 1994 despite a credit balance carried forward from 1993). The economic concessions accorded to Russia, over oil and federal taxation among others, will mean a drastic drop in the standard of living. Officially contributions to the Federation have increased to 25 per cent of the Tatar budget compared to 13 per cent in 1993. Unofficially the estimates are nearer 75 per cent.[22] The price of certain basic commodities increased dramatically the day after the signing of the Treaty. This may strengthen the independence bloc. Corruption, which had been kept relatively discreet until the signing of the Treaty, has since become evident. The government of Tatarstan will not be able to avoid debates on this issue completely. It is common knowledge that the main preoccupation of the government *nomenklatura* now, including the president, vice-president and prime minister, is to finish building their villas before the next political upheaval. There is a re-activation of the KGB and police harassment of the nationalist opposition, short-term arrests and beatings.[23]

## The Role of Islam

After four centuries of religious persecutions, in the name of Orthodox Christianity or atheism, the Volga Tatars have developed an extra-ordinary capacity for surviving as Muslims. Until the collapse of the Soviet Union they provided a relatively high percentage of registered clerics and students attending the two Central Asian *madrasas*.[24] The extraordinary cohesion in the support given by the Tatars – intellectuals, political élites, rural masses and working classes alike – to the anniversary celebrations organised by Mufti Talgat Tajuddin on 18–26 August 1989 in Ufa and Kazan made it clear that Islam and nation are inseparable. Following this initial enthusiasm, the national movement has downplayed the role of Islam in order not to antagonise the Russian population whose support was needed in the struggle for independence. However, Tatarstan like other Muslim regions of the Former Soviet Union, has witnessed a steady although discreet religious revival.

An editorial in the Tatar religious journal *Iman*[25] is indicative of the position of the radical Muslim youth. The article shares most of the ideas of the secular nationalists on the history of the Tatars, but puts the blame for the conquest of Kazan specifically on the Russian Orthodox Church, and recognises Islam as the main obstacle to Russification. It forecasts that democracy will strengthen the influence of religion on politics, and that the alliance of the Russian government with the Orthodox Church will lead to an increase in Orthodox proselytism. *Iman* rejects equal rights for Islam and Orthodoxy in Tatarstan – 'there should be no Russian popes on Tatar lands'. Russians, it writes, are historically experts in forced conversions. The Russian clergy can draw upon a variety of institutional supports to pursue missionary activity – the media and military in particular. *Iman* strongly opposes Christian teaching in Tatarstan's schools and notes that already Russian priests visit schools to baptise children whatever their religious background, despite the official division of state and religion in Tatarstan:

Thus Tatar children who have not yet learned about their own religion are obliged to look up to a Russian priest. Will the Muslim clerics have the same rights and access to the media? Obviously not. In comparison to the activity of the Russian Orthodox churches, the mosques lag far behind. This is not only due to economic pressures ... The stronger the

Russian Church, the easier it will be to keep the empire. Will the Tatar government help the cause of Islam? What is the meaning of our sovereignty? If Orthodoxy wins in Tatarstan, will we have sovereignty? Already the Russian populated regions of Tatarstan have demanded autonomy. If the Tatar homeland becomes Christian will we need sovereignty? ...Will our government be satisfied with a Christian autonomy? Tatarstan must be, before all else, the homeland of the Tatars and of Islam, otherwise Tatars will disappear as a nation.

Despite this criticism, the government of Tatarstan has, unofficially, provided help to the mosques. The number of large mosques in the republic has risen to over 200 from 18 before *perestroika*. If small village mosques are included the number reaches 500.[26] In the past couple of years the yearly number of pilgrims to Mecca was approximately 150, almost the same as before the 1917 Revolution, while between 1944 and 1985 only 45 Tatars went to *hajj* from the RSFSR. Steadily, Tatar clerics are rebuilding the pre-revolutionary religious establishment. They are discarding the administrative structures, copied on the model of the Russian Orthodox churches, enforced in Tsarist and Soviet times to curtail their freedom of action and speech. Although the national political parties are dismissive of the religious leaders, Islam may well become a focus for the disenchanted and provide the necessary framework for future political opposition.

Most importantly, Tatar Islam has revived its most dynamic tradition – *Prosvetitel'stvo*, a word that carries the notion of enlightenment, education and missionary work. It was a feature of Tatar Islam in its 19th century *jadid* heyday when Islam in Russia – still a young and conquering faith – was making rapid progress among the Turkic and Finnish pagan population and Russian rural colonies in the periphery. No other Muslim people has developed this activity in such a systematic nationwide manner. Today Tatar Islam has taken up where it left off in 1917, with evident success. Whole communities of Tatar Staro Kryashens and Novo Kryashens are returning to Islam. Energetic missionary work is conducted among the Chuvash, whom the Tatars consider 'should be a Muslim nation'. This is being done at the request of the Chuvash National Congress. Conversions are also high among the Maris. The Khakass, a small Turkic Siberian nation (around 100,000 people), are the latest candidates for mass conversion to Islam. They have asked the Tatar muftis to send them missionaries.[27]

## CONCLUSION

The situation within the independence movement today is more complicated than at the time of its formation in 1989, when the position between 'us' (Tatars) and 'them' (Russians), was clear. The nationalist parties have been unable to respond to the Treaty. They have lost their influence but this does not mean that nationalism is dead. It is possible that in the short term Tatarstan will experience a 'stagnation' period – parliament will be ineffective, future elections manipulated, the economy overburdened by heavy subsidies to the military-industrial complex which remains in Moscow's control. The nationalists will have to re-assess their tactics, maybe forfeiting the belief that reason, moderation, intellectual discourse and negotiations will ensure success. Today 'the masks are down', and this may play into the hands of the national movement by crystallising positions in the Tatar ranks, forcing a choice and stronger commitment. An added dimension is the fact that Tatars will no longer accept any form of national government such as that in Uzbekistan. Democracy and sovereignty are linked. Tatar society is ripe for democracy.

Although the Treaty was a blow, there is room for optimism in the long term. Many Tatars believe that time is on their side and that full independence will be gained because of the degradation of the Russian Federation from within and its likely collapse as an economic entity. Horizontal economic links, backed by bilateral agreements, are developing in the Volga-Urals and Siberia, with Kazan the communication centre. In autumn 1994 Tatarstan opened its first petrol refining plant, thus it is no longer vulnerable to Moscow's economic blackmail. Despite the present friction with Bashkortostan, the legal and traditional basis for a Tatar–Bashkir confederation exists. There is growing coordination between the nationalists of the other Volga republics, through the Assembly of the Volga–Ural nations, and with Russian separatists in the 'Ural Republic'. Most now favour an independent Volga–Ural confederation as a realistic prospect and alternative to reliance on trade with the centre, whereas a few years ago it was considered a Utopian dream.

The Treaty is undoubtedly a step on the path to independence, but it is not the end of history for the Tatars. It leaves many ambiguities which the Tatars will be able to play to their advantage. The victory that Moscow is confident of having gained may be short-lived, the Tatars having proved over the centuries to be resilient, resourceful and persistent. A more uncompromising and radical national movement may arise. One can also assume that Islam will play a stronger role in the national movement than it has been allowed so far, and that antagonism between Tatars and Russians will sharpen. The struggle ahead may well be intense, as the stakes are high. The Russian empire was built on the ruins of the Kazan Khanate. Both Tatars and Russians know that the 'liberation' of Kazan will herald the end of the empire.

# NOTES

1. S. M. Solov'ev *Istoriya Rossii s drevneishikh vremen* vol. 5–6 (Moscow 1959–1965), p. 467, as quoted by Azade Ayse Rorlich in *The Volga Tatars – A Profile in National Resilience* (Stanford, CA, Hoover Institution Press 1986), p. 16.
2. Alexandre Bennigsen and Chantal Quelquejay *Les Mouvements nationaux chez les Musulmans de Russie. Le 'Sultangalievisme' au Tatarstan* (Paris, Mouton 1960), pp. 22–3.
3. Rorlich *The Volga Tatars*, p. 41.
4. It was estimated by Il'minsky that 200,000 Tatars were converted, 130,000 in the *guberniya* of Kazan alone. However, most of these new converts – Novo Kryashens – remained crypto-Muslims and returned to Islam after 1905.
5. Bennigsen and Quelquejay *Les Mouvements nationaux chez les Musulmans de Russie*, p. 40, gives the following percentage of literacy for 1897: Tatars 20.4 per cent, Russians 18.3 per cent, and, among the other indigenous Volga peoples, Chuvash 8.9 per cent, Mordvins 9.5 per cent, Udmurts 4.8 per cent and Maris 5.8 per cent.
6. L. Trotsky *Staline* (Paris, Grasset 1948), p. 577.
7. There is at present a campaign in Kazan to rehabilitate Sultan Galiev. Several articles have appeared: I. Tagirov 'Kem ul Sultangaliev?', *Kazan Utlary* no. 4, 1989, pp. 163–73 (in Tatar); and B. Sultanbekov 'Sultan-Galiev. Lichnost' i sud'ba' *Sovetskaya Tatariya* 24 May 1989 (in Russian). Sultanbekov's objective article based on new archive material provides information on the later part of Sultan Galiev's life and his death generally previously unknown to scholars in the West.
8. Intervention by Korbut *Stenograficheskii otchet IX-oi oblastnoi konferentsii Tatarskoi organizatsii R.K.P. (b)*, pp. 113–14.
9. Gerhard von Mende *Der Nationale Kampf der Russlands Turken* (Berlin 1936), pp. 158–59.
10. Data provided by D. M. Iskhakov 'Sotsial'no-demograficheskie problemy v Tatarskoi respublike' in *Materialy Uchreditel'nogo s"ezda*, TOTs.
11. *Tezisy k podgotovke platformy tatarskogo obshchestvennogo tsentra*. See *Central Asian and Caucasus Chronicle*, vol. 8 no. 2, (May 1989), pp. 5–9, for an English translation of the manifesto, and 'The Volga Tatars', in *The Nationalities Question in the Soviet Union*, Graham Smith ed., London, Longman, 1990, pp. 283–287.
12. R. Khakimov, 'Avtonomnaya respublika – politicheskii anakhronizm?', *Komsomolets Tatarii*, no. 36 (10 Sept. 1989).
13. Ann Sheehy, 'Tatarstan Asserts Its Sovereignty', *RFE/RL Research Report*, no. 14 (3 April 1992).
14. *Nezavisimaya Gazeta*, 27 and 29 October 1992.
15. *Rossiiskaya Gazeta*, 4 November 1994.
16. *Pravda*, 13 February 1993, and *Izvestiya*, 11 March 1993.
17. *Pravda*, 11 February 1994.
18. *Izvestiya*, 14 December 1993.
19. For a discussion of the treaty see Elisabeth Teague, 'Russia and Tatarstan Sign Power-sharing Treaty', *RFE/RL Research Report*, vol. 3, no. 14, 8 April 1994.

20. Reported in a conversation with the author in July 1994 in Kazan.
21. Shah Ali was the Muscovite candidate during a dynastic succession crisis in the Kazan Khanate which opposed Muscovy to Kazan Tatars allied with the Crimean Khanate. Shah Ali was the nominal military commander during the Russian campaign against Kazan in 1523 which marked the first permanent conquest of the Khanate's territory. He ruled in Kazan twice, in 1518–1521 and 1546. See Jaroslaw Pelenski, *Russia and Kazan. Conquest and Imperial Ideology (1438–1560s)*, The Hague, Paris, Mouton, 1974.
22. Reported to me by a deputy of the Parliament of Tatarstan in July 1994 whose name I prefer not to reveal.
23. These usually go unreported. However, *Nezavisimaya Gazeta*, 5 March 1994, no. 43 (719), reported that 150 people were beaten up and severely injured on 9 March 1994 during a demonstration in Naberezhnye Chelny protesting against the Treaty.
24. Mir-i Arab in Bukhara and Imam Ismail Al-Bukhari in Tashkent.
25. *Iman*, no. 1 (27), 1994, in the Tatar language, published by the religious youth organisation 'Iman'.
26. See M. A. Saidasheva, 'Islam sredi tatar v 20–30 gody', in *Mezhetnicheskie i mezhkonfessional'nye otnosheniya v Respublike Tatarstan*, part 2, IIaLI, AN, Kazan, 1993, pp. 169–170.
27. In their case the incentive is economic – their situation is desperate, with no help from Moscow and massive Russian out-migration. They believe that as Muslims they would benefit from some support from other Islamic nations.

# CHAPTER FIVE

# The Northern Minorities

Piers Vitebsky

## INTRODUCTION

The term 'Northern Minorities' covers a number of diverse native peoples across the sparsely-populated Russian Arctic and Far East. Collectively they number some 184,000 and are currently grouped in the 1989 census under 26 ethnic names. The Northern Minorities speak languages belonging to several language families, none of them related to Russian. Thus, the Evenk and Even languages belong to the Tungus-Manchu family, the Dolgan to the Turkic, and the Khant and Saami to the Finno-Ugric; while the Yukaghir and Chukchi languages are classified as Paleo-Siberian or Paleo-Asiatic and the Ket language has no known relations.[1] A few groups have cousins in neighbouring countries: the Saami in northern Scandinavia, the Eskimo in North America and Greenland, and the Evenk in China and Mongolia.

Linguistic differences are crosscut by differences in economy. Some groups such as the Khant lived traditionally by hunting and freshwater fishing, an activity also important among predominantly reindeer-herding groups such as the Nenets, Evenk or inland Chukchi, while groups on the east coast such as the Eskimo and coastal Chukchi hunt walrus and whale at sea. Though there have been many changes, these activities remain central to the indigenous economy. However, they are extremely vulnerable since they require immense tracts of clean land or water and are opposed in principle to the mineral-extracting economy of the 'Russian' settlers who now far outnumber them on their own territories. For the Northern Minorities today, therefore, issues of ethnic identity are particularly closely tied up with ecological and environmental problems.[2]

From the mid-16th century, Russian traders and adventurers began to penetrate east of the Urals, reaching the Pacific Ocean in 1640. They compelled the small groups of indigenous peoples whom they met to supply them with furs under a fur tax (*yasak*), and at remote frontier markets they traded salt, guns and vodka. The native economy was affected by the shift from hunting large food animals to hunting small fur-bearers, and already in the eighteenth century many forests had been depleted of the latter. There was also considerable social and demographic upheaval.[3] Russian travellers were fascinated by the native form of spirit mediums and gave the term *shaman*, derived from an Evenk word, to the world of comparative religion.[4]

Siberia was ruled by autocratic governors, far from the sight of the central government. In 1822, Count Speranskiy enacted an enlightened 'Code of Indigenous Administration', which attempted to protect the native economy from numerous abuses, and this was updated by a statute in 1892. But there was little machinery, or will, to enforce these and for the most part the administrative condition of the Northern Minorities remained benighted and impoverished, while Russian immigration and expropriation of their territory continued unchecked. The region was also used for banishment of political dissidents from the centre, and exiled scholars contributed greatly to the ethnographic study of the region. By the turn of the 20th century, the Siberian regionalist movement called *oblastnichestvo* called for a separate regional parliament and the establishment of native reserves, on the model of Indian reserves in North America. These demands were not met at the time, nor were they achieved later by the Soviet concept of ethnic territory. However, versions of this idea have resurfaced with some force in the past few years.

It is not possible to do justice to each of these diverse peoples in a short chapter; instead, selected peoples have been presented as examples to illustrate important stages in the history of the Northern Minorities as a whole.[5]


## THE NORTHERN MINORITIES DURING THE SOVIET PERIOD

Communist rule took some time to establish in the remoter northern areas, but its immediate impact was particularly drastic, since it was based on ideologies and introduced structural frameworks that had evolved in the European heartland and were highly unsuited to the distinctive northern economy and society. There was a tension among those in power between two opposed positions. One position argued that the northern peoples should be ruled with a light hand and helped to find their own way forward. This amounted essentially to a programme of protection for indigenous culture, sometimes advocating a policy of native 'reservations'. It was upheld by a group of scholars, led by Vladimir Bogoraz, an anthropologist who had spent ten years of his life in exile among the Northern peoples.[6]

The opposing position maintained that these peoples should follow the same path as all the other populations in the new state and should form part of one 'Soviet people'. This conception amounted to a new ethnic identity and aimed at the homogenisation of diverse cultural forms. Either way, northern natives were generally held to be primitive and inferior to Russians, and the only native voices to be heard were those few that had been trained in Soviet institutions to become agents of Sovietisation in their home communities.

In the relatively liberal 1920s, Bogoraz persuaded the People's Commissariat of Nationalities (NARKOMNATS) to establish a 'Committee of the North'.[7] The Committee's brief included studying indigenous lifestyles, working out policies for their protection and administration, and training native personnel to become teachers in nomadic schools with a curriculum still closely based on native life. But these gentleman-scholars were quickly overtaken by the push for industrial development, as well as by the leftward swing in the late 1920s, in which key figures in northern society, such as shamans and owners of reindeer, were identified as kulaks and class enemies and were persecuted and killed. Collectivisation was particularly destructive here, since northern cultures and economies were based on a delicate adaptation to an exceptionally harsh environment and were still relatively self-sufficient. The norms of peasant cattle pastoralism in European Russia did not make sense in the North, where a family with two hundred reindeer was not rich, but no more than moderately well equipped to survive. When the state tried to confiscate reindeer, there was bitter resistance. Many herders destroyed their animals rather than allow them to fall into the hands of the state,[8] and as late as 1990 it is likely that the number of reindeer had still not returned to the pre-collectivisation level.[9]

As part of their educational and civilising mission, the Committee of the North established 'cultural bases' (kul'tbaz), centres of cultural and medical services, as well as schools, with boarding schools for the children of nomadic herders and hunters. They also developed scripts and produced textbooks in northern languages.[10] Native teachers were trained in various centres and in particular at the Institute for the Peoples of the North (Institut narodov severa) in Leningrad.[11] A northern intelligentsia began to form, with a small number of native writers, administrators and Communist Party cadres. Several small native administrative regions were established. These were abolished in the 1930s; other institutional arrangements remained but were affected by the hardening political climate.

On the economic and demographic fronts, the Soviet period was marked by a massive influx of 'Russian' settlers (i.e. European, actually including many Ukranians, Estonians and numerous other non-northern natives). Especially from the 1930s, the Soviet Union's massive industrialisation programme depended on raw materials from across much of the North. The native, animal-based economy was dwarfed by a new economy based on the extraction of minerals and manned almost entirely by newcomers. Labour was provided by European prisoners in the labour camps of the gulag. Regardless of the ideological reasons at the centre of their deportation, these prisoners were necessary for the economic development of the North (after Stalin's death in 1953, they were replaced by free labour attracted by the lure of high incremental payments and bonuses (*nadbavka*)). With their very limited intelligentsia, the Northern Minorities were relatively uninvolved in the drama of the camps that was being acted out on their territory. Reindeer herders in the Verkhoyansk Mountains used to watch small groups of prisoners being marched across their mountains to a camp with many of them collapsing on the way; the natives were obliged to shoot escaped prisoners, cut off their right hand and take it to the authorities.[12] Power shifted from local soviets to state super-corporations such as Glavsevmorput (the administration of the Northern Sea Route which carries heavy cargo from Murmansk to Vladivostok) and Dal'stroi (the administration of the development of the far North-east).[13]

From the 1930s to the mid-1980s, a succession of policies and developments had an almost unremittingly negative impact on the Northern Minorities. During the 1960s, the world's biggest reserves of oil and gas[14] were found around the territory of the Khant, Mansi and Nenets peoples in west Siberia, gradually extending as far north as the Yamal peninsula. These became the mainstay of Soviet foreign-exchange earnings, severely curtailing any native right to protest. During the 1950s, the partly native-language education of the 1920s and 1930s was replaced by a strong tendency to Russification. Children were punished for speaking native languages at school and parents were instructed not to speak them at home. This age-group today has been characterised by a linguist as a semi-lingual 'broken generation', without full mastery of either their native language or Russian.[15]

But perhaps the most long-lasting blow to northern communities came in the early 1960s. While the earlier process of collectivisation had been quite thoroughgoing, the transition of nomadic populations to a 'sedentary' (*osedlyy*) way of life had often been only partial. It was now, far more insistently than during the 1930s, that all herders were compelled to shift the focus of their lives from the outlying camps to fixed villages. In particular, all herders' children finally left the camps to attend full-time school there. If their mothers chose to remain in the herding camps, for instance with younger children below school age, then these schoolchildren were obliged to live in boarding schools (*internat.*). This policy caused great distress. As a parent later wrote, 'who would choose to tear themselves away from a ten-year-old child? Of course the children come home for the holidays. But they come as if to a strange house and don't feel at home here.' A former boarder remembered, 'I spent ten years in an *internat*. .... I remember my teachers well, and am grateful to them. But I hardly remember my mother.'[16]

A distinction was made between 'production nomadism' (*proizvodstvennoye kochevaniye*) and 'nomadism as a way of life' (*bytovoye kochevaniye*). Production nomadism encompassed the male herders themselves, whose movement with the herds was considered unavoidable. But their women and children, whose company and specialist labour had been such an integral part of nomadism as a way of life, were now to be kept separate in the village. Such people were considered 'unutilised labour resources' and a range of village-based occupations was introduced to keep them busy. The result was a separation of the nomadic men from the village-based women and an alienation of the children in the village boarding school from the activities and specialised knowledge of the men.[17]

The sites of villages were chosen to suit these other activities and with an eye to the development of the region as a whole, with good transport links for import and export. Reindeer herding was firmly put in its place: 'the choice of a site which answers to these requirements is quite difficult enough, and if one adds the further condition that the central village should be near the migration routes of the herders, then it becomes even more complicated'.[18] Small settlements were amalgamated into larger villages on the grounds that they were 'without prospects' (*neperspektivniy*), and their populations were displaced.

The sidelining of native economic activities was matched by a contempt for native culture. 'They told our grandparents that nomadism was backward: "Come on," they were told, "live a settled life, become part of civilisation, of culture".[19] In the late 1950s, the director of a college in Novo-Chaplino burned all available copies of the poems of Yurii Anko, the first literary work in Siberian Eskimo, on the grounds that they 'impeded the arrival of the radiant future, in which Russian would become the single language of the Soviet people'.[20]

## PERESTROIKA

The effect of *perestroika* took some time to reach the Northern Minorities, but led to a high point of activity and optimism between 1988 and 1990. As late as 1987, conservative metropolitan anthropologists were still insisting on the cultural and ethnic 'blossoming' of these peoples under Soviet rule.[21] The tide turned rapidly in early 1988, following the first meeting in Moscow (which the author attended) of a group of radical non-native anthropologists, geographers and other northern experts under the name 'The Unquiet North' (*Trevozhniy Sever*). This led to a highly influential article in the Communist

Party's own journal[22] and was followed by a series of further articles, readers' letters, commentaries, 'round table' meetings and exposés of crisis situations.[23]

The number of these events was small but, given the symbolic importance of the North in Russian public consciousness, their impact was considerable. The impression of innocent primitives, well cared for by a benign state, was replaced by something more complex and almost uniformly disturbing, which indicated a failure of responsibility by the state on a massive scale. This debate crystallised around a number of central themes.

Perhaps the most prominent of these was the issue of environmental degradation. In a *Moscow News* article entitled 'Not by oil alone', the Khant writer Yeremei Aipin described the pollution of his people's fishing grounds near the western Siberian oilfields by oil floating 'two inches thick . . . killing all life along the way', and the extremely low wage labour available as a substitute for fishing: 'And this is happening near the rich oil fields of Samotlor, the flicker of whose flares have been for decades dancing over all this human misery'.[24]

The environment was in any case becoming a major issue throughout the country. But in the North it combined in a unique and distinctive way with native welfare because of the central importance and vulnerability of native economic activities based on animal resources. In the same article, Aipin estimated that recent oil development in Tyumensakaya *oblast'* (district) alone had deprived native peoples of 28 rivers formerly used for commercial fishing, 17,700 hectares of spawning and feeding grounds and 11 million hectares of reindeer pasture. Other prominent cases were the proposal to build a hydroelectric dam across the Nizhnyaya Tunguska river in central Siberia, thereby drowning huge swathes of reindeer pasture and changing the local climate;[25] and the proposal to build ten parallel gas pipelines across the pastures and migration routes of the Nenets reindeer herders on Yamal peninsula.[26]

A further issue was native health and demography. Suddenly it seemed that, far from blossoming, the Northern Minorities were in imminent danger of disappearing altogether. Their rate of growth in the 1970s was five times less than it had been during the 1960s, and seven out of the 26 peoples had declined in numbers. This decline was due to ethnic assimilation and a combination of low birth rates with high death rates. As natives moved into town or married a person from a larger ethnic group, they replaced the old designation in their passport as 'Evenk' or 'Chukchi' by calling themselves 'Russian', both in the census and increasingly in their minds. The traditional family of 3–5 children was moving towards the Russian style of one-child family, while mortality remained extremely high. The average life expectancy turned out to be many years less than among Russians, and under the village-building programme the prevalent tuberculosis and respiratory diseases had been joined in the 1960s and 1970s by a sharp rise in poisonings and woundings. Now, one-third of all deaths were said to have non-medical causes.[27]

A major cause of morbidity and mortality was revealed to be radiation from the atmospheric nuclear tests conducted on Novaya Zemlya in the 1950s, 1960s, and even later. Reindeer herders were particularly vulnerable since dangerous isotopes are heavily absorbed by the lichen on which reindeer feed and concentrated in the reindeers' bodies which form the herders' daily diet.[28] To this day, accurate information is hard to obtain, though even without this it is clear that the problem is widespread and extremely serious. The concentration of public attention on radiation was not always helpful, as it allowed the authorities to pin the disastrous medical state of the Northern Minorities on a single cause that was outside their control, thereby absolving themselves from responsibility for the lamentable provision of day-to-day health care delivery and other public services.[29]

Finally, all of these concerns were brought together in a growing movement towards ethnic revival and local self-government. Here, the desire for ecological control of one's own landscape and economic control of its natural resources were translated into the classic Soviet idiom of territoriality.[30] At the same time, people said openly that the policy of creating a 'Soviet people' had been no more than a screen for Russification. Demands for schooling in native languages became numerous but were hampered by a widespread lack of teachers who knew the languages adequately, since they were themselves the product of the earlier policy of separating children from their roots and sending the more academically inclined ones away for a Russian education.

The old, simple Soviet conception of the 'development' of the Northern Minorities collapsed and gave way to several main viewpoints. These are reminiscent of the language of 'development' in the rest of the world, and in particular of the Canadian and Alaskan North in the 1970s, but they were still novel in the Soviet context. The first viewpoint, endorsed by Soviet anthropologists and many old northern hands, was that the Northern Minorities could adapt to the modern, changing world only through the revitalisation of their own cultures. This approach was oriented towards the rural population and its animal-based economy, especially reindeer herding. An opposed viewpoint, promoted especially by sociologists from Novosibirsk,[31] maintained that the development of the North was inevitable and the northern natives should be brought quickly into the industrial labour force. Between these extremes, it was suggested that the traditional branches of the native economy should be modernised technically and converted into a semi-industrialised form of resource use; or that their economic and social life should be restructured in the spirit of contemporary reforms of society at large through cost-accounting (*khozraschet*) and forms of contract and lease. The most radical view aimed at the development of genuine native autonomy, with the greatest possible growth of local forms of self-government and of the economic and legal independence of each community.[32]

Actual developments followed all these routes to a greater or lesser extent, though the industrial solution was widely rejected by the Northern Minorities themselves. The contract approach was prominent from 1988 to 1990 but finally failed (see below), while the most dynamic thinking centred around ideas of self-government.

Various groups among the Northern Minorities took many initiatives, though always against a background of uncertainty and the expectation of continued official interference. In March 1990, a new Association of Peoples of the North held their inaugural meeting inside the Moscow Kremlin, attended on the first day by President Gorbachev and Prime Minister Ryzhkov.[33] Vladimir Sanghi, the Nivkh writer who was elected president, later claimed that the Congress had been orchestrated by the apparat.[34] But a forceful list of demands and objectives was laid down, including the demand for Soviet ratification of the International Labour Organisation's 'Convention Concerning Indigenous and Tribal Peoples in Independent Countries'.[35]

Similar local organisations sprang up at the same time throughout the North, such as 'Save the Yugra' (the supposed homeland of the Ugrian peoples) among the Khanty and Mansi, the Chukchi Conference, and the Yukaghir Congress. A few days after the Kremlin meeting, the Association of Native Peoples of Yakutiya held their own meeting at the mouth of the river Kolyma in north-east Siberia. This coincided with an updated and officially sponsored version of a traditional spring festival which seemed intended as a festival of folklore and traditional games. But the festival was dominated by the Association's meeting in which speaker after speaker, many in traditional reindeer-fur winter costume, came up to the platform to denounce the government's environmental mismanagement and express anger about pollution, the decline of native languages and the lack of self-government.[36]

Local feeling made its impact on national institutions at the centre. In the 1989 elections of people's deputies, several Northern Minority intellectuals were elected, even in areas where the electorate were mostly 'Russians'. Aipin was elected for the Khanty-Mansiyskiy *okrug*, and indeed his article 'Not by oil alone' served as his manifesto, while in Vladivostok the Nanai anthropologist Evdokiya Gaer defeated the Commander-in-Chief of the armed forces of the Soviet Far East. There were also bids for greater territorial autonomy at the very local scale. In 1988, reformers in a partly Even community in northern Yakutiya campaigned for the restoration of the Eveno-Bytantayskiy rayon, abolished in the 1930s, and by the summer of 1989 they achieved their aim.[37] Two laws passed by the central government in 1990 also lent their weight to the idea of local control, at least in principle.

One stated that mineral exploitation should take place only with the consent of a territory's local council (soviet). The other allowed for the creation of an ethnic territory even where a native people were not in the majority.[38]

Equally significant were the Northern Minorities' new international contacts. In June 1988, the first planeload of Alaskan Eskimo arrived in Provideniya since intermarrying families speaking the same dialect were torn apart with the closing of the border in 1948. Traffic in both directions then became frequent.[39] The younger generation of Eskimo were astonished to find that their elders could use the Eskimo language to converse fluently with fashionably-dressed American citizens while they themselves were tongue-tied. The following term, the level of attention at compulsory Eskimo language lessons rose significantly.[40] In 1989, a delegation of Siberian Eskimo visited Greenland to participate for the first time in a meeting of the Inuit Circumpolar Conference.[41]

However, the pressure for the national exploitation of minerals intensified and some groups among the Northern Minorities were especially affected. On Yamal Peninsula, it emerged that just the disturbance of building ten gas pipelines across the migration routes of the reindeer herded by the Nenets people would make the routes impassable for ten years. After an unprecedented public outcry, the USSR Council of Ministers decided to postpone the project by some 5–7 years, but suspicions lingered that the project was not really being shut down, but only being made less conspicuous.[42]

This debate threw up in an urgent form a question of crucial and growing importance to Northern Minorities: the value of land, and notions of compensation for land taken or ruined. A single community's requirements for hunting, herding and fishing may amount to hundreds of thousands or even millions of hectares. Even after the concept of compensation had been accepted, figures suggested varied from 59 kopecks to 10 roubles per hectare – against a cost in Yamal of 20 million roubles per kilometre for each of the ten parallel pipelines (at 1989 prices).[43] It also remained uncertain how far a local community's 'ownership' of their territory could be construed as extending to the subsurface rights.

At the same time, no system of land use could be made to work without a viable reorganisation of labour at the micro-level of social relationships within the community. The integrity of the Eveno-Bytantayskiy rayon as an economic and political unit foundered on the rock of local factionalism, in particular between conservatives and reformists.[44] With the introduction of market-oriented cost accounting (khozraschet), reindeer herders became free contractors instead of state employees. The 'family contract' was supposed to undo some of the effects of collectivisation and bring members of a family back together again as a unit of production.[45] But the state farm failed to fulfil its part of the contract and, before the end of the Soviet period, herders in this area were anticipating official policy by trying to organise themselves into a 'clan cooperative society' (*rodovaya obshchina*).

## AFTER PERESTROIKA

The heady days of demands and manifestos, the hopes for the Association of Northern Natives, the euphoria of contact with Alaska in Chukotka or with Norway in the Saami village of Lovozero – all these have waned, or become regularised so that they no longer seem to promise magic solutions. In their place, native people face the daunting task of sustaining viable communities with high transport costs and overheads. This is a widespread problem throughout the native Arctic and it afflicts large areas of Greenland, Alaska and Canada. In these countries, whatever natural resources are taken out of the northern regions, native communities are sustained in return by a high level of subsidies and provision of social services. The Northern Minorities in Russia, however, find themselves on the outer edge of an industrial state that either wants the land for other purposes or perhaps is coming to abandon the area altogether.

In the Russian North, the indigenous economy depends largely on reindeer-herding, fishing and hunting. The *perestroika* period revealed all of these to be in severe crisis economically, ecologically and demographically. Meanwhile, more or less centralised oil, gas and mining industries compete on the same land, on behalf of non-native interests.[46]

Though the ecological situation is probably getting worse, environmentalism is a less prominent idiom now than it was during *perestroika*: as in other regions, there is a widespread feeling that good environmental management is an expensive luxury. In many places, people are reduced to an overriding concern with the need to survive each winter as it comes. In northern Yakutia, with the spring break-up of the ice in June 1994, the supply ships did not come along the Northern Sea Route from Murmansk or Vladivostok. The previous year's consignment had not been paid for and there was a shortage of very basic consumer goods for onward distribution to outlying native villages.

Under the Soviet system and into *perestroika*, the power of farm directors and other bosses lay largely in the ability to withhold or grant basic supplies and services such as transport of firewood to the village, clothing, waterproof boots, flour, jobs, a sheet of tin for the roof, places in school for children, or seats on the small planes into town.[47] Today, old power networks remain strong and traditional bosses have adapted their style to remain in power, but they are often in no position to provide for essential needs of their clients. There is thus enormous potential for a reshaping of power relations. It is probably no longer possible to speak of a coherent state policy towards these regions. Rather, there are a number of haphazard sub-strategies, involving various interest groups that include various factions among the native peoples themselves.

The central arena of negotiation is land use and resource management. These are subject to a complex web of separate and conflicting state agencies, so that their actual legal status is uncertain. During *perestroika* there have been major shifts in the relative balance of power between different levels of government, from the village, through provincial, to national level; with the advent of entities such as 'ethnic village councils' (*narodniy sel'sovet*), supposedly having the right to control the exploitation of subsurface minerals, new concepts of ownership, management and use of resources have evolved; with the decay of the state farm and the beginnings of entrepreneurship, new kinds of persons, communities and corporations are coming to enjoy these rights, and on new terms.

The most difficult question is that of privatisation, which has been under discussion for several years. By 1990, the growth of private reindeer herds was already being encouraged. But privatising the pasture remains an intractable problem. Just as an unsuitable European model of collectivisation was imposed on northern native society, so any regime of land and resource allocation that is not to be a disaster must reckon with the extensive land-use pattern of the native economy and with its labour pattern, as well as with the degree of a person's integration into the community. In one village studied by the author, one million hectares are farmed by 90 herders, or 12 per cent of the population. Should the land be given only to these herders, and if not, by what criteria are others to be included or excluded? In another village, it was at first proposed to give the land (in the form of a 'clan society', *rodovaya obshchina*, see below) exclusively to those currently employed by the state farm. This would have given a full share to migrant non-native boilermen, mechanics or cooks in the soup-kitchen, while excluding young native people and even retired reindeer herders.[48]

'Ownership' of land is contested in a variety of ways. The members of one research project have compiled a map of the eastern tip of Chukotka showing sites that were occupied earlier this century. Where the policy of amalgamation (*ukrupneniye*) around the 1960s has left the area with only 14 inhabited villages, the number of such sites identified amounts to 158.[49] The natives of Chukotka are also being helped to re-occupy old territory through a related project to observe the movement of bowhead whales from previously-abandoned look-out points around the coast. Mineral development plans sometimes force the parties concerned into clarifying land rights and even into archaeological and anthropological research, as in an extensive programme that is starting on Yamal peninsula.[50] Different levels of authority may claim the same rights. In 1991 on the island of Sakhalin, conflicting agreements of understanding to oil prospecting and extracting rights were signed by two different levels of government with two rival foreign consortia.

However it is organised, privatisation of land will have a much more severe impact in the North than in European Russia since the alienation of land, either to Russians or to local entrepreneurs, could dispossess much of the indigenous population and disempower them still further. Having never before had a political arena within which to operate, indigenous land claims are likely to be one of the biggest issues of the near future, perhaps modelled partly on aspects of the Alaska Native Land Claims Settlement Act.[51]

For the Northern Minorities, the land and knowledge of how to use it for animal-based economic activities are virtually the only resource available. With the diminishing of any state-maintained infrastructure, people and communities are turning to a mixture of self-help and entrepreneurial activity. These operate at the levels both of production and of marketing.

At the level of production, the state farm (sovkhoz) earlier tried to stamp out family solidarity and there is often little idea now of how the old clan structures worked. But in many regions the farm itself is largely defunct or moribund and herders, fishermen and hunters are finding themselves obliged either to return to their kinship networks or to form other networks of trust and partnership to replace these. In the northern Sakha Republic and no doubt elsewhere, all forms of contract, even the family kind, collapsed around 1990–91 because the state farm did not fulfil its part of the bargain. Currently, many herders have organised themselves into 'clan societies' (rodovaya obshchina), which are notionally free players in a wider market. In the Evenk Autonomous Okrug, these clan societies have been highly developed since 1992 in place of the state farms which, apart from those near the town of Tura, became effectively bankrupt with the withdrawal of state subsidies.[52] But these societies still depend on veterinary and other logistic support that cannot easily be supplied by other, equally free entities. Moreover, local élites change their idiom with the times, rather than their personnel, and sometimes stifle moves towards independence. In its death throes, the sovkhoz may still be able to inflict severe damage on its heirs. Thus, in a Yakutian state farm known to the author in 1990, at a time when government policy was beginning to promote the family contract, one family already formed an effective and viable reindeer-herding team. This family had anticipated government policy and could have been held up as a model success story. Instead, the farm administration took advantage of an outbreak of brucellosis among the deer to destroy the entire herd and redeploy each herder in a different brigade, hundreds of kilometres away from each other. The family was thus broken up economically, socially and morally.[53]

But the situation is far from uniform. On the Taimyr peninsula, the state farm survives and the herders themselves do not want to see it abolished. Here, the highly profitable Noril'sk smelting plant, which supports a town population of some 300,000, also subsidises the 4,000 natives in the hinterland in order to secure a cheap and reliable supply of meat.[54]

The level of marketing presents a serious obstacle because it can render any efforts at production pointless. The state farm no longer offers a guaranteed procurement point. Native herders a few hundred kilometres outside the town of Yakutsk produce reindeer meat but cannot get this to the town in a saleable condition. Instead, town-dwellers buy more expensive meat flown in from Holland, Britain and Australia while heaps of reindeer carcasses rot in the nearby mountains. A similar situation holds throughout much of the North. There is also little to protect producers from the vagaries of the wider world market. Young reindeer antlers were the first commodity to bring any substantial foreign currency to northern native communities. In 1988–90, these fetched a very high price in Korea and among Korean Americans and were far more valuable than the deer on which they grew. But the rush of Russian antlers flooded the market and the price has now slumped.

Though some native communities and individuals are proving quick to learn, entrepreneurial activity, and particularly investment, belong to a very unfamiliar world involving foreign capital, partners and know-how. A small amount of foreign investment can transform local life over a wide area. For example, the US Agency for International Development is now sending Even reindeer herders to Alaska to learn how to package meat and make sausages. An Alaskan Eskimo local council has supplied Eskimo villages in Chukotka with fax machines, as well as sponsoring the whale-watching programme mentioned above. At the other end of the country, Saami communities in northern Norway collect money each winter for food and clothes, which are taken by boat in summer to Naryan Mar for distribution among Nenets communities.

The Association of Northern Peoples is in decline, for reasons that epitomise the difficulties of any concerted action by the Northern Minorities: the fact that the age of manifestos is over; internal friction between personalities and ethnic groups (for example, the Eskimo have strong links to their cousins in North America which are not available to the Chukchi who traditionally dominated them); the high costs of aviation which make face-to-face meetings difficult without a compensatory network of easy telecommunications; and the uneven rate of entrepreneurial contacts as each ethnic group or community develops its own outside links and survival strategy. For all these reasons, local-level associations are often more dynamic.

The international dimension is becoming increasingly significant for many peoples among the Northern Minorities. Though they tend to underestimate the problems of these countries, they are also aware of the constitutional position of corresponding northern minorities in the long-established 'liberal democracies' throughout the non-Russian Arctic and sub-Arctic. Local activists are now firmly in contact with international indigenous rights groups, and their campaigns over what they see as violations of their territory receive extensive coverage abroad.[55] Their opponents, too, are not confined to government departments and corporations inside Russia. In early 1993, after a fierce international campaign, activists among the Nanai and Udeghai won an order from the Russian Supreme Court banning the South Korean company Hyundai from felling forests on their territory behind Vladivostok. In what may become a landmark decision, the Court rejected the argument of the state forestry corporation that the lands had never been formally transferred to the native people in the first place.[56]

The Russian North was designed to be 'plugged into the Soviet economy'.[57] The question now is what other kind of Russian North can come into being. The region's infrastructure originated with the introduction of large-scale European populations, first through the labour camps and later as free workers attracted by high wages and good living facilities (which were generally denied to the natives). With the collapse of the national economy in 1991–92, these incentives have disappeared and there is nothing to keep the Europeans there. In many outlying settlements, the last doctor, vet, book-keeper or mechanic is simply putting his or her family on one of the few remaining flights by an Antonov-2 biplane and leaving. For example, it has been said that the region of Chukotka has lost a quarter of its pre-1990 population, with the village of Provideniya decreasing from some 5,500 to around 3,500.[58]

The centralised Soviet economy and polity created a hinterland that was highly dependent logistically, economically and psychologically on ties with the centre. Social services were provided out of state budgets, often by trained personnel from outside. Though there are some native administrators and specialists, some of the Europeans who are leaving were key representatives of the state. It is not easy to assess what is happening now, let alone predict the future. One perhaps extreme interpretation is to see the withdrawal of the 'Russians' as a withdrawal of the state itself, perhaps comparable to the withdrawal of the Romans from Britain.[59]

The degree of withdrawal by central government presents varying opportunities for native peoples to regain power and makes varying demands on them to work out how to plan their lives. The distinction seems to depend on the scale and utility of mineral resources available for exploitation by the non-native economy, whether in its state or multinational aspect. In areas where the economy is predominantly native, it seems that the bureaucracy is shrinking and the move towards self-help is considerable. In other areas, the withdrawal of the state is less thoroughgoing: while the bureaucracy remains powerful, the balance of power is still shifting. Finally, there are areas where industrial interests are so strong that it is inconceivable that the state, or its private corporate surrogates, could withdraw. Here, the influx of newcomers will continue and the natives' bargaining power will remain severely limited. Obvious examples are the territory of the Khant and Mansi in western Siberia and of the Nenets on Yamal peninsula. With the Russian state's desperate need for foreign currency, the gas project on Yamal has sprung to life again. Here, there is not even an okrug-level local administration, power remains very unequal and any concessions to native communities will still be small and hard-won. However, because of their experiences in the American Arctic, the Western companies now involved are keenly aware of the potential for native and environmentalist law-suits and are setting up environmental impact studies and even archaeological and anthropological research programmes. The Nenets reindeer herders will not have the option of retaining their previous land-use pattern, but they may be able to use new patterns of public opinion at home and abroad to negotiate the best possible terms.

## NOTES

1. This entire region is conventionally often called the 'North', even though in the Far East it may come down almost to the Korean border. Though there is much local variation, there are also many features in common climatically, geographically and politically. In the Soviet period, the 'North' was also classified by degrees of hardship and bonus payments were made to newcomers. The peoples called 'Northern Minorities' here were generally called 'Small Peoples of the North' (*malyye narody severa*). Ethnonyms are not always stable or realistic, and may sometimes be the names of clans or other local groupings.

2. For the environmental history of the Northern Minorities, see Igor Krupnik, *Arctic Adaptations: Native Whalers and Reindeer Herders of Northern Eurasia* (Hanover, NH and London: University Press of New England).

3. For a historical overview, see Terence Armstrong, *Russian Settlement in the North* (Cambridge: Cambridge University Press 1965); James Forsyth, *A History of the Peoples of Siberia: Russia's North Asian Colony* (Cambridge: Cambridge University Press 1992). For demography, see D. B. and E. M. Shimkin, 'Population Dynamics in Northeastern Siberia, 1650/1700 to 1970', *The Musk-Ox* (Saskatoon, Canada), 16 (1975), pp. 7–23.

4. Gloria Flaherty, *Shamanism and the Eighteenth Century* (Princeton, NJ, Princeton University Press 1992).

5. For other recent overviews, see Nikolai Vakhtin, *Native Peoples of the*

*Russian Far North* (London: Minority Rights Group 1992); Gail Fondahl, 'Siberia: Native Peoples and Newcomers in Collision', in Ian Bremmer and Ray Taras, eds, *Nation and Politics in the Soviet Successor States* (Cambridge: Cambridge University Press 1993), pp. 477–510. There are numerous ethnographic studies of individual peoples in Russian which cannot be discussed here. A lengthy but conventionally Soviet treatment of each people is given in English in M. G. Levin and L. P. Potapov, *The Peoples of Siberia* (University of Chicago Press 1964); selected pieces are translated regularly in *Anthropology and Archaeology of Eurasia* (ME Sharpe, Armonk, NY). It is probably not an exaggeration to say that no ethnography of any Northern Minority has yet been published that meets the concerns and interests of modern world anthropology. However, a number of studies are in progress, or have already been written as PhD theses. Those known to be on the way to publication include (provisional titles) Bruce Grant, *Soviet House of Culture: Ethnography, History and the Savage* (on the peoples of Sakhalin island), Stanford University Press; and Piers Vitebsky, *The Message in the Fire: Dreams, Omens and Personal Destiny in Siberia* (on the Even of the northern Sakha Republic (Yakutia)), Manchester University Press.

6. Some of V. G. Bogoraz's own classic anthropological work on peoples of the north Pacific coast has been published in English, e.g. 'The Chukchee', *Memoirs of the American Museum of Natural History*, vol xi, 1904–9. For an overview of the Soviet period, see Kerstin E. Kuoljok, *The Revolution in the North: Soviet Ethnography and Nationality Policy* (Uppsala: Almqvist and Wiksell 1985).

7. Fully entitled the 'Committee for Assisting the Peoples of the Far North' and established in 1924. The Committee published two important journals, *Severnaya Aziya* from 1925 to 1931 and *Sovetskii Sever* from 1930 to 1935.

8. Z. V. Gogolev, *Sotsial'no-ekonomicheskoye razvitiye Yakutii (1917-iyun' 1941)*, Novosibirsk 1972, p. 211.

9. It is extremely difficult to obtain reliable figures for the reindeer population. The study of local statistics can give very varying results. Two versions of aggregate figures are given in Ye. Ye. Syroyechkovskii, *Severnyy olen'*, Moscow 1986, p. 12 and in V. A. Zabrodin, ed., *Severnoye olenevodstvo*, Moscow 1979, p. 13.

10. For a succinct summary by a socio-linguist, see Vakhtin, op. cit., pp. 13–14.

11. This evolved out of the 1925 'workers' faculty' (*rabfak*), was established in 1930, and eventually moved in 1953 to the Hertzen State Pedagogical Institute in Leningrad.

12. Source: author's fieldwork.

13. Among many sources, Vakhtin, op cit., p. 15.

14. David Wilson, 'The Siberian Oil and Gas Industry', in A. Wood, ed., *Siberia: Problems and Prospects of Regional Development* (London: Croom Helm 1987), p. 87.

15. Vakhtin, op. cit., p. 18.

16. For an early discussion of inappropriate education in the Soviet North, see E. Dunn, 'Educating the Small Peoples of the Soviet North: the Limits of Culture Change', *Arctic Anthropology*, 5(1), 1968, pp. 1–31;

E. Dunn, 'Education and the Native Intelligentsia in the Soviet North: Further Thoughts on the Limits of Culture Change', *Arctic Anthropology*, 6(2), 1970, pp. 112–122. The comments quoted come respectively from L. A. Galyan in *Severnyye Prostory* 1987(2), p. 24 and A. Nergaki in *Severnyye Prostory* 1988(3), pp. 25–6.

17. For a full discussion see Piers Vitebsky, 'The Crisis in Siberian Reindeer Herding Today: a Technical or a Social Problem?', in Alan Wood and Walter Joyce, eds, *Modern Siberia: Social and Economic Development*, (London: Routledge 1995). See also articles by Dunn (note 16).

18. B. Lashov, *Nekotorye voprosy razvitiya natsional'nykh rayonov krainego severa*, Yakutsk 1973, p. 98.

19. Spoken by Anatoliy Alekseyev in the documentary film 'Siberia – After the Shaman', by Piers Vitebsky, Graham Johnston and Lindsay Dodd, Channel 4 television 1991 (shown in the series 'Nomads').

20. Yurii Rytkheu in *Ogonyek*, April 1989.

21. Yu. Bromley and I. Gurvich in *Problemy sovremennogo razvitiya narodnostei severa*, Novosibirsk 1987, p. 159.

22. A. Pika and B. Prokhorov, 'Bol'shyye problemy malykh narodov', *Kommunist* 16 (1988), pp. 76–83, translated as 'Soviet Union: Big Problems of Small Ethnic Groups' in *International Work Group for Indigenous Affairs (IWGIA) Newsletter* 57(1989), pp. 122–35 and readers' responses to this gathered under the heading 'Sever oshibok ne proshchayet', *Kommunist* 1989(5), pp. 65–74.

23. Typical journalistic examples are 'Poka ne pozdno!', *Pravda*, 24 December 1988; V. Ledkov, 'Zagovoril sever', *Sovetskaya Rossiya*, 18 June 1989; 'Na perelome', *Sovetskaya Kul'tura*, 11 February 1989; the entire issue of the Salekhard newspaper *Krasnyy Sever* dated 10 December 1988. Examples in the professional literature include Ye. A. Oborotova, 'Narody severa v sovremennom mire: vzglyady i pozitsii', *Sovetskaya Etnografiya*, 1988(5), pp. 146–151; B. Prokhorov, 'Kak sberech' Yamal', *Znaniye–sila*, 1988(7), pp. 1–8, translated as 'How to save Yamal', *IWGIA Newsletter* 58, 1989, pp. 113–128; B. B. Prokhorov, ed., *Regional'nyye problemy sotsial'no-demographicheskogo razvitiya*, Moscow 1987, which despite its title is devoted entirely to the peoples of the North; V. I. Boiko, Yu. P. Nikitin and A. I. Solomakha, eds, *Problemy sovremennogo sotsial'nogo razvitiya narodnostei severa*, Novosibirsk, 1987. See also *Severnyye Prostory*, passim. An important chronology is given in Boris Chichlo, 'La premiere victoire des 'petits peuples'', *Questions sibériennes* 1 (1990), pp. 44–56.

24. Aipin, Ye. A., 'Not by Oil Alone', *Moscow News* 1989(2), reprinted in *International Work Group for Indigenous Affairs (IWGIA) Newsletter* 57(1989), pp. 137–43.

25. S. S. Savoskul and V. V. Karlov, Turukhanskaya GES i sudba evenkii, *Sovetskaya Etnografiya* 1988(5), pp. 166–8.

26. Piers Vitebsky, 'Gas, Environmentalism and Native Anxieties in the Soviet Arctic: the Case of Yamal Peninsula', *Polar Record* 26(156), 1990, pp. 19–26.

27. Information taken from a number of sources and conversations but especially from A. Pika, 'Demograficheskaya politika v rayonakh prozhivaniya narodov severa: problemy i perspektivi', in B. B. Prokhorov, ed., *Regional'nyye problemy sotsial'no-demographicheskogo razvitiya*,

Moscow 1987. However, it is noteworthy that a similar picture emerges from many parts of Arctic Canada, Alaska and Greenland, which suffered similar programmes of village resettlement and boarding-school regimes at around the same period.

28. Because of prevailing winds the impact of the Chernobyl accident, so strong among the Saami reindeer herders of Scandinavia, seems to have been minor here. For the Northern Minorities of Russia, the damage was earlier and far greater.

29. A widely read and extremely alarming article by V. Lupandin and Ye. Gaer in *Moscow News* 34 (1989), entitled 'Chernobyl on the Chukot [*sic*] peninsula', damaged the cause when it was found not to have been based on proper research.

30. Piers Vitebsky, 'Landscape and Self-Determination among the Eveny: the Political Environment of Siberian Reindeer Herders Today', in E. Croll and D. Parkin, eds, *Bush Base, Forest Farm: Culture, Environment and Development* (London: Routledge), pp. 223–46.

31. For example V. I. Boiko, Yu. P. Nikitin and A. I. Solomakha, eds, *Problemy sovremennogo sotsial'nogo razvitiya narodnostei severa* Novosibirsk, 1987.

32. This paragraph is based on Igor Krupnik, 'Arctic Ethno-Ecology: Environmentalist Debates in the Soviet North', trans. P. Vitebsky, in E. Croll and D. Parkin, eds, op cit., pp. 218–22.

33. See Jens Dahl, 'Indigenous Peoples of the Soviet North', *IWGIA Document* 67, 1990; Chichlo, 'La premiere victoire. . .'. Dahl, Chichlo and the author were present at this meeting.

34. *Argumenty i Fakty*, 14(495), 1990, p. 1. This Association is said to have had its origin in a meeting of the Writers' Union of the RSFSR in 1988.

35. This convention had just been published in part in Russian in *Severnyye Prostory*, February 1990.

36. Shown in the author's film 'Siberia – After the Shaman'.

37. For an extensive discussion of the symbolic aspects of this *rayon*, see Vitebsky, 'Landscape and Self-Determination'. In the long run, the outcome was not as successful as they thought at the time and as I portrayed it in that article. This was due largely to clan rivalries and internal factions. For central constraints on local freedom, see Piers Vitebsky, 'Centralised Decentralisation: the Ethnography of Remote Reindeer Herders under Perestroika', *Cahiers du monde russe et soviétique*, XXX1(2–3), 1990, pp. 345–55 (p. 354).

38. Respectively 'On General Principles of Local Self-Administration', 9 April; and 'On Free Ethnic Development of the Citizens of the USSR Living outside their Ethnic Territories or Having no Such Territories within the USSR'; both discussed in Vakhtin, op. cit., pp. 28–9.

39. W. Garrett, 'Air Bridge to Siberia', *National Geographic* 1988, 174(4), pp. 504–8.

40. Nikolai Vakhtin, personal communication.

41. The Inuit Circumpolar Conference brings together people of Inuit origin from Alaska, Canada, Greenland and Siberia. The Canadian term 'Inuit' is the more favoured word for 'Eskimo', which is now considered insulting in some regions though it is still used in Russia.

42. Announcement, *Izvestiya*, 10 March 1989; opposition to project, B. Prok-horov, 'Kak sberech' Yamal', *Znaniye–sila*, 1988(7), pp. 1–8, translated as 'How to Save Yamal', *IWGIA Newsletter* 58, 1989, pp. 113–128. For an overall discussion, see Vitebsky, 'Gas. . .'.

43. Sources in Vitebsky, 'Gas. . .', p. 23.

44. See note 37.

45. Vitebsky, 'The Crisis. . .'

46. Vitebsky, 'Gas. . .'.

47. Analysed for a Buryat collective farm in Caroline Humphrey, *Karl Marx Collective: Economy, Society and Religion in a Siberian Collective Farm* (Cambridge: Cambridge University Press 1983).

48. This represents a microcosm of the problem facing the privatisation of any enterprise in the country. For a view that links the scale of the state farm to that of the giant smelting plant in Noril'sk, see David Anderson, 'The Novosibirsk Stock-Market Boom', *Anthropology Today* 10(4), 1994, pp. 10–16 (p. 12).

49. *Beringian Notes*, National Parks Service (Alaska Region), series 2, No. 2, 7 December 1993.

50. William W. Fitzhugh *et al.*, 'Preliminary Field Report for 1994' ('Living Yamal' Project, etc.), Artic Studies Center, Smithsonian Institution, Washington DC (typescript).

51. Thomas A. Moorhouse, 'Sovereignty, Tribal Government and the Alaska Native Claims Settlement Act Amendments of 1987', *Polar Record* 25(154), 1991, pp. 197–206.

52. David Anderson, personal communication.

53. See Vitebsky, 'The Crisis. . .'; the episode forms a leading story in the film 'Siberia – After the Shaman'.

54. David Anderson, personal communication. This is an example of how versions of the Soviet system replicate themselves on a smaller scale inside the larger system. See also Caroline Humphrey, ''Icebergs', Barter and the Mafia in Provincial Russia', *Anthropology Today*, 7(2), 1991, pp. 8–13, which also discusses protectionism at the level of the ethnic group and of the enterprise.

55. Particularly in IWGIA publications; see also Vakhtin, op. cit.

56. *IWGIA Newsletter* 1993(1):37.

57. The phrase is Nikolai Vakhtin's (personal communication). For the intense fervour and ideological conviction of this process in the 1930s, see H. Smolka, *Forty Thousand against the Artic: Russia's Polar Empire*, London 1937.

58. Estimated figures from Igor Krupnik, personal communication, though some reports (autumn 1994) suggest that Russians are beginning to return as they find no opportunities back home. For population structures in two neighbouring Siberian and US Eskimo settlements, see D. G. Callaway and A. Pilyasov, 'A Comparative Analysis of the Settlements of Novoye Chaplino and Gambell', *Polar Record* 29(168) 1993, pp. 25–36.

59. This view comes from conversations with Igor Krupnik.

CHAPTER SIX

# Buryatiya and the Buryats

Caroline Humphrey

The Buryats are one of the 'quiet' nationalities of Russia. Even during the years of *perestroika* and the subsequent dramatic political events, Buryats were notable for their loyalty to central government and the relative weakness of any political expression of nationalism. In June 1994 they voted overwhelmingly for a President who stood for traditional Communist values. Although they appear Russified in many ways, the Buryats have experienced a remarkable cultural revival in recent years. The effect of this situation is that, in the federal political context, Buryats are joining with the local Russian population to express *regional* interests, while in cultural contexts they maintain a distinctive ethnic identity.

## BACKGROUND

The Buryats are a people of Mongolian descent, language group and culture. The southern border of the Buryat Republic (formerly the Buryat ASSR) forms the frontier of Siberian Russia with Mongolia. The Buryats, however, straddle the various administrative and political units of this region. Some 249,500 of them live in the Buryat Republic (1989 census), i.e. 23.9 per cent of the total population. A further 35,600 Buryats live in Mongolia and between 6,000 and 7,000 in Inner Mongolia in China.[1]

In the medieval period the Buryats were a cluster of tribes living around Lake Baikal. The establishment of a frontier between the Russian and the Manchurian empires in the 1680s created the political conditions in which the Buryats could emerge as a separate people. However, they were not administratively unified in Russia until the Buryatskaya ASSR was created in 1923. The basis of the traditional economy was livestock herding, which was somewhat nomadic in character, particularly to the east of Lake Baikal. The original religion

113

of the Buryats was shamanism, largely replaced by Buddhism in the eighteenth and nineteenth centuries. The Buryats lived in the wooden, eight-sided 'yurta' or in Mongolian-type felt-covered mobile tents. These are the grounds for the Stalin-period view of the Buryats as primitive nomads, but this is not the whole story.

The Buryat tribes were said by Soviet historians to have 'voluntarily' entered the Russian empire in the seventeenth century. In fact they resisted, but having no guns were no match for the Cossack troops sent by Moscow to conquer eastern Siberia. Gradually during the eighteenth century, Russian peasant settlement increased. The Buryats were forced off the best land. They sent several delegations to the Moscow tsars to plead for land rights, but to little avail. By the end of the nineteenth century, and especially with the construction of the Trans-Siberian railway, an increased flow of settlers took over virtually all the fertile riverine land, dividing the Buryats into geographically separate enclaves. The lack of a tradition of political centralisation of the Buryats and their territorial dispersion remain important factors in their situation today.

However, the land reforms proposed by the tsarist government at the turn of the century, whereby all households were to be allotted equal shares of land, irrespective of whether they were peasant farmers or nomadic herdsmen, aroused bitter anger among almost all Buryats, and were the first spur to organised Buryat nationalism. This could occur because the Buryats had by then developed an educated élite, conscious of Buryat history and already engaged in a movement for religious and cultural renewal.[2] The key to this is religion.

The underlying religion of the Buryats was shamanism, based on the idea of spirits in nature that can 'possess' human beings and are to some extent controllable by shamans. However, the missionary efforts of Tibetan and Mongolian Buddhist lamas had great success among the Buryats. The spirits of nature were renamed and classified as Buddhist protector deities. By the end of the nineteenth century there were some thirty-six monasteries in Trans-Baikal, one for each district, and it is estimated that around one-fifth of the adult male population were Buddhist lamas. Pilgrimages were regularly made to Mongolia and Tibet. In the early 20th century Buryat lama reformers alleged that the great economic power of the monasteries and their close ties with the tribal aristocracy had led to degeneration of the ideals of Buddhism. This movement for religious reform aligned with the 'nationalist', anti-Speransky tendency, and the resulting platform – itself internally diverse – was also much influenced by Western liberal ideas.

Right through the tsarist period political exiles had been sent to Buryatiya. The Decembrists in particular are credited by Soviet historians with much educational work. Some Buryats were able to benefit from the mixture of Buddhist and Orthodox schooling available, which resulted in the emergence of notable scholars, such as the orientalist Dorzhi Banzarov (1822–55). By the beginning of this century Buryat intellectual–religious leaders were in contact – even in vogue – with liberal circles in Russia. A Buddhist temple was built in St Petersburg. The independent-minded, radical Buryat intelligentsia, accustomed to acting as intermediaries between the Russians and Mongolians, was determined to preserve and enhance the Buryat language and culture. They were in contact with enlightened Buryat Buddhist lamas, such as Agvan Dorzhiev (1853–1938) who acted as an agent of Russian interests in Tibet, and was one of those who began to advocate a reform of the local monasteries. It was in this international context that, alongside the traditional theological, philosophical, medical, artistic and other schools that had long flourished in the Buryat lamaseries, there suddenly erupted a rethinking of Buddhist culture, and an extraordinary debate on ethics, politics, language, the role of religion in everyday life, and the place of Buryat culture in the context of the Russian Empire.

It is not clear to what extent these new ideas penetrated among the Buryat herdsmen. Certainly they were opposed by the *taisha* (prince) of the Khori clan and his allies. Some of the monasteries, which had always had a tendency to compete with one another at the best of times, stirred into open conflict with the reformers.


## NATIONALITY AS PART OF SOVIET LIFE

The Buryats played little part in the Civil War which established Bolshevik power in eastern Siberia. They were, however, centrally involved in a number of political movements which aimed to set up a 'pan-Mongolian' state in the east. These movements, as far as the Buryats were concerned, were a resurgence of the forces that had been so active at the beginning of the century. Though for some they were envisaged as Buddhist theocracies, for others their real goal was independence of the Mongol peoples from both Russian and Chinese domination. Rapidly swept aside in the military events of the revolutionary period, their place was taken by a grouping of the Buryat intelligentsia with socialist inclinations. The people who formed the Buryat National Committee (Burnatskom) were SRs, not Bolsheviks, and many of them envisaged a socialist state compatible with reformed Buddhism. It was under their aegis that the Buryat-Mongol ASSR was set up in 1923. Its territory was larger than at present and included areas both west and east of Lake Baikal. Its capital was the predominantly Russian trading town of Verkheneudinsk, later re-named Ulan-Ude ('Red Ude').

During the 1920s the leaders of the Burnatskom were gradually ousted by Bolsheviks, both Russian and Buryat. As the Communist policies gradually became apparent (expropriation of monastic lands, annihilation of aristocratic and clan leadership, confiscation of livestock for state purposes, a new territorial basis for administration, and so on), there was a series of mass emigrations of Buryats. Some of them fled to northern Mongolia, others to the Hulun Buir and Shilingol regions of Inner Mongolia in China. In Buryatiya the possibility of a new allocation of lands led to many clashes between Russian peasants and Buryats. In this chaotic situation the redistribution of land did not get very far, but a number of small communes were set up in the 1920s, including some for Buddhist lamas (the latter were regarded with suspicion both by lay believers and by the Bolsheviks). With collectivisation in 1929–32 all such experiments were swept aside. The Buryats suffered greatly in this period and large numbers of the herds were slaughtered. There were armed uprisings in many villages and some monasteries also became centres of resistance. It would not be correct, however, simply to see the new socialist ideas as implemented by Russians in the teeth of Buryat opposition. Many Russian peasants of the region were Old Believers and highly conservative, and many Buryats of the younger generation had become enthused with the new ideology.

At this period the population of the Buryat ASSR was largely rural. Russians and Buryats lived mainly in separate collective farms. During the 1930s engineering and railway repair workshops were established, together with some mining, lumbering and manufacturing. These industries and the towns associated with them were populated almost entirely by Russians, mainly people drafted in from outside the Republic. Rural Buryats were, however, drawn into mass education programmes. Young people, often orphans or those without extensive kin networks, were brought to boarding schools and trained for leadership posts (for instance as Party officials, local administrators and farm leaders). Some of these were young lamas expelled from the monasteries. By 1938 the monasteries were brutally crushed and virtually all of them physically destroyed.

From around 1931 onwards the cultural policy was one of overt Russification combined with moves to detach the Buryats from their Mongolian connections. Histories began to be published portraying the pre-revolutionary Buryats as poverty-stricken, illiterate, tribal people, ground down by extortionate princes, lamas and shamans. Most of the leading figures of the Buryat intelligentsia, branded as 'bourgeois nationalists', disappeared in the purges of the late 1930s. The Mongolian script used to write Buryat was abandoned at the end of the 1920s. An experiment with a Latin script was short-lived and Cyrillic was introduced instead. The 'official' Buryat language, which had been based on the Selenga dialect (i.e. the one closest to Mongolian) was changed to the Khori dialect. This involved a systematic shift of pronunciation away from Mongol, and was difficult for many groups of Buryats to understand. Vocabulary was changed wherever possible to non-Mongol or introduced Soviet terms, and the use of the old words was criticised as 'archaic'. Schooling and textbooks were increasingly in Russian. By the 1950s Buryat oral epics were being denounced as 'feudal', and archaeologists were revealing that the Western Buryats were not really Mongolian at all but originally a Turkic people, subsequently Mongolized. This process culminated in the break-up and renaming of the Buryat-Mongol ASSR. In 1937 the ASSR was much reduced in size: the territory west of Lake Baikal was ceded to the Irkutsk Oblast, with a small Buryat enclave left as the Ust'-Ordynsk National Okrug, and the eastern steppes were relinquished to the Chita Oblast, the Buryat-settled lands of Aga becoming the Aga National Okrug within it. In 1958 the Buryat-Mongol ASSR was renamed the Buryat ASSR.

It does not seem that this reorganisation was simply a 'divide and rule' response by Moscow to a Buryat nationalist move at the period. The Buryats were too subjected and encompassed by the Russian population for that. It seems more likely that the Buryat leaders of the ASSR were attempting to ingratiate themselves with Moscow in the context of demands from the more powerful regions of Irkutsk and Chita. But whatever the reasons, the result was an even greater political fragmentation of the people calling themselves Buryat, a situation that has remained up to the present day. Only around 58 per cent of Buryats live in the Buryat republic, while 20 per cent live in the Irkutsk Oblast, 12 per cent in the Ust'-Ordynsk National Okrug and 9 per cent in the Aga National Okrug.

Nevertheless, the Buryats experienced considerable development in the Soviet period, especially in education. According to local accounts in the early 1980s, of all the nationalities in the USSR (including Russians), the Buryats had the highest level of education after the Armenians. The Buryats play a disproportionately large part in governmental and cultural institutions of the ASSR, and they dominate the rural intelligentsia.

Relatively few Buryats are engaged in industry, mining or lumbering. Many remain in agriculture, especially in livestock farming. The farms of the region were never very successful, but this cannot be attributed to lack of training of the workforce. Rather, it seems to have been caused, as elsewhere, by a combination of inappropriate, over-centralised plans, low prices, neglect of infrastructure, mismanagement and general anomie. In the 1950s large areas of pastures were ploughed up for grain crops; and simultaneously the number of sheep rose greatly. This resulted in disastrous environmental damage to the remaining pastures. Probably the Buryats are no worse off in rural regions than the Russians, who tend to be concentrated in low-paid labouring jobs in agriculture. However, in Ulan-Ude the Buryats, occupied in administration, culture and services, contrast themselves with 'the Russians', who consist of two distinct groups: the old élite of mainly

Jewish families from the pre-Soviet trading days, and the 'black mass' of the working class recently arrived from outside.

Because of the policy of supporting national cadres in the ASSR, Buryats flooded in from the surrounding regions. Western Buryats from the Irkutsk Oblast in particular moved to the ASSR, often abandoning villages to a few remaining families.

Even by the late 1960s the Buryats gave the impression of being very Russified. The traditional pastoral economy had been swallowed up by the collective and state farms with their mechanisation and bureaucracy. At this time, Buryat was abandoned in favour of Russian as the language of instruction in schools. The vast majority of Buryats spoke Russian fluently and over the next two decades young people ceased to acquire their own native language. Indigenous housing had long since disappeared. People lived in long rows of more or less identical houses of the Russian Siberian type. No one except a few old women wore Buryat national clothing. The utensils, books, carpets and furniture used were the standard Soviet issue. Two monasteries had been resurrected after the Second World War, but on a tiny scale, and the lamas had to study Marxism-Leninism before they graduated to religious texts. Any remaining shamans were subject to arrest, and few people dared attend services at the monasteries. Folk ensembles appeared in the most clumsy theatrical approximations to Buryat clothing, which must have been the product of non-Buryat imagination. Yet they were enthusiastically applauded by the shepherds when they portrayed wicked feudal princes, solidarity with Vietnam, and the helping hand of the 'older brother'. People seemed matter-of-fact and secular, if grim and dependent on alcohol, as they struggled to make collectivised agriculture work in the Siberian cold.[3]

But to some extent the impression of Russification, if not Sovietisation, was misleading. People spoke Russian, but they had not forgotten Buryat, nor the domestic side of Buryat culture. Above all, they remembered long genealogies, whole lineages of ancestors, and they still observed the exogamic marriage rules of the clans. Almost everyone knew Buryat myths and legends. Sacred places of the spirits in nature were given surreptitious worship. Ancient burial rites were still practised. With the repression of Buddhism shamanism had re-emerged during the war, and never entirely died out. But all of this was hidden. Only the occasional drunken brawl in the towns, where Russians and Buryats lived in separate quarters, gave an indication that there might be tension under the surface.

## REDISCOVERING THE NATION'S HISTORY

In the *perestroika* period of the late 1980s there was a burst of interest in exploring the Buryat past. This involved first of all Buddhism, and the issue of closer links with Mongolia. Even the official institutions began to change. For years the monastery at Ivolga, re-opened after the Second World War, had been engaged in Soviet-led 'Buddhists for Peace' propaganda movements. But it now became less concerned with condemning imperialism and more involved with religious questions. In 1989 thirty young Buddhists from the USSR, mostly Buryats, were sent to Ulaanbaatar in Mongolia to study to become monks. Soon small new monasteries were founded and funds sought to restore the ruins of famous ancient ones. Aged former lamas were sought out and begged to return to staff the new temples. This movement led to the establishing of contacts with the other Buddhist peoples of Russia, the Tuvinians and the Kalmyks, and more widely with Buryats in Mongolia and China. The visiting Dalai Lama was given a tumultuous welcome. The stadium in Ulan-Ude was engaged for his speech and the entire government appeared on stage to acknowledge him.

Another sign of the redisovery of the Buddhist past is the huge popularity of Tibetan medicine, of which the practitioners are mainly lamas. There is also a Centre of Eastern Medicine in Ulan-Ude. The emphasis in Tibetan medicine on ecological relations between plants, and on the homeopathic balance and individual psychology of the patient, has clearly struck a chord of sympathy with the Buryats and even the Russians.

So thoroughly was knowledge of the Buryat culture heritage erased during the Soviet period that many young Buryats were ignorant of elementary facts about their past. For this reason historical articles published in the *perestroika* years had enormous effect. These ranged from straightforward accounts of the Buryat pilgrims to Tibet, or those who were guides to the Russian explorers of Central Asia, to more sensitive subjects, such as Zhamsaran (Piotr) Badmaev, the Aga Buryat who had been both a Christian and a doctor of Tibetan medicine at the tsarist court in St Petersburg. For decades Badmaev had been reviled as a charlatan, working to cure 'odious types' in the aristocracy. But his name was rehabilitated and his grandson wrote a widely published memoir of him. This described not only the many unfashionable patients in need tended by Badmaev himself, but also how his wife and Buryat lama students carried on his work in Leningrad until 1937–8 when they were arrested. Newspaper accounts of other prominent Buryats unjustly arrested in the 1930s were also published, and readers were asked to contribute photographs and memoires to the Museum of the History of Buryatiya. Over one hundred informal Buryat cultural centres and societies were set up in Ulan-Ude in this period. An example was the Geser Society, named after the famous epic, established to promote interest in Buryat literature.

The recent religious and cultural renaissance has not taken the form of a revival of the 'pan-Mongolian' movements of earlier in the century. This can be seen from cautious Buryat reactions to two issues, one concerning language and the other interpretations of history. One of the most important issues in the *perestroika* period was the decline in knowledge of the Buryat language. By the mid-1980s lobbying had succeeded in having the Buryat language reinstated in all schools, at least as a taught subject, though not as the medium of instruction. It was difficult to find teachers. Many young Buryats in the cities do not know their own language, or else have a much impaired command of it. To help in this situation the newspaper *Pravda Buryatii* started in early 1989 to published an innocuous little column of Buryat conversational phrases, vocabulary, etc. This aroused an amazing degree of controversy. Many Buryats wrote to thank the newspaper and to request the re-publication of Buryat grammars and dictionaries. But Russians wrote to complain about the 'ideological group' behind the column and to ask why they were being 'compelled' to learn a language of such limited usefulness. Other Russians responded that they had lived in Buryatiya for years and were glad to have the possibility of learning the language. Behind all this was the suggestion that Buryat should become the state language, to the exclusion of Russian. In the event, Buryat has become a state language alongside Russian, the latter continuing to be by far the more widely used, even among Buryats.

An article about spying in the late 1930s is interesting in that it enables us to see how far *glasnost'* progressed in relation to Buryat nationalism of the past, and indicates certain limits on wider Mongolian sympathies among Buryats.[4] The author, a Buryat agent of Smersh, went into Mongolia on foot, in a variety of ingenious disguises entirely suitable for a thriller, with the aim of unmasking Mongolians acting as undercover agents for the Japanese. The Mongolians he turned up were followers of De Wang (Prince Demchukdongrub), the nationalist leader of the Inner Mongolian movement for independence from the Chinese. It is true that De Wang, having obtained no support from Soviet-dominated Mongolia, was forced unwillingly to accept Japanese patronage against overwhelming Chinese forces. But the Buryat author had little sympathy for him, even in the changed circumstances of the *perestroika* era. The article calls him a 'Japanese puppet', assumes his followers were working for Japanese imperialism, and says not a word about the Inner Mongolian struggle for independence. We must conclude that Buryat stirrings stop short at the political implications of wider Mongolian sympathies.

## THE BURYATS IN THE *PERESTROIKA* PERIOD AND AFTER

At the end of the 1980s, although Buryats were only 24 per cent of the population of the Republic, they comprised 50 per cent of the obkom (ASSR) Party *apparat*, 45 per cent of the raion and city Party cadres, and 60 per cent of the leading officials in the ministries and ASSR administration.[5] The Party of this period was firmly wedded to a conservative line, and during the *perestroika* period it was unusual even in Siberia in retaining a First Secretary from the pre-Gorbachev era.[6] Warnings were issues that the slogan, 'All power to the Soviets!' should not be taken to moderate the influence of the Party or place its leading role in society in doubt. Speeches gave evidence that the national movements in the Baltic republics and the Caucasus were regarded with fear and suspicion. Sympathy was expressed for the Russians of those regions, and there were constant calls for the renewal of the best traditions of Bolshevism and ideological work to promote the idea of socialism as the pre-eminent way of life.

All this suggests, of course, that alternative views were rife in Buryatiya. It seems that this was expressed partly in a subdued conflict between the Party and the Komsomol, dominated by younger and better-qualified people. This pattern was quite different from that found in the Union republics, and, as Smith has pointed out,[7] could be expected in regions where the nationality had no political coherence before the Soviet era.

During the late 1980s the Party experienced a severe drop in popular esteem and authority. In 1986–7, for example, 1,198 members and candidate members were removed from Party rolls (220 for hooliganism, drunkenness and moral degradation), 269 were punished by the Party, and 630 received sobering-up. Nevertheless, 18 people convicted of crimes and 26 oblast and raion leaders banned from office were found again in leadership roles.[8] It was difficult in some places to find people willing to stand as party secretaries, and members started to complain about the Party dues deducted from their pay.

On the evidence of the elections in 1989, the deputies to the Soviets seemed to arouse as little enthusiasm as their Party counterparts. On their return to Ulan-Ude from the Congress in Moscow they were subject to a barrage of criticism. Why had the 'Buryat' deputies not made speeches? Why had they not spoken up about the ecological damage to Baikal? Why did they vote against Yeltsin? The replies were weak. One deputy, admitting that she had not even applied to speak, responded, 'On such an important occasion one should have something definite and businesslike to propose'.[9] The picture we receive from that period is of the official representatives of Buryatiya (not necessarily themselves Buryat) being unused to taking the initiative in the capital, and incapable of articulating the views of their constituents. This was a problem experienced by many of the non-Russian nationalities of the RSFSR in getting their voices heard at all, a subject of bitter complaint by the few speakers from these groups at the Congress of People's Deputies.[10]

The reaction to the August coup of 1991 was characteristic. Saganov, then Chairman of the Council of Ministers of Buryatiya, is said to have written a telegram to Moscow in support of the 'putchists'. However, the telegram was not actually sent. In this way, Buryats say, Saganov could appear on the winning side whatever happened (either taking the line, 'We composed the telegram but the post office was closed', or, if events turned out otherwise, 'We never sent a telegram').

During the years when the Communist Party was banned, it organised itself 'underground', with cells in many institutions throughout the Republic. It re-emerged as a much smaller Party holding to an orthodox line, now seen as 'far left'. Meanwhile, the political spectrum diversified into a number of new parties, whose differences from one another are by no means clear even to the electorate. Politics centred around personalities. Each of the major figures grouped around himself a number of parties and movements.

Thus, for the elections to the State Duma in December 1993 there were three major blocs, led respectively by Potapov, Saganov and Ivanov. A short discussion of these three figures and their careers shows the degree to which nationalist issues have now disappeared from the political agenda. Potapov is a local Russian but, unusually, he speaks Buryat well. His entire career was spent as a high-ranking Communist official. Though he now espouses a more democratic line, he is widely thought of as a 'Communist', and his bloc includes such conservative elements as the Afghan veterans and the 'Women of Russia'. Saganov is a Buryat. He was an oppositional figure in the Brezhnev period, 'exiled' to North Korea as a second secretary in the Soviet Embassy. In the Gorbachev era he returned to power as Chairman of the Buryat Council of Ministers; seen as somewhat more democratic than Potapov, his links nevertheless are with Khasbulatov in Moscow. Deputies supporting Saganov lost heavily to Potapov's group in the December 1993 elections, and therefore, although Saganov remains as Chairman, he did not stand for the Presidency in the June 1994 elections. Potapov's main rival for the Presidency was Ivanov, who is younger than the other major figures and stands for business interests and democratic policies. Ivanov is half-Buryat, half-Slav, and his career was in engineering rather than politics. In the June 1994 Presidential election the vote was Ivanov 23 per cent, Potapov 77 per cent, reflecting widespread dislike of market-oriented economic policy. It seems that the question of nationality has played relatively little part in recent elections. True, the Zhirinovsky bloc was widely supported by local Russians, while Buryats found its policies frightening, but otherwise Buryats showed no consistent voting pattern. A large number of them have always supported Potapov against the Buryat candidates, Saganov and Ivanov.

Around 1990 there was a move to re-unite the disparate Buryat territories within Russia, i.e. to join the Ust'-Ordynsk and Aga Okrugs to the Buryat ASSR. Also, calls were published in the newspapers for 'Mongol' to be reinstated in the name of the republic, for the Russian terms *raion* and *selo* to be replaced by the native *aimak* and *somon* (used in Mongolia, but discontinued earlier in Buryatiya), and for the parliament to be called by the Mongolian term *hural*. However, apart from the introduction of the term *hural*, these moves have come to nothing. The idea of unification of Buryat territories, only weakly supported for fear of angering local Russians, was definitively scotched when Yeltsin's government raised the status of National Okrugs to equal that of Republics (the former ASSRs) within Russia. Now Ust'-Ordynsk and Aga have every reason to stay separate from Buryatiya, negotiating their own terms with Moscow. Aga in particular has been successful at this, inviting Yeltsin on a visit, acquiring status as a special economic zone for contracts with China, and even suggesting setting up a branch of the Aga bank in Moscow. The proposal to Mongolise names seems to have quietly disappeared. People say they have no energy for such matters now: the focus should be the disastrous state of the economy.

Here, Buryats and Russians alike face a grim prospect. There is little difference between the two nationalities in attitudes to privatisation: both, especially in rural areas, are largely against it. Thus collective and state farms have been retained in Buryatiya. The worse the economic situation, the more determined are people to cling on to collective institutions, as these still are the main providers of essential services (rural housing, distribution of water, fodder, fertiliser, winter fuel, etc., and in many places the support of schools, hospitals, and kindergartens). During 1993–4 many farms were unable to pay their members' wages for months on end, but still the rural population supports them and relatively few have become 'private farmers'. In the cities, however, business enterprise is more widespread, especially it seems among the young, well-educated Buryats. Recently successful entrepreneurs have agitated to obtain seats in the Hural (parliament).

As the disastrous effects of Soviet-era economic policies have become evident, Buryatiya has experienced a strong environmental movement. Ecological issues are rarely seen as a national problem. There is no doubt that the impurity of Lake Baikal and the River Selenga is important in local and regional politics. The problems have been caused in the main by the cellulose industry and effluents from Ulan-Ude and Severo-Baikal'sk. The Buryats might understandably identify the pollution with Russian incomers, but all the evidence is that it is the multinational intelligentsia and Siberian Russians, not Buryats, who are most vocal on this issue. The Russian writer Valentin Rasputin is famous for his publicity on behalf of the purity of sacred Lake Baikal. A multidisciplinary study on the ecology and sustainable development of the Baikal region has been under way since the beginning of the 1990s. This scientific work combines environmental research with geography, experimental medicine, ethnography, economics and new subjects such as 'ethnic ecology' and 'eco-pedagogics'. The point to note here is that what we are seeing here is a *regional* as opposed to national initiative, and this is characteristic of Buryatiya in general.[11] In contrast to the *perestroika* years, the informal societies now being set up in Ulan-Ude are *zemlyachestva* (gatherings based on geographical identities).

## CONCLUSION

The Buryats seem at ease with, or perhaps resigned to, their close relations with the Siberian Russians. Unlike in Tuva in 1990–1, there was no backlash against Russians when the economic collapse hit hard, and unlike in Yakutia there is little attempt to establish their republic as an quasi-autonomous resource base. Apart from the possibility of developing international tourism at Lake Baikal, Buryatiya in fact has few sources of wealth, and its economy is still heavily dependent on central allocations. Established political leaders with good connections in the capital are thus preferred. All the signs are that the Buryats wish to cooperate with Russians in maintaining order and attending to the numerous economic and social problems within the republic. These include public health, a disastrous fall in the birth-rate after 1989,[12] and the urgent need to reorganise land-use, all of which are non-'national' issues. The regional groups of Buryats have not united and seem set to pursue their own interests separately. The idea of uniting with Mongolia, tentatively raised in the Gorbachev years, is now out of the question. The Buryats look at the even more difficult economic situation of Mongols and their reaction is: why should we join up with that?

It would be a mistake, however, to see the Buryats as losing their cultural identity. On the contrary, perhaps because they have strong historical traditions, which were widely publicised from 1986 onwards and have now entered the mainstream of cultural life, the Buryats seem confident of retaining their culture. Indeed they are eager to share it. For example, they are pleased at the large numbers of Russians who become involved with Buddhism, and many Buryats also attend Orthodox church services. Unlike the 'pan-Mongolian' movements of the 1910s and 1920s, the present cultural activities are largely separate from 'nationalism' as locally understood. The Buryats combine regional economic preoccupations with increasing international links (trade with China, religious ties with India). In these circumstances, 'nationalism', in the sense of the political promotion of ethnic Buryat interests, now looks to most people both narrow and extremist.

## NOTES

1. This population figure is uncertain, as the Buryats living in China are classified in statistics as 'Mongolians'.
2. K. M. Gerasimova, *Lamaizm i natsional'no-kolonial'naya politika tsarizma v zabaikalye v XIX i nachale XX vekov* (Ulan-Ude, Filial of the Academy of Sciences, 1957).

3.  C. Humphrey *Karl Marx Collective: Economy, Society and Religion in a Siberian Collective Farm* (Cambridge: Cambridge University Press 1983), pp. 12–22.
4.  Ts. Tserendorzhiev 'Po sledam shpionov' *Pravda Buryatii*, 1 August 1989, p. 4.
5.  *Pravda Buryatii*, 10 September 1989, p. 2.
6.  The First Secretary, A. M. Belyakov, a Russian, was in power since 1984.
7.  G. Smith, 'Gorbachev's greatest challenge: perestroika and the national question' *Political Geography Quarterly* 8 (1) 1989, pp. 7–20.
8.  *Pravda*, 18 June 1988, p. 2.
9.  *Pravda Buryatii*, 16 June 1989, p. 1.
10. O. Glebov and J. Crowfoot *The Soviet Empire: Its Nations Speak Out* (Chur and London: Harwood Academic Publishers 1989), pp. 93–101.
11. An example of the numerous documents produced by this initiative is the complex programme 'Sokhraneniye i vozrozhdeniye prirodnoi i kul'turnoi sredy korennykh narodov Baikal'skogo regiona' (Russian Academy of Sciences, Moscow and Ulan-Ude 1994). In such publications the phrase 'indigenous peoples' refers to Russians as well as Buryats.
12. Goskomstat Respubliki Buryatiya, 'Migratsiya naseleniya v respublike buryatiya', 1992, p. 4.

# PART III

# The Baltic States

The Baltic states of Estonia, Latvia and Lithuania, with a combined population of 8.8 million, are among the smallest of the post-Soviet states (see Fig. 3). They are also unique among these states in having gone through a previous period of sustained independent statehood (1918–40), their national sovereignties coming to an abrupt end following the signing of the Molotov–Ribbentrop Pact between Germany and the Soviet Union on 23 August 1939, which paved the way for their incorporation into the Soviet Union. Although sharing parallel historical experiences, culturally they are very different. Each possesses its own language and literary traditions, Lithuanians their Catholicism, Estonians their Lutheranism, and Latvians a mix of both.

Besides being culturally the most Western of the post-Soviet states, the region is also the most urbanised, with among the highest living standards. It was the Baltic republics, with their unique pre-Soviet experiences of pluralist democracy and *laissez-faire* economies, that were singled out by Moscow as the most likely to embrace *perestroika*. But Gorbachev's programme of *glasnost'* and democratisation in the least Sovietised of the Soviet republics also enabled grassroots-based national movements to arise which, although initially supportive of Moscow-style reforms, became increasingly nationalistic, securing for the Baltic republics the role of pacesetters in challenging the territorial legitimacy of Soviet rule.

Although the post-independence transition to democratic rule has been smoother in the Baltic States than elsewhere, the two most multiethnic republics, Latvia and Estonia, have had difficulties in coming to terms with the presence of large Russian minorities, many of whom settled in the republics during the Soviet period. Unlike the other post-Soviet states, Latvia and Estonia did not grant citizenship to all those living in their national territory at the time of independent statehood, with only citizens of the previous inter-war state and their descendants automatically qualifying. Yet despite fears among the Russian settler community of becoming a new ethnic underclass, the republics have remained ethnically stable.

Figure 3 : **THE BALTIC STATES**

# CHAPTER SEVEN

# Estonia and the Estonians

Riina Kionka and Raivo Vetik

Despite the relatively small size and the disadvantageous geographic position of their homeland, the Estonian people have prevailed for centuries under difficult conditions. Estonians have been under several varieties of foreign rule for over 700 years, and emerged from the mid-1980s to be pacesetters in challenging the continuation of rule from Moscow.

The geographical positioning of the Estonians at the far eastern reaches of the Baltic Sea, neatly sandwiched between the Great Slavic nations of the East and the Germanic nations of the West, has left the territory of Estonia precariously vulnerable to outside influence. That same geostrategic positioning allows Estonia – especially in modern times, with varying degrees of success – to function as a go-between, a kind of conduit, between East and West. The tiny population, having hovered around 1 million in modern times, allows for easy domination by others. And because political and economic domination usually goes hand in hand with cultural domination, the spectre of assimilation, forced or otherwise, has always lurked nearby for the Estonians, be it by Germans, Swedes, Poles or, most recently, Russians.

## BACKGROUND

The Estonians have lived in the territory now known as Estonia for some 5,000 years. Little is known about Estonians in prehistoric times. The Estonian language belongs to the Finno-Ugric language group, which embraces such modern languages as Finnish and Hungarian. The origins of the Finno-Ugric peoples is unclear, but archaeological, linguistic and anthropological evidence points to a westward migration from the middle Volga region, between the Kama and Oka rivers.[1] Most twentieth-century Finnish, Hungarian and Estonian scholars agree that the Finno-Ugric peoples first lived in the forest zone of Eastern Europe just west of the Ural Mountains. Around the third millennium BC they began migrating in a succession of small waves towards the west. One major branch went north to the eastern littoral of the Baltic Sea; the other headed further west into what became modern Hungary.

Agriculture dominated the economy, but the level of technology the Estonians reached before the Middle Ages is unclear. Farmsteads were organised by village, and were almost never individual. Estonian family structure in prehistoric times was probably similar to other nomadic and early agricultural societies, in that extended families, or clans, were the norms. These male-dominated clans were economically self-sufficient units. In the last centuries before German conquest, Estonian society still displayed few differences in wealth or social power, excepting a class of slaves of increasing importance as a source of cheap labour as the nomadic way of life came to an end. On the eve of the Middle Ages most Estonians were small landholders with a measure of societal decision-making that came from owning land and bearing weapons. Politically the Estonians were decentralised, with administrative and political subdivisions emerging on the local level only in the first centuries after the birth of Christ. Estonia was fundamentally independent, with Kievan Russia in the east and the Vikings in the west collecting tribute only occasionally under military duress. Until the German conquest, beginning at the end of the twelfth century, Estonia was not ruled by outsiders.

By the end of the twelfth century, incursions from the west had begun, and with them began the long pattern of foreign domination made attractive by Estonia's convenient location. Estonia was one of the last dark corners of medieval Europe to be Christianised. The German crusading order, the Sword Brethren, were the first outsiders to establish a modicum of control, with Danish help, over northern Estonia at the beginning of the thirteenth century.[2] Under German–Danish conquest, Estonians were Christianised, colonised and gradually enserfed. In the words of one scholar, 'the social dichotomy of lord and peasant was enhanced by an ethnic one as well'.[3]

The Swedes and Russians also became involved at times in the conquest of northern Estonia. In 1236, as a reaction to a serious defeat at the hands of the Lithuanians and Semigallians, the Sword Brethren allied with the military monastic Order of the Teutonic Knights and became known as the Livonian branch of the Teutonic Knights. In 1346 the Danes, finding upkeep of the distant colony too costly, sold their part of Estonia to the Livonian Order of the Teutonic Knights. The Germans ruled Estonia until the Livonian Wars in the middle of the sixteenth century hastened the already advanced demise of German power. Northern Estonia submitted to Swedish authority in 1561, and southern Estonia (Livonia) became part of Lithuania's Duchy of Kurland. Sweden and Lithuania filled the power vacuum until the Russian push to the Baltic Sea in the Great Northern War.

The Treaty of Nystad of 1721 imposed Russian rule in the territory that became modern Estonia – finally with southern Estonia (Livonia) and northern Estonia united. The Baltic German nobility under Russian rule regained many powers over the native peasants that had been lost under Swedish rule, and consequently showed considerable loyalty to Imperial Russia.[4]

The Baltic Provinces were the first in the Russian empire in which serfdom was, by 1819, abolished. By the mid-1800s peasants were able to hold small plots of land, and the abolition of compulsory guild membership spurred Estonian peasants to move to cities. These moves created the economic foundation for the Estonian national cultural awakening that had lain dormant during some 600 years of foreign rule. During the last two decades of the nineteenth century especially, the tsarist administration attempted to assimilate culturally, or Russify, the Estonians. Despite these efforts, Estonia was caught in the current of national awakening (*ärkamisaeg*) that began sweeping through Europe in the middle of the nineteenth century. This first took a cultural form: a movement sprang up to adopt the use of Estonian as the language of instruction in schools; all-Estonian song festivals were held regularly and became, after a time, expressions of national feeling rather than of loyalty to the tsar; and a national literature in Estonian developed.[5] More importantly, the same activists who agitated for a modern national culture began to focus on establishing a modern national state. Another pattern that would later become central to political developments – the use of culture as politics – emerged.

The possibility for the expression of growing political demands for self-determination presented itself as the 1905 Revolution swept through Estonia. Estonians called for freedom of the press and assembly and for universal franchise, and in November an all-Estonian Assembly called for national autonomy. Although Estonian gains were minimal, the 1905 uprisings were brutally suppressed, yet the tense stability that reigned between 1905 and 1917 allowed Estonians to advance the aspiration of national statehood.

A window of opportunity presented itself in the collapse of the German empire in the First World War, and the Russian revolution and subsequent civil war. Russia's Provisional Government granted national autonomy to Estonia, but the internecine struggle mirroring the one in Petrograd continued in Estonia. An autonomous Estonian government (*Maapäev*) was formed but was quickly forced underground by opposing political forces. In the face of the impending German invasion, the Committee of Elders of the underground *Maapäev* announced the Republic of Estonia on 24 February 1918, one day before German troops occupied Tallinn. After the German armistice and subsequent troop withdrawal from Estonia in November 1918, fighting broke out between Bolshevik troops and Estonian partisans. After some fifteen months, the Republic of Estonia and Soviet Russia signed the Peace of Tartu – the Soviet Union's first foreign peace treaty – on 2 February 1920. According to the terms of that treaty, Soviet Russia renounced in perpetuity all rights to the territory of Estonia. The Tartu Peace Treaty was to become a cornerstone in Estonia's struggle under Gorbachev to reinstate Estonia's independence some seventy years later.

Independence lasted twenty-two years.[6] During that time, Estonia underwent a number of economic, social and political reforms necessary to come to terms with its new status as a sovereign state. Economically and socially, the most important step was land reform in 1919. As a result of the sweeping legislation, the large estate holdings belonging to the Baltic nobility were redistributed among peasants and especially among volunteers in the war of independence. Loss of markets in the east led to considerable hardship compounded by the Great Depression before Estonia developed an export-based economy and domestic industries such as oil-shale extraction. Estonia's principal markets became Scandinavia and Western Europe, with some exports to the United States and the Soviet Union.

During independence Estonia also operated under a liberal democratic constitution modelled on the Swiss, Weimar, French and American constitutions. Estonia's first attempt at liberal democracy proved unstable under considerable economic pressures. From 1934 to 1938, partly to guard pre-emptively against a coup from far rightist parties, President Konstantin Päts governed the country by presidential decree. After 1938 a constitutional regime was re-established, which functioned until Soviet annexation in the summer of 1940.

The independence period was one of great cultural advance. Estonian language schools were established, and artistic life of all kinds flourished. One of the more notable cultural acts of the independence period, unique in Western Europe at the time of its passage in 1925, was a guarantee of cultural autonomy to minority groups comprising at least 3,000 persons.

The imminent demise of independence was signalled by the signing of the Molotov–Ribbentrop Non-aggression Pact on 23 August 1939. That agreement's secret clause provided for the Soviet takeover of Estonia, Latvia and part of Finland and, later, Lithuania, in return for Nazi Germany's assuming control over most of Poland. After some diplomatic jockeying, the Soviet Union staged fraudulent elections in June 1940, the Estonian Soviet Socialist Republic was proclaimed on 21 July 1940, and it was formally accepted into the Soviet Union on 6 August 1940.[7]

## ESTONIANS AS PART OF THE SOVIET UNION

The year of Soviet rule that followed was accompanied by the expropriation of property, the Sovietisation of cultural life and the installation of Stalinist communism in political life.[8] Deportations also quickly followed, beginning on the night of 14 June 1941. That night more than 10,000 people, mostly women, children and the elderly, were taken from their homes and sent to Siberia in cattle cars.[9] Thus, when Nazi Germany attacked the Soviet Union on 22 June 1941, the invading troops were received in relatively warm fashion by Estonians.

Most Estonians did not yet know that German plans for the Baltic included annexation to the Third Reich, expulsion of two-thirds of the population and assimilation of the rest with ethnic Germans. The two and a half years of Nazi German occupation gave ample evidence to conclude that German intentions were not much more generous than Soviet intentions. Nevertheless, few Estonians welcomed the Red Army's push west through the Baltic, starting at Narva in January 1944. Some 10 per cent of the population fled to the West between 1940 and 1944, most in the last months of 1944 before Soviet troops pushed through for the last time. By late September, Soviet forces expelled the last German troops from Estonia, heralding a second phase of Soviet rule.[10]

Post-war Sovietisation of life in Estonia continued in 1944 where it had left off in 1941. First and foremost, this meant integrating Estonian agriculture and industry into the all-Union economy. Forced collectivisation did not begin in earnest until 1947, and proceeded slowly until late March 1949. On 25–26 March some 8 to 12 per cent of the rural Estonian population, with estimates ranging from 20,000 to 80,000 people, was deported to labour camps in various parts of the Soviet Union.[11] Within the next month over 56 per cent of Estonian farms were collectivised, over 20 per cent in the first two weeks of April 1949 alone, and the collective farm quickly emerged to become the main form of economic and social organisation in the countryside.

Estonia's industry was also quickly integrated into Stalin's highly centralised economy. Despite the fact that between the wars Estonia's industrial speciality was in light manufacturing and foodstuffs, post-war investment in heavy industry far outweighed that in other industrial branches. Moscow focused on the industries in Estonia that had locally available raw materials, such as oil-shale mining for electricity production and the chemical sector, especially phosphates. Yet one notable characteristic of Estonia's post-Stalin economy is the republic's role as a laboratory for economic experiments. Under Khrushchev and Brezhnev, there was considerable experimentation in industrial management techniques that were implemented sooner and with more success in Estonia than in other regions of the Soviet economy. For instance, in the mid-1960s central authorities began giving greater power to local managers, including the powers to offer incentives for increased workers' productivity and to dispose of profits. By 1969, 84 per cent of the overall Soviet industrial output came from enterprises using this system; in Estonia that percentage reached 96 per cent.[12]

However, the more tightly enmeshed in the Soviet economy Estonia became, the less control republic authorities had over production plans, output disposition or management of local industries. For instance, although Estonia, along with the rest of the Soviet Union, participated in Khrushchev's 1957–65 *sovnarkhoz* experiment to increase regional control over industry, over 75 per cent of Estonia's industrial output, both before and after this temporary reform, was controlled by central authorities.[13] By the mid-1980s central control over the republic's industrial output exceeded 90 per cent.[14]

Post-war political integration into the Soviet Union paralleled economic integration. The Estonian republic underwent several administrative reorganisations during the Stalin years to bring it into accordance with the prevailing Soviet model.

After the war the Estonian Communist Party (ECP) had been gradually transformed from a group of 133 members in spring 1940 into the pre-eminent organisation in the republic. The early post-war years saw a rapid increase in Party membership. Most of these new members were Russified Estonians who had spent most of their lives in the Soviet Union, were assimilated as Russians, and returned to Estonia to make careers only after the Soviet annexation. Not surprisingly, Estonians were reluctant to join the ECP and thus take part in the Sovietisation of their own country. This is reflected in the decreasing ethnic Estonian share of the total Party membership, from some 90 per cent in 1941 to 48 per cent in 1946 to 41 per cent in 1952.[15] The drop in the Estonian share of Party membership by the early 1950s reflects the CPSU's purge of 'bourgeois nationalists' from the ECP in 1950–51. Compared to Stalin's CPSU purges of the 1930s and 1940s, the ECP purge was less bloody, and probably reflected Moscow's unease over an ECP heavily populated by ethnic Estonians with no Soviet training who might be inclined to think 'nationalistically'.

After Stalin's death, Party membership continued to increase and its social bases widened to include more ethnic Estonians, especially during the generally greater optimism of the early 1960s. By the mid-1960s the proportion of ethnic Estonians in the ECP stabilised at around 50 per cent. On the eve of *perestroika*, the ECP claimed about 100,000 members, less than half of them ethnic Estonians, and took in about 1.6 per cent of the republic's population. The upper echelons of the Party, however, continued to be dominated by Russians and Russified Estonians.

Dissent, as the term was understood in the 1970s and 1980s, was largely eliminated in the immediate post-war period by the effectiveness of Stalinist terror. However, another more potent form of protest against Sovietisation, which could hardly be called 'dissent', emerged. From the retreat of Nazi troops in 1944 until as late as 1955, a protracted anti-Soviet pro-independence guerrilla movement existed in the countryside. The movement drew its followers – called 'forest brethren' (*metsavennad*, a popular Estonian term for guerrillas) – from stranded Estonian soldiers who had been mobilised into the Nazi German army, from those seeking to avoid arrest by Soviet security forces or mobilisation into the Soviet army at the war's end, and from those seeking revenge for the mass deportations of 1941 and 1949. The forest brethren worked in groups or alone, and used German and later Soviet equipment that had been left behind. In some areas the guerrillas had effective military control until the late 1940s; in other areas they could only protect themselves and the local population from acts of violence. At the high point of guerrilla strength in 1946–48 there were probably some 5,000 forest brethren. These men did not hope to bring down the Soviet regime by their actions, but evidently expected a restoration of Estonian independence with Allied help, and thus sought to ensure their own survival until such a time came.

More traditional forms of dissent in significant quantity did not appear until the late 1960s. Hopes for systemic reform accompanied the process of de-Stalinisation carried out through the late 1950s and early 1960s. When reform did not materialise and heightened expectations proved groundless, open dissent appeared. This 'quiet dissent' of the 1960s, mostly in the form of protest letters, centred on civil rights issues and was bolstered by the Soviet invasion of Czechoslovakia in August 1968.

By the 1970s national concerns, including concerns about ecological ruin, a consequence of the country's rapid industrialisation, had become the major theme of dissent in Estonia, and the dissenters came increasingly from the ranks of natural scientists and, later, students. A spate of protest letters in the 1970s was followed in each instance by an official crackdown. Despite the authorities' reactions, ranging from arrest and imprisonment to censure, the scope of dissent broadened and the area of concern widened to include worries over cultural autonomy.

By the late 1970s there was growing concern throughout most sectors of Estonian society about the threat of cultural Russification to the Estonian language and national identity. An official Moscow policy implemented in 1978 that sought to increase the role of the Russian language in non-Russian Soviet republics explains a great deal of the worry among Estonians. By 1981, for the first time in the republic's history, Russian was taught in the first grade of Estonian language schools, and was also introduced into Estonian pre-school teaching. Among Estonians, the catch-phrase encompassing this concern was 'Will the people disappear? (kas rahvas kaob?). This widespread concern about cultural survival is responsible for the broadening of the social base of dissent in the late 1970s. In October 1980 some 2,000 secondary school students gathered in the streets of Tartu to protest against Russian rule and call for a free Estonia. Brutal use of police force to suppress this protest prompted forty established intellectuals, among them some leading Communists with impeccable credentials, to sign an open protest letter sent to Moscow and the republic authorities. This 'Letter of the Forty', as it came to be known, decried the increase in ethnic tensions in the republic, precipitated by Russian immigration, and spoke out against the increasing threat to the Estonian language and culture. Such concerns became particularly critical for Estonians due to their demographic position.

Before incorporation, the Estonian proportion of its territory's population was 88.2 per cent, but by 1950 it had dropped to some 76 per cent. It is not surprising that the population of Estonia sank during the war and immediately afterwards to new lows. War losses, the 1941 deportation, and a brain drain of some 10 per cent of the population to the West partially explain the sudden drop in the post-war years, as do territorial changes.[16]

This demographic trend of an ever-decreasing ethnic Estonian share of the total population continued after Stalin's death. According to official census data, by 1960 Estonians made up 74.1 per cent of the total population, in 1970 68.2 per cent, in 1980 64.5 per cent, and by 1989 only 61.5 per cent. There are a number of explanations for this phenomenon. Although from 1953 to 1961 natural increase outstripped net migration increase in the republic, this trend was reversed after 1961 and remained reversed until Estonia once again became an independent state. Since 1962 Estonia's birth-rate has been among the lowest in the Soviet Union.

The low-birth rate is only part of the explanation for the demographic situation. The massive influx of non-Estonians since 1945 is responsible for the precipitous drop in the ethnic Estonian share of the population. The heavy industrial projects developed or augmented in the Stalin era and later required a larger pool of labour than was locally available. Thus, non-Estonian workers came to the republic from other parts of the Soviet Union to staff these industrial projects. These workers, who were attracted by the republic's higher standard of living, paved the way for later waves of immigration. Most were Russians, but a significant minority comprised Ukrainians, Belarusians and other nationalities.

A positive aspect of the post-Stalin era for Estonia was a re-opening in the late 1950s of citizens' contacts with foreign countries. After Khrushchev denounced Stalin's 'two-camp theory' of international relations in favour of 'peaceful coexistence' in his 1956 'secret speech' to the 20th CPSU Congress, it became permissible, to a point, for Soviet citizens to have contacts with foreigners. This move had a tremendous impact on Estonia. For the first time since the Second World War, Estonians were allowed, theoretically, to have contact with their friends and family in the West. Ties were also reactivated with Finland. Contact with Finnish tourists lent Tallinn a cosmopolitan air in keeping with its Western atmosphere, and boosted a flourishing black market. Starting in the middle 1960s, Estonians began watching Finnish television beamed from nearby Helsinki. This electronic 'window on the West' afforded Estonians more information on current affairs and more access to Western culture and thought than any other group in the Soviet Union. This heightened media environment may have been pivotal in preparing Estonians for their vanguard role in extending *perestroika* under Gorbachev.

## ESTONIANS UNDER GORBACHEV

Although the meaning of Gorbachev's terms *perestroika* and *glasnost'* was inexact, Estonians quickly discerned that the new policies could hold very interesting possibilities for the nation. These twin policies had the effect, in Estonia, of catalysing a 'new awakening period' (*uus ärkamisaeg*) that was to lead, as did the first awakening period in late tsarist times, to independent statehood.[17]

The wave of reform began in Estonia with the environmental movement. Vociferous criticism of Estonia's ecological devastation in 1985 was followed by a curious silence in 1986. Later it became clear that despite *glasnost'*, new censorship rules had been implemented in 1986 to quell discussion of pollution. The primary focus of concern was open-pit mining of some of the world's largest phosphate reserves in the north-east of Estonia. Although the issue was an ecological one, it also hinged on demographic concerns. A plan to enlarge the phosphate mining project would have included the in-migration of some 30,000 workers and dependants into Estonia, pushing Estonians into minority status in their own country. Thus, although the debate was environmental in form, it was actually national in content.[18]

The phosphate mining project, along with a host of other highly polluting industrial projects, became the subject of bitter open criticism during 1987. By June 1988 a loose coalition of dissidents, rural inhabitants, workers and intellectuals (including Party intellectuals), all concerned about this double environmental/demographic threat, had successfully consolidated their efforts and succeeded in ending the ten year rule of ECP First Secretary Karl Vaino.

Karl Vaino's demise was a harbinger of the ECP's own gradual loss of influence in the late 1980s. In the early *perestroika* years, the ECP remained stable; the only significant personnel change was the replacement of Aleksandr Kudriavtsev, its Second Secretary, a post traditionally reserved for non-Estonians, by another Russian, Georgii Alyoshin. The Party appeared strong at its 19th Congress in 1986. First Secretary Vaino devoted most of this first *glasnost'*-inspired speech to attacking national culture and Estonians' love of 'Western mass culture' (a clear reference to Finnish television). But by 1988 the ECP's weakness had become clear. In the highly changeable political environment of that year, the Party was unable to assume more than a passive role, and thereby was relegated to a reactive position. Vaino's removal in response to public dissatisfaction indicates how weak the Party had become.

Karl Vaino was replaced by the much more acceptable Vaino Väljas. A number of initial steps by Väljas, including praising the 1980 'Letter of the Forty', enhanced his own and the ECP's reputation, at least for a time. But the Party continued its downward spiral of influence in 1989 and 1990, and began to disintegrate. In November 1989, the Writers' Union Party Organisation voted to suspend its activity and the Estonian Komsomol disbanded. In February 1990 Estonia's Supreme Soviet eliminated paragraph 6 of the republic's constitution which had guaranteed the Party's leading role in society. The final blow came at the ECP's 20th Congress in March 1990 when it voted to break with the CPSU. The Party splintered into three branches, then consolidated into a pro-CPSU and an independent ECP.

As the ECP waned, other political movements, groupings and parties moved to fill the power vacuum. The first and most important of these was the Estonian Popular Front, established in April 1988 in response to appeals made at the Estonian Cultural Union's plenum two weeks earlier. Initially a grass-roots organisation, the Popular Front became a well-organised movement with its own platform, leadership and broad constituency. The Popular Front was followed by the Greens and the dissident-led Estonian National Independence Party, the latter the first to call for full independence in January 1988. By 1989 the political spectrum widened and new parties were formed and re-formed almost daily. Between November 1989 and February 1990 some twenty to thirty parties existed in a republic of 1.5 million people. This frenzied party proliferation stabilised in time for the Supreme Soviet elections of 18 March 1990, where sixteen parties endorsed candidates.[19]

A number of changes in the governance of the republic, brought about by political advances, played a major role in the late 1980s in forming a legal framework for political change. This involved the republic's Supreme Soviet being transformed into an authentic regional law-making body in which key nationally minded leaders, mostly but not exclusively ethnic Estonians, pushed through reformist legislation. This was not always an easy task. Even though the Supreme Soviet, elected in 1985, was nearly 75 per cent ethnic Estonian, it had not traditionally been a medium of reform.

Nevertheless, this relatively conservative Supreme Soviet managed to pass a number of laws. Notable among them was a package of laws that addressed the most sensitive ethnic concerns. The package included the early declaration of sovereignty (November 1988); a law on economic independence (May 1989) that was subsequently confirmed by the USSR Supreme Soviet (November 1989); a language law which made Estonian the official language of the republic (January 1989); and local and republic election laws stipulating residency requirements for voting and candidacy (August and November 1989).

On 18 March 1990, Estonians elected a new Supreme Soviet in the most democratic elections for a republic-level organ since incorporation into the USSR. Following laws making service in the Soviet military voluntary and creating an alternative service (March and April 1990), the new Supreme Soviet quickly established its tenor by declaring the beginning of a transition period to full independence on 30 March 1990. It also chose Popular Front leader Edgar Savisaar as Estonia's first non-Communist Prime Minister. Savisaar in turn chose a moderate cabinet containing very few Communists.

Despite the Estonian Supreme Soviets apparent responsiveness to new conditions, an alternative legislature developed in Estonia in 1990. In February 1990 a body known as the Congress of Estonia was elected in completely unsanctioned unofficial elections. The Congress was organised by a group called the Estonian Citizens' Committees. The Citizens' Committees, acting as an informal body much like the Committees of Correspondence in the American Revolution, registered citizens of the inter-war Republic of Estonia and their descendants with the goal of forming a legally competent citizens' forum. The Congress of Estonia's point of departure was that Estonia remained an occupied country because as Estonia was forcibly annexed by the Soviet Union, the inter-war republic continued to exist *de jure*. Only citizens of that republic and their descendants, argued the Congress, should decide the future of Estonia. The Congress organisers encouraged all non-Estonians who could not claim citizenship to apply for citizenship – and some 60,000 did so. The Congress which met for its initial session in March 1990, showed every sign of becoming a complementary, not competing, political force in relation to the Supreme Soviet.[20]

Reaction to Estonia's interpretation of *perestroika* and *glasnost'* among its 600,000 non-Estonians (about 38.5 per cent of the population) was mixed.[21] In 1988 two groups were formed among non-Estonians in response to the rise of the Popular Front. The International Front and the United Council of Work Collectives had nearly identical constituencies, and together formed 'Intermovement'. Intermovement, a conservative Russian nationalist organisation, was opposed to Estonian-style reform and independence. It was established, ostensibly, to protect the interests of non-Estonians and to further an 'internationalist' (as opposed to a 'nationalist') orientation. Intermovement organised mass demonstrations opposing the republic's Supreme Soviet nationality laws, and asked Moscow to intervene directly on behalf of non-Estonians in the republics' move towards independence.

Potentially the most dangerous moment occurred in May 1990 when hundreds of Intermovement demonstrators attempted to force themselves into the Supreme Soviet building. The attempt was neutralised by thousands of Estonians who immediately arrived after a call of help by the Prime Minister Savisaar on Estonian radio. Fortunately the confrontation did not lead to bloodshed, although it almost did.

Another critical moment was in January 1991 when Soviet troops began 'restoration of order' in the Baltic States. Violent actions were concentrated in Vilnius and Riga, where a number of unarmed civilians defending parliament buildings were killed. Bloodshed was avoided in Tallinn due to the rapid actions of the Estonian leadership following a joint statement with Yeltsin concerning the mutual recognition of all three Baltic States. An important consequence of these events was that such a brutal use of military force against civilians turned many Baltic Russians against Moscow.

Survey data of this period indicate that the non-Estonian population was divided with regard to the independence issue. This was confirmed by the results of the 3 March 1991 national referendum on the independence of Estonia. The question was formulated as follows: 'Do you want the restoration of the independence of the Republic of Estonia?' The total turnout in the referendum was 83 per cent, and 78 per cent of participants voted 'yes'. The results do not indicate directly how particular groups voted, but additional calculations as well as opinion polls of the period revealed that of the non-Estonians, about 30 per cent voted for independence.[22] A survey carried out just before the referendum revealed that three main factors had influenced support for independence among the non-Estonian population: knowledge of the Estonian language, the number of years lived in Estonia, and a perception that standards of living in Estonia were higher than in other Soviet regions.

## NATION-BUILDING AND ETHNIC RELATIONS SINCE 1991

Estonia's independence was secured after an unsuccessful anti-reformist military coup in Moscow in August 1991. On the second day of the coup, 20 August, the Estonian Supreme Council adopted a 'Resolution on the National Independence of Estonia'. On 24 August Yeltsin's Russia recognised Estonia's independence and urged the USSR and the world to follow. By the end of August about forty states had done so. At the same time Estonia became a member of the Conference for Security and Co-operation in Europe, and a few weeks later it was admitted to the United Nations. This meant an end to 47 years of Soviet occupation in Estonia. It is important that, despite all the crimes and hardships of the Soviet occupation, Estonia regained its independence without any politically motivated deaths. In contrast to many other regions of the Soviet Union, Estonia can therefore be viewed as something of a laboratory for the peaceful securing of statehood.[23]

One of the first steps in the new stage of nation-building was to create a new Estonian constitution. On 7 September 1991 a Constitutional Assembly was formed combining 30 members elected by the Supreme Council and another 30 elected by the Estonian Congress. Such a political compromise between the two main groupings in Estonian politics reflected the general aim of the Constitution: to maintain the idea of legal continuity of the Estonian Republic on the one hand and to take account of new realities on the other. The Assembly finished its work by the spring of 1992. According to the Constitution Estonia is a parliamentary state. The President is elected by Parliament, and has a veto on legislation which can be overrided by a simple majority of parliament. The Constitution guarantees basic freedoms, an independent judiciary with a legal chancellor to monitor the constitutionality of laws, and a state audit office to watch over state expenditures.

A referendum on the new Constitution was held on 28 June 1992 in which only pre-occupation Estonian citizens were entitled to vote. This included whether they wished electoral suffrage to include about 10,000 mainly Russian resident non-citizens who had already applied for citizenship. Fifty-four per cent of voters answered 'no' to the question which reflected how closely divided Estonian citizens were on how to handle the citizenship issue.

Parliamentary and Presidential elections were held on 20 September 1992 in which sixty-eight per cent of citizens participated. In the 101-seat Riigikogu the right-wing Fatherland's list won 28 places and formed a coalition government with the Estonian National Independence Party and moderates. The centre-left Secure Home bloc with the Centre Party (a residue of the Popular Front) constituted the core of the opposition. In addition, four smaller electoral coalitions surpassed the 5 per cent popular vote threshold and gained representation in the Riigikogu.

In the Presidential elections two rounds were needed as none of the four candidates – Arnold Rüütel, Lennart Meri, Rein Taagepera and Lagle Parek – received the required 50 per cent of the vote in the first round. In the first round the former Chairman of the Supreme Soviet, Arnold Rüütel, topped the list with 41.8 per cent of the vote. His rivals in the campaign highlighted his Soviet past, and especially the fact that he had been appointed Chairman of the Supreme Soviet in 1983 by Yuri Andropov. This was enough to block him from getting 50 per cent in the first round; and in the second round of the elections to the Riigikogu the Fatherland's candidate, Lennart Meri, received 59 against Rüütel's 31 votes.

After the elections, the Riigikogu stated in the Declaration of 7 October 1992 that the transition period in Estonia had ended and that constitutional power was now fully restored. However, final state sovereignty was only achieved two years later when the last Russian troops left Estonia on 31 August 1994.

A controversial aspect of the legal arrangement in Estonia concerns the question of the status of the immigrants who settled during the Soviet occupation. In February 1992 the citizenship law of 1938 with some amendments was reenacted by the Riigikogu, proceeding from the idea of legal continuity with the earlier Estonian Republic. According to the law only residents who were citizens before Soviet occupation and their descendants are defined as citizens. The law requires two years' residence before a person is entitled to apply for citizenship, and a further one year waiting period before an applicant can be naturalised. In addition, it requires some knowledge of the Estonian language. The most controversial element of the law is that it applies not only to potential immigrants but also to those who have long resided in Estonia.

Such an approach to the citizenship issue was opposed by the majority of the non-Estonian population. Their argument was that as persons who immigrated to Estonia during the Soviet period could not foresee that their legal status could change so fundamentally, a more just solution to the citizenship issue would be the adoption of the so called 'zero option', that is, all those who resided in Estonia when it declared its independence should automatically qualify for Estonian citizenship.[24]

The most dangerous political crisis in respect of these issues occurred in the summer of 1993 when the 'Law on Aliens' was being considered by the Riigikogu. The law was urgent in the matter of determining the legal status of non-citizens in Estonia, in which category about 80 per cent of Estonia's Russian population belonged. The first version of the law was adopted on 21 June. Several of its points met strong criticism from both local Russian leaders and legal experts of several European organisations. The High Commissioner of the CSCE, Max van der Stoel, pointed out that the law did not specify clearly the issue of residence and working permits for non-citizens who had come to Estonia before 1991.[25] After further consultation the Estonian President rejected the law. A new version with considerable amendments was adopted by the Riigikogu on 8 July.

The reaction of non-citizens to the new social and political situation in which they found themselves was twofold. The first reaction was exemplified by their activities in opposing the initial version of the Law on Aliens as well as some other laws of Estonia which they regarded as discriminatory (Language Law, School Law, etc.). As a protest action, Narva City Council held a referendum on autonomy status of the city on 16–17 July 1993. The referendum did not have serious consequences, but indicated a potential threat to Estonia if the authorities could not find a way of resolving the ethnic issue.

A second type of reaction can be seen in the formation of new political organisations to defend the interests of the non-Estonian population. After long negotiations between eight different groups of non-Estonians, the Representative Assembly of the Russian-Speaking Population of Estonia was established on 30 January 1993. Its stated aim is to represent the interests of this section of the population, whose views would otherwise not be heard in Estonia's state institutions.[26] Compared to Intermovement (which was dismantled in August 1991 because of its support for the military coup in Moscow), this organisation took a constructive approach, restricting its activities to constitutional means. For example, in relation to the citizenship issue it was stated in its 'Proposals' of April 1993 that 'one should apply to the full extent the possibilities which are contained in the Citizenship Law of the Republic of Estonia (1938) and abrogate the discriminative restrictions in the Decree on the Enactment of this particular law'.[27] This in effect meant that the Representative Assembly decided not to oppose the fundamental principle of legal continuity of the Estonian Republic, but to act within its established framework and to defend its interests.

Besides the controversies around the citizenship issue, the Estonian authorities undertook several important steps aimed at managing ethnic tensions. First, the new Law on Local Elections was adopted by the Riigikogu on 19 May 1993. In addition to Estonian citizens the franchise was given to stateless persons and citizens of other countries if they had resided in the election area for the last five years and registered themselves on the list of voters. The local elections took place on 17 October 1993 and the Russian-language population took an active part in them. For example, in Tallinn City Council, Russian electoral blocks received 27 out of 64 seats. As a result, an important legal channel for influencing Estonian politics was established for non-citizens.

The next positive step was made through the adoption of the Law on Cultural Autonomy in October 1993. Unlike most systems of autonomy, the Estonian law is based not on the principle of territoriality but on individuality. This avoids the well-known disadvantages of the territorial principle, which often extends little protection to a minority in the territorial subdivision concerned. According to the law, ethnic minorities in Estonia have the right to establish their own educational institutions and local councils to handle cultural problems.

The creation of a Round Table of non-citizens and ethnic minorities under the auspices of the President of Estonia can be viewed in the same spirit. On 10 July 1993 the first session of the Round Table gathered in Tallinn, in which the Representative Assembly, the Estonian Union of Nationalities and several political parties took part. This forum was to play a positive role in mediating tensions between central and Narva city authorities during the period of the referendum issue in Narva in July 1993.

## CONCLUSIONS AND PROSPECTS

The Estonian case can be regarded as an important example of both peaceful methods of struggle for independence and a rather successful management of ethnic tensions in the post-Communist period. Two symmetrical processes can be identified as part of the Estonian strategy of nation-building.

Firstly, the non-Estonian population is adapting comparatively quickly to the new social and political situation and is generally positive towards integration into Estonian society. Thus, an opinion survey carried out in September 1993 revealed that its views gave little sustenance to the forces in Russia that would wish to reclaim the Baltic States. Seventy-four per cent of Russians living in Estonia described current relations between themselves and Estonians as good or very good. An even bigger majority was of the opinion that Russians had far more freedom in Estonia than in the former Soviet Union. In addition, seventy-six per cent said that Estonia offered a better chance for improving their living standards. Fifty-eight per cent indicated their commitment to learning the Estonian language.[28] A very important psychological development is that there is a remarkable difference between how diaspora Russians perceive themselves and how they believe Russians in Russia think about them in respect of the major ethnic issues. A survey of December 1993 indicates that a clear majority of Russian respondents not only identify themselves with Estonia rather than with Russia, but also believe that their opinion differs from that of their one-time co-nationals in Russia.[29]

Secondly, the Estonian authorities have launched several political structures aimed at accommodating ethnic differences. This means that a two-way process is under way in Estonia. In a sense, the logic of political adjustments on the part of the state has been symmetrical to that of the psychological adaptation of the Russian community. In both cases, negative reactions towards the other group were dominant at first, but later gave way to more balanced, positive approaches. The management of this process can be regarded as a possible model for ethnic conflict accommodation in other regions of the post-Communist world and elsewhere.

## NOTES

1. See Toivo Raun *Estonia and the Estonians* (Stanford, CA, Hoover Institution Press 1987); and Evald Uustalu *The History of the Estonian People* (London, Boreas Publishing 1952).
2. Estonia's capital city derives its modern name Tallinn from the Estonian

equivalent of 'Danish citadel', the Danes having enlarged the Estonian fortress during their domination of Tallinn and north-eastern Estonia.

3. Raun *Estonia and the Estonians*, p. 19.
4. See Edward Thaden et al., *Russification in the Baltic Provinces and Finland, 1855–1914* (Princeton, NJ, Princeton University Press 1981).
5. Arvo Mägi *Estonian Literature* (Stockholm, Baltic Humanitarian Association 1968).
6. Georg von Rauch, *The Baltic States: Years of Independence 1917–1940* (Berkeley, University of California Press 1974).
7. William Hough 'The annexation of the Baltic states and its effect on the development of law prohibiting forcible seizure of territory' *The New York Law School Journal of International and Comparative Law*, 6(2), 1985.
8. For a contemporary appraisal of Estonian history from the Stone Age to the present, see Mart Laar, Lauri Vahtre and Heiki Valk *Kodu Lugu I & II* (Tallinn, Loomingu Raamatukogu 1989).
9. Laar et al., *Kodu Lugu II*, p. 54.
10. For a detailed review of the war years, see Raun *Estonia and Estonians*; and Romuald Misiunas and Rein Taagepera *The Baltic States: Years of Dependence 1940–1980* (Berkeley, University of California Press 1983).
11. Parming suggests that 80,000 were deported, Taagepera puts the number at 50,000–60,000, and Laar et al. estimate that nearly 21,000 were deported in late March 1949. Tõnu Parming, 'Population changes and processes' in Parming and Järvesoo (eds) *A Case Study of a Soviet Republic: the Estonian SSR* (Boulder, CO, Westview 1978); Misinunas and Taagepera *Estonia and the Estonians*; Laar et al., *Kodu Lugu*.
12. Raun *Estonia and the Estonians*, p. 198.
13. Elmar Järvesoo 'The postwar economic transformation', in Parming and Järvesoo *A Case Study of a Soviet Republic*; Raun *Estonia and the Estonians*.
14. For a comparison of the effects of Soviet rule on the economies of two comparable societies – Estonia and Finland – see Sirje Sinilind *Viro ja Venäjä* (Helsinki, Alea-Kirja 1985).
15. Raun, *Estonia and the Estonians*, pp. 190–3.
16. In 1945 Estonia lost territories in the north-east and south-east amounting to some 5 per cent of the total inter-war area and possibly encompassing some 70,000 residents. The Narva area in the north-east was joined with the RSFSR, and the Petseri area in the south-east, largely populated by Estonians of the Orthodox faith, was given to the Pihkva Oblast. These alterations in territory and populations, ostensibly made 'for ethnic reasons', also helped to explain the initial increase in the Estonian share of the total in the immediate post-war years.
17. For a descriptive chronological account of events, see Rein Taagepera 'Estonia's road to independence', *Problems of Communism* 38 (6), 1989.
18. Toomas Ilves 'Environmental problems in Estonia', Baltic Area Situation Report, *Radio Free Europe Research*, 6, 1985; and Riina Kionka 'Ecological concern in Estonia,' Baltic Area Situation Report, *Radio Free Europe Research*, 5, 1986.
19. See Riina Kionka 'Estonia, Political Parties in Eastern Europe', *Radio Free Europe Research*, 1990.

20. See Riina Kionka, 'The Estonian Citizens' Committees: an opposition movement of a different complexion', *Report on the USSR*, 1, (6), 1990; and 'The Congress of Estonia', *Report on the USSR*, 2 (12), 1990.
21. Of the 602,393 non-Estonians living in the republic in 1989, some 30.3 per cent were Russians, 3.1 per cent were Ukrainians, 1.8 per cent were Belorussians, and the rest belonged to other nationalities. Estonians made up 61.5 per cent of the population according to the 1989 census (Rahva Hääl, 19 September 1989).
22. See Rein Taagepera 'Ethnic Relations in Estonia' *Journal of Baltic Studies*, vol. 23, no. 2, summer 1991, pp. 121–132.
23. See Andrus Saar 'What did the plebiscite and referendum in Estonia reveal about the statehood of Estonia and the Soviet Union?', *The Monthly Survey of Estonian and Soviet Politics*, March 1991, Tallinn, Panor Press, pp. 12–16.
24. See Raivo Vetik 'Ethnic conflict and accommodation in post-Communist Estonia', *Journal of Peace Research*, vol. 30, no. 3, August 1993, pp. 271–280.
25. Extracts from the Message of Max van der Stoel, CSCE High Commissioner of National Minorities to His Excellency Mr Lennart Meri, President of the Republic of Estonia, *The Monthly Survey of Baltic and Post-Soviet Politics*, July 1993, Tallinn, Panor Press, p. 44.
26. Statute of the Representative Assembly, *The Monthly Survey of Baltic and Post-Soviet Politics*, March 1993, Tallinn, Panor Press, p. 42.
27. 'Proposals for overcoming the crisis situation concerning the citizenship and statelessness in the Republic of Estonia' *The Monthly Survey of Baltic and Post-Soviet Politics*, May 1993, Tallinn, Panor Press, p. 57.
28. See Richard Rose & William Maley 'Nationalities in the Baltic states. A survey study' *Studies in Public Policy*, no. 222, 1994, pp. 39–41.
29. See Raivo Vetik 'Russians in Estonia: new development trends' in Marika Kirch and David D. Laitin, eds., *Changing Identities in Estonia. Sociological Facts and Commentaries* (Tallinn, Estonian Academy of Sciences, 1994), pp. 72–79.

# CHAPTER EIGHT

# Latvia and the Latvians

Graham Smith

The history of the Latvian people has been inextricably bound up with their location at the interface of European and Russian cultural influences and with neighbouring Great Power struggles to establish supremacy over their homeland. During this century Latvians succeeded in achieving national self-determination from Russia in November 1918, only to lose independent statehood two decades later. A brief period of Soviet rule (1940–41) was followed by three years of German occupation until in 1944 Latvia was again incorporated into the Soviet Union. As part of the Soviet federation, the Latvian union republic became one of the most urbanised and multiethnic regions in the USSR, with Latvians by the early 1990s making up 50.7 per cent of the population.[1] Since Latvia's rebirth in 1991, much of the state's political agenda has been dominated by ethno-politics, centring on an underlying tension between the building of a citizen polity on the basis of an ethnic or a territorial commonality.

## THE MAKING OF THE LATVIANS

From the early Middle Ages onwards, succesive invasions, wars and treaties have ensured the division, partition and colonisation of this small country.[2] In the early thirteenth century, western-central Latvia was invaded and brought into the Christian Order of Western Europe by the 'Brethren of the Sword'. The region's conquest was completed by the German Teutonic Knights in 1290 with the enserfment of the Latvian peasantry and the establishment of the Livonian State. In 1561, following the partition of Livonia, south-western Latvia became the hereditary Duchy of Kurland, a successful trading entity under the suzerainty of the Polish monarchy. The rest of Livonia first became a dependency of the Polish Commonwealth, followed by a period under Swedish rule (1629–1721), and by 1721, following the Treaty of

Nystadt, the region was annexed by Russia. Eastern Latvia, known as Latgalia, remained part of the Polish Commonwealth until 1773 when it also was annexed by Russia, with Kurland's incorporation following in 1795. Throughout the nineteenth century, the descendants of the Teutonic Order, the Baltic German nobility (*Ritterschaften*) of western central Latvia (Kurland and southern Lifland), continued to enjoy a special relationship with St Petersburg which gave them considerable economic and cultural autonomy. In contrast, in Latgalia, administered as part of Vitebsk province, the largely Catholic Latvian population remained subservient to a Polish and Russian nobility, developing rural institutions similar to those found in Russia proper. It was not, however, until the second half of the nineteenth century that a Latvian national consciousness was to develop, which was later to spark off demands for political autonomy, culminating in the establishment of an independent Latvia.

For Latvians, the formation and development of a national consciousness are inextricably bound up with these two crucial periods in their pre-Soviet history. The formation of this sense of nationhood paralleled the region's nineteenth-century transition from feudalism to capitalism. From 1804 onwards, a series of local decrees began the gradual process of weakening the hold of the *Ritterschaften* over peasant society, and in 1849 a law granted a legal basis for the creation of peasant-owned farms. Further laws of 1865 and 1866 were to end the exclusive rights of nobles to hold estates. Not only did these changes permit the establishment of a class of Latvian small-scale landed property owners (who by the early 1900s owned around 40 per cent of the land), but also, with the beginnings of the region's industrialisation from the 1860s onwards, the migration of Latvians to the towns, particularly into Riga, resulted in the emergence of an indigenous middle class and industrial proletariat. During this period, the urban share of the region's population increased from 178,800 (or 14.8 per cent) in 1863 to 939,000 (or 38.0 per cent) by the eve of the First World War.[3]

Until the 1860s, there was little sense of a Latvian national identity. Both serfdom and institutional controls to migration and social mobility limited the boundaries of the peasants' intellectual and social geography.[4] Influenced by the Romantic movement's conception of the *Volk* and of a Lutheran religion which held that preaching should be conducted in a people's mother tongue, the Baltic German clergy and literati took a benevolent interest in the distinctive language and culture of the Latvian peasantry, particularly in their oral traditions, such as their folk-songs (*dainas*) and folk-tales, and in promoting the Latvian language. Such attitudes were to ensure that early in the nineteenth century the Latvian tongue became a literary language for a people who, by the time of the 1897 tsarist census, could claim near-universal literacy. It was, however, the newly emergent Latvian intelligentsia who were to become the social bearers of Latvian nationalism. In the 1860s, the Young Latvian Movement was formed among their number, the aim of which was to promote the indigenous language and to counteract and publicise the socio-economic oppression of Latvians, in town and country alike, by the Baltic Germans. This organisation was influential in formulating the ideas behind *Jaunā Strāva* ('New Current'), an organisation set up in the 1890s, which was to give birth to a range of political viewpoints organised along both class and national lines. Attempts by the Russian empire from the 1880s onwards to culturally Russify the region, although initially directed against weakening the privileged position of the Baltic Germans, probably did much in a crucial period in Latvian nation-building to ensure that enmity towards a Russian-dominated state became a feature of the nationalist struggle.

By 1901, *Jaunā Strāva* had evolved into the Latvian Social Democratic Party (LSDP). In advocating greater territorial autonomy for Latvia, the LSDP was conscious of the plight of the region's growing number of minorities, including the cultural particularity of Latgalia. It advocated the transformation of the empire into a federation of democratic states (to include Latvia) and, following the Austro-Marxists, the adoption of a policy of cultural autonomy for its extra-territorial ethnic communities. In 1903, however, the LSDP split into two, with a newly formed Latvian Social Democratic Workers' Party (LSDWP) eventually allying itself with Lenin's Russian Social Democratic Workers' Party, and adopting an internationalist policy. The other political offshoot of the LSDP, the Latvian Social Democratic Union (LSDU), continued to champion national interests and Latvia's national self-determination.[5] There is, however, evidence to suggest that the Latvians were slower than the Ukrainians and Estonians to adopt a platform of national separatism, and even as late as 30 July 1917, at the so-called Riga 'autonomy' conference, also attended by some Bolsheviks, agreement to set up a Latvian National Assembly was not reached.[6] It was not until October 1917, as a result of the efforts of the newly formed Riga Democratic Bloc, which included representatives of all political factions except the Bolshevik wing of the LSDWP, that a resolution was passed demanding the establishment of a fully independent and neutral Latvia.[7] Independence was briefly punctuated by the Red Army's invasion in 1919 and the establishment of a Latvian Soviet republic, but with support from the Western allies it was quickly overthrown by Latvian nationalist troops.[8]

Having obtained independent statehood, in which the Latvians were an absolute majority (making up 75.5 per cent of the 1,960,502 population by 1935),[9] a second important phase in nation-building began. The Latvian language was recognised as the state's official tongue and, with statehood, all the symbols and trappings of successful nationhood were introduced. Cultural autonomy was granted to the country's sizeable minorities, which included the Baltic Germans,

Jews, Russians and Poles.[10] The electoral system, introduced into the Latvian constitution in 1922, also protected minority interests. Based on a complex system of proportional representation, with any five persons being able to register as a political party, it resulted in the representation of a large number of political groupings in the 100-strong Latvian parliament, the Saeima, with political parties reflecting the dominant ethnic, regional, religious and urban/rural divisions in society. However, the Agrarian Bloc, centred on its largest party, the Latvian Peasant Union (LPU), dominated Latvian politics during the inter-war years, and was pivotal in supporting the interests of the socially dominant, rural Latvian population. Agrarian reform ensured the reallocation of land in favour of peasant smallholders, with the individual peasant farmstead (*mājas*) becoming an economic basis and a social symbol of Latvian statehood. Agriculture and rural-related industries received priority, with Latvia becoming a major exporter of agricultural commodities to the West. A series of short-lived coalition governments unable to govern over a politically fragmented Saeima, in combination with a national economy heavily dependent on Western countries now firmly locked into recession, paved the way for the establishment of authoritarian rule in 1934 under Karlis Ulmanis.[11] In emphasising 'national unity as the foundation of the state', Ulmanis nationalised large sections of industry on the pretext that the largely minority-owned trade and industry sector should be under Latvian control.[12] The educational and cultural rights of minorities were also curtailed. Following the Molotov–Ribbentrop Pact of 23 August 1939, Latvia was to share the fate of its Baltic neighbours, coming under Soviet hegemony.

## LATVIA AS PART OF THE SOVIET UNION

As part of Stalin's USSR, the Latvian union republic was subjected to a scale of social and economic reorganisation which rapidly transformed its economy from agriculture to heavy industry, its overwhelmingly ethnically Latvian population into a more multiethnic polity, and its predominantly peasant social structure into a fully urbanised class of industrial workers.[13] However, while Latvians were dislodged from their traditional roles, there is little evidence to suggest that their national consciousness became simply a passive recipient of structural change: it continued to have a proactive capacity to modify and occasionally to resist these changes, most starkly up until the early 1950s in armed guerrilla resistance to Soviet rule.

In their sense of nationhood, the Latvians, unlike most other peoples of the Soviet Union, could draw on a rich variety of pre-Soviet national symbols, including the democratic years of statehood, from which to judge contemporary reality, and an established century-long national culture which was adapted to the new social conditions demanded and produced by Soviet modernity. Such an established set of cultural traditions and values became bound up with dissident politics, occasionally entered the public arena of federal politics (notably during the late 1950s and from the mid-1980s onwards), and was manifested in the reconstituted but never entirely recast national literature and song festivals, as well as finding expression in official Soviet rituals and ceremonies.

The primary objective of the Stalinist state was to 'ensure the transformation of Latvia from an agrarian country into a highly developed industrial–agrarian republic'.[14] Despite its lack of a raw material or energy base (except hydroelectric power and peat), within the first two post-war five-year plans (1946–55) the republic had been transformed into a centre for metal and machine-working and associated heavy industries. By 1960, industrial output had increased to ten times the 1940 level, while the output for metal-building and machine-working and the chemical industry increased by a staggering sixty and fifty times respectively.[15] In contrast, by 1960, agricultural output barely reached the 1940 level.[16]

The republic's rapid industrialisation, it has been concluded, was essentially motivated to ensure the mass immigration of Russian labour and to facilitate cultural assimilation and political stability. Yet the availability of a skilled labour force in a region which by the early twentieth century had already developed a manufacturing base in combination with the beneficial linkage effects of coastal proximity and an already established east–west rail network is as likely to have favoured the adoption of such a strategy, with Slav immigration being more a consequence than the motivating force.[17] From the mid-1950s onwards, however, immigration from other republics, notably from Russia proper, overtook the countryside as the main source of supplemental urban labour and contributed greatly to transforming Latvia from a predominantly pre-war rural society into a country of urban dwellers by the late 1950s.

In contrast, the Latvian countryside did not undergo substantial reorganisation until nearly four years after incorporation. This was partly due to it being perceived as less immediately amenable to structural reorganisation than the city, not least because of the strength of traditional affiliations with nationalism in a countryside that Stalin had regarded as 'the guardian of nationlity'.[18] By 1948, however, collectivisation began, but by January 1949 only 10 per cent of peasant households were collectivised. By the well-tested draconian techniques of Stalinism, which included mass deportations, 98.4 per cent of peasant households had been incorporated into collective farms by the end of 1951.[19] Officially, the richer class of Latvian smallholders – deemed to be the backbone of support for 'bourgeois nationalism' – were blamed for opposing and holding up the process of collectivisation. Yet, in spite of collectivisation, the *mājas*, deemed a 'burdensome heritage of the past' and a major obstacle to the modernisation of the countryside, remained a feature of the rural landscape and an embarrassing symbol to the Soviet authorities, certainly up until the Gorbachev period, of what was once small-scale Latvian agriculture.[20]

Systemic change was facilitated by a republic Party and state apparatus disproportionately made up of 'Russified Latvians' (the so-called *latovichi*); that is, by the Latvians and their descendants that had spent the inter-war years in the Soviet Union and whose only connection with the Latvian nationality was through their passport status. However, with Khrushchev's mid-1950s policy of economic decentralisation, which resulted in the setting up of a Latvian *sovnarkhoz* (or economic council), it was clear that a sizeable section of the republic's Party élite saw in the republic's newly acquired economic powers the means to redress Moscow's standardising policies. At the forefront were members of the Riga Institute of Economics, who argued that the aims of the national economy should be

to develop Latvia's industrial structure and specialisation so that the most rational and economical use of all Latvian natural and labour resources would maximise the Latvian contribution to the development of the USSR's economy as well as the living standards of Latvia.[21]

Preference was to be given to the development of agriculture and consumer industries over outside raw material- and labour-dependent heavy industries.

Prioritising local interests was not, however, limited to the economy; demands were also being made for the promotion of the Latvian language and for Russian migrants to learn Latvian. As one prominent Party official suggested, 'The level of party work would be raised significantly if communists would conduct talks among workers in the language native to the workers.'[22] Action was also taken to increase the number of compulsory hours for the study of Latvian in the republic's schools.

Economic decentralisation therefore provided a way of promoting a particular set of policies more in keeping with the pre-1940 national economy, which was also compatible with limiting immigration. However, political consequences followed which went far further than in any other Soviet republic. Those within the top echelons of public life, which Moscow labelled 'the nationalist group',[23] were duly removed from power. Among those dismissed were Eduards Berklāvs, Vice-chairman of the Latvian Council of Ministers, and Pauls Dzērve, head of Riga's Institute of Economics. Following the purges, the newly appointed First Party Secretary, Arvīds Pelše (1959–66), who replaced Jānis Kalnbērziņš (1940–59), singled out the contested issue of immigration for particular comment:

Some of our comrades, fearing without any basis that our Latvian republic might lose its national identity, wanted to stop the objectively natural process of population shifts. In their speeches they repeatedly maintain, for instance, that the mechanical increase of the population of Riga should be avoided. This attitude is both harmful and politically dangerous. By cultivating national isolationism they identify with bourgeois nationalism, impairing the interests of the peoples of the Soviet Union and endanger also the interests of the Latvian nation.[24]

The return to centralised ministerial control marked an end to experimentation with radical, decentralising reform, but the *sovnarkhoz* episode illustrated how the diffusion of republic economic authority could so easily rekindle territorial and national interests. Throughout the 1960s and 1970s Latvia's political leadership resumed its administration over an economy whose balance and pattern of activity had been primarily determined by Stalin. None the less, considerable strides were made in the development of the electronics and communications industries; compared with the first two decades, agriculture also began to prosper, all of which ensured for the republic's economy a disproportionate role in overall Soviet economic performance. It continued to be a leading net financier to other parts of the Soviet Union, as measured in terms of the small proportion of turnover tax it was allowed to retain for internal consumption.[25] The republic's standard of living also improved immeasurably, with a per capita income generally higher than in Russia proper and second only to Estonia.[26] By 1988, over 28 per cent of Latvia's population earned 200 roubles or more per month (bettered only by Estonia), compared with the all-Union average of 17.2 per cent.[27]

Although Latvia's economic growth targets assigned to industry were among the lowest of any republic during the 1970s and early 1980s, the pattern and tempo of industrial development continued to have profound consequences for the labour supply and for the republic's ethno-demographic composition. Centrally determined sectoral priorities and outmoded practices continued to ensure an insatiable demand for outside labour in spite of limits being set to the overall size of enterprise workforces and in spite of earmarking the capital city, Riga, for limited industrial growth. Largely oblivious to attempts to manage the labour supply, all-Union ministries and their plant managers continued to increase the size of their labour force, to the extent that such practices were publicly condemned by First Party Secretary Augusts Voss (1966–84).[28]

Immigration, primarily from the Russian republic, continued to account for the major part of population growth. The attractions of higher living standards and Western lifestyles motivated much immigration. This accounted for over two-thirds of Latvia's demographic increase throughout the 1970s.[29] By the early 1980s, in part due to lower rates of planned industrial growth for the republic, immigration had slowed down, but from the mid-1980s it again increased.[30] Labour shortages were exacerbated by the republic's low birth-rate, which, by 1980, had reached the all-time low of 14 per thousand population.[31] With the level of natural increase only slightly recovered from the 1980 level of 1.3 per thousand, there remained concern about the republic being able to replace its increasingly ageing population naturally. Consequently, from Latvians constituting 62 per cent of the population in 1959, in the 1989 census they made up a bare majority within their own homeland (50.7 per cent).

It was the social consequences of Russian immigration in combination with policies that challenged the institutional supports enjoyed by the native language and culture that many Latvians feared would further erode the benefits of being Latvian in their native homeland. Yet there is little evidence to suggest that cultural assimilation was occurring during the Brezhnev years. In terms of declared native language, for Latvians probably the most important criterion of nationhood, in 1979, 97.8 per cent of the titular nationality affirmed Latvian as their native language, compared with 98.4 per cent in 1959.[32] The vast majority of Latvians continued to have the opportunity to attend either native or mixed-language (as opposed to Russian) schools, while provision for the native language in the media and institutional support for it as the medium of Latvian culture ensured that it remained pivotal to the Latvian way of life. Although knowledge of Russian continued as a precondition for entrance into higher and specialised education, urbanised Latvians did not need to assimilate into the Russian language and culture in order to gain position and status in the republic.[33] Latvians were well represented in administration, economic management and the professions. Moreover, their over-representation in the 'creative' professions in comparison with most other Soviet nationalities no doubt played an important part in preserving and promoting the native culture.

These opportunities reflected the significance of republic status in providing employment for those with a vested interest in the production and reproduction of the native culture. Such social opportunities for the indigenous population were more broadly reflected in the benefits of being officially designated as 'Latvian' within the Latvian republic. Terenteva's study showed that, when having to choose the nationality of either a Latvian or a Russian parent, sixteen-year-olds preferred the titular nationality.[34] A combination, therefore, of sense of attachment to being Latvian and the material and status privileges that republic designation brings meant that few Latvians either adopted Russian cultural attributes or left their homeland (over 93 per cent of Latvians in the USSR resided in their native republic, which made them one of the most rooted of the major nationalities).[35]

None the less, both institutional and migrational pressures continued to facilitate the spread of the Russian language, so challenging the dominance of the native language and culture. Knowledge of Russian increased: in 1970, 45.3 per cent of Latvians declared a knowledge of Russian compared with 58.3 per cent by 1979.[36] Of equal concern was the reluctance of incoming Russians to learn the indigenous language (by 1979 only 19 per cent knew Latvian, and in 1970 18 per cent).[37] Moscow's renewed emphasis from the late 1970s on expanding the teaching of Russian in schools and universities came as further evidence, particularly to the intelligentsia, of the threatened position of the Latvian language, although the republic's then Minister of Education warmly supported such measures on the grounds that they were promoting the language of internationalism.[38] First Party Secretary Augusts Voss, however, adopted a more cautious approach. At an all-Union scientific conference in Riga in June 1982, he spoke of the need to promote bilingualism in Party work, noting that the attention given to promoting the Russian language should not deflect from the need to ensure the promotion of the indigenous tongue.[39]

Throughout the Brezhnev years organised dissent tended to couch its appeal in the collectivist language of the nation, in which demands for individual freedoms were presented as being bound up with the national right to self-determination. Russification, in particular, was singled out as the greatest threat to the nation, in which the preferred solution to policies of Soviet statism was the re-establishment of a Latvian state. Dissident groups, however, tended to have a limited lifespan. But dissent was not exclusively outside the Party. The most widely publicised dissent came from a document signed by seventeen alienated Latvian Communists which was sent to sister organisations in the West and provided details of the republic's systematic Russification, including, it was noted, that of the political leadership.[40] Although national dissent throughout the Brezhnev years was more evident in Latvia than in most other republics, it was more subdued than in Latvia's Baltic neighbours. Latvia possessed neither the strong mobilising and organisational role that religion played in Lithuanian dissent nor a republic leadership, as in Estonia, willing on occasion to take a firmer stance in support of local interests.

## THE TRANSITION TO STATEHOOD

The opening-up of Latvian society (*glasnost'*) was to provide the first real acid test since 1959 not only of how easily a national consciousness could find its way into the political arena of public life but also of whether, despite nearly half a century of Soviet rule, such a sense of nation-ness was still bound up with a people's imagination of again being sovereign. Although Latvia was to emerge among the pacesetters in translating this sense of national consciousness into demands for independent statehood, as with separatist movements elsewhere this did not occur overnight. Three phases in the transition to statehood are discernible: a period of national reawakening (1985–88) followed by the emergence and consolidation of a grassroots-based nationalist movement (1988–90) and finally, following the marginalisation of the local communist party as the basis of Moscow's political power, support by the Latvian government for independent statehood (1990–91).

Even before Gorbachev's rolling agenda of reforms got under way, there were already signs of the beginnings of a national reawakening. Anti-Russian demonstrations and riots took place in Riga on 9 and 15 May 1985, followed by further demonstrations in late December 1986. 1987 was to be a year of public displays of defiance against past Soviet practices and current policies on a scale previously unknown in the republic's post-war history. These demonstrations focused on a series of symbolically important key dates and events in Latvia's history: successive, cumulative woundings to the nation (for example, commemorations of the anniversaries of the Secret Molotov–Ribbentrop Protocol (23 August) and Stalin's deportations (14 June)) and events associated with Latvian statehood (such as the proclamation of Latvia's independence on 18 November 1918). These so-called 'calendar demonstrations', not least because of their scale, received considerable coverage in both the republic and all-Union press but were largely dismissed as being provoked by 'Western and émigré interference', while the historical actions of the Soviet state in 1939 and 1941 were fervently defended.[41] The republic press, however, conceded that some current grievances were justifiable – notably, ignorance among elements of the republic's Russian community of the titular language and culture – and acknowledged that this had contributed to fuelling tensions. It was admitted that as a legacy of Stalinism, 'blank spots' existed in Latvia's 'tragic history', but it was claimed that these were too readily exploited by Latvian nationalists.[42]

At this stage, oppositional politics was usually of the single-issue type, in which organised opposition was mobilised against specific developmental projects which carried, in particular, environmental ramifications. This included plans to construct a hydroelectric power station on Latvia's Daugava river and proposals to construct a subway in Riga. As with other issues, however, such as those linked to human rights or religious freedoms, oppositional politics contained a strong national and symbolic content bound up with the implications of such issues for the well-being of the Latvian nation and homeland. Overall, the political actions in which Latvian society engaged displayed only limited inter-group coordination and organisational capability. This was a product of a society experimenting with the politics of the possible, in which particular issues, actions and agendas were judged less likely to result in retribution by either Moscow or the local party–state machine.

The second phase (1988–90) marked a period of political take-off linked to the establishment of the Latvian Popular Front. That Moscow's reform-minded leadership was prepared not only to allow but to openly encourage the development of a grassroots-based national movement was bound up with its perception that Latvia (along with its Baltic neighbours), because of its enterprise culture and pre-Soviet experience of pluralist democracy, was likely to be the most receptive to its proposed package of reforms. Gorbachev's five-day 'meet the people' visit to Latvia and Estonia in February 1987, which included visits to experiments where cooperatives, private enterprises and new work practices were already successfully in place, must have underlined this for the General Secretary. Indeed, on his return to Moscow, Gorbachev drew on what he had witnessed in his Baltic visit – in what was labelled his 'revolution of expectations speech' – to warn of the dangers of expecting too much too quickly from the reform programme.[43] There were already clear signs, despite the Latvian leadership's endorsement of *perestroika*, that the gap was growing within the republic over the remit and tempo of reform.

Latvia's intelligentsia – Gorbachev's natural constituency of support in the republic but also the traditional bearers of Latvian nationalism – seized the opportunities opened up by *glasnost'* and by the setting-up of Estonia's Popular Front in May 1988 to recast and to revitalise the agenda for reform in the republic.[44] They were led by the Writers' Union and its chairman, Janis Peters, whose call for the republic's autonomy had already received coverage in the national press.[45] At the early June Plenum of the Latvian Writers' Union, the local party and government came in for particular criticism over their slow handling of *perestroika*. In the same month, Latvia's Cultural Unions passed a resolution, later submitted to the CPSU June Conference, calling, among other things, for Latvian to be made the state language, the republic to be represented in certain international organisations, publication of the secret Molotov–Ribbentrop protocol, and steps to be taken to prevent ecological catastrophe caused by the republic's accelerated industrialisation.[46] The authorities were quick to respond, and on 1 July the Presidium of the Latvian SSR Supreme Soviet acknowledged the need to establish a pro-*perestroika* movement in the republic.[47] By 19 July, events had moved so quickly that the newspaper of the Young Communist League, *Padomju Jaunatne*, also joined in condemning both the government and Party of Latvia over their handling of *perestroika*.[48] The paper demanded that the authorities give priority to securing the economy's restructuring and democratisation, which included economic sovereignty and statehood, and introduce concrete measures to safeguard Latvia's environment. In response to the summer of demands, a movement in support of *perestroika*, the Latvian Popular Front, was formed.

Moscow opted to accommodate such developments. The visit of Gorbachev's emissary, Politburo member Alexandr Yakovlev, to Latvia in August 1988 provided an opportunity for Gorbachev to be briefed on developments in the republic and for both the fledgling Popular Front and Latvia's leadership to get a response from Moscow on the scope for manoeuvrability. In a candid speech to representatives of Latvia's intelligentsia, Yakovlev warned of confrontationism of the intelligentsia and mass media against the local party apparatus, and against ideas of redefining the notion of republic citizenship based on 'selectiveness, exclusion or isolationism'.[49] Although emphasising unity and patience, in paraphrasing Lenin, he seemed to leave the republic in little doubt of what a reconstituted relationship between Latvia and Moscow could mean in the foreseeable future; 'a state in the form of a union must have a common defence and foreign policy. All the rest. . .ought to be the prerogative of the republics'.[50]

With the setting up of the Popular Front, a wide range of previously fragmented environmental, human rights, religious and nationalist groupings were brought together and united with radicals from within the Latvian Communist Party. This included representatives of the Latvian National Independence Movement (set up in June 1988 and headed by the leader of the so-called 'nationalist group' of 1959, Eduards Berklāvs), the Environmental Protection Club, members of the human rights organisation Helsinki-86, and the religious group Rebirth and Renewal (formed in 1987 from among the Latvian Lutheran clergy).[51] At the Front's inaugural congress, held in Riga on 8–9 October 1988, in which calls for Latvia's economic sovereignty and statehood were adopted,[52] its overwhelmingly Latvian membership stood at 120,000, a third of whom were Party members. By the end of 1988, the Popular Front had emerged to become a truly mass organisation, with a membership of around 250,000.[53]

In contrast with the other two Baltic republics, no major purge of the republic leadership followed, probably because of the speed with which Latvia's leadership responded positively to demands for the formation of a popular movement and by the way in which it had avoided challenging head-on the Popular Front (as in Lithuania) and political controversy (as with Estonia's First Party Secretary over the phosphorite affair). The promotion of the First Party Secretary, Boris Pugo (1984–88), to Chairman of the CPSU Central Committee Party Control Committee on 30 September and his replacement by Jan Vagris, previously Chairman of the Presidium of Latvia's Supreme Soviet, who in turn was replaced by Anatolii Gorbunovs, also made the republic's movement to accommodate the Popular Front a far less traumatic affair. Once in place, the republic's leadership tended to follow Estonia's lead in initiating far-reaching socio-economic reforms, although, given the multiethnic composition of the republic and the proportionately higher representation of Russians in Latvia's

Supreme Soviet and Party, change tended to be slower. On 29 September 1988, the Latvian language was designated the state language of the republic, and the symbols of national independence, the flag and national anthem, could be flown and sung in public. In May 1989, the Latvian Communist Party also gave its backing to a law making the Latvian language (rather than Russian) the language of business and government, which was later endorsed by Latvia's Supreme Soviet. And in June 1989, a decree was issued reversing decades of claims that the mass deportations of 14 June 1941 were justified.

It was, however, in the economic arena that the Latvian Party and government leadership was prepared and found it easiest to go furthest, often adding the republic's own character to *perestroika*. Plans were implemented to move towards total economic self-management, a mixed economy and a republic fiscal policy, as outlined in the law on economic independence, which reformists in Moscow saw as an important experiment in giving a more realistic meaning to the Soviet Federation.[54] Much was also made in the republic's press of having to redress the imbalances in the economy and in particular of the 'unjustified priority development of industrial production over agricultural production'.[55] In attempting to redress this imbalance, reminiscent of 1958–59, agriculture and rural development were not only to receive a higher investment priority, but, as a result of legislation passed by Latvia's Supreme Soviet on 6 May 1989, the countryside was to be reorganised along more private and cooperative lines, a policy in keeping with recreating a country of small farmers. The peasantry were to be allowed to lease land for an indefinite period of time and were to be provided with bank credit for housing and other construction needs. Much interest was also being shown, in official republic circles, in making Latvia part of a Special Economic Zone to attract foreign capital, possibly along Chinese lines.[56]

It became quickly apparent that for the Popular Front, especially the organisations within its ranks that advocated a more radical stance on national self-determination, what was at stake was not simply the republic's democratisation and economic restructuring, but the possibility, for the first time in half a century, of 'home rule'. No doubt during these early months the more moderate stance taken by the Popular Front on national sovereignty was in part conditioned by tactical limitations. Certainly from its formation, many of its leaders had clearly set their sights on achieving nothing short of independent statehood.[57] By August 1989, spurred on by developments in neighbouring Estonia and in eastern Europe, the Popular Front had acquired sufficient confidence to call publicly for independent statehood. Although this inevitably fuelled tensions with its own reform-minded but still pro-federal republic government, it was now evident that the Popular Front's views on secession had gained mass support. That support for secession received such a powerful endorsement was strengthened by three issues in particular.

The first centred on the myth of voluntary incorporation into the Soviet federation. In August 1989, in an unprecedented show of solidarity between Latvia and its two Baltic neighbours, the Popular Fronts organised up to two million people to form a human chain stretching from Estonia to Lithuania to show their condemnation of the Molotov–Ribbentrop pact. Such a powerful weapon for mobilising support behind independent statehood provided a major boost a few months later with an official endorsement by the Latvian Supreme Soviet that Latvia's incorporation had no political or legal legitimacy. Soon after, the Congress of People's Deputies in Moscow declared the secret protocols as 'legally untenable and invalid from the moment they had been signed'.[58] Thus for the secesionist cause there was a sense that history was again on its side, based on an appeal to rectificatory justice.

Secondly, there was the issue of the viability of economic self-determination and the benefits that might accrue to Latvia with independent statehood. The notion of economic sovereignty was exploited to the full by the Popular Front, linked to the notion of reconnecting with the form of economy that existed in the inter-war years, emphasising in particular the benefits of rejoining a trading regime of European partners. It was a vision of economic well-being that contrasted sharply with the increasing inability of Moscow's reform programme either to produce successful economic change or to redress falling living standards. An economically faltering Soviet federation, unable to provide the resources or leadership necessary to guarantee material prosperity, must therefore have acted as an important catalyst in swaying particularly those who did not readily identify with the idea of an independent Latvia to the perception that materially they were likely to be more secure in an independent and more Westward-oriented and reform-minded state than as part of a Soviet Union.

The third and most problematic secessionist issue centred on the question of cultural self-preservation. It was based on the simple notion that the most effective way of protecting and regenerating the core national culture was to establish a protective ring-wall in the form of Latvia's own polity. In one way or another, in relation to centralised control, industrial development, environmental degradation, language or immigration, the nationalist movement effectively linked the self-preservation of the Latvian national culture and way of life with greater control over their own political, economic and cultural affairs. It was more problematic, however, to convince non-Latvians within the republic of the benefits of greater autonomy, if not independent statehood. The Popular Front itself was divided on the question of how best to handle the issue of the republic's multiethnicity, reflecting two identifiable modes of national consciousness, each struggling to secure the high ground. On the one hand, there was a brand of nationalist politics that took the form of an *ethnic* nationalism and based its appeal on a primordial sense of nation-ness. Grounded in abstract notions of 'the people' and in 'blood notions' of genealogical descent, it reflected a desire to obtain, as nearly as possible, a coterminous nation-state. The need to introduce such measures as restricting citizenship to the core nation based on the argument of cultural self-preservation was combined with often uncompromising language in which the republic's Russian community were referred to as 'the civil garrison' of 'the occupying power', as 'colonists' and as 'rootless migrants'. One resolution passed by the Latvian Popular Front described the Russian settlers as 'a huge mass of badly qualified and uncultured people' who threatened to swamp the ancestral territory of the Latvian peoples,[59] with a handful of delegates even going so far as to advocate the repatriation of Russians.[60] This was precisely the position taken up by the more fundamentalist-minded Latvian Citizens' Committee in early 1989, which argued that only citizens of the pre-1940 republic and their descendants should have the right to a stake in their nation's future.

The above conception of nation-ness contrasted with a *civic–terri-torial* nationalism. In keeping with the 1920s tradition in Latvia of pluralist citizenship and tolerance towards cultural difference, emphasis was placed as much on the importance of individual as of national rights. It was an inclusionary conception of community, designed to mobilise all those who lived and worked within the territory of the republic, and to signal that a multicultural society could be commensurate with national self-determination. It was reflected in efforts by moderates within the Popular Front to de-emphasise national exclusivism, which included establishing pluralistically-structured cultural associations within the movement, with the explicit aim of broadening membership to include ethnic minorities. Yet despite efforts by the Popular Front to project the idea of moving towards a multiethnic polity, the Russian community remained decidedly uneasy about supporting a nationalist cause whose rhetoric reflected concern about their presence in an alien homeland.

It was in part because of the Front's inability to appeal to a broader mass-based constituency that a second, officially backed movement in support of *perestroika* was set up towards the end of 1988.[61] Although it called itself the International Front (or Interfront), its 300,000 estimated membership[62] was drawn largely from Latvia's 821,000-strong Russian-speaking community (which made up a third of the republic's population), with only about a tenth of its members being Latvian.[63] As an organisation, it showed itself to be far less supportive of economic sovereignty, and keen to ensure that the interests of Latvia's Russian community were safeguarded, particularly following a new language law that threatened to marginalise members of the Russian community with no knowledge of the titular language.[64] Above all, however, it was a movement whose members were associated with those political and economic institutions – such as the party, KGB and economic ministries – that had long since served as important arms of central control. For the Popular Front, this conservative pro-federal movement symbolised at best an attempt to halt the securing of greater political autonomy and at worst a return to Brezhnev-style rule. Yet there is evidence to suggest that, certainly by 1990, what support existed among the Russian community for Interfront was giving way to support for independent statehood.[65] Despite fears of becoming 'second class citizens' in a Latvian-dominated polity, many Russians had come round to the view that life in a Western-style economy was preferable to remaining part of a Soviet Union unable to guarantee employment, basic services and decent housing.

The final phase in Latvia's transition to independent statehood (1990–91) was characterised by members of the Popular Front gaining control of the republic Supreme Soviet and the peripheralisation of the Latvian Communist Party. On 4 May 1990, the Latvian Supreme Soviet, following Estonia's lead, declared its intention to re-establish the Latvian state. Like Estonia, however, Latvia was not prepared to go as far as Lithuania's declaration of unilateral independence, in part fearing that economic sanctions by Moscow would follow. But such a reluctance was also conditioned by Latvia's multiethnic composition reflecting a far more powerful strand of support in the republic, especially from Russians within the old-style Communist Party and its allied institutions, for reinstating centralised control over the republic. Indeed the last-minute attempt by conservative forces in January 1991 to regain control of the republic through the use of OMON troops, and the street violence that followed, did much to strengthen distrust among Latvian nationalists not only of Moscow but also, given the high profile of Russians in the Communist Party, of the Russian community generally.

## THE MAKING OF AN ETHNIC DEMOCRACY

Rather than resolving how best Latvia should deal with both the aspirations of Latvian nation-builders and safeguarding the interests of a multiethnic society, independent statehood merely sharpened the ethno-political agenda, bringing to the fore the highly contested issue of who should or should not be included within the citizen-polity. In part due to the increasingly nationalistic stance taken by its policy-makers towards the largest Russian-settler community in the Baltic States, Latvia was far more reluctant than either Lithuania or Estonia to finalise the citizenship question. Although a more accommodative stance was eventually adopted as set out in its citizenship law of July 1994, the issue of whether Latvian nation-building is compatible with moving towards structuring a politically stable democracy remains uncertain.[66]

That Latvia initially edged towards a less compromising position on the issue of citizenship reflected a detectable switch in emphasis towards national exclusivism, directed particularly against a settler community whose identification with and loyalty to the Latvian state were widely questioned. Initially, the state proposed to grant automatic citizenship to pre-1940 nationals and their descendants. For the rest, a resolution demanded a 16 year length of residency requirement (later reduced to ten years), and a test of competence in the Latvian language. Since an *ethnic* over a *civic-territorial* conception of citizenship was emphasised based on the premise that the republic was not the legal successor of the USSR, it followed that the Latvian state was under no obligation to accommodate those who had settled in Latvia during Soviet rule. As a consequence about thirty per cent of Latvia's population – primarily Russians who settled during Soviet rule – became non-citizens. Any other course of action, for radically minded nationalists, would merely have legitimised half a century of Soviet occupation. However, as part of the 1994 citizenship law the previously proposed quota system, whereby only 2000 non-citizens could gain citizenship each year, was revised, ensuring that most applicants, provided they meet the laws on length of residency and language capability, have at least the prospect of naturalisation by 2005.

Geopolitics played an important part in shaping the 1991–94 citizenship debates and in influencing their eventual outcome. For its part, Russia's parliament, concerned about its Russian diaspora and their marginalisation, declared its intention in 1992 to take up the cause of ethnic Russians living in Latvia and Estonia. It was a cause not wholly motivated by humanistic concerns: the emergence in Russia of a neo-nationalism unable to come to terms with loss of empire in part explained this policy shift, as did recognition that the plight of the settler community could provide a useful negotiating weapon in securing Russia's geopolitical and economic interests in the region.[67] Yeltsin thus purposely linked Russian troop withdrawal to Latvia taking a more accommodative stance on citizenship, something the Latvian government interpreted as an interference in its sovereign right to practise national self-determination. As Yeltsin made clear, 'Russia has no intention to sign any agreement regarding the withdrawal of Russian troops from Latvia or Estonia until these countries bring their legislation into line with international standards'.[68] Latvian politicians, however, quickly countered such accusations of human rights violation, laying the blame for the fate of Latvia's Russian minority with the parliament of the Russian federation: 'At the moment Russia is demonstrating a cynical reluctance to withdraw its troops. If Europe demands liberalism without demanding that Russia speed up the withdrawal of troops, then that could generate among the people unnecessary radicalism and lack of confidence in European structures.'[69] The Latvian government was therefore faced with a dilemma concerning geopolitical security: to stand steadfast and so allow the greater likelihood of Latvia remaining a military-subject state, or to acquiese on citizenship by incorporating a large section of a settler community into the body politic, with the prospect of threatening the newly established national hegemony that independent statehood had secured for the Latvians. Although agreement was eventually reached on 30 April 1994 on Russian troop withdrawal, and despite the more accommodative stance adopted by the Latvian parlament towards the settler community two months later, Latvia's powerful neighbour continues to take an uncompromising line, threatening again to use economic sanctions to secure a satisfactory conclusion to what is described as Latvia's 'national intolerance, raised to the level of official policy'.[70]

Western governments and organisations have also exerted considerable pressure on the Latvian state to adopt a more accommodationist position. Anxious to be accepted as a Western-style democracy and to secure economic and geosecurity benefits from the west, the fledgling state has been especially sensitive about accusations of intolerance. Supra-state organisations, notably the Council of Europe and the CSCE, were especially critical of Latvia's early stance on citizenship,[71] barring the way to its membership of the Council of Europe until February 1995. Economic organisations, such as the European Bank for Reconstruction and Development, also linked the prospects of developmental aid to the adoption of a more compromising stance. Concerned that Latvia's programme of economic recovery would be stillborn as a consequence of the West's imposing conditions on reconnecting Latvian markets and investment opportunities, Latvia's more liberally minded politicians were particularly active in arguing that failure to come to a satisfactory resolution of the citizenship question would 'bring about very grave difficulties in both our internal and external affairs'.[72]

It is too early to determine what impact Latvian nation-building will have on shaping ethnic relations. It seems that although the formula Lativa has adopted does not lend itself to easy classification, its political system come closest to resembling what a number of commentators in similar multiethnic societies have labelled an ethnic democracy. This encapsulates three central features.[73] Firstly, an ethnic democracy accords an institutional superior status to the core nation beyond its numerical proportion within the state territory. Secondly, certain civil and political rights are enjoyed universally. These can include the right of assembly and association, freedom of the press, an independent judiciary, a multi-party system, and a change of government through fair elections. And thirdly, certain collective rights are extended to ethnic minorities. In combining some elements of civil and political democracy with explicit ethnic dominance, an ethnic democracy attempts to preserve ethno-political stability based on the contradictions and tensions inherent in such a system. For a multiethnic polity like Latvia emerging from coercive rule, and where the transition to democracy is unlikely to be automatic or easy, the adoption of such a model has its own inner logic. As Smooha and Hanf note, 'Since nationalism in eastern Europe tends to be integral and exlusionary as opposed to western nationalism which tends to be open, inclusive and coterminous with citizenship, there is a strong possibility for some of the democratising states there to become ethnic democracies'.[74]

The scope of political rights and language legislation has been crucial in safeguarding the institutional hegemony of what is enshrined in the 1994 citizenship law as the goal of seeing the 'development of Latvia as a single nation-state'. Without citizenship, permanent residents do not have the right to vote in national elections. Consequently, ethnic minorities are grossly under-represented: in the 1993 national election, for instance, only seven ethnic Russians were elected to Latvia's parliament (a 100-member legislature). At the local–municipal level, where the right to local political representation does exist for permanent residents, the situation is marginally better: 10 per cent of Riga's municipal council is Russian (although over half the population is non-Latvian) and in Daugavpils non-Latvians make up 50 per cent (although 87 per cent of the city's population).[75] Moreover, despite the existence of a flourishing multi-party political system, the right to form or join a political party is not extended to all domiciled in the republic. Language legislation also favours the core nation. For many Russian speakers, of whom nearly four-fifths do not possess a knowledge of the local language, the new language policy will act as a major obstacle to participation in the body politic and as a brake on social mobility, especially to membership of the public sector-based professions. Consequently, language not only will function as a key resource for the strengthening and reproduction of the core culture but is also likely to facilitate the establishment of a new ethnic division of labour in which Russians unable or unwilling to meet the language requirements may find themselves becoming a new urban underclass. Social stratification along ethnic lines is likely to be reinforced within the arena of property rights in which, following legislation on privatisation, only citizens of the republic will have the right through the distribution of vouchers to buy companies, land and housing, with extra vouchers made available to restitution claiments and political victims of Soviet rule. Within the arena of cultural rights, there is greater accommodation: minorities have the right to their own language, schools, and newspapers, access to television programmes in their own language, and cultural associations.

Whether Latvia has the confidence to move from an ethnic to a pluralist democracy based on majoritarian or consociational rule still remains uncertain. Much will depend on the success of its transition towards securing an economic prosperity in which both Latvians and non-Latvians can reap the rewards of statehood. The attitude of Latvia's powerful geopolitical neighbour will also be crucial. If Latvia does not move towards a more accommodating position with regard to its non-citizens, the prospects for ethno-stability characteristic of the early years of statehood are less likely to be sustained.

## NOTES

The author wishes to thank the British Academy for its financial support.
1. *Dzimtenes Balss* 11 May 1989.
2. For general histories and geographies of Latvia, see A. Bilmanis *A History of Latvia* (Washington, DC, 1951); A. Drizula *Istoriya Latviiskoi SSR* (Riga 1971); J. Rutkis *Latvia: Country and People* (Stockholm, Latvian National Foundation 1967).
3. Rutkis, *Latvia*, p. 292.
4. A. Plakans 'The Latvians' in E. C. Thaden (ed.) *Russification in the Baltic Provinces and Finland 1855–1914* (Princeton, NJ, Princeton University Press 1981), pp. 207–86.
5. U. Germanis 'The idea of an independent Latvia and its development in 1917' in A. Sprudzs and A. Rusis *Res Baltica* (Leyden 1968), pp. 27–87.
6. A. Ezergailis 'The Latvian "autonomy" conference of 30 July 1917' *Journal of Baltic Studies* vol. 8, no. 2, pp. 162–71.
7. Germanis 'The idea of an independent Latvia'.
8. S. Page 'Social and national currents in Latvia, 1860–1917' *American Slavonic and East European Review* vol. 9 (1949), pp. 25–36.
9. G. E. Smith 'Soziale und geographische veranderungen in der bevolkerungsstruktur von Estland, Lettland und Litauen 1918–40' *Acta Baltica* vol. 19/20 (1979/80), pp. 118–81.
10. See, for example, G. Von Rauch *The Baltic States: The Years of Independence, 1917–1940* (London, G. Hurst & Co. 1974).
11. J. Rogainis 'The emergence of an authoritarian regime in Latvia, 1932–34' *Lituanus* vol. 17, no. 3 (1971), pp. 61–85.
12. Ibid.
13. For accounts of socio-economic and political developments since 1944, see E. Allworth (ed.) *Nationality Group Survival in Multi-ethnic States: Shifting Support Patterns in the Soviet Baltic Region* (New York, Praeger 1977); J. Dreifelds 'Latvian national demands and group consciousness since 1959', and J. Penikis 'Latvian nationalism: preface to a dissenting view' in J. Simmonds (ed.) *Nationalism in the USSR and Eastern Europe in the Era of Brezhnev and Kosygin* (Detroit, University of Detroit Press

1977), pp. 136–56 and 157–61; G. E. Smith, 'The impact of modernisation on the Latvian Soviet republic' *Co-existence* vol. 16 (1979), pp. 45–64; G. E. Smith, 'Die probleme des nationalismus in den drei baltischen sowjet republiken Estland, Lettland und Litauen' *Acta Baltica* vol. 21, pp. 143–77.

14. I. K. Lebedev *Bol'sheviki Latvii v bor'be za razvitie promyshlennosti* (Moscow 1949), p. 12.

14. Tsentral'noe statisticheskoe Upravlenie pri Sovete Ministrov Latviiskoi SSR, *Narodnoe Khozyaistvo Latviiskoi SSR v 1976 godu* (Riga, Liesma 1977).

16. Ibid.

17. T. Parming 'Population processes and the nationality issue in the Soviet Baltic' *Soviet Studies* vol. 32, no. 3 (1980), pp. 398–414.

18. J. Stalin *Marxism and the National and Colonial Question* (London 1936), p. 110.

19. K. Ya. Strazdin *et al. Istoriya Latviiskoi SSR* (Riga 1942–58), vol. 3, pp. 549–52.

20. L. Terent'eva *Kolkhoznoe krest'yanstvo Latvii* (Moscow, Izdatel'stvo 1960).

21. *Padomju Latvijas Komunists* no. 1 (Jan. 1960), p. 11.

22. *Sovetskaya Latviya* 26 Jan. 1958.

23. *Sovetskaya Latviya* 18 Nov. 1961.

24. *Padomju Latvijas Komunists* no. 9 (Sept. 1959), pp. 7–14.

25. D. Bahry *Outside Moscow: Power, Politics and Budgetary Policy in the Soviet Republics* (New York, Columbia University Press 1987), p. 56.

26. See, for example, A. Bohnet and N. Penkaitis 'A comparison of living standards and consumption patterns between the RSFSR and the Baltic republics' *Journal of Baltic Studies* vol. 19, no. 1 (1988), pp. 33–48.

27. A. Kovalev 'Kto i pochemu za chertoi bednosti' *Ekonomischeskaya gazeta* vol. 25, p. 11.

28. *Pravda* 27 Feb. 1981.

29. P. Zvidrinysh *et al. Naselenie Sovetskoi Latvii* (Riga, Zinatne 1986), p. 33, provides the following five-yearly figures on net migration and its percentage contribution to the republic's population growth: 1951–55: 16,900, 26%; 1956–60: 58,000, 47%; 1961–65: 78,000, 58%; 1966–70: 66,300, 63%; 1971–75: 63,900, 65%; 1976–80: 40,000, 71%; and 1981–84: 40,800, 62%.

30. For 1987 it has been estimated that net migration reached 18,800. See *Literaturnaya Gazeta* 19 July 1989, p. 10.

31. Latvijas PSR Centrala statisikas parvalde *Latvijas PSR tautas saimnieciba 1985 gada* (Riga, Avots 1986), p. 23.

32. Yu. V. Arutunyan *et al. Sotsial'no-Kul'turnyi oblik Sovetskikh Natsii (po materialam etnosotsiologischeskogo issledovaniya)* (Moscow, Nauka 1986).

33. Yu. V. Arutunyan *et al.*, ibid., p. 66; M. Kulichenko *et al. Natsional'nye otnosheniya v razvitom sotsialesticheskom obshchestve* (Moscow, Mysl' 1977), p. 97.

34. L Terent'eva 'Kz divautu gimenes jauniesi izskir savu tautibu' *Zinatne un Tekhnika* no. 8 (Aug. 1970), p. 12.

35. Arutunyan, op. cit., p. 32.

36. *Vestnik Statistiki* no. 10 (1980), p. 72.
37. Ibid., p. 72.
38. *Sovetskaya Latviya* 6 June 1979.
39. *Sovetskaya Latviya* 29 June 1982.
40. 'Letter by Seventeen Latvian Communists' in G. Saunders (ed.) *Samizdat* (New York 1974), pp. 427–40.
41. *Komsomolskaya Pravda* 26 Aug. 1987.
42. *Sovetskaya Latviya* 30 Aug. 1987.
43. *Tass* 25 Feb. 1987.
44. For accounts of developments over the summer of 1988 leading to the formation of Latvia's Popular Front, see D. Bungs 'The national awakening in Latvia' *Radio Free Europe*, RAD/175, 1988; J. Dreifelds 'Latvian national rebirth' *Problems of Communism* vol. 38, (1989) pp. 77–94; and O. Rozitis 'The rise of Latvian nationalism' *Swiss Review of World Affairs* (Feb. 1989), pp. 24–6.
45. *Pravda* 16 Sept. 1987; *Literaturnaya Gazeta* 18 Nov. 1987.
46. *Literatura Maksla* 10 June 1988.
47. *Cina* 3 July 1988.
48. *Padomju Jaunatne* 19 July 1988.
49. *Sovetskaya Latviya* 12 Aug. 1988.
50. Ibid.
51. For an account of Rebirth and Renewal, see M. Sapiets '"Rebirth and Renewal" in the Latvian Lutheran Church' *Religion in Communist Lands* vol. 16, no. 3 (1988), pp. 237–49.
52. The draft programme of the People's Front appeared in *Sovetskaya Moldodezh* 8 Sept. 1988.
53. *Literaturnaya gazeta* 19 July 1989, p. 10.
54. The details of this law are laid out in *Sovetskaya Latviya* 7 July 1989, p. 2.
55. A. Kalninsh, head of the Latvian Komsomol Report Group on Latvia's socio-economic development to the year 2000. *Sovetskaya Molodezh* 7 Sept. 1988.
56. See, for example, the interview with the Chairman of Latvia's State Planning Committee, in *Izvestiya* 4 Aug. 1989, p. 2.
57. Personal interview with Romualdas Razukas, later Chairman of the Popular Front, Riga 15 September 1992.
58. *Vestnik Ministerstva Inostrannykh del SSSR*, No. 2 (60), 31 January 1990, pp. 7–16.
59. Resolution no. 8 as cited in E. Rudenschiold, 'The ethnic dimension in contemporary Latvian politics: focusing forces for change' *Soviet Studies*, vol. 44, no. 4 (1992) p. 613.
60. Ibid.
61. *Pravda*, 14 Dec. 1988.
62. *Literaturnaya gazeta*, 19 July 1989, p. 10.
63. Ibid.
64. Ibid.
65. Rudenschiold, *op. cit.*
66. See for example A. Lieven *The Baltic Revolution. Estonia, Latvia, Lithuania and the Path to Independence* (New Haven, CT, Yale University Press 1993); G. Smith (ed.) The *Baltic States. The National*

*Self-Determination of Estonia, Latvia and Lithuania* (London, Macmillan 1994).

67. See for example the statement by Migranyan, Yeltsin's advisor and member of the Presidential Council, concerning the geopolitical and economic importance of Latvia to Russia *Nezavisimaya gazeta*, 12 and 18 January 1994.
68. *The Baltic Observer* 15 Oct. 1992.
69. FBIS-SOV-92-083:72.
70. *Baltic Independent* 12–18 Aug. 1994.
71. FBIS-SOV-93-032:58.
72. FBIS-SOV-92-199:69.
73. See for example S. Smooha 'Minority status in an ethnic democracy: the status of the Arab minority in Israel' *Ethnic and Racial Studies*, vol. 13, no. 3 (1990) pp. 389–413.
74 S. Smooha and T. Hanf 'The diverse modes of conflict regulation in deeply divided societies' in A. Smith (ed.), *Ethnicity and Nationalism* (Leyden 1992), p. 32.
75. *Baltic Independent*, 25 June–1 July 1993, p. 5.

# CHAPTER NINE

# Lithuania and the Lithuanians

Alfred Erich Senn

'Lithuania', as an ethno-territorial designation, refers to a region on the south-east coast of the Baltic Sea, between 'Latvia', 'Poland' and 'Belarus'. The boundaries of this territory have been the subject of disputes, since Belarusians, Poles, Jews and Russians have all challenged the Lithuanians' claim to the region's history. A multinational Grand Duchy, led by Lithuanians, arose here in the 13th century, entered into union with Poland in 1386, and ceased to exist as a result of the 18th century partitions of the Polish–Lithuanian Commonwealth. Poles have considered Lithuania to have been Polish in culture; Belarusians have viewed it as populated mostly by Slavs; a significant percentage of the Jews in the world today can trace their ancestry to this region; Russians have claimed the land as part of historic '*Rus*'.

The Lithuanians speak a Baltic language, akin to Latvian but nothing like the Slavic languages spoken by other neighbours, and in religious preference they are overwhelmingly Roman Catholic. Because they were the last pagan people in Europe, baptised in the 14th century but fully converted probably only in the 16th, the culture of the Lithuanians bears many traces of their pagan ancestry. The earliest written texts in Lithuanian date from the 16th century, and a secular literature developed only in the 18th and 19th centuries. From 1864 to 1904 the Russian authorities tried to convert the language to Cyrillic characters, but they failed as the Lithuanians smuggled books from East Prussia. Lithuanian linguists used the time to plan the conversion of the language from the Polish alphabet to a new one based on the Czech alphabet.

The modern Lithuanian national movement, which began in the 19th century when most of the region was a part of the Russian Empire, demanded the liberation of Lithuanian culture from both Polish and Russian domination. After the First World War the Lithuanians established a national state, which existed until the early stages of the Second World War. The major question in Lithuanian foreign policy in the 1920s and 1930s focused on the possession of the city of Vilnius/Wilno, which the Poles had seized in 1920.[1] In 1940 the Soviet Union, acting in concert with Nazi Germany, incorporated Lithuania as a constituent republic; and finally, in 1990 and 1991, the Lithuanians 're-established' the independent national state that had existed in the 1920s and 1930s.

The region lacks extensive natural resources, and in the past it specialised in food production and industrial crops such as flax. Under Soviet rule industry developed, including a chemical complex and an atomic energy plant, but industrial production dropped severely in the post-Soviet years. Any listing of the country's resources, however, must also mention its intellectual and sporting accomplishments – the achievements of Lithuania's writers, artists, and scientists, not to mention its athletes, were notable even under Soviet rule.

## LITHUANIA UNDER SOVIET RULE

In 1940 the Soviet Union sent troops into Lithuania and incorporated the republic into the USSR. Although Soviet historians called this a 'popular revolution', there was significant opposition to Soviet rule, and in June 1941 the Soviets carried out mass deportations. A week later, when Nazi Germany attacked the Soviet Union, Lithuanian nationalists tried to re-establish an independent government, but the Germans soon suppressed their efforts. After the war Lithuanian armed resistance, despite new mass deportations, lasted into the early 1950s.

Three factors reinforced the Lithuanians' national consciousness under Soviet rule: the role of the Lithuanians as the major Catholic people in the Soviet Union, the existence of a substantial *émigré* community in Western Europe and in North America, and the policy decision of the United States and other Western governments not to recognise the USSR's incorporation of Lithuania and its two Baltic neighbours. Soviet propaganda denounced these factors as part of a coordinated anti-Communist campaign, but even Moscow recognised their significance.

In 1940 the US government had called the Soviet incorporation of Lithuania illegal, and had insisted that the Lithuanian state continued to exist even though it had no government. During the Second World War, the Americans were on the verge of accepting Stalin's rule in the Baltic, but with the coming of the Cold War they offered clandestine aid to the Lithuanian resistance. When diplomatic relations between Washington and Moscow stabilised, the US government shaved the meaning of this policy of 'non-recognitiion', but even in the 1980s it remained a factor in US–Soviet relations.[2]

The Lithuanian emigration, which dated from the late 19th century, expanded significantly in the aftermath of the Second World War when many Lithuanians fled Soviet rule in their homeland, thereby becoming 'displaced persons'. *Emigré* leaders organized their own quasi-government, the Supreme Committee for the Liberation of Lithuania (VLIK), which at first tried to coordinate the clandestine Western aid to the resistance but then became basically an *émigré* organisation, keeping alive a vision of independence.

There were only a handful of Catholic churches in the USSR outside Lithuania, but over 600 churches were still functioning in the republic in the 1980s. The Catholic Church, although closely regulated by the Soviet authorities, provided a rallying point for people resisting the Soviet order. Many dissidents even found it difficult to separate their religious values from their national feelings – for them the two were virtually identical. The Catholics in fact provided the major *samizdat* publication in Lithuania, *The Chronicle of the Catholic Church in Lithuania*.[3]

The Soviet regime actually left little space in which people could try to resist. Demonstrations of defiance could be the work only of individuals, not of groups. Open dissidents at the very least had to forsake any sort of intellectual position for their beliefs. An intellectual might dare to work in the underground, but exposure would mean loss of his or her job. The deportees who were able to return from Siberia in the 1950s and 1960s had to commit themselves to silence. The Soviet KGB maintained its watch through an elaborate network of agents and informants aimed at identifying and punishing 'unreliable' elements in the society.

In the first years after the Second World War many Lithuanians viewed the Soviet order as an occupation regime, and refused to cooperate with it. After the Soviet authorities had suppressed the resistance, and of course after Stalin's death in 1953, Lithuanian national consciousness could take either of two forms: a type of personal self-deprivation, refusing to accept the rewards the Soviet system offered, or a pragmatic style of working within the system. While the deep-seated resentment resulted in spectacular actions, such as the defection of the sailor Simas Kudirka and the self-immolation of Romas Kalanta, the pragmatic behaviour eroded the Soviet system from within.[4]

By the late 1950s, the younger generation was more ready to take intellectual and scientific positions in the system and even to join the party. Although they constituted about 80 per cent of the population, Lithuanians became a majority in the Lithuanian Communist Party only in the late 1950s. In the late 1980s, some Soviet commentators asked whether the Soviet government had been too generous in allowing the Lithuanians to develop their own national intelligentsia.[5] In mediating between the system and the mass of people living under it, the intellectuals brought a considerable admixture of Lithuanian culture and ways into the public life of the republic.

The secretary of the LCP, Antanas Sniečkus, embodied these developments in a unique way. In Stalin's time he was the only Baltic party leader who belonged to the eponymous nationality, and he ruled Lithuania from 1940 to his death in 1974, in the Brezhnev era. In the first half of his 'reign' he sternly executed orders from Moscow, but in the second half he defended his position against the Centre and thereby helped Lithuanians to strengthen their own positions *vis-à-vis* the central authorities.[6]

Sniečkus's successor, Petras Griškevičius (1974–1987), followed Moscow's orders much more obediently; the building of a giant atomic energy plant in the north-eastern Lithuanian region of Ignalina exemplified this subservience. When Lithuanians could freely discuss the plant, many argued that Sniečkus would never have accepted this project, which not only raised questions of life and death for Lithuania in its use of the faulty design of the Chernobyl plant but also brought an influx of Russian workers that reduced the Lithuanians to a minority in that part of the republic. The development of a giant chemical complex in the centre of Lithuania raised similar concerns.

In the 1980s Lithuanians also feared the inroads of Russian language and culture into their lives. Many, for example, looked at the requirement that doctoral dissertations be written in Russian as a threat to the future of Lithuanian as a vehicle for critical, scientific thinking. The Soviet policy of bilingualism, providing children with structured education in Russian before they could study Lithuanian, also threatened the language's future.[7]

Nevertheless, in the early 1980s Lithuania appeared to be quiet. Individual Lithuanians might freely tell foreign friends about their dislike of the Soviet regime, but no significant organised opposition could exist in the republic. The small group of public dissidents was well known, but many outsiders feared that the KGB had infiltrated its ranks and was using it to entice others to display their anti-establishment sentiments. The public distrust fostered by the practices of the Soviet order would long poison the atmosphere in post-Soviet Lithuania.[8]

Lithuania entered the Gorbachev era as a productive republic, providing agricultural products, some important industrial goods, and even athletes for the Soviet system. (Lithuanians took great pride in the fact that at one point in the Soviet victory over the United States in Olympic basketball in 1988, there were four Lithuanians on the court at the same time; at the 1992 Olympics the Lithuanians won the bronze medal in basketball.) Below the surface there was considerable discontent and restlessness, but in the oppressive atmosphere of the Soviet order it could bubble to the surface only in isolated incidents.

## THE GORBACHEV PERIOD

The Lithuanian challenge to the Soviet system arose from Mikhail Gorbachev's ideas of decentralising the Soviet apparatus, of allowing greater freedom of criticism to Soviet citizens, and of establishing a 'state ruled by law'. These aims released local forces, previously quiet and disorganised, throughout the Soviet empire, and the Soviet state, with its repressive apparatus weakened, suddenly had no clothes.

Lithuanians now point to the dissidents' demonstration of 23 August 1987, denouncing the Molotov–Ribbentrop pact of 1939, as the beginning of the 'rebirth' of Lithuanian national feeling, but 'reformist' efforts, aimed at improving life under Soviet rule, had preceded that action. Gorbachev's encouragement of local initiatives allowed the Lithuanian Writers' Union to protest against planned oil drilling in the Couronian Sound as a danger to the region's picturesque and fragile ecology. Telephone calls poured in to the union's headquarters asking how they dared to lead such action, but the old mould had been broken. In the spring of 1988 the Lithuanians began to question the safety of the Ignalina atomic energy plant.

The Writers' Union also attacked Soviet cultural policies. The writers of course had a vested interest in the preservation and development of the language, and they began to challenge the historians of Lithuania to write the 'real history' of Lithuania. In this context the demonstrators on 23 August 1987 were adding their own demand for the re-establishment of a national Lithuanian history. The party leadership found that under Gorbachev's new practices it had to use words rather than force, and being unprepared for such open competition, it soon lost control of the situation.

The party still seemed in charge in February 1988 when Lithuanian nationalists marked the 70th anniversary of the Lithuanian State Council's declaration of independence in 1918. Moscow flew in foreign correspondents who duly reported home that they saw little, and the authorities claimed that the people had rejected the siren calls of 'foreign voices', meaning especially Voice of America and Vatican radio.

New currents were nevertheless taking form. Informal associations were discussing previously forbidden subjects, and on 3 June representatives of several such groups gathered to form the Initiative Group of the Lithuanian Movement for Perestroika (*Lietuvos persitvarkymo sajudis*) or, as it became better known, Sajudis. The group consisted of 35 persons, and included artists, writers, musicians, economists, and philosophers – but no historians. Nineteen were party members. The group refused an invitation to serve the party in an advisory capacity, and instead organised public meetings that gave birth to a mass movement demanding that Lithuanians take control of their own lives.

Sajudis's first programme eschewed political goals, focusing instead on strengthening the place of the Lithuanian language in the administration of the republic's affairs, on protecting the environment, and on gaining greater control over the republic's economy, which was essentially run from Moscow. In the autumn, when Gorbachev announced his plans to amend the Soviet constitution, Sajudis leaders understood this as a step toward re-establishing the Centre, and they redirected their energies toward political goals.[9]

In origin the Sajudis Initiative Group consisted exclusively of Vilnius intellectuals, but when the movement's constituent congress in October 1988 elected a Seimas, a sort of unofficial legislature, which in turn elected a Council, Sajudis's leadership base broadened significantly. The decision of Sajudis leaders not to make the movement a closed-membership organisation opened the way for people from other parts of Lithuania, especially from the 'second city' of Kaunas, to join and to voice more radical demands, denouncing the Soviet system altogether and raising ever more daring calls for independence.

As Sajudis moved into a more radical path, the Lithuanian Communist Party entered the flow of reform. In August Aleksandr Iakovlev had come to Vilnius to hear party leaders' complaints and had told them to make their peace with Sajudis, but the old party leadership could not make the adjustment. Reformers in the party then forced Moscow's viceroy, Nikolai Mitkin, out of his post as Second Secretary of the LCP, and installed their own candidate, Algirdas Brazauskas, as the new First Secretary.

Brazauskas had the approval of Sajudis leaders, but he urged moderation. At the Sajudis congress he tried to remind the delegates of the place and time in which they lived; when he subsequently refused to support a move to make Lithuanian laws superior to Soviet laws, Sajudis leaders turned against him. Sensitive to his position between Vilnius and Moscow, Brazauskas remained conciliatory toward the Centre until the spring of 1989 when Sajudis achieved an overwhelming victory in the election of deputies to the new USSR Congress of People's Deputies. Brazauskas then moved close to Sajudis.

Sajudis, on the other hand, encouraged national movements in other parts of the Soviet Union. It helped Belarusians, Crimean Tatars and Moldovans. In May 1989 it financed a meeting of representatives of the three Baltic national fronts, and on 23 August, on the anniversary of the Molotov–Ribbentrop pact, it joined with the Latvians and Estonians in a show of Baltic solidarity by forming a human chain reaching from Vilnius to Tallinn, the capital of Estonia.

The conservatives in the CPSU Politburo looked askance at the developments in Lithuania, and on 26 August they warned that if Communist leaders in the Baltic did not control their nationalists, the three nations would face dire consequences.[10]

Times, however, had changed drastically since the days when a threat from Moscow sufficed to bring deviators into line. Lithuanians rallied behind Brazauskas to defy the Centre, and Soviet leaders beat a hasty embarrassed retreat from their threat.

The drive for Lithuania's independence had essentially conquered the nation by the autumn of 1989, and political leaders were focusing their attention on the republican elections, scheduled for February and

March 1990. After the devastating electoral defeat that the CPSU had suffered throughout the USSR in March and April 1989, Moscow had postponed local elections, originally scheduled for the autumn, and now Brazauskas's LCP faced a daunting task in building a new constituency among the Lithuanian electorate.

For Lithuanians the question concerning independence was now 'when', not 'whether'. Brazauskas advocated a cautious programme, 'step by step', which spoke of 'sovereignty' rather than 'independence' and, it was hoped, would arouse a minimum of opposition from Moscow. Radicals, on the other hand, declared that Moscow's opposition was a given and that therefore the nation should demand independence immediately. From these differences arose a new political struggle: Sajudis radicals declared that they would support Brazauskas only in so far as he opposed Moscow, and they expressed doubts that he was sincere in his public stance on behalf of Lithuanian 'sovereignty'.

The political struggle in Lithuania also drove institutional changes. As an integral part of his appeal for a genuine voter constituency in the republic, Brazauskas advocated pulling the LCP free of CPSU control and ending the LCP's position of dominance in Lithuanian society. The latter proposal took the form of altering Article 6 of the Lithuanian constitution to abolish the position of the LCP as 'the leading and guiding force' of society. Gorbachev and the conservatives vigorously denounced Brazauskas's intentions, but the Lithuanians realised both goals in December 1989.[11]

In an effort to stop the processes in Lithuania, Gorbachev visited Vilnius in January 1990 with the intention of persuading the population to rebel against Brazauskas. He patently failed, and in February, under pressure from the CPSU Central Committee, which was itself frightened by the execution of the Romanian Communist dictator Nicolae Ceausescu, Gorbachev denounced Brazauskas. Not recognising that Brazauskas was dealing with a considerably more radical constituency than he was, Gorbachev now essentially abandoned the last traces of his vision of *perestroika* in Lithuania.[12]

When Lithuanians went to the polls in February 1990 to elect a new Supreme Council,[13] confrontation with Moscow loomed, and the electorate returned a two-thirds majority of Sajudis-backed candidates to the legislature. On 11 March the parliament elected Vytautas Landsbergis, who had been the president of the Sajudis Council, as the chairman of its presidium, essentially the head of the Lithuanian state, and it declared that Lithuania was again an independent state as it had been in 1940 before the occupation by the Soviet army.

The parliament's action rested on a complicated set of decisions. It declared that the Soviet years constituted an occupation by a foreign power and that the constitution of 1938 was still operative. Since, however, the Sajudis majority in parliament did not want to re-establish the institution of the presidency – Brazauskas was still the most popular political figure in Lithuania – it then suspended the 1938 constitution and adopted a new constitution based on the constitution of the Lithuanian SSR. This kept Landsbergis in office as a chief of state elected by a parliament, and Landsbergis then directed the Lithuanian stand in the ensuing confrontation with Moscow.

After the Lithuanians had rejected Gorbachev's demand that they rescind their resolutions of 11 March, the Soviet leader imposed a blockade on the republic, denying it goods that he claimed the Soviet Union could sell on the international market for hard currency but nevertheless allowing the Lithuanians about 20 per cent of their normal natural gas supply. The latter, plus the electrical production of the Ignalina atomic power plant, helped the Lithuanians to resist Gorbachev's pressure, and after two months the Soviet leader essentially gave in, ending the blockade when the Lithuanians promised to declare a moratorium on implementation of their declaration of independence when direct negotiations commenced between Moscow and Vilnius. (Since the negotiations never formally began, the Lithuanians never effected a moratorium.)

Conservative forces in Moscow now forged other plans for the re-establishment of Soviet control of Lithuania. In March the head of the Soviet land forces, General Valentin Varennikov, had already proposed military intervention, but in the autumn the new CPSU Secretary for organisational matters, Oleg Shenin, began to organise Russian and Polish sympathisers in Lithuania under the leadership of the Lithuanian Communist Party-CPSU, a rump organisation that had broken away from Brazauskas's LCP to remain loyal to Moscow.[14]

The situation came to a head in January 1991 when Moscow loyalists in Vilnius attempted to stir up ethnic conflict; after that had failed, Soviet troops attacked selected buildings, especially those housing the media and Lithuania's rudimentary police and defence force. The worldwide negative publicity when Soviet tanks attacked the television tower in Vilnius caused Gorbachev quickly to back away from the adventure.[15] He was apparently supposed to proclaim 'presidential rule' (martial law) in Lithuania, but in the end he refused, claiming that he knew nothing about the actions of the Soviet army in Lithuania.

The 'January days' of 1991 sealed the fate of the Soviet Union and of Gorbachev's political career. The 'coup-plotters' behind the 'August putsch' of 1991 in Moscow had almost all been involved in the failed action in Vilnius. On the other hand, the military force that had taken the television tower in Lithuania refused to follow orders to seize the 'White House' in Moscow in which Boris Yeltsin had taken refuge. (Even the defence of the Russian White House resembled the Lithuanian defence of the parliament building in Vilnius in January.) When the August putsch failed, Lithuania, Latvia and Estonia won general diplomatic recognition as independent states, and the Soviet Union collapsed soon after.


## LITHUANIA AS A NATION-STATE

After September 1991, as rulers of a nation-state, the Lithuanians had to deal with a new set of problems, not the least of which was living with the other peoples inhabiting their state.[16] Lithuanian government leaders had little doubt that their state existed to serve the interests of their nation, but the role of the other nationalities remained to be defined. The boundaries of the republic were the same as those of the Lithuanian SSR, and in this territory Lithuanians themselves in 1989 constituted 79.6 per cent of the population. Russians represented 9.4 per cent and Poles about 7.0 per cent. The rest of the population included Belarusians, Ukrainians, Tatars, Latvians and Jews.

In the unprecedented new atmosphere of free discussion and debate, conceptions of Lithuania's past wove into modern politics to form a seamless fabric, as each of the minorities represented both domestic and international problems for the Lithuanian state. From the Lithuanians' point of view, the Polish question was the most sensitive in domestic politics, the Russian question remained relatively quiet, and the Jewish question, which focuses on Lithuania's history, became the most delicate one in Lithuania's international standing. (In 1994, of these three groups, only the Poles had representation in the Lithuanian parliament.)

The tension began to develop in 1988 when the leaders of the LCP accepted Lithuanian as the official language of the republic. Russians and Poles, many of whom displayed disdain for the Lithuanian language, objected; many Polish families were in fact sending their children to Russian schools in the belief that Russian was the vehicle for making careers. The Moscow authorities added their own explosive spice to the mixture by encouraging Russians and Poles to rally together in an organisation called *Edinstvo* (Unity, *Jedność* in Polish).[17]

In November 1989 the Lithuanian Supreme Council (then still representing the authority of the LCP) committed the republic to the 'zero option' alternative in extending the right of citizenship to 'persons who on the day of the enactment of this law have been continuously living on the territory of the republic and have here a continuing place of work or a continuing legal source of existence. These persons may freely opt for citizenship within two years from the day of the enactment of this law.'[18] The vast majority of non-Lithuanians in the state took advantage of the opportunity.

After March 1990, Lithuanian officials tended to view the other nationalities of the republic as separate communities of citizens, and they established a Council of Nationalities, later renamed the Department of Nationalities, to deal with them. This practice encouraged the communities to produce their own leaders, and the competition between leaders would of course intensify each group's politics.

Gorbachev did what he could to stimulate national antagonism in Lithuania. When he imposed his blockade on Lithuania in the spring of 1990, he made exceptions to supply the Polish and Russian inhabitants of eastern Lithuania with the essentials of life. At the same time, Moscow loyalists demanded that autonomous Polish districts be established in parts of Lithuania. (One Polish leader called for the establishment of a Polish SSR as a constituent republic of the USSR.) Belarusians also raised territorial demands on Lithuania, often claiming the same regions that Poles did. During the stalemate that lingered after the January Days of 1991, pro-Moscow sources freely spoke of dismembering Lithuania.

When the Lithuanians became the masters of the house in September 1991, one of the Supreme Council's first acts was to suppress local government in two districts of south-east Lithuania where it claimed that local CPSU-loyalists had even supported the August putsch in Moscow. The local officials in those regions had clearly opposed Lithuanian independence, and now having lost their source of support in Moscow, they appealed to Warsaw for sympathy and help. The Lithuanians themselves displayed considerable clumsiness and insensitivity by sending in administrators who spoke Russian but not Polish.

The Lithuanians also faced a worldwide avalanche of criticism because of an article in *The New York Times* charging them with indiscriminately rehabilitating war criminals who had participated in the killing of Jews in Lithuania.[19] Although only some 12,000 Jews were still reportedly living in Lithuania in 1989, the historical question of the Holocaust was still very much alive, and it threatened to destroy the sympathy that the Lithuanians had won in the West in the course of their struggle with Moscow. Jewish leaders in Vilnius have publicly declared that there is no official anti-Semitism in Lithuania, but even US Senators have made clear that their attitude towards the Lithuanian republic is conditioned by their perception of Lithuanian attitudes toward the Jews.[20]

The Lithuanian government, both under Landsbergis and under Brazauskas, has made public statements regretting the mass killing of the Jews, but the controversy continued unabated. In September 1994, when Prime Minister Adolfas Šleževičius spoke of the imperative to find and prosecute the still surviving persons guilty of the killings, *The New York Times* reported that according to Jewish critics he was underestimating the number of guilty persons; at the same time Lithuanian critics complained that the government must find and prosecute the KGB and other officials who had participated in the mass killings and deportations of Lithuanians.[21]

In another example of the role of history in post-Soviet politics, Poles nurtured deep-seated grievances about the way the Soviets had occupied Vilnius (in Polish, Wilno) in 1939 and had turned the area over to the Lithuanians. During World War II, local Polish partisans in the region, AK (Home Army) units, had fought in the name of Poland against the German occupation and, as the Lithuanians saw it, against Lithuanian sovereignty. In the 1990s, Lithuanian war veterans bitterly recalled the experiences of wartime and opposed the efforts of the Poles of Lithuania to win recognition for the work of the AK, and nationalists in Lithuania opposed the signing of treaty of friendship with Poland until the Poles apologised for seizing Vilnius in 1920.

The Polish community formulated its own set of contemporary demands, calling for the establishment of a Polish university in Vilnius, for the holding of masses in Polish in the Vilnius cathedral (Lithuanian churches held masses in Polish even under Soviet rule), for restoration of property to Polish pre-war organisations in the Vilnius region, and for limiting the settlement of Lithuanians in the region surrounding the city of Vilnius. The Polish embassy in Vilnius has strongly supported the development of the Polish community, and as more Polish families send their children to Polish instead of Russian schools, the politics of the Polish minority will probably intensify.[22]

The experience of the Russians in Lithuania has been markedly different. Under the terms of the Lithuanian citizenship law, Russians received investment cheques, and many used these to buy their apartments. Those wanting to move to Russia could sell this property, thereby acquiring a nest-egg to carry with them. Partially as a result of this situation, Russians have declined since 1989 to below 9 per cent of the population. Moscow has exerted relatively little pressure on behalf of this group, and the basic problems would seem to be mainly ones of daily life – the use of language, school textbooks, border crossings and, of course, the question of who speaks for the Russians.[23]

The politics of Lithuania's minorities developed against a background of considerable institutional confusion within the ranks of the Lithuanians themselves. In the aftermath of independence, Sajudis's parliamentary majority, which had been disintegrating ever since the debate over moratorium in the summer of 1990, crumbled, and Sajudis itself became a more narrowly based nationalist organisation. Declaring that the parliament was unable to function, Landsbergis demanded the establishment of a strong presidency. When the Supreme Council objected, Sajudis forced the holding of a referendum in May 1992. The referendum failed, and Landsbergis then called for new parliamentary elections.[24]

Landsbergis expected to win the elections, scheduled for October

1992, and he strengthened his position in September when he reached agreement with the Russian government on the withdrawal of Russian troops from Lithuania by 31 August 1993. Also included in the voting was the adoption of a new constitution that would create a strong presidency, which Landsbergis's supporters presumed he would occupy.

In the elections Brazauskas's Lithuanian Democratic Labour Party (LDLP, the heir of the former independent LCP) unexpectedly won an overwhelming victory, and the voters adopted the new constitution. (The minorities of Lithuania generally supported the LDLP.) Stunned by the defeat, Landsbergis declined to enter the subsequent presidential race, and in February 1993 Brazauskas defeated Stasys Lozoraitis, the Lithuanian ambassador in Washington, to become Lithuania's first popularly elected president.

The political right in Lithuania at first looked at the LDLP victory as something akin to a restoration of the Soviet order. Some commentators wanted to discuss the meaning of the 1926 coup in Lithuania when a military coup ousted a leftist government that had relied on the support of the minorities, but that mood eventually passed. Nevertheless the self-styled 'patriotic' press has repeatedly charged that the Brazauskas government was soft, if not treasonous, in dealing with Moscow and was making undue concessions to the Poles in particular. (Needless to say, Polish spokespersons complained that the Brazauskas government was not living up to its promises.) Brazauskas's opponents spoke of the desirability of holding new parliamentary elections ahead of schedule – the parliament was to serve until 1996 – but they were unable to muster the support for a referendum to force the issue.

In its first two years in power, the LDLP accomplished much in establishing institutions of government and in introducing a seemingly stable currency, the litas.[25] On the other hand, the Gross Domestic Product continued its decline of the post-Gorbachev years. The LDLP majority in the parliament remained stable, despite predictions that it might split into a conservative and a liberal wing, but the cabinet of Adolfas Šleževičius, installed in March 1993, changed more than half its members in its first 18 months in office.

## CONCLUSION

Although the Western press frequently refers to it as 'tiny', Lithuania is larger than Belgium, Denmark, the Netherlands or Israel. Its population is of course lower than any of these four, and its geopolitical position on the western edge of the remnants of the Soviet empire make it appear smaller than it is. The Lithuanians have displayed a strong national consciousness; there can be no doubt that most of them support independence; there is no marked desire to rejoin any new confederation or union of Eurasian republics. The Brazauskas administration has worked to bring the country into NATO and other Western European organisations. Lithuania's future will nevertheless depend to a great extent on general developments in eastern Europe.

# NOTES

1. See Alfred Erich Senn *The Great Powers, Lithuania, and the Vilna Question, 1920–1928* (Leiden: E. J. Brill 1966).
2. See Robert Vitas *The United States and Lithuania: The Stimson Doctrine of Nonrecognition* (New York: Praeger 1990).
3. See *Chronicle of the Catholic Church in Lithuania* (Chicago, IL: Loyola University Press 1981).
4. On Kalanta, see Alfred Erich Senn 'Pokalbis su Romo Kalanto šeima' *Akiračiai*, 1989, vol. 5, pp. 8–9.
5. See *Sotsial'no-politicheskie problemy mezhnatsional'nykh otnoshenii v SSSR: teoriia i praktika* (Moscow: Institute of Marxism-Leninism 1989), pp. 41–46.
6. See the account of Sniečkus's work in Vytautas Tininas *Sovietine Lietuva ir jos veikejai* (Vilnius: Enciklopedija 1994), pp. 250–63. When I first visited Vilnius in 1960, I found Russian more useful than Lithuanian in getting around the city. On my return in 1970, Lithuanian served me everywhere.
7. See Alfred Erich Senn *Lithuania Awakening* (Berkeley, CA: University of California Press 1990), pp. 7–10.
8. Since the authorities controlled the admissions to the single seminary educating priests in Lithuania, there were also fears that the KGB had infiltrated the clergy.
9. See my *Lithuania Awakening*.
10. See *The New York Times*, 27 August 1989.
11. I discuss this in detail in *Gorbachev's Failure in Lithuania* (New York: St. Martin's Press 1995), chapters 7 and 8.
12. See *Materialy plenuma Tsentral'nogo Komiteta KPSS 5–7 fevralia 1990 g.* (Moscow: Politizdat 1990).
13. Until March 1990, the legislature was called the Supreme Soviet in English; although the Lithuanian name, *Aukščiausioji Taryba*, did not change, Lithuanians henceforth insisted that the English form should be 'Supreme Council'.
14. I discuss these plans in *Gorbachev's Failure in Lithuania*, chapter 11.
15. For an eyewitness account of the violence in Vilnius, see Alfred Erich Senn *Crisis in Lithuania, January 1991* (Chicago, IL: Akiraciai 1990).
16. A useful account of conditions in Lithuania in 1991–1992 can be found in *Lithuania: An Economic Profile* (Springfield, VA: National Technical Information Service 1992).

17. On the KGB's role, see See Vadim Bakatin, *Izbavlenie ot KGB* (Moscow: Novosti 1992), p. 49. Anatole Lieven's 'belief that three-quarters of the Polish Lithuanian "problem" could be solved by a handful of symbolic gestures on the Lithuanian side' (Anatole Lieven, *The Baltic Revolution* (New Haven, CT: Yale University Press 1993), p. 172) seems far too simplistic.

18. *Lietuva–Litva–Lithuania* (Vilnius: Atgimimas 1989), p. 35. This quotation is translated from the Russian edition.

19. See *The New York Times*, 5 September 1991.

20. See the report of the hearing on the nomination of James Swihart as the new ambassador to Lithuania in August 1994, in *Lietuvos rytas*, 12 August 1994.

21. See *The New York Times*, 23 September 1994; when Lithuanian President Algirdas Brazauskas visited the United States in October 1994, the question about the KGB surfaced at every press conference.

22. Lithuanians frequently respond to questions about the situation of the Poles with complaints that the Lithuanians living across the border in Poland live in far worse conditions than the Poles in Lithuania.

23. At a grievance meeting between Russians and representatives of the Department of Nationalities in June 1993, Russian Orthodox Archbishop Chrisostom walked out when he was not permitted to make a preliminary statement.

24. Landsbergis won 69.4 per cent of the vote, but less than 50 per cent of the voters turned out. *Lietuvos aidas* 27 May 1992.

25. In August 1994 a referendum to 'index' savings accounts, an idea that IMF specialists called 'inflationary' and Brazauskas labelled 'nonsense', failed because only some 30 per cent of the voters went to the polls.

# PART IV

# The South-Western Borderlands

The three states of the south-western borderlands (see Fig. 4) are Belarus, Moldova and Ukraine, which together have a population of 66.2 million. The Ukrainians and Belarusians have most in common. They share with the Russians their East Slav origins from which their languages are also derived. Their religion is grounded in Byzantine Christianity, while historical roots in the medieval state of Kiev-Rus are another important link with a common past.

Granted union republic status as part of the 1922 Soviet Federal Treaty, both Ukrainians and Belarusians, relative to the other non-Russian nationalities, benefited in a number of ways from their common Eastern Slav origins. In contrast to the other non-Russian nationalities, they enjoyed greater upward mobility beyond the boundaries of their namesake republics, and advanced in significant numbers into the central élite and served in important positions. Close cultural affinity, together with a large Russian presence in both republics, also facilitated linguistic Russification, with Ukrainians and Belarusians having by far the highest proportion of Russified, non-native speakers among the union republic nationalities.

For the post-Soviet states, Ukraine's relationship with Russia is of particular importance, not least because of its 11 million Russian minority. Although Ukraine has adopted a concept of citizenship based on territoriality rather than on ethnic or cultural criteria, many Ukrainian nationalists would prefer to see nation-building playing a more central part in the process of state-building. This has manifested itself in a territorial dualism that has dominated Ukraine's politics since 1991: between a predominantly agricultural west which has become a power base for Ukrainian neo-nationalism, and the industrial east where Russians are concentrated and demands for reintegration with Russia have been voiced.

The third republic, Moldova, has since independence been plagued by ethnic violence. Following the ending of the Soviet Union, Moldova faced a unique choice reflecting two nationalist modes of Moldovan identity: between irredentism (joining up with their one time co-nationals in neighbouring Romania) or separatism (forming a Moldovan state). Opting for the latter did not ease relations with their large, predominantly Russian, settler community who were quick to break away and set up their own Transdniester Republic. Even more than in Ukraine, relations with Russia have deteriorated. Both situations contrast sharply with Belarus, which has among the most cordial relations with Russia of the post-Soviet states.

Figure 4 : **THE SOUTH-WESTERN BORDERLANDS**

# CHAPTER TEN

# Ukraine and the Ukrainians

Peter J. S. Duncan

Ukraine is the largest country in eastern Europe after Russia, in both territory and population (51.9 million), and the Ukrainians were the second largest nationality, after the Russians, in the USSR. The Eastern Slavs who formed the State of Kievan Rus' in the ninth century are seen by Russian historians as the ancestors of the Russians, Ukrainians and Belarusians. In the tenth century the Kievan princes accepted Christianity from Byzantium. After the Tatar invasion of the thirteenth century, the southern and western parts, including what became Ukraine, gradually fell under the control of Lithuania and then Poland.

The name *Ukraina* means borderland, and Ukraine for most of its history has lacked independent statehood. Its institutions have usually been imposed from outside, mainly from Poland or Russia, as the border between these two countries has shifted. In 1596, under the Union of Brest, the Polish government forced the Orthodox Christians of Ukraine and Belarus into union with Rome. This was done by establishing the Uniate, or Ukrainian Catholic, Church, which maintained the Eastern rite but recognised Papal supremacy. Ukrainian discontent led to the national revolution of 1648 against Poland and the Polish landlords, and then to the Treaty of Pereyaslavl of 1654. Under this the Ukrainian Cossack hetman Bohdan Khmel'nyts'kyi recognised the suzerainty of the Muscovite Tsar in return for protection against Poland. In 1663, however, Muscovy divided Ukraine with Poland, regaining control of the whole country (except Galicia in the west) by the partitions of Poland in the eighteenth century. Peter the Great began the process of abolishing the distinctive Ukrainian institutions, and of integrating Ukraine into the Russian Empire.

While the Russians looked on Ukraine and Belarus ('Little Russia' and 'White Russia') as organically linked to Russia, differing from her only by the dialect of their inhabitants, the Ukrainians felt themselves to be different. The Ukrainian national revival came, as elsewhere in eastern Europe, in the nineteenth century. The poet

Taras Shevchenko (1814–1861) created a Ukrainian literary language. Small underground nationalist groups called for Ukrainian autonomy, often in the context of a Slav federation. Indeed the influential publicist Mykola Kostomarov (1817–1885) contrasted the individualism and federalism of the Ukrainians with the collectivism and centralism of the Russians. The Tsarist Empire reacted to the Ukrainian movement by banning the use of the Ukrainian language in the education system and in print, from 1876 up to the 1905 revolution. Only in Galicia was there a Ukrainian Press over this period, allowed by the Habsburgs. After 1905, Nicholas II legalised the Ukrainian Press, but the victory of reaction led to a return to Russification. This in turn encouraged the growth of the Ukrainian nationalist movement, up to 1914.

## THE UKRAINIANS IN THE SOVIET UNION

Following the Bolshevik Revolution, a German-backed Ukrainian government, the Rada, declared Ukraine independent. Between 1918 and 1921 Russians, Poles and Ukrainians, Red and White, fought over Ukraine in a devastating civil war. The new Polish State gained western Ukraine, including the city of Lvov. The rest of the country became the Ukrainian SSR. Although formally independent, it was ruled by members of the Russian Communist Party (Bolsheviks), which was centrally controlled from Moscow. In 1922 the Communists brought form into line with substance and made Ukraine, together with the Russian republic, Belarus and Transcaucasia, one of the founder republics of the USSR.[1]

The wealth of Ukraine traditionally lay in its agriculture, and later also in its raw materials. Its fertile Black-Earth lands had made it the breadbasket of tsarist Russia. Bolshevik support in Ukraine, as in the other Russian borderlands, was weak in the peasantry and concentrated among the industrial workers, who were mainly of Russian nationality. From 1923, Moscow adopted a policy of nativization (*korenizatsiya*), promoting leaders from the indigenous nationality and developing the local language. This policy was nowhere taken further than in Ukraine. Ukrainian Communists worked together with nationalist leaders, brought back from exile to promote 'Ukrainianisation'. The Ukrainian language became the language of politics, economics and most of the press.

Rapid industrialisation created an ethnic Ukrainian working class; by 1930 over half the industrial workers in Ukraine were Ukrainians. A further reflection of the growth of nationalist feeling was the formation of the Ukrainian Autocephalous Orthodox Church in 1921, from within the Russian Orthodox Church. The authorities forced this back into the Russian Church in 1930 because of its Ukrainian nationalism.

Meanwhile, Stalin grew suspicious about the increasing tendency of the Ukrainian Communists, especially the education commissar Mykola Skrypnik, to act independently of Moscow's wishes. He forced the policy of collectivisation on Ukraine and imposed excessively high demands for grain delivery from the republic to the centre. The result of these policies was the 1932–1933 grain famine in which perhaps over seven million people died. Millions died in other parts of the Soviet Union as well, but in Ukraine the famine appears to have been deliberately engineered to destroy Ukrainian nationalism and its peasant base.[2] The results of the 1937 census were suppressed as they revealed a catastrophic decline in the Ukrainian population.

The unsuccessful efforts of Skrypnik and the Ukrainian Communists to counter the famine led to Skrypnik's suicide in 1933. Stalin reimposed Moscow's control, purged the Ukrainian leadership on charges of 'bourgeois nationalism' and ended Ukrainianisation. The role of the Ukrainian language was reduced, and in 1938 Russian became a compulsory subject in schools in Ukraine, as throughout the USSR. The history books were rewritten to reflect the Stalinist conception of history: the non-Russians had not been forcibly incorporated into the Russian Empire but had voluntarily joined it. The nationally-minded Ukrainian intellectual élite was destroyed in the purges by the end of the 1930s.[3]

In view of Stalin's treatment of Ukraine, it is not surprising that there was some collaboration between Ukrainians and the Nazis, who occupied the republic during the Second World War. The great majority of Ukrainians fought on the Soviet side. In recognition of the destruction suffered during the war, Ukraine and Belarus were allowed to become founder members of the United Nations. The moving west of the Soviet border after the war reunified the more nationalist Western Ukraine with the rest of the country. Attempting to weaken Ukrainian nationalism, Moscow ordered the Russian Orthodox Church to absorb the Uniate Church, which was strong in this area and itself linked with nationalism. This was accomplished with the aid of the secret police. Nevertheless, the Organisation of Ukrainian Nationalists and the Ukrainian Insurgent Army waged an armed struggle for independence into the early 1950s.

The death of Stalin in 1953 and Khrushchev's denunciation of him in 1956 made possible the revival of Ukrainian political and cultural life. The top positions in the republic were again given to Ukrainians, and writers began to develop a new wave of literature in the Ukrainian language. At the same time, a new development appeared under Khrushchev which lasted up to the end of Brezhnev's rule:

Ukrainians, and Russians from Ukraine, came to occupy prominent positions in the USSR outside Ukraine. If the Russians were the 'elder brother' among the Soviet nationalities, the Ukrainians were the 'junior elder brother'.

While in the 1980s many of the most prominent Ukrainians were replaced by Russians, it remained the case in both the Party apparatus and the Council of Ministers that the Ukrainians were the only non-Russian nationality to have significant representation. This situation gave ambitious Ukrainians the opportunity to aim to achieve high rank outside their republic in a way not easily open to non-Slavs. A precondition for this was their willingness to work entirely in the Russian language, and many Ukrainian parents preferred to send their children to Russian-language schools to enhance their career opportunities.

The relationship between the Ukrainians and Russians and the development of Ukrainian national feeling has been fashioned by demographic factors. According to the 1989 census, of the 44.1 million ethnic Ukrainians in the Soviet Union, 37.4 million lived in the Ukrainian SSR. The population of Ukraine was 72.7 per cent Ukrainians (down from 76.8 per cent in 1959), 22.1 per cent Russians, 0.9 per cent Jews, 0.9 per cent Belarusians, 0.6 per cent Moldavians (Romanians) and 2.8 per cent other nationalities. As a nation, the Ukrainians are now barely reproducing themselves.

The immigration of Russians (especially manual workers) and the emigration of Ukrainians (including skilled workers and specialists) to other parts of the Soviet Union added to Ukrainian worries. The proportion of Ukrainians in the USSR speaking Ukrainian as the mother tongue fell from 87.7 per cent in 1959 to 81.1 per cent in 1989. Less than half the Ukrainians outside the republic, lacking native-language schools and largely deprived of a Ukrainian-language Press, retained the language as a mother tongue. In Ukraine, the proportion of Ukrainians reporting Ukrainian as their mother tongue fell from 93.5 per cent in 1959 to 89.1 per cent in 1979. Russians and Russified Ukrainians are most strongly concentrated in the Crimea and in the cities of the east and south of the republic.

The key feature of demographic change is urbanisation. In the mid-1960s the size of the urban population overtook the rural population, and reached 67 per cent of the whole population in 1989. This process was mainly a movement of ethnic Ukrainians from the countryside to the cities. This has included a move from the rural provinces of the more nationalist Western Ukraine to the most industrially developed cities in Eastern Ukraine. At the same time, with Russians in Ukraine not under pressure to learn Ukrainian, but with 56.2 per cent of Ukrainians claiming bilingualism in 1989, the normal language of work in Ukrainian cities up to independence was Russian. In the capital Kiev, where the Russian population was just under a quarter of the total in

1979, the Russian language was used throughout the university except in philology. In the republic, Ukrainians were less likely than Russians to go to university or to have white-collar jobs.[4]

The fall of Khrushchev was followed by the arrest and sentencing in 1965–1966 of at least thirty of the most active defenders of the Ukrainian language. The new Moscow leadership seemed bent on increasing the role of Russian. The First Secretary of the CPU Central Committee, Petro Shelest, was under pressure from both Moscow and the political and cultural forces in Ukraine that were resisting Russification. He apparently gave protection to some of the nationally-minded intellectuals. He circulated Ivan Dzyuba's *samizdat* book, *Internationalism or Russification?* (1965), an attack on Russification couched in Leninist terms, to CPU provincial secretaries.[5] In 1966 he called for more works to be written in Ukrainian, and allowed leading writers such as Oles' Honchar and Vitalii Korotych to call for the publication of suppressed works. Shelest was unable to maintain his position, however. In the late 1960s, a human rights movement developed in Ukraine, protesting against the repression of intellectuals. The *samizdat Ukrainian Herald* (*Ukrains'kyi visnyk*) appeared in 1970, chronicling dissent and the authorities' response. In 1972 Moscow acted on its fears of resurgent Ukrainian nationalism and replaced Shelest by the Ukrainian Prime Minister, Volodymyr Shcherbyts'kyi.

Shelest was accused of idealising the Ukrainian past and over-estimating the Ukrainian contribution to the USSR in his 1970 book, *Ukraino, nasha radyans'ka* (O Ukraine, Our Soviet Land). Before Shelest's fall, a wave of arrests, labour camp sentences and incarcerations in psychiatric hospitals was unleashed in Ukraine, and this continued under Shcherbyts'kyi. There were at least a hundred victims, including the mathematician Leonid Plyushch, the writers Valentyn Moroz, Vyacheslav Chornovil, the editor of the *Ukrainian Herald*, and Dzyuba. The last subsequently recanted and was released. Shcherbyts'kyi also purged the Party leadership of those considered to be supporters of Shelest's line. At Moscow's behest, the use of Russian was stepped up in the Press, the schools and finally even the nursery schools. Numerous historical studies in the Ukrainian language that were in the pipeline were denied publication. Symbolically, whereas Shelest had addressed the CPU Congress in Ukrainian, Shcherbyts'kyi used the Russian language. The propaganda organs repeated themes about the historical friendship of the Russian, Ukrainian and Belarusian peoples – described as 'peoples of one blood' (*edinokrovnye*). Ukrainians feared that Moscow seemed to be building up a Russian-speaking East Slav bloc of these nations, to resist centrifugal forces in the Soviet Union. In 1976 Mykola Rudenko and Oleksii Tykhyi established the Ukrainian Helsinki Group, to highlight violations of the Helsinki Final Act in Ukraine. With the support of the Moscow Helsinki Group, they succeeded in drawing worldwide attention to

Russification and repression in Ukraine. Both the leaders were arrested and sent to labour camps the following year.[6]

It was probably in order to undercut the potential appeal of the Helsinki Group that Shcherbyts'kyi tried to come to terms with the Ukrainian intelligentsia in the late 1970s. Scholars were allowed to study more closely the prerevolutionary history of Ukraine.[7] But for those who stepped beyond the permitted lines, the political climate was not merciful. In the clampdown on dissent that began throughout the Soviet Union in 1979, and continued for the next five years, Ukrainians made up a high proportion of the new labour camp prisoners. In 1984 Tykhyi and two other Ukrainian activists died in the camps. In September 1985, soon after Gorbachev had come to power, Vasyl' Stus died after torture and illness in a special regime camp.

## UKRAINE UNDER GORBACHEV

The single most important event in the life of the Ukrainians in the 1980s was the tragic explosion of a nuclear reactor at Chernobyl, near Kiev, in April 1986. Although only about thirty people died in the immediate aftermath of the explosion, the reluctance of the authorities to admit first to the event and then to the dangers from the leak of radiation caused unnecessary delay and then panic evacuation from the affected area. It is impossible to estimate the total damage caused, in terms of the poisoning of the water supply, the effect on the soil in this important agricultural zone, and the future deaths from cancer. In the conditions of *glasnost'* emerging in Moscow, the disaster was widely reported by the Soviet media. This gave a fillip to feelings of concern about the environment and to a greening of politics throughout the Soviet Union. Nationally-minded Russians and non-Russians, and especially Ukrainians, saw the model of industrial development and the political system that had allowed the disaster as threats to the ecological survival of their peoples.

The most striking feature of Ukrainian political life in this period was Shcherbyts'kyi's ability to remain in his post for so long. His survival was not due to his zealous promotion of *perestroika*; there was virtually no change from above in Kiev. While naturally Shcherbyts'kyi paid lip service to Gorbachev's line, he made few concessions to the rising tide of demands emanating from the Ukrainian intelligentsia. These demands focused on the publication of banned works; an investigation into the 1932–1933 famine; the defence of the Ukrainian language; opposition to the expansion of nuclear power; and permission for the formation of a Popular Front, along the lines of those existing in the Baltic republics.

The demands were articulated mainly by members of the Union of Writers of Ukraine (UWU). As in other republics, the Ukrainian writers assumed a responsibility to defend national interests which extended beyond purely cultural concerns. *Literaturna Ukraina*, the Ukrainian-language weekly newspaper of the UWU with a circulation of 60,000, was the main vehicle of these demands.

It is likely that Gorbachev originally planned to remove Shcherbyts'kyi, as he removed Brezhnev's other cronies from leading positions, but found him to be in a particularly strong position in the Party. By the middle of 1988, however, Gorbachev may well have decided to keep Shcherbyts'kyi in his post for the time being. The evidence of the aspirations of the Baltic peoples for autonomy and the outburst of conflict between Armenians and Azeris highlighted the dangers involved in loosening the reins in the non-Russian republics. A political explosion in Ukraine could well have meant the end of *perestroika*. Shcherbyts'kyi would not reform Ukraine, but he had sixteen years' experience of working with the KGB to maintain political stability.

In spite of the lack of change at the top in Kiev, the Ukrainian intelligentsia took the rise of *glasnost'* in Moscow as a signal to make demands on the local leadership. Pressure mounted for the truth to be told about the history of Ukraine, in the pre-revolutionary and especially the Soviet period. In 1987 and 1988 the Moscow magazine *Ogonyok*, then edited by Korotych, published suggestions that the 1932–1933 Ukrainian famine had been created artificially. After this *Literaturna Ukraina* (18 February 1988) published a long speech by the writer Oleksa Musienko. He portrayed the history of Ukraine under Stalin and Brezhnev as one of crimes committed by Moscow against Ukrainians, including the famine. At the 19th Conference of the CPSU in June 1988, Borys Oliinyk called for an enquiry into the famine in the context of Stalin's crimes and was applauded. Demands came also for the publishing of banned literary works.

The major concern of the Ukrainian writers, however, was with the future status of the Ukrainian language. At the UWU Congress of June 1986, Honchar attacked Ukrainians who held their own language in contempt, and called for the defence of the 'linguistic environment'. Oliinyk at the USSR Writers' Congress in the same month was careful to blame not Moscow, but Ukrainians who behaved like Russian chauvinists in promoting the Russian language and thereby violating Leninist nationality policy. From then on, writers regularly expressed their concern at the fate of Ukrainian. They saw the problem as particularly acute in the education system: nearly half of all schoolchildren in the republic studied in Russian, and some knew no Ukrainian at all.

In July 1987, the UWU plenum passed a resolution making a comprehensive series of demands on language. These included giving the Ukrainian language official status in the republic; the compulsory study of Ukrainian in all schools; increasing the use of the language in the media and in films; and its widespread use in State and public organisations and workplaces. The following month the CPU Politburo passed a resolution calling for more attention to be given to the teaching of both the Ukrainian and Russian languages, but making no significant concessions to the Ukrainian intellectuals.[8] Shcherbyts'kyi was prepared to go no further, and at the January and October 1988 CPU Central Committee plenums he attacked writers for continuing to protest about the language situation. On the other hand, late in 1988 cultural centres for Ukrainians were opened in Moscow and Leningrad, and Radio Kiev expressed support for cultural rights for Ukrainians outside the republic.

Another issue that inflamed Ukrainian national feelings was the plan to expand the generation of nuclear power, in spite of the Chernobyl catastrophe. In 1987 a protest movement against plans to build new sites and expand the Chernobyl facilities developed under the leadership of Honchar and other writers and scientists.[9] In April 1988 a demonstration of 500 people, organised by the unofficial Ukrainian Culturological Club, was prevented from marching through Kiev, but in June a petition against nuclear power was sent from Ukraine to the 19th Party Conference, bearing 4000 signatures. Since the nuclear power industry is run from Moscow, not Kiev, the issue pitted the Ukrainian intellectuals directly against the centre. With environmentalist feeling growing in Moscow, it began to seem that the Kremlin might not force the expansion of nuclear power in Ukraine. The UWU, meanwhile, established an ecology commission to watch over environmental issues in the republic.

The amnesty of political prisoners in 1987, introduced by Gorbachev in the spirit of *glasnost'*, returned to Ukraine most of the well-known dissidents who had been sentenced under Brezhnev. As in the Russian republic, a parallel phenomenon was the development of a wide variety of unofficial organisations known as 'informal groups', in which Brezhnev-era dissidents participated together with a younger generation of citizens.

The *Ukrainian Herald* resumed publication, again under the editorship of Chornovil. The first issue contained a major section on the Ukrainian Culturological Club. This informal group was formed in Kiev in summer 1987 and was concerned with language, environment and history, especially the famine. In March 1988 the Ukrainian Helsinki Union (UHU) was relaunched, and the *Herald* became its official organ. The UHU called for a new constitution for the USSR and the republics, with the aim of transforming the Soviet Union into a confederation of independent States. Ukraine would have its own citizenship and immigration controls, and Ukrainian would be the official language. The Crimean Tatars, expelled by Stalin from the Crimea at the end of the Second World War, would be allowed back, and the Crimean autonomous republic would be re-established within Ukraine.[10] In

June 1988 the Native Language Society in Lvov organised a meeting about the 19th Party Conference. It was addressed by Chornovil and attended by 6,000 to 8,000 people. Five days later a follow-up meeting was not allowed to take place, although the numbers turning up had reportedly risen to 50,000. Placards supported the Ukrainian language and the legalisation of the Uniates.

During the summer of 1988, unions to support *perestroika* were established in Kiev, Odessa and Lvov – in the last case at least, out of a coalition of informal groups. After three mass meetings in Lvov, the authorities moved from criticising the organisers through the Press to large-scale arrests. Ivan Makar was arrested in August, and against the normal trend of the time, was held for several months for his part in arranging a demonstration. In October the Kiev Popular Union was allowed to hold a meeting, but the Shcherbyts'kyi leadership was making it clear that a Ukraine-wide popular front on the Baltic model would not be permitted. The demand for such an organisation could only be put forward in Moscow. In January 1989 Ivan Dzyuba (despite his earlier renunciation of his previous activities) called in *Moscow News* for a Ukrainian Popular Front to help fight the 'spiritual Chernobyl' threatening the republic.[11]

The situation began to change in February 1989, coinciding with the visit of Gorbachev to Kiev. On 16 February *Literaturna Ukraina* published the Draft Programme of the 'Popular Movement (*Rukh*) of Ukraine for *Perestroika*'. This recognised the leading role of the Communist Party, but demanded that Ukrainian be given the status of the state language of the republic and called for religious freedom. Shcherbyts'kyi's media reacted with hostility. In the elections to the USSR Congress of People's Deputies in March–April 1989, many officials were elected without opposition being permitted, but some freely contested elections led to victories for radicals. In June the Donbass miners went on strike over industrial and social issues, weakening Shcherbyts'kyi's position. In September the Ukrainian leadership was finally forced to allow *Rukh* to hold a Ukraine-wide founding conference. Nationalists from Galicia and cultural figures from Kiev were joined by Russian-speaking Donbass miners, all under the leadership of the writer Ivan Drach.

In the same month, Shcherbyts'kyi was ousted and replaced as First Secretary by Vladimir Ivashko. Gorbachev now wanted to promote *perestroika* in Ukraine. Late in 1989, Ukrainian Catholics seized control of many churches in Western Ukraine. Unlike in Lithuania and Armenia, religion in Ukraine has historically been a divisive factor, the East being Orthodox and the West Uniate. The representatives of the Moscow Patriarchate in Kiev protested to the local authorities, but to little effect. It appeared that prior to Gorbachev's visit to the Pope, the Soviet government had assured the Vatican that the situation of the Uniates would improve. In November 1989, Ukrainian was declared the official language of the state. This led over the next year to its increased use in the schools and administration. In January 1990 *Rukh* organised a million-strong human chain from Kiev to Lvov.

The elections to the Ukrainian Supreme Rada (Supreme Soviet), held in March 1990, took place in considerably freer conditions than those of the previous year. *Rukh* formed an electoral alliance, the Democratic Bloc, with other opponents of the apparatus. This succeeded in winning about one quarter of the seats in the Supreme Rada, and, as was expected, achieved its greatest support in the more nationalist Western Ukraine. *Rukh* also made important gains in the local elections, sweeping the board in the Lvov City Soviet and also doing well in Kiev. Former dissidents who now led independent political movements found themselves in high elected office: Chornovil, for example, became Chairperson of the Lvov *Oblast'* Soviet, confronting the bitter resistance of the Communists. Environmental problems were a factor in the success of the democrats, with new revelations emerging about the damage inflicted by the Chernobyl radiation on the health of the population, the extent of the cover-up and the failure of the authorities to protect the victims.

Gorbachev's decision to end the 'leading role' of the Communist Party in the USSR, implemented in March 1990, legitimised political pluralism in Ukraine, promoted the disintegration of the CPU and gave a major boost to the national–democratic movement. Large demonstrations with Ukrainian blue-and-yellow flags became a feature of life not only in Western Ukraine but also in Kiev. Under the impact of the nationalist victories in the elections in the Baltic States, the Lithuanian declaration of independence and the declaration of state sovereignty of the RSFSR, the Ukrainian Supreme Rada passed its own sovereignty declaration almost unanimously on 16 July 1990. This proclaimed the supremacy of Ukrainian law over USSR law and committed Ukraine to being a neutral state without nuclear weapons.

Ivashko's promotion to Moscow led to his replacement by Stanislav Hurenko as First Secretary, and Leonid Kravchuk, the CPU ideology secretary, became Chairperson of the Supreme Rada. In October 1990 a mass movement of students, including a two-week hunger strike, forced the resignation of the Chairperson of the Council of Ministers, Vitalii Masol. Opposition parties began to be formed: the UHU became the Ukrainian Republican Party (URP), the reform Communists in the Democratic Platform established the Party of the Democratic Revival of Ukraine (PDRU) and some cultural leaders from *Rukh* established the Democratic Party of Ukraine (DPU). Kravchuk sought to contain the burgeoning national movement, imprisoning the radical people's deputy Stepan Khmara, but pursued the challenge to the Gorbachev centre on his own terms. In November 1990 Kravchuk and Yeltsin as leaders of Ukraine and the RSFSR signed a treaty recognising each other's territorial integrity and promising to develop bilateral relations without the centre.

The growth of Ukrainian nationalism alarmed the leaders of the Crimea. This was the only *oblast'* in Ukraine with a Russian majority (67 per cent in 1989, with 26 per cent Ukrainian). Moreover, under Nikolai Bagrov the *oblast'* soviet was a bulwark of Communist conservatism. The region's resorts were favourite summer haunts for the Soviet élite. In January 1991 the *oblast'* voted by 93 per cent in a referendum to seek the status of an Autonomous Soviet Socialist Republic within Ukraine. Kravchuk accepted this and allowed the new republic its own constitution, with Russian as the state language.

Also in January 1991, Soviet forces attempted to crack down on supporters of independence in Vilnius and Riga. This split the Ukrainian Communists, with Hirenko favouring a hard line but Kravchuk backing the Baltic governments. A large minority of the Communists in the Supreme Rada backed Kravchuk, who proceeded to build a new coalition of these 'national Communists', favouring Ukrainian sovereignty, and the national–democratic opposition (then known as the People's Council).

Seeking a renewed mandate, Gorbachev held a Union-wide referendum in March 1991 on whether the USSR should continue. Kravchuk's coalition succeeded in posing a second question on the ballot paper, asking whether Ukraine should belong to the Union on the basis of the Ukrainian sovereignty declaration. On an 83 per cent turnout, 70.5 per cent said that they favoured maintenance of the Union, while 80 per cent expressed their support for the sovereignty declaration. This result was open to misinterpretation, but it is clear that while it was a victory for advocates of Ukrainian sovereignty, the majority of the population wished to remain in the Soviet Union. An exception to this was Galicia, where a third question was posed, showing 88 per cent in favour of independence. Thereafter, in the negotiations between Gorbachev and nine Soviet republics over a new Union Treaty, Ukraine argued for a maximum of decentralisation, with the republics taking over Union property and having their own armies, and the Union being denied the right to raise its own taxation.

## INDEPENDENT UKRAINE UNDER KRAVCHUK

Kravchuk avoided condemning the August 1991 Moscow coup until it appeared likely to be defeated, and he came under fire for his hesitation from nationalists and democrats in Ukraine. On 24 August, however, three days after the collapse of the coup, he organised the passage through the Supreme Rada of a Ukrainian declaration of independence, conditional on its confirmation in a referendum on 1 December. The end of the coup was the signal for declarations of independence by nationalists in the Baltic States and by Communists in Central Asia and Azerbaijan. The latter hoped to hang on to power in their own republics even while the Communists were defeated in Russia itself. Kravchuk's stance seemed to have parallels with this, although he banned the CPU and continued his alliance with moderate Ukrainian nationalists. From 24 August onwards Kravchuk rejected any attempt to recreate either a political or an economic union to replace the USSR. Thus he not only opposed Gorbachev's efforts to create a Union of Sovereign States, but also ensured that the Supreme Rada repudiated the plan for an economic union which was initialed by the Chairperson of the Council of Ministers, Vitold Fokin, on 6 November.

Elections for the new post of President of Ukraine were held on the same day as the referendum. Like Yeltsin and unlike Gorbachev, Kravchuk sought to gain the legitimacy conferred by popular direct election. He won easily with 61.6 per cent; his nearest rival was Chornovil, the official *Rukh* candidate, with 23.3 per cent. In the independence vote, an overwhelming 90.3 per cent voted 'Yes'. The turnout of 84 per cent in the election and referendum reflected the high level of political mobilisation. Every *oblast'* voted 'Yes'; even the Crimea voted 54 per cent for Ukrainian independence, while the next lowest 'Yes' vote was Lugansk *oblast'*, which despite its 45 per cent Russian minority voted 83 per cent for independence.[12]

The attraction of ethnic Russians to the banner of independence was due to Kravchuk's promotion of a territorial and non-ethnic form of nationalism; it was the Ukrainian state that was being built up, and membership of the state was open to all nationalities: Ukrainian, Russian, Jewish or any other. Unlike Estonia and Latvia, but like the majority of the post-Soviet states, in October the Supreme Rada gave Ukrainian citizenship to all Soviet citizens residing in the republic. The Declaration of the Rights of the Nationalities of Ukraine, passed in November, promised official status for the language of ethnic minorities (including Russians) in selected territories.[13] Preparations for the establishment of Ukrainian armed forces began with the August declaration of independence. It was symptomatic of the non-ethnic nature of the Ukrainian state that the first Ukrainian Minister of Defence, Konstantin Morozov, appointed on 4 September, was a Russian, as indeed was the Chairperson of the Council of Ministers, Fokin. Nor was there any attempt to promote the Ukrainian language in the Crimea or in the eastern parts of Ukraine where the Russian language was dominant.

Kravchuk's victory reflected several other factors. He had stolen the programme of his nationalist rivals; he was actually implementing what Chornovil had called for. Chornovil, although respected for his suffering in Brezhnev's labour camps, was seen by many voters as too extreme, while Kravchuk, the former Communist ideologist, was seen as a pragmatist. Coming as he did from the Western Ukraine, it was probably easier for him to make the transition to a nationalist position. Most importantly, Kravchuk was able to use the traditional Communist means of control over the mass media, especially television, to ensure support for himself and his programme of independence. It is difficult to believe that without this control of the media it would have been possible to transform the clear (albeit qualified) support of the population for the Union, expressed in March 1991, to the dramatic support for independence in December.

At the same time Kravchuk made skilful use of, as well as being genuinely alarmed by, a growing Russian nationalism emanating from Yeltsin's circle: Russia taking over Union property, its insistence on naming key USSR ministers, and the statement by Yeltsin's press secretary, Pavel Voshchanov, in August 1991 that Russia would reserve the right to revise its borders with any republic (other than the Baltic States) that left the USSR. This veiled threat to the Crimea encouraged Ukrainians to rally round Kravchuk. Further, the economic chaos in the Soviet Union over the previous years which had inevitably engulfed Ukraine made independence enticing. Nor should one underestimate the role played by Ukrainian émigrés, brought up in Canada and the USA, who returned to Ukraine and argued that the republic would be economically better off if it were free of 'exploitation' by Russia. This argument focused on the richness of Ukrainian agriculture, but paid little attention to Ukraine's energy dependence on Russia. In reality the economies of both Russia and Ukraine had suffered by the distortions imposed by central planning and the priority of the defence industry.

As late as 25 November 1991 Gorbachev had declared: 'I cannot imagine a Union Treaty without Ukraine'.[14] Nor would Yeltsin's Russia accept a Union that included the less developed Central Asia but not Ukraine; it would imply an orientation away from Europe to Asia. On 5 December the Supreme Rada renounced the 1922 treaty that had created the USSR. The Ukrainian events transformed the situation in Moscow. Despite Yeltsin's proclaimed commitment to the Union, on 8 December he, Kravchuk and the Belarusian leader Stanislau Shushkevich announced the end of the USSR and the formation of the Commonwealth of Independent States. While the power struggle in Moscow between Yeltsin and Gorbachev was perhaps decisive in this process, the Ukrainian referendum at least served as a catalyst. Debate will continue as to the relative importance of Gorbachev's incompetence, Yeltsin's ambition and Kravchuk's cunning in the fall of the USSR. Gorbachev at the time accused Yeltsin of 'playing the Ukrainian card' to remove the central Union structures. It was clear, however, that whatever Yeltsin may have wished, Ukraine would not accept anything less than full independence. Kravchuk made it clear that the CIS could be neither a federation nor a confederation, but an association, a mechanism for civilised divorce; in February 1992 he called it 'a committee to liquidate the old structures'.[15] Since this time Ukraine has been the least enthusiastic member of the CIS (excluding Azerbaijan, which did not ratify its membership); through 1992 it opposed the setting-up of permanent structures, thus weakening the association, until a majority of the other members decided to draw up a security treaty and a Charter without Ukraine. On the other hand, Ukraine regularly attended the meetings of the CIS heads of state and heads of government. Kravchuk was having to balance between those in Ukraine who wanted to preserve as many of the economic links with the other CIS members as possible, and the nationalists, such as *Rukh*, the URP and DPU, who saw Ukraine's very membership in the Commonwealth as a betrayal of its independence.

The agreement to establish the CIS gave a boost to the development of what seemed to be the most prominent symbol of Ukrainian statehood, the armed forces. On 12 December 1991 Kravchuk nationalised the parts of the Soviet Army based in Ukraine, other than strategic forces; from January 1992 soldiers were required to swear an oath of loyalty to Ukraine. Less than half of these were ethnic Ukrainians, and over half the officers were ethnic Russians. Nevertheless the great majority swore the oath. For those who came from outside Ukraine, their shift in allegiance was undoubtedly due to the better housing and pay that Kravchuk promised, the fear of being involved in Caucasian wars if they transferred to CIS forces, and even the milder climate. None of these factors guaranteed their emotional loyalty to Ukraine, particularly in the event of a conflict with Russia. It was hardly surprising, then, that the Organisation of Officers of Ukraine, created in July 1991 by Ukrainian nationalist officers, called for the recruitment of ethnic Ukrainian officers serving outside Ukraine to join the Ukrainian Army and replace the non-Ukrainians. In response to this pressure, Kravchuk appointed ethnic Russians to leading posts in the Ministry of Defence, although Morozov was retained as Minister.[16]

In the economy, the Ukrainian government announced in October 1991 that Ukraine would assert its statehood by introducing its own currency, the *hryvnia*, the following year. As an interim measure, a coupon known as the *karbovanets* was introduced in January 1992. The introduction of the new currency was postponed because of the lack of reserves of foreign currency. Meanwhile, the Ukrainian economy could not fail to be affected by the Russian price liberalisation of January 1992, which threatened to suck in goods from, and export the rapid Russian inflation to, Ukraine. Output in Russia continued to fall; difficulties over payments between the two states disrupted trade and accelerated the fall in production in both countries. Ukrainian nationalist politicians advocated reducing economic links with Russia and leaving the rouble zone; but Western pressure at that time prevented the latter, while the former was happening despite the government's intentions. Fokin promised privatisation and liberalisation of the economy, and Ukrainian prices did follow Russian prices upwards, but the government was in reality unwilling to allow large enterprises to close.

The lack of adequate financial controls meant that the *karbovanets* was too weak to protect Ukraine from the consequences of Russian inflation. The Russian rouble ceased to be legal tender in Ukraine by autumn 1992, but the *karbovanets* fell against the dollar even faster than the rouble did in 1992–93. Indeed Ukraine was probably the only country in the world where the rouble was considered a hard currency. The market for Ukraine's arms industry was collapsing with the end of the USSR and there was little demand for Ukraine's agricultural produce, while on the other hand Ukraine was heavily dependent on Russia as a source of energy. With Russia moving towards world prices in its exports, Ukraine's economy was increasingly uncompetitive. Fokin's replacement by the missile factory director Leonid Kuchma as Prime Minister in September 1992 did not result in economic radicalism, as the political system became deadlocked between the President, the Prime Minister and the Supreme Rada. In November, however, Ukraine did leave the rouble zone.

Politically, from August 1991 Kravchuk relied for support in the building of Ukrainian statehood on a bloc composed of the bulk of the old *nomenklatura* – the national Communists – together with the more moderate parts of the former nationalist opposition. He succeeded in splitting *Rukh* by co-opting the more moderate wing. The national Communists, who renounced socialist ideas, were the dominant partners. The conservative or internationalist Communists formed the Socialist Party of Ukraine (SPU) in October 1991. For the moderate nationalists, the creation of a Ukrainian state was more important than the purging of the old Communists, and this led them to support Kravchuk while pushing him in a more nationalist (and anti-CIS) direction. The main moderate nationalist parties, the URP and the DPU, formed the Congress of National Democratic Forces (CNDF) in August 1992. A liberal bloc, New Ukraine, also for a time formed part of Kravchuk's coalition. Led by the PDRU and created in January 1992, this attracted support from the Russian technical intelligentsia and favoured the continuation of the CIS. In June 1992, however, it went into opposition over the slow pace of economic reform, forming a new alliance with *Rukh*. In February 1993 *Rukh* itself, under Chornovil's leadership, was registered as a political party, the largest in Ukraine. An interesting feature of this period was that, like Yeltsin in Russia, Kravchuk lacked a 'Presidential party' (although the CNDF was sometimes described as this); also like Yeltsin, he sought to replace the banned Communist apparatus in the *oblasti* by a network of prefects, appointed by himself. It was typical of Kravchuk's approach that the bulk of these people came from the old apparatus. At the same time, he attempted to build up a spiritual base by supporting the Ukrainian Catholics and the movement for Ukrainian autocephaly within the Orthodox Church.

Although the draft constitution published in July 1992 rejected the view of Chornovil, New Ukraine and some ethnic Russian leaders that Ukraine should become a federation, Kiev continued to promise to guarantee the rights of minorities. Leaving aside Western Ukraine, where differences with the rest of Ukraine are cultural and religious rather than ethnic, the regions where minorities are concentrated are Transcarpathia, Chernovtsy (Bukovina), the southern and eastern parts of Ukraine and the special case of Crimea. The Transcarpathian and Chernovtsy *oblasti* both voted in the December 1991 referendum for greater regional autonomy, while overwhelmingly backing Ukrainian independence. In Transcarpathia the sense of separate Ruthenian (Rusyn) identity continues to be strong, although there is little support for full independence or unification with Slovakia. The Beregszasz district of Transcarpathia, dominated by ethnic Hungarians, voted in favour of becoming a Magyar district. In September 1991 the Chernovtsy *Oblast'* Soviet had decided to allow the large Romanian (Moldavian) minority to use its native language in certain areas, but this has not undermined a degree of support for Romanian claims on Northern Bukovina.

In Southern and Eastern Ukraine (other than the Crimea) there is a Ukrainian majority but the urban Ukrainians are mainly Russian-speaking. Attempts to create a regional 'Novorossiia' identity in Odessa and southern Ukraine have fallen on deaf ears, while the SPU has had rather more support in the Donbass for its demands for protection of the rights of the Russian language and for regional autonomy. Russians form nearly half the population of the Donetsk and Lugansk *oblasti* in the Donbass, and dominate the towns.[17] Since there has been no threat from the centre to the use of the Russian language, and indeed ninety per cent of schoolchildren in the Ukrainian Donbass are taught in Russian,[18] the chances of the SPU's front organisations to mobilise the Russians on a cultural basis are limited. In June 1993, however, in response to a wave of price increases, Donbass miners and other workers went on strike, demanding a referendum of confidence in Kravchuk and the Supreme Rada and regional autonomy for Eastern Ukraine. A rally in Lugansk demanded the unification of Ukraine and Russia.[19] Kravchuk and the parliament were forced to agree to hold a confidence referendum.

Ethnic relations in the Crimea since August 1991 have been compli-cated by the support of leading Russian politicians, including Vice-President Aleksandr Rutskoi and the Russian Supreme Soviet, for the return of the Crimea to Russia, and by disputes between Russia and Ukraine over the future of the Black Sea Fleet, based in Sevastopol in the Crimea. The Crimean leadership responded to Ukrainian independence by declaring Crimean sovereignty in September 1991, while the Republican Movement of the Crimea advocated independence. Concessions from Kravchuk laid the basis for the approval of Ukrainian independence by a small majority in the Crimea in December, but Kravchuk's subsequent watering-down of these concessions under nationalist pressure led Bagrov to declare independence on 5 May 1992. This marked a major political crisis for Ukraine. Kravchuk ignored nationalist calls for the forcible dissolution of the Crimean Supreme Soviet, but threats of economic pressure made the Crimean leadership back down. Nevertheless on 21 May the Russian Supreme Soviet declared that Khrushchev's transfer in 1954 of the Crimea from the RSFSR to Ukraine was 'lacking juridical force'. This claim did not have the backing of Yeltsin and the Russian government; it was intended to embarrass them. It seems that when Yeltsin and Kravchuk met at Dagomys in June, they agreed that the Crimea would remain in Ukraine. After this a new *modus vivendi* was found between the Crimea and Kiev: the Crimea was allowed to have its own citizenship and flag and control over its resources, remaining a republic within Ukraine. Meanwhile, the Crimean Tatar Milli Majlis has become aligned with the Ukrainian side. In October 1992, following the destruction by the Crimean authorities of a Tatar shanty-town, 6,000 Tatars attacked the Supreme Soviet building in Simferopol.[20]

The Ukrainian claim to the Black Sea Fleet was a highly visible issue in Russian–Ukrainian relations after independence. The January 1992 agreement that 'strategic' forces would go to the CIS and 'non-strategic' to Ukraine foundered on disagreement on the meaning of 'strategic'. Yeltsin claimed that the Black Sea Fleet had always been Russian. The Ukrainian government tried to persuade crews to swear loyalty to Ukraine, but the commander and most of the fleet refused to do so. Most officers and men were Russians or Russified Ukrainians. Various agreements made by Yeltsin and Kravchuk in 1992 and 1993 on the division of the fleet encountered the resistance of the majority of the sailors, who wanted the fleet to remain united. There was talk of the possibility of dual citizenship for the sailors. In July 1993 the Russian Supreme Soviet declared that Sevastopol was legally part of the Russian Federation. Yeltsin and the Russian Foreign Ministry joined the Ukrainians in rejecting this declaration.[21]

The repeated claims on the Crimea made in Russia, although denounced by Yeltsin, have played into the hands of Ukrainian nationalists. Many Russians have found it difficult to accept the reality of Ukrainian independence; many, including part of the leadership, expect that Ukraine and Russia will reunite in the future. Russians who believe that the Crimea should be part of an independent Ukraine are in a minority. Ukrainian suspicion of Russia and the fear that Moscow may in future turn more aggressive have led the Supreme Rada to reconsider the non-nuclear status of Ukraine.

The Minsk agreement of 30 December 1991 stipulated that nuclear weapons in Ukraine would be under joint CIS control, with tactical weapons to be removed by July 1992 to Russia for dismantling, and strategic weapons by the end of 1994. In May 1992 the four former Soviet republics with nuclear weapons on their soil – Russia, Ukraine, Belarus and Kazakhstan – and the United States signed the Lisbon Protocol. Under this, Ukraine, Belarus and Kazakhstan agreed to sign the nuclear non-proliferation treaty (NPT) and to ratify the Strategic Arms Reduction Treaty (START-I) signed in 1991 by US President George Bush and Gorbachev. Afterwards, however, Ukraine met the deadline for the removal of tactical nuclear weapons but had second thoughts about its non-nuclear status. Although Belarus and Kazakhstan signed the NPT and ratified START-I, Ukraine held back. This caused anxiety in the West and in Russia. Some Ukrainian leaders appeared to be using the strategic missiles as a bargaining chip in the hope of attracting foreign aid. Others believed that Ukraine could increase its security and influence in Europe by holding on to the weapons. Ukrainian scientists were reportedly trying to discover the means to make the weapons operational without reference to Moscow.

## CONCLUSION

*Perestroika* unleashed the national–democratic movement in Ukraine and split the Ukrainian Communists. After the failure of the August 1991 Moscow coup, the national Communists declared the independence of Ukraine, in alliance with moderate nationalists. Like many of the former Soviet republics, Ukraine in the first years of independence remained under the domination of people from the former Communist *nomenklatura*. The new leaders, being pragmatists, defined Ukrainian statehood and citizenship on a territorial and non-ethnic basis. The policy of ethnic accommodation kept the national minorities quiescent and even supportive. In this and the avoidance of ethnic violence, Ukraine provided a positive model, in contradistinction to the wars breaking out elsewhere in the former Soviet Union and the disenfranchisement of Russian minorities in Estonia and Latvia.

Certainly, unlike the Estonians and Latvians, the Ukrainians never faced being outnumbered in their own republic by immigration. The spread of the Russian language has been halted, as Ukrainian has become the main language of political life in Kiev. On the other hand there has been no attempt by the Ukrainian leadership to exclude the use of the Russian language in areas where Russian-speakers form a majority. If this policy were to change, discontent would be likely among Russians and Russian-speaking Ukrainians. Assimilation into the Ukrainian nationality seems an unlikely outcome.

A more serious danger to ethnic relations is posed by the continuing economic crisis. The Ukrainian élite has maintained social peace by avoiding radical economic reforms of the type that would cause closure of the inefficient Soviet-built industries. The Donbass coal mines, in the context of the USSR, faced shutdown because of their high cost in comparison with those of Western Siberia. Unwilling to alienate the Russian miners, independent Ukraine kept them open. It seems inevitable, however, that with the danger of hyperinflation in Ukraine, Kiev will have to begin to implement a more radical programme. If, however unjustly, unemployment were perceived to be a consequence of independence, Russians in Ukraine might begin to agitate for either the partition of Ukraine, with certain regions joining Russia, or the unification of Ukraine as a whole with Russia. In view of the close cultural affinity between Russians and Ukrainians, it seems plausible that many Ukrainians, too, may come to question whether the cost of independence is too high.[22] It was partly to reduce these dangers, as well as to restore the Soviet-era economic links, that Kuchma in July 1993 agreed with the Russian and Belarusian prime ministers on the need for a 'common economic space' for the three Slav republics. Their declaration called for the free movement of goods and people between their countries.

In place of the promised referendum on confidence, Kravchuk and the Supreme Rada agreed to hold early parliamentary and presidential elections in 1994. The electoral law for the parliamentary vote, based solely on single-mandate constituencies, required a 50 per cent turnout and the winning contender to achieve a majority of votes cast in the first or second round. These stringent conditions meant that one quarter of the seats were left vacant after the elections, held in March and April 1994. Although just over half of the deputies stood as Independents, the elections were a victory for the parties of the Left, who accounted for two-thirds of the successful candidates proclaiming party allegiance. Within the Left, the dominant force was the Communist Party of Ukraine (CPU) which had only been allowed to form in October 1993. Openly committed to the restoration of the USSR, and appealing to Russians and Russian-speaking Ukrainians, the CPU won three-fifths of the seats in the Donbass and did well in other parts of Eastern Ukraine. The CPU cashed in on the backlash against the failure of Kravchuk's economic policy, on nostalgia for the relatively prosperous days of the Soviet period, on the view that Russian should be the second state language of Ukraine and on the desire for closer relations with Russia. Meanwhile the Ukrainian nationalists maintained their support in Western Ukraine.[23]

The principle challenger to Kravchuk in the presidential elections held in June and July 1994 was the former Prime Minister Kuchma.

Advocating the reintegration of the Ukrainian economy in the CIS and calling for Russian to be made an official language of Ukraine, Kuchma succeeded in winning 52 per cent of the vote in the second round against Kravchuk. Geographically, Ukraine was again deeply split, with the East supporting Kuchma and the West supporting Kravchuk. Russians and Russian-speakers were strongly in support of Kuchma.[24]

In power, however, Kuchma defended Ukraine's sovereignty within the CIS and further conciliated Western Ukraine by downplaying the role of the Russian language and himself speaking Ukrainian (which he had learned very quickly). Ukraine's international position had improved with the agreement in Moscow in January 1994 at a trilateral summit of Kravchuk, Yeltsin and US President Bill Clinton that Ukraine would give up all its nuclear weapons in exchange for Western aid. This agreement was ratified by the new parliament and in December 1994, at the Budapest summit of the Organisation for Security and Cooperation in Europe, Kuchma signed the nuclear non-proliferation treaty. Together with the trade and partnership agreement signed with the European Union, and Kuchma's commitment to beginning economic reform, this opened the way to expand Ukraine's westward economic and political links.

Strengthened internationally, Kuchma turned to the growing challenge from the Crimean Republic. Yuri Meshkov, elected President of the Crimea in January 1994, and the Crimean Supreme Soviet were seeking to upgrade Crimean autonomy and transform the relationship with Kiev into one based on bilateral treaties. In April 1995 Kuchma issued a decree taking over control of the Crimean government. Until then the Russian authorities had refused to intervene, but the head of the Crimean Supreme Soviet Sergei Tsekov came to the Russian State Duma to ask for support.[25] Following this, Yeltsin announced that he would not sign the friendship treaty between Russia and Ukraine until the autonomy of the Crimea was restored.

The attitude of Russia will also be important in the future of ethnic relations in Ukraine. It is unlikely that serious people in Moscow would wish to annex the Donbass, but the Crimea is a more attractive target. Undoubtedly, as long as Ukraine remains independent, and as long as the Crimea remains part of it, there will always be politicians in Russia who will seek to make political capital out of the Crimean question. It is entirely possible that a future Russian government will seek the return of not only Sevastopol but the Crimea as a whole. Such a situation would require not only the United Nations and European security structures to function better than they have been doing, but also the continuation of the tactful policies of the Ukrainian leadership towards the ethnic minorities.

# NOTES

1. For a historical overview see R. Szporluk 'The Ukraine and Russia' in R. Conquest (ed.) *The Last Empire: Nationality and the Soviet Future* (Stanford, CA: Hoover Institution Press 1986) pp. 151–182.
2. See R. Conquest *The Harvest of Sorrow: Soviet Collectivization and the Terror-Famine* (London: Hutchinson 1986).
3. J. E. Mace 'Famine and Nationalism in Soviet Ukraine' *Problems of Communism*, 33, No. 3 (May–June 1984), pp. 37–50.
4. *Vestnik statistiki* 1980, Nos 2 and 8; B. Krawchenko 'Ethno-Demographic Trends in Ukraine in the 1970s' in B. Krawchenko (ed.) *Ukraine after Shelest* (Edmonton: Canadian Institute of Ukrainian Studies, University of Alberta 1983), pp. 101–119; B. Lewytzkyj, *Politics and Society in Soviet Ukraine 1953–1980* (Edmonton: Canadian Institute of Ukrainian Studies, University of Alberta 1984), ch. 6; R. Szporluk 'The Ukraine and the Ukrainians' in Z. Katz (ed.) *Handbook of Major Soviet Nationalities* (New York: Free Press 1975), pp. 31–34.
5. I. Dzyuba *Internationalism or Russification?* (New York: Monad 1974).
6. Chornovil *The Chornovil Papers* (New York: McGraw-Hill 1968); M. Hayward (ed.) *Ferment in the Ukraine* (Woodhaven, NY: Crisis Press 1973); K. C. Farmer *Ukrainian Nationalism in the Post-Stalin Era: Myth, Symbols and Ideology in Soviet Nationality Policy* (The Hague: Nijhoff 1980); R. Solchanyk 'Politics and the National Question in the Post–Shelest Period', and B. Nahaylo, 'Ukrainian Dissent and Opposition after Shelest', in Krawchenko, *Ukraine after Shelest*, pp. 1–29 and 30–54; Lewytzkyj, *Politics and Society*, passim.
7. Bilinsky 'Shcherbytskyi, Ukraine and Kremlin Politics' *Problems of Communism*, 32, No. 4 (July–August 1983), pp. 1–20.
8. For the proceedings of the UWU Plenum and the Politburo resolution, see *Soviet Ukrainian Affairs*, Vol. 1, No. 3 (1987), pp. 8–27.
9. B. Nahaylo 'Mounting Opposition in the Ukraine to Nuclear Energy Program', *Radio Liberty Research Bulletin*, RL Supplement 1/88 (16 February 1988).
10. For documents of the UHU, see *The Ukrainian Review*, 36, No. 4 (Winter 1988), pp. 72–86.
11. Dzyuba 'A Time to Gather Stones' *Moscow News*, 15 January 1989.
12. Andrew Wilson 'Ukraine' *Russia and the Successor States Briefing Service*, Vol. 1, No. 1 (February 1993), p. 11.
13. B. Nahaylo, 'Ukraine' *RFE/RL Research Report*, Vol. 1, No. 27 (3 July 1992), p. 54.
14. M. S. Gorbachev *Dekabr'-91. Moia pozitisiia* (Moscow: Novosti 1992), p. 15.
15. Quoted in R. Solchanyk, 'Kravchuk Defines Ukrainian-CIS Relations', *RFE/RL Research Report*, 1, No. 11 (13 March 1992), p. 9.
16. Wilson, 'Ukraine', p. 29.
17. *Ibid.*, pp. 18–23.
18. R. Solchanyk, 'The Politics of Language in Ukraine', *RFE/RL Research Report*, 2, No. 10 (5 March 1993), p. 3.
19. J. Meek, 'Ukraine Strike Opens up Divisions', *The Guardian*, 14 June 1993.

20. Wilson, 'Ukraine', pp. 20–21.
21. Oborona Sevastopolia', *Nezavisimaia gazeta*, 13 July 1993.
22. V. Vyzhutovich, 'The National-State Idea is Collapsing in Ukraine', *Moscow News*, 23 July 1993.
23. This draws from D. Arel & A. Wilson, 'The Ukrainian Parliamentary Elections', *RFE/RL Research Report*, Vol. 3, No. 26 (1 July 1994), pp. 6–17.
24. D. Arel & A. Wilson, 'Ukraine under Kuchma: Back to "Eurasia"?' *ibid.*, No. 32 (19 August 1994), pp. 1–12.
25. P. Zhuravlev, 'Sergei Tsekov vozzval k Dume', *Segodnya*, 15 April 1995.

# CHAPTER ELEVEN

# Belarus and the Belarusians

Ralph Clem

The Belarusian people, who since medieval times have inhabited the region that bears their name today, were one of the largest ethnic groups in the former Soviet Union, yet also one of the least known.[1] To a large extent the relatively low visibility of Belarusians can be attributed to historical and geographical circumstances which combined to retard their coalescence into a modern nation. In the present century, however, despite the trauma of revolution and war, the Belarusians underwent a profound ethnogenesis and developed into one of the major nationalities of the USSR, a process that to an appreciable – although perhaps unintended – extent resulted from the manner in which the Soviet government dealt with the question of ethnicity. Now, having emerged from the disintegration of the Soviet Union with a sovereign state, Belarus, the Belarusians are entering yet another phase in their long and often difficult history, a phase in which the opportunities and costs of independence will condition their further ethno-cultural growth.

## BACKGROUND

Belarus' location has influenced its historical, political and social development, and not always positively. Bordered on the east by Russia, on the south by Ukraine, on the west by Poland, and on the north by Lithuania and Latvia, Belarus has been at one of the crossroads of European history and has suffered accordingly. Thus situated among more powerful and often aggressive neighbours, Belarus is also positioned on one of the principal East–West transportation routes (Warsaw and Vilnius through Minsk to Smolensk and on to Moscow); Napoleon invaded Russia by this route in 1812, as did Guderian and his panzers in 1941.

The indigenous people of this region, the Belarusians, are descended from Slavic tribes that migrated into the area from Central Europe, apparently during the sixth century AD. By the ninth century, principalities subordinate to the Kievan state (in what is now Ukraine) had been established in Belarus; internecine conflict among these was characteristic of the era. The Mongol invasion of the mid-thirteenth century destroyed Kiev, and in the power vacuum that followed Belarus was annexed by the Grand Duchy of Lithuania to the north. Thus began a period of over 400 years during which Belarus was dominated by Lithuania and – after their union in 1569 – by Poland. This separation of Belarus from Slavic lands to the east (Russia) and south (Ukraine) began a long process of divergent linguistic and cultural development which ultimately led to the evolution of the Belarusians as a distinct ethnic group.[2]

With the rise of Russian hegemony in the late eighteenth century, Belarus found itself at the mercy of its expansionist neighbour to the east. During the reign of Catherine the Great, a weakened Polish state was dismembered in a series of partitions (1772, 1793 and 1795), with Russia obtaining all the Belarusian provinces. Incorporated into the Russian empire, Belarus became an integral part of the tsarist state, and was subject to the influence of the Russianisation policies of the time.[3] From 1859 to 1906 Belarusian language publications and the use of Belarusian as the medium of instruction in schools were banned. As a consequence, Belarusian cultural activities were poorly developed in the last years of the *ancien régime*, although the poets Yanka Kapala, Yakov Kolas and others laid the foundation for a national literature, and at least one newspaper in the Belarusian language was in publication.[4] Furthermore, the social and agrarian economic order that had existed in Belarus was largely intact; although Russians had assumed a greater role in the Belarusian provinces, Poles and Jews predominated in the cities, while ethnic Belarusians remained almost exclusively peasants.[5]

The evolution of modern Belarusian nationalism is closely linked to the unsettled political conditions in eastern Europe and Russia in the early twentieth century, and to the ethnic stratification system which placed the indigenous Belarusians at the bottom of the socio-economic ladder and largely outside the small modernising sector of their homeland. Although it is clear that some indicators of Belarusian ethnogenesis were in evidence by the turn of the century (for example, the beginnings of a national literature), it was only in 1902 that a small political organisation was founded (the Belarusian Socialist Hromada) which espoused Belarusian autonomy.[6] During the chaos of the First World War, Russian Revolution and Civil War, and the Russo-Polish War of 1919–20, the Belarusian nationalists were overwhelmed by events, having found it impossible to establish a viable ethnic separatist movement in the face of military occupation by German, Polish and Red forces and the manoeuvring of larger political parties (especially the Russian Communists). Although a Belarusian nationalist council (the Rada) came into existence in the summer of 1917, it had little popular support and its declaration of independence in December 1917 was of no real importance.[7]

In a penetrating analysis of the antecedents of Belarusian nationalism, Stephen Guthier demonstrated that the socio-economic and demographic conditions in Belarus during the late nineteenth and early twentieth centuries contributed to this lack of enthusiasm for the Belarusian nationalist cause.[8] Although a large number of people (5.7 million) identified themselves as speakers of the Belarusian language in the 1897 tsarist census (there was no question in this enumeration about ethnic affiliation *per se*), and despite the fact that Belarusian speakers composed a majority or plurality in several provinces and districts, the Belarusians were not well positioned for the development of a national consciousness of sufficient strength to withstand the external pressures occasioned by the troubled times.[9] Significantly, because virtually all (98 per cent) of Belarusians were rural or small town dwellers, they were isolated from the politically dynamic urban environment. Furthermore, in their own homeland Belarusians were vastly under-represented in the skilled professions and intelligentsia (which typically provides the core of nationalist movements), and very few Belarusians could read and write (which cut off the majority from ethnic literature and newspapers). Finally, Belarus itself lacked a political centre (or primate city) to act as a focal point for the nationalist cause.[10]

Out of the upheavals of the first quarter of this century, however, emerged a geographical entity that would at last provide a framework within which a Belarusian identity could coalesce. At the conclusion of the Russo-Polish War, the Treaty of Riga (1921) divided Belarusian lands between a newly independent Poland and the fledgling Soviet state. In the following year, the establishment of the Union of Soviet Socialist Republics as a federation of ethno-territorial units brought into existence the Belorussian Soviet Socialist Republic (BSSR); in the next few years the territory of the BSSR was expanded to include almost all areas of Belarusian settlement in the part of Belarus that was then within the USSR. The geographical denouement of the BSSR occurred in 1939 when the western part of Belarus (which had been ceded to inter-war Poland) was annexed by the Soviet Union (and retained by it as part of the BSSR following the Second World War).

The period between the wars witnessed the gradual development of an indigenous socio-economic infrastructure in Belarus, and not coincidentally, the growth of a Belarusian ethnic identity. The principal reason for the increased vitality of Belarusian nationalism was the existence of a legitimate ethno-territory (the BSSR) and a primate city (the capital, Minsk), coupled with official approval and even encouragement of non-Russian ethnic consciousness in the USSR during the 1920s. For example, between 1927 and 1938 the number of books published in the Belarusian language increased from 1.3 to 12.3 million, and was accompanied by a rise in literacy.[11] Even though the 'nativisation' and 'flowering of nationalities' policies were later reversed in the Stalin era, the effect was to abet ethnic groups (such as the Belarusians) in their critical formative stage.

In demographic terms, the number of Belarusians grew comparatively little between the tsarist census of 1897 (5.7 million) and the first Soviet census, conducted in 1926 (6.1 million), although it should be noted that both figures are tainted by technical problems.[12] Ethnic Belarusians in the USSR were overwhelmingly concentrated in the BSSR territory (81.2 per cent in 1897 and 82.9 per cent in 1926), where they composed just over 71 per cent of the population in 1897, a figure that declined to about 66 per cent by 1926.[13] Jews were a major presence in Belarus in 1897 and 1926, especially in urban areas (where they accounted for about half of the population), and Poles were also prominent in the region's population. Significantly, by 1926 the Belarusian share of the urban component of the BSSR had almost doubled since the late nineteenth century, reflecting the initial stage of the formation of a modernised Belarusian population. Nevertheless, the overall level of urbanisation for the Belarusians was still far below the national average, both because the BSSR itself was relatively unurbanised and due to the presence of large numbers of Jews, Poles, and Russians in the cities of the republic. In terms of other socio-economic characteristics, Guthier points to a pronounced increase in literacy among Belarusians in the 1897–1926 period, as well as their further integration into the professions.[14]

The interval between the censuses of 1926 and 1939 is of considerable interest as regards the maturation of the Belarusian ethnic group, because during this time the processes of industrialisation and urbanisation were accelerated by the Soviet Five Year Plans, which in turn set in motion massive social change. Data from the 1939 census indicate that the changes underway in the 1920s continued through the remainder of the inter-war years, with further increases in the level of urbanisation among Belarusians and in literacy (especially in rural areas of the BSSR).[15]

## DEMOGRAPHIC AND SOCIO-ECONOMIC TRENDS IN BELARUS IN THE WAR AND POST-WAR ERA

Both the ravages of the Second World War and rapid post-war economic development were to alter the socio-economic and ethno-demographic landscape of Belarus, the latter propelling the Belarusian people towards a more modernised status (with all that that implies for their future evolution as a nationality).

It is not possible to state with any precision the magnitude of population losses that occurred in Belarus or among the Belarusian people during the Second World War. The entire territory of the BSSR was held by German forces for almost three years, and suffered considerably in both human and material terms from combat action and a protracted partisan campaign. It was feasible, however, to estimate the demographic impact of the war in absolute numbers and relative to other areas of the USSR. Soviet sources put the population of the BSSR in 1939 (in current borders) at 8.9 million, and gave the 1951 population for the same area as only 7.8 million.[16] If one projects the 1939 population forward to 1951 at the growth rate that obtained between 1926 and 1939, then a shortfall of approximately 2.7 million persons results between the expected and observed figures. Looked at another way, the BSSR did not regain its 1939 population until 1969. Owing to the effects of the war, Belarus lost a greater percentage of its population than any other region of the USSR; between 1939 and 1951, the population of Belarus declined by 12.7 per cent, while that of Ukraine dropped by 8 per cent and that of the entire USSR fell by 4.7 per cent.[17]

As a result of the severity and atrocities of the German occupation, as well as population movements that followed the realignment of international borders in eastern Europe after the war, the ethnic composition of Belarus was radically altered. First, the once large Jewish population was virtually annihilated by the Germans or, in lesser numbers, was evacuated to other areas of the Soviet Union.[18] Second, many Poles moved from western Belarus (formerly part of inter-war Poland) to Poland proper as the Soviet–Polish border was shifted to the west. Also, at the same time some ethnic Belarusians probably migrated from Poland and Lithuania to the BSSR. Finally, many more Russians moved into the BSSR in the post-war period to take up positions vacated by those that were killed or displaced and to serve as cadres for the recovery effort (and perhaps also to provide an ethnic Russian presence in this important non-Russian frontier region of the USSR).

Consequently, by 1959 (the first post-war census in the USSR) the Belarusians composed a much larger share of the population of the BSSR than had been the case in the pre-war era. Conversely, the proportion of Jews and Poles declined precipitously. These changes were even more pronounced in cities of the republic, where Belarusians increased from about a third to over two-thirds of the urban population, with the Russians accounting for another fifth.

After 1959, as the pace of economic development quickened in Belarus, the Belarusian people were drawn increasingly into the republic's modernised sector. The best evidence of this phenomenon is the continued growth of the urban population of the BSSR and of the proportion of Belarusians living in cities. In the first instance, the level of urbanisation in the BSSR rose at a rate higher than the national average from 1959 to 1970 and again from 1970 to 1979.[19] Likewise, the data for the Belarusian ethnic group indicated intensified urbanisation (in 1959, about a third of Belarusians were urban, whereas by 1979 over half lived in cities) and further growth in their share of the BSSR's urban population.[20] Guthier attributed these trends to a strong demand for labour in the cities generated by rapid economic growth (industrial output expanded three-fold from 1959 to 1970) and the vacuum created by the loss of the urban Jewish population, a demand that attracted hundreds of thousands of ethnic Belarusians from the countryside.[21]

The development of Belarus' economy also produced changes in the workforce and occupational characteristics of the Belarusian people. As recently as 1959, well over half of all Belarusians were collective farmers, a figure that declined to under a fifth by 1979. In comparison with Ukrainians and Russians, over this period the Belarusians overtook the former and closed the gap on the latter in terms of social class distribution.[22]

The final aspect of social change among the Belarusian people that we shall examine is educational attainment. Although they have shown marked improvement in recent decades, the Belarusians did not fare as well in education as have many other nationalities of the former Soviet Union. Despite ranking seventh among the fifteen union republic nationalities in the increase in level of schooling achieved from 1959 to 1979, the Belarusians remained in tenth place in educational attainment in 1979 (they were tied with the Uzbeks for ninth in 1959). Thus, although the Belarusians may have made progress in education, they only just kept pace with the rising national average and remained below it as of 1979. This situation was unlikely to change dramatically in the 1980s due to the chronic under-representation of Belarusians in higher education institutions. In 1970, age-adjusted data for participation in higher education in the USSR revealed that the Belarusians ranked 14 out of 15 union republic nationalities, with only about half the rate of the highest ranking group (Georgians).[23] However, Belarusians were much better represented in specialised secondary schools in the 1970s.

In summary, the period following the Second World War was one in which the BSSR and the Belarusian people underwent large-scale modernisation and social change. Of particular note were the rapid changes in urbanisation and social class composition for both the republic and the Belarusian ethnic group. In other aspects of socio-economic status, such as participation in the specialised workforce and education, the Belarusians made major strides, but lagged behind other regions and nationalities. The overall record was thus mixed, but certainly attested to the advancement of the Belarusians and their position in Soviet society.

# ACCULTURATION AND ASSIMILATION OF BELARUSIANS

Just as the maturation of a modern Belarusian nationality was tied to the existence of a political entity within which the group could modernise and develop the sustaining elements of a viable ethnic identity, the post-Second World War era has also been one in which the Belarusians have been increasingly subject to the ethnically disruptive forces of rapid social change. Many analysts view the situation in the 1960s and later as another watershed for Belarusian nationalism, pointing to steady – or possibly accelerating – erosion of ethnic cohesion (i.e. acculturation) among Belarusians since that time, an erosion which, if unchecked, leads to the loss of individuals through ethnic re-identification (or assimilation). Indeed, it appears from the available evidence (which is incomplete) that large numbers of Belarusians assimilated to the Russian nationality in the first half of this century.[24] Most recently, the relatively strong propensity for Belarusians to acculturate and assimilate became extremely important demographically because losses from ethnic re-identification compound the already low rate of natural population growth characteristic of the group.

It is generally believed that the linguistic and cultural affinity between Belarusians and Russians facilitated the acculturation and possibly the assimilation of the former by the latter during the Soviet period. Soviet census figures on native language adherence, often employed to study acculturation trends, indicated that Belarusians had the lowest level of native language loyalty among the fourteen non-Russian union republic nationalities, and also ranked first in knowledge of Russian as a second language. Furthermore, the extensive social mobilisation experienced by Belarusians had, ironically, often resulted in their acculturation through the effects of urbanisation and migration to areas outside Belarus; these two tendencies led to greater inter-ethnic contacts and higher rates of inter-marriage with non-Belarusians, both of which are linked to acculturation.[25] During the Soviet period, acculturation was also typically more in evidence among younger Belarusians, which suggests that the phenomenon was progressing as the generations changed.

# BELARUS IN THE 1980s; PROSPERITY AND DISCONTENT

The 1980s witnessed both a continuation of the rapid socio-economic modernisation of Belarus and the emergence in that republic of an incipient nationalist movement, the latter having been something of a surprise in the light of the supposed relatively inert status of ethnic consciousness among Belarusians.

Belarus was one of the leading economic growth regions of the USSR during the 1980s. In terms of growth in produced national income per capita, the BSSR ranked first among the fifteen republics for the decade of the 1980s.[26] Perhaps even more importantly, Belarus ranked third (behind Estonia and Latvia) in the growth of labour productivity in the 1980s, a significant point given the needed emphasis in the late Soviet period on productivity growth as a means of compensating for declining capital investment.[27] The relative strength of Belarus' economy in the 1980s was due to several factors; the republic received comparatively large amounts of capital investment; its industry mix (machinery, chemicals, textiles, electronics and computers) was more favourable for a technologically modernising economy than in most areas of the USSR; its central location vis-à-vis eastern Europe (a disadvantage in earlier, unsettled times) and the densely populated and developed western and Baltic regions of the USSR; and an extensive transportation network (railroads and pipelines in particular), all served to promote development in the BSSR.

These positive economic indicators translated into beneficial trends for both wages and the standard of living in Belarus: whereas the republic was previously disadvantaged in these respects, major gains were made in the 1980s. For example, in 1960 Belarus ranked fourteenth and fifteenth among the republics in blue-collar and white-collar wages in the urban and rural sectors; by 1987 its position had improved to eighth and seventh respectively.[28] In terms of living standards, Gertrude Schroeder found that Belarus had made tremendous strides forward, moving from ninth place among the fifteen republics in real per capita consumption in 1960 to sixth place in 1985, with consumption in the BSSR above the national average for the first time.[29] Demographic evidence also attested to Belarus' improved circumstances: in 1990, the BSSR had the second lowest infant mortality rate in the USSR.[30] The level of urbanisation continued to grow rapidly, such that by 1991 over two-thirds of the republic's population lived in urban areas.[31] Also, the republic changed from a negative to a positive migration balance in the 1980s, a reflection of the greater demand for labour created by the economic growth mentioned above, the low rate of increase in the indigenous workforce, and the general tendency for people to move to or remain in regions of relative prosperity.[32]

Somewhat paradoxically, as the economic situation in Belarus improved into the late 1980s, the first evidence of a revitalised Belarusian nationalism came to light, manifesting in the same manner as had similar movements elsewhere in the USSR (albeit later). Under the more permissive social and political climate engendered by the Gorbachev administration (i.e. the politics of glasnost' and democratisation), informal (or 'patriotic') groups with varying agendas sprang up in Belarus, espousing linguistic, cultural, historical, environmental, and other concerns. Foremost among these organisations were Talaka (Mutual Aid) and Tuteishyia ('the Locals', a term used in tsarist times to refer to the inhabitants of Belarus) which, together with smaller groups, sought to promote a revival of the Belarusian language, literature, and ethnic consciousness.[33] Individual groups typically adopted specific causes, ranging from the posting of signs in Belarusian in the Minsk metro to the termination of nuclear power station construction (Belarus was severely affected by the Chernobyl reactor accident, with large areas contaminated by radioactivity and resultant serious health problems among the republic's population), but the issues raised had in common the theme of greater involvement of the Belarusian people in the affairs of their nationality homeland. One prominent example of how these unofficial groups brought to the public eye matters of popular concern was the exposure of crimes of the Stalin era, notably the uncovering of mass graves of as many as 30,000 victims of the NKVD in the Kurapaty woods; many of those killed were prominent Belarusian writers and intellectuals, whose demise is now portrayed as an atrocity against the Belarusian people.[34]

Though small in membership, these informal associations, composed mainly of young people and members of the intelligentsia, exerted a significant influence on the social and political life of the republic. Initially, the authorities took a strong stance against the proliferaion of unofficial groups, and suppressed the first such club, *Spadcyna* ('Heritage') in December 1986.[35] Subsequent attempts to stage public rallies in Belarus were blocked or disrupted by the police or those presumed to be acting on their orders (sometimes violently). Likewise, when Belrusian independent youth organisations attempted to arrange a conference in Minsk in January 1989, officials restricted their use of facilities and otherwise obstructed their plans to the point that the organisers moved the meeting to Vilnius, where they were welcomed by the Lithuanian *Sajudis* popular movement.[36]

In this particular case, the authorities no doubt erred in forcing the issue, as the effect of their intransigence was to facilitate greater interaction between the Belarusian groups and those in more politically active Lithuania. In fact, Belarusian informal groups were represented for the first time at the fifth meeting of representatives of non-Russian national–democratic movements in Vilnius in late January 1989, an indication of the growing ties between popular front organisations in Belarus and those in other republics.[37]

A significant occurrence in this unfolding drama took place in February 1989, when over 50,000 people attended a rally in Minsk organised by the Renewal Belarusian Popular Front for Perestroika, a confederation of informal organisations. On this occasion the event proceeded peacefully amid the display of the traditional Belarusian national flag and the nationalist 'Pahonya' symbol (a mounted knight). Although much smaller than similar demonstrations in the Baltic and Caucasian republics at the time, the rally proved that there was sufficient interest in the cause of Belarusian ethnicity to mobilise an appreciable number of people in a direct challenge to the political leadership of the republic.[38] Yet, as the Soviet Union entered the 1990s destablised by events in the Baltic republics and in Moscow itself, Belarus was certainly not in the forefront of the movement for change. Regardless, it would be swept along by the current and into the post-Soviet era.

## INDEPENDENCE AND ITS IMPLICATIONS

In the pivotal year of 1991, the dramatic political changes wrought by the unleashing of nationalism in the USSR brought to the fore the question of independence for Belarus, but not without considerable hesitancy and mixed results. As central authority steadily eroded in the USSR of 1990–91, the Belarusian leadership remained one of the most resistant to reform, and evidence of large-scale support for independence was clearly lacking; in the all-Union referendum of March 1991 on the preservation of the USSR, 83 per cent of those voting in the BSSR favoured maintaining the status quo.[39] However, later that spring the steadily deteriorating economic conditions brought on by Gorbachev's reform measures triggered numerous strikes and protests against rising prices, and the public mood shifted rapidly against the government. As the disgruntled workers organised and began to press for major demands, including an end to the monopoly of power by the Communist Party, the authorities responded by increasing wages and successfully blocked action against the Party in the republic's Supreme Soviet.[40]

The aborted coup of 19 August 1991 was a catalyst for change in Belarus, as it was everywhere in the USSR. The conservative Communist leadership in Belarus vacillated sufficiently to enable their political survival once it was clear that the coup attempt had failed, and then positioned themselves for the transition to independence by embracing Belarusian statehood. The Supreme Soviet of Belarus declared its independence on 25 August, adopted the new name Republic of Belarus on 19 September, and in quick succession passed a new law on citizenship and elected Stanislav Shushkevich, a moderate nationalist, as chairman of the Supreme Soviet. However, the Belarusian government continued to be dominated by former Communists, including Prime Minister Vyacheslav Kebich, and as a consequence remained closely tied to Russia and later was instrumental in the establishment of the Commonwealth of Independent States.[41]

For the foreseeable future, the key political issue for Belarus will be the nature of its relationship with Russia. Nationalists and democrats, still in a minority in the Supreme Soviet, urge a more independent stance, while the former Communists favour close ties. Belarus has since its independence sought greater integration into European affairs and has expanded its diplomatic links both in Europe and elsewhere.[42] But in light of the difficult economic situation, in September 1993 Belarus entered into a pact with Russia and Ukraine to establish an economic union, suggesting that necessity dictates the maintenance of a pro-Russian alignment.[43] A substantial ethnic Russian minority in Belarus (13.2 per cent of the 1989 population) is another factor in this calculation, although the Russian irredentist issue has not yet materialised to the degree that it has in Estonia, Ukraine or Kazakhstan. A secondary but critical concern is the need to legitimise the political system, since both the government and the Supreme Soviet are largely relics of the Soviet period. Finally, the slow pace of economic reform, understandable in light of the continuing presence of so many former Communists in the government, means that whereas Belarus has experienced less of a decline in its economy than the other countries of the former Soviet Union, it has not yet taken the painful steps required to make the transition to a market economy. Whether this strategy will be more successful than the 'shock therapy' programme begun in Russia (and later reined in) remains to be seen.[44] The ousting of Shushkevich in January 1994 and his replacement by Mechislav Grib, a former security official, presages a major retreat from reform and suggests that even closer economic and military ties with Russia will soon be in place.

Yet the future of Belarus and of the Belarusian people remains tied in the first instance to the question of its legitimacy as a state, especially to whether or not the concept of a nation-state is viable in the minds of its citizens. That remains an open question, in contrast to the Baltic countries, or Russia, or even Ukraine, and at this juncture one cannot rule out an eventual political reunion with Russia should independence prove unsatisfying politically and economically. Over the course of this century the Belarusian people have endured considerable hardship and emerged from the Soviet era with a separate but perhaps not vibrant ethnic identity. The strength of this identity will now be tested in the crucible of economic crisis and political uncertainty.

## NOTES

1. In keeping with the usage adopted after independence in 1991, the terms Belarus and Belarusians are used throughout in place of the former Belorussia and Belorussians, except where reference is made to the former Belorussian Soviet Socialist Republic. The term 'Belarusian' or 'Belorussian' literally means 'White Russian', but should not be confused with the 'White' (i.e. counter-revolutionary) element of the Russian Civil War period. The Belarusian language belongs to the Slavonic group and is linguistically akin to Russian and Ukrainian. See Bernard Comrie *The Languages of the Soviet Union* (Cambridge, Cambridge Univeristy Press 1981), pp. 144–46.
2. Jan Zaprudnik 'Belorussia and the Belorussians' in Zev Katz (ed.)

*Handbook of Major Soviet Nationalities* (New York, Free Press 1975), pp. 50–2.

3. Hugh Seton-Watson *The Russian Empire, 1801–1917* (Oxford, Oxford University Press 1967), pp. 45–6, 49–50, 191.

4. Zaprudnik 'Belorussia and the Belorussians', *The Russian Empire*, p. 609; Roman Szporluk 'West Ukraine and West Belorussia' *Soviet Studies* 31 (1) (Jan. 1979), pp. 89–90.

5. Steven L. Guthier 'The Belorussians: national identification and assimilation, 1897–1970' *Soviet Studies* 29 (1) (Jan. 1977), pp. 40–8.

6. Richard Pipes *The Formation of the Soviet Union* (New York, Atheneum 1968), pp. 11–12.

7. Ibid., pp. 71–5. See also Nicholas Vakar *Belorussia: The Making of a Nation* (Cambridge, MA, Harvard University Press 1956), pp. 93–106.

8. Guthier, *op. cit.*, pp. 37–61: and in *Soviet Studies* 29 (2) (April 1977), pp. 270–83.

9. Robert A. Lewis, Richard H. Rowland and Ralph S. Clem *Nationality and Population Change in Russia and the USSR* (New York, Praeger 1976), p. 279.

10. Guthier, *op. cit.*, p. 43.

11. Ibid., Table 14, p. 59.

12. For a discussion of the enumeration procedures used, see Brian D. Silver 'The ethnic and language dimensions in Russian and Soviet censuses', in Ralph S. Clem (ed.) *Research Guide to the Russian and Soviet Censuses* (Ithaca, NY, Cornell University Press 1986), pp. 70–97. Population figures for 1897 and 1926 are from Lewis, Rowland, and Clem, *op. cit.*, p. 279.

13. Ibid., p. 412.

14. Guthier, *op. cit.*, pp. 54–5.

15. A. A. Isupov *Natsional'nyi Sostav Naseleniya SSSR* (Moscow, Statistika 1961), pp. 27–42; Guthier, *op. cit.*, p. 60.

16. USSR, Tsentral'noe Statisticheskoe Upravlenie, *Naselenie SSSR, 1973* (Moscow, Statistika 1975), pp. 10–11.

17. Calculated from *Naselenie, 1973*, pp. 10–11.

18. Eugene M. Kulischer *Europe on the Move* (New York, Columbia University Press 1948), p. 109, mentions that large numbers of Jews migrated from Belorussia to other areas of the USSR prior to the German invasion and may have, depending on their destination, survived.

19. The figures for Belarus are: 31% urban in 1959, 43% in 1970, and 55% in 1979.

20. By 1970 Belarusians accounted for 69% of Belarus' urban population.

21. Guthier, *Soviet Studies* 29 (2) (April 1977), 272–74.

22. Yu. V. Arutyunyan and Yu. V. Bromlei *Sotsial'no-Kulturnyi Oblik Sovetskikh Natsii* (Moscow, Nauka 1986), p. 55.

23. Ellen Jones and Fred W. Grupp 'Measuring nationality trends in the Soviet Union: a research note' *Slavic Review* 41 (1) (Spring 1982), Table 2, p. 117.

24. A Soviet study concluded that about 60,000 Belarusians living outside the BSSR may have assimilated to Russian nationality between 1926 and 1959. See A. A. Rakov *Naselenie BSSR* (Minsk 1969), p. 91, cited in Guthier, *Soviet Studies* 29 (2) (April 1977), pp. 276–77. See also Lewis, Rowland and Clem, *op. cit.*, p. 222.

25. Robert J. Kaiser 'National territorality in multinational, multi-homeland states: a comparative study of the Soviet Union, Yugoslavia and Czechoslovakia', Unpublished PhD dissertation, Columbia University, New York, 1988, pp. 310–34 and Appendix E, p. 390.
26. USSR, Goskomstat *Narodnoe Khozyaistvo SSSR b 1990 g.* (Moscow, Finansy i Statistika 1991), p. 12.
27. Ibid., p. 13.
28. USSR, Goskomstat *Trud v SSSR* (Moscow, Finansy i Statistika 1988), pp. 156–57.
29. Gertrude E. Schroeder 'Nationalities and the Soviet Economy' in Lubomyr Hajda and Mark A. Beissinger (eds) *The Nationalities Factor in Soviet Politics and Society* (Boulder, CO, Westview 1990), pp. 43–71.
30. USSR, *Narodnoe Khozyaistvo 1990*, p. 92.
31. 67.1%; Ibid., p. 71.
32. Projecting the BSSR's population forward based on birth and death rates in the republic indicates an apparent reversal of net migration from outward to inward around 1985. See Richard H. Rowland 'Union republic migration trends in the USSR during the 1980s' *Soviet Geography* 29 (9) (Nov. 1988), pp. 809–29.
33. Bohdan Nahaylo 'More signs of greater national assertiveness by Belorussians' *Radio Liberty Report* 22/88, 18 Jan. 1988.
34. Bohdan Nahaylo 'Political demonstration in Minsk attests to Belorussian national assertiveness' *Radio Liberty Report* RL 481/87, 26 Nov. 1987.
35. Ibid., p. 5.
36. 'They didn't reach agreement' *Pravda* 17 Jan. 1989, p. 3, translated in *Current Digest of the Soviet Press* 41 (3) (15 Feb. 1989), pp. 26–7.
37. Bohdan Nahaylo 'Non-Russian national-democratic movements adopt charter and issue appeal to Russian intelligentsia' *Report on the USSR* 1 (8) (24 Feb. 1989), pp. 15–17.
38. Kathleen Mihalisko '"Renewal" Belorussian Popular Front for Perestroika' *Report on the USSR* 1 (10) (10 March 1989), pp. 28–9. See also 'Belorussian "informal" groups gather in Minsk' *Krasnaya Zvezda* 22 Feb. 1989, p. 4, translated in *FBIS-Soviet Union Daily Report*, 9 March 1989, pp. 56–60.
39. Kathleen Mihalisko, 'The All-Union referendum in Belorussia' *Report on the USSR* 3 (13) (29 March 1991), pp. 7–9.
40. Kathleen Mihalisko 'Belorussia: Setting Sail Without a Compass' *RFE/RL Research Report* 1 (1) (3 Jan. 1992), pp. 39–41.
41. Ibid., pp. 40–41.
42. Kathleen Mihalisko 'The Outlook for Independent Belarus' *RFE/RL Research Report* 1 (24) (12 June 1992), pp. 7–13.
43. 'Heads of Government of Three Slavic Republics Agree on Integration Once Again' *Izvestiya* 13 July 1993, pp. 1–2, translated in *Current Digest of the Soviet Press* 45 (28) (1993), pp. 12–13.
44. James H. Noren 'The FSU Economies: First Year of Transition' *Post-Soviet Geography* 34 (7) (Sept. 1993), pp. 419–452. Of the 15 newly independent countries of the former USSR, Belarus had the third-smallest decline in industrial production, but did considerably worse in agriculture.

# CHAPTER TWELVE

# Moldova and the Moldovans

Jonathan Eyal and Graham Smith

The area between the Pruth, Danube and Dniester rivers, the territory of Bessarabia, was part of historic Moldova, one of the Danubian principalities overwhelmingly inhabited by Romanians. Moldova was traditionally disputed by the Ottoman and Russian empires: for the tsars, it meant access to the Danube and to the Balkans; for Constantinople it entailed a last line of defence against the traditional enemy to the north. On one issue, however, tsar and sultan were agreed: the Romanian population should not be allowed to have its own nation-state. The fact that this state did finally come into existence in the second half of the last century is due in no small measure to the ingenuity of Romanian nationalists, who were able to play off one neighbour against another and benefit from cessions of territory from all.

Bessarabia could not escape the Romanian struggle for independence and unity. Its acquisition by Russia in 1812 (when the Moldovan principality was still under nominal Ottoman suzerainty) was intended to be but the first step in a broad Russian plan to 'liberate' the Balkans.[1] Historical circumstances, however, dictated otherwise, and Bessarabia remained the only territory inhabited by Romanians under Russian control after Romania's independence. Although the territory of current Moldova does not correspond to the boundaries of historic Bessarabia, one factor remains unchanged: the majority of Moldova's inhabitants are still ethnic Romanians.

To be sure, the ethnic characterisation of any group is always a hazardous undertaking, for it depends on a multitude of factors which may converge into a separate ethnic identity. Yet in the case of the Moldovans, there can be no doubt, for, according to any conceivable definition of a nation, they can only be considered Romanians: they share exactly the same language, practise the same faith and have the same history. At every conceivable opportunity (in the 1870s, in 1918 and in 1941) the inhabitants of Moldova freely opted for union with Romania and considered themselves as Romanian. Furthermore – and despite persistent Russian or Soviet attempts to prove the contrary – Moldovans never sought nor achieved an independent existence as a state until it was thrust upon them following the USSR's disintegration in 1991. For all Moldovans, there were therefore only two historic experiences: either union with Romania or Russian rule. Moldova (known as Moldavia during the Soviet period) was, therefore, the only republic in the USSR that had a nation-state outside the country's boundaries; it was a territory without its own, separate nation, a political notion rather than an ethnic reality.[2]

## HISTORICAL BACKGROUND

Both Russian and Soviet policies were also primarily influenced by this basic fact. Throughout the last century – and once it became clear that a Romanian national state would ultimately come into being – the Russian government encouraged the dilution of Bessarabia's Romanian character through the settlement of other ethnic groups. Jews who migrated to the province were granted exemption from military service and the usual discriminatory legislation that applied in other parts of the empire; Bulgarians and Gagauz (a Christian Turkic group) were granted land and financial inducements to settle in the strategically sensitive south of the province. The Orthodox church (whose initial loyalty was to Constantinople) was taken over by the Russian church, and Bessarabia's hugely profitable farms were distributed among the neighbouring Russian nobility which, by the turn of the century, dominated the cultural and political life of the province. This systematic policy of de-nationalisation had one consequence still evident in Moldova today. The region's cities became dominated by other ethnic groups (usually Jews in the capital of Chisinau and in Cahul and Balti, sometimes Germans and more often Russians and Ukrainians), while the local Romanians remained confined to the villages. Most of the commercial activities were handled by Jews, most administration by Russians, and the largest share of higher education establishments was frequented by Germans and Jews. From representing roughly 80 per cent of the population in 1812, the Romanian share of Bessarabia's inhabitants sank to 56 per cent a century later. Nevertheless, nationalist stirrings did take place. During the 1905 Russian revolution, the first Romanian-language publications appeared and, concomitantly, the first indications that a Romanian intelligentsia still existed started to be felt. The truth was that, regardless of Russia's policies, Romanian culture continued to exist in neighbouring Romania, and the city of Iasi (the capital of historic

Moldova, only 50 kilometres from the border with Bessarabia) became a Mecca of Romanian culture.

The 1917 upheavals in Russia immediately sparked off a nationalist uprising in Bessarabia as well. However, due to the province's particular circumstances, the Bessarabian revolt was not led by intellectuals, but by peasants and soldiers defecting from the front, and initially assumed the character of a social revolution. For most of the soldiers and peasants who declared an independent 'Moldavian Republic' in 1918, unity with Romania was a poisoned chalice, for the neighbouring state was still ruled by a coalition of boyars and a royal court, a cabal of politicians who represented no one and who only a decade before had suppressed a peasant uprising with great bloodshed.

The revolutionary committees in Chisinau therefore established a parliament, the Sfatul Tarii. Yet this parliament quickly discovered that promises of social reform could not contain nationalist aspirations. Opposition of the local Russian nobility and church was only to be expected; the designs of the Ukrainian leaders (who also engaged at the same time in a fight for the independence of their own state) was not, and came as a great surprise. Torn between the territorial designs of neighbouring Ukraine, the threat of Bolshevik and White Guard forces – both of whom refused to accept Bessarabia's independence – and a state of internal anarchy from other unruly ethnic groups in the province, Sfatul Tarii ultimately asked for Romanian protection. This came in the shape of a massive deployment of troops and, after a short interval, Bessarabia's parliamentary assembly voted for union with Romania.

Much has been written about the significance of this union: official Soviet history claims that the union was 'illegal' since it was decreed by an 'unrepresentative' assembly; Romanians, on the other hand, have always claimed that the union was an 'expression of popular will'.[3] Both views are mistaken. In the atmosphere prevailing throughout Russia at the time, no 'national assembly' could be regarded as wholly representative of the popular will. At the time, it is equally clear that most Bessarabian Romanians accepted the union as legitimate and never questioned it.

Needless to say, difficulties arose: throughout the 1920s and 1930s Bessarabians accused other Romanians of failing to fulfil their initial promise to create a democratic state; Romanians in other provinces regarded the Bessarabians as uncouth and simple peasants who should not be taken seriously. Nevertheless, no one considered the Bessarabians as anything but Romanians.

The Soviet leaders always refused to recognise the union of Bessarabia with Romania, and Moscow's demands for the return of the province poisoned relations between the two states throughout the inter-war period.[4] Negotiations between the two neighbours were held at various locations in the 1920s and 1930s, but all of them failed and, on the eve of the Second World War, Bessarabia remained a contested land.[5] As part of the secret protocol attached to the Nazi–Soviet Pact of 1939, Bessarabia was assigned to the Soviet sphere of influence[6] and, on 24 June 1940, a Soviet ultimatum was delivered to Romania demanding the immediate cession of the territory. Although Romania did recover Bessarabia in 1941 (when it invaded the USSR on the coat-tails of the German armies), the province was lost again in 1944 and remained under Soviet control until 1991.

## SOVIET POLICIES IN MOLDAVIA

Stalin's policies in Soviet Moldavia (Moldova) were ostensibly very similar to those implemented in other republics at the end of the Second World War. The negation of national culture and the destruction of any form of social organisation outside the Communist Party; the deportations, arrests, executions, deliberately induced famines and other acts of brutality were applied in Soviet Moldavia as well with a rigour that probably claimed the life of one Moldavian out of ten between 1945 and 1953.

However, some features of Soviet policies in the republic were unique, specifically tailored for Moldavia's particular circumstances. The most important was Soviet policy towards the definition of Moldavia's 'nation'. There is considerable evidence that immediately after the incorporation of Bessarabia into the USSR in 1940, the Soviet authorities toyed with the idea of incorporating the territory into the Ukraine; the Ukrainian Communist Party certainly argued that this would provide a solution to Moldavia's problems and many people in Moscow favoured it too. For reasons that are still unclear, Stalin decided otherwise and a Moldavian republic was formed. However, once this decision was taken, the question of the republic's ethnic make-up had to be faced and Stalin opted for nothing less than the creation of a separate 'Moldavian' nation. This appeared to promise several long-term advantages: first, it delineated the Moldavian republic from the Ukraine and thus justified the latter's independent existence. More importantly, the 'creation' of a separate Moldavian nation could sever the connection with neighbouring Romania for good. Finally, the classification of Moldavians as a separate nation answered another Stalinist policy: that of incorporating only entire nations into the USSR.[7]

As any ethnographer could have suggested, a new nation cannot be created overnight. But ethnographers were not much in demand in Stalin's USSR and, as long as sheer force was what kept the Moldavians under control, the manipulation of their ethnic identity was merely a feeble justification, rather than the rationale of Soviet policies. The nexus of this justification concentrated on the language, as the most perceptible ingredient of any nation. In order to differentiate the Romanian spoken in Moldavia from that spoken in Romania the Latin alphabet in which Romanian is written was supplanted by the Cyrillic. Indeed, according to the authorities, only the Cyrillic was 'natural' to Moldavian,[8] and literary figures who persisted in using the Latin alphabet were promptly punished for seeking to 'Romanise'[9] a language that they regarded as Slavic in origin.[10]

In cultural affairs, Moldavia was also subjected to some particular policies, all of which were intended to highlight the republic's separate existence from Romania. Like all other Soviet republics, local culture and customs were relegated to a secondary importance, frozen in a showcase of 'folklore' which had little to do with genuine Moldavian traditions. Few dance groups and popular music bands were allowed to operate, and Russian culture was elevated to the role of supreme importance. The republic was portrayed in the official propaganda as the ideal holiday resort, a land of cheap and plentiful wine, merry girls, sun and simple peasants. Chisinau's cultural life was dominated by Russian-language theatres, and Pushkin (who spent a short time in Moldavia) was particularly favoured precisely because he appeared to provide a bridge between Moldavia and Russia's cultural traditions.

However, the authorities in Chisinau had another difficulty: across the frontiers, in independent Romania, indigenous literature continued to be published. Should this be available to the Moldavians, the entire Soviet policy of creating a separate Moldavian nation could have collapsed. For this reason, the importation of Romanian books was strictly controlled. During the period of de-Stalinisation and even during Brezhnev's rule the ban on Romanian literature was relaxed to a certain extent. However, there never was any question of just importing Romanian books, for that would have contradicted the authorities' claim that Moldavian was a separate language. Instead, Romanian authors were selectively published in Moldavia, in the Cyrillic script and only after a political decision at the highest level.[11] History was equally heavily controlled and rewritten. Here, again, the Soviet aim was not simply to show that Moldavia belonged to the USSR. Much more importantly, official historiography sought to 'prove' that Moldavians had nothing to do with neighbouring Romania. Thus, paradoxically, while in many other republics Moscow usually sought to play down their previous independent existence, in Moldavia the authorities fought hard to buttress it.

The fact that these attempts were undertaken in the one republic that was never truly independent only made them more ironic. According to the official history, Moldavia had never been part of Romania: it was occupied by Ukrainians, Poles and Turks and ultimately 'liberated' by Russians in 1812. The tsarist rule may not have been benign, but it was, on the whole, 'beneficial' by raising local standards of literacy and by laying the foundations of local industry. These industrial enterprises led to the formation of a 'working class' who seized power in 1917, only to be crushed by Romanian 'occupiers'. After twenty years of this occupation and at the first possible moment, the first workers' state came to the 'liberation' of the province, and the 'Moldavian' nation had lived happily ever after.[12]

To any experienced observer, it should have been clear that the attempts to create a nation with its own language, history and identity could not succeed under the best of circumstances. However, the clumsy application of the Soviet policies in Moldavia made their failure clearly inevitable. In reality, Moscow was pursuing not one, but two inherently contradictory aims. On the one hand, it sought to buttress the Moldavians' sense of identity, as the only means for severing their connection with Romania. Yet at the same time, the authorities could not forget that the creation of a strong local identity might not, after all, be to their advantage either. In this sense, therefore, Moldavia was squeezed between two Soviet policies: the traditional one of suppressing any national consciousness as much as possible, and the particular one of encouraging Moldavian peculiarities at the expense of the Romanian connection. As a result, none of the Soviet policies in Moldavia were implemented to their logical conclusion.

In language questions, for instance, the imposition of the Cyrillic was coupled with a steady reduction in the teaching of Romanian in all the republic's schools and the elimination of the language from the republican administration. As a result, more than 40 per cent of those who claimed to speak 'Moldavian' also admitted that they did not have complete command of the language, according to the preliminary figures of the 1989 census. Moldavia's cultural policies also displayed the same 'stop–go' mentality. The availability of Romanian literature was heavily restricted while, at the same time, local Moldavians were discouraged from publishing their works. The result was a domination of everything Russian: not even one Moldavian dramatist could be found to grace with his name one of the local theatres; in the republican Central Library (inelegantly named Krupskaya) not more than one-third of all holdings had anything remotely to do with local culture and literature,[13] while regional libraries often had not even one Moldavian book.[14]

Finally, the rewriting of history was equally stunted: while the authorities remained eager to emphasise that Moldavia was not part of the territories that ultimately formed independent Romania, they were also keen to show that the 'Moldavians', on whose behalf the republic was ostensibly created, were themselves not the first inhabitants of the land. Strikingly, the entire history of the area was written not by local Moldavians but by Russians or Ukrainians, whose personal, stereotyped perceptions served as the icing on layers of mystifications. Thus, Moldavian children learned at school that their republic was a land of migrants, of boorish peasants and superstitious priests, a *tabula rasa* of civilisation saved only with the arrival of Slav settlers. Russians and Ukrainians dominated the Moldavian Academy of Sciences and its History Institute, and the best professional position for a young Moldavian historian was a country primary school. Only in Moldavia was it still possible as late as 1988 to write a historical thesis based on no primary sources and without the slightest knowledge of the local language; only in Moldavia was it still normal to encounter during the 1980s official historians who fervently argued that their republic was 'multi-national' even before the political concept of the nation became a consideration in international relations.

The disastrous results of this haphazard policy of encouraging and at the same time discouraging the creation of the Moldavian nation were not immediately apparent for three reasons. First, as long as neighbouring Romania was ruled by a Communist regime that was equally subservient to Moscow's interest, Moldavians were kept in check by the Russian rulers and their ostensible nation-state at the same time. Second, as long as local cadres continued to be imported from Russia and the Ukraine and the majority of Moldavians remained confined to their villages, the possibility of an organised opposition remained remote. Finally, as long as Moscow's rule in the republic was conducted with an iron fist, any opposition could be crushed immediately.[15] Yet the greatest failure of the authorities was not to realise that none of these three facts was immutable or permanent, and that in the absence of any alternative policy, the moment Moldavians were allowed their say there would be a veritable social explosion.

Soviet control over Romania was the first to go: in the 1960s, Romania's Communists (for reasons quite independent of the Moldavian question) initiated a policy of differentiation from the Soviet Union and an opening to the West. President Nicolae Ceauşescu's rule remained that of a particularly vicious and nepotistic Balkan family, but it was remarkably effective in manipulating Romanian nationalism in general and traditional hatred of the Russians in particular. Romania's challenge was never considered serious enough to merit a Soviet invasion, precisely because Ceauşescu's policies never seriously challenged the rule of the Party in that country or Moscow's interests in eastern Europe. Nevertheless, the estrangement between the two states meant that Romanian nationalism became a force to be reckoned with in Soviet Moldavia, where it found a more receptive audience. Throughout Brezhnev's rule more and more Moldavians migrated to the towns, and, especially in the 1970s, the local press and literary life were slowly 'nationalised'. However – and unlike the case of other republics – this process continued by default in spite of, rather than because of, a conscious official policy. Moldavian intellectuals started to emerge; Moldavian economists and skilled labourers left the land and found opportunities in towns. Yet they could not be accommodated in the republic's administration, which remained firmly under Russian and Ukrainian control. By the early 1980s it was clear that nationalist grievances, combined with economic difficulties, had created a potentially explosive situation, but the local Party leadership did nothing until Mikhail Gorbachev removed the third and last instrument in their traditional policy: that of the persistent use of coercion.

Unlike any other republics in the former Soviet Union, the Moldavian leadership was bereft of any vehicle for conducting a dialogue with its population: it could not encourage Moldavian nationalism, for it feared that this would spill into demands for unification with Romania; it could not encourage purely regional pride, for Moldavia was never an independent state and therefore had none. The Moldavians were left in a state of limbo, a dead end that precluded any compromise but also offered no alternative. Moldavia had the dubious distinction of having been governed by two men who subsequently became the USSR's leaders,[16] and the local Party, commonly entitled the 'Moldavian Mafia', was assumed to have good contacts in Moscow. It was not only the collapse of Brezhnev's cabal in 1985 that stunned the Moldavian leaders; much more important for them was the fact that Gorbachev's policies were demanding a dialogue with the local population. Chisinau deemed this impossible and actually dangerous, and it is clear that Simeon Grossu, the republican party leader, remained in power until 1989 precisely because Moscow was persuaded that Moldavia might be a special case best treated by old, Brezhnevite hands.

## MOLDAVIA UNDER GORBACHEV

### The Rise of Organised Opposition

It is undoubtedly true that Moldavia was one of the last republics to stir under Gorbachev's policies. This is due to many factors, among which the republic's continued agricultural character, the comparatively low number of Moldavian intellectuals and the ethnically mixed nature of the republic's urban areas are clearly important. Nevertheless, by the end of 1987 some members of the local Writers' Union put forward vague demands for political liberalisation which, although quickly brushed aside, ultimately created the mass opposition movement during the summer of 1988.[17] One of this movement's most striking features is not that it started by advancing cultural and political demands (for this was the case in most other republics), but rather that demands for changes in the economic mechanism were entirely absent from its platform.

The reasons for this are clear enough: while the opposition movements in the Baltic republics knew very well from the start that only by controlling their economy, environment and political administration would they stand a chance of prising power from Moscow, their Moldavian counterparts had a much simpler aim. The aim was nothing less than the destruction of Moscow's artificial creation of a Moldavian nation, and this was achieved in a very simple and effective way. Essentially, all the opposition movements did was to turn their rulers' justifications against them: if the Moldovans had their own language, why should this not be the state language in the republic and why should this not be the state language in the republic and why should it not be taught at all levels? And, if Moldovans were indeed a nation, why should their right to their land be doubted and their culture circumscribed? There is no doubt that the Moldovan intellectuals understood very well the difficulties hiding behind their seemingly naïive questions. In essence they were challenging the entire official policy of forty years, which was based on a delicate balance between the appearance of a nation and the reality of Russian domination. And in reality, Moldovans were convinced that whichever tactic Chisinau ultimately adopted, the result would be the same: a reassertion of their true ethnic identity.

It cannot be assumed that, at least at the beginning of their struggle, the Moldovan activists had any clear idea of what that ethnic identity would entail. Rather, their demands were much more basic and entailed the affirmation of their attributes as a nation. However, once these were obtained, it quickly became clear to most opposition groups that their nation and their republic could not be defined without a reference to the Romanians and their independent state. The same process operated in East Germany as well and essentially for the same basic reason: in the search for obvious attributes of their separate nations, both the East Germans and the Moldovans discovered – sometimes to their dismay – that these simply did not exist.

Thus, although the Moldovan popular movement of opposition started by borrowing freely from the political platforms of its counterparts in other Soviet republics, it ended up with a policy entirely its own. From the viewpoint of the authorities, therefore, the worst had happened: far from acquiring a new pride in their republic, the Moldovans were drawn to everything Romanian. Yet the responsibility for this phenomenon was squarely that of the Soviet authorities, who never considered it necessary to fill their fiction of a 'Moldovan' nation with any real content.

### The Battle for a Language and Culture

It was to be expected that the issue of the language should provide the first conflict with the authorities. Language policies were at the heart of Soviet attempts to create a separate nation, and the language has always provided the most potent rallying symbol for all Romanians.

By 1988, the Moldovan opposition groups advanced three demands: that Romanian should be recognised as the state's language; that it should again be written in the Latin alphabet; and that the government should acknowledge that 'Moldovan' and Romanian are one and the same tongue.

The first skirmish was conducted along predictable lines: the government asserted that a return to the Latin alphabet was unnecessary and unworkable; the opposition replied that only the Latin alphabet could render the language's sounds accurately. Yet both protagonists knew only too well that their clash was hardly a linguistic one: its essence was the definition of the nation, a definition on which everything else would ultimately depend. At the beginning, Simeon Grossu reacted to these demands in a predictable manner, by accusing the opposition groups of 'nationalism', 'separatism' and other heinous crimes and by refusing to contemplate any change.[18] However, his position quickly changed when it became clear that some concessions would have to be made. As a consequence, the reintroduction of the Latin alphabet was accepted, but the adoption of Romanian as state language continued to be rejected, with an explanation that revealed the true extent of the leadership's fears. According to Grossu, Romanian could not be considered a state language, for the Moldavian republic was 'multi-national', and any move according preference to any tongue would automatically discriminate against others.[19] To the Moldovan opposition movement Grossu's stance was clear enough: just when the population started taking the government's concept of the Moldovan nation seriously, the government tried to discard it.

The bitter conflict that developed was not without its irony for, of the opposition's three linguistic demands, the adoption of Romanian as a state language was certainly not the most provocative from the government's viewpoint. Much more serious was the demand for an official acknowledgement that 'Moldovan' and Romanian are one and the same language. Yet it was precisely on this issue that government and popular opposition managed to reach a swift compromise. The reasons why this compromise could be reached are clear enough: once the use of the Cyrillic alphabet was discarded, it was obvious that the fiction about the existence of a 'Moldovan' language could simply not be maintained. At the same time, leading members of the opposition were also aware of the fact that to extract an official admission from the government on this point was of little practical value and amounted to a dissipation of their energies. The 'linguistic identity' question (as it came to be known) was essentially won by the opposition, and all that remained was to create a suitable mechanism through which the government could accept defeat without undue loss of face.

The 'identity issue' was therefore assigned to a special committee of the Moldavian Academy of Sciences, who reported, to no one's surprise, that 'Moldovan' and Romanian were, indeed, identical.[20]

However, since this report was not presented to the Supreme Soviet, and did not form part of the language legislation, it allowed the government to continue referring to the 'Moldovan' language rather than to Romanian. The final version of the Languages Law mentions 'the Moldavian–Romanian linguistic identity which really exists'. As part of the compromise, this statement is contained in the preamble to the Act. The government later tried to dismiss the importance of the clause by suggesting that it applied only to 'the Moldavians in the republic and the Romanians resident elsewhere in the USSR';[21] Moldovan intellectuals, well aware that their authorities were merely hiding behind an even bigger nonsense that before, were happy to ridicule this stance and refer to their language as Romanian.[22]

Yet, on the subject of the state language, the battle continued throughout 1989 and led to a progressive radicalisation of all ethnic groups in the republic. For an increasingly desperate leadership, this question was its last stand. Once it became clear that the notion of a Moldavian nation would actually mean something, the authorities in Chisinau therefore rushed to limit its consequences, and the official assertions about the need to protect the rights of other 'nations' in the republic grew in direct proportion to the opposition's linguistic demands. By the summer of 1989, Chisinau was confronted with a veritable surge of dissent and a united Moldovan Popular Front which included not just urban intellectuals but also workers. On 28 August 1989 they filled the streets of the capital. The presence of half a million demonstrators surprised even the opposition.

No compromise – even one offered by Gorbachev on the telephone to members of the republic's Supreme Soviet, which by then was in almost permanent session – seemed to work. The debates in the Supreme Soviet encapsulated the entire problem: while Eugen Sobor, Moldavia's Culture Minister, spoke of the imperative to respect the language of the nation that 'gave its name to this republic',[23] Russian deputies complained against discrimination of 'other nations, living in compact formations throughout Moldova'.[24] After a few weeks when the republic seemed to be slipping out of anyone's control, the Supreme Soviet ultimately voted a law that enshrined Romanian as the state language while according other ethnic groups the right to use their own language in regions in which they live. Nevertheless, all members of the administration and of local authorities would be obliged to learn Romanian and speak it at all times. There is little doubt that the Moldovans had won their most important victory. This had little to do with the language issue *per se*; rather, it amounted to extracting an open admission from their government that the republic was theirs and theirs alone, and that all other ethnic groups in Moldova were not 'nations', but rather ethnic minorities whose rights should be respected but whose claims could not be considered equal to the interests of the majority. The concept of a 'Moldovan' at last had a meaning.

## *The Disintegration of Party Control*

The prolonged dispute over language questions affected all political bodies in the country. Simeon Grossu, the Party leader who swore not to consider Romanian a state language and who claimed that to return to the Latin alphabet would render the entire population illiterate, was thoroughly discredited in the eyes of everyone. The Moldovans considered him beyond the pale; the Russians regarded his climb-down as little short of treason. In the cities of Tiraspol and Bender – major centres for ethnic Russians in the republic – general strikes were declared. The Russians openly declared their strikes to be political and the local soviets in the two cities vowed not to apply the language law, with the unreserved support of the regional Party leader. Chisinau, however, did nothing, and the pace of protests accelerated, with the Moldovans concentrating on the rehabilitation of their literature and history. The Popular Front began demanding that restrictions on the importation of Romanian literature be rescinded and that their republic's history should not be falsified. The government responded with a pledge to enact a 'complex plan of cultural development' which, by the year 2005, would supposedly answer all the population's needs.[25] Yet Moldova's intellectuals quickly perceived that, irrespective of their government, they did have an alternative route to speed up their cultural revival.

Unlike the citizens of any other Soviet republic, the Moldovans did not have to revive an indigenous culture, nor wait for years until local writers saw their works in print; they could simply publish Romanian literature, easily accessible across the border. And, since the authorities continued to refuse any direct importation of Romanian books, either by pleading poverty[26] or by citing 'technical difficulties',[27] Moldovans simply started publishing them in their literary periodicals. A poem by Mihai Eminescu, Romania's foremost poet, was published in all its versions not merely once but many times,[28] and in most periodicals as well.[29] The poem, imbued with hatred of anything foreign and particularly anything Russian, needed no explanation and remained one of the most evocative symbols of Romanian unity. In effect, the Party lost control over the entire press: the Russian and Romanian-language versions of the Party daily were constantly at loggerheads with each other, representing diametrically opposed views on almost any subject; the majority of the other papers devoted the greater part of their issues to nationalist and religious symbols. No amount of warnings against 'undue interest in foreign countries' – a jibe clearly aimed at Romania – worked and, most spectacularly, Grossu even failed to dismiss the adventurous editor of the Party daily when the latter published the text of an opposition letter without explicit permission.[30]

Yet even the restoration of Romanian literature was insignificant compared to the attacks of the opposition against the official interpretations of Moldova's history. The quest to establish the 'truth' about Moldova's past could only lead – as everyone was perfectly aware from the start – to questioning of the incorporation of the republic into the USSR. Similar movements took place throughout the union, but in Moldova's case the demands for the rewriting of history were particularly strong because they were led by a large number of young and competent historians who were constantly deprived of useful employment and scholarly pursuits. They rebelled not only against the falsehoods advanced by the authorities as historical facts, but also against the entire historical establishment in the republic which, as already noted, was dominated by members of other ethnic groups. Disoriented and unable to offer any clear response, the Moldovan authorities sought to deflect this movement by rehabilitating former Communists exterminated by Stalin during various purges and re-working arcane explanations about the 'development of social classes in Moldavia'.[31] Yet this failed to project an image of change, for the simple reason that the overwhelming majority of the Moldavian Communists before the Second World War were members of other ethnic groups and usually had little connection with the republic. The rehabilitation of people unknown to anyone born in the last forty years was therefore no substitute for what the Moldovan historians really wanted discussed: how was their territory incorporated in the USSR and how was the local population treated under Soviet rule?

The crucial conflict revolved around the interpretation of the Molotov–Ribbentrop Pact. On this issue, Chisinau's predicament was ostensibly eased by the Kremlin's decision in the summer of 1989 to admit that a secret protocol dividing European territories had actually been signed between Nazi Germany and the Soviet Union fifty years earlier. However, this official admission, far from allowing the Moldavian leadership room for manoeuvre, actually compounded its difficulties. Moscow could admit to the existence of this protocol and still claim that the Baltic states freely joined the USSR; the same argument could not be applied to Moldova, which was never an independent state and which therefore could never be considered as having 'opted' for incorporation into the USSR. But there was worse to come. Essentially, the Soviet ultimatum delivered to Romania in 1940 did not speak of 'Moldovans' at all. Instead, it referred to the inhabitants as 'basically Ukrainians' whose 'wish' to be united with their brethren in Ukraine would be satisfied through the cession of the Bessarabian territory. Furthermore, the ultimatum also demanded half of the Romanian province of Bukovina – which was never part of the Russian empire – not for ethnic or historical reasons, but simply as a compensation that Romania had to pay for its twenty year 'occupation' of 'Soviet territory in Moldavia'. Finally, the territory seized from Romania in 1940 did not coincide with the final frontiers of the Moldavian republic: northern and southern parts were annexed to neighbouring Ukraine and the latter ceded some territory to Moldavia. In sum, therefore, the 1940 Soviet ultimatum demanded Romania's territory on behalf of a nation which at the time the Kremlin did not believe existed, and led to the creation of a republic that should never have been there and did not correspond to Moldavia's current frontiers. No wonder Chisinau resolved to say nothing on this matter, for no reasoning could have explained these uncomfortable truths.

The government's inability even to begin confronting its historical legacy led to the creation of a unique Moldavian dissident organisation: the Association of Historians, which sought to open the state archives and publish the 'historical truth'.[32] As a result, Moldova was presented with two histories: the official one which remained unchanged and the unofficial one, published in instalments in the literary press. Chisinau continued to attack 'falsifiers of history', threatening dissidents with KGB action,[33] while the independent historians continued to publish previously forbidden documents, all of which challenged the presence of Soviet power on their land.[34] And, whereas in most other Soviet republics access to archival material improved, in Moldavia restrictions intensified. Items locked away included all the Romanian-language newspapers published between the wars and even the most ephemeral papers of Moldova's short-lived parliament, the Sfatul Tarii.[35] Knowing that there could be no going back to the old historical justifications but unable to contemplate any change, the government essentially retreated into its shell: it did not refute the historical studies put forward by Moldavians, but nor did it accept them.

The same attitude was adopted towards the problem of the republic's flag and national symbols. One of the first demands of the Popular Front was for a change in Moldova's flag, from the stereotyped Soviet version bequeathed by Stalin to all republics to a flag that would represent the Moldovans' true 'heritage'. The Popular Front had no doubt which flag could achieve this aim: none other than the Romanian vertical tricolour of red, yellow and blue. Romanian tricolours started appearing in the late spring of 1989 and, very quickly, spread throughout the republic. Displayed on lapels, cars, buildings and present at all demonstrations, the tricolour became the most visible symbol of dissent and at the same time the most potent example of Moldova's historic connection with Romania.

At least on this issue, the authorities moved quickly and established a special committee in order to discover Moldova's 'real' flag. The committee searched through historical documents at home and as far afield as Greece and Austria, yet in vain: according to all available evidence, Moldova had never had a flag of its own; it employed either the Romanian flag or the Soviet one. Yet this did not prevent the government from offering various compromises. One such compromise promised the adoption of the red and blue only;[36] another suggested retaining the current flag with the addition of yellow (in order to answer the opposition's demands for the inclusion of all three colours).[37] Needless to say, this 'multi-chrome policy' was nothing but a belated attempt to sustain the former policy of differentiation. Indeed, Moldovan officials were even terrified of mentioning the name of Romania in public. During a televised discussion on the subject, officials merely argued that they could not accept the tricolour as Moldova's flag, for 'it already represented another sovereign state'. Asked by the television presenter – with some mischief in mind – which state that might be, the official quickly obliged: it was 'the African republic of Chad'.[38]

Most Moldovans understood that they had reached yet another stalemate. And so, having had two interpretations of the Moldovan nation and two versions of its history, Moldova also acquired two flags: the one flown by the government from public buildings and the one flown by most people during their activities. The disjunction between the official and the real was complete, and it had catastrophic effects in the life of the republic. In one year, Moldova's crime rate climbed to the highest in the USSR; its economic performance plummeted to tenth place in the union and barely above that of the Asian Soviet republics.[39] After lengthy strikes and factory lockouts, all production plans were in tatters and all Moldova's ethnic groups decided to take matters into their own hands. The small Gagauz minority, emboldened by the government's assertions that it was a separate 'nation', promptly declared the Gagauz an 'autonomous republic'[40] and the Russians followed suit by establishing their claim to a 'Dniester republic'.

The government, meanwhile, continued to behave as though nothing was happening: it ordered a military parade for the October Revolution day, and was genuinely shocked to find that this resulted in widespread riots for days after.[41] Having survived longer than any other Brezhnevite republican leader but failing to quell the nationalist unrest, Simeon Grossu was clearly a spent force. Yet Moscow's choice for his replacement was not another man from the republic: aware that the Moldovan leadership was hopelessly split and discredited and remembering the sensitivity of the Moldovan question, the Kremlin imposed Petru Luchniskyi, an ethnic Moldovan who spent most of his political career in other parts of the USSR.

## THE QUESTION OF REUNIFICATION

Nothing prepared Party leader Luchniskyi or his masters in Moscow for what followed in December 1989. The Romanian Revolution started with the removal of Nicolae Ceauşescu's dictatorship in that country; its long-term effect would be the elimination of Communism in Romania and the re-emergence of the 'Moldovan question' as an important dispute between the two neighbouring states.

In every irredentist situation, there are three actors: the nation-state (Romania), the unredeemed ethnic group (Moldovans), and the state which possesses the unredeemed territory (USSR). The last is usually reactive: it is interested in limiting as far as possible the contacts between its unredeemed people and their nation state, and it therefore pursues an essentially defensive policy intended to preserve a territorial status quo. This is precisely the policy the Soviet Union undertook under Gorbachev. And, as long as Nicolae Ceauşescu ruled in neighbouring Romania, it was also the policy the Romanians adhered to. Despite his increasingly shrill attacks against Gorbachev's economic and political reforms, the former Romanian ruler was careful to distance himself from any claims on Moldova, for obvious reasons. First, it was clear that if Romania advanced any such claims, Moscow could encourage the Hungarians to advance similar claims to Romanian territory in Transylvania. More importantly, the nationalism Ceauşescu practised was one guided from above and manipulated by his regime. Yet the nationalism the Moldovans promoted was one that grew from below, with strong religious and popular overtones, precisely the kind that Ceauşescu always repressed. Finally, the Romanian ruler understood perfectly well that the Moldovans were not only challenging Russian rule; they were also attacking dictatorial methods of government and Communist power. For all these reasons, Ceauşescu's Romania simply ignored the rebirth of Moldovan nationalism and actually rebuffed Soviet offers to open the borders between the two states.[42] Romania also reduced its imports of Moldovan literature and a veritable 'Great Wall of China' went up on the Romanian border, frustrating any Moldovan attempt to establish better contacts with their kith and kin.[43] Ceauşescu's stance changed only when the Romanian leader became isolated both at home and abroad. Thus, at his Party Congress in November 1989, Ceauşescu openly called for the elimination of the 'consequences' of the Molotov–Ribbentrop Pact, a clear reference to the redrawing of frontiers between his state and the USSR.[44] Yet, even this reference hardly amounted to a change of heart, for Ceauşescu still viewed Moldova as essentially an instrument – rather than an object – in his wider battle with the Soviet Union.

These considerations were wiped out with the Romanian Revolution in December 1989. The overthrow of Ceauşescu evoked an instant response in Moldova, whose citizens sent vast quantities of food and medical aid to the Romanian revolutionaries. Furthermore, in the heat of the revolution, many Moldovan nationalists crossed the river separating the two states, and immediately voiced demands for unification with Romania.[45] The provisional authorities in Bucharest –

realising how sensitive the issue was – remained noticeably coy about mentioning such developments, preferring instead to refer to broad Soviet support for their struggle against the dictator. Nevertheless, the newly freed Romanian press had no such compunction and news items from neighbouring Moldova became a regular feature.[46] And, despite the fact that from Bucharest's viewpoint the issue of Moldova could only complicate Soviet–Romanian relations at a time when Soviet economic support was needed most, it was obvious that no Romanian government would be able to prevent the conflict from being raised. Political activists in the Romanian city of Iasi considered this issue most important, and intellectuals in most other Romanian cities had already drafted proposals for union with their brethren in the Soviet Union.[47]

The Soviet authorities, realising that the problem of Moldavia could no longer be avoided, resolved instead to meet it head on. Thus, while promising the Romanian revolutionary government additional financial and technical support (and thereby reminding Bucharest of its economic dependence on its mighty northern neighbour), Moscow also lessened travel restrictions at its frontiers and promised to allow Moldovans greater cultural rights. These measures were essentially only palliatives, intended to stabilise rather than solve an explosive situation, for the truth was that neither Moscow nor Bucharest could control the Moldovan problem any longer. Short of the use of force, it was clear that the initiative was in the hands of the Moldovans themselves.

Throughout 1990 support within Moldova for 'reconnecting up' with post-revolutionary Romania was voiced through the activities of the Moldovan Popular Front. Within local policy-making circles nation-building policies were also geared towards the republic's Romanianisation. The Romanian language continued to be promoted amongst the largely non-Moldovan regions of the South (Gagauz-inhabited region) and East (Trans-Dniester). On 5 June 1990, in a highly symbolic act of territorial and historical connection with its western neighbour, Chisinau changed the name of its republic from Moldavia to Moldova after the medieval principality, a large part of which was in Romania. Following the failure of the August 1991 coup in Moscow and Moldova's declaration of statehood a few days later on 27 August, there was every indication to suggest that statehood would mark a brief transitional period in paving the way to eventual reunification. Although far from categorical in its intentions, the Moldovan parliament declared the republic's statehood, 'in awareness of the one thousand year existence of our people and its uninterrupted statehood within the historical and ethnic boundaries of its national formation'.[48] Furthermore, the territorial divisions of both 1775 and 1812 were considered as 'acts in contravention of the historical and national rights and legal status of the Moldovan principality.'[49]

Despite the widely held expectation that reunification with Romania would follow, it faded as a political issue whilst the idea of Moldovan statehood took shape and became increasingly acceptable to Moldovans.

By 1994 there was little political support for abandoning Moldovan independence. In the February elections of that year, the Moldovan Popular Front, repackaged as the Christian Democratic Popular Front (the only Party campaigning on the question of reunification), was able to secure a mere 7.5 per cent of the popular vote. A referendum on reunification the following month was unequivocal in its rejection of reunification, with three quarters of voters favouring the continuation of an independent Moldova.[50] This *volte-face* can be attributed to various reasons. Compared with Moldova, progress on democratisation in post-revolutionary Romania was considered to be far less certain. Moldovans had also begun to question the rosy memory of their past associations with pre-1939 Romania and whether the neglect of the region's interests during the inter-war period would again return in a post-1989 regime that had already displayed insensitivity to regional concerns. Then there was the issue of the high economic costs to the highly specialised and agrarian-orientated Moldovan economy consequent to becoming part of Romania, compared with what seemed to be a much lower-risk strategy of building upon well-established trade relations with Russia and the other post-Soviet countries that a Moldovan state (as a member of the CIS) could enjoy. Support for the benefits of a re-establishment of trade relations within the CIS received a further political boost in the February 1994 elections, when pro-CIS parties secured 84 out of the 105 seats in the national legislature. Moreover new and highly prestigious occupational niches were created for Moldova's intellectual elites with statehood who realised that their interests would be best served through securing the survival of an independent Moldova. Furthermore, although reunification remains a central platform for the more vociferous Romanian nationalist parties and has continued to be supported by the Romanian Orthodox Church, it is no longer considered by Bucharest as a priority objective, only as a distant goal. Indeed the Romanian leadership is more concerned to ensure the territorial integrity of its own polity, and to contain regional separatism amongst its Translyvanian–Hungarian minority. Finally, Moldova's government has become increasingly sensitive to the issue of ethnic stability within its own borders, and to accommodating the wishes of its non-Moldovan population. To the Russian minority of the Trans-Dniester region and the Gagauz in the South the idea of reunification is even more unacceptable than it is to the other regions of Moldova.

## THE ETHNOPOLITICS OF TRANS-DNIESTER

The greatest challenge to Moldova's political legitimacy and territorial integrity has come not from the supporters of reunification but from regional separatists. Indeed it has been the Trans-Dniester conflict, erupting into widespread ethnic violence and eventual Civil War, that has dominated the political agenda of the fledgeling Moldovan state[51].

The establishment of a Dniester republic, in September 2nd 1990, which was committed to remaining part of the Soviet Union, was not only a reaction to fears that Moldova would eventually join with Romania but was also a refusal to become part of a more sovereign Moldova. A regionalist movement emerged whose support-base was primarily ethnic Russian. Although Russians constitute only a quarter of the region's 740,000 inhabitants, discontent with Chisinau's policies in the region is more widespread, with support also to be found amongst the heavily russified Ukrainians and some of the Moldovan population, which, unlike their west bank co-nationals, were heavily influenced by Slavic culture. Substantial concerns exist in the region, not to mention fears of the imposition of a Romanian linguistic hegemony. In a March 1991 referendum, 93 per cent of the voters of Trans-Dniester endorsed the move to remain part of the Soviet Union[52].

Despite Moldova adopting an inclusionary citizenship policy in June 1991, whereby all residents on Moldovan territory were granted the right to citizenship, tensions between Chisinau and Trans-Dniester continued to intensify. The failure of the right-wing coup in Moscow in August 1991, supported by the Trans-Dniester rebels, turned what had been an irredentist movement into a movement now demanding the establishment of a Trans-Dniester republic. By the Spring of 1992, centre-regional tensions had escalated into civil war. Although Russia officially distanced itself from the war, it remains unclear what support was given by the Russian 14th Army already stationed in the region, which at the very least supplied the breakaway republic with arms, with some of its commanders actively supporting the republic during the hostilities. Less ambiguous was the public support given by right-wing nationalists in Russia and of the participation in the war by cossacks from Russia fighting on the side of the Trans-Dniestrians. Anxious to secure a conclusion to the conflict, Moldova and Russia signed a bilateral agreement in July 1992 that laid a framework for normalising the situation.

Accordingly, a multinational peacekeeping force drawn from Russia and Moldova was established, and a timetable set for the 14th Russian Army's withdrawal from the region. It was also agreed that should Moldova's status as a sovereign state be changed, Trans-Dniester would be guaranteed the right to national self-determination and thus, if it so wished, to secede. The left bank was also to be granted special regional status although its exact form was only fully elaborated upon in April 1994 at a CSCE organised conference between Moldova and Trans-Dniester. Substantial autonomy is to be granted to the region, although the adoption of proposals supported by Trans-Dniester to transform Moldova from a unitary to a confederal state still remain inconclusive.

## CONCLUSIONS

Given the geopolitical pressures for unification and regional-secessionism, few commentators could have predicted in the Autumn of 1991 that Moldova had a future as a sovereign state. Instead the idea of statehood has become acceptable to Moldovans who have adjusted in a remarkably short period to a duality of identity in which there no longer seems to be a major tension between being culturally Romanian and politically Moldovan. What remains more problematic is whether Moldovan statehood can accommodate a multiculturalism that safeguards the interests of both the core nation and the population of Trans-Dniester. It may well be that a confederation still offers the best prospects for ethnic stability in the region.

## NOTES

1. G. F. Jewsbury 'An overview of the history of Bessarabia' in M. Manoliu-Manea (ed.) *The Tragic Plight of a Border Area: Bessarabia and Bucovina* (Humboldt State University Press, CA, 1983), pp. 1–18.
2. In this chapter, the terms 'Moldavian' or 'Moldavia' are used purely for reasons of brevity.
3. I. G. Pelivan *The Union of Bessarabia with the Mother Country* (Paris 1920). This work was prepared for the Paris Peace Conference which met at the time.
4. See, for example, V. V. Tilea *Actiunea Diplomatica a Romaniei* (Sibiu, 1925), pp. 221 ff.; for a rather subjective discussion of the legal ramifications of the problems, see A. Popovici *The Political Status of Bessarabia* (Washington, DC, Randsdell, 1931).
5. The most promising attempts at mediation between the Soviet Union and Romania are documented in W. M. Bacon *Behind Closed Doors: Secret Papers on the Failure of Romanian–Soviet Negotiations, 1931–1932* (Stanford, CA, 1979).
6. Despite the recent revelations in the Soviet press, the fullest documentation is still US Department of State *Nazi–Soviet Relations, 1939–1941: Documents from the Archives of the German Foreign Office* (Washington, DC 1948).
7. The union of all strands of the Ukrainian nation under Soviet control was one of the principal reasons for Stalin's annexation of Czechoslovak, Hungarian and additional Romanian territory in 1945.
8. See *Nistru* Nov. 1988.
9. *Moldova Socialista*, 17 June 1989.

10. A. Lazarev, *Moldovanskaya Sovetskaya gosudarstvenost i Bessarabskiy vopros* (Chisinau, Cartea Moldoveneasca 1974), pp. 739–42.
11. For an example of the selection, see G. Cozonac and A. Borodin (eds) *Literatura artistica editata in RSS Moldoveneasca, 1924–1964* (Chisinau, Cartea Moldoveneasca 1967).
12. *Kommunisticheskoye Podpolyie Bessarabyii (1914–1944 gg). Sbornik dokumentov ii materialov* (Chisinau, vol. 1, 1987; vol. 2, 1988); and *Sovyetskaya Moldavyia* 21 June 1988.
13. *Invatamintul Public* 29 Sept. 1989.
14. *Moldova Socialista* 2 Sept. 1988.
15. N. Lupan *Basarabia: Colonizari si Asimilare* (Madrid, Editura Carpati 1979), pp. 17– 0; M. Bruchis *Nations–Nationalities–People: A Study of the Nationalities Policy of the Communist Party in Soviet Moldavia* (New York, Columbia University Press 1984), p. 91.
16. Leonid Brezhnev ruled the republic as First Secretary in the early 1950s; Konstantin Chernenko was Moldavia's chief ideological secretary for a long period.
17. B. Nahaylo 'National ferment in Moldavia' *Radio Liberty Research*, RL 32/88, 24 Jan. 1988.
18. *Moldova Socialista* 11 Nov. 1988.
19. J. Eyal 'Soviet Moldavia: history catches up and a "separate" language disappears', Radio Liberty, *Report on the USSR*, vol. 1 (8), 24 Feb. 1989, pp. 25–9.
20. *Limba si Literatura Moldoveneasca* no. 2 (April–June 1989), p. 15.
21. *Moldova Socialista* 3 Sept. 1989.
22. *Literatura si Arta* 13 July 1989, p. 8.
23. *Moldova Socialista* 5 Sept. 1989.
24. *Moldova Socialista* 29 Aug. 1989.
25. *Moldova Socialista* 9 Oct. 1988.
26. A paltry additional sum of only 32,000 roubles was allocated for the purchase of Romanian literature for the whole of 1989: *Literatura si Arta* 29 June 1989.
27. *Nistru* April 1989, pp. 85–7.
28. *Nistru* June 1989, pp. 33–43.
29. See, for instance, *Tinerimea Moldovei* 10 Sept. 1989.
30. *Literatura si Arta* 25 May 1989.
31. *Comunistul Moldovei* April 1989, pp. 92–4.
32. *Invatamintul Public* 21 June 1989.
33. *Orizontul* Aug. 1989, p. 69.
34. On the events of 1812, see *Literatura si Arta* 10 Aug. 1989; on 1918, see *Moldova Socialista* 16 Aug. 1989; on the interwar period, the most notable articles were published in *Moldova Socialista* 18 and 27 Aug. 1989; on the events of 1940, see ibid., 23 Aug. 1989 as well as every issue of *Literatura si Arta* since August 1989.
35. *Tinerimea Moldovei* 8 Sept. 1989.
36. *Moldova Socialista* 16 April 1989.
37. *Moldova Socialista* 28 July 1989.
38. *Literatura si Arta* 13 July 1989. Chad does, indeed, have an identical tricolour flag.
39. *The Economist* 23 Sept. 1989, p. 70.

40. *Moldova Socialista* 6 Dec. 1989.
41. *Moldova Socialista* 9 and 11 Nov. 1989.
42. *Moldova Socialista* 11, 24 and 27 May 1989; *Nistru*, April 1989, pp. 79–80.
43. *Literatura si Arta*, 17 Aug. 1989.
44. *Scinteia*, 21 Nov. 1989.
45. *Le Monde*, 3 Jan. 1990.
46. *Scinteia Poporului*, 23 Dec. 1989; *Romania Libera*, 27 Dec. 1989.
47. *The Times*, 5 Jan. 1990; *The Independent*, 8 Jan. 1990.
48. *Deklaratsiya o nezavisimosti Respubliki Moldova*, Chisinaw, 27 August 1991.
49. *Ibid.*
50. Mark, R, Moldova. Progress and Crisis *Transitions* (Open Media Research Institute, Prague), February 1995, pp. 57–9.
51. Kolsto, P. (1993) The Dniester Conflict: Between Irredentism and Separatism, *Europe–Asia Studies*, vol. 45(b), pp. 973–1000.
52. *Ibid.*

# PART V

# Transcaucasia

Transcaucasia is a small but relatively densely populated area separated from Russia by the Caucasian Mountains and bordered on each side by the Black and Caspian seas (see Fig. 5). It is divided into three states: Armenia, Azerbaijan and Georgia. Although formed as individual republics in 1920, in March 1922 all three were incorporated into the newly established Transcaucasian Socialist Federative Soviet Republic, which lasted until 1936, after which each constituted a separate union republic until 1991.

Culturally the region can legitimately claim to contain the most ancient cultures of Northern Eurasia. Each of the three major nationalities, the Armenians, Azerbaijanis and Georgians, have their own distinctive language; whereas Armenians and Georgians have been Christian since the third century, the Turkic-speaking Azerbaijanis are Shiite Muslim. Transcaucasia's geo-strategic location at the crossroads of Asia and Europe has resulted in subjugation to Persian, Turkish and Russian rule. As part of the Soviet federation, the region's economic development was achieved without the runaway industrialisation experienced by many other union republics, which also limited Russian immigration, making the now sovereign states among the least ethnically Russian.

Transcaucasia is also the homeland to a number of other nationalities, including the Abkhazians and South Ossetians, as well as the Adzarians (Muslim Georgians). Present ethnic tensions in the region are, however, in part a product of a Soviet nationalities policy in which national boundaries were not necessarily drawn according to ethnic criteria. Consequently, the predominantly Azerbaijani community of Nakhichevan, which is part of Azerbaijan, is an enclave within Armenia while the Armenian minority of Mountainous Karabagh (or Nagorno-Karabakh) falls within the sovereign boundaries of Azerbaijan. National, ethnic and religious rivalries fuelled by territorial claims are longstanding, notably between Muslim Azerbaijanis and Christian Armenians, between Georgians and Abkhazians and between Azerbaijanis and Georgians.

Since 1988, the region has been subject to ethno-communal violence which has escalated with the end of Soviet rule. Transcaucasia provided the first major test for the Gorbachev administration of how to handle the national question, with the region experiencing a series of general strikes and demonstrations and a level of ethnic violence previously unknown in Soviet history. At the forefront was the issue of territorial ownership of Nagorno-Karabakh, triggered in February 1988 by the Nagorno-Karabakh Soviet calling for its enclave's accession to Armenia. Civil war continues to rage in Georgia, where the rights of its minorities are seen by Georgian nation-builders as an obstacle to the full realisation of Georgian sovereignty.

Figure 5 : **TRANSCAUCASIA**

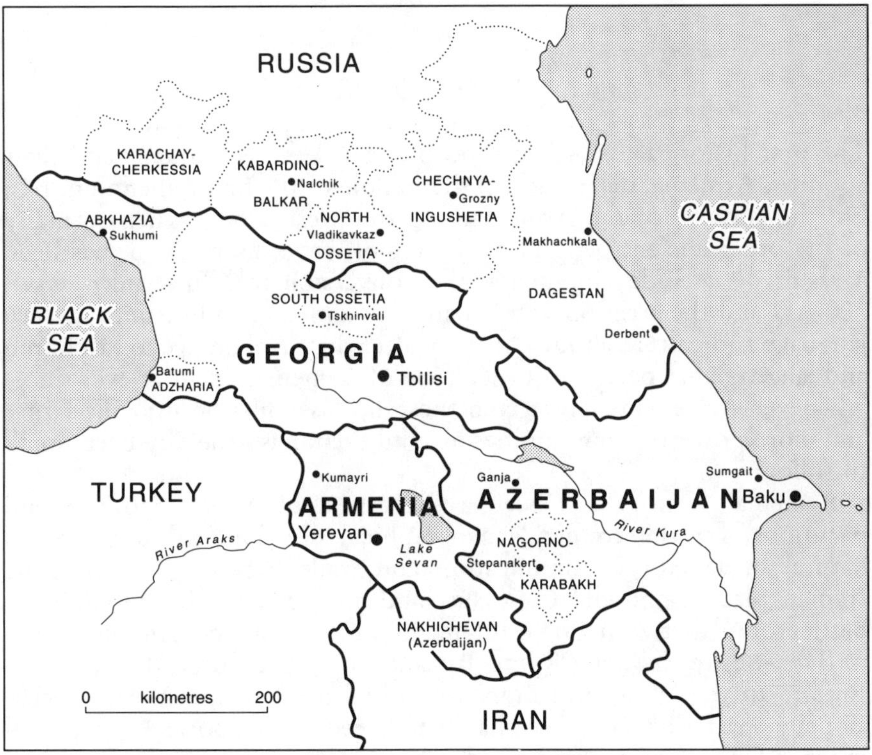

# CHAPTER THIRTEEN

# Armenia and the Armenians

Edmund M. Herzig

## BACKGROUND

The first historical record of a people called the Armenians and their country, Armenia, dates back to the middle of the first millennium BC, but the survival of the Armenians to the present day, when so many of the other ancient peoples of the region have disappeared, has been a result of later developments: the conversion to Christianity about 300 AD and the creation of an Armenian alphabet and distinct literary language and culture about a century after that. Adherence to its church and language has been the cornerstone of Armenian identity ever since; whenever Armenians have given these up, assimilation into the larger and more powerful communities around them has generally been quick to follow.[1]

Armenia's history has been a succession of wars, conquests and partitions, for the country's geographical position makes it both a natural bridge for communication and trade between Anatolia, the Iranian plateau and the Caucasus, and an inevitable borderland and battleground between powerful neighbours: Iran under a succession of dynasties to the East; Rome–Byzantium succeeded by the Ottoman Empire to the West; and more recently Russia to the North. Occasionally parts of Armenia have achieved a temporary or partial independence, but such interludes have been rare and mostly short-lived. Rome and Sasanian Iran fought over and partitioned Armenia, then it was controlled by Byzantium and the Islamic Empire of the Ummayad and Abbasid caliphates, before the Seljuk Turks conquered the whole region in the eleventh century. Thereafter there was no independent Armenian state in historic Greater Armenia until 1918. The Seljuk armies were followed by those of Genghis Khan and Timur, each bringing new massacres, the flight or deportation of more of the Armenian population and the immigration of growing numbers of Turkish nomads, many of whom later settled on the land.

Between the sixteenth and eighteenth centuries Ottoman Turkey and

ARMENIA AND THE ARMENIANS

Safavi Iran fought over Armenia and divided it into western and eastern halves (Treaties of Amasya, 1555 and Zuhab, 1639), a division that led to the development of distinct Modern Western and Modern Eastern Armenian languages. The first stirrings of a renewed consciousness of Armenian identity and nationhood can also be detected in this period, mainly among the diaspora communities most directly in touch with Europeans: Venice, Amsterdam and India (Madras and Calcutta).[2]

In the early nineteenth century Tsarist Russia took eastern Armenia from Iran and later a part of western Armenia from the Ottomans. As the century progressed, the fragile and complex ethnic jigsaw of the Ottoman Empire and Russian Transcaucasia began to be pulled apart by emerging Western-style secular nationalism among Turks, Armenians and the other peoples of the region. Over the years and under the influence of events elsewhere the new nationalisms became increasingly radical in mood and political in their demands, most significantly in territorial ambitions to secure national homelands. Nineteenth century Armenian nationalism remained largely the property of the educated and progressive élites of the big cities, particularly Istanbul and Tiflis (Tbilisi). It emphasised the religion (though this figured less prominently on the agenda of the more radical and revolutionary groups), language, culture and ancient history of the Armenian people, and its prime objective was the liberation of historic Armenia from Ottoman oppression. Armenian nationalists were strongly influenced by the example of the Balkan independence movements, by an awareness of the comparative freedom of Armenians under Russian rule, and by contemporary European political ideas and developments in general.[3]

Armenian and Turkish nationalism and Armenia's sensitive position on the border between an expansionist Russia and a weak and defensive Ottoman Empire gave rise to competing claims, mutual antagonism and eventual conflict; there were widespread massacres of Ottoman Armenians in 1895–6. The violence of the years before the First World War was, however, overshadowed by the national catastrophe of 1915, which Armenians invariably refer to as the Genocide. The tragic events of that year and their causes are keenly disputed by Armenian and Turkish historians, and the Turkish archives for the period are yet to be fully opened, but this much seems clear: in 1915 a Turkish government desperate in the face of Russian invasion decided to prevent the Armenians on its eastern borders from assisting the advancing enemy by removing or eliminating them once and for all. As many as one and a half million may have died through execution, massacre, and starvation and exhaustion on forced marches to concentration camps in Northern Syria. Tens of thousands more fled to Russian-controlled eastern Armenia, the Middle East, Europe and America. The western part of historic Greater Armenia was emptied of its Armenian population and remains so to this day, while the Armenian diaspora communities expanded greatly. The experience and memory of the Genocide have left an ineradicable imprint on modern Armenians' self-perception, indeed the Genocide has in part, especially among the survivors and their descendants, replaced religion and language as the central element in Armenian identity.[4]

Today there are probably about six million Armenians scattered across the globe. The great majority live in what used to be the Soviet Union: according to the 1989 census there were 4.6 million Armenians living in the Soviet Union, 3.1 million in the Republic of Armenia, where they constituted about 93 per cent of the population of 3.3 million. Armenia's principal minorities were Azerbaijanis (85,000), Kurds (56,000) and Russians (52,000). By 1989 the Azerbaijani minority was already considerably reduced and has since shrunk to almost nothing. There has also been a continuing stream of Armenian immigrants from Azerbaijan. The population of the Armenian capital, Erevan, is 1.2 million – over a third of the Republic's total.[5] Demographic data on the Armenian diaspora are not full or reliable, but there are probably some two million Armenians in the diaspora communities outside the former Soviet Union: about half a million each in the Middle East and North America, between a quarter and half a million in Europe, and smaller communities in Latin America, the rest of Asia and Australia.[6]

# THE INCORPORATION OF ARMENIA INTO THE SOVIET UNION

In the aftermath of the 1917 February Revolution, Transcaucasia was effectively cut adrift from Russia and left to sink or swim. The years from then until the establishment of Soviet power in 1920–1 were a period of continuous acute crisis for Armenia.[7] Initially Transcaucasia was nominally united in a single Republic, but in May 1918 the Assembly of the Republic dissolved itself and Georgia declared itself an independent state. Azerbaijan and a reluctant Armenia had no choice but to follow suit. The Republic of Armenia was much the weakest of the three new states and lacked any powerful protector (Georgia had Germany and Azerbaijan Turkey). Its territory was based on the old Tsarist governorship of Erevan, a small, mountainous, backward and impoverished area – for although Armenians possessed considerable wealth and economic power in Transcaucasia, these were concentrated not in Armenia itself but in Tbilisi and Baku, also the centres of Armenian political and cultural life. Erevan, with a population of thirty thousand (a tenth the size of the other two new capitals), was a minor provincial centre with none of the resources or administrative machinery to govern an independent state.[8]

These underlying disadvantages facing the government formed by the nationalist and socialist Dashnak party were greatly exacerbated by the problems created by the years of war and the continuing turbulence in the region. Before 1914 Armenia had imported much of its food, but the new Republic was landlocked and had no reliable line of supply to receive imports, nor indeed the resources to pay for them. Agricultural production had fallen drastically during the war years, and of a population of 750,000 as many as 300,000 were refugees from western Armenia. They needed to be fed and sheltered, but initially could make little contribution to the national economy. It has been suggested that as many as twenty per cent of the population died of famine and disease in the first eighteen months of the Republic's existence.[9]

To add to its internal difficulties, the Republic of Armenia was born into a state of war with Turkey (rapidly brought to an end by the humiliating treaty of 4 June 1918) and soon became involved in territorial and ethnic clashes with Georgia and Azerbaijan. These were mostly suspended after the British military intervention in autumn 1918 following Turkey's surrender at the end of the First World War, but the British did nothing to solve the underlying sources of conflict. As soon as they departed in summer 1920 the fighting broke out again and Armenia was soon at war with Turkey, now led by Kemal Atatürk. The campaign was a disaster and at the end of 1920 the Dashnak government made way for the Bolsheviks without resistance, preferring a Soviet takeover to annihilation by the Turks.[10] There was some resistance to the Bolsheviks, but it was relatively short-lived and ineffectual, though the Dashnak party (*Dashnaktsutiun*) remained an important political force in the Armenian diaspora, where it continued to espouse the cause of an independent non-communist Armenia throughout the Soviet period. Since independence it has again become a major political force in Armenia itself.

## THE SOVIET ACHIEVEMENT

Armenia in 1920 was a devastated and desperate land and the Soviet achievement must be measured against this background. With thousands dying of starvation, the first need was to provide food; within six years agricultural land under cultivation had risen from about thirty to ninety per cent and food production to nearly seventy-five per cent of pre-war levels. Work began on several major irrigation projects and there was progress in repairing and extending the road network. Industrial reconstruction was slower and unemployment remained a serious problem throughout the 1920s, aggravated by the large number of refugees and the influx of peasants into the cities.[11] During the first ten years of Soviet rule economic reconstruction took priority over other considerations and there was little progress towards the ideal of a new Soviet urban social order. The great majority of the population remained rural, with less than thirteen per cent classed as proletarians.[12]

The real revolution came only after 1929, when Armenia was forced through the traumatic upheaval of collectivisation and industrialisation. The human and material costs were immense, but the achievement undeniable: in 1929 just 3.7 per cent of peasant households were in collectives, by 1936 the figure was eighty per cent. By 1931 unemployment was eradicated (at least officially) and the gross product of industry in 1935 was 650 per cent that of 1928, raising industry's share in the value of total economic production from 21.7 to 62.1 per cent. Social change accompanied economic revolution, and family and village – the traditional units of rural life and agricultural production – had to accommodate the collective. In the towns a new sovietised proletariat came into existence.[13]

The social and economic progress so violently initiated in the early 1930s continued in subsequent decades, though not at the same breakneck pace. Two-thirds of Armenia's young and fast-growing population were now urban and in 1975 thirty-eight per cent of the labour force were industrial workers, forty-two per cent worked in the service sector and only twenty per cent were employed in agriculture and forestry.[14] Education, health care and standards of living all improved markedly in the post-Second World War period. The economy continued to develop rapidly, though the per capita rate appeared less impressive because of the vigorous demographic growth. By most indicators, however, Armenian living standards continued to lag behind average Soviet levels, let alone those of the West. Such indicators did not, of course, take into account the role of the thriving black economy, which made a significant contribution to the living standards of many Armenians.[15]

## ARMENIAN NATIONALISM IN THE SOVIET PERIOD

National consciousness was already highly developed among educated Armenians by the time of the 1917 Revolution. Armenia's painful history and the century-long division between the Russian Empire and Ottoman Turkey did much to shape Armenians' self-image. Pro-Russian sentiment was strong, since Armenians under Russian rule were generally better off than those in the Ottoman Empire and because Russia was widely perceived as a Christian protector. Most Armenians rejected (and by and large still do reject) the Middle Eastern elements in their heritage, choosing to see themselves as an island of civilised Christian 'Europeans' in a hostile sea of barbarous Muslim Asiatics.[16] This self-image, already evident in past centuries, was deeply scored into the Armenian psyche by the Genocide of 1915, leaving a traumatised historical consciousness: a continuing sense of outrage at the Genocide, made more bitter still by the lack of any acknowledgement of guilt or reparation on the part of Turkey and by the betrayal of the Western Allies, who reneged on promises of compensation and an independent Armenian homeland after the First World War.[17] Nationalist aspirations have since largely been directed towards avenging 1915, gaining international and Turkish recognition of the Genocide and achieving retroactively a territorial settlement more in line with Armenian claims and the Allies' promises. All strands of Armenian nationalism are to some extent irredentist: all consider the territory currently occupied by the Republic of Armenia to be only a fraction of what Armenians can legitimately claim and nurture hopes of one day recovering some of the land lost to Turkey, Georgia and Azerbaijan.

From a nationalist viewpoint, incorporation into the Soviet Union had both positive and negative aspects. At the time the overriding consideration was that Soviet Russia had rescued Armenia in the hour of need. The price, however, was the loss of full independence and of much of the territory to which Armenians laid claim. The Bolsheviks renounced all Tsarist gains from Turkey in western Armenia and were, moreover, broadly sympathetic towards Kemalist Turkey, which they perceived as a natural ally in the struggle of the oppressed peoples against Western imperialism. Armenian hopes of Western support and a mandate for Armenia were completely out of line with the Bolsheviks' international position.[18] The territorial settlement in 1921 between the Soviet Union and Turkey (Treaties of Moscow and Kars) entailed giving up not only the Armenia proposed at the Treaty of Sèvres (1920) and the western Armenian provinces that had been a part of Russia since 1878, but also the Surmalu district of Erevan (Russian since it was ceded by Iran in 1828) in which stands Mount Ararat, the most potent symbol of the Armenian homeland. It was further agreed that Nakhichevan should form a part of the Azerbaijani Republic though they were separated by Armenian Zangezur. Other border disputes with Georgia and Azerbaijan were also settled to Armenia's disadvantage, most notably that over Mountainous Karabagh.[19]

In Armenia, as in other parts of the Union, Soviet cultural policy was ambivalent towards nationalist expression. In the 1920s pragmatic communists accepted the fact that 'the international outlook is the future ideal, not the immediate one'. National homelands, that is to say territories whose inhabitants mainly belonged to a single ethnic group defined in terms of language, economic life and culture, constituted the basic administrative divisions of the Union and the Soviet government did not initially perceive any inherent threat to its authority from the development of separate national identities among the various peoples of the Union. The policy of 'nativisation' (*korenizatsiya*) was pursued simultaneously with the reconstruction programme, and there was toleration of the overtly nationalist aspirations of the intelligentsia. Thus Armenian was made the official language of the Republic, employed in government, administration and all schools except those for the ethnic minorities. Armenian art and culture were promoted and, until the later 1920s, the communists showed restraint in their dealings with the Armenian church.[20]

This period of toleration came to an abrupt end in the mid-1930s. During the Great Purge of 1936–8 the ranks of the Armenian political leadership, Communist Party and intelligentsia were decimated, most of the victims being charged with nationalism. Control from Moscow tightened and no deviation from the strict party line was permitted. Later, during the war years, the aspects of national culture and consciousness that were felt to be a source of patriotic loyalty were again encouraged, but from 1947 to 1953 the policy changed again and 'bourgeois nationalism' was again subjected to violent attack.[21]

In the years between Stalin's death and Gorbachev's election as Party General Secretary, greater tolerance returned and official encouragement was given to many manifestations of Armenian national consciousness. This leniency did not, however, extend to nationalists who challenged the Soviet status quo; the borderline between officially approved national expression and unofficial dissident nationalism was shifting and ill-defined. In general, Armenian nationalism retained its Russophile character: few dissidents called for secession from the USSR and probably most Armenians felt that the benefits of belonging to the Union – principally security and socio-economic development – outweighed the sacrifice in autonomy.[22] Two important issues, however, remained controversial: language and historical–territorial questions.

While Armenian was the official language of the Republic, there was widespread anxiety that Russian was steadily gaining ground. A good knowledge of Russian came to be a prerequisite for career success and therefore many parents sent their children to schools where Russian, not Armenian, was the principal language of instruction. The language issue occasionally became the subject of active protests: for example, when the new Republican Constitution of 1978 was being drawn up, a proposal to remove the clause guaranteeing Armenian as the official language had to be dropped following a demonstration in Erevan.[23]

The other issue that never ceased to stir strong passions was the historical question of the Genocide and the loss of territory that Armenians believe should belong to them. There was a demonstration in Erevan in 1965 to commemorate the fiftieth anniversary of the Genocide, and since then the anniversary has been celebrated officially and a monument erected to the victims.[24] It was the historical–territorial issue that erupted with such force in the Gorbachev period.

# THE GORBACHEV PERIOD

When Gorbachev launched his programme of reforms in the mid-1980s, many voices, critics inside the Soviet Union as well as foreign commentators, predicted difficulties over the nationalities question, but the sudden growth of a radical, popular national movement in Armenia was unexpected. The Baltic republics, the Ukraine and 'Muslim' Central Asia all had traditions of anti-Russian nationalism, but Armenia had always appeared politically docile and conscious of the debt it owed its Russian 'liberators'. What happened there in the last few years of the 1980s can be understood only in relation to the central motivating issue: the question of Mountainous Karabagh.

The Autonomous Oblast of Mountainous Karabagh[25] is 4,400 square kilometres in area; its population in January 1990 was recorded as 188,000, the great majority of whom were Armenians, whose numbers had been swollen by immigration from Azerbaijan, while many of the Azerbaijani inhabitants had left.[26] The region has been disputed for centuries and Armenian and Azerbaijani historians and ethnographers keep up a fierce debate over whether the region was 'originally' Armenian or a part of the long-vanished country of Caucasian Albania.[27] In the early medieval period the Albanians gradually assimilated with the neighbouring peoples, losing any distinct linguistic, religious or cultural identity; those who did not convert to Islam merged with the Armenians, who also took over the Albanian church. From the time of the Seljuk conquest in the eleventh century a Turkish element was introduced into the predominantly Armenian population of Mountainous Karabagh. Despite occasional periods of partial independence, Karabagh was at least nominally a part of some larger Islamic state throughout the medieval period, until Iran ceded the territory to Russia in 1813. After the Russian Revolution it was disputed by the independent Republics of Armenia and Azerbaijan and finally, in the 1920s, declared an Autonomous Oblast within the Republic of Azerbaijan.

There are a number of reasons for Karabagh being what a historian writing in 1983 described as 'the single most volatile issue among the Armenians'.[28] The first is that Armenian nationalists have tended to equate the Azerbaijanis with the Turks of Turkey and to see Azerbaijan's possession of Mountainous Karabagh as a symbol of the Turks' success in 'getting away with' the 1915 Genocide and the occupation of Armenian lands.[29] Second, Mountainous Karabagh's incorporation into Azerbaijan was facilitated by the British occupying forces in 1918 and therefore reminds Armenians of the Allies' betrayal of their cause after the First World War.[30] Third, Karabagh epitomises the unsatisfactory resolution of international and republican boundaries at the outset of the Soviet period: the day before independent Armenia's government stepped down, Narimanov – the Bolshevik chief in Baku

255

– sent a telegram to the incoming Soviet government of Armenia ceding Mountainous Karabagh (doubtless in order to sweeten the Armenians' acceptance of Soviet power).[31] This cession was never put into effect, however, and in 1921 a plenary session of the Caucasian Bureau of the Central Committee of the Communist Party decided (apparently on Stalin's insistence and reversing a decision reached by majority vote the day before) that, 'considering the necessity of national harmony between Muslims and Armenians, the economic linkage between upper and lower Karabagh, and its permanent ties to Azerbaijan, Mountainous Karabagh should be left within the boundaries of the Azerbaijani Soviet Socialist Republic while declaring it an Autonomous Oblast . . .'; Mountainous Karabagh was formally incorporated into Azerbaijan in July 1923.[32] Furthermore, since medieval times the mountains of Karabagh have been a centre for the survival of Armenian folk traditions and culture. These, and the future of the Armenian language in Karabagh, were threatened by the discriminatory policies and poor development of the Oblast under Azerbaijani rule.[33] Finally, nationalist aspirations have focused on Karabagh because it is the only part of the Armenian *irredenta* that has a majority Armenian population and that there is a real possibility of recovering.[34]

Agitation for a reconsideration of the Karabagh question intensified soon after Gorbachev came to power. Late in 1987 there were demonstrations in Erevan on environmental issues as well as Karabagh, and clashes between Armenian and Azerbaijani villagers in Karabagh itself. Early in 1988 a petition bearing some 75,000–100,000 signatures demanding the transfer of Karabagh to Armenia was presented to the authorities in Moscow.[35]

This simmering local dispute was transformed into a major crisis after 20 February 1988, when the Mountainous Karabagh Soviet passed an unprecedented resolution demanding a transfer to Armenian jurisdiction.[36] Armenians demonstrated in support of the resolution in Karabagh, in Erevan and other Armenian towns, and even in Moscow. The first demonstrations numbered a few thousand, but in the course of a week hundreds of thousands were participating in enthusiastic daily demonstrations in the Armenian capital. Participants and observers describe the mood of this first week as spontaneous, optimistic, idealistic and generally loyal to Soviet authority. The targets were the historic wrongs committed against the Armenians in the time of Stalin or before, the corrupt Armenian and Azerbaijani Communist Party leaderships in general, and the maladministration of Karabagh in particular. At this stage the Azerbaijani people as a whole were not the object of animosity. The demonstrators looked to Gorbachev and his reforms to set right past wrongs and reform the local leadership. They were not yet ready to take the law into their own hands nor looking for confrontation with Moscow; in fact many emphasised their Soviet patriotism by carrying placards of Gorbachev and the flag of Soviet Armenia.[37]

The initial government response was fairly muted. The Central Committee of the Communist Party of the USSR rejected the Karabagh Soviet's request for transfer and tried to place the burden of responsibility for resolving the situation on the shoulders of the Armenian and Azerbaijani leaderships. At the same time high-ranking party officials were sent from Moscow to the Caucasus to monitor the situation and help suggest solutions. Troops were also despatched to Erevan, though not deployed against the demonstrators. None of this, nor appeals for calm from Demirjian (Armenian Party Secretary) and the Catholicos (head of the Armenian church) had any effect, and the mass demonstrations subsided only after two leading Armenian intellectuals returned from an unannounced meeting with Gorbachev and called for a month's suspension of demonstrations on the basis of a promise that the issue would be investigated at the highest level. Gorbachev himself broadcast a message to the Armenian and Azerbaijani peoples in which he accepted that mistakes had been made, but emphasised the need for maturity and restraint in tackling complex issues.

The proposed breathing-space was shattered only two days later by the outbreak of anti-Armenian violence in Sumgait, an industrial town in Azerbaijan. These racist attacks and the apparent negligence or complicity of the security services led, overnight, to a sharp change of mood in Armenia. The official version of events, which suggested a death toll of thirty-two, was widely disbelieved and rumours of hundreds if not thousands of victims have circulated ever since. For Armenians Sumgait seemed a reminder of what their parents or grandparents had suffered at the hands of the Turks in 1915, and of their continuing vulnerability as a minority everywhere outside the Republic of Armenia. In an atmosphere of escalating racial hostility large-scale emigrations from both Azerbaijan and Armenia began. By the end of 1988 more than 200,000 refugees (more than the total population of Mountainous Karabagh) had crossed between the two republics. The often harrowing stories of the persecution and atrocities suffered by these refugees were seized on by the Armenian and Azerbaijani media and played an important part in forming public opinion in both republics and keeping emotions and fears running high. The treatment of the issue in the central Soviet press also contributed to the increasingly radical and rebellious mood in Armenia. While acknowledging the complexity of the issue and criticising past and present republican and local leaderships, the Moscow media, reflecting the views of Gorbachev, branded the Karabagh campaigners as opportunist nationalist extremists, stooges of foreign powers and 'anti-*perestroika* forces', even going so far as to suggest that the demonstrations in Erevan had been orchestrated by external enemies.[38] The Sumgait massacre, the growing refugee crisis and Moscow's unsympathetic response led to a rapid hardening of attitudes in Armenia. With the raising of the spectre of massacre at the hands of Turks, Armenians' resentments and hostility began to focus on Azerbaijan and the Azerbaijanis in general, rather than just on the Communist Party leadership. Faith in Gorbachev and Moscow faded rapidly.

In spring and summer 1988 the popular movement in Armenia developed from a series of spontaneous mass demonstrations to a coordinated network of activists in factories, institutes and offices across Armenia. A Karabagh Committee with about a dozen members, most of them intellectuals, including several current or former members of the Communist Party, began to provide active leadership for the movement.[39] The agenda was also undergoing changes: many still favoured a single issue campaign directed towards the transfer of Mountainous Karabagh, but others were interested in a broader nationalist campaign covering issues such as international recognition of the Genocide, reparations from Turkey, measures to reinforce the Armenian language and steps to discourage Armenian emigration while promoting links with the diaspora. Still others looked on the movement as part of a broader struggle for democracy and reform sweeping the whole Soviet Union, and emphasised the environment, civil rights and other issues.

With no progress on the Karabagh question and little evidence of sympathy or responsiveness from either the republican or the Moscow leadership, the mood of the protesters in Erevan became increasingly impatient and radical, while Armenians in Mountainous Karabagh went on general strike. On 15 June 1988 the Armenian Supreme Soviet succumbed to pressure and endorsed the Karabagh Armenians' request to transfer to Armenian jurisdiction. Two days later the Azerbaijani Supreme Soviet rejected the demand, bringing the governments of the republics into direct confrontation. The republican communist leadership were clearly incapable of resolving the issue; any solution would have to come from Moscow. On 18 July, after months of intense anticipation, the Presidium of the Supreme Soviet of the USSR flatly rejected the transfer of Mountainous Karabagh to Armenia. Gorbachev particularly emphasised that the decision on Karabagh would set a precedent for other national and territorial disputes within the Union and, in the light of this, the refusal to redraw boundaries was scarcely surprising, but with little on offer in the way of positive measures – a special commission was set up with a remit to submit proposals to the Supreme Soviet in due course – the decision provided no solution to the conflict. The Karabagh Armenians now dug their heels in to resist, while in Armenia the nationalist movement grew still more anti-Soviet, developing a radical agenda at the top of which was the demand for full democracy and independence. The Supreme Soviet decision left the Armenian communists paralysed, caught between the conflicting demands of loyalty to their people and to Moscow.

At the end of the year, on 7 December 1988, the north-western part of Armenia was struck by a devastating earthquake, which completely destroyed the town of Spitak (population 25,000) as well as most of the housing in Armenia's second city, Leninakan. In all about 25,000 lost their lives and some half a million were left homeless.[40] The death and destruction were undoubtedly exacerbated by the poor design and construction of the blocks of flats in which many of the victims lived. The cost of reconstruction was subsequently put at six billion roubles. The enormity of this disaster and the massive national and international relief operation briefly distracted attention from the political crisis, but far from being brought together by the tragedy, the nationalist movement and the communist government were soon at loggerheads again, accusing each other of inefficiency, self-interest and deliberate obstruction in the relief work. Nor did the huge Soviet investment in relief and reconstruction lead to any reconciliation with Moscow. On the contrary, proposals to resettle some of the earthquake orphans in other republics caused an outcry, as Armenians were reminded of the fate of the orphans of the 1915 Genocide – adopted and assimilated into foreign homes.

At the beginning of 1989 Moscow at last took decisive measures to try to break the deadlock over Karabagh. Following the report of the special commission, local and republican government was suspended and the Oblast put under temporary direct rule from Moscow in the shape of a special committee headed by Arkadii Volskii. At about the same time the members of the Karabagh Committee, leaders of the nationalist movement in Armenia, were arrested and held in prison until the end of May. For a few months there were some signs of a return to normality in Karabagh, but then matters deteriorated, with both Armenians and Azerbaijanis accusing the Russians of favouring the other side, and withdrawing their support. A general strike in Stepanakert lasted from May to August, when the Karabagh Armenians elected their own National Council, which announced the Oblast's secession from Azerbaijan and began to function as a shadow government.

In autumn 1989 Azerbaijan initiated a blockade of road and rail links and energy supplies to both Mountainous Karabagh and Armenia. With brief interruptions this blockade has remained in force ever since, with disastrous consequences for Armenia's economy. Azerbaijan was the main channel for trade with other Soviet republics and Armenia's industry was very heavily dependent on this trade both for raw materials and other supplies and for markets for its products. Azerbaijan was also a vital channel for energy supplies, particularly since the closure of Armenia's nuclear power station following the earthquake. Efforts to develop alternative routes have met with little success. Transport and energy lines through Georgia have been increasingly subject to disruption, while trade and energy routes through Turkey and Iran have remained insignificant – in the former case because of Turkish cooperation in Azerbaijan's blockade of Armenia, in the latter because the existing infrastructure is inadequate and requires heavy investment before it can make a serious contribution. As a consequence of the blockade many of Armenia's industries have shut down or been reduced to working at a fraction of their capacity.[41] Domestic users have been reduced to a couple of hours of electricity per day and almost no heating, and transport and other services have been severely disrupted. The blockage has also slowed earthquake reconstruction to a crawl: by December 1990 only seven to eight per cent of the housing projected for the first two years of the programme had been completed and no major enterprises rebuilt. Construction and relief teams from other Soviet republics and abroad left one by one in the face of impossible working conditions.[42]

In the face of the blockade and the withdrawal of cooperation by both sides, Volskii was forced to concede that the Special Committee could achieve little.[43] The special administration was brought to an end and Mountainous Karabagh restored to Azerbaijani control. The next eighteen months, until the attempted coup in Moscow in August 1991, saw a clear alignment of Gorbachev and Moscow with the Communists in Baku against the increasingly independence-minded Armenians. Moscow's new stance followed the events in Baku of January 1990, when after several days of rioting, and the killing and wounding of a number of Armenians, the Soviet army intervened, bloodily suppressed the Azerbaijani Popular Front and reinforced Azerbaijan's Communist government. In the same month the members of the Karabagh National Council were arrested and the Azerbaijani authorities, backed by Soviet Interior Ministry (MVD) troops, attempted to reimpose their authority over the Karabagh Armenians. In autumn 1990 and spring 1991 MVD troops participated in barely disguised ethnic cleansing operations in Armenian villages within and outside the Mountainous Karabagh Oblast.[44] From the end of 1990 conditions in Mountainous Karabagh became desperate: Stepanakert was under siege, with power, water and other essential supplies frequently cut off and continual rocket and artillery bombardment from the Azerbaijani forces in Shusha a few miles away.[45] At times there was a real danger of the conflict escalating into all-out war: in the spring of 1990 there was fighting across the Armenian–Nakhichevan Autonomous Republic border and in the summer of the same year there were hostilities along the length of the Armenian–Azerbaijani border. Irregular forces and later the fledgling Armenian and Azerbaijani national armies seized or purchased arms from Soviet police and army arsenals. Casualties and damage increased with the growing use of rockets, artillery, armoured vehicles and eventually even aircraft in the conflict.

Moscow's new pro-Azerbaijani line provoked strong reactions in Armenia. In spring 1990 demonstrators damaged the KGB headquarters in Erevan and there were nine deaths when they attacked MVD troops at Erevan railway station.[46] The nationalist opposition, although consisting of a number of distinct groups and parties, combined under the umbrella of the Armenian Pan-National Movement (APNM), led by Levon Ter-Petrosian, former leader of the Karabagh Committee. When the APNM won a majority in summer elections to the Soviet or Parliament, Ter-Petrosian became chairman of the Parliament, and Vazgen Manukian, another former Karabagh Committee member, Prime Minister. The new government declared its intention of turning Armenia into a fully independent sovereign state incorporating Mountainous Karabagh.[47]

## INDEPENDENCE

It was not until September 1991 that Armenia had the chance to vote for independence in a referendum – the result was ninety-nine per cent in favour[48] – and Ter-Petrosian was not elected president until the following month, but the APNM successes in the elections of summer 1990 ended communist rule in Armenia and mark the beginning, if not of full independence, at least of a government committed to it and determined to pursue its own policies independent of Moscow.

The problems facing the new government were immense: an economy in ruins, a crippling long-term blockade by Azerbaijan, a chronic energy crisis, a state of virtual war with Azerbaijan, a heavy drain of resources to support the Karabagh Armenians, serious unrest in Erevan, where well-armed irregular militias and gangsters were refusing to accept any form of control, and threats from Moscow of military intervention if all such irregular formations were not disarmed. Gorbachev was also exerting strong political pressure as he sought to salvage the Soviet Union through a new Union Treaty. Armenia, like the Baltic Republics, Georgia and Moldova, refused to negotiate or hold a referendum on the new treaty, which further soured relations with Moscow. These became so strained that on 6 May 1991 Ter-Petrosian stated that: 'To all intents and purposes, the Soviet Union has declared war on Armenia'.[49] Moscow's stance changed only after the failed coup of August 1991. The Azerbaijani Party leader Mutalibov had welcomed the coup, so Yeltsin's Russia adopted a more pro-Armenian policy, especially as Ter-Petrosian was from the start a supporter of the new Commonwealth of Independent States (CIS).[50]

Karabagh has remained the central nationality issue, indeed the single most important issue, in Armenian politics since independence. At the same time as Armenia's referendum on independence, Mountainous Karabagh declared itself an independent republic, but in November Azerbaijan abrogated the Oblast's autonomous status, leaving the two sides further apart than ever.[51]

Fighting intensified with the withdrawal of Soviet forces in early 1992, and until the spring the Armenians were mainly on the defensive. Thereafter, however, they managed to seize the initiative and scored a number of successes, assisted by Azerbaijan's military disorganisation and political upheavals. In May they took Shusha, the Azerbaijanis' main stronghold in Mountainous Karabagh, giving them control of the whole territory of the Oblast. Soon after they opened a land corridor at Lachin to link Mountainous Karabagh with Armenia, greatly facilitating communications and supplies. The military successes of 1992 were continued in spring and summer of 1993, when the Karabagh Armenians took advantage of the virtual collapse of the Azerbaijani army to open a second land corridor at Kelbajar and then to occupy a large swathe of Azerbaijani territory around Mountainous Karabagh, including all the land to the South and West of the Oblast as far as the Armenian and Iranian borders, extending as far East as Horadiz. These victories have boosted Armenian morale and provided a welcome respite for the Karabagh Armenians, but most analysts believe that in the long run Azerbaijan's superior resources will tilt the military balance in its favour.[52] Moreover, international perceptions of the Karabagh Armenians have been altered by their military successes; the shift began with the killing of numerous Azerbaijani civilians at Khojaly in February 1992 and has continued with the capture of territory outside Mountainous Karabagh and the creation of tens of thousands of new Azerbaijani refugees. No longer viewed as the victims of the conflict, the Armenians are now often seen rather as the aggressors, and United Nations resolutions have called on the Armenian forces to withdraw from occupied Azerbaijani territory. Relations with Iran have also been severely strained by the military activities on the border and the new refugee crisis. Numerous attempts at mediation by Russia, Kazakhstan, Iran and the CSCE were eventually rewarded with a lasting ceasefire in May 1994, but it is proving difficult to convert the ceasefire into peace. The gulf between the Karabagh Armenians' insistence on their right to self-determination and the Azerbaijani's determination to maintain their territorial integrity remains.

Levon Ter-Petrosian's government has attempted to steer a diplomatic course, acknowledging its material and moral support for the Karabagh Armenians, but denying any direct military involvement. Talk of political union between Armenia and Karabagh has been dropped and the Armenian government has not even recognised the self-declared independent republic of Mountainous Karabagh, stating that it will recognise any agreement reached between Azerbaijan and the Karabagh Armenians. This stance represents a significant step down from earlier positions and has led to occasionally strained relations with the Karabagh leadership, especially during 1992, when the leader in Karabagh was a member of the radical nationalist Dashnak party. In spite of the government's attempts to distance itself, Karabagh remains the central issue in Armenian politics, the question that must be solved before there can be progress in other areas.

In politics the stability of Ter–Petrosian's presidency and the success of his generally moderate and pragmatic policies depend on the Karabagh Armenians at least maintaining their position. The president has no parliamentary majority and the opposition regularly criticises his lukewarm support of the Karabagh cause. So far he has survived votes of confidence, but the opposition parties' ability to make political capital out of the Karabagh issue represents a clear threat to his position.

There are other nationality-related issues, but Armenia has few minorities and those that remain, predominantly Kurds and Russians, neither voice serious dissatisfaction with their situation nor present any serious threat. Nevertheless, there can be no doubt that Armenia today has a more assertively and self-consciously Armenian feel than in the Soviet period and this is not congenial to all. Russian-speaking Armenians, as well as the minorities, feel alienated. The debate over a new constitution introduced in 1994, revolved largely around the citizenship question: should the basic criterion be residence in the Republic of Armenia (as proposed in the government's draft) or Armenian ethnicity (as demanded by the nationalist opposition). Another potentially dangerous issue is posed by the sizeable and concentrated Armenian minority in Georgia; it has shown some signs of wishing to assert its autonomy or even to seek reunification with Armenia (there is another long-standing border dispute at issue here). The language question is also still alive, but since the collapse of the Soviet Union there is no longer any real sense that Armenian is threatened by Russian.

One other nationality issue particular to the Armenians is that of relations with the diaspora. While Armenians in Armenia are generally keen on promoting relations with the diaspora and acting as a cultural and national homeland for all Armenians, and while they appreciate the considerable donations and investments made by the diaspora, there have been tensions. North American and European Armenians have sometime caused resentment by their perceived condescension. Their readiness to preach the virtues of a free market irks a people suffering rocketing inflation and shortages of basic commodities, and the uncompromising stance advocated by some on relations with Russia and Turkey can sound hollow to those who will have to live with the consequences of such policies.

Such issues are insignificant compared to Karabagh, however. Without peace with Azerbaijan the blockage will continue, condemning Armenia's economy to stagnation for want of supplies, energy and access to its traditional markets in the CIS. The government's economic programme of privatisation, market and financial reform and increased trade with neighbouring countries cannot make real progress under current conditions. Reconstruction after the 1988 earthquake and provision of housing and services for the hundreds of thousands of refugees from Azerbaijan are also stalled.

Armenia's foreign relations are also dominated by Karabagh. Ter-Petrosian's government is committed to establishing normal neighbourly relations with both Turkey and Iran, but while there has been some progress on the diplomatic level, Turkey has so far stopped short of opening her border with Armenia in any significant way because of strong popular support for Azerbaijan. Relations with Iran are not haunted by the same ghosts as those with Turkey and have traditionally been better, but these too have been put under strain by developments in the Karabagh war. Until a lasting peace settlement is agreed, it will remain difficult for Armenia to convince Western countries and international bodies that it should be given the loans and investment it desperately needs, to build or rebuild housing and infrastructure, and to start new and modernise old enterprises. Only relations with Russia have improved with a growing perception of shared interest vis-à-vis Azerbaijan, Turkey and the Turkic and Islamic 'crescent'.


## CONCLUSIONS AND PROSPECTS

Considering the extraordinarily difficult circumstances in which Armenia became independent, the achievements should not be underestimated. So far Armenia has avoided all-out war with Azerbaijan; indeed the current government has succeeded in at least partially distancing itself from the struggle. Relatively speaking, Armenia has also achieved remarkable political stability in a democratic framework. The government enjoys unchallenged control over the whole territory of the Republic (though on a local level the old Soviet *nomenklatura* still occupy many of the positions of power), and the institutions of democratic government and civic society are functioning, if not without certain strains. Ter-Petrosian has been accused of undemocratic or even dictatorial tendencies and the suspension of the Dashnak party and closure of its newspapers in December 1994 lend weight to those accusations, but by comparison with Georgia, Azerbaijan and many other post-Soviet republics Armenia appears a model of political stability and legitimacy. Nevertheless, the slow pace of progress in the new Constitution and other important legislation as well as the growing public apathy and disenchantment with politics in general pose serious problems for future political development.

There have also been some positive economic indications. The privatisation process is well-advanced and 1994 saw real economic growth for the first time since independence, as well as a significant decline in the rate of inflation. The IMF rewarded Armenia with credits and loans. These limited economic successes come, however, after years of near-complete economic collapse and a steep decline in standards of living. If the Karabagh peace negotiations make progress and the Azerbaijani and Turkish blockade is lifted, there is clear potential for further economic growth, but if the present stalemate continues the prospects appear bleak for domestic politics, the economy and international relations. The past six years of Armenia's history have been dominated by this conflict: Karabagh provided the focal point for the independence movement and the testing ground for the new generation of politicians; it also clearly revealed the inability of the communist leadership, *glasnost'* and *perestroika* notwithstanding, to resolve the nationalities problems and contradictions embedded in the Soviet system. Now it presents independent Armenia's government with a tough set of choices and challenges. Karabagh will continue to exert a powerful influence over Armenian politics and national debate for some time to come.

## NOTES

1.  On the history of Armenia and the Armenians down to the coming of Islam see: I. M. Diakonoff *The Prehistory of the Armenian People*, trans. L. Jennings (Delmar, NY: Caravan Books 1984); C. Burney and D. M. Lang *The Peoples of the Hills: Ancient Ararat and Caucasus*, (London: Weidenfeld and Nicolson 1971); N. Adontz *Armenia in the Period of Justinian: the Political Conditions based on the* naxarar *system*, translated and revised by N. G. Garsoian, 2 vols (Louvain: Imprimerie Orientaliste 1970); G. Dédéyan (ed.) *Histoire des Arméniens*. (Toulouse: Editions Privat 1982) chapter 1–4; G. A. Bournoutian, *A History of the Armenian People, Volume 1: Pre-history to 1500 A.D.* (Costa Mesa, CA: Mazda Publishers, 1993).
2.  On Armenian history from the advent of Islam to the nineteenth century, see: Dédéyan, *op. cit.*, chapters 5–11; Bournoutian, *op. cit.*
3.  See: Dédéyan *op. cit.*, chapter 12; L. Nalbandian *The Armenian Revolutionary Movement. The Development of Armenian Political Parties through the Nineteenth Century* (Berkeley, CA: University of California

Press 1963); R. G. Suny *Looking towards Ararat. Armenia in Modern History* (Bloomington and Indianapolis, IN: Indiana University Press 1993), chapters 3–5.

4. For a narrative account of the Armenians in the Ottoman Empire up to 1915, see C. J. Walker *Armenia. The Survival of a Nation*, revised second edition (London: Routledge 1990) chapters 4–7. On the Genocide see R. G. Hovannisian (ed.) *The Armenian Genocide. History, Politics, Ethics* (London: St Martin's 1992); R. G. Hovannisian (ed.) *The Armenian Genocide in Perspective* (New Brunswick, NJ: Transaction 1986); R. G. Suny *op. cit.*, chapter 6.

5. *Vestnik statistiki*, 1990, no. 3, p. 79; 1990, no. 10, p. 69; 1991, no. 5, p. 78.

6. Demographic data on the Armenians of the diaspora are often unreliable and out of date, so the figures suggested are only rough approximations. For an idea of the wide discrepancies between sources see, Suny, *op. cit.*, pp. 270–1, note 3 (citing N. B. Schahgaldian, 'The Political Integration of an Immigrant Community into a Composite Society: the Armenians in Lebanon, 1920–74', PhD dissertation, Columbia University, 1979, p. 47) and D. M. Lang and C. J. Walker *The Armenians*, fifth edition (London: Minority Rights Group 1981), p. 11.

7. On the events of the period from the First World War to the establishment of Soviet power, see: F. Kazemzadeh, *The Struggle for Transcaucasia (1917–1921)* (New York: Philosophical Library 1951); Dédéyan (ed.), *op. cit.*, chapter 13; Walker, *op. cit.*, chapter 8; Suny *op. cit.*, chapter 7; S. Afanasyan *L'Arménie, l'Azerbaidjan et la Géorgie: de l'indépendance à l'instauration du pouvoir sovietique 1917–23* (Paris: Editions l'Harmattan 1981); R. G. Suny, *Armenia in the Twentieth Century* (Chico, CA: Scholar's Press 1983). The most detailed account is in R. G. Hovannisian's *Armenia on the Road to Independence, 1918* (Berkeley, CA: University of California Press, 1967) and his *The Republic of Armenia*, 2 vols, (Berkeley, CA: University of California Press 1971–82), whose third and final volume is yet to appear.

8. R. G. Hovannisian 'Caucasian Armenia between Imperial and Soviet Rule: the Interlude of National Independence', in R. G. Suny (ed.) *Transcaucasia. Nationalism and Social Change* (Ann Arbor, MI: University of Michigan Press 1983), p. 260; Afanasyan, *op. cit.*, pp. 56–9.

9. Hovannisian, 'Caucasian Armenia', p. 270; Suny, *Armenia*, p. 29; M. K. Matossian, *The Impact of Soviet Policies in Armenia* (Leiden: E. J. Brill 1962), p. 26.

10. Hovannisian, 'Caucasian Armenia', pp. 261, 268–9; Afanasyan, *op. cit.*, pp. 72, 88; Suny, *Armenia*, pp. 26–7; A. H. Arslanian, 'Britain and the Transcaucasian Nationalities during the Russian Civil War', in Suny (ed.), *Transcaucasia*, pp. 293–304; A. Nassibian, *Britain and the Armenian Question 1915–1923* (London and Sydney: Croom Helm 1984).

11. Matossian, *op. cit.*, pp. 53, 57–8.

12. Ibid., pp. 59–60, 62.

13. Ibid., pp. 102–16.

14. *Vestnik statistiki*, 1990, no. , p. 79; Suny, *Armenia*, p. 75.

15. G. E. Schroeder, 'Transcaucasia since Stalin: the Economic Dimension', in Suny (ed.), *Transcaucasia*, pp. 397–416. See also C.-S. Mouradian, *De*

*Staline à Gorbachev: histoire d'une republique sovietique: l'Arménie* (Paris: Editions Ramsay 1990).

16. Suny, *Armenia*, pp. 10–11.
17. Walker, *Armenia*, pp. 263–7, 276–7, 280–1, 291–2.
18. Suny, *Armenia*, pp. 23–4; Afanasyan, *L'Arménie*, pp. 88–97.
19. Hovannisian, 'Caucasian Armenia', p. 291; Afanasyan, *L'Arménie*, p. 181, 199.
20. Matossian, *Impact*, pp. 78–81, 90–5.
21. Ibid., pp. 127, 141–7, 155–69, 194. Suny, *Looking toward Ararat*, chapter 9.
22. Suny, *Looking toward Ararat*, chapters 10 and 11; N. Dudwick, 'Armenia: the Nation Awakes', in I. Bremmer and T. Taras (eds.), *Nations and Politics in the Soviet Successor States*, (Cambridge: Cambridge University Press, 1993), p. 267–73; Mouradian, *De Staline à Gorbachev*.
23. Dudwick, 'Armenia', p. 269–70; Suny, *Looking toward Ararat*, p. 188.
24. Ibid., pp. 186–91.
25. In Russian, *Nagorno-Karabakhskaya Avtonomnaya Oblast'* (NKAO) or *Nagornyi Karabakh*. The name is probably of mixed Turkish–Persian origin: T. *kara* meaning black (probably in the sense of dark, lush, fertile) and P. *bagh* meaning garden or orchard. 'Mountainous' or 'Highland' distinguishes this from 'Plains' or 'Lowland' Karabagh to the North, whose principal city is now known again by its Medieval name of Ganje (it was Kirovabad in Soviet and Elizavetpol in Tsarist times). Armenians frequently use their ancient name Artsakh instead of Karabagh. On the etymology of the name, see *Encyclopaedia of Islam* vol. 4 (new edition, Leiden: E. J. Brill 1978) entry 'Karabagh'; Ananias of Širak *The Geography of Ananias of Širak* (Ašxarhacoyc). *The Long and Short Recensions*, Introduction, translation and commentary by R. Hewsen, Beihefte zum Tübinger Atlas des Vorderen Orients Reihe B (Geisteswissenschaften) no. 77 (Wiesbaden: Dr Ludwig Reichert 1992), pp. 193–8; C. J. Walker (ed.) *Armenia and Karabagh. The Struggle for Unity* (London: Minority Rights Publications, 1991) pp. 69–72.
26. *Vestnik statistiki*, 1990, no. 3, p. 78. In 1979 the population had been 162,000, with 76 per cent Armenians and 23 per cent Azerbaijanis (B. S. Mirzoyan, 'Nagornyi Karabakh', *Lraber Hasarakakan Gitutyunneri*, 1988, no. 7, p. 43).
27. On this debate, see N. Dudwick, 'The Case of the Caucasian Albanians: Ethnohistory and Ethnic Politics;, *Cahiers du monde russe et soviétique*, 31/2–3 (1990), pp. 377–84; R. H. Hewsen, 'Ethno-history and the Armenian Influence upon the Caucasian Albanians', in T. J. Samuelian (ed.), *Classical Armenian Culture*, University of Pennsylvania Armenian Texts and Studies 4, (Philadelphia, PA: University of Pennsylvania Press 1982); C. J. Walker (ed.), *Armenia and Karabagh*, chapter 9; F. Mamedova, 'Le problème de l'*ethnos* albano-caucasien (sur la base des recherches de Ju. V. Bromlej sur la théorie de l'*ethnos*)', *Cahiers du monde russe et soviétique*, 31/2–3 (1990) p. 385–94.
28. Suny, *Armenia*, p. 80.
29. See, for example, G. J. Libaridian (ed.), *The Karabagh File. Documents and Facts on the Region of Mountainous Karabagh 1918–88* (Cambridge, MA and Toronto: Zoryan Institute 1988), pp. 76–7.

30. A. H. Arslanian, 'Britain and the Armeno-Azerbaijani Struggle for Mountainous Karabagh, 1918–19', *Middle Eastern Studies*, 1 (1980), pp. 92–104.
31. Libaridian, *Karabagh File*, p. 34.
32. Ibid., pp. 36–7: Walker (ed.) *Armenia and Karabagh*, pp. 105–11.
33. See, for example, the report of the Special Commission of the Supreme Soviet *(Current Digest of the Soviet Press* (hereafter *CDSP*), vol. 40, no. 51 (1989).
34. Libaridian (ed.), *Karabagh File*, pp. 69, 73–4.
35. Ibid., pp. 88–9.
36. Ibid., pp. 90.
37. This account of the February demonstrations is largely drawn from articles in *Armenian Reporter* – particularly the 21 July 1988 issue. For a synopsis of the coverage in the Soviet press see *CDSP*, vol. 40 (1988).
38. See, for example, the articles in *Pravda*, 21 March and 4 April 1988. Some reports were more perceptive, for example *Izvestiya*, 24 March 1988.
39. *CDSP*, vol. 40, no. 30 (1988); *Armenian Reporter*, 8, 15 and 29 September 1988.
40. *CDSP*, vol. 41, no. 1 (1989), p. 18.
41. On the Armenian economy see: IMF *Economic Reviews: Armenia*, prepared under the direction of J. Odling-Smee (Washington, DC: International Monetary Fund 1993); Economist Intelligence Unit, quarterly *Country Report. Armenia*.
42. *CDSP*, vol. 42, no. 49 (1990) pp. 25–6.
43. *CDSP*, vol. 41, no. 49 (1989), p. 19.
44. *CDSP*, vol. 43, no. 18 (1991), p. 9 and no. 26 (1991) pp. 7–8; C. Cox and J. Eibner, *Ethnic Cleansing in Progress. War in Nagorno Karabakh* (Zürich, London, Washington DC: Institute for Religious Minorities in the Islamic World 1993) p. 41, 45–50.
45. *CDSP*, vol. 42, no. 50 (1990) p. 16.
46. *CDSP*, vol. 42, nos 15 and 22 (1990).
47. *CDSP*, vol. 42, no. 34 (1990) p. 15; Suny, *Looking toward Ararat*, p. 240.
48. *CDSP*, vol. 43, no. 38 (1991) p. 33.
49. Suny, *Looking toward Ararat*, p. 243.
50. *CDSP*, vol. 44, no. 14 (1992) p. 25.
51. *CDSP*, vol. 43, no. 36 (1991) p. 37 and no. 48 (1991) p. 22.
52. J. Aves *Post-Soviet Transcaucasia*, (London: Royal Institute of International Affairs 1993) pp. 36–7.

# CHAPTER FOURTEEN

# Azerbaijan and the Azerbaijanis

Tamara Dragadze

At the beginning of 1988 Azerbaijan was propelled into world focus as a result of the dispute over Nagorno Karabagh, the ensuing communal conflict having become one of the hallmarks of Gorbachev's term of office. The determination of the Azerbaijanis to retain their territorial integrity, as established when they were incorporated into the Soviet Union, was one of the most intractable problems Gorbachev had to face. The desire of the now independent Azerbaijan to retain both its independence and its territorial integrity are issues that many within governmental circles in Post-Soviet Russia have also been reluctant to come to terms with.

## BACKGROUND

The Azerbaijanis inhabit a land along the Eastern edge of the Caspian Sea, sharing borders with Iran, Armenia, Georgia and Daghestan. Southern Azerbaijan, with its capital Tabriz, is in Iran and for the whole of the Soviet period it had been more or less constantly cut off from Northern Azerbaijan which formed Soviet Azerbaijan, now the Azerbaijan Republic, despite linguistic, cultural and kinship links between the two halves. Today the Azerbaijan Republic covers a territory of 86,000 square kilometres and boasts a rich and varied countryside with high mountains along the Great Caucasian Range and a tropical micro-climate to the south of the republic.

The Azerbaijanis view themselves as the direct inheritors of the many cultures and civilisations that thrived on their land over the centuries. Undoubtedly, as in other parts of the Caucasus, the territory witnessed very early human habitation, with rock carvings in Gobustan and evidence of Zarathustrian worship being a source of national pride. Its location provided a crossroads between East and West which was enjoyed by scholars and merchants in antiquity and in the Middle

Ages, but coveted by powerful conquerers from the neighbouring areas. Thus the Medians were succeeded by the Aechemenid State in what is now Southern Azerbaijan, but by the 2nd century AD the Caucasian Albanian Kingdom began to establish itself in the Northern areas in whose name outstanding Christian churches were later to be built, whose origins are now fiercely disputed by the Armenians. Turkic-language tribes began to settle in the area from around the 2nd century, but Azerbaijanis today insist that they assimilated with the native peoples and only the settlers' language type came to dominate and not their population or culture.[1]

By the end of the 7th century AD much territory came under the rule of the Arab Caliphates. Islam became the predominant religion although Christianity and other religions persisted among some sections of the population. There subsequently flourished a series of Islamic cultural centres where poets such as Nizami of Ganja, Fizuli and others, whose poetry is now recited at public meetings, made their names. The more independent State of Shirvan was established and is said to have fiercely resisted the invasions first of the Seljuk Turks and then of the Mongols. Later the Safavids were to unite Azerbaijan before a series of small feudal states were established, under a Persian sphere of influence.

The turning point in modern Azerbaijani history came with the entry of Russia into the Caucasian arena, Russia's Caucasian frontier with Iran being 'in many ways as important an arena of 19th century Great Game as British India's frontier with Afghanistan'.[2] The first accords with Persia, the Treaty of Gulistan in 1813 and the Treaty of Turkmanchay in 1828 resulted in Azerbaijan being divided in two, with Northern Azerbaijan being ceded to Russia, establishing the political pattern that has continued to this day.

The economic and cultural consequences of Russian colonisation have bred in today's post-Soviet Azerbaijanis an ambivalence towards Russia: on the one hand Russia opened the door to Europe in the 19th century, bringing industrialisation and new ideas to the region. On the other hand the Azerbaijanis lost control of their own destiny and their resources, a theme we shall return to below.

## THE AZERBAIJANI NATION IN MODERN TIMES

By the end of the 19th century, Azerbaijani intellectuals had turned Baku into an important centre of modern Muslim culture. Thus Azerbaijanis can boast that the first modern theatre in the Muslim world and the first Muslim opera were opened in Baku. In the 19th century there were already several newspapers and a growing native literature.[3] A few Azerbaijanis had grown oil-rich, along with a greater number of West Europeans, Armenians and Russians. The Azerbaijani magnate Taghiyev subsidised every kind of cultural activitry, including a grammar school for Azerbaijani girls. The cultural universe in Baku at the time extended to Istanbul and Tabriz, to Kazan (where Tatar intellectuals had devised their own form of Jaddidism and called for cooperation and a union of Russian Muslims), to Moscow and St Petersburg, Paris and Berlin. A literary language had to be devised that would cater for some of the political ideas afloat at the time, which focused on integrating the majority of the rural population into mainstream Azerbaijani progress. This inevitably led to reflection on Azerbaijani ethnic identity,[4] as did the development of yearnings for independence from Russian colonial rule. The tactics through which this was to be achieved centred on the choice of three options: Pan-Turkism, Pan-Islamism or Azerbaijani nationalism.

By the early 20th century colonisation of Azerbaijan also resulted in a shift in the ethnic composition of the population, especially in the urban centres, although Russia had already used rural areas as a dumping ground for Russian dissident sectarian communities. Inevitably, with subtle intervention from various political groups as well as even subtler encouragement, occasionally, from the Russian government, ethnic conflict erupted between Azerbaijanis and Armenians, the latter numbers in the area having increased since Russian colonisation. Political allegiances were also to develop along ethnic lines, Bolshevism in particular was to be dominated by non-Azerbaijanis.

With the collapse of the Tsarist government in late 1917 the question became even more urgent as to whether the Azerbaijanis were to express their nationhood culturally or territorially.[5] This was no parochial question, since Baku was a leading world oil-supplier whose fate could affect Russian and Western interests. The complexities of Turkey's involvement in the peace talks at the end of the First World War only added to the conflicting loyalties of the powers involved in deciding the Azerbaijanis' fate. A multinational working class population in Baku provided fertile ground for Bolshevik recruitment, not so in the countryside, however. The heightened tensions and further misguided intervention from external interested parties undoubtedly contributed to a massacre by Armenians of Azerbaijanis in March 1918, followed by a revenge massacre of Armenians in September of the same year. Amidst the affray the Baku Commune was established[6] in the capital, whose business was carried out in Russian and whose aims were 'internationalist'. A section of the indigenous population and many leading native intellectuals doubted the system's capacity to serve their interests as effectively as would a sovereign Azerbaijani nation. With the collapse of the Commune and the flight of the Baku commissars, few of whom were Azerbaijani, an independent Republic of Azerbaijan was declared in 1918, as were Republics in the other two Trans-Caucasian nations. Largely tolerant of political diversity and dominated by a benevolent bourgeoisie, a government led by the Azerbaijani Mussavat (literally Equality) Party was established. Immediately, the attributes of a national culture befitting an independent country were also created, such as the University of Baku in 1919. This brief period of independence fired the imagination of Azerbaijanis in Gorbachev's time. The national flag resurfaced as an emblem[7] and the 11th Division of the Red Army, whose entrance in April 1920 brought about the end of Azerbaijani independence and established Soviet rule, was sometimes referred to in *samizdat* as an army of occupation.[8]

In the process of the carving out of the three Caucasian republics by the Bolsheviks, Azerbaijan was seen by Georgia and Armenia to have gained territorially relative to themselves, notably, for the Armenians, by the allocation of Nagorno Karabagh to the Soviet Azerbaijan Republic.[9] Yet the Azerbaijanis are resentful of the divisive 'autonomous region' status accorded to Nagorno Karabagh and of the fact that their province of Nakhichevan is isolated by Armenian territory since Zangezur was allocated to Armenia, again by the Caucasian Bureau in which there was only one Azerbaijani.[10] Other members of the KavBureau, as it was called, were denounced as enemies of the Azerbaijani people at the November 1988 demonstrations, in particular Armenian Bolsheviks such as Shaumian. The leading Azerbaijani Bolshevik convert, Nariman Narimanov, died in 1925 in what Azerbaijanis today see as sinister circumstances. The events of 1920 and 1921 that accompanied the establishment of Soviet power in Caucasia were at the centre of most national debates up to the end of 1991, when Azerbaijan gained independence. Today, as the republic struggles to maintain it, the debates are more about the strength or weakness of the UN as a guarantor of national sovereignty and whether there is a real chance for Azerbaijan to find relief from economic hardship through the republic becoming a modern oil-rich sovereign state.

## AZERBAIJAN UNDER SOVIET RULE

The Sovietisation of Azerbaijan had a two-pronged thrust: first, to harness its economic resources so as to serve the interests of the Soviet Union as a whole and, concurrently, to create as elsewhere in the USSR through both terror and reward, an acquiescent, loyal population. As for all Soviet nationalities that were Muslim had and used the Arabic script, the alphabet for writing Azerbaijani was changed from Arabic script to Latin and then to Cyrillic. The influence of the Azerbaijani language beyond the borders of the Republic into neighbouring Daghestan, for example, was abandoned.[11] Under Stalin, the border with Iran was closed and Azerbaijanis with Iranian passports were expelled in 1938, thus completing the process of isolating Soviet Azerbaijan. Likewise, in 1937 many surviving intellectuals were imprisoned or executed. The countryside was collectivised, nomads were forcibly sedentarised and an anti-religious campaign was unleashed. Thus, historical sites with religious significance were destroyed: for example the shrine of Bibi Eybat outside Baku, whose natural spring had been legendary for more than a millennium, was dynamited and covered over, ostensibly to make way for the building of a road. Under Stalin too, deportations of whole populations took place. Thus, in 1948, around 100,000 Azerbaijanis were deported from Armenia.[12] In a polemical speech, Gorbachev once reminded the Armenians that before the Revolution Azerbaijanis had formed 43 per cent of the population of Erevan.[13]

The population of Azerbaijan had in-built complexities because of the large national communities living within its borders. In 1979, the population of Azerbaijan stood at 6,025,500. The ethnic composition was said roughly to be: Azerbaijanis, 4,708,000; Armenians, 475,000; Russians, 475,300; Daghestanis, 205,100; Jews, 35,500; Tatars, 31,400; Ukrainians, 26,400; Georgians, 11,400; others, 57,100.[14] It should be pointed out, however, that successive local governments in Azerbaijan have been nervous of potential claims by ethnic minorities for 'autonomous region' status. As a result, scant attention was paid to the separate identity of the Talysh, the Tats, Muslim Georgians (but not Christian Georgians) and other minorities who until recently had to declare themselves 'Azerbaijani'.

It was under Gorbachev that these issues came to be discussed publicly, and not without acrimony. The recent armed conflict in and around Nagorno Karabagh resulted in important adjustments to ethnic population figures because of the influx of new Azerbaijani refugees from Armenia and the departure of Armenians from Azerbaijan, which will be discussed below. The rights of ethnic groups to schools and culture in their own language have been officially enshrined in recent government decrees. At the same time Azerbaijanis assert that their own language and culture should be recognised as dominant in the Azerbaijani republic as it would be in any other nation state, although little fuss is made about the use of Russian even to conduct official business.

As elsewhere in the Soviet Union, the population was declared to be 100 per cent literate, which was hailed as a great Soviet achievement. Today there are several establishments of higher education, including a national university, a polytechnical institute and an Academy of Sciences of Azerbaijan. However, during the Soviet period there were other establishments that would have been less likely to be found in the other two Caucasian Republics, such as a branch of a technical institute of Odessa. There is more teaching in the Russian language in Azerbaijan, which cannot be explained only by the large non-Azerbaijani population in Baku. Azerbaijani intellectuals who have greater facility in thinking aloud in Russian than in Azerbaijani are more numerous, perhaps, than those of the titular nationalities in the other two republics. During the Soviet period in the country at large there had been a greater, or at least more successful, effort to obtain acceptance of Azerbaijan's union with Soviet Russia through the use of particular symbols. Thus one saw in the countryside a proliferation of Russian names for State Farms, such as Kallinin or Sverdlov or Kirov, which the other two republics had largely avoided.

Industrialisation under the Soviets increased by expanding the already established enterprises and work force in Baku. In the post Second World War period large new industrial towns such as Sumgait and Ali Baramly were built which absorbed not only part of the growing Azerbaijani rural population but also immigrants from elsewhere as well as, in the case of Sumgait, large numbers of prisoners serving their sentences through active labour.

At the same time, although non-Azerbaijanis were less likely to benefit from patronage, the diverse ethnic groups lived relatively peacefully, racially motivated murder was rare, and the Houses of Friendship large and the lip-service to inter-ethnic harmony loud and clear. Certain sections of the population today look back at these aspects of the period with nostalgia and regret.

The political history of the local leadership has been chequered, and some writers have judged discriminatory many policies carried out in Azerbaijan by the Moscow authorities.[15] Undoubtedly, however, under the Brezhnev regime a successful *pax sovietica* was established in which dissident nationalist elements were ruthlessly suppressed, largely by a local leadership eager to retain the *status quo* through which relatively lavish lifestyles could be maintained through local networks of corruption.[16] Haidar Aliev became Communist Party First Secretary in Azerbaijan in 1969. He won Moscow approval by expanding the sectors of the economy that were deemed to be of 'all-Union significance'. In the countryside vast territories that had previously served the local population in fruit and vegetables were turned over to mono-culture, such as to vineyards whose produce was almost entirely exported from Azerbaijan. The number of enterprises run entirely as subsidiaries of Russian factories or by ministries in Moscow increased. Aliev succeeded, however, in obtaining a virtual monopoly in the whole Soviet Union for Azerbaijan to produce air-conditioners and in several oil-related industries. On the whole, he was seen to be a 'strong leader', and through an elaborate patron–client system was able to bring, through informal channels, stability despite a population increasingly divided between the privileged and those who were not.

# AZERBAIJAN UNDER GORBACHEV; THE STRUGGLE FOR INDEPENDENCE

If for centuries the Azerbaijanis have pondered which way to express their ethnic identity and sense of nationhood, under Gorbachev this aspect unequivocally found its expression for a majority of the population in the strongest sense of territoriality yet documented. Apart from difficulties of a more political nature linked to local party inertia and national conflicts over territory, Gorbachev was faced with particular problems in Azerbaijan because of the effects of a growing population with increasing awareness of their economic deprivations.

The population of Azerbaijan in 1987 had reached 6,811,000 and the excess of births over deaths had been 2.9 per cent in the past two years. From 1970 to 1985 the rural and urban populations had been equal, but the past two years had witnessed an increase in favour of urban dwellers (54 per cent urban, 46 per cent rural).[17] This growing youthful population demanded education (further education usually is seen as the way to better jobs) and employment. Increasingly more rural people looked for both in the cities. There was a sharp increase in unemployment (unofficially 14 per cent), although reliable statistics are hard to come by. They believed that the racist attitudes of other peoples of the USSR towards them increased and this promoted a greater reluctance in the population to seek work outside Azerbaijan. Urban housing problems also grew in consequence, the number of factory workers living in hostels and families living in virtual shacks at the edge of the cities becoming larger than ever. In rural areas the land available varied sharply but gainful employment was hard to acquire for schools leavers in a system that remained inflexible and gave little scope for improvement. The leasing system in farming promoted by Gorbachev had hardly begun and was rigidly controlled. The state still forbade movement away from mono-cultures such as cotton or grapes. Choice in the use of pesticides was also not allowed, and such decisions had an increasingly disastrous effect on animal husbandry and soil quality.

The economy, according to official statistics, would be seen to have grown impressively, although in demonstrating this the authorities had to resort to devices such as using base dates like 1913 or 1940 to show recent growth in relation to those earlier times and to conceal more recent trends.[18] The Five-Year Plan of 1980–5 was nevertheless demonstrated to have increased to 116.4 million roubles in overall production compared to the 1976–80 period, which yielded 85.9 million roubles.[19] In the very new climate of media openness that began in Azerbaijan only in September 1989, a new picture emerged. Between 1980 and 1988, it is claimed, one-fifth of annual production was wasted each year.[20] More damning, however, was the alleged fact that no other republic was afflicted by such disproportions.

The lagging behind the rest of the USSR in all indices of economic welfare of the Azerbaijani population grew from 1.7 to 2 times in the same period (1980–8). It was revealed that the Republic held one of the last places in the Soviet Union for levels of social and cultural benefits. *Per capita* use of national income was only 62 per cent of the average level for the rest of the Soviet Union, there was only 65 per cent use of average Soviet social funds and only 59 per cent of consumer goods compared to the overall average in the Soviet Union. The same article, published in the Communist Party's official papers (*Kommunist Azerbaijan* in Azerbaijani; *Bakinskiy Rabochiy* in Russian) declared that the average *per capita* income in Azerbaijan was 75 roubles per month, whereas such a low wage was received by only 12.6 per cent in the rest of the country. Whereas those in the Soviet Union receiving more than 200 roubles per month formed 17.2 per cent of the whole, in Azerbaijan only 6.3 per cent of the population benefited in this way.

Thus, the Azerbaijanis asked why they should occupy this humiliating position, having supplied the world and the Soviet Union in particular with oil for a century. Even though Siberian oil resources and petroleum products gained in importance and their own diminished towards the end of the Soviet period, they pointed to other mineral resources and even to their export of agricultural produce as having significance. Why should so many Moscow ministries control such large sectors of industrial production if Azerbaijani wealth were so small? This last question, however, led to the riposte of the newly formed Popular Front of Azerbaijan, subsequently adopted by the local Communist Party too: most of the gross national product of Azerbaijan was deemed to leave the republic. The Popular Front said 93 per cent of GNP was expropriated, and only portions of this were returned annually in unpredictable handouts from the centre. In consequence, Gorbachev had to face in Azerbaijan one of the most forceful demands for economic independence in the Soviet Union. The transition to self-financing and self-accounting encouraged by the centre was transformed locally into serious demands for control over all production on the territory of the Azerbaijan Republic. Insistance from the centre that 'production of all-Union significance' should be excluded from local control was met with fierce resistance. Whereas the Baltic republics demanded the same firmly but quietly, the Azerbaijani population was viewed by the centre as volatile. The Azerbaijanis appeared so disgruntled that they claimed to be willing to take untold risks to achieve this aim. It must also, and importantly, be said that the majority of the working class was Azerbaijani and that initially it participated more than in any other Union republic in the organisation and expression of national dissent.

Economic grievances, however, had sharpened the division between the local Azerbaijani Communist Party and the majority of the population, who regarded it as a bastion of privilege paid by subservience to the centre. The Popular Front was recognised officially only in September 1989, and it was only force of circumstances, in particular the growth of industrial unrest, that finally forced the local Communist Party to agree to consult the Popular Front and to join it in the struggle for republican sovereignty, particularly in the economic sphere.

To begin with, the Popular Front of Azerbaijan achieved unprecedented local prestige and influence in a rapid reversal of fortune in September and October 1989. As described below, the way this happened reflected some of the new democratic elements in the Gorbachev era: the direct use of television, mass demonstrations and strikes.

As elsewhere in the Soviet Union, groups of intellectuals had gathered informally, particularly since the mid-1960s, to discuss ways of gaining concessions from the government for personal liberty and, in the case of the minority republics, for national self-determination. The restoration of national monuments, the concern for the ecological devastation caused by mindless policies and other similar issues had always been at the forefront of these mostly clandestine discussions: under Gorbachev they gathered momentum and were expressed more openly. On the fringes of open dissent in Azerbaijan there had been members of the intelligentsia who maintained their distance overtly, as a tactic in order to act as mediators with the local party who at first had been totally hostile. Exceptionally in Azerbaijan, however, the initiative for the organisation of dissent through mass demonstrations was taken by the working class, notably in November 1988, which at first distanced itself from the intelligentsia whose members it deemed to be mainly corrupt in their pursuit of personal wealth.[21] On that occasion, nearly a million people gathered in the main square in Baku, with workers being joined by students and other citizens. The initial impetus was to protest about Moscow's handling of the Nagorno Karabagh affair and the Armenian hostility, but very soon protests were to centre on economic mismanagement and workers' rights. Workers from the podium tightly controlled the meetings, suppressing what they deemed to be provocative actions such as the shouting of anti-Armenian slogans. They organised campfires for warmth in the November chill and distributed food to the demonstrators after insisting that the Russian soldiers who stood surrounding them be fed first.[22] The central authorities, however, became nervous after the tenth day and finally, after repeated and clear warnings about their plans, moved in troops and tanks and cleared the relatively small number of people who had remained in the square, arresting the leaders, among whom was Neimat Panakhov, at the time dubbed the 'Lech Walesa of Azerbaijan'.[23] In an interview with the author, Panakhov affirmed his belief that it was the authorities' fear of an Azerbaijani democratic workers' movement that had motivated their inaction to stop the Armenian irredentist movement, which they knew full well would be highly provocative for the Azerbaijanis. In his view, the November meeting had started spontaneously but could have been disbanded easily had the government agreed to a genuine dialogue on worker grievances (the local and Moscow officials refused to appear in public at the time). It must be said, however, that in 1990 the workers' movement disintegrated rapidly and has not played a part in Azerbaijan's politics since then. In a document dated 30 October 1989, a member of the Popular Front voiced concern at the possibility of a rift between the moderate intellectuals (and a minority of moderate workers) among the few Popular Front leaders and the militant workers on whose support the Popular Front movement depended.[24] Later, in 1990, Neimat Panakhov had to go into hiding, having been successfully discredited as an irresponsible leader whose overzealousness provoked in part the massacre by Soviet troops of innocent civilians on 20 January 1990.

It is important to pay attention to the role of the Popular Front of Azerbaijan during its apogee in 1989. Much of its activity had been devoted to finding ways of solving the Nagorno Karabagh dispute yet, interestingly, the programme of the Popular Front of Azerbaijan did not specifically mention Nagorno Karabakh at all.[25] First, the programme declared that the aim of the 'Popular Front of Azerbaijan (PFA) is to support perestroika as a general social movement aiming to improve and democratise all spheres of our lives'.[26] It supported the objective that the 'social, economic and political norms and practices correspond in spirit and in letter to the basic law of the Constitution of the Soviet Socialist Republic of Azerbaijan'.[27] The PFA 'absolutely condemned the use of force in political struggle'; its founding values were 'humanism, democracy, pluralism, internationalism and human rights'.[28] It did not differentiate 'according to social group, Party membership, nationality or religion'. However, more difficult for Gorbachev was its declaration that 'The main task of the PFA is to achieve political, economic and cultural sovereignty for the Republic of Azerbaijan', including independent representation abroad in the UN and UNESCO. It also supported the abolition of political barriers that impeded the development of economic and cultural ties with Southern Azerbaijan, 'while recognizing the indisputable borders between the USSR and Iran'. The programme also advocated that peasants, 'the true owners of the land', should have the land handed back to them for unlimited use, to have complete freedom to cultivate it as individual farmers or in a collective. The PFA also noted that the slogan 'Factories and plants to the workers' could be put into action only by endowing the council of workers' collectives with rights in the managing of enterprises and by ensuring that 'competent managers are in charge of enterprises through free and democratic elections'. The PFA programme had a strong component on human rights: 'Freedom and not just well being' as the highest universal good. It also opposed participation in any military action not declared under international law. On ethnic relations it declared that 'The Azerbaijanis as the dominant ethnic group in the republic are responsible for ethnic relations' and that 'the PFA aims for the creation of the best conditions for the preservation and the encouragement of the language, culture and national traditions of the ethnic minorities living in the Azerbaijan SSR'. It also wanted to encourage broad cultural links with the peoples of the world, but in particular with the peoples 'who historically formed the cultural region of the Near and Middle East'. It hoped to spread a new attitude towards Islamic religion and culture 'so that it should no longer be subjected to the ignorant attacks of philistines'. As elsewhere under Gorbachev, the local Communist Party had been weakened and here it commanded authority and respect only when it echoed the Popular Front's uncompromising stance on Nagorno Karabagh and relations with Moscow.

Another factor in the new political movements at the time was that a significant number of Azerbaijanis listened to foreign broadcasts, in particular the Azerbaijani language programmes of Radio Liberty and Voice of America, which themselves were in direct contact with the dissident community in Azerbaijan. Thus, in remote rural areas as elsewhere, the masses appeared to be well informed and, until the press became more open, relied more on these sources of information than other media. Yet it is typically a trait of the Gorbachev era that television acquired exceptional influence, especially for the urban population.

Following mass meetings and occasional stoppages in August 1989 which elicited no response from the local government, the Popular Front called a national meeting for 2 September 1989 to be followed by a national strike two days later – the first in 70 years (according to Leila Iunusova)[29] – if the local government refused to meet their main demands. These included having an unscheduled meeting of the Supreme Soviet of the Azerbaijan SSR to discuss matters of sovereignty, of normalisation in Nagorno Karabakh, the release of political prisoners, the recognition of the Popular Front of Azerbaijan and other issues. They demanded that there be direct transmission by television of the Supreme Soviet session, open voting and televised recognition of the PFA. As tension mounted, new words entered the political vocabulary of Azerbaijan, according to PFA member Leila Iunusova[31] 'tatil' (strike) and 'iste'fa' (resign). These words were chanted during speeches at the meetings organised continually in the open air in Baku from precisely 6 to 10 p.m., at which the national flag of the 1918–1920 independent government was displayed. It was nostalgia for that period and not Islamic revivalism, as was sometimes mistakenly reported, that brought the crescent emblem on the flag back into the streets.

Dialogue began between the Azerbaijani government and the PFA. To demonstrate this, the second secretary of the Communist Party in Azerbaijan, V. Polyanichko (Moscow usually appointed non-native, invariably Russian or 'Russianised' Ukrainian, second Party secretaries in the Union republics) appeared at a mass meeting and announced that a special session of the Azerbaijani Supreme Soviet would take place on 15 September, to which the PFA would be invited. However, the PFA leaders announced at the same meeting that if at precisely 8.30 p.m. on 10 September someone from the PFA leadership did not appear on television to call an end to the strike, people were to resume it on 12 September.

Indeed, three PFA members and three officials did appear on television together and the strike was halted. The next day, however, A. Vezirov, the First Secretary of the Communist Party in Azerbaijan, flew back from Moscow and was displeased, apparently, with what had taken place in his absence.[31] This was seen as an indication of how local leaders were under the thumb of the central government in Moscow.

The PFA called a meeting on 13 September at which allegedly half a million people were present, and announced that Vezirov had till 9 p.m. that evening to sign the prepared protocol to avoid a renewal of the strike, which he did. Two days later, the Extraordinary Session of the Supreme Soviet of Azerbaijan was covered by direct television broadcast. Crowds nevertheless stood outside the building as heated discussions took place inside, culminating in high tension when the exasperated PFA turned to the television cameras and announced their wish that the strikes resume. It was one o'clock in the morning and masses of people still stood outside. Sensing the gravity of the situation, Vezirov asked for a 15 minute break that turned into two hours, after which concessions were made to the PFA. Shortly afterwards, the press agreed to publish the discussion papers for drafting laws on economic and political sovereignty.[32] The PFA from now on, instead of being subject to sporadic arrest and harassment, was officially recognised. The Azerbaijani government leaders appeared on television from time to time to state that the yearnings of the PFA for sovereignty as well as an end to the conflictual situation in Nagorno Karabakh were identical with their own wishes.

In early 1990, the PFA was eclipsed and, even though its chairman later became president of the republic for a year, it never again represented the full unity of purpose and decisive strength of the period just described.

Any desire for a gradual transition to self-rule evaporated rapidly after a dramatic event which, through its large scale, made Azerbaijan unique in the whole of Soviet history. January 1990 has been dubbed 'Black January' in Azerbaijan. Tensions had been growing with every new wave of refugees from Armenia and there was an increasing sense of frustration with Moscow over negotiations for sovereignty. From 13 to 15 January 1990, roving bands started to raid Armenian homes and commit atrocities. Inexplicably, large numbers of former prisoners had been released just before, and, at the same time, the forces of law and order abstained entirely from taking any action during the three days of violence. Alleged perpetrators of violence who were brought to the police stations and army stations were immediately released. It was mainly Azerbaijani volunteers who provided escorts for the Armenians fleeing from Baku. Elsewhere and in rural areas in particular it was often Russian army units that rounded up Armenians and forcibly escorted them out of the country. Thus, a tragedy of huge proportions took place, when the entire populations of Armenians and Azerbaijanis in each other's countries left their homes to become refugees elsewhere. A region that for centuries had been characterised by heterogeneous populations suddenly, at the end of Soviet rule, changed its character in what probably will be an irreparable way.

Several days after the departure of the last Armenians, on 19 and 20 January 1990, an event occurred that has become inscribed on the consciousness of Azerbaijanis for the foreseeable future: Russian-manned Soviet tanks drove into the streets of Baku killing people indiscriminately, with unconfirmed figures of around two hundred dead and several hundred wounded. According to General Yazov, the deployment of troops in Baku had the purpose of 'upholding Soviet power', to dismantle the power of the PFA and restore it to the local Communist Party. Azerbaijanis could not at the time understand Western governments' gullability at having believed Gorbachev's initial excuse that the massacre was a humanitarian effort to save Armenians, when none had been killed for several days. He was to be contradicted by his own military officials, who said the action was directed at Azerbaijani political attempts to leave the Soviet orbit.

There was much acrimony. The Communist government in Azerbaijan was unanimous and bitter in its attack against Moscow, but it was able to discredit the PFA for having lacked caution. Vezirov was dismissed for inaction and replaced by Ayaz Mutalibov, who became one of the First Party Secretaries subsequently to be President of his republic. After the coup attempted in Moscow in 1991, about which he was somewhat silent, Ayaz Mutalibov directed his government to declare sovereignty but his own position was that Azerbaijan would have to seek true independence only gradually, given her dependence on Russian supplies in the economic field. By the end of the year Azerbaijan found itself an independent republic, part of the free-fall experienced by the Union republics when the Soviet Union fell apart. This was not what Gorbachev and his entourage had planned, but it was certainly what Azerbaijan had fought for.

# NAGORNO KARABAGH

Since May 1994 there has been a ceasefire between the Armenian and Azerbaijani forces, but no government in Armenia or Azerbaijan settled the issue of Nagorno Karabagh. That the Armenians' demands from late 1987 onwards to administer the region from Erevan should have met with such fierce reaction from the Azerbaijanis can be explained in several ways. First, the Azerbaijanis learned to think of their nationhood in territorial terms. It would have been seen by the Azerbaijanis as the ultimate insult if the Soviet authorities ordered them to hand over territory they had thought was their 'unalienable resource' at a time when they had become increasingly aware of the way they had been economically exploited by the centre. Second, they could not accept the legitimacy of Armenian demands on historical, statistical or political grounds. Third, they perceived that the outside world had interpreted their refusal to concede the territory as provocation accepting minority Armenian views that dismissed the Azerbaijanis as aggressive barbarians. Fourth, and this has come to the forefront recently, the crisis of Nagorno Karabagh is seen to be an instrument manipulated by a particular Russian grouping in order to establish its hegemony over the region again.

The original decision taken in 1921 on the republican borders had been ceaselessly disputed, however discreetly at times.[33] When Gorbachev came to power, many Armenians in the enclave of Nagorno Karabagh had become exasperated by what they believed was the deliberate mismanagement of their region by Baku. Some Azerbaijanis today say those Armenians were not alone in suffering the consequences of bad administration, and that corrupt government should have been eliminated rather than allowing nationalist diversions to develop.[34] Instead, indecision in Moscow was the result, it is thought, of a policy of seeking piecemeal measures to encourage Armenian nationalist interpretations of events and to create instability in order to gain greater control over the republics at a later stage. Conspiracy theories abounded in Azerbaijan as a result of each concession Moscow is perceived to have made to Armenian sentiment, which made it more difficult for Gorbachev to reach an understanding with the Azerbaijanis.

After independence at the end of 1991, Russia insisted on being the main mediator in the dispute, although lip-service was paid to the efforts of the CSCE. Neither Armenia nor Azerbaijan can contest this, since Russia is virtually the sole supplier of weapons to both sides in the conflict and so any agreement excluding Russia would be meaningless.[35] Furthermore, with what the Azerbaijanis see as a *de facto* recognition by the United States and Western Europe of the Caucasus as being within the 'Russian sphere of influence', it is unlikely that the call for international peacekeepers and monitors will be given high priority in the West.

The Nagorno Karabagh affair can be divided so far into four phases, the first beginning in November 1987, the second in September 1989, the third in 1992 and the fourth in 1994.

Most articulate Azerbaijanis claim that the issue of Nagorno Karabagh started in November 1987 when Agabegyan, one of Gorbachev's economic advisors who is of Armenian ethnic origin, declared that he believed that Nagorno Karabagh should be handed over to the administration of the Armenian Soviet republic.[36] In view of the system of personal patronage, there was nervousness at the thought that someone so close to the General Secretary of the Soviet Communist Party should be of that opinion. The Azerbaijani version of events obviously differs from the Armenian version, more familiar to the West. Azerbaijanis nearly all believe that the mass protests in Nagorno Karabagh by the Armenian population were organised not by local inhabitants but by leaders from the Armenian republic with the active connivance of elements of the Russian KGB, who at the time would still have been able to stop them had they wished to.[37] They point to the resentment felt by the majority of Armenians who lived in Baku at the risks they were being exposed to by the protests in Stepanakert, capital of the Nagorno Karabagh enclave and in Erevan, capital of Armenia. When spirits became heated in both Erevan and the enclave, two Azerbaijani youths were killed in early 1988 and others fled from the area. Up to 2,000 Azerbaijanis from Armenia were said to have arrived then in Sumgait. Baku radio, allegedly believing it could calm the fervent spirit of the Armenians by telling them of the risks involved in their movement, announced the deaths of the two Azerbaijani youths, thinking this would make the Armenians regret their actions. Instead, the announcement allegedly backfired: the Azerbaijani population, hearing the news, was outraged and the massacre of Sumgait took place, in which a disputed number of Armenians lost their lives in the most macabre of circumstances.

The events in Sumgait form a landmark in Gorbachev's rule – ethnic violence on a scale unknown by his immediate predecessors. The massacre in Sumgait is also a turning point in the history of the modern Azerbaijani nation, for it is the event that brought this previously lesser known nation to world attention, and gave it a reputation the Azerbaijanis resent. The social and ecological conditions in Sumgait were regrettable, Azerbaijanis explained to the author, with 20 per cent of its population being prisoners in forced labour and one of the highest infant mortality rates because of pollution. Many Azerbaijanis felt obliged to ask the world not to condemn a whole nation because of the atrocities, however horrific, committed by a small number of mostly very young men. They also wished to refute the stereotypical image of themselves as 'wild Turks' whom the Armenians have likened to the Western Turks responsible for the massacre of Armenians in 1915. They pointed to inexplicable circumstances, such as an Armenian video-cameraman ready to record the violence as soon as it began. Moreover, Moscow, although perhaps not Gorbachev alone, was perceived to have handled the situation in a way that would, at the time, alienate the Azerbaijanis further. As public sympathy rose for the Armenian cause, the Azerbaijanis argued that they were not given a chance to get equal media coverage for their version of events or for the violence to which they too fell victim.

There was a rapid escalation of terror immediately after the events of Sumgait. The Azerbaijanis insist that they suffered more deaths than the Armenians. The dramatic exchange of population between the Soviet Republics of Armenia and Azerbaijan mentioned above, with some refugees arriving in Azerbaijan apparently not even fully dressed, caused a public outcry that the authorities and eventually martial law attempted to diffuse. When direct rule was imposed in Nagorno Karabagh by a special committee set up by decree on 12 January 1989, the Russian commander in chief A. Volsky, in the interests of security, asked all 16,000 Azerbaijanis to leave the regional capital Stepanakert, an act interpreted by a majority of Azerbaijanis as blatant anti-Azerbaijani bias. More worrying, however, was the portrayal of the special administrative arrangement as a first step towards the rulers in Moscow conceding Nagorno Karabagh to Armenia. At the Communist Party level there were also resolutions and counter-resolutions between the Soviet republics of Armenia and Azerbaijan (see chapter 13), resulting in the kind of deadlock uncharacteristic of totalitarian communist rule. The second phase in the Nagorno Karabagh debacle began in September 1989, when reports that started in June reached the rest of Azerbaijan that not only were Azerbaijani villages near Shusha in the southern part of Nagorno Karabagh still cut off after more than a year from water and electricity supplies, but the remaining Azerbaijanis were being threatened by armed bands of Armenians whom the forces under Volsky had ignored. As this was the period when the Popular Front was seen to be more vociferous than the local Communist Party and was gaining momentum, the former proposed a railway blockade of goods destined for Armenia.

The blockade (called an 'embargo' by the Popular Front) was thought to demonstrate two factors: first, that Azerbaijani railway workers and even Azerbaijani passengers were not receiving sufficient protection from Soviet forces directed from Moscow or the forces of either republic against alleged attacks when travelling through Armenian territory. Second, the blockage was supposed to serve as a demonstration to the world that Armenia was dependent on Azerbaijani goodwill to receive the goods it so badly needed, and, by implication, that having refrained from such action in the past had demonstrated Azerbaijani restraint and good manners. The outcry following the news that badly needed materials for the reconstruction of parts of Armenia so adversely affected by the earthquake in December 1988 were being withheld or deliberately ruined was met with a certain amount of indifference among the Azerbaijani popular leadership. Never had the fact been released that the first Soviet plane to crash (with the loss of around 70 lives) bringing relief to earthquake-stricken Armenia had actually come from Azerbaijan. They had instead been accused of having been jubilant when the earthquake took place in Armenia. Azerbaijanis constantly deny this.

A new decree from Moscow on 28 November 1989 dissolved the special commission ruling Nagorno Karabakh and returned its administration to Azerbaijan. Rumours, increasingly frequent, spread through the rest of the country that the Armenian armed guerrillas were going to seize by force the enclave and the two regions separating it from the borders of the Armenian republic. An Azerbaijani 'voluntary militia' was established and skirmishes began between protagonists from both republics. Fighting also took place north of the enclave and along the borders between Nakhichevan and the Armenian republic. In protest, Azerbaijani crowds in southern Nakhichevan claimed land along the border with Iran usually kept as a no-man's land for Soviet military use. They also demanded the right to visit relatives in Iran and the opening of the border in the way the Berlin Wall had been breached in Germany. The lack of resistance by the Russian border guards was surprising and later interpreted by the Azerbaijanis as a deliberate passivity in order to discredit them and to justify the armed intervention against crowds in Baku in January 1990.

The third phase in the Nagorno Karabagh debacle began in the aftermath of the collapse of the Soviet Union. This phase involved two characteristics: (1) the fate of politicians in Azerbaijan began to be decided more or less locally rather than in Moscow and the issue of Nagorno Karabagh became one of the most important factors for their success; (2) a military solution to the problem became the approach preferred by both sides, which exposed them to manipulation by Russia, the sole supplier of weapons to both sides.

First in February 1992, President Ayaz Mutalibov, who had resisted the formation of a national army although Azerbaijan was fully independent, was ousted in the wake of the massacre of refugees fleeing Kelbajar, a town the Armenian forces had taken with the help, the Azerbaijanis maintained, of the 366th Russian Regiment (of the 23rd Division) still stationed in Nagorno Karabagh. In June 1993 when President Abulfaz Elchibey was in turn ousted, one of the many reasons given was his failure to win the war.

The military solution was disastrous for the Azerbaijani army, which consisted of unorganised and uncoordinated Azerbaijani battalions run by warlords, with the dubious assistance of a handful of Afghan mercenaries and others alongside untrained young Azerbaijani men. The net result of their defeats has been that up to 20 per cent of all Azerbaijani territory is occupied by Armenian forces and there are officially up to 1 million refugees and displaced persons, i.e. one in 7 citizens of Azerbaijan, creating a terrible burden. The conquests have permitted the Armenians to gain control of land linking the republic directly to Nagorno Karabagh as one land mass, and much of the Azerbaijani border with Iran. According to Azerbaijani sources the scorched earth policy of the occupying forces will make it difficult for the Azerbaijani population, if it ever returns, to start normal life again.

The fourth phase in the Nagorno Karabagh debacle began in May 1994 with a declaration of a ceasefire by both sides which has been maintained for over six months at the time of writing. A political solution is still being sought, but at least the fighting, which has resulted in around 20,000 deaths on both sides, has stopped for the moment.

## AZERBAIJAN SINCE INDEPENDENCE

Towards the end of the Soviet period under Gorbachev, foreign oil companies were invited to negotiate joint ventures with the Azerbaijan Republic. After independence, the Azerbaijan State Oil Company had the right to negotiate on its own and, in turn, had to reorganise itself to take on the decision-making functions that previously had been placed in Moscow. The result of the four years of negotiations has been that Azerbaijan is becoming known worldwide for its oil even more than its past fighting with Armenia since the reserves in the Azerbaijan sector of the Caspian Sea are considerable. On 20 September 1994, an agreement was signed between Azerbaijan and a consortium of 10 foreign oil companies to develop two offshore oil fields. Interestingly, however, a week before the contract was signed by the former President Elchibey, the Russian barracks in Gandja, the second largest city in Azerbaijan, was evacuated in the dead of night, without the Russian forces informing the central government in Baku. The local warlord, Suret Huseinov, popular for his exploits in Karabagh and for his business acumen which had provided sufficient profits for his own battalion to be well clothed and fed, took possession of the intact weapons and provisions the Russians had left and mounted a coup against the president in Baku. To avoid bloodshed and recognising his government's loss of popularity, President Elchibey fled without a fight but not before calling on Haidar Aliev, former strongman in Soviet times, to take over from him. Aliev, however, had torn up his Communist Party card, spent some time in his native province of Nakhichevan and decided it was important for Azerbaijan to maintain its independence from Moscow and control its own resources. He was now seen as an elder statesman with experience and authority. He agreed that Azerbaijan should become a member of the Commonwealth of Independent States to achieve some concessions from Russia, but pledged himself to stand firm in all matters concerning the economic and political sovereignty of Azerbaijan. Elections were called rapidly and his position as president was confirmed in October 1993. Suret Huseinov was given the coveted position of Prime Minister but within months Azerbaijan had lost territory to the Armenian forces and the economy began a downward spiral that only foreign investment will be able to stem. Within days of the signing of the oil agreement Suret Huseinov was again implicated in an attempted coup against the government of which he was a member, the aim of this coup possibly being to bring Ayaz Mutalibov, who now lives in Moscow, back to power. Haidar Aliev, through appealing to popular support and relying on international backing for his country's independence and right to control its own oil, survived the attempt to oust him. He united the opposition, the regions and the business community in support for his position.

The Russian Foreign Minister's spokesman, two hours after the oil contract signature, objected to Azerbaijan's claiming that the Caspian Sea had been divided into sectors since the 1970s and demanded that Russia be consulted before any commercial contracts were signed. When Haidar Aliev came to power, the Russian company Lukoil was given a 10 per cent stake in Azerbaijan's own share and the right to participate in the collective decisions taken by the production team consisting of themselves – Azerbaijan and Russian – with British, American, Turkish, Norwegian and Saudi Arabian companies. This has pushed Azerbaijan into the international arena in a way that it hopes will be irreversible. Unless moderates in Russia prevail over the forces there bent on restoring hegemony in the former Soviet republics, the issue of defending Azerbaijan's rights to forge its own economic policy, including foreign investment, could possibly force the Western-led international community into choosing whether or not to confront Russia over Azerbaijan. Iran and Russia share a reluctance to see Azerbaijan achieve full independence underpinned by oil-rich prosperity, whereas Turkey sees Azerbaijan as an arena in which to demonstrate its own importance in the region through its offers of aid, support and advice. Because of its oil reserves, therefore, Azerbaijan hopes to resist absorption into a wholly Russian orbit although, at the time of writing, this is not a foregone conclusion.

Azerbaijan has also had the experience of receiving aid for its refugees from many international charities, although it believes more could be achieved if more political support were forthcoming as well. The

Council for Security and Cooperation in Europe set up a 'Minsk initiative group' first with an Italian and then with a Swedish chairman to mediate and negotiate a settlement to the conflict in Karabagh. Although itself a member of the 'Minsk initiative group', the Russian government appointed its own special envoy who has conducted parallel negotiations. No attempts have succeeded so far in getting the parties to the conflict to negotiate outside the Russian mediation, which would involve the placing of Russian peacekeeping troops, who would not be under the command of any international body, along the outside edge of the occupied territories most detrimental to Azerbaijan's position. It is also assumed that the reopening of Russian military bases in Azerbaijan would have to be accepted as well. The Armenian side is also not entirely convinced that its role as a pawn in Russia's wider geopolitical strategy would be generally beneficial in the long term. Except for the ceasefire, not much has been achieved as yet in the peace process, although informal meetings between the two Caucasian sides are increasingly frequent.

## PROSPECTS

Azerbaijan stands at the crossroads. Since 1992 it has achieved diplomatic recognition in the international community, and through its oil negotiations has entered the international economy also. This has made it more vulnerable on two counts: (1) it is difficult for Russia to come to terms with an oil rich country on its presumably vulnerable Southern flank eschewing control by Moscow; (2) with the potential wealth that oil transactions can bring, Azerbaijan's political stability may become hostage to individual ambitions seeking to profit, while the legislation that could prevent this is incomplete and unlikely to be implemented in the short term. Electoral reform, privatisation legislation and other markers required for a transition to democracy and a market economy are developing at a slow pace, partly because of the political upheavals and the time lost over the conflict in Karabagh. With an ever increasing diplomatic corps and business community in Baku, Azerbaijan is seeking outside help in modernising and internationalising its education system and economy. There is, however, always the possibility that the rural areas, given their deeply deprived state will become volatile and that external forces will take advantage of the discontent before the economic benefits of oil development start to be redistributed among the population at large.

# NOTES

1. Guliev, Dj. B., (ed.) *Istoria Azerbaijana* (The history of Azerbaijan) (Baku: Elm Publishers 1979).
2. Tapper R. (ed.) *The conflict of tribe and state in Iran and Afghanistan*. (London: Croom Helm; New York: St. Martin's Press 1983).
3. Swietochowski, T. *Russian Azerbaijan 1905–1920: the shaping of national identity in a Muslim community*. (Cambridge: Cambridge University Press 1985).
4. Ibid.
5. Swietochowski, T. 'National Consciousness and Political Orientations in Azerbaijan, 1905–1920' in Suny, R. (ed.) *Transcaucasia: nationalism and social change*, (MI, Michigan Slavic Publications 1983).
5. Ibid.
6. Kazemzadeh, F. *The Struggle for Transcaucasia 1917–1921*, (New York/Oxford: the Philosophical Library 1951); Swietochowski, T. 1985 op. cit., Suny, R. G. 'The Baku Commune 1917–1918', *Class and Nationality in the Russian Revolution*, (Princeton, NJ: Princeton University Press 1972).
7. Iunusova, L. 'The end of the ice age; Azerbaijan August–September 1989' in *Central Asia and Caucasus Chronicle* Vol. 8 No. 6 (Dec. 1989/Jan. 1990).
8. Bunyatov, Z. Istoricheskaya nauka v Azerbaijane na rubezhe dvukh stoletii; sostayanie i perspektivi (Historical science in Azerbaijan on the frontiers of two centuries; conditions and perspectives) in *Elm*, 24 September 1988, (Baku: Academy of Sciences News Publishers), Samizdat paper 'Dirchalish' (Revival) May 1989, Baku.
9. Dragadze, T. 'The Armenian-Azerbaijani conflict; structure and sentiment', in Third World Quarterly Vol. 11, No. 1, Jan 1989, London.
10. Swietochowski 1985 op. cit.
11. Crisp, S. 'Language policy in Daghestan'. Paper read at a conference in London on 'The Russian advance towards the Muslim world and the barrier of the North Caucasus', (London: Society for Central Asian Studies 1988).
12. Tabrizli, A. *Histoire du Daglig(haut)-Garabagh a la lumiere de documents historiques*, (Strasbourg: Dagyeli Publishers of the Association Culturelle Azerbaidjanaise a Strasbourg 1989).
13. *Pravda* 11 July 1988; Suny R. 1983 op. cit. p. 77.
14. Narodnoe Khozaistvo Azerbaijanskoi SSR k 70 letiyu velikogo oktyabrya 1987 (National economy of the Azerbaijani SSR towards the 70th anniversary of Great October) *Gosudarstvenniy komitet Azerbaijanskoy SSR po statistike* Baku; Azerbaijanskoe gosudarstvennoe izdatelstvo.
15. Alstadt, A. L. 'Nagorno-Karabagh, "Apple of Discord" in the Azerbaijan SSR', in *Central Asian Survey* Vol. 7 No. 4, London 1988.
16. Smith, G. 'Gorbachev's greatest challenge: perestroika and the national question', in *Political Geography Quarterly*, Vol. 8, No. 1, January 1989, pp. 7–20 1989.
17. Derived by author from Narodnoe Khozaistvo 1987, op. cit.
18. Narodnoe Khozaistvo 1987, op. cit.
19. Ibid.
20. *Bakinskiy Rabochiy*, 21 Sept. 1989, Baku.

21. Dragadze, T. Interview with Neimat Panakhov, in *Central Asia and Caucasus Chronicle*, Vol. 8, No. 5, London 1989.
22. Ibid.
23. Ibid.
24. Iunusova, L. op. cit.
25. Programme of the Azerbaijan Popular Front, 1989 in *Central Asia and Caucasus Chronicle* Vol. 8, No. 4, August.
26. Programme of the Azerbaijan Popular Front op. cit. Ibid.
27. Programme of the Azerbaijan Popular Front op. cit. Ibid.
28. Programme of the Azerbaijan Popular Front op. cit. Ibid.
29. Iunusova, L. op. cit.
30. Ibid.
31. Ibid.
32. Ibid.
33. Kocharli, T. Neobkhodimoe utochnenie (Necessary clarification). In *Bakinskiy Rabochiy* 8 June 1989, Baku.
34. Dragadze, T. Interview with Neimat Panakhov, op. cit.
35. *Jane's Intelligence Review*, T. Dragadze, 'The conflict in Transcaucasia and the importance of inventory' February 1994.
36. *L'Humanite*, November 1987, Paris.
37. Source: Author's interviews in 1989 and January 1990.

# CHAPTER FIFTEEN

# Georgia and the Georgians

Stephen Jones and Robert Parsons

## BACKGROUND

Sakartvelo, the land of the Kartvelians (as the Georgians call themselves), lies between the Black and Caspian seas and on the southern flanks of the main Caucasian range. A naturally abundant land, it has always attracted the attention of its more powerful southern and northern neighbours. As a consequence, its history, apart from brief interludes of peace, has been a long struggle for survival.

Georgia has been exposed to a wide range of cultural influences: classical, Byzantine, Persian, Turkish and, more recently, Russian, but the single most important moment in the early beginnings of national identity was Georgia's conversion to Christianity in the fourth century AD.

As Islam spread rapidly through Asia Minor, Georgia, like Armenia, began to forge an identity that marked it off from the surrounding Persian and Arab worlds. With the collapse of the last Armenian state on the Armenian plateau in the eleventh century, Georgia was left as a solitary outpost of Christianity. Yet it was just at this moment that the Georgian state reached the peak of its powers. From the eleventh century, the term 'Sakartvelo', describing all the land occupied by the Georgians, entered into common usage and, for the first time, all the Georgian lands, stretching from the Black Sea to the Caspian and south into present-day Turkey and Iran, were united under one ruler.

Against a background of political unity, economic prosperity and military success, Georgian culture flourished until the Mongol invasions of the mid-thirteenth century shattered the power of the central state. Fractured by the rivalries of its feudal princes and constantly invaded by the Mongols, Persians and Turks, Georgia entered into a long period of decline that lasted well into the eighteenth century.

In 1783, however, King Irakli II, who had successfully reunited the eastern half of the Georgian state, concluded the Treaty of Giorgievsk with Russia. By its terms, Georgia ceded control of foreign and defence policy to the Russian crown, but retained sovereignty over its internal affairs. It was to prove to be the first step on the road to incorporation into the Russian empire. In 1801, Tsar Paul abrogated the terms of the treaty by forcibly annexing the Kingdom of Kartl-Kakheti (East Georgia).

Over the ensuing sixty years, Russia took over piecemeal most of the remaining Georgian territories, until by the conclusion of the Russo-Turkish war in 1878 much of the medieval Georgian state had been reunited under its control. But, although Georgians were grateful to the Russians for protecting them from their Muslim neighbours and regaining their lost territories, they bitterly resented the division of Georgia into separate administrative provinces and the persistent denigration of their culture and language. It is an ambivalence towards the Russian presence that persists to this day.

By the late nineteenth century, opposition to the Russians had led to the formation of a national liberation movement among the Georgian intelligentsia. But what began as a student movement had by the turn of the century spread to the peasantry and working class. The main beneficiaries were the socialists, who were quick to exploit a coincidence of class and nationality: whereas the bourgeoisie was predominantly Armenian and Russian, the Georgians comprised the peasantry, working class and increasingly destitute aristocracy. Within years, the Georgian socialists, as members of the Menshevik wing of the Russian Social Democratic Party, had created a mass organisation with branches all over the country.

In 1917 the openness and minimalist aims of the Georgian Mensheviks brought them into conflict with the Bolsheviks. Noe Zhordania, the leader of the Georgian party organisation, refused to recognise the legality of the October Revolution, preferring instead to lead Georgia to independence.

## GEORGIAN INDEPENDENCE 1918–21

The reluctance of the Georgian Social Democrats to separate from Russian proved short-lived. In his declaration of Georgia's independence on 26 May 1918, Zhordania abandoned the ideas of class struggle in favour of national unity and relegated socialism to the status of a distant goal.

But the new government faced enormous problems. Years of exploitation under the tsarist administration had left the Georgian economy unbalanced and unprepared for self-rule. Regarded primarily as a supplier of raw materials, its industrial development had been even slower than that of central Russia, producing in 1915 to the value of

10 roubles of factory-made goods per capita a year.[1] By 1918 war and revolution had undermined even that modest achievement.

Independence, while enthusiastically welcomed, was achieved against a background of economic collapse, sudden loss of the crucial Russian market and Turkish invasion. Communications between the capital, Tbilisi, and the outlying districts were almost non-existent, food was scarce and the administrative infrastructure had collapsed, leaving few with the experience to fill the role of the Russian bureaucracy.

Nor did the end of the war bring relief. Despite its neutrality, both sides in the Russian Civil War were hostile to Georgia. The Whites sought on several occasions to seize parts of its territory, while the Bolsheviks helped organise uprisings in the national minority areas of Abkhazia and South Ossetia. But the Russians and Turks were not the only threat: in December 1918 the Armenians invaded following a futile dispute over the border regions of Lore. Only British intervention brought the conflict to an end.[2]

Against this background the Georgian Social Democratic Party (GSDP) began increasingly to stress the urgency of active popular support for the state, a difficult task in a country where there was no recent history of a united, independent state structure and where the peasantry had grown used to regarding the state as alien and hostile. They saw mass participation in the electoral process and a programme of Georgianisation as the keys to overcoming popular indifference.

Local government elections in 1918 were followed in 1919 by national elections. Under a system of proportional representation, the GSDP won convincingly, securing 109 of the 130 seats in the Georgian Constituent Assembly. Remarkably, 70 per cent of the rural electorate turned out to vote.[3]

Electoral reform was accompanied by a national education programme. Georgian became the official medium of instruction and a crash programme was undertaken to build schools and libraries in the villages. The first Georgian university opened in January 1918. Yet, like so many of the reforms in 1918–21, they were never fully realised. Because of the economic crisis, teachers were badly paid, often close to destitution, and schools had few textbooks. Moreover, the reorganisation of education and the new status of Georgian demanded the creation of an entirely new syllabus and set of textbooks. Neither of these existed by the time of the Russian invasion in 1921.[4]

For all the problems, however, many had believed in 1920 that the worst was over. The Social Democrats still commanded enormous support, particularly among the working class and peasantry, and Soviet Russia had signalled its readiness to recognise Georgia's independence.[5] On 7 May 1920 Lenin signed a treaty renouncing Soviet Russia's claim to Georgian territory and any right to interfere in Georgia's internal affairs. But less than a year later, on 11 February 1921, on the pretext of an uprising in the neutral zone of Lore between Georgia and

Armenia, the Red Army invaded. Six weeks later Georgia's short-lived independence was at an end.[6]

## THE GEORGIANS AS PART OF SOVIET LIFE

As Soviet historians later admitted, the invasion was no more than a localised protest among Armenian peasants, engineered by the leader of the Caucasian Bolsheviks, Sergo Ordzhonikidze, a close associate of Stalin.[7] The poor standing of the Bolsheviks in Georgia fell even lower as a consequence of the invasion. Its membership in the countryside still numbered fewer than 6,000 by 1924. Most of the new recruits, moreover, were poor, uneducated peasants.[8] But the government faced more than just an ideological struggle. The economy was in ruins, with industrial output in 1921 a mere 13.8 per cent of its 1913 level and inflation spiralling out of control.[9]

Industrial reconstruction in the 1920s moved slowly. Despite investment in several major hydroelectric projects and the creation of a number of large-scale industrial associations, output in 1925 had still reached only 86.4 per cent of its pre-war level, while unemployment remained high.[10]

Georgia was a predominantly rural society. Some 70 per cent of its national income was derived from agriculture and 85.5 per cent of the population lived in the countryside.[11] The Bolshevik land reform of April 1921, which brought Georgia into line with Soviet Russia, did little to improve life, partly because the independent Georgian government's own land reforms had already redistributed most of the available land and partly because of the overall shortage of land. At 40.1 persons per square kilometre, Georgia had one of the highest population densities in the USSR in the 1920s. The all-union average was 7.3.[12]

The Party authorities continued to regard the peasantry as a threat to their authority throughout the 1920s, always fearful that national and economic grievances could fuse into armed resistance. Despite the Party's failure to win active support, however, the stability brought by the first years of Soviet power proved enough to win the peasantry's acquiescence. By 1926, agricultural output was back to 85.5 per cent of its 1913 level.[13]

The change in regime did little to alter established demographic patterns. As a result of the pro-Georgian policies of the GSDP government, independence had witnessed a rise in the Georgian share of the population from 67.7 per cent in 1917 to 71.5 per cent in 1922–23, a development that was partially reversed as Armenians and Russians returned to Georgia after the invasion. By 1989 Georgians comprised 70.1 per cent of the population of 5,448,600.[14]

Political opposition to Moscow continued at least until 1925 from the defeated Georgian intelligentsia, supported to some extent by the working class and peasantry, and, more surprisingly, from the Georgian Communist Party leadership, which resented the attempts of the centre to limit its autonomy. This inner party issue focused on a bitter dispute between the 'national deviationists', led by Budu Mdivani, and the Caucasian Buro, led by Ordzhonikidze, about the pace of the socialist revolution in Georgia and the question of whether Georgia should be incorporated into the USSR as a separate republic or as part of a Transcaucasian federation. In December 1922, the Georgian Bolsheviks were forced to concede defeat. Georgia entered the USSR as a part of the Transcaucasian Socialist Federal Soviet Republic (ZSFSR). The arrangement not only granted the ZSFSR powers to establish overall economic plans for the area and the right to overrule any republican decision, but also deprived the republics of their separate right to secede. That was now invested in the ZSFSR as a whole. The defeat of the 'national deviationists' brought a new centralist Party leadership into power and heralded the beginnings of tougher policies in the republic.

The resistance of the nationalist opposition to Soviet power crumbled with the defeat of a popular uprising in August 1924. As many as 4,000 people were subsequently executed.[15] It was a forewarning of the fate that awaited Georgia in the 1930s. The collectivisation and industrialisation of 1928–32 were followed in 1936–38 by political purges that cut a deep swathe through the intelligentsia and wiped out almost the entire Georgian Party leadership.

The full force of collectivisation hit the republic between October 1929 and March 1930. In just four months the number of collectivised families rose from 3.4 per cent to 65.2 per cent.[16] In March, however, the campaign suddenly slackened in response to Stalin's 'Dizzy with success' article in *Pravda*. By the beginning of 1932 the number of collectivised farms had fallen to 36.1 per cent of the total.[17] But the financial penalties of remaining outside the collectives began to have the same effect as the violence of the initial campaign. By the end of the decade 92.3 per cent of agriculture had been collectivised.[18]

The transformation of agriculture was accompanied by an equally dramatic transformation of industry. The total value of production reached 503 million roubles in 1932, almost thirteen times its pre-war level, and then more than doubled in the second five year plan to reach 1,047 million roubles in 1937, 75.2 per cent of the national product.[19] By 1940 industrial output had increased 670 per cent over 1928. Between 1930 and 1934 the size of the industrial workforce grew by 40.5 per cent, while by 1939 the population of Tbilisi had swollen to 519,000, some 225,000 more than in 1926.[20]

The violent economic revolution was matched by brutal purges of the intelligentsia and Party and government apparatuses, orchestrated by Lavrenti Beria, who became First Secretary of the Georgian Party in 1931 and simultaneously head of the Transcaucasian Party in 1932. A cleansing of Party ranks in 1933 was followed in 1934 with a series of attacks on the cultural intelligentsia. In 1936–37 countless Georgian writers, poets, artists, scientists and others were executed or perished in exile. Far from benefiting from Stalin's patronage, it is probable that proportionately Georgia suffered more than any other republic during the purges.[21]

The new constitution in 1936 restored republican status to Georgia but did nothing to restore its former autonomy. As if to underline the point, Budu Mdivani, who had been leader of the Georgian Party during its feud with Ordzhonikidze and Stalin, was arrested and shot in 1937.

By the end of the decade Georgia's social and economic life had been violently transformed. Thousands of peasants had been forced to take up collectivised farming. Thousands had been executed, sent into exile or simply disappeared. Thousands more had abandoned their villages to seek work in the urban factories. In the towns, the old intelligentsia, the product of the greatest flourishing of Georgian artistic talent since the Middle Ages, had either been exterminated or cowed into silent obedience. The new intelligentsia was the product of the Soviet education system, owed nothing to the past and everything to Stalin and Beria, while the old working class, which had jeered Stalin when he came to Georgia after the invasion of 1921, was now either dead or submerged by the new tide that had flooded into the towns with industrialisation. Increasingly few Party members had taken part in the revolution and most of the 18,555 who had joined since 1936 were fully conscious that they owed their careers to the purges.

The upheavals of the 1930s marked another turning point in Georgia's history and the starting point for the pattern of socio-economic development of the next fifty years. By January 1989, the population had grown to 5,448,600, 55.6 per cent of whom lived in towns. Over a million people are concentrated in the overcrowded capital, Tbilisi.[22] Despite this, and the destruction of rural life in the 1930s, traditional values and customs continue to influence Georgian cultural preferences.

Somewhat paradoxically, Soviet policies also appear to have strengthened Georgian national identity. *Korenizatsiya* and the importance attached to spreading literacy in the native languages has created a generation that is better educated and read in the Georgian language than any of its predecessors and more conscious of its history and culture. By the end of the Soviet period Georgian theatre, film and literature flourished and, in many instances, received international acclaim.

Economic expansion continued, though not at the break-neck speed of the 1930s. In addition to manganese and coal mining and its traditional industries of wine, tea, tobacco and citrus fruit, Georgia now produces a wide range of industrial and consumer goods. Industrial output rose by 240 per cent between 1940 and 1958 and by 1979 53.3 per cent of the workforce was employed in industry and only 16 per cent as collective farmers.[23] Georgia had more doctors per head of the population than anywhere else in the Soviet Union, and by 1979 had proportionately more people with a higher education than any other republic (150 in every 1,000).[24] Yet it was evident that the Georgian economy was not performing well. Industrial output in 1960–71 was the third lowest of any union republic and, despite some recovery while Edward Shevardnadze was Georgian Party First Secretary (1972–85), was struggling to achieve any growth by the end of the 1980s.[25]

## GEORGIAN NATIONALISM

At the time of the Russian invasion in 1921, Georgian national consciousness was high and cultural activity well developed. Initially the invasion strengthened national sentiment, although subsequently a combination of physical elimination of opponents and a conciliatory cultural policy won the acquiescence of the Georgian people without ever undermining their underlying attachment to the nation.

In the pre-Gorbachev period, Georgian nationalism manifested itself on several occasions, notably in 1924, 1956 and 1978, usually with bloody consequences. The attempt in 1924 to restore independence was crushed and led to severe repression; in 1956 Georgian protests against Khrushchev's 20th Congress speech on Stalin assumed a vaguely nationalist character, and in 1978 thousands defied armed troops in Tbilisi to demand that Georgian be reinstated as the state language of the republic.

The motives behind the 1956 demonstration are far from clear. Some were simply responding to a sense of injured national pride – they saw Khrushchev's attack on Stalin as an attack on the Georgian people as a whole; others, reflecting a view widely held throughout the USSR, were protesting against the denigration of a man they had grown up to believe was beyond criticism; while others simply took the opportunity to express themselves freely for the first time in their lives. For them it was the first chink of light. The consequences were tragic; many tens of people were killed when troops fired without warning. The incident left a deep mark on the consciousness of the post-war generation of Georgians and reinforced national distrust of the Soviet state.

Unlike 1956, the demonstrations in Tbilisi in 1978 passed without violence and for that reason alone marked an important stage in the recovery of national confidence and the development of the current national movement. Even more importantly, the party authorities gave way to the demonstrators' demands.[26] The status of the Georgian language, resistance to Russification and the defence of national rights became the rallying points of the Georgian intelligentsia's opposition to Moscow through the 1970s and early 1980s.

The effects of *perestroika* were at first slow to reach Georgia, dripping through the filter of conservative Party opposition until popular opinion, encouraged by awareness of what was happening elsewhere in the Soviet Union, began to put pressure on the leadership for faster change. Patiashvili, the man suddenly called on to replace Shevardnadze as First Secretary of the Georgian Party when the latter moved to Moscow as Foreign Minister in July 1985, appeared uneasy in his new post, unsure of how to respond to the demands of the time. While *perestroika* deepened in parts of Russia and the Baltic republics, Patiashvili railed against economic sabotage, moral degeneration and a growing private property mentality.[27] Despite public statements in favour of *perestroika* and *glasnost'*, for his first two years in office Patiashvili was preoccupied with weeding out Shevardnadze's protégés and building up his own power base. By 1987, at least eight former close associates of the Foreign Minister had been dismissed, and some of them imprisoned on corruption charges.[28] But Georgia was not immune to the changes taking place elsewhere in the Soviet Union. The party's daily Georgian-language paper, *Komunisti*, began to run a series of investigations into the corrupt practices of the Ministry of the Interior,[29] and at the end of 1986, Tengiz Abuladze's film *Monanieba* (Repentance) and the subsequent public discussion broke one of the taboos of Georgian life and so removed one of the psychological barriers to the re-examination of Georgian history that was soon to follow.

In early 1987, frustration at the slow pace of *perestroika* began to form around a number of key issues. The first of these was ecology, a response not just to the wanton damage to the countryside, but also to people's lives. In March 1987 many blamed the heavy avalanches and consequent loss of life in the mountainous area of Svaneti on the construction of too many hydroelectric stations. Whether they were right or not mattered little. The common perception was that the authorities paid no attention to people's needs, were contemptuous of public opinion and more concerned with private gain than with the welfare of the nation.

This was what lay at the heart of the opposition in 1987–88 to a plan to build a railway across the Caucasus linking Georgia directly with Russia. The scheme would have been the most expensive in Georgia's history. Not unusually, it went ahead without public consultation or regard for potential pitfalls. The project brought into focus a number of issues that Georgian dissidents had been protesting about over the previous decade: damage to the environment, pollution and the destruction of historical monuments, many of which lay in the line's path. It was to prove the catalyst for the formation of the national movement.

By the summer the dispute over the railway had given rise to a vituperative debate in the republican press – the first real evidence of *glasnost'*.[30] The temperature rose still higher as the public became aware that Soviet troops were using one of Georgia's most ancient monasteries – Davitgaredzha – for artillery practice. The disputes over the environment and the destruction of historical monuments and spiritual values gradually brought *glasnost'* to the Georgian media. By the end of 1987, the press had caught up and was calling for a re-examination of the blank spots of Georgian history.

In the face of official procrastination over the demands for an end to work on the Caucasian railway and removal of the firing range, opposition to the authorities expanded to encompass wider issues. At the end of 1987, several prominent dissidents formed the Ilia Tchavtchavadze Society, named after the founder of the nineteenth-century national liberation movement. It demanded, among other things, that all matters concerning the future of Georgia be settled in accordance with the wishes of the Georgian people, that Georgian became the state language of the republic, that fundamental importance be attached to improving the study of Georgian language, history and geography at school and that Georgians be allowed to perform their military service in Georgia.[31]

But an influential and more radical wing broke away in early 1988 to set up a loose alliance of groups united in their rejection of compromise with the authorities. Initially at least, this included the Georgian Helsinki Group, the National Democratic Party, the Georgian National Justice Union and the Georgian National Independence Party, all of whom regarded any form of cooperation with the state, even when there was potential advantage to be gained, as a form of moral compromise. All, to one degree or another, stressed the importance of the close association of the future independent state with the Georgian Orthodox Church.[32] This overtly religious strand in the outlook of the opposition groups struck a chord with young Georgians who led a religious revival as thousands were christened in mass baptisms in different parts of the country.

Despite making a number of gestures in 1988 to win popular support, the Party failed to curb the growing influence of the unofficial organisations, and in the summer was forced to bow to public pressure on the Caucasian railway. With the Party on the defensive, a series of demonstrations in September called for the closure of the firing range and the rapid extension of democratisation. The September demonstrations marked a watershed in the development both of the national movement and of the attitude of the Party towards it. By its repeated attempts to marginalise the opposition groups and its failure to follow the example of the Baltic Party organisations in co-opting the reform movements, the Party missed an opportunity to bridge the gulf between itself and society. Devoid of any coherent policy and bereft of moral authority, the Georgian Party became increasingly confused in the face of the growing challenge to its authority.

Complaints began to be voiced about discrimination against Georgians in the Abkaz Autonomous Republic in north-west Georgia and the republic's demographic situation. In contrast to the Baltic republics, Georgians were not complaining about Russians, who make up less than 8 per cent of the population, but about the rapidly expanding Azeri population in south-west Georgia and the Armenians in the southern regions of Akhalkalaki, Akhaltsikhe and Bogdanovka. What made matters worse was that corrupt Georgian party officials had been illegally selling state land to Azeris, many of them settlers from neighbouring Azerbaijan. With land at a premium because of the population density, Georgian nationalists began to call for the expulsion of Azeri settlers and the establishment of a pro-Georgian demographic policy.[33]

By denying legal outlets to dissident opinion and by doing nothing to increase the involvement of the people in the political process, Patiashvili widened the gulf between state and society at a time when *perestroika* was supposed to be narrowing it. Nothing illustrated this better than the Georgian leadership's conduct of the March 1989 elections to the USSR Congress of People's Deputies. What was intended as an example of the democratisation of Soviet society in Georgia merely confirmed how little had changed: 57 per cent of the constituencies had only one candidate, far above the Soviet average, and the turnout was claimed to be an absurdly high 97 per cent.[34]

Against this background, the political situation deteriorated in March, when ethnic tension between the Abkhaz and Georgians spilled over into violence. Calls by Abkhaz nationalists, among them senior Party members, for separation from Georgia brought a furious response throughout the republic and were the direct cause of the demonstrations the following month in Tbilisi. But what began as an anti-Abkhaz protest evolved into a massive demonstration for independence.[35]

With factories coming out on strike, the transport system paralysed, peasants pouring in from the countryside, vast crowds choking the centre of Tbilisi and over 100 people on hunger strike on the steps of the government building, Patiashvili called on Moscow to grant him the use of special troops to disperse the crowd. Permission was granted. Gorbachev and Shevardnadze were absent on state visit to Britain.[36] Early in the morning of 9 April, airborne troops joined special and regular Interior Ministry units in what the commissions investigating the tragedy have described as a 'punative operation' against a peaceful demonstration.[37] Nineteen people were killed, sixteen of them women.

More than 4,000 people were treated for injuries and over 500 were hospitalised. Two more people were killed by troops later the same day.[38]

Although ultimate responsibility for the use of the troops rested with senior Politburo members and ministers in Moscow – notably Ligachev; Chebrikov, the former head of the KGB; Yazov, the Minister of Defence; and Colonel-General Radionov, the Commander-in-Chief of the Transcaucasian Military District, Patiashvili was seen as responsible for the chain of events that led to the April tragedy during the previous year.[39] But if the attack was intended to intimidate the Georgians, it clearly backfired. Instead, it radicalised popular opinion and greatly boosted the standing of the leaders of the national movement. According to a poll carried out by the Georgian Supreme Soviet Commission investigating the events of 9 April, 79 per cent of the Georgian population felt the unofficial groups represented the national interest, while 71 per cent had a 'negative attitude' towards the former leadership.

9 April was seen by Georgians as yet another national trauma which, like those of 1921, 1924, and 1956, was created by the colonial power in Moscow. It accelerated the collapse of communism in the republic, and symbolised the hollowness of *perestroika* and the illegitimacy of Moscow's rule. It allowed myriad new parties to set the political agenda despite the policy of the new communist leadership under Givi Gumbaridze which followed the strategy of the Lithuanian communist party by incorporating nationalist demands into its programme. In September 1989, Gumbaridze, who had briefly been Georgia's KGB chief before his promotion to first party secretary in April 1989, published a new version of the Georgian party's programme which called for national sovereignty, including the supremacy of Georgian law over all-Union law, Georgian citizenship, the separation of powers, multiparty elections, and an end to the Party's monopoly.[40] By the following summer, the communist-dominated Georgian Supreme Soviet had passed laws enhancing Georgia's sovereignty, and the Georgian government had approved policies of Georgian settlement in minority areas, pressured Soviet troops to abandon military bases (notably in Mtskheta), promoted the Georgianisation of place names and a new national history in the schools, and established a commission to explore a judicial mechanism for the formal separation of Georgia from the Union. But Gumbaridze's policy of political reform and openness only revealed the depths of Georgian estrangement from the system, as professional organisations from trade unions to the republic's football league broke with their all-Union counterparts and announced their independence from the Communist Party. The Georgian Communist Party could not compete with the shining moral authority of the new parties, the most prominent of which was the Round Table group under Zviad Gamsakhurdia, former dissident and

301

the son of one of Georgia's greatest patriotic novelists, Konstantine Gamsakhurdia.[41]

The formal end to communist power came in October 1990 with elections to the new Georgian Supreme Soviet. Despite controversy surrounding the electoral law, which limited candidacies to residents of ten years, disenfranchised the Soviet military and forbade the registration of parties 'whose activity does not extend over Georgia's entire territory' – thus excluding ethnic and regional parties – the election was conducted fairly and based on a mixed system of majority and proportional representation. Of the six parties and five electoral blocs that took part, the radical nationalist Round Table–Free Georgia bloc led by Gamsakhurdia secured 155 seats out of 250 (54 per cent of the vote). The Georgian Communist Party, with most of its support in rural and ethnically non-Georgian areas, came next with 64 seats (29.6 per cent of the vote), and the Popular Front was third with 12 seats (1.93 per cent).[42] The result was greeted with jubilation, although in retrospect it determined many of the problems that were to follow. None of the blocs representing moderate intelligentsia opinion were successful in the elections, and ethnic minorities were hardly represented at all. The Supreme Soviet was polarised between a majority of deputies who proudly dubbed themselves the 'irreconcilables', well-versed in the popular politics of the street and full of bellicose rhetoric about the coming battle with Moscow, and the minority of communist deputies unprepared for opposition politics, viewed as a fifth column.

## THE GAMSAKHURDIA ERA

Gamsakhurdia's period in office was characterised by political violence, economic decay, social polarisation, international isolation, and finally war. But Gamsakhurdia, who was incompetent, naive, authoritarian and prone to self-aggrandisement and paranoia, was only part of the tragedy that brought Georgia to a military takeover in December 1991. Georgian society, as I have argued elsewhere, was ripe for Gamsakhurdia. His militant populist themes of national unity, direct action, mass participation, anti-élitism, traditionalism and heroism appealed to a population that was deeply nationalistic, embittered with the Soviet system and all it represented, and undergoing the trauma of rapid economic and political change.[43] But Gamsakhurdia's success – and his final downfall – cannot be understood apart from the legacy of both Georgian and Soviet political cultures. The Soviet system produced the social and institutional structures ideal for Gamsakhurdia's branch of populism. It stunted social and political differentiation, prevented the growth of autonomous interest groups and parties, and undermined a sense of political efficacy and political accommodation. Politics was personalised, revolved around top leaders, and its language was reduced to Manichaean choices of 'good and bad', or 'them and us'. The state was authoritarian and promoted generally egalitarian expectations. At the same time, despite the early years of rapid social mobility, Soviet policies left multiple divisions between a small politico-cultural élite and a large socially undifferentiated mass, between urban and rural populations (particularly between Tbilisi and the provinces), and between Georgians and non-Georgians, all of which Gamsakhurdia successfully exploited in his claim to represent the 'voice of the people'.

But it was not Soviet political structures alone that provided Gamsakhurdia with his populist base. He benefited from Georgian cultural values such as the hagiographic view of native writers and leaders, mystification of the past and support for conservative family values, all of which, paradoxically, were encouraged by the Soviet system itself.[44] The Soviet system also forced Georgians, due to the inefficacy of formal structures, to develop their traditional reliance on personal loyalties and nepotistic networks, and it produced an intelligentsia largely untouched by the constant revision, critique and renewal that characterises its Western counterparts. This left it with a belief in moral certainties and in its own culture's neglected superiority, a view it communicated to the majority of the population. Gamsakhurdia, with his policies of Georgianisation, glorification of the national past, state paternalism and intolerance of challenges to national unity, was representative of this way of thinking. In the May 1991 Presidential elections, Gamsakhurdia won 87 per cent of the vote.[45] Gamsakhurdia, like most Georgians, believed that independence (declared 9 April 1991), elections and a multiparty legislative body were sufficient for democracy. Concepts such as the protection of minorities, cooperation between competing élites and procedural norms limiting executive power guaranteed by the rule of law were poorly understood. Within a short period Gamsakhurdia had introduced a legislative programme which represented, on paper at least, a *Rechtstaat*: laws on the freedom of the press, an independent judiciary, political parties, religious and economic freedom, and the separation of powers.[46] But the basic democratic thrust of these laws was flawed by omission or vagueness, and undermined by other less democratic ones like those on the Prefecture and Presidency. These laws, along with a new constitution, preserved a highly centralised system with enormous powers in the hands of the President and his appointees. Arguably these powers, such as his right to appoint and dismiss Prime Ministers, cabinets and top army officers, or to dissolve the parliament, call a referendum and declare a state of emergency and rule by decree, were similar to those of the French President. But Gamsakhurdia's Presidential preeminence was heightened by his power to suspend the force of laws and decrees passed by the legislatures of autonomous republics and regions in Georgia and by his right to serve unlimited terms. He could only be impeached by three-quarters of the parliamentary vote for an act of treason.[47]

But the real problem was not the legislation, rather its irrelevance. Gamsakhurdia's obsessive emphasis on national unity led him to a number of conclusions: ethnic minorities were dangerous, the state should be active and vigilant, the media and the opposition were factional and potentially disloyal. Gamsakhurdia's own rejection of 'prudence' and 'compromise' in relations with the opposition, and his lack of understanding for institutional and normative boundaries in the political arena, led to an association of himself and his allies with the state. His populist style, with its emphasis on referenda, rallies, letter-writing campaigns and glorification of the leader, created a highly charged emotional atmosphere in which 'enemies of the nation', 'Judases' and 'red intelligentsias' figured prominently.

By the summer of 1991, the national consensus that Gamsakhurdia so desperately sought was disintegrating. The inordinately influential cultural intelligentsia of Tbilisi was deeply resentful of Gamsakhurdia's attacks on its authority and his heavy-handed manipulation of cultural institutions through intimidation and personnel changes. Parliamentarians including members of Gamsakhurdia's own bloc and sacked former colleagues were alienated by his cavalier manipulation of procedure, endless revisions of the constitution, and frequent use of dubiously legitimate Presidential decrees.[48] Finally the extra-parliamentary opposition, excluded from all political consideration by Gamsakhurdia and with some of their leaders in prison, expressed their opposition to Gamsakhurdia through street rallies, hunger strikes and paramilitary activity. But crucial to the opposition's success was the August 1991 putsch in Moscow. Gamsakhurdia's response was perceived as weak, and his decision to demote the Georgian National Guard by putting it under the control of the Georgian Ministry of Interior was taken as submission to the Moscow conspirators' demands.[49] The majority of the National Guard, the only effective military force in Georgia apart from Soviet forces, followed its commander, Tengiz Kitovani, into opposition. From August until the end of the year when Gamsakhurdia was overthrown by a coup led by the National Guard and paramilitary groups of the extra-parliamentary opposition, Georgian political life was characterised by parades, demonstrations, barricades and occupations. Gamsakhurdia's decision to put all the power ministries under direct Presidential control, his expulsion of the entire communist party bloc from parliament, and his attempt to mobilise the rural population in his defence proved fruitless. Soviet troops secretly supported the opposition with arms and the population was too exhausted to take sides.

## THE SHEVARDNADZE ERA

In January 1992, a Military Council came to power, led by the triumvirate of Tengiz Kitovani, Tengiz Sigua, Gamsakhurdia's former prime minister, and Jaba Ioseliani, leader of the powerful paramilitary organisation *Mkhedrioni* (Horsemen). The Council declared its aim to be the restoration of democracy and created a Provisional Government and a Political Consultative Council consisting of all the major political parties. But despite its policy of national reconciliation, the Military Council proved incapable of restoring civil order or of ending the republic's international isolation. In March the Military Council invited Eduard Shevardnadze to resume his leadership of the Georgian republic, and the short interregnum of praetorian guardianship came to an end.[50]

Shevardnadze inherited a state, that, in the strict Weberian sense of the word ('an organisation which monopolises legitimate violence over a given territory'), no longer existed. There were two wars, one with the South Ossetian secessionists, the other with the ex-President's supporters in Mingrelia, western Georgia. Both the southwestern autonomous republic of Adzharia under Aslan Abashidze and the Abkhazian autonomous republic under the leadership of Vladislav Ardzinba were out of Tbilisi's control. The Armenian- and Azeri-populated regions on the republic's southern borders had established ethnocratic heirarchies which effectively ran themselves. There was no army responsible to a legitimate executive power, rather a number of competing paramilitary groups, and the structures of government had ceased to function. Of the multiple and interrelated tasks that Shevardnadze faced, the most pressing were an end to the wars in South Ossetia and western Georgia, accommodation with Georgia's ethnic minorities, the re-establishment of civilian control over the paramilitaries and the restoration of some normality in economic life. At the same time Shevardnadze, who had replaced a legitimately elected President removed by a military coup, needed to seek popular and international legitimacy through a revived democratic system.

Shevardnadze's period in office has brought mixed results in all areas, and many of the problems remain unresolved. He has been dogged by powerful paramilitaries unwilling to cede their power, Russian military intervention in Abkhazia and to a lesser extent in South Ossetia, devastation of the economic and political infrastructures, and a population severely hampered by its Soviet mentality.[51] Despite these obstacles, Shevardnadze's realism and his willingness to compromise brought the conflict in South Ossetia to an end within three months of his arrival. Within seven months in October 1992 he had established a newly elected parliament and temporary power structure, with himself popularly elected as both Chairman of Parliament and Head of State.[52] The appeasement of Gamsakhurdia's followers and the national minorities proved less easy. In June 1992 Shevardnadze withstood a feeble coup attempt by Gamsakhurdia's supporters in the centre of Tbilisi, but far more threatening was the war in western Georgia where Gamsakhurdia had extensive support among the local Mingrelian population.[53] The war lasted until the autumn of 1993, when Gamsakhurdia's forces, after almost capturing the western Georgian regional capital of Kutaisi, were defeated by a combination of Georgian and Russian forces. In January 1994 Gamsakhurdia was dead, either by suicide or at the hands of his own followers, which brought an end to the armed revolt. But it did not heal the bitter regional and political divisions that Gamsakhurdia's rule had exacerbated in Georgian society.

The civil war and a more prolonged war with Abkhazian separatists, which broke out in August 1992 and ended in Georgia's defeat in September 1993 with the loss of the Abkhazian autonomous republic and over 20,000 lives, undermined Shevardnadze's attempt to rebuild Georgian institutions and 'civilianise' the Georgian paramilitaries. The permanent military crisis increased the power of the paramilitaries, particularly in the absence of a regular army. Shevardnadze was forced to indulge in a careful balancing act between the two military leaders, Tengiz Kitovani and Jaba Ioseliani, commanders of the National Guard and *Mkhedrioni* respectively. It was only in May 1993 that he was able to remove the impetuous Kitovani as Minister of Defense. Kitovani had already disobeyed Shevardnadze a number of times, including unsanctioned military action against the Abkhazians which had led to the 13 month war. Ioseliani proved politically more flexible than Kitovani but, despite persistent attempts by Shevardnadze to integrate Ioseliani's militia into the regular armed forces, he still commands it like a personal army.[54] While the possibility of violence continues in Abkhazia, South Ossetia and the southern regions populated by Armenians and Azeris, Shevardnadze needs Ioseliani. Ioseliani remains unpredictable, and his assertions of independence from Shevardnadze and his government have led to serious political crises on a number of occasions.[55] But at the same time Ioseliani's *Mkhedrioni* has frequently saved Shevardnadze from military defeat. Thus despite protests from the Georgian parliament, which points to Ioseliani's criminal background and involvement in the black market, Shevardnadze continues to employ him in responsible positions such as chairman of the delegation conducting peace talks with Abkhazian separatists in Geneva and Head of the State of Emergency Provisional Committee set up in October 1993. Ioseliani, through his informal network of clients who control *Mkhedrioni*, large sections of the economy and government ministers, remains one of the most powerful men in Georgia, but his unpopularity with the Georgian population has encouraged him to maintain his alliance with Shevardnadze.

The war, as well as providing paramilitaries with their *raison d'étre*, increased the crime rate as armed soldiers returned home to joblessness, and undermined the legal power structures set up by the temporary Law on State Power in November 1992.[56] The parliament, due to a bad electoral law designed to prevent a repeat of the single-party monopoly of the legislature under Gamsakhurdia, comprised twenty-six fractious parties. The inexperience of the new politicians, the limited power given to the Speaker and parliamentary authorities to control the conduct of debates, the newness of procedure and a traditional Georgian nihilism towards rules were not unsurmountable barriers to an effective legislature. But fluctuation in the fortunes of war, mistakes in its conduct and condemnation of Shevardnadze's policy of 'capitulation' to the Russians, who eventually forced Georgia back into the CIS in October 1993 and extracted military basing rights in return for their arbitration in the conflict,[57] led to a hysterical legislature in which opponents labelled one another traitors. Such highly charged partisanship prevented compromise, sabotaged the parliament's legislative programme and undermined public confidence in parliamentary politics. Parliamentarians ceased to attend legislative committees, neglected constituents' local needs, and created regular crises with demands for Shevardnadze's resignation. Bitter distrust between the parliamentary opposition and Shevardnadze grew as the latter ignoring parliament's sensibilities, gained and used emergency powers to resolve Georgia's military, financial and political crises. A weak and disorganised parliament suited Shevardnadze, but it undermined a central pillar of the new constitutional structure, and has done great damage to the long-term health of Georgian democracy.

The war undermined the Georgian economy, already devastated because of the breakdown of supplies, particularly energy, grain and raw materials for manufacturing from the former USSR. All resources were devoted to the war effort, economic reform was postponed indefinitely, and following Georgia's defeat in Abkhazia the state was burdened with a quarter of a million refugees. Shevardnadze cannot be blamed alone for the 1993 levels of GDP, industrial and agricultural output and labour productivity, which have fallen to the levels of the 1960s, nor for the devastation of war or the 9,000 per cent inflation, but his passivity in the area of economic reform and commitment to a National Bank policy of massive credit emissions contributed to the permanent economic catastrophe in he republic. Until September 1994, when under pressure from the World Bank and IMF the first steps were taken to implement economic reform, there had been no effective privatisation, total confusion in land redistribution, continued massive price and employment subsidies, an absence of revenue collection and hence an uncontrolled budget deficit. This led to a massive decline in living standards and unprecedented levels of poverty as the salaries paid by the government in official 'coupons' became totally worthless. The average monthly salary of one half million coupons (approximately

50 cents) can be used to buy rationed bread, pay for certain utilities and public transport. The remainder of the economy functions in roubles or dollars, currencies that are not taxed and have to be earned by moonlighting, trading or borrowing. The absence of economic restructuring, which preserved an incompetent ministerial structure that discouraged foreign investment and prevented revenue earnings, increased Georgia's dependence on Russian energy and contributed to the misery of Georgian winters, during which most domestic consumers were deprived of heat, electricity and hot water.[58]

Shevardnadze has responded to the war and to the accompanying economic and political crisis with caution. His personnel policies have demonstrated a particular weakness for balance and continuity at the expense of change. Almost all of Shevardnadze's cabinet are former *apparatchiki*, such as Prime Minister Ot'ar Patsatsia and deputy Prime minister Avt'andil Margiani, appointed for their regional political bases rather than their commitment to reform.[59] While useful in a system based on clients and personal networks, they are a brake on the transition to a leaner, better-managed bureaucracy and an independent economy.

## CONCLUSIONS

Georgia continues to exist, as one Georgian scholar put it to me, in a state of 'stable catastrophe'. Shevardnadze has made some progress in reducing crime and, since the appointment of Vardik'o Nadibaidze as Defence Minister in April 1994, has begun to restore a regular military under civilian control. He has improved relations with Georgia's national minorities and preserved basic civil liberties despite the pressures of a state under siege. He has ended Georgia's international isolation and brought relations with strategic neighbors Russia, Armenia and the North Caucasus onto a more even keel. But the concentration of enormous powers in his own hands, his indifference to the self-destruction of the Georgian parliament, his promotion of conservative *apparatchiki* to policy-making positions, and his neglect of the economy have undermined popular faith in the institutions of democracy and the market. His dogged commitment to peaceful resolution of conflicts with the Abkhazians, Ossetians and Russians has brought him limited success. Both Abkhazia and South Ossetia remain outside Georgian control, and despite a signed agreement with the Abkhazian separatists in May 1994 for the return of refugees, very few had been resettled six months later. In order to bring peace to Georgia, Shevardnadze sacrificed Georgian sovereignty. Russia exercises the greatest influence in Abkhazia and South Ossetia, and in return for its arbitration of the separatist conflicts it had militarily supported it was granted three military bases, joint use of all Georgia's ports and airfields and supervision of Georgia's borders. Georgia is not a client state, but Russia has taken it well beyond the limits of Finlandisation. More than anything else, events in Russia will determine Georgia's political future.

Shevardnadze managed to save the Georgian ship of state when it was perilously close to sinking, but has given it very little direction. His attempts to reassert political authority and end the 'feudalisation' of politics, characterised by geographic and political regionalism, the rise of unaccountable economic and political barons, and a system of informal and uncodified obligations and rules, are constantly underlined by Shevardnadze's own political practice. He continues to concentrate powers in his own hands, promote old clients, ignore the legislature and stall on major economic change. But as yet there is no credible alternative to Shevardnadze, and until there is, it seems likely that Georgia will continue its laggardly transition to democracy and the market.

# NOTES

1. K. Kandelaki *Sak'art'velos Erovnuli meurneoba, dsigni meore* (Paris, Institute for the Study of the USSR, 1960), p. 87. Output per capita in Russia as a whole was 30 roubles.
2. J. W. R. Parsons *The Emergence and Development of the National Question in Soviet Georgia, 1801–1921*, Unpublished Ph.D. thesis, University of Glasgow, 1987, pp. 522–26; R. G. Hovannisian *The Republic of Armenia*, vol. 1 (Berkeley, 1971), p. 115.
3. Parsons *The National Question*, pp. 529–30.
4. Ibid., pp. 512–13.
5. C. Kandelaki *The Georgian Question Before the Free World (Acts, Documents, Evidence)* (Paris 1953), pp. 182–90.
6. N. Zhordania *Chemi Dsarsuli* (Paris 1953), p. 157.
7. S. F. Jones *Georgian Social Democracy: In Opposition and Power, 1892–1921*, Unpublished Ph.D thesis, London School of Economics 1984, pp. 542–43.
8. Stephen Jones 'The establishment of Soviet power in Transcaucasia: the case of Georgia, 1921–1928' *Soviet Studies* XL, (4) (Oct. 1988), p. 617.
9. I. Katcharava 'Sabtchot'a erovnuli sakhelmdsip'oebriobis shek'mna da sakhalkho meurneobis aghdgena sak-art'veloshi (1921–1925 ds.ds)' in I. Katcharava (ed.) *Sak'art'veloshi istoriis narkvevebi T.7* (Tbilisi, Sabtchot'a Sak'art'velo 1976), p. 155.
10. *Ocherki Istorii Komunisticheskoi Partii Gruzii, 1883–1970* (Tbilisi 1971), pp. 460–62.
11. Steven Jones, *op. cit.* p. 618.
12. Katcharava 'Sabtchot'a erovnuli', pp. 130–32.
13. Ibid., p. 137.
14. *Komunisti*, 13 Jan. 1990, and Stephen Jones, *op cit.*, p. 617.

15. Until recently the 1924 uprising was one of the many 'blank spots' in Georgian history. Since 1988, however, it has become the subject of numerous articles in the Georgian press, and, already, a novel, *Siskhlis Dsvimebi* by Guram Gegeshidze, serialised in the monthly *Mnat'obi* 3,4,5 (1989).
16. *Komunisti* 25 Feb. 1930.
17. T'. Zhghenti 'Kolmeurneobat'a sameurneo-organizatsiuli ganmtkitseba' in *Sak'art'velos istoriis narkvevebi T.7* (Tbilisi, Sabtchot'a Sak'art'-velo 1976), p. 644.
18. I. Chik'ava 'Sabtchot'a sak'art'velo sotsialisturi sazogadoebis ganvit'arebisa da ganmtkitsebis periodshi, 1937–1941 ds.ds.', in *Sakart'velos istoriis narkvevebi T.7* (Tbilisi, Sabtchot'a Sak'art'velo 1976), p. 780.
19. N. Makharadze 'Meore khut'dsliani gegmis shesrulebis shedegebi. Sotsializmis gamardzhveba. Akhali konstitutsiis migheba' in *Sak'art'velos istoriis narkvevebi* (Tbilisi, Sabtchot'a Sak'art'velo 1976), p. 675.
20. R. Klimiashvili *K'alak' T'bilisis demograp'iuli protsesebis sotsialuri p'ak'torebi* (Tbilisi, Metsniereba 1974), p. 38.
21. This is a point strongly made by many Georgian writers, who feel that an attempt is being made in the Russian media to attribute Stalin's excesses to his Georgian birth and, at the same time, to suggest that he protected Georgia from the worst excesses of the 1930s. In an open letter to Gorbachev, published in the literary paper *Literaturuli Sak'art'velo* on 21 April 1989, more than 200 writers argued that the bloody action taken by Soviet troops against Georgian demonstrators earlier that month was the 'logical conclusion and crowning of the general denigration of the Georgian people sparked off in the central press, radio and television'. One writer, Guram P'andzhikidze, pointed out in *Literaturuli Sak'art'velo*, 21 and 28 October, 1988, that aside from the repressions of 1924 and 1937, Georgia also suffered in 1951 when thousands were taken from the Tbilisi intelligentsia overnight and exiled to Central Asia. He noted too that Georgia suffered more than 380,000 losses during the war, over 10 per cent of the population and proportionately higher than any other republic.
22. *Komunisti* 15 June 1989.
23. *Vestnik Statistiki* 1 (1981), p. 67.
24. Ibid., 4 (1981), pp. 69–72.
25. Shevardnadze did for a while achieve notable results in revitalising the Georgian economy, although from a relatively low base. In his first two years, industrial output grew by 9.6 per cent and agricultural output by 18 per cent. Georgia was one of only four republics to fulfil the tenth five year plan targets. But today the Georgian economy, like that of the rest of the former USSR, is struggling to achieve any growth at all.
26. J. W. R. Parsons 'National integration in Georgia' *Soviet Studies* 34 (4) (Oct. 1982), pp. 556–57.
27. *Komunisti* 6 Aug. 1989.
28. Saliko Khabeishvili, the former Central Committee Secretary for Industry, had worked with Shevardnadze since their time together in the Georgian Komsomol in the 1950s. In February 1987 he was sentenced to fifteen years' imprisonment on charges of corruption. See *Komunisti* 22 Feb. 1987.

29. Major-General Guram Gvetadze was forced out of office after a series of articles critical of him and his ministry in *Komunisti* in late 1985 and early 1986. Among other things, it was revealed that convicted criminals were living in luxury in corrective labour camps and continuing to direct their activities from behind bars. The author of the articles was Nugzar Popkhadze, at that time head of the Central Committee Agitation and Propaganda Department. Popkhadze stood firmly behind Patiashvili's opposition to dialogue with the so-called 'informal organisations' and was one of the first to be dismissed when Patiashvili lost his post in April 1989.

30. See S. Jones, 'The Caucasian Mountain Railway Project a Victory for *Glasnost?*' *Central Asian Survey* 8 (2), 1989, pp. 47–59.

31. *Iveria*, 7 (June 1988), pp. 4–5. *Iveria* is one of the publications of the Ilia Tchavtchavadze Society.

32. The main part of the programme of the Georgian National Democratic Party (Sak'art'velos erovnul-demokratiuli partia) states, for instance: 'The ideological basis of our party is theo-democracy, which, aside from traditional democratic values, means granting the church the leading role in the moral issues of the nations.' See *Moambe* 10 (1989). *Moambe* is one of the party's regular publications.

33. *Literaturuli Sak'art'velo* 11 Nov. 1988.

34. Ibid.

35. Ibid.

36. Ibid.

37. Three official investigations were conducted by the Georgian Supreme Soviet, the SSR Congress of People's Deputies, and the USSR Military Procurator's Office. Only the last justified the action as a necessary military operation, contradicting the conclusions of the previous two commissions. For a fuller analysis of the events that led up to 9 April, see Stephen F. Jones 'Glasnost, Perestroika and the Georgian Soviet Socialist Republic,' in *Armenian Review*, Summer/Autumn 1990, Vol. 43, Nos. 2–3/170–71, pp. 127–52.

38. Ibid.

39. Ibid.

40. *Komunisti*, 17 Sept. 1989, pp. 1–3.

41. For a close investigation of Gamsakhurdia's personality and politics, see Stephen F. Jones 'Populism in Georgia: the Gamsakhurdia Phenomenon' in Donald Schwartz and Razmik Panossian (eds), *Nationalism and History: the Politics of Nation Building in Post-Soviet Armenia, Azerbaijan and Georgia* (University of Toronto, 1994), pp. 127–49.

42. The full election results were as follows:

| | |
|---|---|
| Round Table–Free Georgia bloc | 155 deputies (53.9 per cent) |
| Georgian Communist Party | 64 deputies (29.57 per cent) |
| Georgian Popular Front | 12 deputies (1.93 per cent) |
| Democratic Georgia | 4 deputies (1.65 per cent) |
| All Georgian Rustaveli Society | 1 deputy (2.32 per cent) |
| Liberation and Economic Rebirth | 1 deputy (1.46 per cent) |
| Independents | 9 deputies |

The remaining parties failed to reach the 4 per cent cut-off. In Abkhazian and Ossetian districts there was a boycott or low turnout. Judging from names alone, the ethnic minorities were poorly represented, with only two Armenians, one Azeri and one Russian. The total turnout was just under 70 per cent. For a full breakdown of the election results by district see *Akhali Sak'art'velo* 16 November 1990, p. 3 and *Zaria Vostoka*, 9 and 14 November 1990.

43. Jones, 'Populism in Georgia', *op. cit.*

44. For a more detailed discussion of this curious paradox in the Georgian context, see Stephen F. Jones 'Old Ghosts and New Chains: Ethnicity and Memory in the Georgian Republic' in Rubie Watson (ed.) *Memory, History and Opposition under State Socialism* (Santa Fe, NM: School of American Research Press 1994), pp. 149–65.

45. For the Presidential election results, see *Foreign Broadcast Information Service Daily Report: Soviet Union* (henceforth *FBIS-SOV*), 91–159, p. 148.

46. For a more detailed discussion of Gamsakhurdia's legislative record, see Stephen F. Jones 'Georgia: a Failed Democratic Transition' in Ian Bremmer and Ray Taras (eds), *Nations and Politics in the Soviet Successor States* (Cambridge, Cambridge University Press 1993), pp. 288–310.

47. See *Sak'art'velos respublikis konstitutsia*, as amended until October 1991 (no listed publishers, 63 pp.). The author has a copy.

48. An example of his disregard for the law was his expulsion of the Communist Party deputies from the legislature shortly after the August 1991 putsch and his nationalisation of the party's property. Between October 1990 and 1991, using his majority in the parliament, Gamsakhurdia pushed through twenty amendments to the constitution with little discussion and almost no consultation with the broader public.

49. For Gamsakhurdia's official response to the putsch, see *Sak'art'velos Respublika*, No. 163, 21 August 1991, p. 1.

50. Eduard Shevardnadze was First Party Secretary of the Communist Party of Georgia from 1972 to 1985, when he was appointed Soviet Foreign Minister.

51. For a discussion of Russian military involvement in Caucasia in the post-Gorbachev period, see Thomas Goltz 'Letter from Eurasia: the Hidden Russian Hand' *Foreign Policy*, No. 92, Fall 1993, pp. 92–116.

52. For a detailed description of this law and institutional power relations in Georgia under Shevardnadze, see Stephen F. Jones 'Georgia's Power Structures' *Radio Free Europe/Radio Liberty Research Report*, Vol. 2, No. 39, 1 October 1993, pp. 5–9.

53. Zviad Gamsakhurdia was himself of Mingrelian origin, although he spent his life in Tbilisi and did not speak the Mingrelian language.

54. In September 1993 a cabinet shake-up gave *Mkhedrioni* official status as the Georgian Rescuers' Corps with its own state Committee led by Giorgi Gelashvili. This had been one of Ioseliani's demands in return for *Mkhedrioni*'s participation in the war against Abkhazia. The organisation remains under Ioseliani's personal control, based on a system of personal loyalty to the leader.

55. For example, Ioseliani's accusations of dictatorship, leveled at Shevardnadze during a parliamentary debate concerned with granting additional state of emergency powers to the Head of State in September 1993, led to Shevardnadze's brief resignation.

56. For a description of this law, see Jones 'Georgia's Power Structures', *op. cit.*

57. See *The Caucasian Chronicle*, October 1993 issue, pp. 7–8, and 'Russian–Georgian Troop Agreement Signed', in *RFE/RL Daily Bulletin*, No. 196, 12 October 1994.

58. For a review of the Georgian economy in 1992–93, see *Georgia: a Blueprint for Reforms* World Bank Country Study, Washington, DC, 1993.

59. Ot'ar Patsatsia was an enterprise manager in Mingrelia and from April 1992 the Governor of Mingrelia's regional capital, Zugdidi. He is Mingrelian in origin and was appointed Prime Minister to appease the Mingrelian supporters of ex-President Gamsakhurdia. Avt'andil Margiani was briefly Communist Party boss in Georgia after Gumbaridze's resignation in December 1990, but Margiani's primary service to Shevardnadze in his ability to influence the republic's Svan population. Margiani is, in origin, a Svan.

# PART VI

# Muslim Central Asia

Besides having a common religion, the eponymous peoples of the five Central Asian states of Kazakhstan, Uzbekistan, Turkmenistan, Kyrgyzstan and Tajikistan share a Turkic ethnic background (except for the Tajiks, who are Iranian) (see Fig. 6). The region, known in Tsarist times as Russian Turkestan and the Steppe Region, remained relatively isolated from Russian influences until the latter half of the nineteenth century when it was absorbed into the Russian empire. Until 1923, however, parts of the region, namely the Emirate of Bukhara and the Khanate of Khiva, although under Russian suzerainty retained a nominally independent status. In 1924, Turkestan (based on Tashkent) and the Khorazmian and Bukharan Soviet Socialist Republics were dissolved, and the region was divided into the union republics of Turkmenistan and Uzbekistan (within which the Tajik ASSR was included), with Kyrgyzstan becoming an autonomous republic (ASSRs) within the Russian union republic in 1926. In 1929, Tajikistan was upgraded from autonomous republic status (in which it had been included with the Uzbek SSR) to a full union republic, as were Kazakhstan and Kyrgyzstan seven years later. Although nationality group criteria was adopted in Central Asia's administrative partitioning, which by and large Moscow succeeded in making coterminous with the new administrative boundaries, there seems little doubt, given the strength of pan-Turkic and pan-Islamic sentiments in the region, that Central Asia's Balkanisation was motivated by geopolitical considerations. Such a divide-and-rule strategy circumvented mobilisation along Islamic lines among peoples whose sense of individual national identity at that time was very rudimentary.

With the exception of Kazakhstan, whose northern half is industrialised and economically similar to adjacent regions of Russia, Central Asia remains predominantly rural and largely underdeveloped, with some of the lowest standards of living in the post-Soviet states. Compared with educational and social levels in neighbouring Muslim countries to the south, however, considerable material benefits accrued to Central Asians from Soviet power. This, combined with conservatively-minded republic leaders and a civil society with no tradition of pluralist democracy or of nation-statehood, made Central Asians the least reluctant to challenge Soviet rule. Statehood was in effect thrust on Central Asians, who had neither asked nor struggled to secure it.

In these post-Soviet states, two ideologies have emerged to occupy the space vacated by communism: 'democratic' authoritarianism coupled with gradual government controlled economic reform. Although they are anxious, not least for reasons of economic dependency, to establish cordial relations with Russia, tensions exist, particularly over the flight of many Russian settlers fearful of worsening economic conditions and the loss of their privilege status and over Russia's interventionist role in the region's political and ethnic flashpoints, as in the Tajik civil war (1991–93).

Figure 6 : **MUSLIM CENTRAL ASIA**

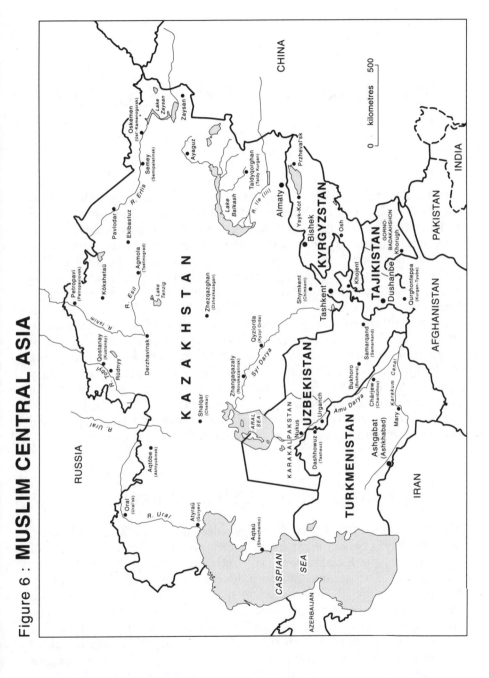

CHAPTER SIXTEEN

# Kazakhstan and the Kazakhs

Ingvar Svanberg

On 16 December, 1991 Kazakhstan declared itself an independent republic, and on 21 December it joined the Commonwealth of Independent States. Although Kazakhstan had been the scene of the first overt protests against central Moscow rule five years earlier, the republic refrained from declaring independence until the very end of the Union.[1] Its economic and structural dependence meant that the country had little to gain from the dissolution of the Soviet Union. More than any of the Soviet republican leaders, Kazakh President Nursultan Nazarbaev was faithful to Gorbachev until the very end. In the summer of 1991 he was the first to approve Gorbachev's proposal of a new union treaty, and remained a consistent proponent of preserving the USSR as a loose federation after the unsuccessful attempted military coup in August 1991. At the same time he is an independent, strong and genuinely popular leader in his own country. He is the head of a nation with access to nuclear arsenals and a country that is a potential power centre in the borderland between Asia and Europe.[2]

## KAZAKHSTAN UNDER SOVIET RULE

The Kazakhs speak a Turkic language belonging to the Kipchak branch. The ethnonym *Qazaq* came into use around 1520. At the beginning of this century, the Kazakhs were still referred to as Kirghiz or Kirghiz-Kazakhs in Russian and Western literature. In 1926 the ethnonym Kazakh was officially introduced in the Soviet Union in keeping with the policy of naming people according to their own ethnonyms. The transcription from Russian has been kept in most Western literature. A more correct spelling in English would be Kazak rather than Kazakh.[3]

The Kazakhs have a complex ethnic history and trace their origins back to various nomadic tribes that lived on the steppes of Turkestan during the days of Chinggiz Khan. Towards the end of that period, in the late 15th and the early 16th centuries, these nomadic tribes were united in a political confederation known as Kazakh Orda.[4] From this tribal confederation the Kazakhs emerged as a consolidated ethnic group. During the 16th century the Kazakhs enlarged their territory on the Central Asian steppes. Although they were united under Qasim Khan and partly during the reign of his successor Tahir Khan, they soon split into smaller nomadic tribal federations. The nomadic groups were politically unified in three large, territorially based tribal federations or Hordes known as the Larger, Middle and Lesser Hordes (*Ulu, Orta* and *Kishi Jüz*). The Larger Horde lived in the area known today as Dzhetisu (Semirechie) in the north-east, the Lesser Horde were to be found in Western Kazakhstan in the south-west, and the Middle Horde lived in between, in what today constitutes Central Kazakhstan. This division persists and is an important dimension in contemporary Kazakh identity. The Kazakh Hordes are subdivided in patrilateral lineages that remain a significant cultural factor in their social life. The exogamous lineages not only provide a chart for identifying individuals according to heritage, but also establish the rules for much social behaviour. A correct understanding of the force of lineages is vital when interpreting contemporary Kazakh society.[5]

As a result of the expansion of the Oirat Mongols in Central Asia in the 18th century, Kazakh tribes began to seek the protection of the Russian tsar. The first to do so was the khan of the Lesser Horde in 1731, followed by the khan of the Middle Horde in 1740 and part of the Larger Horde in 1742. When the Oirat Mongols were finally crushed and dispersed by the Qing army in 1756, the most potent enemy of the Kazakhs was destroyed.[6] With Russian control Islam gained firm roots in the area, as the tsarist government encouraged the Tatars to proselytise in the steppe region.

The Kazakhs became a buffer between Russia and China, the two expanding empires of Inner Asia. Nominal Russian sovereignty existed without any real Russian interference on the steppes, and the khans continued to control the plain. In the 1820s, under Tsar Aleksandr I, a new system of administration was introduced in Kazakh territory. Hitherto the Middle Horde had been ruled by two khans, but after their deaths their power was abolished by the tsarist authorities. In 1822 the territory of the Middle Horde Kazakhs was divided into Russian administrative units, and Russian military jurisdiction was introduced for criminal offences. The Kazakhs were no longer allowed to acquire serfs. The same process was carried out in 1824 for the Lesser Horde Kazakhs. These changes in tsarist policy led to revolts among the Kazakhs, but the tsarist authorities continued their colonial policy towards the nomads. New taxation methods were introduced, and from the 1830s onwards Kazakhs were no longer allowed to cultivate land. In 1847 the Larger Horde finally lost its independence when forced to pledge allegiance to the tsarist government.

After the abolition of serfdom in Russia in 1861, peasants started to move eastwards to settle and cultivate land on the Kazakh plain. The increasing number of Russian and Ukrainian peasants led to the emigration of the Kazakhs eastwards into Chinese territory. More than 500 villages were established on the steppe by the end of the 19th century. An 1895 tsarist Russian commission reserved land for new settlers in areas that had been used mainly by the Kazakh nomads.[7]

During the so-called Stolypin agrarian reform between 1906 and 1912, when 19 million hectares of land on the Kazakh plain were set aside for farming, a new mass settlement of Russian peasants took place.[8] The increasing pressure of Russian colonists also paved the way for Kazakh nationalism among the Kazakh élite that had traditionally been sympathetic to Russian culture.

In 1916 the tsarist government decided that Kazakhs, who traditionally had been exempted from military service, should be drafted into labour units. This led to a revolt on the steppe and in the Ferghana Valley. More than 50,000 rebels took part in the uprising. As a punishment, General Koropatkin, the Governor-General of Turkestan, decided to drive the nomads who participated in the revolt from their lands and to make the territory immediately available for Russian settlers. During the February Revolution of 1917 under the leadership of Alikhan Bukeikhan, the Kazakhs formed a semi-independent state called Alash Orda, whose autonomy came to an end in 1920 when the Bolsheviks finally took control of the Kazakh steppe. Kazakhstan was incorporated as the Kirghiz Autonomous Soviet Socialist Republic on 26 August, 1920 (renamed Kazakh ASSR in 1925) as part of RSFSR. Kazakhstan became a Union Republic in December 1936 and received the official name the Kazakh Soviet Socialist Republic.[9]

The collectivisation programme in Soviet Central Asia and Kazakhstan in the late 1920s led to conflict and great difficulties for the nomads. The Kazakhs were forced to settle and many nomadic families saw their herds starving on pastures that could no longer sustain them. Thousands of Kazakhs fled to Xinjiang in China and to Afghanistan. There are several estimates of the number of victims killed in the famines that occurred in conjunction with collectivisation, and this is one of the many cases in which the Soviet government was apparently guilty of attempted genocide. Indigenous Kazakh scholars have also recently begun to publish figures: according to a Kazakh historian, almost 1.7 million Kazakhs (40 per cent) perished in this period, while a demographer estimates the loss as between 2.5 and 4 million.[10] The 1926 census reported 3,968,300 Kazakhs; by 1950 the figure was still only 3,621,600. The long unpublished 1937 census cites 2,182,000 Kazakhs in Kazakhstan in that year.[11]

The Soviet Union continued to encourage settlement of Russian peasants in the post-Second World War period, especially in the 1950s, when many farmers moved into the republic. Under the Virgin Lands

Campaign initiated by Khrushchev, vast grazing lands were to be put under the plough and opened up for colonisation. Moscow encouraged thousands upon thousands of Russian and Ukrainian farmers to settle there, which caused protests among the Kazakhs. Due to difficulties with developing projects in Kazakhstan, Leonid Brezhnev was sent there to act as party leader in 1954. When Brezhnev's skill was needed elsewhere in 1956, a Kazakh, Dinmukhamed Kunaev, was named First Secretary. Due to economic shortcomings in the republic, Khrushchev criticised Kunaev so heavily that he was forced to resign. Kunaev was, however, back in power in 1964 and later became the first Kazakh to become a full member of the ruling Politburo of the Soviet Union. Under Brezhnev it became a tradition that the First Secretaries of the Union republics should be recruited among the natives; Kunaev was one of Brezhnev's men. The policy under Kunaev brought good living standards to Kazakhstan. Reforms in higher education allowed a higher percentage of the indigenous nationalities to attend universities and to take advantage of better job opportunities. The capital Almaty (formerly Alma Ata) grew to a large city during his years in power and became a monument to Kunaev's strength, with many prestigious government and official buildings.[12] The pre-modern pattern of the lineage system still worked during the Kunaev era. The Communist party was dominated by people belonging to lineages within *Ulu Jüz*, mostly from southern Kazakhstan.

Little is known about ethnic unrest during Kunaev's period in office up to the 1980s. Some disturbances near the Chinese border were noted in the early 1960s, when increasing tensions between China and the Soviet Union led to open dispute. Sharing its border with China, during the 1960s and 1970s Kazakhstan was a centre for Soviet anti-Chinese propaganda. Border clashes occurred several times, and Kazakh infiltrators were sent to neighbouring Xinjiang to spread propaganda among the Chinese Kazakhs. The Soviet propaganda in Xinjiang and the harsh economic situation caused unrest among Kazakhs and other nationalities in China, leading to a major influx of Kazakh and Uighur refugees in Kazakhstan in 1961 and 1962; a total of about 120,000 were reported to have refugees in the early 1960s settled in East Kazakhstan Oblast.

One of the first outbreaks of nationalistic unrest under Gorbachev occurred in Almaty on 16 December, 1986, when Kunaev was replaced by an ethnic Russian, Gennadii Kolbin. The latter was sent to clean up the corruption and economic mismanagement that had marked Kunaev's regime. There is no question that Kunaev was a very corrupt leader, even if the 1989 investigations exonerated him from many charges. The Alma Ata events, in which according to some unofficial estimates over 200 people were killed, were officially reported to have resulted in two deaths 1,722 injuries and about 8,500 arrests. Yet they came as a surprise to both Moscow and many foreign observers.[13]

A number of his associates, many of whom were related to him, met a similar fate in the wake of Kunaev's dismissal. They were removed from their posts for permitting nepotism and taking bribes. Officials in the provinces were also fired and even put on trial. Many people came under scrutiny. Kolbin presented a plan for setting up a body to ensure fair ethnic representation in all institutions, and steps were taken to reform the administrative system. However, the open criticism against Kolbin increased and his situation in Kazakhstan became untenable. In 1989 Kolbin was ordered to return to Moscow and was replaced by Nursultan Nazarbaev, an ethnic Kazakh. Many of Kolbin's reforms were annulled, and to a certain degree Kunaev was restored, with the Kolbin period soon becoming an almost forgotten interlude in the history of Kazakhstan. In May 1992 a foundation was formed to commemorate the significance of the events of December 1986.

While the Alma Ata incidents were caused by dissatisfaction with Moscow's interference in local affairs, ethnic conflicts surfaced among workers from an oil refinery in a small town in western Kazakhstan. A wave of violence swept over Novi Uzen during the summer of 1989. On 17 June a gang of Kazakh youths were reported to have attacked cooperatives and set fire to vehicles, following the closure of the oil factory that had brought the Lezghins into the area. The Kazakhs who took part demanded that the Lezghins and other immigrant workers in the area be expelled in order to free jobs for the locals. They accused the Lezghins of taking their jobs, and the stores run by Caucasian immigrants of overpricing commodities. The disturbances spread northwards to most other towns on the Mangyshlak Peninsula. By 26 June five people had been killed and 118 injured during the clashes. About 3,500 people were reported to have fled the area, mostly to Daghestan. Minor protests and disturbances also occurred in other Kazakh cities. These riots should not be interpreted as national manifestations against Moscow, but rather as what Ottar Brox calls 'structural fascism', i.e. victims of the same system engaging in internal conflicts.[14] At the same time these events contributed to a consolidation of nation-ness among the Kazakh people.[15]

## NURSULTAN NAZARBAEV, 'THE ENLIGHTENED LEADER'

National presidential elections were held on 1 December 1991 and won by the sole candidate, Nursultan Nazarbaev.[16] Nazarbaev belongs to *Ulu Jüz*, a tribal federation that dominated politics in Kazakhstan during the Communist era.[17] He has sought close ties with Europe and the United States, and visited various countries and received delegations from Western governments. He also maintains close ties with Russia and has acted as negotiator in several conflict areas of the former

Soviet Union, notably in Bashkortostan, Tatarstan and Transcaucasia. His emphasis on external affairs has led to criticism at home, where it is claimed he neglects domestic problems, not least the economic conditions in Kazakhstan. One strategic problem that has facilitated this role is his country's geo-political location between the nuclear powers of Russia and China. Within the CIS, Kazakhstan is the third largest holder of nuclear weapons, and in 1994 had over 1,000 warheads and 100 long-distance missiles. Its nuclear arsenal is currently in the process of being sent to Russia for eventual dismantling. Swift progress is being made and the country could be non-nuclear by 1996.

Nazarbaev has avoided forming a coalition with the established political organisations of Kazakhstan. *Azat, Jeltoqsan* and the illegal ultranationalist *Alash* organisation are Kazakh and nationalistic, while the Socialist party is dominated by Russians and Russified Kazakhs (other Russian parties include *Edinstvo* and *Pamyat'*). Nazarbaev seems to be in favour of the People's Congress of Kazakhstan, a multiethnic umbrella organisation founded by the authors Olzhas Süleimenov and Mukhtar Shakhanov. However, Nazarbaev does not tolerate public criticism and several journalists have been arrested for writings that allegedly damage the honour of the president. On 28 January 1993 the Supreme Kenges (parliament) adopted a new Constitution for Kazakhstan. This defines the authority of the President, who must be a Kazakh speaker, and who is allowed to appoint the prime minister, interior ministers, the chairman of the National Security Council, and all the ambassadors of the republic.

## ETHNIC RELATIONS IN KAZAKHSTAN

Although the new Kazakh nationalism is characterised by an increasingly chauvinistic ideology, Kazakhstan is a multiethnic society with two dominant ethnic groups and a larger number of minorities. According to the 1989 Soviet census the Kazakhs made up 39.7 per cent of Kazakhstan's population and the Russians 37.8 per cent. However, the Russians' birth rate is significantly lower than that of the Kazakhs, and large numbers of the former moved out during the 1980s. Although the Kazakhs were outnumbered by the Russians in 1979, the higher rate of natural population increase among the Kazakhs and the large Russian out-migration during the 1980s and 1990s have led to an equalisation of the two groups. Kazakh population experts maintain that the Kazakhs now clearly outnumber the Russians (44.3 per cent as opposed to 35.8 per cent in 1994).

Despite its multiethnic character, there were few mixed marriages in the republic. They were most common in northern Kazakhstan, with its numerous Russian and other Western immigrants. The Kazakhs prefer endogamous marriages (92.5 per cent in 1988). Mixed marriages were more likely to occur with other Turkic peoples than with Russians.[18]

So far, Nazarbaev has managed to balance the two major ethnic groups and in many aspects Kazakhstan can be regarded as a dual society. Political power resides mainly with the indigenous Kazakhs, while the industrial and educational focus rests with the Slavs. While the Kazakhs to a large extent possess an oriental cultural heritage, the Slavs are more Western-oriented although the Russian population is far from homogeneous. It consists of recent immigrants as well as people whose forebears have resided in Kazakhstan for generations and who consider it their homeland. Moreover, despite ethnic labels, many of the immigrants representing over 100 minor ethnic groups are Russophiles and Russian-speaking. Descendants of Ural Cossacks living in Kazakhstan have revived their organisation and have political aspirations of clear pro-Russian orientation. The geographical distribution of the Russians also has certain geo-political implications. The Russians dominate the agricultural districts in the northern part of Kazakhstan, adjacent to Russia. The whole of northern Kazakhstan therefore is a potential flashpoint between Russia and Kazakhstan. However, relations with the country's Russian population remained peaceful until December 1992, when Russian demonstrators in Öskemen (formerly Ust'-Kamenogorsk) called for concessions on citizenship and language laws. Consciousness of the rising tensions is evident in Nazarbaev's public exhortations for tolerance among peoples, and he has repeatedly pointed to the former Yugoslavia as a deterrent.

However, the question of citizenship has not been a major issue in Kazakhstan. It has generally been the consensus that all persons, regardless of their ethnic origins, who were permanent residents of Kazakhstan in March 1992 should be considered citizens of the republic. However, the estrangement of the many ethnic groups due to Kazakh nationalism and to increased nationalism in the former 'homelands' of the immigrant groups has developed rapidly, and numerous non-Kazakhs now prefer to emigrate.

While the Russians and other Slavic peoples settled in Kazakhstan as a result of agricultural colonisation and later industrial exploitation, particularly of the oil fields, other groups arrived as refugees or as a result of deportation. Three of these groups are significant in number and have either a demographic or a cultural centre in Kazakhstan: the Uighurs, the Germans and the Koreans, who constituted 7% of the population in 1989. The Uighurs, as well as the Dungans, came as refugees and immigrants from Chinese Turkestan (present-day Xinjiang) chiefly during the 1880s while the Volga Germans, Balkars, Lezghins, Chechens, Ingush, Finns, Karachais, Ossetians, Crimean Tatars, Moldavians, Bulgarians, Meskhetian Turks, Greeks, Kurds, and Koreans belong to the peoples deported to Kazakhstan before or in connection with the Second World War. The deportations were probably a way to compensate for the decline of the indigenous population in the early 1930s. Most of the Caucasian people returned after rehabilitation in 1957, while others remained in the republic. Since independence, however, there has been an exodus of Lezghins and Chechens due to increasing harassment from the local population. An infamous decision was reached by the local authorities in Öskemen in November 1992 to get rid of the immigrated Lezghins, an act with a clear racist flavour. The legitimacy of their right to be in Kazakhstan is now in question, and they have become scapegoats for economic and social problems within the republic.

The Uighurs are spread throughout Kazakhstan, but are primarily urban dwellers. Uighur merchants have probably always been active in Central Asia, but the first movement into the Semirechie area occurred in 1881. More than sixty refugee settlements were established of which 45 still exist. The first refugees who arrived were from Ili Valley in western Xinjiang, while later arrivals have come from other areas. At the turn of the century the Uighurs in Kazakhstan were usually called Taranchi or Turpanlyk and Kashgarlyk, names derived from their places of origin. However, in 1921 they were categorized as Uighurs, a term earlier used for an ancient Turkic folk. It was in the 1930s that the name Uighur first gained a foothold in China. According to the 1990 Chinese census, there are 7,214,431 Uighurs in that country.

The latest movement of Uighurs to Kazakhstan occurred in the 1960s, when, together with a large group of Kazakhs, they fled the political chaos and economic catastrophe that followed the failure of the Great Leap Forward in China. With the improvement in relations with China at the end of the 1980s it has again become possible for them to visit relatives in China, and many Uighurs now travel to Xinjiang to conduct business and maintain contacts with the former homeland.[19] The Dungans are Chinese-speaking Muslims, usually called *Hui* in China, who also emigrated in the 1880s to the Chu Valley in Kazakhstan. They originated from colonisers with roots in Shenshi province in China, whose dialect is still the native language of the Dungans of Kazakhstan.

Kazakhstan's Germans are mainly the descendants of the Volga Germans who settled agricultural lands in the Volga region in the time of Catherine the Great (see Chapter 23). When Nazi Germany attacked the Soviet Union in 1941 the Germans living in the Volga Republic were deported to Siberia and northern Kazakhstan. Today they are concentrated in the city of Karaganda, where they make up 11.5 per cent of the population.[20] The Volga Germans accounted for 5.8 per cent of the total population of the republic, according to the 1989 census, but a considerable number have emigrated since then.

Since the late 1980s demands have been made for the formation of a German autonomous republic within Kazakhstan, a proposal that has caused tension among the Kazakhs, but the potential conflict has been averted by the rapidly increasing stream of Germans leaving the East for the West, an emigration movement that also includes Kazakhstan's Germans. Since 1989 many have left Kazakhstan, some for Germany, others for European Russia. In the nearby Russian district of Altai a German national district was re-established in July 1991. German law guarantees Germans the right to immigrate, but considering the size of the German minorities in Siberia and Kazakhstan the government in Bonn is anxious to solve the problem within Russia and Kazakhstan. Germany has therefore promised to start joint ventures in areas inhabited by Germans.[21]

The Koreans migrated to the present-day Vladivostock area of the Russian Far East primarily in 1869 and after the annexation of Korea by the Japanese empire in 1910; the Korean population left between 1906 and 1937, when they were forcibly relocated to Central Asia where a Korean border population was located. After the Revolution a Korean national area was created on the Pos'yet. Due to the sharp conflicts between the Russians and the Koreans in connection with collectivisation and later also influenced by strategic considerations as the Japanese expanded in Asia, between 1928 and 1937 the Koreans were banished to Kazakhstan, Kyrgyzstan and Uzbekistan. However, even before the mass transfer Koreans were living in Kazakhstan. Most of the Koreans in Kazakhstan are located in the Kyzylorda district and in Almaty.[22] Although the Koreans have experienced a cultural revival and once again are allowed their own schools and religious and ethnic organisations, many are discussing the possibility of moving back to their former homeland.

## THE LANGUAGE QUESTION

The spoken language of contemporary Kazakhs is either Kazakh or Russian. The status of the Kazakh language within the Republic was a hotly debated question during the 1980s. Linguistic Russification is strong. In 1989 60.4 per cent considered themselves to be bilingual, one of the highest of the union republic nationalities (see Table 4) and 97 per cent of Kazakhs regarded Kazakh as their first language. The Kazakh élite, however, is generally more at home with Russian than with its mother tongue. Many younger urban Kazakhs prefer to speak Russian due to the educational and urban values of their families. Those who have received a university education have been instructed in Russian and follow events in the Russian media. Furthermore, as Almaty is primarily a Russian city both culturally and linguistically, there is less need to use Kazakh. During recent years numerous letters have been sent to newspapers complaining about the misspelling of Kazakh signs and place names. Kazakh leaders and cultural personalities have also received their share of criticism when they and other Kazakh intellectuals have preferred Russian to Kazakh in various situations. A new language society in Kazakhstan, *Qazaq Tili Qoghamï*, works for the preservation of the language, and key members of the Kazakh élite take part in the society's work. The most revolutionary decision that has been taken regarding the language concerns the return to the Latin alphabet, which is regarded as a way of approaching the Western world. In the new Constitution for Kazakhstan of January 1993, Kazakh was declared the state language of the republic, while Russian was given special status as 'the social language between peoples'.

## CULTURAL REVIVAL

Consciousness of and interest in the Kazakh national culture has grown since the late 1980s. Symbols of Kazakh national identity have been created and used in the ongoing process of cultural renewal. One important demand of the awakened Kazakh nationalism is a new written history,[23] as filling the blank spots of their history has become an important goal of Kazakh intellectuals. The old Soviet street names of Almaty are gone and have been replaced by new Kazakh-oriented ones.[24] As in other Central Asian republics, the celebration of the Persian New Year, *naurïz*, has been taken up in some parts of Kazakhstan. Nazarbaev has maintained that the Kazakh people would want to orient themselves towards a modern and global culture, rather than fastening onto a backward-looking national chauvinism.

Traditionally Kazakhs have been, at least nominally, Sunni Muslims of the Hanafi juridical school. Islam was brought to the masses in the 18th century, (by itinerant Tatar mullahs who built mosques and opened Quramic schools). This was encouraged by the tsarist administration as part of the policy of establishing a Muslim barrier against the expanding Chinese Empire. In the mid-1990s, however, the percentage of religiously indifferent people is probably much higher than among other native populations of Central Asia. Knowledge of the *Quran* is very limited, and very few Muslim practices are observed. The only traditional Muslim manner followed is the circumcision of boys, a widely observed custom, even among urbanites and agnostics. Funeral customs also generally follow the Muslim pattern. Kazakh women have traditionally been more independent then their sedentary Muslim sisters. However, most Kazakhs still identify themselves as Muslims, although Islam until recently had a very low profile in the Republic. The Muslims of Kazakhstan are under the jurisdiction of the Spiritual Directorate of Kazakhstan, which was created in 1990. This reorganisation is officially supported by Nazarbaev and may be seen as part of the creation of a state-controlled Islamic organisation following the Turkish model. At the same time Nazarbaev has stressed that religious freedom exists in Kazakhstan and believes that there is little danger that Islamic fundamentalism will gain a foothold. By the beginning of 1992 there were 250 functioning mosques in Kazakhstan. The number is growing steadily, and there is extensive building, especially in Almaty.[25]

## ECONOMY AND ENVIRONMENTAL ISSUES

The economy of Kazakhstan is still based on agriculture. Within the Soviet Union Kazakhstan was one of the most important producers of meat. During the great settlement projects of the 1950s much land came under cultivation and was converted to arable, especially in the north, where significant amounts of grain are produced. Kazakhstan raised one-third of all wheat within the former Soviet Union. Industrialisation has primarily concentrated on mining, with the extensive exploitation of minerals.

Following its independence, Kazakhstan has begun to move away from central planning, with privatisation and the free market beginning to play an important part in the overall economy. Yet, as is the case in other republics, Kazakhstan is struggling with considerable economic problems. Already prior to independence more than half the population lived below the official poverty line. Few consumer products are produced in Kazakhstan, and the country is highly trade-dependent. Yet, as Prime Minister Sergei Tereshchenko stated in early 1993, nearly all Kazakh production could not be sold on the international market, because of its inferior standard. In his efforts to privatise and transform Kazakhstan into a market economy, Nazarbaev has called in foreign experts, including Americans and South Koreans. Foreign investors have also been attracted to Kazakhstan, mainly from the Far East, with numerous joint-venture agreements being signed with South Korea, Japan, and China. Turkey has also emerged as pivotal, primarily because it offers a window on the West, and several agreements on cultural exchanges have been signed.[26] However, Kazakhstan has far to go. Much hope is placed on the international community, with little happening at the local level, where bureaucrats and traditional élites still maintain control.

The most serious problem is the growing threat to the environment and the ecological catastrophe with which Kazakhstan is faced. This is a question of both pure destruction of the environment and the consequences of nuclear tests carried out during the Soviet period. Such concerns became an important issue in the late 1980s, and were bound up with the politicisation of ethnic and national issues. Local environmental issues also became focused around the Nevada-Semey movement in 1988 and its concern with the continuing testing of atomic weapons. With independence, the movement took on a strong anti-Russian character. Nazarbaev closed the test sites in Semipalatinsk in August 1991; in June 1992 the government declared the area around the site an ecological disaster zone.

## THE INTERNATIONALISATION OF ETHNIC TENSIONS: RUSSIA AND CHINA

As a result of independent statehood, Kazakhstan has also had to define its relations with its two most powerful neighbours, Russia and China, both of which involve an ethnic dimension. The Russians have settled mainly on the plains in northern Kazakhstan along the Russian border. It is a traditionally Kazakh area which Russian colonisers claimed from the nineteenth century onwards, first for agricultural purposes and later for industrialisation. In September 1990 the Russian exile author Solzhenitsyn published an article in which he advocated an expansion of the Russian borders at the expense of Kazakhstan; this led to extensive demonstrations in Almaty. Even a press aide to Yeltsin expressed similar ideas following the Moscow coup of August 1991, although Yeltsin promptly disavowed the statement. Nazarbaev immediately declared that any attempt to realise such claims would mean war. Opinion polls in the autumn of 1991 in Kazakhstan showed that neither the local Russians nor Kazakhs wanted a revision of the boundary. Yet it is possible that this border will remain unstable and a source of potential conflict with Russia.

A latent conflict is the unresolved border between Kazakhstan and China, resulting from the concession made by the Qing government to tsarist Russia in the late 19th century. The Ili Valley has traditionally been the gateway to China, and from the end of the nineteenth century until the 1950s trade was extensive. During the 1940s and 1950s the Soviet Union exerted strong influence in the Chinese Xinjiang province. Many Kazakhs who fled from Kazakhstan in the 1930s had settled in the Ili district in China. The area had a strong orientation towards Kazakhstan, and many received their higher education in Alma Ata. During the 1940s a short-lived, Soviet-supported 'independent' state, the Ili Republic, mostly inhabited by Kazakhs, was set up along the Soviet border in Xinjiang.[27] The break between Peking and Moscow put an end to previous good relations, and led to open hostility. When cordial relations were resumed in the 1980s, cross-border travel again became possible and the border to Xinjiang was opened up through the Ili Valley in 1987. Many Kazakhs and Uighurs from Kazakhstan made visits to their relatives, border trade became lively, and cultural groups visited Xinjiang. Since then almost twenty border points have been opened up between Kazakhstan and Xinjiang. China, which has its own dissatisfied Turkic-speaking Islamic population in Xinjiang, has watched with great unease the transition toward independence in Kazakhstan. However, it was very quick to recognise the new Central Asian republic, while at the same time denying that Xinjiang is part of Central Asia. In the beginning of 1992 an agreement was reached with China which provided for the settlement of some Kazakhs from Xinjiang in Kazakhstan. In February 1992 Kazakhstan's Prime Minister Tereshchenko paid an official visit to Peking and signed a pact allowing for increased economic cooperation between the countries. The Chinese leaders hope that such a strategy will dampen nationalistic sentiments among the Uighurs and Kazakhs in Xinjiang. However, in the summer of 1992, a political party calling itself 'For a Free Uighuristan' was founded in Bishkek by Uighurs from Kazakhstan and Kyrgyzstan, a development that is likely to complicate relations between China and these two neighbouring republics.

## ACKNOWLEDGEMENTS

I am grateful to Mr Abdulvahap Kara (Munich), Ms Aisulu Sopieva (Bishkek) and Ms Jarmila Durmanová (Department of Eastern European Studies, Uppsala University) for providing references and material, as well as Marie Clark Nelson (Department of History, Uppsala University) and my research assistant Karin Borevi (Centre for Multiethnic Research, Uppsala University).

## NOTES

1.  M. B. Olcott 'Central Asia's Catapult to Independence' *Foreign Affairs* 71:3 (Summer 1992), pp. 108–130.
2.  See for example I. Svanberg 'Contemporary Changes among the Kazaks,' pp. 83–101 in I. Svanberg (ed.) *Ethnicity, Minorities and Cultural Encounters*, Uppsala Multiethnic Papers 25 (Uppsala, Centre for Multiethnic Research 1991).
3.  See the discussion in L. Benson and I. Svanberg 'The Kazaks in Xinjiang,' in L. Benson and I. Svanberg (eds) *The Kazaks of China. Essays on an Ethnic Minority*, Studia Multiethnica Upsaliensia 5 (Uppsala, Almqvist & Wiksell International 1988), p. 2.
4.  For a general survey on the history of the Kazakhs, see L. Krader and I. Wayne *The Kazakhs. A Background Study for Psychological Warfare*. Human Resources Research Office, Technical Report 23 (Washington, DC 1955), and the well-researched book by M. B. Olcott, *The Kazakhs*, Studies of Nationalities in the USSR Series (Stanford, CA, Hoover

Institution Press, Stanford University 1987). The most recent developments are dealt with in G. Imart, *From 'Roots' to Great Expectations. Kirghizia and Kazakhstan between the Devil and the Deep.* Papers on Inner Asia 12 (Bloomington, IN, Indiana University 1990), I. Svanberg 'Kazakstan' in S. Gustavsson and I. Svanberg (eds) *Gamla folk och nya stater. Det upplösta Sovjetimperiet* (Stockholm, Gidlunds Bokförlag 1992), pp. 350–368, M. B. Olcott 'The Future of Central Asia', *The Harriman Institute Forum* 6:2 (October 1992), pp. 1–10 and M. B. Olcott 'Kazakhstan: a republic of minorities', in I. Bremmer and T. Taras (eds) *Nations and Politics in the Soviet Successor States* (Cambridge, Cambridge University Press 1993), pp. 313–330.

5. For details on traditional social structure among the Kazakhs, see Kh. Argïnbaev *Qazaq khalqïndaghï sem'ya men neke (Tarikhi-etnografïyalïq solu)*, (Almatï, Gïlim 1973) and I. Svanberg 'Xinjiang Kazak Adoption Practices', in K. Borevi and I. Svanberg (eds) *Ethnic Life and Minority Cultures*, Uppsala Multiethnic Papers, 28 (Uppsala, Centre for Multiethnic Research 1992), pp. 41–48.

6. The Oirat Mongol sphere of influence in Central Asia is erronously referred to as the Dzungarian Khanate in Soviet literature. For a discussion, see J. Miyawaki 'Did a Dzungar Khanate Really Exist?' *Journal of the Anglo-Mongolian Society* 10 (1) (1987), pp. 1–5.

7. On the Kazakh frontier in Russian colonial policy, see R. S. Clem 'The Frontier and Colonisation in Russian and Soviet Central Asia', in R. A. Lewis (ed.) *Geographic Perspectives on Soviet Central Asia* (London & New York, Routledge 1992), pp. 28–33.

8. G. Demko *The Russian Colonization of Kazakhstan, 1896–1916.* (Bloomington, IN, Mouton 1969).

9. S. Blank 'Ethnic and Party Policy in Soviet Kazakhstan, 1920–1924', *Central Asian Survey* 10:3 (1991), pp. 1–19; M. B. Olcott 'The Emergence of National Identity in Kazakhstan', *Canadian Review of Studies in Nationalism* 8:2 (1981), pp. 285–300.

10. Zh. B. Abïlkozhyn, M. K. Kozybaev and M. B. Tätimov 'Kazakhstan-skaya tragediya', *Voprosy Istorii* 1989–7, pp. 53–71; A. Nove 'How Many Victims in the 1930s?' *Soviet Studies* 42:2 (1990), pp. 369–373; R. Conquest 'Excess Deaths and Camp Numbers: Some Comments', *Soviet Studies* 43:5 (1991), pp. 949–952; R. J. Rummel *Lethal Politics, Soviet Genocides and Mass Murder 1900–1987* (New Brunswick, NJ, Transaction Books 1991), p. 86; N. Diuk and A. Karatnycky *New Nations Rising. The Fall of the Soviets and the Challenge of Independence* (New York/Chichester/Brisbane/Toronto/Singapore, John Wiley & Sons 1993), p. 196.

11. '1989 Census Documents', *Journal of Soviet Nationalities* 1:2 (Winter 1990–1991), p. 160.

12. P. A. Goble 'Gorbachev and the Soviet Nationality Problem', in M. Friedberg and H. Isham (eds) *Soviet Society Under Gorbachev, Current Trends and the Prospects for Reform* (New York, M.E. Sharpe 1987), pp. 78–100; H. Krag 'Kunajev fyrte Kazakernas kulturtradition til Moskva', *Information* 23 Dec. 1986, p. 2.

13. I. Svanberg 'Kazakstan', in S. Gustavsson and I. Svanberg (eds) *Gamla folk och nya stater. Det upplösta Sovjetimperiet* (Stockholm, Gidlunds

Bokförlag 1992), p. 359. The author Mukhtar Shakhanov headed a commission to investigate the events on the Government Square in December 1986. According to the report (*Almatï Jeltoqsan 1986*, Almatï 1991) 99 people were put on trial and nearly 300 students were dismissed from their universities. How many people were killed has not been determined. However, four Kazakh fatalities and one Russian are named in the report.

14. O. Brox *Strukturfascismen och andra essäer. En vetenskapligt skolad socialist analyserar människans maktlöshet i nutidens samhälle*. Verdandi-debatt 65 (Stockholm, Bokförlaget Prisma 1972), p. 9.

15. H. Carrère d'Encausse *La gloire des nations ou la fin de l'Empire soviétique* (Paris, Fayard 1991), pp. 63–87.

16. Many portraits of him have recently been published. See V. Kiyanitsa 'Nursultan Nazarbayev', *Moscow News Weekly* no. 3, 1992; G. Bahro 'Nursultan Abischewitsch Nasarbajew', *Orient* 32:4 (1991), pp. 509–514; J. Critchlow 'Kazakhstan and Nazarbaev: Political Prospects', *RFE/RL Research Report* (January 1992), pp. 31–34; V. Morozov 'Nursultan means enlightened ruler', *New Times International* no. 4 (January 1993), pp. 14–17. Nazarbaev describes his life in the book *Ädiletin aq joli* (Almatï 1991).

17. M. B. Olcott 'Central Asia's Post-Empire Politics,' *Orbis* 36:2 (Spring 1992), p. 258.

18. R. Karklins *Ethnic Relations in the USSR. Perspectives from Below* (Boston, MA, Allen & Unwin 1986), p. 156; 'Data on Ethnic Inter-marriages', *Journal of Soviet Nationalities* 1:2 (Summer 1990), pp. 160–169.

19. J. Rudelson *Bones in the Sand. The struggle to create Uighur nationalist ideologies in Xinjiang, China*. PhD thesis, Department of Anthropology, Harvard University, 1992.

20. On Germans in Kazakhstan, see B. Dietz and P. Hilkes *Russlanddeutsche: Unbekannte im Osten, Geschichte, Situation, Zukunftsperspektiven*. Geschichte und Staat, Bd. 292 (München, Günter Olzog Verlag 1992); I. Trutanow, *Russlands Stiefkinder. Ein deutsches Dorf in Kasachstan* (Berlin, Basis-Druck 1992).

21. Ch. Pan '"Bleiben" oder "Gehen" als Dilemma der Russlanddeutschen', *Europa Ethnica* 50:1–2 (1993), pp. 65–68; J. Kearney, 'Kazakhs in search of the Fatherland. After 200 years in the east, ethnic Germans are going home', *The European* 143 (Feb. 4–7, 1993), p. 12.

22. S. Kho *Koreans in the Soviet Central Asia*. Studia Orientalia 61 (Helsinki, The Finnish Oriental Society 1987).

23. A renewed interest in the tribal structure of the Kazakh social organisation has resulted in publications like *Shejire, Qazaqtïng rutainalïk qürïlisï* (Almatï, Rauan 1991).

24. M. B. Olcott 'Central Asia on its own', *Journal of Democracy* (January 1993), p. 99.

25. I. Svanberg 'Kazakstan,' in S. Gustavsson and I. Svanberg (eds) *Gamla folk och nya stater. Det upplösta Sovjetimperiet* (Stockholm, Gidlunds Bokförlag 1992), p. 365. On contemporary Islam in Kazakhstan, see K. Borevi and I.Svanberg 'Kazakstan, Kirgizistan och Uzbekistan', in I. Svanberg and D. Westerlund (eds) *Majoritetens islam* (Stockholm, Arena Förlag, forthcoming.)

26. R. Menon and H. J. Barkey 'The Transformation of Central Asia: Implications for Regional and International Security', *Survival*, 34:4 (Winter 1992–93), pp. 68–89.
27. L. Benson *The Ili Rebellion. The Moslem Challenge to Chinese Authority in Xinjiang 1944–1949* (Armonk, NY, M.E. Sharpe 1990).

# CHAPTER SEVENTEEN

# Uzbekistan and the Uzbeks

Shirin Akiner

## BACKGROUND

The Uzbeks are a people of predominantly Turkic origin, with a significant admixture of Iranian and Turkicised Mongol elements. They speak Uzbek, a language that evolved out of Chagatai, the chief literary medium of the eastern Turkic world (a contemporary and counterpart to Ottoman Turkish). The Uzbeks are Sunni Muslims of the Hanafi school, as are the majority of former Soviet Muslims, and also of Muslims outside the Soviet Union.

The Uzbeks, who were by far the largest group of Muslims in the former Soviet Union, today number some 17 million. Over 14 million, approximately 85 per cent of the total, live within Uzbekistan; a further 7 per cent, some 1.2 million, in Tadzhikistan; 3.5 per cent, approximately half a million, in Kyrgyzstan, and close on 2 per cent each, some 332,000, in Turkmenistan and Kazakhstan.[1] There used to be a colony of some 1.5 million Uzbeks across the border to the south, in Afghanistan; many of these fled to Pakistan during the Soviet occupation of 1979–89, and some moved still further afield, to begin new lives in Turkey. Few have so far returned to Afghanistan. There are another 20,000 Uzbeks to the west, in the Xinjiang-Uighur Autonomous Region of the People's Republic of China. Cross-border contacts have become easier in recent years, but are still fairly limited and are restricted, in the main, to close blood relations.

The Uzbeks are descendants of the nomadic tribes of the Golden Horde who settled in Transoxiana in the 15th–16th centuries and there intermingled with the sedentary population (mostly Iranian peoples and descendants of earlier Turkic invaders). After the disintegration of the Timurid empire in the 15th century, independent local khanates emerged, the most powerful of which came to be centred on Bukhara, Khiva and Kokand. Tsarist troops invaded the region in the second half of the 19th century. They met with little resistance from the local rulers who, distracted by internecine struggles, were unable to present a coordinated resistance. Bukhara became a Russian Protectorate in 1868, Khiva in 1873; the khanate of Kokand was abolished and its territory fully incorporated into the Russian empire in 1876. However, Russian rule proved to be less onerous than that of most other colonial regimes, and, for the most part, the indigenous population continued to live much as before.[2] The social and material changes introduced by the Russians were relatively few, and limited to the main urban centres. Nevertheless, they provided a channel for new ideas into a society that had previously been isolated and closed for many centuries. Moreover, once part of the empire, the Central Asians came into close contact with other 'Russian' Muslims, notably the Tatars of the Volga and Crimea, and the Azerbaijanis. Far more progressive than the Central Asians, it was they who introduced the *jadid* (reformist) movement to Central Asia. They pioneered a more modern type of education. Many of the privately-owned vernacular newspapers that appeared in Central Asia from 1905 onwards were *jadid* publications.[3]

Tsarist rule in Tashkent was replaced by Soviet in late 1917, and in April 1918 the Turkestan ASSR was proclaimed (within the RSFSR), comprising most of Soviet Central Asia. Meanwhile, however, a fierce struggle was still being waged between Bolshevik and anti-Bolshevik forces, interventionists and disparate native bands of *basmachi* (literally 'raiders'). Soviet rule was not finally consolidated until the early 1920s. The former Protectorates of Bukhara and Khiva were transformed into nominally independent People's Soviet Republics in 1920, then incorporated into the Soviet Union in 1923–24.[4]

## SOVIETISATION OF THE UZBEKS

While the Tsarist administration consciously restricted its efforts to change Central Asian society, the Soviets, by contrast, sought drastically to remould it. The first and most fundamental innovation was the creation of national administrative units. These were based on ethno-linguistic divisions. It would be an exaggeration to say that such divisions did not exist (though this is indeed a view held by some), but certainly prior to this they had had no political significance. Traditionally, clan, region and religion had provided the key elements in self-definition. The ethnonym 'Uzbek' was not often used by the local population: the most common terms of identification were those derived from place-names, e.g. *Namanganlyq* 'someone from Namangan'. The colonial administration referred to the native sedentarised population as *Sart*, a word of Sanskrit origin meaning 'trader'. By the early years of the 20th century a handful of intellectuals had begun to raise the question of ethnic identity, but in a vague, tentative way. There was nothing in their discussions, nor in the subsequent turmoil of civil war, that in any way prepared the ground for the National Delimitation of the Central Asian Republics of 1924–25, as a result of which the Uzbek SSR and other Central Asian republics were created. Far from being a response to a popular, indigenous demand, the Delimitation was an administrative decision imposed on the region from the centre, the result, some would say, of a 'divide and rule' policy.[5]

The Uzbek SSR, which came into being on 27 October 1924, encompassed the districts of Amu Darya, Syr Darya, Samarkand and Ferghana, part of the former Bukharan state, and part of the Khorezm (Khivan) state. It included the Tadzhik ASSR until 1929, when this acquired full union republic status; it acquired the Karakalpak ASSR (originally part of the RSFSR) in 1936. Uzbeks represented 66 per cent of the total population (cf. approximately 70 per cent today).

## Language and literacy

The creation of separate administrative units was but the first step in the process of nation-building. The development of distinctive national literary languages, literatures, histories, rituals, symbols and art forms helped to consolidate the new national identities. So much of the Central Asian heritage was common to the whole region that efforts to parcel it up into 'nationalist' packages led to distorted and grossly anachronistic interpretations of history (including fierce rivalries over the supposed ethnic origins of medieval scholars). However, artificial though they were, in time these devices achieved a measure of success, and a degree of national pride, even of nationalism, was born. The Uzbeks, for example, have come to believe that they have a unique hereditary claim to the brilliant achievements of ancient Transoxiana. This, along with their numerical superiority, has reinforced their view of themselves as the natural leaders of Central Asia today. The neighbouring republics regard this cultural aggrandisement as an expression of 'great Uzbek chauvinism'.

Easily comprehensible literary languages, full literacy, and a plentiful supply of printed material were required in order to reach out to the masses, to communicate the new ideology to them and to involve them in the new political system. The Uzbeks, unlike some other peoples of Central Asia, already had their own literary language, Chagatai (also known as Old Uzbek). However, it was a refined, learned medium, far removed from the spoken dialects of the region. Moreover, and perhaps more importantly, it was firmly associated with the pre-revolutionary period. In the 1920s there was a struggle between the so-called 'bourgeois nationalists', who mostly supported the continued use of Chagatai, and the pro-Russian group, who were in favour of developing a new literary form based on the dialects of Tashkent and Ferghana.[6] These were the dialects of the economic and political centres of the new republic, and also of the burgeoning print language. They were untypical of the main body of Uzbek dialects in that they were highly Iranised and had lost much of their vowel harmony, the most distinctive feature of the Turkic languages. Nevertheless, they were adopted as the base for the national language. Terms drawn from Russian were introduced to convey new concepts in such fields as ideology, technology, and the general Soviet 'way of life'. The change of scripts gave visual emphasis to the new orientation. The Arabic script continued to be used up to 1930, when it was replaced by the Latin. This in turn was superseded by the Cyrillic in 1940.

One of the chief reasons advanced for the abolition of the Arabic script was that it was an impediment to the spread of literacy. That is a debatable point, but it is undeniable that the literacy level rose with astonishing speed under Soviet rule. According to the 1926 census, literacy among Uzbeks stood at a mere 3.8 per cent; by 1932, 52.5 per cent of the population were said to be literate. The curve continued to rise until today it is claimed to be over 99 per cent. There may be some exaggeration in this, but what has been achieved is remarkable, and far outstrips literacy rates in neighbouring countries such as Pakistan, Afghanistan and Iran. It required an extraordinary level of organisation and coordination, since virtually everything had to be created from scratch, from the construction of school buildings to the training of teachers, from the compilation of basic textbooks to the provision of paper and printing facilities.[7] Yet there were also losses. The changes of script have meant that the Uzbeks were bereft not only of the whole of their pre-revolutionary written culture but also of first-hand acquaintance with sources relating to the formative first decades of Soviet rule. Literacy has given them access to only a small and carefully edited segment of their history.

## Islam

In November 1917 the Soviet government issued a declaration 'to all the toiling Muslims of Russia and the East' that henceforth their beliefs with customs would be considered 'free and inviolable'.[8] At first this promise was fulfilled reasonably well. By the end of the 1920s, however, the situation had changed. In Uzbekistan, as in other parts of the Soviet Union, a fierce anti-religious campaign was unleashed. Muslim schools and courts were phased out (initially, since there were few secular alternatives, they had been allowed to continue functioning); mosques were closed, often to be turned into clubs or cinemas, religious literature confiscated and destroyed, religious functionaries persecuted. The Arabic script, which had been used for the literary languages of Central Asia for close on a thousand years, and has a special significance for Muslims all over the world because it is the script in which the *Qur'an* was originally recorded, was replaced by the Latin. In short, as far as possible all visible signs of the religion were wiped out and it became dangerous to even admit to being a Muslim.

However, it was impossible to eradicate overnight something that had for centuries been the very essence of life. Quite apart from the role that religion had played in shaping the culture and history of Central Asia, almost every custom and tradition had its roots in Islam. To have abandoned such markers of identity as, for example, circumcision and Islamic burial rites, would have been to cut oneself off from one's ancestors, to become an isolated individual rather than a member of a living community linked to past, present and future generations.[9] During and after the Second World War the government adopted a slightly more conciliatory attitude towards Islam. Four regional Muslim Spiritual Directorates were created, to regulate such formal aspects of Islam as were allowed to reappear at this time. The largest and most important Directorate had its seat in Tashkent, the Uzbek capital. The first two (and until 1989 the only) *madrasa* ('religious college') in the Soviet Union were reopened in Bukhara and Tashkent. A small number of mosques were also gradually reopened and a few religious publications were sanctioned, although their print runs were tiny and their circulation tightly controlled. Some 20–30 carefully chosen pilgrims (drawn from the whole of the USSR) were allowed to make the annual *hajj* ('pilgrimage') to Mecca, one of the basic duties of a Muslim. These changes were mostly cosmetic and did little to bring greater freedom of worship to ordinary believers. Their primary purpose was to impress foreign Muslims, thereby to pave the way for better relations with Muslim states in Africa and Asia.

## Social and economic change

Soviet rule brought drastic changes to the social and economic life of the Uzbeks. Under the Tsarist administration there had been some industrial development of Central Asia (chiefly the extraction of petroleum, coal and copper), also a substantial expansion of the cultivation of cotton. Short staple native cotton had long been grown locally, but it was the introduction of higher yielding American strains in 1884 that revolutionised production and transformed the region into the principal supplier of raw material to the Russian textile industry (the simultaneous extension of the railway system solved the transport problem). The 'great leap forward' in economic development, however, was initiated during the first two Soviet five-year plans (1928–1938). In order to accomplish this, large numbers of professionals and skilled technicians were brought in from other parts of the Soviet Union. By the 1930s, some 85 per cent of the industrial workforce was composed of immigrants from European Russia. During the war years, a number of industrial enterprises from the western parts of the Soviet Union were relocated in Central Asia, over 100 in

Uzbekistan alone; this further helped to accelerate the economic development of the region (and brought in yet more immigrants). After the war, the industrial growth rate remained high for a time, but by the mid-1950s it had begun to decline sharply. This downward trend has since continued, occasioned to a large extent by the lack of sufficient capital investment in the post-war years. There was, however, a temporary upturn in the 1970s; this was closely related to an increase in cotton production from 1965 onwards.[10] In 1980 Uzbekistan was said to have produced over 6 million tonnes of raw cotton; in 1983 it apparently almost rivalled the output of the whole of the United States of America. Official figures for this period, however, were notoriously unreliable. Over the last few years there has been a decrease in production. It now accounts for something under 5 million tonnes.

The workforce in the cotton fields is entirely Uzbek. Despite all the hardships and lack of facilities in the rural areas there has as yet been very little urban drift; the great majority of the population have remained in their ancestral villages. This has been a very important factor in preserving the traditional way of life, at least within the confines of the family. In the late 1920s there was a vigorous campaign to emancipate women; known as *hujum* ('attack'), its aim was to draw women out of the home, to educate them (only 1 per cent were literate in 1926), and to turn them into independent wage earners. It encouraged women to abandoned symbols of male domination, including the wearing of the heavy, all-enveloping veil that was traditional in the cities of the south. The *hujum* had a lasting effect on the lives of urban women, many of whom now work outside the home, some as highly qualified professionals. In the villages, however, there has been little real change. The feeling of hopelessness engendered by the dreary, poverty-ridden conditions in rural areas is one of the chief reasons why several hundred women a year commit suicide by self-immolation.[11]

## UZBEKS IN THE GORBACHEV PERIOD

*Perestroika* and *glasnost'* were slow to come to Uzbekistan. There was confusion and uncertainty about the intentions of the 'centre'. Also, Central Asian society was by nature highly conservative. Criticism of those in authority, the *aqsaqaly* ('whitebeards'), was considered unseemly, no matter how justified it might be. This attitude, when combined with a system that provided few checks and controls on those in power, had encouraged the emergence of an élite who were rarely called to account for their actions. Nepotism, protectionism, bribe-taking and other forms of corruption were rife. The word 'mafia' came to be used of the ruling cliques in Uzbekistan, not least by the Uzbeks themselves. Virtually every organisation and every neighbourhood was plagued by this phenomenon. *Perestroika* was powerless to break the stranglehold of these networks on society. Consequently, even the modest moves towards democratisation that were taking place elsewhere in the Soviet Union at this time hardly made an appearance in Uzbekistan.

Nevertheless, from 1989 onwards there was slightly greater freedom of the press and slightly more opportunity to raise publicly subjects that were formerly forbidden. It was mainly the writers who led the struggle for greater openness, but academics, painters, film-makers and other creative artists also made an important contribution. It came as a painful shock to many to discover how grave were the problems that confronted the republic. They included serious shortcomings in health care and housing in rural areas (where some 80 per cent of the Uzbeks live); a greater incidence of disease, malnutrition and poverty than had previously been acknowledged; a lopsidedly colonial-type economy that produced raw materials which were purchased by the state at prices far below the world market level, then exported to other parts of the Union for processing. There was growing indignation over the extent to which the indigenous culture and history had been distorted and manipulated. As in other parts of the Soviet Union, there was a demand for the rehabilitation of those liquidated in the purges of the 1930s; also, for the filling-in of the 'blank spots' of history. Yet by no means was everything open for discussion; the *jadid* period – the period of the first stirrings of political awareness in the early years of the 20th century – remained a sensitive topic. So did the establishment of Soviet power in the region, the incorporation of the Bukharan and Khivan states into Turkestan, and the whole of the civil war period.

One of the issues that attracted particular attention in the second half of the 1980s was the state of the Aral Sea. The flow of the two main rivers, the Amu Darya and the Syr Darya had been so reduced by the demands of irrigation schemes that by this period they no longer reached the Sea, which was now drying up at an ever-increasing rate. In recent years small but significant climatic changes have been observed, caused by the shrinking of the Sea; dust storms, fiercer and more frequent now, scoop up salts from the exposed seabed and scatter them far and wide, hastening the process of desertification. Highly toxic and non-biodegradable, these salts are the residue from the fertilisers and pesticides used to boost the cotton crop. The effects of long-term exposure to these chemicals is, in the opinion of some local physicians, similar to that caused by exposure to radiation. Political activists in the 1980s began to speak of genocide. Evidence of this catastrophic state of affairs had long been available to the authorities, yet they chose to ignore it. A Society for the Protection of the Aral Sea was created under the auspices of the Writers' Union in 1989. It did much to raise public awareness of the disaster. Solutions to the problem, however, were more difficult to find. To date there has been little progress in this direction.[12]

The plight of the Aral Sea, like so many of Uzbekistan's problems, has its roots in the monoculture of cotton. The drive for higher productivity, initiated by Khrushchev in the 1950s, developed a mad momentum of its own during the Brezhnev era. The strain on the republic was unbearable and every aspect of life suffered. Precious water resources were squandered with no thought for sustainable development. It is now acknowledged that the monoculture of cotton has been responsible for some of the worst health problems of the republic. As more land was turned over to cotton, other forms of agriculture were neglected. Crop rotation was abandoned, leading to an impoverishment of the soil. Less space was available for the cultivation of fruit and vegetables; pasture land, too, was reduced. Basic foodstuffs became scarce and expensive, and the diet of the population suffered accordingly. Vitamin, protein and iodine deficiencies are widespread, resistance to infection is low, especially among children; the official infant mortality rate in the Aral Sea region is 118 per 1,000 live births, but the actual rate is probably higher (cf. the Soviet average of 25.4).

Further health hazards are created by the vast quantities of chemical fertilisers and pesticides that are used on the crop (according to Uzbek scientists, some 54 kg per hectare). These have seeped into the soil and the water supply, and so into the food chain; in many parts of the republic there is no clean drinking water. Butyfos, the most dangerous of the defoliants, was banned in 1987, but others, almost as lethal, are still legal and continue to be used. Women and children, who in some areas still harvest the crop by hand, are exposed without any form of protective clothing to the full force of these chemicals. The harm they do in the short term is all too obvious, but it is feared that the long-term effects will be even more serious.[13]

## First stirrings of political opposition

In the second half of the 1980s the first stirrings of political opposition began to appear. *Birlik* ('Unity'), the first socio-political movement in Central Asia, was founded in Tashkent in November 1988 by a group of Uzbek intellectuals. It was closely modelled on 'popular front' movements in other parts of the Soviet Union, in particular *Sajudis*. The movement grew rapidly under the chairmanship of Abdurahim Pulatov, a lecturer and research scientist in cybernetics at Tashkent University. The struggle to obtain legal recognition for Uzbek as the state language of the republic provided the movement with its chief platform. They had anticipated a long struggle. However, the government ceded this point almost immediately. Legislation enshrining this in the Constitution was passed in October 1989. *Birlik*, robbed of this focus for its activities, soon began to disintegrate. To some extent this was the result of personality clashes within the leadership, but collapse was undoubtedly hastened by the machinations of the authorities, who sometimes invited cooperation from *Birlik* members, sometimes clamped down on them, often intimated that official registration of the movement was imminent, but constantly postponed the granting of it. The consequence of this policy was to produce rifts within the movement, as some members were persuaded that cooperation with the government was possible, and were therefore prepared to make concessions in order to secure the good will of the authorities, while others suspected a trap and refused to compromise on even the smallest points of contention. In 1990 a splinter group was formed under the leadership of the poet Muhammad Salih. It adopted the name *Erk* ('Freedom/Free Will'), but it was in fact, initially at least, more compliant than *Birlik*. The latter came to be regarded as an extremist nationalist movement and rapidly lost public support. *Erk* retained its popularity for a year or two, but failed to establish a firm constituency and in time it, too, was marginalized, outflanked by the government.

## Islam

Official attitudes towards Islam during the 1980s were ambivalent. In the press, especially in organs of the centre, and even in statements from the senior leadership, including those of Mr Gorbachev himself, there was not infrequently a critical, almost derogatory, approach to the religion. In practice, however, there was improvement in working relations between the state and the Muslim community. The clearest intimation of change came in March 1989, when a new mufti was elected to head the Muslim Spiritual Directorate of Central Asia and Kazakhstan. The post was of more than regional importance, since the incumbent at that time was mouthpiece of official Soviet views on Muslim affairs for those within the USSR, as well as for those abroad. Previously, three generations of the Babakhanov family had fulfilled this function, and had proved themselves to be dependable allies of the secular authorities. However, such blatant collusion was no longer acceptable in the freer climate of the *perestroika* era. Shamsuddin Babakhanov, elected in 1982, became an embarrassment to all concerned, not least to the policy-makers in Moscow. Yet there was no formal mechanism by which he could be relieved of his duties. The problem was solved when the Muslim community held an unprecedented 'spontaneous' public demonstration in Tashkent, accusing him of licentious and un-Islamic behaviour and demanding his resignation. Their voice was heeded; a few weeks later the Rector of

Tashkent *madrasa*, 37-year-old Muhammad Sadyq Mahammed Yusuf Hoja-ogli, was installed in Babakhanov's place. Trained in Libya, he was generally regarded as a sincere believer, well versed in Islamic scholarship.

Shortly after his appointment, a number of dramatic concessions were made towards the Muslims. More mosques were opened over the next few months than had previously been permitted in several years. A new edition of the *Qur'an* was promised, its 50,000 copies to be the first step towards fulfilling Mufti Muhammad Sadyq's publicly expressed hope that there would soon be a copy of the Holy Scripture in every home. An Uzbek translation of the *Qur'an* was commissioned and extracts soon began to appear in print. Perhaps the most potent symbol of the 'new thinking', and the one that touched believers most deeply, was the return of the Othman *Qur'an* to the safekeeping of the Muslims. Believed by Central Asians to be a 7th century manuscript, copied soon after the death of the Prophet, it is one of the holiest treasures of Islam. It was taken to St Petersburg by the Tsarist administration, returned to Central Asia by the Soviet government, but kept for most of the past 70 years in the custody of the civil authorities.

Not every obstacle to Muslim worship was removed, but by 1990 it was easier to practice Islam in Uzbekistan than at any time since the founding of the republic. The general mass of believers welcomed these developments, which did much to enhance Mr Gorbachev's popularity. However, the new freedoms placed new responsibilities on the Muslim leaders. They were expected to give moral direction to the community, to act as a counterbalance to 'undesirable phenomena' ranging from hooliganism to nascent fundamentalism. Mufti Muhammad Sadyq was elected (the single, unopposed candidate in his ward) to the Congress of People's Deputies in March 1989. Thereafter, the government encouraged him to speak out on matters of law and order as, for example, during the communal violence in Ferghana in June 1989. He and the other *ulama* ('religious scholars'), however, had for so long been accustomed to a marginal role in society that it was not easy for them to find a common language with the community at large. The new mufti, like his predecessors, was soon reduced to the status of a government functionary. His moral authority was soon being challenged by independent revivalist movements that began to appear in the Ferghana Valley. Dubbed 'Wahabbis' by the Soviet press (although originally they did not appear to have had links with foreign Muslims and it was unlikely that they received any support from Saudi Arabia), they preached strict adherence to Muslim values. They eschewed politics and, as far as possible, avoided direct contact with the state. By the end of 1989 they numbered some 8,000–10,000; however, their sphere of influence was far wider than their actual numbers suggested, since they were admired by many who, though not active believers themselves, admired the uncompromising piety of these Muslims.


## THE ROAD TO INDEPENDENCE

The anti-corruption campaigns of the 1980s revealed the labyrinthine complexity of 'mafia' activities in Uzbekistan. It was by no means only Uzbeks that were involved; many highly placed officials in Moscow were also implicated. However, Uzbeks were made the scapegoats for shortcomings that, to a greater or lesser extent, were endemic throughout the Soviet Union. This caused anger and deep resentment in Uzbekistan. Coupled with other factors, such as the emergence of embryonic opposition movements and the beginnings of an Islamic revival, this marked a turning point in the relationship between the Uzbeks and the 'centre'. Some intellectuals began to speak of a 'national awakening'. It was against this background of incipient alienation that in 1990 the First Party Secretary of Uzbekistan, Islam Karimov, following Mr Gorbachev's example, assumed the title of 'President' (the first of the republican leaders to adopt this course of action); a few months later, Uzbekistan declared its sovereignty. The constitutional implications of this move were not, however, clarified (though they certainly fell far short of secession), and in the all-Union referendum on the future of the Soviet Union, held on 17 March 1991, the Uzbeks voted overwhelmingly in favour of preserving the Union.

The attempted coup of August 1991 to unseat President Gorbachev found widespread support in Uzbekistan. When it failed, President Karimov rapidly distanced himself from Moscow by declaring full independence. Again, the constitutional situation remained vague and most Uzbeks assumed that it implied greater autonomy, but certainly not a severing of links with the 'centre'. The collapse of the Soviet Union in December of that year was wholly unexpected. Uzbekistan, along with the other Central Asian republics, joined the Commonwealth of Independent States at the Almaty summit meeting of 21 December 1991.

Political independence was in itself no guarantee of economic independence and there were doubts as to whether the Central Asian republics could constitute viable state entities. However, within a surprisingly short period independent national institutions began to emerge. Some degree of economic restructuring has now been introduced, including the liberalisation of prices, the initiation of a privatisation programme, and the launching of a national currency (the sum-coupon)

Inevitably, close economic, defence and communications links have been maintained with Russia. At the same time, however, Uzbekistan has developed diplomatic and commercial contacts with over 100 countries in the Middle East, the Far East, South Asia, Europe, North America and Africa. It has joined a number of international organisations, including the UN (in March 1992) and the CSCE. Direct air links have been established with a number of major foreign cities and telecommunication networks have been upgraded. Thus, although the process of transition to genuine independence is still far from complete, considerable progress has been made in this direction.

The collapse of the Soviet Union has had not only political and economic consequences, but also psychological and cultural repercussions. These have been particularly acute in the Central Asian republics. Their nationhood, and even their modern sense of identity, were created within the Soviet framework. The sudden disintegration of this ideological context has left a spiritual vacuum. Traditional values have been undermined to such an extent that if they are to play an active role in contemporary society they must be consciously recultivated. Islam is an important element in this process of the redefinition of identity. In Uzbekistan, the government is actively promoting the Islamicisation of society, albeit in a moderate, tightly controlled manner. The conflict in Tadzhikistan has aroused fears that Uzbekistan, too, might be afflicted by religious extremism. Any manifestation of fundamentalist (or independent) Muslim activity is therefore repressed as harshly as during the Soviet period. The Islamic Revival Party, which developed out of the so-called 'Wahabbi' movement, is proscribed. Even secular opposition groups such as *Erk* and *Birlik* are accused of fundamentalist leanings; both have now been suspended.

The tentative 'national awakening' of the 1980s was concerned with questions of Uzbek identity and political status. Today, a more pressing problem is the creation of a concept of citizenship that gives due emphasis to the culture and traditions of the titular people, but at the same time ensures equal civil rights for all, regardless of ethnic background. The legislation on citizenship is liberal in its formulation, but many of the minority groups currently domiciled in Uzbekistan fear that Soviet domination will soon be replaced by Uzbek. There has already been a sizeable exodus of Slavs and other non-Uzbek peoples. It will take much patience and goodwill on the part of the majority if confidence is to be restored.

The outlook for Uzbekistan in the near future is fraught with problems of every description. In the longer term, however, it is possible that a degree of prosperity and stability will be achieved. The republic has rich human and material resources and if it succeeds in consolidating its economic as well as its political independence, there is every chance that it will become a significant regional power. The chief danger lies in the gulf that is already widening between the 'haves' and the 'have-nots'. If this is not bridged, it will inevitably lead to disillusionment, alienation and ungovernable frustration.

## NOTES

1. According to the 1989 census, the regional distribution of Uzbeks within the USSR was as follows:

   | | |
   |---|---|
   | Total number of Uzbeks | 16,697,825 |
   | in UzSSR | 14,142,475 |
   | In KazSSR | 332,017 |
   | In KirSSR | 550,096 |
   | In TurkSSR | 317,333 |
   | In TadzhSSR | 1,197,841 |

   Source: *Vestnik statistiki*, 1990–1991.

2. There are several accounts of life in Central Asia under the Tsarist administration. Of particular interest are those by the American consul in Moscow, E. Schuyler, *Turkistan: Notes of a Journey in Russian Turkistan* ... (London: Sampson Low, Marston, Searle & Rivington, 1876), and F. H. Skrine (of the Indian Civil Service) and E. D. Ross, *The Heart of Asia: A History of Russian Turkestan and the Central Asian Khanates from the Earliest Times* (London: Methuen, 1899), pp. 238–428.

3. For a review of the pre-revolutionary press in Central Asia see A. Bennigsen and Ch. Lemercier-Quelquejay, *La Presse et le mouvement national chez les musulmans de Russie avant 1920* (Paris, the Hague: Mouton, 1964); T. Ernazov, *Rastsvet narodnoj pechati v Uzbekistane* (Tashkent: Uzbekistan, 1968).

4. The best study to date of the Khanates in the Tsarist and early Soviet period is S. Becker, *Russia's Protectorates in Central Asia: Bukhara and Khiva, 1865–1924* (Cambridge, MA: Harvard, 1968).

5. Cf. A. Bennigsen, 'Islamic, or Local consciousness Among Soviet Nationalities?', in *Soviet Nationality Problems* (New York: Columbia University Press, 1971), pp. 168–82; T. Zhdanko, in I. R. Grigulevich and S. Ya. Kozlov (eds), *Ethnocultural Processes and National Problems in the Modern World* (Moscow: Progress, 1979) pp. 133–56; R. Vaidyanath, *The Formation of the Soviet Central Asian Republics: A Study in Soviet Nationalities Policy, 1917–1936* (New Delhi: People's Publishing House, 1967).

6. A useful discussion of the political currents underlying the changes of script etc. is given in E. Allworth, *Uzbek Literary Politics* (The Hague: Mounton, 1964) pp. 169–200; see also S. Akiner, 'Uzbekistan: Republic of Many Tongues', in M. Kirkwood (ed.), *Language Planning in the Soviet Union* (London: Macmillan, 1989), pp. 100–122.

7. See W. K. Medlin, W. M. Cave and F. Carpenter, *Education and Development in Central Asia* (Leiden: Brill, 1971); also T. N. Kary-Niyazov, *Ocherki Kul'tury Sovetskogo Uzbekistana* (Moscow: AN SSSR, 1955) pp. 55–68, 334–60.

8. 'Obrashchenie Predsedatelya Soveta Narodnykh Kommissarov V. I. Lenina i Narodnogo Kommissara po Delam Natsional'nostei I. V. Stalina k vsem trudyashchimsya musul'manam Rossii i Vostoka, 20 noya. (3 dek.) 1917g.', *Dokumenty vneshnoi politiki SSSR*, vol. 1 (Moscow: Gos. izdatel'stvo politicheskoi literatury, 1957) pp. 34–35.
9. The fullest Western study of Islam in the Soviet Union, though now somewhat out of date, is A. Bennigsen and Ch. Lemercier-Quelquejay, *Islam in the Soviet Union* (London: Pall Mall, 1967); cf. *Islam v SSSR*, E. G. Filimonov (responsible editor) (Moscow: Mysl', 1983).
10. See further A. R. Khan and D. Ghai, *Collective Agriculture and Rural Development in Soviet Central Asia* (London: Macmillan, 1979).
11. For two contrasting views of the lot of women in Soviet Central Asia see G. Massell, *The Surrogate Proletariat* (London: Princeton University Press, 1974); B. P. Pal'vanova, *Emansipatsiya musul'manki* (Moscow: Nauka, 1982). There have been several reports in the press on self-immolation, e.g. 'The Flames of Feudalism' by E. Gafarov, Head of Burns Unit, Civic Hospital, Samarkand, *International Pravda*, vol. 2, no. 7, 1988, p. 24.
12. *Sud'ba Arala*, R. Ternovskaya (ed.) (Tashkent: Mekhnat, 1988), a collection of some 20 essays by journalists, academics and politicians, presents a survey of the current thinking on the problem; see also 'Aral'skaya Katastrofa', *Novyi Mir*, no. 5, 1989, pp. 182–241.
13. See for example the reports in *Ogonek* by A. Minkin, no. 13, March 1988, 'Zaraza ubiistvennaya', p. 26; and no. 33, August 1988, 'Posledstviya zarazy', p. 15.

# CHAPTER EIGHTEEN

# Turkmenistan and the Turkmen

Annette Bohr

Turkmenistan appears to be a bastion of calm amid the rising storm of interethnic conflict and nationalist agitation that has been sweeping Central Asia since the mid-1980s. Following the collapse of the USSR in 1991, the tentative stirrings of political pluralism that had been ushered in by Gorbachev's reforms were quickly and effectively silenced by the establishment of an authoritarian regime under President Saparmurat Niyazov, the chief designer of Turkmenistan's independence. Niyazov's style of rule, a curious mixture of pro-investment economic gradualism, state nationalism, populism, and oriental despotism, has given rise to a lavish personality cult that has made itself felt in every part of this remote desert nation of 3.83 million inhabitants.[1]

Several factors account for the failure of democratic ideas to have taken hold during the *perestroika* period, the first of which is rooted in pre-Soviet Turkmen history. Before the establishment of Soviet rule, the largely nomadic Turkmen tribes never formed a national state and were often divided among different powers, such as the Iranian empire, the Khivan khanate and the Bukharan emirate. The territory that constitutes present-day Turkmenistan, which stretches from the Caspian Sea in the west to the Amu Dar'ya river in the east and from Kazakhstan and Uzbekistan in the north to Iran and Afghanistan in the south, was the last Central Asian territory to be brought under the control of tsarist Russia. When tsarist annexation of the Turkmen region was completed in 1884–85, the tribe represented the highest form of political and economic power.[2]

At present, Turkmenistan in many respects still constitutes more of a tribal confederation than a modern nation. The largest tribes are the Tekke in central Turkmenistan, the Ersary near the region of the Turkmen–Afghan border, and the Yomud in western Turkmenistan. Although the tribes have been steadily losing their economic power since the early Soviet period, tribal loyalties still exercise a strong influence on the Turkmen, and are reinforced by rules of endogamy and the persistence of dialects. In fact, tribal loyalties are stronger in

Turkmenistan than in any other Muslim area of the former USSR, impeding the development of a cohesive and homogeneous Turkmen nation capable of pushing for greater political freedom and civil rights. As one Turkmen journalist put it: 'Feuds between tribes are a ruinous occurrence in our life that hamper the development of the republic and often lead to tragedy'.[3]

Second, the low level of economic and social development in Turkmenistan has thwarted the growth of opposition movements such as those seen in the Baltic republics or even in Kyrgyzstan and Belarus. Turkmenistan was among the very poorest of the Soviet republics in terms of per capita income, and had the USSR's highest rate of infant mortality as well as its lowest rate of life expectancy. Whereas the largest and most influential of the Soviet Union's popular movements were urban-based, Turkmen society is predominantly rural, with only 45.3 per cent of the population residing in cities as of the beginning of 1989. Wedged in the southernmost corner of the former Soviet Union, Turkmenistan is also geographically severed from the momentous political changes that have been shaking the other Soviet successor states.

Third, the role of the Turkmen intelligentsia has been limited by its small size and its difficulty in articulating the interests of Turkmen society, mobilising the population, and effecting democratic change.

Fourth, traditional culture in Turkmenistan, which emphasises respect for elders and deference to authority, is at odds with fundamental modern democratic ideals, such as freedom of speech and political pluralism.

## TURKMENISTAN UNDER SOVIET RULE

The forging of the Turkmen into a modern nation – albeit one with a rather weak sense of unity – has perhaps been the single greatest achievement of Soviet rule in the region. It is therefore ironic that this national identity was created inadvertently, following the delimitation of Central Asian territory along national lines (*razmezhevanie*) in the first years of Soviet rule. At that time, Central Asia was divided up into distinct nations according to Stalin's four criteria: unity of economy and culture, territory and language. Soviet leaders clearly hoped that these new creations would undermine Pan-Islamic and Pan-Turkic sentiments, thereby forestalling any aspirations to Central Asian unity. Consequently, an autonomous Turkmen region was created in 1921, followed by the establishment of the Turkmen Soviet Socialist Republic on 27 October 1924.

The consolidation of Soviet power in the Turkmen region, however, did not occur without a struggle. Turkmen participated in the *basmachi* guerrilla revolt that swept Central Asia following the Bolshevik revolution. Led by Muhammad Qurban Junayd Khan, Turkmen tribes successfully took the Khivan capital in 1918 and established their leader in power. A Red Army detachment drove him into the desert early in 1920, where he and his followers continued to fight for several years as part of the *basmachi* resistance.[4] The essence of *basmachestvo* was to expel rural and urban settlers and to protect the traditional way of life threatened by Western civilisation. The collectivisation drive begun in Central Asia in 1929 was particularly traumatic, as it forced many Turkmen, Kazakh and Kyrgyz nomads to settle and join collective farms. Turkmen resistance fighters waged war in the area of Krasnovodsk and the Kara-Kum desert throughout the early 1930s, with the last battle fought in 1936.[5]

Peaceful resistance to Soviet rule was offered by the nascent Turkmen intelligentsia. A Provisional Turkmen Congress was formed in Ashgabat following the 1917 October Revolution that later merged with the Whites late in 1918 to form a Transcaspian government. This government, with limited British assistance, managed to hold off Bolsheviks for a year before succumbing to Soviet rule. It was between 1930 and 1935, however, that the Turkmen intelligentsia was most vocal, going so far as to demand political autonomy and the abandonment of the Turkmen language in favour of Anatolian Turkish or Chatagai, a Turkic language with deep literary roots in Central Asia. Soviet authorities began purging Turkmen intellectuals on a large scale in 1934, soon widening the purges to include Turkmen government leaders. In 1937–38, the chairman of the Turkmen Supreme Soviet, Nederbai Aitakov, was executed, and with him perished the last of a generation of Turkmen nationalists.[6]

In 1928, Soviet authorities launched an anti-religious campaign with the aim of completely eliminating Islam among the Turkmen. This campaign was perhaps the harshest of all the anti-Islamic offensives simultaneously begun in all the republics of Central Asia. Of the approximately 500 mosques that were functioning in the Turkmen territory in 1917, only four were still operating in 1979: two in Mary Oblast in the villages of Bairam Ali and Iolatan, and two in Tashauz Oblast in the cities of Tashauz and Ilialy.[7] As in the rest of Central Asia, all Islamic courts of law, *waqf* holdings (Muslim religious endowments that formed the basis of clerical economic power), and Muslim primary and secondary schools had been liquidated in Turkmenistan by the end of the 1920s.

On the other side of the coin, the strongly developed compulsory school system that replaced the religious schools, together with the mass campaigns against adult illiteracy, produced truly impressive results, although not as great as Soviet figures indicate. (Official statistics claim that the literacy rate in Turkmenistan jumped from 2.3 per cent to 99 per cent between 1926 and 1970, but this percentage apparently included a large number of people able only to sign their names and spell a few words.) Literacy rates appear especially impressive given that Soviet authorities changed the alphabet used by the peoples of Central Asia and Azerbaijan twice within a period of twelve years, creating overnight illiteracy for millions of Soviet Muslims. In March 1926, the Congress of Turcology meeting in Baku decided to replace the Arabic alphabet by the Latin, thus breaking Central Asian ties with the language of Islam and the Arabic world. This change, however, provided an undesirable link with Turkey, and in 1939 the Latin alphabet was replaced by the Cyrillic and the teaching of Russian was made compulsory.[8] Although the alphabet changes were to have disastrous consequences for the study of Central Asian history and literature, there was little opposition to the move as it occurred at the height of the Stalinist purges when much of the Central Asian intelligentsia had already perished.

During the Second World War, Stalin suspended the war on Islam in order to secure greater support for the war effort among Soviet Muslims, as among other believers in the USSR. An official Muslim organisation was established in 1942, consisting of four 'spiritual directorates' of Muftats. Of the four, the Muslim Religious Board for Central Asia and Kazakhstan, seated in Tashkent, was the most important and had jurisdiction over approximately 75 per cent of the country's more than 50 million Muslims.[9] A *kazi* served as the leading representative of the official Islam in each Central Asian republic. After the war, persecution of religion was resumed although the official Islamic establishment remained. Particularly under Brezhnev, the Soviet regime found the official Islamic establishment to be a convenient instrument with which to advance its interests in the international Muslim community.

Following the Islamic revolution in Iran and the Soviet invasion of Afghanistan, anti-Islamic propaganda in the USSR took an especially vicious turn. Distrust of official Islam among Soviet Muslims and the paucity of officially recognised mosques and clerics forced Islam to establish itself underground, where it thrived in the post-war period and in recent decades in particular. In Turkmenistan, as in the rest of Central Asia, the number of mosques operating illegally far outstripped those operating on an official basis.[10] The observance of certain rituals associated with Islam – such as circumcision, religious weddings and burials, and the celebration of the religious festival of Kurban Bairam – was nearly universal among the native population even at the height of the Soviet anti-religious campaign.

## Soviet rule and the development of the Turkmen economy

Before the revolution, the Turkmen region was already beginning to abandon the production of foodstuffs in favour of producing cotton. In

1912, the tsarist Minister of Agriculture had declared cotton a strategic crop, stating that 'it is better to supply this region with imported cereals even if they are more expensive, and make its irrigated land available for cotton cultivation'.[11] Soviet authorities perpetuated this trend by embarking on a policy of cotton monoculture. Those Central Asian farmers who opposed the sharp reduction in the amount of arable land available for the production of food were branded kulaks and saboteurs. Due to this policy, the USSR became self-sufficient in cotton for the first time in 1931, and a net exporter in 1937.[12] In the post-war years, cotton production in the republics has grown by an astonishing 450 per cent, primarily owing to the construction of elaborate irrigation projects in the region, such as the Kara-Kum Canal, the USSR's single largest irrigation project.

It was not until the first years of Soviet rule that Turkmenistan entered the industrial age, for tsarist Russia had made little attempt at its industrialisation. Soviet central authorities earmarked hefty sums of the all-Union budget for the industrialisation of the republic, and also sent a large number of skilled Slavic workers to facilitate the process. By the end of the 1920s, a number of industrial enterprises had been established, including those for the manufacture of textiles, silk and confections.

From the 1930s onward, however, Turkmenistan's industry grew at a snail's pace; in fact, the growth of industrial production in the republic between 1940 and 1950 and between 1960 and 1970 was the slowest of any Union republic except Azerbaijan.[13] At the time of the collapse of the USSR, the industrial enterprises established in Turkmenistan in the 1920s accounted for virtually all light industry in the republic.[14] Most heavy industry in the republic is geared towards the exploitation of Turkmenistan's large oil and gas deposits, with the exception of the Kara-Bogaz chemical works industry. The latter, however, has been threatened in recent years by the environmental disaster set in motion when the strait between the Kara-Bogaz Gulf and the Caspian Sea was dammed in 1980.[15]

The lack of industry in Turkmenistan, together with its orientation towards cotton production, has meant that the indigenous population has remained overwhelmingly concentrated in the least modernised sectors of the economy: the agriculture and service occupations. The problem grew more acute during the last decades of the USSR's existence as Turkmenistan's labour force expanded disproportionately to that of the rest of the country. Whereas the population of the USSR as a whole grew by less than forty per cent between 1959 and 1989, the population of the Turkmen SSR increased by 139 per cent. These large increases made themselves felt primarily in the rural regions of the republic where the majority of Turkmen resided.

Turkmenistan's Russian population, by contrast, has remained highly urban and concentrated in professional, administrative, and managerial occupations. Given the privileged status of the Russian language and culture during the Soviet era, there was little incentive for Russians to integrate into Turkmen society or to learn the local language. According to the 1989 census, a mere 2.5 per cent of Russians residing in Turkmenistan claimed a knowledge of the local language as a second language – a far lower percentage than in the other Soviet republics, Kyrgyzstan and Kazakhstan excepted.

Despite this apartheid-like arrangement, the final decades of Soviet rule in Turkmenistan were characterised by a remarkable social and political stability. While making outward displays of fealty and appearing to comply with the norms set down by officials in Moscow, however, many Turkmen political leaders were in fact managing clan-oriented fiefdoms involving massive amounts of embezzlement and graft. Dissent took a more open form for the vast majority of Turkmen: they simply refused to assimilate into Russian culture, steadfastly retaining their traditional social structure and way of life.

## TURKMENISTAN UNDER *PERESTROIKA*

Democracy had its heyday in Turkmenistan during the Gorbachev era, fleeting and unremarkable as it was. Despite the absence of informal organisations with a large following and mass demonstrations in the republic, the collective national consciousness grew significantly from 1987 onwards, as evidenced by increasing demands for an improvement in the status of the native language, for a reexamination of Turkmen history without ideological constraints, and for a halt to environmental damage and its concomitant health risks.

Encouraged by *glasnost'*, members of the intelligentsia and politicians alike began to describe their republic's relationship with Moscow as colonialist in essence. As support for their argument, they pointed to an investment policy geared towards the export of massive amounts of raw cotton and natural gas from their republic at artifically low prices and which neglected the development of industry. The emphasis on primary production in the republic led to an excessive degree of dependency on Russia proper and other regions for imports of textiles and food, and also exacerbated burgeoning unemployment. As a result of growing calls for greater economic sovereignty, Moscow took certain steps to correct the one-sided economic relationship between centre and periphery, such as reducing the amount of land under cotton cultivation and raising state procurement prices for raw cotton and natural gas.[16]

Turkmenistan's leadership was silent during the momentous events of August 1991, neither publicly condemning nor condoning the actions of the hard-line communists in Moscow until it had become clear that the coup was doomed to failure. A Turkmen deputy later attempted to justify the leadership's delayed reaction by claiming that news of Yeltsin's defiance had been slow in reaching Ashgabat.[17] Members of Turkmenistan's small opposition, however, maintained that the failure of the republican leadership to denounce the State Committee on the State of Emergency (GKChP) constituted a tacit approval of the junta's actions. They buttressed their argument by pointing out that the government had not only ordered the republican media to publish all the GKChP's directives, rescinding them only on 22 August, but had even managed to have portraits of Gorbachev removed from the buildings of the republican's oblast and raion Party committees.[18]

As the republics of the USSR began declaring their independence one after another following the failure of the Moscow coup, Turkmenistan's leadership decided to put the question of self-rule to a national referendum, which was held in October 1991. Despite the Turkmen population's having voted overwhelmingly in favour of preserving the Soviet Union (98 per cent of all ballots cast) in a similar referendum held only seven months before, 94.1 per cent of the electorate cast their ballots for independence – the domestic press, television, and even the religious authorities having made it clear during a pre-referendum media blitz which way the population was expected to vote. Thus, on 27 October 1991 – exactly sixty-seven years after the creation of the Turkmen Soviet Socialist Republic – the independent state of Turkmenistan was founded.

## INDEPENDENT TURKMENISTAN: THE MAKING OF AN AUTHORITARIAN REGIME

On 26 August 1991, following the example set by neighbouring Uzbekistan only a few days before, Party First Secretary Niyazov announced that the Communist Party of Turkmenistan was to be renamed the People's Democratic Party of Turkmenistan. By the time the new name was eventually adopted at the party's Twenty-fifth Congress in December 1991, however, it had been shortened to the Democratic Party of Turkmenistan (DPT). The change was a purely cosmetic one: Niyazov was confirmed in the post of chairman, and the old communist power structure remained essentially intact.

On 18 May 1992, Turkmenistan's parliament adopted a new constitution after only two hours of discussion, making it the first Central Asian state to adopt such a document following the dissolution of the USSR.[19] A popular presidential election was held on 21 June 1992 under the new constitution, although Niyazov had been directly elected to the presidency by popular ballot only twenty months before in October 1990.[20] Never having relaxed his grip on political life or allowed an opposition to form, Niyazov was once again the sole candidate and won a tidy victory: according to official results, voter turnout was 99.8 per cent, with 98.5 per cent of all ballots cast in favour of Niyazov. In January 1994, a nationwide referendum was carried out which automatically prolonged Niyazov's presidential mandate until the year 2002 without his having to submit to another popular election.[21]

The new constitution provided for the replacement of the local soviets by the more conservative Councils of Elders. Rather than elaborate policy, these bodies convene merely to approve the course already set by Niyazov; All-Turkmen Congresses of representatives of the Councils of Elders are inevitably accompanied by a large dose of ceremony and media fanfare.[22] A Turkmen Cabinet of Ministers was formed on 26 June 1992, replacing the Presidential Council.[23] Unsurprisingly, the president was elected to serve as chairman of the new Cabinet. Thus, Niyazov at present holds the posts of head of state, head of government, chairman of the renamed Communist Party, and supreme commander-in-chief of the Turkmen National Armed Forces. Additionally, decrees issued by the Turkmen president carry the force of law.

The most original ruling organ created by Niyazov during his reorganization of the political structure in May and June of 1992 was the *Khalk Maslakhaty* (People's Council), a body that is intended to hark back to the Turkmen 'national tradition' of holding tribal assemblies to solve the most pressing problems.[24] According to the Constitution, the *Khalk Maslakhaty* is the supreme representative organ of power in the country. Its members include the president, the members of parliament, the chairmen of the Supreme Court and the Supreme Economic Court, the prosecutor general, the members of the Cabinet of Ministers, the heads of the five national regions (*velayats*) and sixty elected officials from the nation's districts (*etraps*).[25] The Cabinet of Ministers led by its chairman, Niyazov, is required to accept the Council's decisions for mandatory implementation, although Turkmen officials claim that the *Khalk Maslakhaty* is neither an executive nor a legislative body.[26] The rather nebulous powers of the *Khalk Maslakhaty* also supersede those of the legislature. In fact, both the *Khalk Maslakhaty* and the parliament (renamed *Mejlis*) act as little more than vehicles to promote Niyazov's personal rule. One of the *Mejlis*'s first resolutions, for example, adopted in the spring of 1992, deemed 'expedient the production of portraits of the president of Turkmenistan and their unlimited sale to the population'.[27]

## Nationalism as an official ideology

President Niyazov has skilfully used burgeoning national sentiment to bolster his undemocratic regime, while carefully controlling the ways in which this sentiment has been allowed to develop. The adoption of a new oath on Niyazov's initiative at a plenum of representatives of the official clergy illustrates the extent to which Turkmen citizens are expected to subordinate personal interests to the national cause: 'If my actions are injurious to Turkmenistan, may my arm wither and fall off; if I bring harm to Turkmenistan, may my arm and leg wither and fall off; and if I betray Turkmenistan, may my life wither away'. Old and young are obliged to recite this invocation after meals, and teachers are obliged to teach it to their pupils. Similar words are said to open and close the main Turkmen news broadcast *Vatan* (homeland).[28]

Niyazov's status as an inadvertent founding father of an independent country has required him to transform himself from a loyal communist *apparatchik* into a proud nationalist. The memory of those who died during the battle for the fortress of Geok Tepe in 1881, which finally broke the stubborn Turkmen resistance to tsarist Russian forces and decided the fate of the rest of the Transcaspia, is still sacred for a great number of Turkmen. Although discussions of Geok-Tepe – denounced as 'reactionary' under official Soviet dogma – were strictly taboo as late as the mid-1980s, the Turkmen President recently renamed the battle the 'People's Patriotic War'. With the help of the French, Niyazov has undertaken the building of a memorial complex at the site of the fortress of Geok-Tepe, complete with a large mosque.[29] President Niyazov has also revived certain folk traditions, sometimes by presidential decree. Such was the case with 'Good Neighbourliness Day', a nationwide festival celebrated on the first Sunday in December at which 'neighbours are to share bread and salt, smiles, and courtesies'.[30] The Turkmen president has even imbued melon with national meaning, declaring the second Sunday in August as 'Turkmen Melon Day' and remarking that 'all measures should be taken to rehabilitate the bygone glory of melon, which is inseparably linked to the fate of the Turkmen people'.[31]

The success of Soviet nationalities policy in fostering separate national identities in Central Asian well exceeded Stalin's plan for the republics to be merely 'nationalist in form, socialist in content'. In comparison with clan and tribal attachments, which are restricted by their nature, nationalism has the advantage of being a broader notion while still being confined to a particular territory, i.e. the homeland. Despite the development of a national identity, however, subnational loyalties on the level of tribe and clan remain an integral part of the social fabric in Turkmenistan. In a speech urging the Turkmen to eliminate old tribal ways and to put a stop to any intrigues on tribal grounds, President Niyazov recently declared: 'No matter what tribes we come from, we remain sons of the Turkmen people'.[32] At the same time, aware of the important role tribal identities continue to play in society, the Turkmen president decided to place the emblems of five Turkmen tribes on the new state flag.[33]

In the few years that Turkmenistan has existed as an independent state President Niyazov has managed to build a cult of personality to rival or even exceed that of dictator Joseph Stalin. In seeking to equate his personal leadership with the welfare of the nation as a whole, the personality cult can be viewed as a major component of Niyazov's larger effort to strengthen his autocratic regime. The title 'Turkmenbashi', meaning 'head of the Turkmen', has been unofficially conferred on Niyazov. The Turkmen president has stated that this title symbolises the nation's unity and cohesion at a time of trial, adding that he has 'no right to object to it if it helps to strengthen peace in the country'.[34] Visitors to the country now arrive at Saparmurad Turkmenbashi Airport, students attend Saparmurad Turkmenbashi University, and ships dock at the western port city of Saparmurad Turkmenbashi (formerly Krasnovodsk). Lenin Avenue in Ashgabat and the Karakum Canal have also been renamed in his honour. His portrait is omnipresent and can even be found on the new national banknotes in the tradition of medieval Central Asian rulers.[35] The Turkmenbashi's birthday has been declared a national holiday. Newspapers are full of panegyric letters to him, and even a mild case of tonsilitis elicits copious amounts of letters from well-wishers.[36]

The removal of Russia's moderating influence following the collapse of the USSR brought an end to the nascent efforts of opposition groups in Turkmenistan to introduce democratic reform. President Niyazov has openly opposed the creation of political parties on the grounds that Turkmen society is not yet ready for political pluralism.[37] No opposition movements or parties are officially registered in the country, and hunger strikes and demonstrations have been prohibited. Censorship is extremely stringent, private publishing houses are banned, and the local correspondents of Russian newspapers are forced to wait months for official accreditation, when they receive it at all.[38]

Opposition movements, which appeared in Turkmenistan in 1989, managed to play only a limited role there before Niyazov's policy of systematic harassment drove their most active members into exile. Moreover, the Turkmen leader has stayed several steps ahead of his opposition, often directly stealing the latter's platform. Such was the case with Turkmenistan's first and most significant popular movement, *Agzybirlik* (Unity), whose programme focused on national revival – a concept soon appropriated by the Turkmen president. The first major public effort launched by *Agzybirlik* was the staging of a demonstration on 14 June 1990 at Geok-Tepe, the site of the historic last stand of Turkmen resistance to Russian rule (see above). Despite official warnings to stay away, nearly 10,000 people gathered to commemorate those who had died in the famous battle for the fortress of Geok-Tepe in 1881. The following day, 15 January 1990, the Turkmen authorities banned the opposition movement.

Despite the ban, at the beginning of August 1991, *Agzybirlik* joined with two small opposition parties, the Democratic Party (not to be confused with the DPT headed by Niyazov) and the Movement for Democratic Reform, to form *Genesh*, a coalition of democratic forces. Unrelenting harassment on the part of the Turkmen authorities, however, ultimately splintered the groups and drove their leading members into exile in Moscow, where they have continued to agitate against Niyazov's regime. Currently, the Turkmen president's most visible challenger is Avdy Kuliev, the former Turkmen minister of foreign affairs (1990–1992) and the present leader of the Turkmenistan Fund for Cultural and Business Cooperation, an opposition group in support of democratic reform in Turkmenistan that was registered in Moscow in August 1993.

## A New Era for Islam

President Niyazov's religious policy seeks to keep the growth and expression of Islam within officially designated boundaries while simultaneously exploiting the upsurge in religious belief to enhance his own popularity.

In order to better control religious sentiment, he has created a council for religious affairs that operates within the presidential apparatus. Its members include Turkmenistan's highest religious authority, *kazi* Nasrullo ibn Ibadullah, who acts as chairman; the head of the Orthodox church in Turkmenistan, who acts as co-chairman; and state officials, who act as watchdogs 'to ensure the observance of the law'.[39] Furthermore, the *kaziat* appoints Islamic clerics in all rural areas, thereby allowing the state to exert control on 'the Islamicisation of the population' right down to the village level.[40]

Cloaking himself in the mantle of Islam, the Turkmen president has sponsored the rapid building of mosques, the refurbishment of holy places, and the restoration of Islamic holidays on the one hand, while banning all religious parties on the other. Whereas in 1987 there were only four functioning mosques in the Turkmen SSR (and none in the capital city of Ashgabat), that number had risen to eighty-three by 1992, with another sixty-four mosques under construction.[41] Furthermore, five mosques have been opened to serve the country's relatively small Shiite community, which consists primarily of Kurds and Azerbaijanis. In 1991 Turkmenistan's first madrassah was founded in Dashhowuz (formerly Tashauz) to help alleviate the country's acute shortage of trained religious clergy.[42] Making full use of the Islamic card to win support among believers at home, the Turkmen president made a pilgrimage (*hajj*) to Mecca and Medina during an official visit to Saudi Arabia in March 1992, thereby adding the new title of *haji* to his already long list of distinctions.

Islam is a force that has been working side by side with nationalism throughout the newly independent states of Central Asia. One notable example is the way in which many religious Turkmen have begun to question the dominant role played by the country's Uzbek population in Turkmenistan's official religious establishment. The *kaziat* is located in Dashhowuz Oblast, where the Uzbek population is highly concentrated, although Dashhowuz is situated more than 500 kilometres from the nation's capital. The majority of the country's officially appointed religious clerics are Uzbeks, as is the *kazi* himself.[43] In an interview published in the Russian newspaper *Nezavisimaya gazeta*, the outspoken imam-khatib of the Khezret-Omar Mosque in Ashgabat even called for the *kazi*'s removal on the grounds that the latter is an 'Uzbek, who does not fully understand the traditions, way of life, and culture of the Turkmen people'.[44]

Over a period of centuries, Islam in Turkmenistan has become a unusual blend of orthodox Islam, Sufi mysticism, and shamanistic practices. The cult of ancestors is still observed, and reverence for members of the four holy tribes (the *Awlad*) is still strong. The veneration of holy places, which are generally tombs connected with Sufi saints, mythical personages, or tribal ancestors, continues to play an active role in the preservation of religious feeling among the population; these places are more numerous in Turkmenistan than in the old sedentary territories of Central Asia. The most celebrated holy place in the country is the tomb of Najmuddin Kubra (sheikh Kebir Ata) in Kunya-Urgench, which is regularly frequented by pilgrims.[45] Hundreds of pilgrims are also reported to visit the mausoleums of Muhammad ibn Zeid and Sultan Sanjar in Bayramaly, to name but a few of the country's many places of pilgrimage.[46] *Kazi* Ibadullah, who is young, well-educated, and a modernist in his approach towards Islam, periodically condemns the making of pilgrimages to 'holy places' other than Mecca. Given the resilience of the holy places, however, which acted as real centres of religious life in the absence of functioning mosques during the Soviet period, they are sure to remain an important part of worship in Turkmenistan even under Niyazov's iron-fisted rule.

### *'Open doors and positive neutrality'*

Aware of his nation's premature birth, President Niyazov lost little time in setting about the twin tasks of seeking international recognition of Turkmenistan's status as an independent state and emerging from economic isolation. To further these ends, he adopted two new policy initiatives: 'positive neutrality' and 'open doors'. The first declares Turkmenistan's official policy of non-interference and opposition to membership in any international economic or military alliances – including participation in CIS peacekeeping forces – that could lead to an infringement of its sovereignty. The second calls for large-scale foreign investment in Turkmenistan's oil, gas, and other natural resource sectors.

In the early months of 1992 Turkmenistan was admitted to the United Nations, the Commission on Security and Cooperation in Europe, the International Monetary Fund, and the Economic Cooperation Organization (ECO).[47] Membership of the World Bank and the European Bank for Reconstruction and Development, granted in the second half of the year, has brought tangible benefits. In August 1994, the EBRD agreed to give Turkmenistan $30–35 million in credit to develop small and medium-sized businesses, and the World Bank made public its decision to give the state $25 million in credit, to be paid back over the next twenty years.[48] In June 1994, Turkish President Suleyman Demirel announced that Turkey's Export–Import Bank would offer a credit line of $90 million to Turkmenistan to promote trade between the two countries.[49]

While setting out to establish Turkmenistan in the world arena, Niyazov never lost sight of the fact that he now headed a country whose economy was fully interwoven with those of its neighbours. In order to preserve and regulate its interregional economic ties in the absence of a centre, Turkmenistan hastened the process – begun in 1990 – of signing bilateral agreements with other post-Soviet states. Preferring bilateral relations and rejecting the creation of supragovernmental coordinating structures, Turkmenistan together with Moldova and Ukraine have been 'non-signers' of the agreements endorsed by the majority of the other CIS member states, including those on collective security and the creation of an interstate bank.[50]

Once one of the poorest Soviet republics, Turkmenistan was the only CIS state to yield a positive economic indicator for the rate of change of national income produced in 1993 over 1992. It was also the most successful of the CIS states by far in reversing its decline in industrial output in 1993.[51] One of the most important post-independence developments for Turkmenistan was the agreement reached with Russia in December 1991 to allow Turkmenistan to export a limited amount of natural gas to Europe through Russian pipelines in exchange for hard currency calculated at world prices. Turkmenistan's wealth in natural resources has enabled President Niyazov to indulge in certain populist measures – in particular, the population has been supplied with water, gas, and electricity free of charge since June 1993. Moreover, the Turkmen leader has managed to introduce price liberalisation at a snail's pace, even reintroducing price controls on certain foodstuffs when he deemed it necessary.

The Achilles' heel of the Turkmen economy, however, is the present system of shipping the country's natural gas through Russia, which gives Moscow considerable leverage over Turkmenistan and locks it into selling its main commodity to impoverished, unreliable clients, i.e. Ukraine, Azerbaijan and Georgia. As of 1 September 1994, Ukraine owed $855 million to Turkmenistan for supplies of gas received in 1993–1994 alone; Georgia's unpaid bill for Turkmen natural gas supplies received in 1993 was $200 million.[52] Consequently, Turkmenistan has placed great hopes on its multi-billion dollar project to construct an alternative pipeline via Turkey and Iran to ship gas to Western Europe. Iran and Turkmenistan have also signed a document declaring their intention to build an oil pipeline between the two countries. Financing remains a major problem, however, since few Western banks are willing to extend credit for a venture involving Iran.[53] Another major project under consideration – considered Utopian by many outside observers – is the construction of a gas pipeline from Turkmenistan via China to Japan, which Chinese Premier Li Peng has dubbed 'the project of the century'.[54]

### Relations with the Russian Federation

'We cannot conceive of a future without the closest of relations with the Russian Federation, including mutual, fraternal support in all economic and political questions.'[55] Such was President Niyazov's assessment of his country's relationship with its most important ally, on which the Turkmen depend for the bulk of their foreign trade, the export of their natural gas and oil, their transportation and communications networks, and their military security.

In June 1992, Turkmenistan concluded a bilateral military accord with Russia under which a Turkmen national army was created on the basis of the Kushka and Kyzyl Arvat Divisions and several other detachments of the former USSR Armed Forces. The forces were put under joint Russo-Turkmen command, except for air defence and some strategic air force units, which remained solely under Russian command.[56] While ethnic Turkmen constituted 70 per cent of the army, they made up only 15–20 per cent of the officer corps.[57]

On 1 January 1994, all troops under joint Russo-Turkmen command were transferred to the sole command of Turkmenistan. A special agreement had been concluded on 1 September 1993 governing the status of Russian soldiers serving in the Turkmen National Armed Forces and formally guaranteeing them certain rights and privileges. Turkmenistan is at present the only former Soviet republic with a full set of military agreements with Russia that the latter regards as favouring its interests.[58] In actuality, however, many provisions of the agreements remain unfulfilled, resulting in great consternation among the Russian officers corps in Turkmenistan. Following the introduction in November 1993 of the Turkmen national currency, the manat, living standards for Russian officers in Turkmenistan were reported to have fallen sharply, prompting a group of them to threaten to take their case to the United Nations.[59] This same group of Russian officers has pointed out that the transfer of command of forces to Turkmenistan has led to a sharp decline in the state of military readiness, with even the most essential spare parts and equipment reported to be unavailable.[60]

In addition to its unique military arrangement with the Russian Federation, Turkmenistan is so far the only successor state to have concluded an agreement on dual citizenship with that nation. At a meeting of the heads of CIS states in Ashgabat on 24 December 1993, President Niyazov symbolically issued Russian President Boris Yeltsin with a new Turkmen passport, declaring him an honorary Turkmen. The leaders of the other Central Asian states have all rejected the institution of dual citizenship in their countries, arguing that it would give rise to divided loyalties among their respective Russian populations. The Russian Federation, on the other hand, considers the introduction of dual citizenship one of its main goals in the 'near abroad' and its most reliable instrument for defending the interests of the Russian populations living there. According to the Decree on the Main Directions of the State Policy of the Russian Federation towards Compatriots Living Abroad, published on 11 August 1994, Russia also regards agreements on dual citizenship as serving to 'strengthen trust between states'.[61]

In opting to implement dual citizenship, the Turkmen leadership hopes not only to fortify its relationship with Russia but also to achieve the more practical aim of curtailing the exodus of its Russian inhabitants, which in 1989 constituted 9.5 per cent of Turkmenistan's total population. Turkmen leaders are well aware that the Russian population take badly needed professional and technical skills with them when they leave: In 1993, members of the titular nationality made up only 9.5 per cent of all industrial workers in Turkmenistan, although they accounted for over seventy per cent of the total population.[62] According to preliminary data, between 1989 and 1993 a net total of 29,500 Russians (the number leaving Turkmenistan less the number arriving) or 8.8 per cent of Turkmenistan's Russian population emigrated to Russia.[63] While substantial, this percentage is significantly smaller than the corresponding percentages for the other Central Asian republics, Kazakhstan excepted.[64] Whereas Russians from neighbouring Kyrgyzstan and Tajikistan have cited interethnic conflict and severe economic decline as their primary reasons for leaving those states, Russian emigrants from Turkmenistan have pointed to limited prospects for professional advancement owing to language and other barriers; inferior educational possibilities; and a creeping sense of cultural alienation.[65]

## CONCLUSIONS

Turkmenistan is poised uneasily between the lure of modernisation and the forces of tradition. In order to realise his goal of making Turkmenistan a 'new Kuwait with gas', President Niyazov is endeavouring to revolutionise industry and introduce free trade while bypassing a social revolution. Presenting himself as the principal champion of the Turkmen national cause, he has succeeded in both exploiting and controlling national and religious sentiment to a remarkable degree. Moreover, much to the envy of several of his counterparts in other newly independent states, he has thus far avoided outbreaks of violence on ethnic or other grounds, with the exception of the riots that took place in the Turkmen cities of Ashgabat and Nebit-Dag in May 1989.[66]

Although the fledgling state has managed to conclude an impressive number of economic deals with foreign states and has begun to receive a limited amount of hard currency for its exports, it is still beset by serious economic problems – namely, an underdeveloped infrastructure, scarce water resources, food shortages, inflation, and growing unemployment. Perhaps Turkmenistan's greatest vulnerability is its dependence on its economic ties with the republics of the former Soviet Union, and in particular on Russia.

None the less, given Turkmenistan's tremendous natural resources and small population, its economic situation is unlikely to take a significant downturn in the near future. Virtually everything that the nation produces (cotton, gas, oil, horses, carpets, etc.) can be sold on world markets for hard currency. President Niyazov has so far been able to direct a large part of the country's profits from sales of gas, oil, and cotton towards protecting the living standards of the population. Furthermore, although the cult of personality surrounding Niyazov derives in part from official efforts to generate public support, the 'Turkmenbashi' does enjoy a good deal of genuine popularity – especially among those who credit him with having saved the nation from economic disaster and civil strife à la Tajikistan. Ultimately, however, Turkmenistan's success in establishing itself as an independent state is likely to be measured by the degree to which it is able to diversify its markets and increase its manufacturing capabilities while preserving social stability, ethnic harmony, and close ties with Russia.

## NOTES

1. The Kara-Kum desert makes up 90 per cent of the country's total area. Figures for population are mid-1993 estimates from the Bureau of the Census, Center for International Research, Washington, DC.
2. Mehmet Saray *The Turkmens in the Age of Imperialism: a Study of the Turkmen People and their Incorporation into the Russian Empire* (Ankara, Turkish Historical Society Printing House 1989), pp. 8–13, 23–61. See also Alexandre Bennigsen and S. Enders Wimbush *Muslims of the Soviet Empire* (Bloomington, IN, Indiana University Press 1986), p. 95.
3. 'Iz plena ambitsii', *Turkmenskaya Iskra* 5 May 1988.
4. Aman Berdi Murat 'Turkmenistan and the Turkmens', in Zev Katz (ed.)

*Handbook of Major Soviet Nationalities* (New York, Macmillan 1975), p. 265.

5. Chantal Lemercier-Quelquejay 'Muslim National Minorities in Revolution and War', in S. Enders Wimbush (ed.) *Soviet Nationalities in Strategic Perspective* (New York, St Martin's Press 1985), p. 54.

6. Helen Carrere D'Encausse 'The Russian Revolution and Soviet Policy in Central Asia', in Gavin Hambly (ed.) *Central Asia* (New York, Delacorte Press 1969), p. 238.

7. Bennigsen and Wimbush, *op. cit.*, p. 101.

8. Edward Allworth *Uzbek Literary Politics* (The Hague, 1964), pp. 169–78.

9. In 1990 Kazakhstan broke away from the Muslim Religious Board for Central Asia and Kazakhstan to form its own sovereign religious board, based in Almaty. In 1990 the Muslim Religious Board for the North Caucasus ceased to exist, having splintered into several religious boards.

10. *Literaturnaya Gazeta*, 18 May 1988, p. 10.

11. Geoffrey Wheeler *The Modern History of Soviet Central Asia* (New York, Praeger 1964), p. 157.

12. Violet Conolly *Beyond the Urals* (London, Oxford University Press 1967), pp. 91–3.

13. Murat, *op. cit.*, p. 263.

14. *Ashkhabad* no. 5, 1989, p. 61.

15. *Izvestiya* 15 Jan. 1988.

16. *Turkmenskaya iskra* 20 August 1989, *Izvestia* 7 February 1991 and *Economicheskaya gazeta*, No. 12, 1989, pp. 10–13.

17. Central Television, 27 August 1991, cited in Bess Brown 'Central Asia and the Coup' *Report on the USSR*, RFE/RL Inc., No. 36, 6 September 1991.

18. Address of the Consultative Council of Democratic Movements of Turkmenistan *Genesh* to the USSR Supreme Soviet, 23 August 1991.

19. *Srednyaya Aziya: Spravochnye Materialy* (Moscow, Institute for Humanitarian and Political Research 1992), p. 89.

20. The October 1990 elections were the first in the USSR in which a president of a Union republic of the USSR was directly elected by popular ballot. The all-Union press paid relatively little attention to them, however, owing to their lack of democratic substance and their predetermined outcome.

21. *Ostankino Novosti* 17 January 1994.

22. *ITAR-TASS* 8 September 1994.

23. *ITAR-TASS* 26 June 1992, in FBIS SOV 29 June 1992.

24. *ITAR-TASS* 24 November 1992, in FBIS SOV 25 November 1992.

25. *Nezavisimaya gazeta*, 20 October 1992.

26. *Nezavisimaya gazeta*, 17 December 1992. An expert group of the Turkmenistan Fund, an opposition organisation based in Moscow, has maintained that the *Khalk Maslakhaty* constitutes *de facto* a fourth branch of government, thereby contravening Article Four of the Turkmen Constitution, which allows for only three branches of government. They have further argued that the *Khalk Maslakhaty* not only weakens the legislative powers of the *Mejlis* but renders impossible any theoretical system of checks and balances.

27. *Komsomolskaya pravda* 17 Oct. 1992, in FBIS SOV 20 October 1993.

28. *Byulleten' Obshchestva sodeistviya soblyudeniyu prav cheloveka v Tsentralnoi Azii* (Moscow, No. 8, 10 May 1994 in *Prava Cheloveka* 23 May 1994.
29. *ITAR TASS* 1 July 1994.
30. *ITAR-TASS* 6 December 1992, in FBIS SOV 7 December 1992.
31. *Izvestia* 18 July 1984.
32. *Rossiiskie Vesti* 12 January 1992, in FBIS SOV 13 January 1993.
33. The five symbols chosen by Turkmen officials have bewildered experts in Turkmen tribal heraldry. Whereas the emblems of the Tekke and Yomud tribes are easily discernable, it is not completely clear to which tribes the other three emblems on the flag belong. Moreover, the emblem of the Ersary tribe is missing altogether, a circumstance that is reported to have caused some consternation among members of that tribe living in Germany and Sweden.
34. *ITAR TASS* 9 December 1992, in FBIS SOV 19 December 1992.
35. Edward A. Allworth *The Modern Uzbeks* (Stanford, CA, Hoover Institution Press 1990), p. 297.
36. Reuters, 23 March 1993.
37. Reuters, 16 March 1993.
38. *Izvestia* 4 March 1994, *The Christian Science Monitor* 25 March 1993, *Prava Cheloveka*, No. 26, 5 July 1994, and *ANI*, 1 July 1994.
39. *Novaya ezhednevnaya gazeta*, 15 July 1994 in *Prava Cheloveka* No. 30, 2 August 1994.
40. *Byulleten' Obschchestva sodeistviya soblyudeniyu prav cheloveka v Tsentralnoi Azii* (Moscow), No. 8, 10 May 1994 in *Prava Cheloveka* 23 May 1994.
41. Alexander Verkhovsky (ed.) *Islam i politicheskaya bor'ba v stranakh SNG* (Moscow, Panorama 1992), p. 27.
42. *Ibid.*, p. 28.
43. *Srednyaya Aziya: Spravochnye Materialy* (Moscow, Institute for Humanitarian and Political Research 1992), p. 96.
44. *Nezavisimaya gazeta* 8 July 1992.
45. Verkhovsky, *op. cit.*, p. 29.
46. *The Washington Post* 1 April 1993.
47. The ECO is an intergovernmental association that since 1992 has included the five states of Central Asia, Azerbaijan and Afghanistan in addition to its three founding members (Iran, Turkey, and Pakistan). Viewing it as the core of a possible future Islamic Common Market, the ECO's founding members hoped to revitalise the body by inviting the newly independent states to join; however, little progress in this direction has been made.
48. *ITAR-TASS* 29 August 1994.
49. *RFE/RL News Briefs*, 21 June 1994.
50. Ann Sheehy, 'Seven States Sign Charter Strengthening CIS', *Report on the USSR*, RFE/RL Inc., No. 9, 26 February 1993. See also 'Ashgabat's Gas 'Pressure'. Why Turkmenistan did not sign the CIS Charter' *Komsomolskaya pravda*, 29 January 1993.
51. Eric Whitlock, 'The CIS Economies: Divergent and Troubled Paths', *Report on the USSR*, RFE/RL Inc., No. 1, 7 January 1994.
52. *ITAR-TASS* 7 September 1994 and 18 September 1994.

53. Reuters, 6 April 1994. AFP 13 February 1995. The Turkmen-Iranian gas pipeline is expected to extend 5,200 kilometers, cost 8–10 billion dollars and require over ten years to construct.
54. Reuters, 21 April 1994.
55. *ITAR-TASS*, 14 June 1994.
56. *Interfax* 16 July 1992.
57. *Armiya* No. 10, 1994, p. 20.
58. Ibid, p. 22.
59. *Izvestia* 11 February 1994.
60. Ibid.
61. See *Pravda* 18 August 1992 and *Rossiiskaya gazeta* 22 September 1994.
62. *Vostok* No. 6, 1993, p. 77.
63. This percentage has been calculated on the basis of 1989 census data and preliminary figures – likely to be underestimates – provided by the Russian Federal Migration Service. *Vek* No. 28, 29 July–8 August 1994, p. 7.
64. Between 1989 and 1993, the Russian population in Tajikistan decreased by 35.9%; in Kyrgyzstan, by 15.6%; in Uzbekistan, by 12.2%; and in Kazakhstan, by 4.4%.
65. *Komsomolskaya pravda* 25 May 1994.
66. See Annette Bohr 'New Information of May Riots in Ashkhabad and Nebit-Dag', *Report on the USSR*, RFE/RL Inc., No. 29, 21 July 1989.

# CHAPTER NINETEEN

# Tajikistan and the Tajiks

John Payne

## BACKGROUND

The Tajiks speak a language that belongs to the Iranian family and is very closely related to the modern forms of Persian spoken in Iran and Afghanistan. They are therefore linguistically quite distinct from the other main national groups of Central Asia, whose languages (Uzbek, Kirgiz, Turkmen, Kazakh) belong to the Turkic family.

Iranian peoples have been settled in Central Asia since ancient times, predating the Turks by at least a millennium. During the seventh–sixth centuries BC, the territory to the north of the Oxus river (Amu-Darya), which forms the present Tajik and Uzbek Republics, was already occupied by East Iranian peoples: the Bactrians, the Sogdians and the nomadic Sakas. In the sixth century BC, the early independent states of Bactria and Sogdiana were incorporated into the Persian Empire by Cyrus the Great, the founder of the Achaemenian dynasty. At this time, the town of Marakanda (modern Samarkand) in Sogdiana was already an important trading centre.

From the fall of the Achaemenians in the fourth century BC until the Arab conquest at the beginning of the eighth century AD, Bactria and Sogdiana were subjected to a variety of non-Iranian influences. The first of these was Alexander the Great's invasion in the fourth century BC, followed after Alexander's death by the dismemberment of the Greek Empire and the eventual formation of an independent Graeco-Bactrian state in the middle of the third century BC. Greek rule was ended in the middle of the second century BC by the arrival from the north of the nomadic Yüeh-Chi. One Yüeh-Chi dynasty, the Kushans, founded the Kushan state which at the height of its power (first–third centuries AD) included much of the territory of Afghanistan and northern India as well as Bactria and Sogdiana. As the power of the Kushan state declined, the influence of Persia again briefly asserted itself as the Sassanian dynasty seized control over Bactria. However, the attempts of the Sassanians to maintain control over their Central Asian territories

367

were thwarted by yet more nomadic incursions from the north, those of the Hephthalites and other Hunnish tribes in the mid-fifth century AD, followed by those of the first clearly Turkic tribes in the mid-sixth century AD.

By the time of the Arab conquest of Central Asia, the original territory of Bactria and Sogdiana seems to have been divided into a number of small kingdoms. Despite the admixture of non-Iranian populations, Eastern Iranian languages were still predominant: Sogdian indeed served as the lingua franca of the silk route from Samarkand into northern China. However, the uniting of the Iranian world under the Arab Caliphate led to the gradual displacement of the original Eastern Iranian languages by Persian. Persian (Persian name *parsi*, later Arabicised as *farsi*), which by contrast belongs to the Western Iranian language group, was the main language of the Sassanian Empire in Iran and northern Afghanistan. The Arab armies that originally subjugated Central Asia were to a significant extent composed of Islamicised Persians from Khorasan (north-west Iran). Persian subsequently served as an important instrument of Arab propaganda, and Arab power was based on largely autonomous Persian-speaking ruling dynasties. By the time of the Samanid dynasty (tenth century AD), the large towns (such as Bukhara, which was the Samanid capital, and Samarkand) were essentially Persian-speaking, and an extensive literature in Persian had been developed. The poets Rudaki and Firdousi belong to this period.

The name 'Tajik' which is currently used for the Persian-speaking population of Central Asia is based on an Arabic tribal name, 'Taiy'. This name was widely used by other peoples to describe the Arabs: for example, the Arabs were known by this name to the Chinese as early as the first century AD. In the Sogdian form '*tazik*' it was used as a name for the Arab invaders of Central Asia, and then by extension applied at the end of the tenth or the beginning of the eleventh century to the Islamicised Persian-speaking population.

The eleventh to the sixteenth centuries in Central Asia were marked by successive invasions of Turks and Mongols, beginning with the establishment of the Karakhanid dynasty in the eleventh century and ending with the arrival of the Uzbeks in the early sixteenth century. During this period, as the originally Iranian-speaking populations to a large extent assumed the languages of their Turkic overlords and neighbours, the present national groupings in Central Asia were essentially formed. Persian, however, retained its status as a literary language, for example in the works of the poets Omar Khayam and Hafiz, and was maintained as the main spoken language for the majority of the population in the area that constitutes modern Tajikistan. In addition, Persian survived as the language of significant minorities in Bukhara and Samarkand. The old Eastern Iranian languages seem to have been preserved only in a few remote areas by relatively small groups: a dialect of Sogdian, now called Yaghnobi, was spoken in the Yaghnob valley in the high Zeravshan (now central Tajikistan), and other Eastern Iranian dialects, now called the Pamir languages, survived in the inaccessible western valleys of the Pamir massif (now the Gorno-Badakhshanskaya Avtonomnaya Oblast').

At the beginning of the nineteenth century, after centuries of conflict between rival khanates, rule over the territory of modern Tajikistan was divided between the Emirate of Bukhara and the Khanate of Kokand. Kokand fell militarily to Tsarist Russia in 1866, and in 1876 was formally incorporated into the General-Governorship of Turkestan which had been established in 1867 to consolidate Russian military power in Central Asia. A treaty between the Tsar and the Emir of Bukhara in 1868 ceded to Russia many of the Emirate's northern territories, including some areas that are now in northern Tajikistan. By the same treaty, the rump of the Emirate of Bukhara (including the territory that is now central and southern Tajikistan) became a Russian Protectorate. The Eastern Pamir, occupied by nomadic Kirgiz, was incorporated directly into the Tsarist Empire as part of the Kokand Khanate. However, the Western Pamir, which was divided into semi-independent feudal khanates, was incorporated into the Emirate of Bukhara only following discussions in 1895 between England and Russia on the demarcation of the borders of Afghanistan.

Under Tsarist rule, some degree of economic development was brought to the essentially feudal Muslim regions that made up the General-Governorship of Turkestan, including the territories that now form part of northern Tajikistan. Railways were built, and in order to ensure supplies of cheap raw materials for the Russian textile industry, particular attention was paid to the production of cotton. Small factories were set up by Russian industrialists in and around Khodzhent (in the Soviet period renamed Leninabad), and the mineral resources of the area, including coal, began to be exploited. At the same time, Russian settlements began to develop, often with forced expropriation of land. Economically and politically, the Bukharan Emirate was rather more backward, and many of its artisans turned to Russian Turkestan for employment, where the wages could be up to three times as high.

## THE TAJIKS IN THE SOVIET UNION

The Tajik towns that belonged to Russian Turkestan were the first to be affected by the events of 1917. Following the February Revolution, Soviets were quickly established in all the major centres including Khodzhent, Ura-Tyube and Kanibadam. However, these were composed primarily of Russian railway workers, miners and factory employees, rather than native Tajiks. During the summer of 1917, as opposition to the Provisional Government grew in strength, some

Tajik groups emerged, for example the 'Union of Muslim Workers' in Xodzhent. These were persuaded to support the Bolsheviks, who finally took control in Khodzhent in November 1917. Despite resistance from anti-Bolshevik forces in other areas, notably Ura-Tyube, Kokand and the Pamir, the northern and eastern territories of Tajikistan were effectively under Bolshevik control and had been administratively incorporated into the newly-formed Turkestan ASSR by the end of 1918.

By contrast the Emir of Bukhara, whose army consisted of nearly 95,000 men including 13,000 cavalry, was not overthrown until 1920. The first attempt at Soviet intervention in February 1918, in support of a revolutionary group called the 'Young Bukharans', ended in military failure. Only after Soviet power had been consolidated in the rest of Turkestan, and after the fall of the Khanate of Khiva in February 1920, did the Red Army again intervene in Bukhara under the command of M. V. Frunze. After a four-day battle, the Emir was driven out of Bukhara in September 1920 and the Bukharan People's Soviet Republic was declared. However, resistance by the remanants of the Emir's forces continued in Eastern Bukhara (central and southern Tajikistan), where a number of armed anti-Soviet groups known as the Basmachi eventually joined forces under such commanders as the Turkish general Enver Pasha. By the end of 1921, Enver Pasha had 20,000 men under his control, and he remained undefeated until the summer of 1922. Despite this setback, Basmachi resistance to Soviet power continued until 1926, and even in 1929 and 1931 isolated incursions were made into Tajikistan by Basmachi bands based in Afghanistan.

Tajikistan only became a political entity in the delimitation of Central Asia which took place in 1924. Prior to this, 47.7 per cent of all Tajiks in Soviet Central Asia were living in the Turkestan ASSR (403,700 people), and 52.3 per cent were living in the Bukharan People's Soviet Republic (420,100).[1] The new boundaries proposed by the Central Executive Committee of the Turkestan ASSR and the All-Bukharan Soviet of People's Deputies envisaged that Tajikistan would be merely an Autonomous Region within the new Uzbek SSR; however, the 2nd session of the All-Russian Central Executive Committee overruled this decision, giving Tajikistan the status of an Autonomous Soviet Socialist Republic within the Uzbek SSR. The Republic was formally proclaimed on 15 March 1925, with its capital in the town of Dushanbe.

At the time of its formation, the Tajik ASSR had a population of 739,500 (135,700 from the Turkestan ASSR and 603,800 from the Bukharan People's Soviet Republic).[2] The borders were mostly drawn in such a way as to include all the districts with a majority of Tajiks. However, the Tajik and Uzbek populations were so interwoven that the new Tajik ASSR nevertheless contained a sizeable Uzbek minority. For the proportions, the *Tadzhik Soviet Encyclopaedia* suggests figures of 65.4 per cent Tajiks and 32.4 per cent Uzbeks.[3] However, later figures from the 1926 census present a slightly different picture, with a total population of 827,100 (74.6 per cent Tajiks, 21.2 per cent Uzbeks, 1.4 per cent Kirgiz, 0.7 per cent Russians, 0.5 per cent Turkmen, 0.2 per cent Kazakhs, 0.1 per cent Ukrainians and 1.1 per cent other nationalities).[4]

At the same time, a sizeable proportion of the total number of Tajiks (36.9 per cent according to the 1926 census) remained outside the Tajik ASSR, primarily in the neighbouring regions of the Uzbek SSR including Samarkand, Bukhara and Xodzhent. In October 1929 the district of Khodzhent, which despite its Tajik majority had remained in the Uzbek SSR, was transferred to the Tajik ASSR, raising its population to 1,200,000 (901,400 Tajiks (78.4 per cent) and 206,300 Uzbeks (17.9 per cent)).[5] More or less simultaneously, on 16 October 1929, the Tajik ASSR was raised to the status of a full Soviet Republic, becoming the Tajik SSR.

The establishment of Soviet control in Tajikistan, as in the other Central Asian republics, led to the gradual elimination of illiteracy. A number of serious problems had to be overcome: the opposition of the mullahs to the development of a secular education system, the reluctance of Muslim women to attend schools, and the shortage of teachers, buildings and textbooks. In addition, a major difficulty was presented by the divergence of the spoken Tajik dialects from the classical Persian literary language, both in grammar (the dialects had developed a number of new grammatical forms, with the northern dialects in particular being influenced by the neighbouring Uzbek language), and in vocabulary (the classical language contained a large proportion of Arabic words). Some pre-revolutionary Tajik authors, notably Ahmadi Donish, had attempted to bring the spoken forms into the written language, and this movement was continued by the Soviet Tajik author, Sadriddin Aini, whose early stories and novels, *Odina* (1925) and *Dokhunda* (1927), based on the dialects of Bukhara and Samarkand, served as the model for the new Tajik standard language. By the end of 1927, 175 'Likbez' (*Likvidatsiya Bezgramotnosti*, Liquidation of Illiteracy) schools had been set up in the Republic, with the primary aim of training party cadres. This figure had expanded by the 1932–33 school year to 4,069 schools with over 140,000 pupils, including 25,314 women, and by 1939 the official literacy rate for the whole population had reached 71.7 per cent.[6] In 1927 a decision was taken to replace the Arabic alphabet of the classical language with an adapted version of the Latin alphabet. The Latin alphabet was used until 1940, when in its turn it was replaced by the present Cyrillic-based alphabet.

The drive towards the elimination of adult illiteracy was accompanied by the development of a system of education for school-aged pupils, and eventually a full system of higher and technical education. The number of schools rose from 382 in 1928–29 to 2,628 in 1940–41, with 303,500 pupils.[7] Universal secondary education was developed in the post-war years: in 1949–50 Tajikistan moved towards a universal seven-year education, this being extended to eight years in 1959–60. Official Soviet figures claim that by 1976, 90.3 per cent of the young population were in secondary schools, rising to 99.7 per cent in 1980.[8]

The first pedagogical institution to open was the Pedagogical Tekhnikum in Dushanbe (1926), followed at the beginning of the 1930s by similar technikums in Kurgan-Tyube, Kulyab, Nau, Ura-Tyube, Kanibadam, Pendzhikent, Khorog and Yangi-Bazar (later Ordzhonikidzeabad). In deference to Muslim prejudices, the student population initially consisted only of males: separate female teacher-training institutes or colleges were established in Dushanbe, Leninabad and Kanibadam. Other important centres were founded in the pre-war years, for example the Medical Institute in Dushanbe in 1939. However the main expansion of higher education, like that of secondary education, took place in the post-war period. The Tajik State University was opened in 1948, and the Tajik branch of the USSR Academy of Sciences, originally established in 1932, was formed into the Tajik Academy of Sciences in 1951. In 1984 the Academy consisted of 16 research institutes with a total of 1,389 workers.[9]

Modern figures for the participation of women in education show that, despite the dramatic increases since the 1950s (when Asian girls represented only 19 per cent of those enrolled in the final three years of secondary schooling)[10], Tajikistan still lagged to some extent behind the rest of the USSR, including the other Central Asian republics. This can be seen especially in the proportion of women enrolled in higher and special secondary institutions: at the beginning of the 1986–87 academic year, the proportion of women enrolled in higher education was 42 per cent, compared with 56 per cent for the USSR average, 59 per cent for Kirgizia, 56 per cent for Kazakhstan, 46 per cent for Uzbekistan, and 44 per cent for Turmenistan. The figures for the proportion of women in special secondary education was similar: Tajikistan 44 per cent, USSR average 58 per cent, Kirgizia 59 per cent, Kazakhstan 58 per cent, Uzbekistan 51 per cent, and Turkmenistan 49 per cent.[11] At the highest level, 28 women in Tajikistan held the degree of doctor of science in 1986, compared with 6,112 for the USSR as a whole. This is a proportion of 0.77 per cent, while the female population of Tajikistan represents 1.63 per cent of the total female population of the USSR. The total number of women engaged in academic work was 3,627 in 1986, 0.61 per cent of the USSR total of 598,057.[12]

In the field of the economy, the main thrust of the Party's activity in Tajikistan was the collectivisation of agriculture and the increasing development of cotton as the republic's main contribution to the total USSR economy. The process of collectivisation was slower than in the central USSR, especially in the remoter mountain regions, and seems to have met with considerable resistance. By 1932, collectivisation had encompassed 41.9 per cent of all peasant households (USSR total 61.5 per cent) and 65.3 per cent of the agricultural land (USSR total 77.7 per cent).[13] These figures, however, conceal a large discrepancy between the collectivisation of cotton-growing areas, which were made into a USSR priority and selectively resourced, and the collectivisation of lands devoted to grain production and livestock rearing. By 1932–33, 84.2 per cent of the cotton-growing land had been collectivised, compared with 26.5 per cent of the land for grain production and livestock rearing.[14] The mass collectivisation of these remaining areas took place in 1937–38. Table 19.1 gives the absolute growth in the area of cultivated land during the early Soviet period, together with the relative increase in the area devoted to cotton production. Although Tajikistan with its relatively small area had a lesser acreage under cotton cultivation than the neighbouring republic of Uzbekistan, the cotton yield per acre in Tajikistan was the highest in the USSR.

The overall growth rate for Tajikistan over the Soviet period was very high, starting from a relatively low base. However, industrial development was concentrated in urban areas, especially around the major cities of Dushanbe and Leninabad, and the relative weight of the republic in the USSR national economy remained lower for the majority of products than the relative size of its population, which like that of the other Central Asian republics had been growing at a very high rate. The main exceptions reflect the status of Tajikistan as a cotton-growing republic, and traditional specialisms such as silk. Almost half the territory of Tajikistan lies at a height of over 3,000 metres, and within the Central Asian economic region it became an important source of hydroelectric energy (see Table 19.2).

The general picture of Tajikistan in the period 1917–85 was therefore one of considerable development, both in the field of education and in the economy. However, given the rapid increase in the population, this development was not sufficient to raise Tajikistan to average USSR levels. The main role of Tajikistan in the USSR economy was as a supplier of raw cotton, only a relatively small percentage of which was converted into textiles within the republic.

Table 19.1   Area of cultivated land (1000 hectares) in Tajikistan (1913–80)[15]

|  | 1913 | 1940 | 1950 | 1960 | 1970 | 1980 |
|---|---|---|---|---|---|---|
| Total cultivated land | 494.3 | 807.1 | 836.9 | 724.3 | 764.9 | 763.3 |
| Grain | 437.8 | 567.4 | 551.5 | 360.6 | 320.5 | 195.0 |
| Cotton | 26.7 | 106.1 | 126.0 | 172.4 | 254.0 | 308.5 |
| Vegetable oil | 10.4 | 51.2 | 96.3 | 40.7 | 7.8 | 3.7 |
| Animal feed | 13.4 | 55.3 | 48.9 | 131.2 | 150.8 | 217.0 |

Table 19.2   Relative weight of Tajikistan in the USSR economy and in the
Central Asian economic region (1940–1980, percentage)[16]

|  | 1940 | | 1970 | | 1980 | |
|---|---|---|---|---|---|---|
|  | In USSR | In Central Asia | In USSR | In Central Asia | In USSR | In Central Asia |
| Population | 0.78 | 14.1 | 1.21 | 14.6 | 1.5 | 15.0 |
| Electrical energy | 0.13 | 0.92 | 0.48 | 14.0 | 1.0 | 21.5 |
| Cement | – | – | 0.92 | 20.0 | 0.84 | 14.4 |
| Coal | 0.12 | 12.1 | 0.14 | 10.2 | 0.11 | 7.8 |
| Cotton fibre | 7.2 | 8.8 | 11.0 | 12.0 | 10.3 | 11.7 |
| Raw silk | 14.0 | 21.5 | 10.6 | 17.3 | 9.5 | 14.3 |
| Cotton textiles | 0.0 | 0.01 | 1.3 | 30.0 | 1.3 | 25.7 |
| Silk textiles | 2.1 | 25.2 | 3.3 | 38.6 | 3.3 | 31.0 |
| Leather goods | 0.02 | 9.3 | 0.9 | 17.0 | 1.05 | 7.02 |
| Canned goods | 0.04 | 22.5 | 1.6 | 29.0 | 1.75 | 22.6 |

# TAJIKISTAN IN THE GORBACHEV ERA

The most striking feature of Tajikistan in the Gorbachev era was undoubtedly the open expression, under the policy of *glasnost'*, of Tajik nationalist sentiment. However, this sentiment did not immediately result in the kind of popular demand for political independence, or even for total secession from the USSR, that was seen to develop in such republics as Lithuania and Moldavia. Unlike the Baltic states, Tajikistan did not have have any recent history of independence, and indeed owed its existence as a separate republic to the decision of the early Soviet leadership not to treat the Tajiks as an ethnic minority within Uzbekistan. Also, unlike Moldavia, Tajikistan had not had any recent political ties with states outside the USSR. The link with the Persian-speaking populations of Iran and Afghanistan had for centuries been linguistic and cultural rather than political.

Instead, the main issue that initially aroused nationalist passions in Tajikistan was the increasing dominance of the Russian language. In 1926, the Russian and Ukrainian population of Tajikistan was still extremely small at 6,700 (0.8 per cent of the total population). By 1939, this figure had increased to 153,000 (10.3 per cent), and by 1959 to 289,500 (14.6 per cent). Since then, the absolute numbers of Russians and Ukrainians have continued to grow (to 375,800 in 1970 and 430,900 in 1979). Because of the very high Tajik birth rate, the overall proportion of Russians and Ukrainians in the republic had in fact been slightly decreasing in the later Soviet years (to 13.0 per cent in 1970 and 11.3 per cent in 1979).[17] However, the main Tajik (and Uzbek) population growth took place in the rural areas, while the Russian and Ukrainian population was concentrated in the towns and cities. Russians represented 30 per cent of the total urban population, and in the capital, Dushanbe, the proportion of Russians was even higher (see Fig. 7).[18]

The increasing dominance of the Russian language, and the consequential decline in the status of Tajik, was catalogued in an important article in the local press (19 February 1989) by four leading Tajik intellectuals: M. Shukurov, R. Amonov, Sh. Rustamov and A. Sayfullaev.[19] The first three were heads of department in the Rudaki Institute of Language and Literature of the Tajik Academy of Sciences, and the fourth a doctor of philological sciences. Shukurov and his co-authors attributed the decline of Tajik to the post-war period, blaming the command administrative system for enforcing a policy under which Russian was the language of administration, the language of the workplace, and the language of instruction in the majority of institutes of higher and secondary education. Only Tajiks who were educated in Russian-language primary schools and became bilingual could progress to higher levels. The result was that Tajik was not used, even between native Tajiks, in the medical, agricultural, polytechnical and other institutes, or as a working language in the research institutes of the Tajik Academy of Sciences (with the exception of the Rudaki Institute of Language and Literature, the Oriental Institute and the Philosophy Department). The complaint was made that standards of literacy in Tajik were generally low, that Tajik was becoming restricted in its sphere of usage to the home and to Tajik-language schools, and that there might even eventually be a danger of total language loss if nothing were done.

The measures proposed by Shukurov and his co-authors were analogous to those pioneered in the 'Laws of Language' already under discussion or adopted by the Baltic Republics, Georgia and Moldavia. Tajik, they suggested, should be named as the 'state language' of Tajikistan, while Russian should be given the status of a language for 'communication between nationalities'. The naming of Tajik as the state language should not 'lead to discrimination against the other nationalities, peoples and national groups of Tajikistan or to the infringement and restriction of their language rights'. A detailed codex would be necessary to determine exactly where Tajik alone should be used (in legislation, official records, official correspondence within the republic, national pre-school establishments, secondary professional and higher education, etc.), where Tajik and Russian should be equally used (in sessions of the Supreme Soviet and in local Soviets), and when Russian alone was appropriate (in technical documents, in communications with other republics, in official communications between predominantly Russian-speaking collectives within Tajikistan, etc.). In order to achieve these goals, the higher education system should train highly-qualified teachers to run Tajik-language courses in the Republic's institutions, organisations and enterprises. Financial

Figure 7 : **ETHNIC DISTRIBUTION OF MINORITIES IN TAJIKISTAN**

**ETHNIC COMPOSITION OF TAJIKISTAN**
1989 Census

TAJIKS* - including Pamir ("mountain")
Tajiks (speakers of Pamir languages)

OTHERS - include: Tatars, Kyrgyz,
Germans, Ukrainians, Turkmen,
Kazakh and others

OTHERS
6.6%

RUSSIANS
7.6%

TAJIKS*
62.3%

UZBEKS
23.5%

CHINA

GORNO - BADAKHSHON

AUTONOMOUS OBLAST

YAZGHULANI
ROSHANI
BARTANGI
ROSHORVI
SHUGHNI
WAKHI
ISHKASHMI

• Khorog

AFGHANISTAN

Sources :
*Tadzhikskaya Sovetskaya Sotsialisticheskaya
Republika* (section "Naselenie"), Glavaya
Nauchnaya Redaktsiya Tadzhiksko : Sovetsko :
Entsiklopedii, Dushanbe, 1984;
*Atlas Tadzhikskoi SSR*, Glavnoe Upravlenie
Geodezii i Kartografii pri Sovete Ministrov SSSR,
Dushanbe-Moskva, 1968.

KYRGYZSTAN

T A J I K I S T A N

• Adrasman
Taboshar •
• Kanibadam
• Isfara
Buston • Obburdon
Leninabad • Kairakkum
Gafurov • Proletarsk
Nau • Ura-Tyube

UZBEKISTAN

• Pendzhikent

Tursunzade •
Gissar • DUSHANBE
• Ordzhonikidzeabad
Yavan • • Nurek
Dangara • Kalinabad
Kurgan-Tyube • Kulyab
• Vose
Moskovsky •
Kolkhozabad • Parkhar •
• Shaartuz

0    kilometres    100

Areas with highest
Uzbek population

Other minorities
Russians          R
Tatars            T
Kyrgyz            K
Germans           G
Ukrainians        U
Turkmen           Tu
Kazakh            Kz
Yaghnobi          Y

Pamir languages

376

incentives should be provided to non-Tajiks who learned Tajik well, for example 20 per cent or 10 per cent increases in salary for those who achieved an examination mark of 'excellent' or 'good'. Realistically, an equal knowledge of Tajik could not be expected from all social groups within the non-Tajik population. However, officials should be able to converse in the language of their subordinates and visitors, shop assistants should speak the language of their customers, doctors should speak the language of their patients, etc. The time scale envisaged for the conversion of all official communications into Tajik was three to ten years.

Not all Tajik intellectuals shared these views.[20] R. Khashimov, a member of the 'Language and Society' research unit in the Institute of Language and Literature, pointed to the polarisation that had occurred between Russians and Estonians when the Estonian Supreme Soviet voted on the Estonian 'Law on Language' (see chapter seven): the Russian delegates refused to take part in the vote and left the hall. 'Are such extremes necessary?', Khashimov asked. Declaring Tajik as the state language went counter to Lenin's view (expressed with respect to the Soviet Union as a whole) that there should be no single state language in a multilingual state, and might also conflict with the Universal Declaration of Human Rights, which *inter alia* forbids discrimination on the basis of differences in language. In a counter-proposal, Khashimov suggested that the status of Tajik should be improved by making it the 'means of communication between different nationalities within the Republic'. However, recognising the relative weight of the different nationalities in the Republic, all three major languages (Tajik, Russian, Uzbek) should be equally regarded as official 'working' languages of the Republic, and in areas where there were compact groups of various minority languages (Kirgiz, Kazakh, Tatar, German, Turkmen, various Pamir languages), these too should be considered as working languages in those areas. Official interpreters should be available to enable all citizens to use their native language when they wished.

The view that Tajik should be the single state language was, however, officially accepted by a government anxious to espouse what seemed a less dangerous nationalist issue and to maintain some degree of local support as the influence of the central USSR authorities waned. A special commission set up by the Praesidium of the Tajik Supreme Soviet recommended in February 1989 that a corresponding 'Law on Language' should be drafted,[21] and this draft law was ratified during the 10th session of the Supreme Soviet in July 1989.[22] Both meetings seem to have been accompanied by large demonstrations in Dushanbe. For example, on 24 February 1989 hundreds of students were reported to have gathered in Lenin Square in the centre of the city shouting slogans such as: 'Tajik should be made the state language!', 'We demand the renaissance of the ancient Tajik culture!', and 'We support *perestroika*!'.

The local newspaper applauded the decision of senior officials and academics (for example, G. P. Pallaev, then President of the Praesidium of the Supreme Soviet, M. Kanoatov, the First Secretary of the Union of Writers, A. Tursunov, director of the Oriental Institute of the Academy of Sciences, and M. Asimov, member of the Praesidium of the Academy of Sciences) to take an active part in the demonstration by reporting the decisions of the special commission to the crowd. Although passions were aroused, this crowd seems to have dispersed without any major disorder.[23] More disturbing, however, were verbal reports from the same period that gangs of Tajik youths, were beating up visitors to cinemas showing Russian-language films.

The effects of the new language law were already becoming visible towards the end of the Gorbachev period. Most noticeably, the name of the Tajik language was altered in the official press to the 'Tajik (Farsi) language', emphasising its closeness to literary and spoken Persian. School timetables were changed to give greater emphasis to Tajik language and literature, including classical Persian texts in Arabic script. Children in Russian-language schools were to study Tajik from the first to the eleventh class, beginning at age seven.[24] From 1 January 1990, doctors would be required to write case histories in Tajik rather than Russian. Surnames began to lose their Russified -ov and -ova endings, the names of a number of towns and provinces reverted to their pre-Soviet forms (e.g. Leninabad again became Khojand), and Soviet street names in Dushanbe were changed. It was already becoming clear in 1991, however, that some of the early momentum for language reform was slowing down in the face of lack of hardware, teachers and materials.[25]

Despite the efforts of the government to channel manifestations of nationalism in this manner, concern with language reform was soon to be overtaken by more serious problems. Already in 1988–89, there was evidence that the increase in Tajik national sentiment was being accompanied by increased tensions between the nationalities. Russian workers were reported to be leaving Tajikistan, and the opera house in the centre of Dushanbe, which used to carry a banner with the leading political slogan of the day, carried the slogan: 'Russians, do not leave!'. A press report dealt with a certain I. S. Makhmudov, a Tajik industrial worker from Kanibadam, who was convicted under article 71 of the Tajik legal code ('The Infringement of National and Racial Equality') for hanging anti-Russian posters outside local cinemas. A violent land dispute was reported in the summer of 1989 between Tajik and Kirgiz collective farmers on the border between the two republics.[26] Complaints were voiced by Tajiks about the treatment of the Tajik minority living in Uzbekistan, for example the reduction during the Brezhnev years of the number of shcools and classes in which Tajik was the language of instruction, and the unavailability of Tajik television in Bukhara and Samarkand. Some segments of the

Tajik intelligentsia referred to the 'assimilation' of the Tajiks in Bukhara and Samarkand provinces, and tried to question some of the historical aspects of the territorial demarcation of the Central Asian republics in 1924. In an attempt to improve relations, high-level bilateral contacts between Tajikistan and Uzbekistan had been taking place.[27]

Beginning in 1989, certain manifestations of Islamic fundamentalism were also reported in the Tajik press. Anonymous leaflets were distributed calling on parents to educate their children according to Islamic law, and demanding that Tajik girls abandon their European clothing. The distributors of the leaflets ranged from unemployed workers to schoolboys and students.[28] One consequence seems to have been an increase in the number of cases of self-immolation by Tajik girls who were criticised for their European behaviour, or more seriously, were prevented by their fathers from attending school and required to marry against their will.[29] 'Self-appointed mullahs' were reported to be travelling around the villages in Kurgan-Tyube province, reading the Koran. Special criticism was directed against a certain Abdullo Saidov, a driver and geodetic engineer, who as 'mullah Abdullo' called on collective farm workers to support the creation of an Islamic state in Tajikistan.[30] The purveyors of fundamentalist Islamic ideas were accused by the authorities of 'playing with fire'. Official Islamic figures, by contrast, mostly gave tacit support to the authorities.

Fundamentally, the most serious problem facing the Tajik government during the Gorbachev era seems to have been the increasing level of unemployment and housing difficulties as the growth in population and labour resources outstripped the growth in employment opportunities. Table 19.3 illustrates the growth of the Republic's population, compared with the growth of the city of Dushanbe.[31]

From 1979 to 1989, there was an increase of 34 per cent in the population of Tajikistan, the highest population growth rate in the USSR (compare Uzbekistan 29 per cent, USSR average 9.3 per cent). This growth took place primarily in rural areas, leading to an unemployed total of 234,000 in 1986 (219,000 women and 15,000 men; 77.1 per cent in rural areas and 22.9 per cent in urban areas).[32] In his speech to the Plenum of the Central Committee of the CPSU on

Table 19.3   Population of Tajikistan and Dushanbe
(thousands)

| Year | Tajikistan | Year | Dushanbe |
|------|-----------|------|----------|
| 1940 | 1525 | 1939 | 83 |
| 1959 | 1981 | 1959 | 227 |
| 1970 | 2900 | 1970 | 374 |
| 1979 | 3801 | 1979 | 494 |
| 1987 | 4807 | 1987 | 582 |
| 1989 | 5112 | 1989 | n.a. |

20 September 1989 (the Plenum devoted to the nationalities question), K. M. Makhkamov, First Secretary of the Tajik Central Committee, complained that the USSR authorities had as a rule ignored requests for the construction in Tajikistan of cotton-processing and other light industrial plant which might mop up this pool of unused labour. Instead, 90 per cent of the cotton produced in Tajikistan was processed outside the Republic, and the price received for the raw product was miserable by modern standards. If Tajikistan were to move towards the self-management and self-financing envisaged under *perestroika*, the basic conditions under which its economy operated would have to be put on a more equal footing.[33]

The spark that triggered the first serious violence in Dushanbe in mid-February 1990, leading to the imposition of a state of emergency, was a (false) rumour that thousands of Armenian refugees fleeing the Nagorno-Karabakh conflict were to arrive in Dushanbe and would be given priority in housing and employment. It now seems plausible that the events which followed represent a carefully planned unsuccessful *coup d'état* against the Makhkamov regime by individuals within the Communist government, supported by a variety of other disaffected groups and carefully timed to precede the forthcoming elections of people's deputies on 25 February.[34] Extensive rioting over the period 11–15 February, in which the Central Committee and neighbouring buildings were attacked, seems to have been initially contrived by those responsible for the attempted coup, with busloads of rioters brought in from the southern regions. The riot, however, rapidly grew out of control, resulting, according to official figures, in twenty-two dead and many hundreds of injured civilians, police and Interior Ministry forces.[35] During the riot, a newly formed committee named *Va'dat* ('Unity') led by the Deputy Chairman of the Council of Ministers, B. Karimov, demanded the resignation of the government. In the face of the uncontrollable violence, this request was initially acceded to, but on 14 February troops of the Soviet Interior Ministry moved into Dushanbe and by 15 February the city was back under the control of the government. In the aftermath of the coup attempt, Makhkamov was able to consolidate his power by merging the positions of Communist Party First Secretary and Chairman of the Supreme Soviet. Finally, in November 1990, Makhkamov also became President, symbolising the Party's hold over the country as movement towards independence gathered pace.

One immediate consequence of the February coup attempt was the emigration of many non-Tajiks from Dushanbe, in particular Russians, Germans, Armenians and Bukharan Jews. Some estimates put this emigration as high as 100,000 by late 1990.[36] The potential for further confrontation was increased by the refusal in May 1990 to register non-Communist opposition groups such as the largely secular *Rastokhez* ('Renaissance'), a movement whose members were largely drawn from the Tajik intelligentsia (some of whom had compromised their democratic ideals by joining the Va'dat committee), and the largely rural and fundamentalist Islamic Party of Renaissance. As a result, the Democratic Party, with a rather more antagonistic approach towards Marxism-Leninism and the existing regime, was founded on 10 August 1990, drawing many members from Rastokhez, and the Islamic Party of Renaissance continued to grow in strength.

## INDEPENDENCE AND CIVIL WAR

The attempted hard-line coup against President Gorbachev in August 1991 and the subsequent break-up of the Soviet Union soon led to changes in Tajikistan. Inevitably, the Republic moved towards independence in December 1991, but remained within the CIS and maintained the Russian rouble as its currency.

Between late August and October 1991, as the imams of the southern provinces of Garm, Karategin and Kuljab decided to support the Islamic Party, there were mass anti-Communist demonstrations, but these were largely free of violence. President Makhkamov was succeeded in an orderly fashion by the former communist Rahmon Nabiev. However, the tribal and political divisions in Tajik society which had remained largely suppressed throughout the Soviet period did not take long to re-emerge.

The beginnings of the Tajik civil war can be dated to March 1992, triggered by an incident in which the Speaker of the Parliament, Safarali Kenjaev, a Kuljabi, attacked the Minister of Internal Affairs, Mahmadayaz Navjavanov, a Pamiri, alleging financial impropriety. The meeting of the Supreme Soviet at which this attack took place was relayed on television, and on the following day a group of about fifty Pamiri youths gathered on Shakhidon Square in Dushanbe to call for an apology. The Pamiris were soon joined by supporters of the Democratic and Islamic Parties, as well as by members of Rastokhez and the Pamiri grouping 'La'li Badakhshon'. Gradually, agricultural workers from the south began to arrive in Dushanbe in support of Navjavonov, beginning a two-month encampment in the square. Soon the original cause was forgotten and demands were made for the resignation of the President and the Government. A rival pro-communist meeting was organised in the neighbouring Ozodi Square.

In response to the threat, which soon became very serious as the opposition became armed with heavy weapons, President Nabiev turned to a charismatic figure from Kulyab, the former prison camp inmate Sangak Safarov, who had served twenty-two years before being released in 1976 and had become a legendary figure for his resistance to the camp authorities. As pointed out by the Russian journalist V. Medvedev, there are striking parallels between the involvement of Sangak Safarov at this time and the role of Ishan Sultan, a member of the same family, in the Basmachi resistance after the defeat of Enver Pasha by the Red Army.[37] Ishan Sultan, who like Sangak Safarov was a Seyid, claiming direct descent from the prophet Mohammed, was one of the first Basmachi commanders to make terms with the Bolsheviks.

The pro-Communist faction was armed by the Government in May, leading to heavy clashes and scores of dead. The fighting in the capital was resolved when President Nabiev agreed to form a coalition government including his opponents, but was soon resumed in the south of the country as the opposition obtained weapons by making a levy on each family and selling the resulting goods in Afghanistan. The fighting began in the Vaksh valley in the south as opposition forces used terror tactics to drive Uzbeks and Kuljabis from the Kurgan-Tyube district. Tens of thousands of refugees fled to Kuljab and Dushanbe. Eventually, after several abortive ceasefires and brutal killings of political leaders on both sides, the opposition succeeded in forcing the resignation of President Nabiev on 7 September 1992. The presidency was taken over by Akbarsho Iskandarov, Chairman of the Supreme Soviet. This opposition success, however, was short-lived. After a tactical retreat, the pro-Nabiev forces, assisted both actively and tacitly by Uzbekistan and Russia, managed to regain control by the end of November 1992. Emomali Rakhmonov, the Chairman of the Kuljab Executive Committee, became the new leader.

It is easy to see the reasons for Uzbekistan's intervention: the Uzbek leader, Islam Karimov, had himself managed the transformation from Communist leader to national president, and did not wish to see an anti-Communist coalition of Islamic, nationalist and democratic forces take power in the neighbouring country. Russia, too, did not look forward to the possibility of an Islamic state on its southern border with close connections with Afgahanistan, and took over legal control of the border forces in August 1992.[38] However, the difficulties on the Afghan border remain. As a result of the pro-government advance, large numbers of refugees (an estimated 350,000) fled towards the south and into Badakhshan. Approximately one quarter of this total is thought to have crossed into Afghanistan, where they are being trained and armed by the fundamentalist Afghan leader, Gulbuddin Hekmatyar. The Afghan border in addition provides an easy crossing point for Afghan drugs into Tajikistan and thence into Russia and Europe.

Despite the continuation of factional murders and border incursions, some stability returned to Tajikistan in 1993 and 1994. As in the aftermath of the February 1990 riots, activity by the opposition parties (Democratic Party of Tajikistan, Islamic party of Renaissance, Rastokhez, La'li Badakhshon) was banned.[39] The economic consequences of the civil war have, however, been devastating, and will take years to overcome. Preliminary calculations for the first quarter of 1993 showed that the gross national product had fallen by almost a third compared with the same quarter in 1992.[40] Agriculture in particular suffered heavy losses. Particularly hard-hit was the Kurgan-Tyube province where much of the fighting took place, and bread shortages were reported even in the capital Dushanbe. This picture can, however, be expected to improve as long as stability is maintained.

Tajikistan is now relatively firmly back in the same political mould as before the civil war, with Uzbek and Russian support. The situation on the border with Afghanistan is still not completely stable, and political murders continue. Some progress is, however, being made towards economic recovery. Ecologically, Tajikistan is in a much better position than some of the other Central Asian republics. Even though the Pamir glaciers are reported to have been affected by wind-borne pesticides from the Aral basin, Tajikistan appears to have been relatively untouched by the disaster of over-irrigation and rising water-tables that has affected the lower-lying areas of Turkmenistan and Uzbekistan, leading to the disappearance of much of the Aral Sea.

# NOTES

1. *Tadzhikskaya Sovetskaya Sotsialisticheskaya Respublika* (Dushanbe: Glavnaya Redaktsiya Tadzhikskoi Sovetskoi Entsiklopedii, 1984), p. 103 (henceforth *TSSR*).
2. *TSSR* p. 104.
3. Ibid.
4. *Vsesoyuznaya perepis' naseleniya 17 dekabrya 1926 goda* (All-Union Census of the Population of 17 December 1926) (Moscow, 1929). Cited by S. Akiner, *Islamic Peoples of the Soviet Union* (London, Boston, Melbourne and Henley, Kegan Paul International 1983), pp. 307–8.
5. *TSSR* p. 108; Z. Katz (ed.), *Handbook of Major Soviet Nationalities* (New York, Free Press 1975), p. 325.
6. *TSSR* p. 113.
7. *TSSR* p. 260.
8. *TSSR* p. 261.
9. *TSSR* p. 271.
10. *Kommunist Tadzhikistana* 26 Aug. 1953. Cited by Katz, *op. cit.*, p. 342.
11. *Zhenshchiny v SSR 1988, Statisticheskie Materialy* (Moscow, Finansy i Statistika, 1988), p. 16.
12. Ibid., p. 14.
13. *TSSR* p. 111.
14. *TSSR* pp. 111, 115.
15. *TSSR* p. 205.
16. *TSSR* p. 201.
17. Katz *op. cit.*, p. 325; Akiner, *op. cit.*, pp. 307–8.
18. *TSSR* p. 54.

19. *Kommunist Tadzhikistana* 19 Feb. 1989, p. 2.
20. Ibid.
21. A full account of this meeting is given in *Kommunist Tadzhikistana* 25 Feb. 1989.
22. *Izvestiya* 23 July 1989. English resumé in *Current Digest of the Soviet Press* XLI (29) 1989.
23. *Kommunist Tadzhikistana* 26 Feb. 1989.
24. *Kommunist Tadzhikistana* 20 July 1989.
25. John R. Perry, Tajikistan's Language Law Two Years On. *Bulletin of the Association for the Advancement of Central Asian Research* 5 (2) 1992, pp. 3–4.
26. *Kommunist Tadzhikistana* 28 June 1989. English resumé in *Current Digest of the Soviet Press* XLI (28) 1989.
27. *Pravda* 25 June 1988. English resumé in *Current Digest of the Soviet Press* XL (25) 1988.
28. *Kommunist Tadzhikistana* 19 Sept. 1989.
29. *Komsomol'skaya Pravda* 8 Aug. 1987. English resumé in *Current Digest of the Soviet Press* XLIX (32) 1987.
30. *Kommunist Tadzhikistana* 31 Jan. 1987. English resumé in *Current Digest of the Soviet Press* XXXIX (9) 1987.
31. *Narodnoe Khozyaistvo SSSR v 1987g* (Moscow, Finansy i Statistika 1988). Preliminary report of 1989 census in *Izvestiya* 28 April 1989.
32. *Kommunist Tadzhikistana* 20 Jan. 1987. English resumé in *Current Digest of the Soviet Press* XXXIX (14) 1987.
33. *Izvestiya* 22 Sept. 1989.
34. *Kommunist Tadzhikistana* 15 Feb. 1990. A. Niyazi, The Year of Tumult: Tajikistan after February 1990. In V. Naumkin (ed), *State, Religion and Society in Central Asia. A Post-Soviet Critique* (Reading, Ithaca Press 1993), pp. 262–289.
35. Eyewitness accounts of the February events are collated by V. Medvedev, Prazdnik Obshchei Bedy. *Druzhba Narodov* 8 1990, pp. 197–222.
36. M. Atkin, Tajikistan: ancient heritage, new politics. In R. Bremner and I. Tares (eds) *Politics and Nations in the Soviet Successor States* (Cambridge, Cambridge University Press 1993), pp. 361–383.
37. V. Medvedev, Saga o bobo Sangake, voine. *Druzhba Narodov* 6 1993, pp. 187–204. This contains an interview with Sangak himself in Kurgan-Tyube.
38. *The Independent* 17 February 1993 (Report by Hugh Pope from Dushanbe).
39. *Narodnaya Gazeta* 25 June 1993.
40. *Narodnaya Gazeta* 6 May 1993.

# CHAPTER TWENTY

# Kyrgyzstan and the Kyrgyz

Annette Bohr and Simon Crisp

Kyrgyzstan is the seventh in size of the Soviet successor states, with an area of 198,500 square kilometres, and ranks tenth by population (4,291,000, according to the census of January 1989). Situated at the north-eastern extremity of Central Asia, it has borders with Kazakhstan, Uzbekistan and Tajikistan, and with the Xinjiang-Uyghur Autonomous Region of China. Kyrgyzstan is a predominantly mountainous region with significant mineral deposits, and the fast-flowing mountain rivers have enabled hydroelectric power to be developed. Agriculture is mostly concentrated in the lowland areas, although livestock breeding is a traditional occupation in all areas of the republic. Modern industrial centres are located around the capital city of Bishkek in the north of Kyrgyzstan and Osh in the south-west.[1]

The overwhelming majority of the Kyrgyz (88.2 per cent in 1989) live on the territory of their nation, with smaller communities in Tajikistan, Uzbekistan, China and Afghanistan. The figures for out-migration of the Kyrgyz were among the lowest in the USSR.[2] There is a sizable European immigrant population, predominantly Russians, concentrated mainly in the cities of Kyrgyzstan.

The early history of the Kyrgyz is complex, and their origin is disputed. Most scholars, however, believe them to be of mixed Mongolian, Eastern Turkic and Kypchak descent, with an identity formed gradually over the course of many centuries. Indeed, sub-national loyalties at the level of tribe and clan persist to the present day, though the formation of the Kyrgyz as a distinct people is reckoned to have been completed by the sixteenth century.[3] In the following century their territory came under the control of the Jungarian Oirots, a Mongol people against whom the Kyrgyz waged a protracted struggle until the overthrow of the Oirot empire by the Manchus in 1758. The Kyrgyz at this time were loosely organised under their local rulers, but in the early nineteenth century parts of their territory were taken over by the Khanate of Kokand. During the same century the Kyrgyz came under the influence of the Russian empire: groups of Kyrgyz took oaths of allegiance to Russia at various times in the mid-nineteenth century, while southern Kyrgyzstan was incorporated into the empire in 1876 together with the Kokand Khanate, to which it belonged.[4] The latter years of the century were marked by a number of Kyrgyz uprisings and the emigration of part of the population to the Pamirs and Afghanistan; in 1916 a serious revolt broke out in connection with the mobilisation by the tsarist authorities of the indigenous Central Asian population for non-combatant duties, and the suppression of this revolt caused large numbers of Kyrgyz to leave for China. After the Revolution and a bloody period of civil war, Soviet power was effectively established in Kyrgyzstan in 1919–20.

Partly because they came into contact with Muslim states at a relatively late date, the widespread conversion of the Kyrgyz to Islam dates only from the second half of the seventeenth century, and the place of Islam in their ethnic self-consciousness has traditionally been somewhat ambiguous. Nowadays, however, the Kyrgyz are wholly Muslim, and there is every indication that their religious feeling is strong.[5]

## KYRGYZSTAN IN THE SOVIET PERIOD

Kyrgyzstan entered the Soviet period as one of the least agriculturally, industrially and culturally developed regions of the country. Tsarist colonial rule had done little to improve the material standard of living or the general cultural level of the local population. The period of civil war, also, had caused severe damage to the local economy. The first large-scale measure of the new Soviet government, the land reform of 1920–21, was in part an attempt to redress past injustices by returning to the Kyrgyz population lands taken from them; it also, however, represented the first stage of a move to restructure the rural economy along lines more acceptable to the central authorities by encouraging a move away from pastoral nomadism towards more permanent agricultural settlements. Subsequent reforms followed the same pattern, notably the further land reform of 1927–28 in southern Kyrgyzstan and the collectivisation drive of the early 1930s which radically altered the traditional structures of agriculture and the way of life of the rural population.[6]

In the modern period approximately 30 per cent of the republic's economy is derived from agriculture; of this, 54.5 per cent comes from stock-breeding (mainly sheep, cattle and horses) and 45.5 per cent from crop-growing (above all, the so-called technical crops like cotton, tobacco and sugar beet).[7] The main industries are engineering and metal-working, construction, mining (Kyrgyzstan has some of the most important deposits of non-ferrous metals in the former USSR), production of electricity and food. The growth of industry has coincided with that of the towns:[8] between 1939 and 1959 the urban population of Kyrgyzstan increased from 18 to 34 per cent, though the rate of growth has slowed somewhat since then (37 per cent in 1970, 39 per cent in both 1979 and 1989).[9] As in other parts of Central Asia, the proportion of non-Kyrgyz in the republic's towns and among industrial workers is considerably higher than in the population as a whole.[10]

Before the twentieth century Kyrgyzstan was to some extent isolated from the cultural and political movements taking place in the Russian empire, even elsewhere in Central Asia. In the first decades of this century, however, the pan-Turkic Jadidist movement penetrated Kyrgyzstan and generated a certain amount of literature and the formation of local organisations, though most political and cultural activisits from northern Kyrgyzstan joined the Kazakh national movement Alash Orda.[11] The first years of Soviet power saw, as in other regions, a number of concessions to national feeling: the appointment of important figures from the national intelligentsia like Kasym Tynystanov to influential positions in the administration, respect for traditional Kyrgyz culture and way of life, and the creation of a Kyrgyz Autonomous Oblast as a national administrative unit in 1924.[12]

The 1920s also saw the beginnings of a truly national literature, based in the first instance on the rich traditions of Kyrgyz epic poetry, and the formation of a vernacular standard language. The reform of the Arabic alphabet in 1923 allowed the representation in writing of the specific sounds of Kyrgyz (notably the rich system of vowel harmony), and the number of publications in the language increased dramatically, helped to some extent by the introduction of a Latin-based script in 1928 which, while it marked a forced break with the existing literary tradition in the Arabic script, did allow the wider introduction of typographical processes.[13] The first Soviet schools were opened in the early 1920s (by 1923 there were 327, including 251 Kyrgyz schools, with a total of 20,000 pupils). The level of literacy, however, especially among women, remained low until the concerted literacy drive of the early 1930s.[14]

Despite the general atmosphere of tolerance for national traditions and the prevailing policy of the adaptation of Soviet power to local conditions, relations between the Kyrgyz intelligentsia and the central authorities in the 1920s did not follow an entirely smooth path. The Basmachi movement of armed opposition to Soviet power in Central Asia was largely put down in the early years of the decade, but surfaced again during the drive for collectivisation and de-nomadisation of the migrant Kyrgyz herdsmen. And although the national Communist movement was not as strong in Kyrgyzstan as in some other regions of the country, there were a number of attempts by the local élite to gain a greater role for the native Kyrgyz leadership.[15] The leaders of such movements were excluded from the Party and in some cases exiled or imprisoned, a process that gained momentum during Stalin's notorious purges of the native élites during the late 1930s; their sacrifices in Kyrgyzstan included not only most of the local Party leadership but also the most prominent cultural figures of the time.[16]

Industrial and cultural development continued apace during the 1930s, but the basis for this development had changed from one of local concessions to overt centralism: the building of 'socialism in one country' left little or no room for concessions to local conditions, in Kyrgyzstan as elsewhere. The increased pace of industrialisation meant a continued influx of mainly Slav workers from western parts of the Soviet Union and a fundamental change in the structure of the republic's economy; the gradual introduction of universal compulsory schooling meant that a new generation could increasingly be educated along politically acceptable lines; and the adoption in 1941 of the Cyrillic script for Kyrgyz brought the language firmly within the orbit of Russian influence.[17] Even in the post-Stalin 'thaw' the scale of rehabilitations in Kyrgyzstan was notably less than in other Central Asian republics.[18]

Despite a lengthy period of pressure towards uniformity and the creation of a new 'Soviet Man', it is clear that Kyrgyz national aspirations remained largely intact. There is evidence from before the recent period of Kyrgyz nationalist tendencies in literature and in historical scholarship;[19] furthermore, the criticism of the Kyrgyz national epic *Manas* during the course of a concerted campaign against the Central Asian epics in the early 1950s met with spirited local opposition.[20] In addition, although the prevailing line in language policy until very recent times has been to stress the importance of a good knowledge of Russian, voices were occasionally raised to point out the negative effects of this policy on the knowledge of Kyrgyz,[21] and at the end of the 1950s a number of changes to the school curriculum in the republic gave a more prominent place to the study of Kyrgyz language and history.[22]

Changes in the local Party hierarchy reflected tensions in Kyrgyz relations with the centre[23] and also a degree of in-fighting at the local level – notably in the mysterious murder of the Chairman of the Kyrgyz Council of Ministers, Sultan Ibraimov, in December 1980.[24] And even in the early 1970s a number of Kyrgyz legal specialists published articles in the local press demanding more explicit recognition of the constitutional rights of the republic.[25] There is thus a good deal of evidence that the concerns expressed in the new atmosphere generated by *glasnost'* reflected issues that had always been close to the heart of the local political and cultural leadership, even during the years now known as the time of the cult of personality and the period of stagnation.

# KYRGYZSTAN UNDER *PERESTROIKA*

While Kyrgyzstan may initially have been slower than some other republics to take advantage of the new political atmosphere under Gorbachev, the processes of *glasnost'* and *perestroika* worked analogously to developments elsewhere in the Soviet Union: a thorough shake-out of the local leadership, renewed interest in the history and cultural heritage of the Kyrgyz, and the beginnings of a demand for greater economic and linguistic autonomy.

The first signs in Kyrgyzstan of a new openness in the political sphere occurred in the spring of 1985 when the first secretary of the Kyrgyz Communist Party, Turdakun Usubaliev, went into print with some rather sharp criticisms of shortcomings in political work in the republic.[26] The severity and wide-ranging nature of those criticisms, coupled with their author's rather studied claim about the degree of openness they represented, led at least one observer to conclude that the first secretary might be concerned about the security of his own position[27] – and so indeed it turned out, for Usubaliev retired from his post on 2 November 1985, a few days before his sixty-sixth birthday.[28]

The new first secretary, Absamat Masaliev, immediately replaced the second secretary, all three Central Committee secretaries and the first secretaries of two of the republic's four oblasts.[29] At the Eighteenth Congress of the Communist Party of Kyrgyzstan, held on 23–24 January 1986, he launched an outspoken attack on his predecessor's record, accusing Usubaliev of nepotism and cronyism and of creating an atmosphere of servility and sycophancy while monopolising the processes of decision-making.[30] The fate of the former first secretary is a particularly clear case of a policy decision from above coupled with local in-fighting, but the replacement of personnel in key positions was to be a constant feature of the next few years under Gorbachev's rule.

Alongside these numerous personnel changes there was a noticeable change in the cultural climate. The question of Kyrgyz ethno-genesis came in for re-evaluation (see note 3), as did the 1916 uprising, which had had such a devastating effect on the Kyrgyz population.[31] Several speakers at a plenum of the Kyrgyz Writers' Union held in June 1987 criticised their colleagues for neglecting the Kyrgyz cultural heritage – specifically, the language, historical origins, epic poetry, and national–religious customs of the Kyrgyz.[32] A new and more open attitude to the study of Kyrgyz history was displayed by the newly elected director of the Institute of History of the Kyrgyz Academy of Sciences, Salmorbek Tabyshaliev, who singled out the questions of ethnic origin, survivals of the tribal past, and the role of the Russian language for the Kyrgyz as being in need of major revision.[33]

The language question, indeed, became one of the key issues in the cultural field. Prior to the Gorbachev period the main emphasis had been – as throughout the Soviet Union – on ensuring a prestigious role for Russian and developing a high level of bilingualism,[34] but this policy began to change at the Eighteenth Kyrgyz Party Congress when the new first secretary devoted considerable space in his report to the need to improve the teaching of Kyrgyz.[35] Subsequently, the cause of the Kyrgyz language was taken up by scholars, who criticised shortcomings in the existing orthography and the huge number of superfluous loan words from Russian;[36] and by literary figures, who engaged in a sharp debate over the need for specific measures to enhance the status of the Kyrgyz language – namely, by increasing the number of Kyrgyz language schools.[37]

One more striking result of *glasnost'* in Kyrgyzstan was the marked change in the treatment of Islam. It was not that the hostile attitude of the authorities towards religion changed; on the contrary, the flow of anti-religious propaganda continued as strongly as ever,[38] but evidence of the continued strength of religious observance became much more plentiful. The tone was set, once again, at the Eighteenth Congress of the Kyrgyz Communist Party, when the new first secretary Masaliev painted a much more candid picture of the persistence of religion than had his predecessor.[39] Although Islam came relatively late to the Kyrgyz and the official religious establishment is rather small,[40] the connection between Islam and the preservation of traditional national values was clearly felt by a sizeable proportion of the population. There were numerous reports of Muslim observances by Party workers and other dignitaries,[41] and accounts of a flourishing, unregistered 'parallel Islam'.[42] One very clear case was the rise in popularity of the Takht-e Suleiman shrine near Osh, one of the most important religious sites in Central Asia, as a place of pilgrimage.[43]

Expressions of nationalism had begun to appear in the cultural sphere even before the advent of *perestroika*. As early as 1981–83 an ethnographical survey conducted among the rural Kyrgyz population showed a marked preference for national literature, films and plays and above all for the traditional bards.[44] The importance of the epic poetry declaimed by those bards – and specifically of the saga *Manas* which had been criticised in the 1950s – was underscored by the Kyrgyz Writers' Union in June 1987 in the context of a debate recognising the need to pay more attention to the Kyrgyz national heritage (see above). Finally, an event of some importance was the rehabilitation after a protracted struggle of the Kyrgyz writers Moldo Kylych and Kasym Tynystanov, the latter of whom in particular played a crucial part in the formation of Soviet Kyrgyz language and culture.[45] The publication in 1989 of the decree rehabilitating Tynystanov and a number of other Kyrgyz political figures from the early Soviet period was a fitting symbol of the changes that had been taking place in Kyrgyzstan in the years following Gorbachev's ascent to power.

# FROM *PERESTROIKA* TO INDEPENDENCE

The eruption of violent disturbances in January–February 1990 in Bishkek (then Frunze) catalysed the organisation and consolidation of the independent political groupings that had begun to form in 1987–89 to oppose communist rule. Mass demonstrations, prompted by rumours that Armenian refugees from the Nagorno-Karabakh crisis would be resettled in Bishkek, grew into a general confrontation with Kyrgyz authorities over the issues of housing and the immigration of non-Kyrgyz into the republic. Tensions over housing shortages had been steadily building since May 1989, when inhabitants of Bishkek began to seize parcels of public land on the capital's outskirts in order to build homes for themselves. City officials, recognising that a solution to the housing crisis could not be found in the near term, allowed the squatters to keep the plots.[46]

By May 1990 the burgeoning national–democratic opposition had united with Russophone informal groups to form the umbrella opposition organisation *Democratic Kyrgyzstan*. While it included virtually all independent political and social movements extant at the time, its main members were the groups *Ashar* (Mutual Aid), *Asaba* (the Kyrgyz warrior banner), *Atuulduk demilge* (Citizens' Initiative), and the republican division of the all-Union Russian-speaking organisation *Memorial*. When bloody interethnic clashes broke out between Kyrgyz and Uzbeks in Osh Oblast one month later, in June 1990 (see below), *Democratic Kyrgyzstan* was able to play a constructive role in resolving the related disturbances occurring concurrently in Bishkek, thereby greatly enhancing the organisation's authority at the popular level. As a result, in October 1990 *Democratic Kyrgyzstan* successfully exerted pressure on the republican Supreme Soviet to elect the reform-minded Askar Akaev over the reactionary Masaliev to Kyrgyzstan's first presidency.

A physicist and the former head of the Kyrgyz Academy of Sciences, Akaev is currently the only Central Asian head of state who is not a former top Communist Party *apparatchik*, having joined the upper echelons of the party leadership only in July 1990. Following his surprise victory, he moved swiftly to separate the leadership of the state from the Communist Party; another of his first acts as president was to drop the words 'Soviet' and 'Socialist' from the republic's official title, renaming it the Republic of Kyrgyzstan in December 1990.

The attempted coup launched by hard-line communists against Soviet President Mikhail Gorbachev in August 1991 prompted a showdown between Akaev and Kyrgyzstan's own conservative forces in a scenario similar to that played out by Boris Yeltsin in Moscow. For three days and nights military helicopters flew over Akaev's residence; entrances to the radio and television center, telegraph office, and the Central Committee building were barricaded; and the commander of the Turkestan Military District threatened to send troops and tanks into the republic.[47] Akaev's deft handling of the crisis assured him a decisive victory over his communist opposition: within twenty-four hours of the coup's resolution he had put most of Kyrgyzstan's Communist Party leaders under house arrest,[48] and within a few days he had banned all political party organisations from operating in state organs and nationalised the Central Committee building and the Lenin Museum in Bishkek.[49] On 31 August 1991, Kyrgyzstan banned the Communist Party and declared itself an independent state, the eighth of the USSR's fifteen constituent republics to do so in the wake of the failed Moscow coup.

## INDEPENDENT KYRGYZSTAN: ACCOMMODATING ETHNIC INTERESTS

Like the other Central Asian states, the Kyrgyz have been recreating themselves as a nation through a combination of refound history and newly coined traditions. The new nationalism is in part a reaction to Russification and in part an indictment of the Soviet past; hence, assertive efforts to legislate the reinstatement of national traditions and the use of Kyrgyz in public life have been viewed as necessary in the immediate post-independence period in order to compensate for past injustices. Many ethnic Kyrgyz also point to the fact that the Russian population never learned the local language as evidence of the latter's colonial attitude (only 1.2 per cent of the Russian population in Kyrgyzstan claimed a working knowledge of Kyrgyz in 1989, as compared to 33.5 per cent of Lithuania's Russian population, for example).

Against this backdrop of ethnic resentment, it was not surprising that the umbrella opposition movement *Democratic Kyrgyzstan*, which had propelled Akaev to power in 1990, broke apart along ethnic lines once the old power structures had fallen and the common Communist enemy had been vanquished. Many Kyrgyz nationalist forces, regarding *Democratic Kyrgyzstan* as too moderate in its demands, broke away to form more radical groups. The leadership of the Russian-speaking group *Memorial* also withdrew from *Democratic Kyrgyzstan*, while the party *Slavic Fund* busied itself with emigration issues.[50] The communists managed to reconstitute themselves in the meantime as the *Party of Communists of Kyrgyzstan* (PKK), which was registered by the Ministry of Justice on 15 September 1992.[51]

Newly-formed nationalist forces maintained that the Republic of Kyrgyzstan was the Kyrgyz 'national homeland' and therefore belonged to them; consequently, they argued, their interests should take precedence over those of other ethnic groups. President Akaev countered the nationalists by pointing out that an exclusively pro-Kyrgyz agenda could not be pursued in a country where the ethnic Kyrgyz constituted a bare majority of the total population (in 1989, Kyrgyz made up 52.4 per cent of the population; Russians, 21.5 per cent; and Uzbeks, 12.9 per cent).

The passing of a new constitution in May 1993, which was accomplished only after months of wrangling, proved to be the acid test of Akaev's leadership, since nationalist groups and communists alike insisted on putting nearly every phrase to a vote. For example, the original version put forward by parliament declared that the president of the country must be an ethnic Kyrgyz, a stipulation that Akaev successfully fought to eliminate from the final version.[52] Particularly problematic was a land reform bill passed by the parliament in April 1991 which declared that 'the land is the property of the Kyrgyz'. In a small, mountainous country where land is at a premium, the formulation threatened to aggravate already strained relations with the Uzbek population and possibly even reopen the conflict between Kyrgyz and Uzbeks in Osh Oblast. Akaev vetoed the bill and put forward the alternative formulation 'the land is the property of all the peoples of Kyrgyzstan', which was accepted by parliament in September 1991.

Kyrgyz nationalist parties had their own legislative victories, however. In 1993 they succeeded in changing the country's name from the 'Republic of Kyrgyzstan' to the more ethnically-charged 'Kyrgyz Republic'. More importantly, they helped to consolidate public opinion against the introduction of dual citizenship in Kyrgyzstan, an idea that had been informally proposed for the Russian and German population of the republic. Unlike in some Baltic states, citizenship legislation in Kyrgyzstan does not require a knowledge of the local language. Consequently, the requirements to obtain national citizenship have never really been at issue; rather, the merits and demerits of granting dual citizenship to certain ethnic groups only has been under debate. In addition to vague apprehensions about the creation of potential fifth columns, the main argument against dual citizenship is that it would grant rights to some ethnic groups above and beyond those enjoyed by others and, in the process, directly contravene Article 15 of the Kyrgyz Constitution which ensures the equal treatment of all citizens. This implied double standard has created consternation not only among the ethnic Kyrgyz majority but also among Jews, Koreans and even Uzbeks, all of whom have 'historic homelands'.

## The Russian Reaction

Since the collapse of the USSR, much of the Russian diaspora has keenly felt the loss of its privileged status as the 'elder brother' and the 'first nation among equals'. Although many Russians look with understanding on the struggle of the ethnic Kyrgyz to regain their cultural heritage, others consider it a violation of their human rights that they must now learn Kyrgyz to keep their jobs in the public sector and that they do not enjoy the same cultural advantages as their kinsmen in Russia. At the far end of the reactionary spectrum, a few extreme Russian patriots regard the denial of dual citizenship to ethnic Russians in Kyrgyzstan as an 'offence to those who worked for 150 years with their own hands to transform the region of the nomads into a modern state'.[53]

Rather than go to battle with nationalist forces, however, many Russians have chosen the path of least resistance: emigration to Russia. Russians have been leaving the country at an unprecedented pace, taking with them valuable professional and technological skills. The out-migration of the non-Kyrgyz population – in particular, Russians, Germans, Jews, Uzbeks, and Dungans – has led to acute shortages of trained workers in the construction, machine-building, electronics, defence and cotton growing sectors during the crucial transition period to a market economy. Even key supporters of Akaev's reform programme in the executive and legislative branches have joined the ranks of emigrants, including former Deputy Prime Minister German Kuznetsov, who at the time of his departure in July 1993 was the highest-ranking Russian official in the country. According to preliminary data, between 1989 and 1993 a net total of 143,300 Russians (the number leaving Kyrgyzstan less the number arriving) or 15.6 per cent of Kyrgyzstan's Russian population emigrated to Russia.[54] In comparative teams, Kyrgyzstan has experienced the largest decrease in its Russian population in the past five years of all the Central Asian states, Tajikistan excepted.[55] Russian emigrants have cited the economic decline and the sharp drop in living standards as their main reasons for leaving, followed by the preferential treatment accorded to ethnic Kyrgyz, particularly in the workplace; the declaration of Kyrgyz as the state language; increasing Islamicisation; and the looming possibility of interethnic unrest.

Referring to the departure of the Kyrgyz Slavs as his 'main sorrow',[56] Akaev has pushed through several concrete measures aimed at curbing the tide of emigration. Foremost on the list is the allocation of $60 million from the International Monetary Fund to the restructuring of the country's industry, the revitalisation of which the president has declared the main condition for curtailing emigration.[57] Second, on 8 September 1994 Kyrgyzstan became the first CIS country to officially declare Russian the second state language.[58] According to the decree published by the government, office work in all state agencies, organisations and institutions as well as all technical, planning, and financial documentation may be carried out in the Russian language. Official bilingualism is to remain in effect until 1 January 2005. Lastly, a Kyrgyz–Slavic University financed by both governments has been opened in Bishkek. The programme launched by the authorities to persuade the non-native population to stay in the country appears to have borne fruit: according to the Kyrgyz National Statistics Committee, the number of out-migrants leaving the country in the first half of 1994 by some twenty per cent compared with the figure for the first half of 1993.[59]

## The Russified Kyrgyz: Cultural Misfits

An especially delicate dilemma is presented by the large number of Russified Kyrgyz, who generally reside in urban areas side by side with the country's Slavic population but do not feel at home in either of the main ethnic camps. The emergence of an indigenous class of educated élites in Soviet Kyrgyzstan coupled with the tendency of parents to send their offspring to Russian-language schools engendered a class of ethnic Kyrgyz whose outlook and behaviour are informed by Russian language and culture. Among the post-Soviet states, this phenomenon is most common in Central Asia in general and in Kyrgyzstan and Kazakhstan in particular, where the Russian-speaking diasporas are exceptionally large.

The Russification of the native intelligentsia during decades of Soviet rule has created difficulties for nationalists who now seek to make Kyrgyz the sole language of use in the public sector. The chairman of the Kyrgyz language society, *Kyrgyz tili*, complained that the implementation of the state language law has been obstructed by 'certain parts of the native population who do not want to learn their own language', particularly within the Kyrgyz Academy of Sciences.[60]

Recognising that their superficial knowledge of Kyrgyz had placed them in a cultural no man's land, the russified Kyrgyz were among the original supporters of the state language law, viewing it as an opportunity to improve their knowledge of their native language and culture. It was not long, however, before the demands and criticisms of more fervent nationalists created resentment among the russified Kyrgyz, many of whom began to feel like cultural misfits in their own country. As a result, a part of the native intelligentsia has withdrawn its support for the nationalist cause and disappeared from the political arena – the so-called 'nationalist boomerang syndrome'.[61] One Kyrgyz philologist summed up the quandary of the Russified Kyrgyz in the following way: 'The Jews have Israel, the Germans have Germany, and the Russians have Russia. But whither the Europeanised Kyrgyz? Many have simply gone underground, removing themselves from the sociopolitical fray.'[62]

## PRESERVING STABLE BORDERS

Kyrgyzstan's geopolitical location between powerful China, volatile Tajikistan and domineering Uzbekistan is an unenviable one; moreover, it has running border disputes with the first two states and has experienced interethnic violence on its border with the third.

The most serious outbreak of civil unrest in Kyrgyzstan's recent history took place in June 1990 in Osh Oblast on the Kyrgyz–Uzbek border, leaving more than three hundred dead and several hundred injured. Fighting broke out between Kyrgyz and Uzbeks after some Kyrgyz were allotted housing plots and Uzbeks received none; the violence quickly escalated to the point where it became necessary to close all border crossings between the two republics and suspend all flights between Bishkek and Tashkent. Despite these measures, several thousand Uzbeks, armed with makeshift weapons as well as guns, clamoured for several days to get across the border and participate in the struggle.

Although the initial violence was precipitated by the distribution of land, the roots of the conflict went much deeper. When the Fergana Valley was carved up in 1924 and divided among Uzbekistan, Tajikistan and Kyrgyzstan, large numbers of each ethnic group were left outside their titular republics. The relatively recent population explosion in the region and the consequent shortage of jobs, land, and other resources have engendered frictions between the ethnic Kyrgyz, many of whom view the non-native population as 'foreigners' and therefore as having lesser rights; and the country's minorities, who believe that their rights are being infringed by the dominant nationality. Furthermore, the Kyrgyz have traditionally been wary of what they perceive as the Uzbek quest for hegemony in Central Asia, especially given that Uzbek President Islam Karimov appears to regard himself as the self-appointed guardian of the large Uzbek diasporas in neighbouring states.[63] Tensions have been exacerbated by the irredentist claims of some Uzbek groups to some parts of the Fergana Valley, namely the cities of Osh and Uzgen in Kyrgyzstan.[64]

In addition to the explosive border with Uzbekistan to the west, Kyrgyz leaders must keep a watchful eye on the country's southern border with Tajikistan, particular in the area of Isfara Raion, which was the scene of a violent clash between Tajiks and Kyrgyz in July 1989. Thousands of villagers clashed over the right to use land and water, resulting in several deaths and numerous injuries.[65] The dispute has never been settled, despite the attempts of various government commissions over the past five years to find a solution, including the launching of land and river reclamation work.[66]

There is also some cause for concern that the civil war that has sundered Tajikistan could spill across the border into Kyrgyzstan. Kyrgyz Foreign Minister Roza Otunbaeva were stated that there are some 5,000 ethnic Kyrgyz refugees from Tajikistan in the southern regions of Kyrgyzstan, which had precipitated social tensions there.[67] More ominously, armed formations from Tajikistan have appeared in Kyrgyzstan's Osh and Jalal-Abad Oblasts;[68] President Akaev has speculated that some 'Afghan Islamic elements' would like to penetrate into Tajikistan through Kyrgyzstan by taking advantage of mountainous border areas that cannot be fully controlled.[69]

Kyrgyzstan also has outstanding border disputes – inherited from the USSR – with China to the east, although significant progress towards resolving the differences has been made and negotiations are reported to be proceeding in a 'constructive and neighbourly' fashion.[70] Kyrgyzstan's border with China lies along the Kashgar area of the Xinjiang–Uyghur Autonomous Region (XUAR), which has traditionally been a hotbed of Uyghur separatism. Hence, a crucial concern of the Chinese authorities is Kyrgyzstan's approach to the actions of the latter's Uyghur minority (37,000 in 1989), and in particular to a small but vociferous group within it which has demanded autonomy for kinsmen in Xinjiang.[71] To the satisfaction of Chinese officials, in 1992 Kyrgyz authorities refused to register the party Uyghur Organisation for Freedom and officially warned its organisers to discontinue their activities. The official explanation given by the Ministry of Justice was that the party's objectives as expressed in its charter promoted interference in the internal affairs of a sovereign state – namely, its stated aims 'to expose the colonial policy of the Chinese leadership towards Uyghur and other Chinese national minorities' and 'to further the restoration of the independence of Uyghurstan by separating the XUAR from China and establishing it as a separate state'.[72]

As the Kyrgyz leadership has become more cognizant of the country's security needs, its relationship with the Russian Federation – its closest foreign partner and the guarantor of its Soviet-era economic ties – has grown even more important. Initially, President Akaev announced that the new nation would not create its own army, declaring that a national guard of 9,000 men plus 4,000 border guards would suffice; he also called for an early withdrawal of Russian forces.[73] The turn of events in Tajikistan, however, forced the Kyrgyz government to rework its military doctrine, and in July 1992 it endorsed a plan to create a national army.[74]

On 4 March 1994 Kyrgyzstan became the second Soviet successor state (following Turkmenistan) to conclude an agreement with the Russian Federation regulating the service of Russian citizens in the armed forces of Kyrgyzstan. According to this document, Russian servicemen are to sign individual contracts with Kyrgyzstan's Ministry of Defence, and on the expiration of those contracts the Ministry is obliged to purchase housing for them in the Russian city of their choice save Moscow and St Petersburg.[75] As of July 1994, Kyrgyzstan's army consisted of some 15,000 men; some seventy per cent of those were ethnic Kyrgyz, although they made up only thirty per cent of the officer corps.[76]

## A NEW ERA FOR ISLAM

Islam came late to the Kyrgyz, penetrating the territory of the present-day republic in the latter half of the sixteenth century through the Fergana valley in the south; the central and northern areas became Muslim only in the early eighteenth century.[77] As a consequence, Islam played a less direct role in the lives of the Kyrgyz nomads than in those of the sedentary peoples residing in what are today Uzbekistan and Tajikistan. At present, northern Kyrgyzstan is still only superficially Islamicised, while religious feeling in Osh Oblast and the western part of Naryn Oblast – where the majority of Kyrgyzstan's Uzbek population is settled – is significantly stronger.

Islam in Kyrgyzstan tends to be based more on ritual and the perpetuation of customs than on doctrine, and elements of idolatry, polytheism, and totemism are still in evidence. In the opinion of Kyrgyzstan's highest religious authority, *kazi* Kimsanbai Abdurakh-manov, the unorthodox admixture of Islam and pre-Islamic rituals combined with the 'comparatively shallow attitude of the Kyrgyz towards religion' has rendered Kyrgyzstan infertile ground for the advances of fundamentalists in neighbouring southern countries.[78] In March 1991 an attempt was made in Osh Oblast to establish a local branch of the all-Union Islamic Renaissance Party (the same organisation that was to play such a crucial role in the Tajik civil war one year later), but the authorities quickly succeeded in closing it.[79]

The process of national reawakening that has been taking place in the whole of Central Asia has been closely linked to the general upsurge in religious belief, inasmuch as each nation considers Islam to be an integral part of its heritage; as such, Islam has served as an important means for ethnic Kyrgyz to identify with their nation and its history. The strengthening of national identity has meant that Kyrgyz Muslims, like other Central Asians, now make greater distinctions between themselves and their Muslim brethren in neighbouring states. In fact, although Islamic dogma assigns no importance to the nationality of the believer, a *de facto* delimitation of the Central Asian Muslim community along ethnic lines has been occurring. Evidence of this is provided by the protests of members of the Kazakh, Tajik, Turkmen and Kyrgyz *kaziats* since the late *perestroika* period against Uzbek hegemony of the Muslim Religious Board for Central Asia and Kazakhstan (MRBCAK), which is seated in Tashkent. In 1990 Kazakhstan broke away from the MRBCAK to form its own religious directorate, based in Almaty; in 1992 Khojent and Kulyab Oblasts splintered off the Tajik kaziat to create independent *kaziats.*

In Turkmenistan and Kyrgyzstan, calls to form independent religious directorates have so far been overruled – an unsurprising development given that ethnic Uzbeks constitute a large percentage of the members of both *kaziats*. However, the Kyrgyz *kaziat* was beset by a serious conflict in 1990 when a segment of the clergy, led by former *kazi* Sadykjon Kamalov, attempted to detach the *kaziat* from its parent body in Tashkent.[80] The leadership of the MRBCAK managed to quell the mini-uprising and subsequently replaced Kamalov with Kimsanbai Abdurakhmanov, who, like Kamalov, is an ethnic Uzbek.

In March 1990 Kamalov established the Islamic Cultural Centre, which united more than one hundred mullahs from rural mosques. Although the stated aims of the centre are to minister to the needs of Kyrgyz believers and foster ties with Arab countries, it has participated in political events in conjunction with the popular movement *Democratic Kyrgyzstan*. Consequently, in August 1992 the Kyrgyz Ministry of Justice refused to register the Islamic Cultural Centre as an independent organisation on the grounds that it is forbidden for religious organisations to engage in political activity.

With the exception of a few radical elements, the Kyrgyz religious élite has come to terms with the establishment of a secular state that guarantees basic religious freedoms. Moreover, the construction of new mosques and the restoration of old ones has been proceeding with great rapidity, especially in southern Kyrgyzstan, where their number has more than doubled in recent years. Additionally, Kyrgyzstan's first *madrassah* (religious educational establishment) was opened in Bishkek in 1990 to alleviate the shortage of trained imams to serve in the country's mosques. Candidates wishing to gain a place in the *madrassah*, which had some 150 students in 1992, must demonstrate a knowledge of Arabic and the Koran's teachings.[81]

Although careful not to offend Muslim sensibilities, President Akaev has shown less zeal than most of his Central Asian counterparts to re-dress himself in Islamic garb – except when confessional ties can be used to economic advantage. Before leaving on a scheduled trip to Saudi Arabia in October 1992, Akaev told the press that he would include a *hajj* to Mecca and Medina in his itinerary 'without a moment's hesitation' if it would help him to obtain a credit of $100 million from his hosts.[82] He subsequently completed a pilgrimage to the holy places, although King Fahd turned out to be less generous than it was originally hoped. Similarly, Kyrgyzstan became a member of the Economic Coordination Council[83] in 1992, although it stopped short of joining the Islamic Conference Organisation on the grounds that membership was restricted to Muslim nations.

## ECONOMIC DECLINE

The shattered economy of independent Kyrgyzstan vividly demonstrates that the introduction of market reforms and civil liberties in a post-communist state does not necessarily go hand in hand with economic growth. The other newly independent Central Asian states, which have less democracy but more natural resources and have adopted authoritarian gradualistic approaches to reform, have fared better economically. In fact, in 1993 Kyrgyzstan was competing with two war-torn countries – Tajikistan and Armenia – for the poorest economic performance in the CIS.[84] Indicators for national income, industrial output, and the production of consumer goods have all plummeted, although Kyrgyzstan is the only CIS state to have fulfilled the requirements set out by the International Monetary Fund (IMF) and the World Bank for the transition to a market economy.[85] Moreover, President Akaev has strictly adhered to economic reform in two key areas: the liberalisation of prices, ninety per cent of which had been decontrolled by January 1992;[86] and privatisation, with ninety per cent of the country's smaller enterprises and twenty-six per cent of all state property in private hands by September 1993. By the end of 1994 the Kyrgyz national currency had stabilized and inflation had dropped substantially.

Despite its forward-looking economic policies, Kyrgyzstan has suffered unduly from the loss of transfers from the former Union and from disruptions in inter-republican trade, since it imports virtually all its consumer goods, grain and industrial supplies; moreover, unlike Kazakhstan and Turkmenistan, it cannot meet its own energy needs and was therefore hit particularly hard by increases in the prices of petroleum products. The small nation has also experienced a series of landslides and earthquakes in recent years, which have contributed to the general economic decline. The departure of skilled personnel, particularly Slavs and Germans, owing to the closure of industrial enterprises and the 'squeezing-out' of the non-native population from senior positions in the state sector has added to economic woes.

A primary goal of the Kyrgyz leadership has been to secure aid and credit to develop the social safety net for the inevitable losers of reform; at present, one-third of the population is reported to be living below the poverty line.[87] To this end, Akaev has pleaded with World Bank officials to reclassify the country from one with a middle income (annual per capita income of between $676 and $2,965) to a developing country in order to obtain credit on more favourable terms.[88] Arguing that it is unjust to lump Kyrgyzstan in one group with Kazakhstan, Uzbekistan, and Turkmenistan, the Kyrgyz president has pointed out that the 'Turkmenbashi [Turkmen President Saparamurad Niyazov], who is swimming in petroleum dollars, can afford to build himself a palace at a cost of $400 million, while I have only been able to collect $500 million from all of Europe to support a three-year reform programme in the republic'.[89] Under pressure from the IMF, Kyrgyzstan was the first Central Asian country to leave the rouble zone. On 10 May 1993, it replaced the rouble with its own currency, the som, in part to shield the nation from the rampant inflation of the rouble zone and to settle its existing debt with Russia; the primary reason for launching the som, however, was to secure support development from the IMF, which had been encouraging Kyrgyzstan to introduce its own national currency.[90]

The appearance of the new currency has had social as well as economic implications in that it has shed light on the divisions between the country's main ethnic groups. Drawing on national symbols (banknotes depict a legendary Kyrgyz warrior on a rearing horse), according to public opinion polls the som was welcomed by a majority of ethnic Kyrgyz, whereas a majority of ethnic Russians disapproved of the introduction of a national currency.[91] More than two-thirds of the ethnic Uzbeks surveyed endorsed this latest move towards full independence, however, although they believed that the som would fall in relation to the rouble.[92] Kazakh and Uzbek authorities reacted angrily to the reform, fearing that their regions would be inundated with unwanted roubles; President Karimov even ordered an immediate cut-off of gas and telephone lines. Akaev immediately set about making amends to his neighbours, travelling to Tashkent and Almaty to apologise for having introduced the new currency without due consultation. After Kyrgyzstan promised to settle its existing debt with Uzbekistan on mutually agreeable terms, relations between the two states quickly improved.

By January 1994 the governments of Kazakhstan, Uzbekistan and Kyrgyzstan had formed an economic union with the aims of permitting the free circulation of capital, goods and labour and establishing common policies on credit, prices, taxes, customs and hard currency.[93] In a historic move, on 1 February customs posts on the common borders of the three states were removed,[94] and on 8 August it was decided to create a Central Asian bank for cooperation and development.[95] It was only by leaving aside political concerns and concentrating on economic issues that these Central Asian states were able to take concrete steps in each other's direction, and all three appear fully resolved to continue the process of regional integration.

## POLITICAL CURRENTS

The first years of Kyrgyzstan's independence were politically tumultuous, as the fractious parliament waged a series of protracted battles with the executive branch. Strong and divergent political forces continually blocked the implementation of legislation elaborated by

President Akaev, and the government twice resigned in its entirety (in December 1993 and September 1994). Meetings of parliament became little more than long-winded talking-shop sessions and a forum for political intrigues. Hours were spent discussing fringe issues, such as whether or not to eliminate the statute in the Criminal Code forbidding polygamy – a proposal that was only narrowly defeated.[96]

During his first year as president, the national–democratic groups that had brought Akaev to power grew disenchanted when he failed to champion a specifically pro-Kyrgyz agenda; by mid-1992 some of them were calling for his resignation.[97] On the other side of the political spectrum, the reconstituted communists made persistent attempts to undermine the president's authority and thwart his political initiatives. During Kyrgyzstan's first popular presidential elections, which were held on 12 October 1991, Akaev managed to win a resounding victory with 95.3 per cent of the vote, having run for re-election unopposed on a platform of democracy and market reforms. Although he had a popular mandate bolstering him against vestiges of the old-guard communists, the 'leftover *apparatchik*' parliament – elected while Kyrgyzstan was still under the Soviet system – continued to stymie both Akaev's reform programme and the adoption of a new constitution.

In September 1994 the political crisis reached its apogee when a majority of deputies announced their refusal to attend a scheduled legislative session, arguing that the present parliament had outlived its usefulness and was suffering from a crisis of legitimacy since it had failed to disband itself after the adoption of a new constitution in May 1993.[98] Akaev responded by issuing a decree at the end of September announcing that elections for the country's first post-independence parliament would be held in a few months time.[99] Furthermore, in a nationwide referendum held on 22 October 1994, he asked voters to approve the creation of a bicameral parliament of 105 deputies to replace the Soviet-era, unicameral parliament of 350 deputies; with a turnout of 87 per cent, nearly 73 per cent voted in favour of the proposal.[100] A second question on the ballot asked citizens to allow changes to the constitution by means of referendum; this proposal was endorsed by three-quarters of the voters.[101]

Two rounds of voting for deputies to the new parliament took place in February 1995, both of which were charged with irregularities. The first round produced only 15 clear victors, owing to the large number of candidates in many districts. Less than a fifth of all candidates were members of Kyrgystan's 12 registered political parties; the majority were independents or nominated by various organisations, which attested to the apparent strength of regional and clan ties. While the new legislature is not dominated by the old Soviet-era nomenclatura, President Akaev is sure to face an active opposition led by the former communist officials, including two former republican communist party secretaries.

The first chamber of the new parliament is to consist of 35 full-time professional deputies who will be permanently in session, while the second chamber is to have seventy deputies elected on a territorial basis to ensure that the country's regions are represented at the highest level of state power. Akaev had been pressing for the creation of a second chamber over the objections of his opposition on both the left and right as a means of diffusing political tensions at the regional level. 'If we are to be honest', he asserted, 'all intragovernmental conflicts in the post-Soviet states have been precipitated by the struggle of the regional élite for power. So let the battlefield be the parliamentary chamber rather than the whole country.'[102]

## CONCLUSION

Three distinct forms of nationalism have emerged in Kyrgyzstan in the post-independence years: the inclusive state nationalism endorsed by the leadership, which seeks to encourage certain forms of national pride while ensuring the equal treatment of all citizens; the more virulent strain of nationalism promoted by radical groups, such as *Free Kyrgyzstan* and *Asaba*, which equates the nation with the dominant ethnic group; and the reactive nationalism of Russians and other minorities, which is prompted by their perception that they are the targets of discrimination. Rather than form countermovements, however, members of the non-Kyrgyz population who are disgruntled with the creeping 'Kyrgyzification' of the country have generally preferred to emigrate to their ethnic homelands.

The collapse of the USSR has exposed and deepened the ethnic divisions in Kyrgyz society. There is an ethnic component to virtually every major sphere of state activity, ranging from political wrangling in parliament and the establishment of foreign policy priorities to the introduction of a national currency. One of President Akaev's primary tasks has been to balance the interests of the country's main ethnic groups, taking care to safeguard the rights of minorities while conceding certain rights to the ethnic Kyrgyz majority, especially in the area of culture. Despite the extensive measures taken by the Kyrgyz leadership to accommodate the interests of ethnic minorities, however, the Slavic population has demonstrated little interest in learning Kyrgyz or in accepting the young nation as the 'Kyrgyz homeland' – a circumstance that does not augur well for harmonious ethnic relations in the future. In addition to ethnic divisions, the Kyrgyz leadership must take care that the disparate levels of development between the wealthier northern and the disenfranchised southern regions do not impede national cohesion, as was the case in Tajikistan.

On a more positive note, the emigration of the non-native

population from Kyrgyzstan has been slowing; there are signs that the economy will take an upturn in the near future; and a new, bicameral legislature was elected in February 1995. Despite the closure by Akaev in August 1994 of two newspapers which had been critical of him,[103] democratic principles have taken firm root in Kyrgyzstan. Political parties have been allowed to multiply and flourish, and the US State Department has stated that Kyrgyzstan has the best human rights record of any Soviet successor state.

These advances all attest to the fact that Kyrgyzstan has made significant strides towards becoming a fully independent nation. Yet, in order to ensure that the ongoing process of nation-building does not lead to mass emigration or civil unrest, it is essential for the young state to preserve ethnic stability and fixed, peaceful borders – two problems that its predecessor, the USSR, proved unable to solve.

## NOTES

1. Basic geographical information on Kyrgyzstan may be found in K. O. Otorbaev and S. N. Ryazantsev (eds) *Sovetskii Soyuz: geograficheskoe opisanie, Kirgiziya* (Moscow, Mysl' 1970); and in *Kirgizskaya SSR. Entsiklopediya* (Frunze, Glavnaya Redaktsiya KSE 1982).

2. Detailed figures for the Kyrgyz population residing outside the USSR are given in Guy Imart, *Le chardon déchiqueté: être Kirghiz au XXe siècle* (Aix-en-Provence, Université de Provence 1982), pp. 42–3. Figures for Kyrgyz migration are found in ibid., p. 49.

3. On the formation and early history of the Kyrgyz, see S. M. Abramzon *Kirgizy i ikh etnogeneticheskie i istoriko-kul'turnye svyazi* (Leningrad, Nauka 1971), pp. 10–70; *Istoriya Kirgizskoi SSR* vol. 1 (Frunze, Kyrgyzstan 1984), pp. 47–50, 408–41; for recent criticism of the standard account, see Joseph Seagram 'Question of Kirgiz ethnogenesis being reassessed' *RL* 6/87, 30 Dec. 1986. The most likely etymology of the term 'Kyrgyz' is Turkic kyrk + yz, 'The forty (clans making up a tribal confederation)' (Imart *Le chardon déchiquetée*, p. 208, note c). Because of a terminological inexactitude the term 'Kyrgyz' was used prior to 1925 to refer either to the Kazakhs or to the Kyrgyz and Kazakhs together, and so the two peoples have been confused in a number of sources (see Ronald Wixman *The Peoples of the USSR: An Ethnographic Handbook* (London, Macmillan 1984), pp. 107–8. On the contemporary tribe and clan structure of the Kyrgyz, see Alexandre Bennigsen and S. Enders Wimbush *Muslims of the Soviet Empire: A Guide* (London, C. Hurst & Co. 1985), pp. 78–80.

4. The official (and officially celebrated) date for the 'voluntary incorporation' of Kyrgyzstan into Russia is October 1863. See V. M. Ploskikh 'Golos sud'by' *Sovetskaya Kirgiziya* 26 and 28 Oct. 1988.

5.   Guy Imart 'the Islamic impact on traditional Kyrgyz ethnicity' *Nationalities Papers* 14 (1–2) (1986), pp. 65–88; Bennigsen and Wimbush *Muslims of the Soviet Empire op. cit.*, pp. 80–3.

6.   The standard account of the early Soviet land reforms and collectivisation in Kyrgyzstan is given in *Istoriya Kirgizskoi SSR* vol. 3 (Frunze, Kyrgyzstan 1986), pp. 260–89, 397–432.

7.   Data from *Kirgizskaya SSR*, op. cit. pp. 192 and 211–12.

8.   On the industrial growth of the capital Bishkek, see *Central Asian Review* 2 (3) (1954), p. 244.

9.   Figures from *Naselenie SSSR 1973: statisticheskii sbornik* (Moscow, Statistika 1975), pp. 12–13. The more recent figures are given by Ann Sheehy 'Preliminary results of the All-Union census published', *Report on the USSR*, RFE/RL Inc. (19 May 1989), p. 4.

10.  See John Soper 'Nationality issues under review in Kirgizia' *RL* 49/88, 29 Jan. 1988, pp. 4–5.

11.  *Central Asian Review* 5 (3) (1957), pp. 243–44; Allen Hetmanek, 'Kirgizstan and the Kirgiz' in Z. Katz (ed) *Handbook of Major Soviet Nationalities* (New York: Free Press 1975), p. 240.

12.  The Kyrgyz Autonomous Oblast became an Autonomous Soviet Socialist Republic on 1 Feb. 1926, and was upgraded to Union republic status on 5 Dec. 1936.

13.  On Kyrgyz alphabet reform, see S. Kudaibergenov 'Sovershenstovanie i unifikatsiya alfavita kirgizskogo naroda' in N. A. Baskakov (ed.) *Voprosy sovershenstvovaniya alfavitov tyurkskikh yazykov narodov SSSR* (Moscow, Nauka 1972), pp. 93–8.

14.  The relevant figures on education and literacy in the early Soviet period are conveniently summarised in *Kirgizskaya SSR*, pp. 266–67.

15.  Hetmanek 'Kirgizstan and the Kirgiz' p. 241.

16.  The basic Soviet account of Stalin's purges in Kyrgyzstan may be found in *Istoriya Kirgizskoi SSR* vol. 2, part 2 (Frunze, Kyrgyzstan 1968), p. 70; a more extensive treatment published in the West is Azamat Altay 'Kirgiziya during the Great Purge' *Central Asian Review* 12 (2) (1964), pp. 97–107. The names of those purged are conveniently listed in Imart, *Le chardon déchiqueté*, pp. 103 and 214 (note bc).

17.  Imart, *Le chardon déchiquetée*, gives an exhaustive account of the creation and maintenance of a standard Kyrgyz language, emphasising that from the very beginning the so-called literary standard was somewhat artificial.

18.  Jane P. Shapiro 'Political rehabilitations in Soviet Central Asian Party organizations' *Central Asian Review* 14 (3) (1966), pp. 201–3.

19.  See, for example, *Central Asian Review* 1 (2) (1953), pp. 42–7; ibid. 11 (4) (1963), pp. 331–32.

20.  Ibid. 4 (1) (1956), pp. 68–9.

21.  Ibid. 13 (2) (1965), p. 183; Hetmanek 'Kirgizstan and the Kirgiz', p. 257.

22.  Hetmanek 'Kirgizstan and the Kirgiz', p. 256.

23.  *Central Asian Review* 9 (3) (1961), pp. 226–27.

24.  See Bess Brown 'Chairman of Kirgiz Council of Ministers reported murdered' *RL* 469/80, 9 Dec. 1980; *idem* 'Deceased Kirgiz Premier receives belated honors' *RL* 223/86, 6 June 1986; *idem* 'Soviet journal

publishes story about murder of Kyrgyz Prime Minister' *Report on the USSR* RFE/RL Inc., (14 April 1989), pp. 33–5.

25. Hetmanek, 'Kirgizstan and the Kirgiz', pp. 257–58.
26. *Pravda* 7 June 1985.
27. Bess Brown 'Party Chief of Kirgizia Acknowledges Problems in the Republic', *Radio Liberty* 238/85, 2 July 1985.
28. 'Kirgiz Party Chief Usubaliev Retires', *Radio Liberty* 368/85, 7 November 1985.
29. Bess Brown 'New Kirgiz First Secretary Cleans House', *Radio Liberty* 15/86, 31 December 1985.
30. 'Eighteenth Congress of the Communist Party of Kirgizia: An Attack on the Past', *Radio Liberty* 88/86, 20 February 1986.
31. *Kyrgyzstan Madaniyaty* 23 June 1988.
32. John Soper 'Kirgiz Intellectuals Chided for Neglect of Heritage', *Radio Liberty* 331/87, 18 August 1987.
33. *Sovetskaya Kirgiziya* 26 June 1988.
34. See, for example, *Sovetskaya Kirgiziya* 11 August 1982 and 8 Feb 1985; *Izvestiya* 6 January 1986. A wealth of earlier material is entertainingly surveyed by Isabelle Kreindler 'Teaching Russian Aesthetics to the Kirgiz' *Russian Review* 40 (3), July 1981, pp. 333–38.
35. *Sovettik Kyrgyzstan* and *Sovetskaya Kirgiziya* 24 January 1986.
36. Joseph Seagram 'Need for Changes in Kirgiz Language Discussed', *Radio Liberty* 141/86, 21 March 1986; 'Further Momentum in Kirigiz Language Reform', *Radio Liberty* 8/87, 31 December 1986; and John Soper 'Kirgiz Intelligentsia Seeking to Lessen Russian Influence on Native Language', *Radio Liberty* 412/87, 24 September 1987. The poor state of the contemporary Kyrgyz standard language is convincingly documented in Guy Imart *Le chardon déchiqueté: etre Kirghiz au XXE siecle* (Aix-en-Provence, Universite de Provence 1982). Its virtual total exclusion from prestigious social functions can be seen from recent Soviet survey data in A. Orusbaev *Yazykovaya politika KPSS i razvitie kirgizsko-russkogo dvuyazychiya* (Frunze, Ilim, 1987).
37. John Soper 'Kirgiz Writers Express Concern over their National Language', *Radio Liberty* 142/88, 17 March 1988; see also *Central Asian Newsletter* 7 (5–6) December 1988 to January 1989, p. 16. The issue of Kyrgyz language schools was discussed in detail during 1986–87 (see John Soper 'Nationality Issues', pp. 5–10). An outcome of this debate was an announcement by Radio Moscow on 6 July 1989 that the teaching of Kyrgyz in the republic's schools was to increase greatly from September 1989 (see *Report on the USSR*, 14 July 1989, p. 34).
38. A number of recent examples of the genre are summarised in *Central Asia and Caucasus Chronicle* 8 (1), March 1989, p. 5.
39. *Sovettik Kyrgyzstan* 24 January 1986; see the commentary by Joseph Seagram 'The Status of Islam in the USSR as Reflected in Speeches at the Republican Party Congresses', *Radio Liberty* 120/86, 7 March 1986, p. 1.
40. In an interview in *Sovettik Kyrgyzstan* on 11 March 1988 the *Kazi* of Kyrgyzstan, Sadykjon Kamalov, gave the total number of 'working' mosques in the republic as thirty-four.
41. *Leninchil Zhash* 4 July 1987; *Propagandist-Agitator Kirgizstana*, 2, 1988,

pp. 2–16; see also *Central Asian Newsletter* 7 (1) April 1988, p. 11 and (2) May 1988, pp. 11–12.

42. Sh. Bazarbaev 'Kayra kuruu zhana ateisttik ish' *Kyrgyzstan Kommunisti* 10 (1987) pp. 58–62.
43. *Central Asian Newsletter* 6 (5) Oct, 1987, pp. 5–6, and 6 (6) December 1987, pp. 10–11.
44. A. Asankov 'Izmeneniya v kul'turnoi zhizni sel'skogo naseleniya Kirgizskoi SSR' *Sovetskaya Etnografiya* 1, 1984, pp. 90–8.
45. For earlier unsuccessful attempts to rehabilitate Moldo Kylych and Tynystanov, see Ann Sheehy 'Renewed Attempts to Rehabilitate the Works of Two Important Kirgiz Literary Figures Fails', *Radio Liberty* 98/87, 9 March 1987; and John Soper 'Status of Two Kirgiz Literary Figures Being Reluctantly Restored', *Radio Liberty* 405/88, 31 August 1988. The decrees rehabilitating Moldo Kylych, K. Tynystanov, Yu. Abdrakhmanov and D. Mambetaliev were published in *Sovetskaya Kirgiziya* 4 January 1989.
46. Bess Brown 'Ethnic Unrest Claims More Unrest in Fergana Valley', *Report on the USSR*, RFE/RL Inc., 15 June 1990.
47. *Molodezhnaya gazeta* 28 August 1991.
48. Reuters, 13 October 1991.
49. TASS, 23 August 1991.
50. Alexander Verkhovsky, *Srednyaya Aziya i Kazakhstan: Politicheskii Spektr* (Panorama, Moscow, 1992), pp. 27–30.
51. *Slovo Kyrgyzstana* 24 November 1992.
52. *Kyrgyz Rukhu* No. 2, 2 December 1992, pp. 2–3.
53. *Rosiiskaya gazeta* 9 June 1994.
54. This percentage has been calculated on the basis of 1989 census data and preliminary figures – likely to be underestimations – provided by the Russian Federal Migration Service. *Vek* No. 28, 29 July–8 August 1994, p. 7.
55. Between 1989 and 1993, the Russian population in Tajikistan decreased by 35.9%; in Uzbekistan, by 12.2%; in Turkmenistan, by 8.8%; and in Kazakhstan, by 4.4%.
56. *Izvestia* 5 October 1994.
57. Ibid.
58. *Kommersant* 9 September 1994 and Radio Rossiya, 7 September 1994.
59. *Prava Cheloveka* No. 39, 4 October 1994.
60. *Slovo Kyrgyzstana* 27 November 1992.
61. Brat ty mne ili ni brat?' *Vechernii Bishkek* 2 September 1994.
62. Ibid.
63. Karen Dawisha and Bruce Parrott, *Russia and the New States of Eurasia: The Politics of Upheaval* (Cambridge, Cambridge University Press 1994), p. 86.
64. Ibid., p. 53.
65. *Pravda* 15 and 16 July 1989.
66. *RFE/RL Daily Report* No. 142, 29 July 1991; and *RFE/RL News Briefs* 11–15 January 1993.
67. *Slovo Kyrgyzstana* 3 September 1994 and *ITAR-TASS* 19 August 1994.
68. *Slovo Kyrgyzstana* 3 September 1994 and *ITAR-TASS* 23 September 1994.

69. *Interfax* 24 February 1993 in *FBIS-SOV* 25 February 1993.
70. *ITAR-TASS* 21 and 24 April 1994
71. *Slovo Kyrgyzstana* 27 August 1994. See Keith Martin, 'China and Central Asia: Between Seduction and Suspicion', *RFE/RL Research Report*, 24 June 1994.
72. *Srednyaya Azia: Spravochnye Materialy* (Moscow, Institute for Humanitarian and Political Research 1992), p. 43.
73. 'Slavyanskii faktor v armiyakh musulmanskikh gosudarstv SNG' *Armiya* No. 10, 1994, pp. 20–26 and 'Kyrgyzstan Hopes to Build a Switzerland in Central Asia' *The Guardian* 19 March 1992.
74. *FBIS-SOV* 3 June 1992.
75. *RFE/RL Daily Report* 7 March 1994.
76. *NT Segodnya* 21 July 1994 and *Armiya, op. cit.*
77. Alexandre Bennigsen and S. Enders Wimbush *Muslims of the Soviet Empire* (Bloomington, IN, Indiana University Press 1986), pp. 80–81.
78. *Slovo Kyrgyzstana* 17 August 1994.
79. Alexander Verkhovsky (ed.) *Islam i politicheskaya bor'ba v stranakh SNG* (Moscow, Panorama, 1992), p. 24.
80. Ibid., p. 23 and *Srednyaya Aziya: Spravochnye Materialy, op. cit.*, p. 53.
81. Alexander Verhovsky, *op. cit.* p. 24.
82. *Komsomolskaya pravda* 17 October 1992.
83. The ECO is an intergovernmental association that since 1992 has included the five states of Central Asia, Azerbaijan and Afghanistan in addition to its three founding members, Iran, Turkey, and Pakistan; the last three appear to view the ECO as the core of a possible future Islamic Common Market.
84. Erik Whitlock 'The CIS Economies: Divergent and Troubled Paths', *RFE/RL Research Report* 7 January 1994.
85. ITAR-TASS 1 January 1994.
86. *Economic Review: Kyrgyzstan* (Washington, DC, International Monetary Fund), p. 8.
87. *RFE/RL News Briefs* 5–8 July 1994.
88. *ITAR-TASS* 10 June 1994.
89. Ibid.
90. See the excellent analysis by Eugene Huskey 'Kyrgyzstan Leaves the Ruble Zone', *RFE/RL Research Report* 3 September 1993, p. 39 and Reuters 10 May 1993.
91. Ibid., p. 41.
92. Ibid., p. 41.
93. Bess Brown 'Three Central Asian States Form Economic Union', *RFE/RL Research Report* 1 April 1994 and *ITAR-TASS* 8 July 1994.
94. *ITAR-TASS* 1 February 1994.
95. *Ostankino* 5 August 1994.
96. Alexander Verhovsky, op. cit., p. 24.
97. Akaev is often accused by his opposition of having a 'pro-Russian orientation', especially since he frequently states that St Petersburg, where he lived for seventeen years, is his 'second homeland', *Izvestia* 5 October 1994.
98. *Slovo Kyrgyzstana* 17 September 1994 and *Izvestia* 5 October 1994.
99. *Interfax* 30 September 1994.

100. 'The Reliable Referendum', *The Economist* 29 October 1994.
101. Ibid.
102. *Slovo Kyrgyzstana* 27 September 1994.
103. Akaev closed the parliamentary newspaper *Svobodnye gory* and the independent newspaper *Politika*, stating that they 'allow ugly and inexcusable attacks on foreign governments and their symbols' – i.e. on Israel and China.

# PART VII

# The Diaspora Nationalities

There are a number of nationalities whose members are scattered throughout the Post-Soviet states and have become physically separated from their alleged or 'historical' homeland. The most notable cases include the Crimean Tatars, Jews, Volga Germans, Poles, Meskhetian Turks and, since 1991, Russians in the non-Russian states of the former Soviet Union. Often denied the benefits of territorial or cultural autonomy, the diaspora nationalities have had most to fear concerning the reproduction of their national cultures. While the goals of diaspora movements are similar in that they include the right to resettle in the national homeland, for some during the Soviet period this meant leaving the USSR, whereas for others it entailed both the right to resettlement and the creation or recreation of homelands within the territories of the former Soviet Union.

Since the late 1980s, some diaspora demands have been accommodated. In the case of Jews and Volga Germans, this has resulted in a major exodus from the former Soviet Union. There has also been a major repatriation of Crimean Tatars from Russia and the other post-Soviet states to the Crimean homeland from which they were deported during the Second World War. Likewise, many Russians living outside Russia, ill at ease with having become a diaspora overnight without any sense of having emigrated, have resettled in Russia, primarily from the Central Asian states. The future of the twenty-five million strong Russian diaspora that remains is inextricably bound up with Russia's relations with the other Post-Soviet states, and with how the borderland states will respond to growing demands among the Russian communities for greater territorial and cultural autonomy.

# CHAPTER TWENTY-ONE

# Crimean Tatars

Edward J. Lazzerini

## BACKGROUND

Most of the ethnic groups in the post-Soviet states are numerically small (typically well below one million members), and played roles in the evolving Soviet experience consistent with their size. For reasons that defy convincing analysis but have much to do with episodes of extraordinary assault on the core cultural identifiers of particular groups, a very few have adopted a posture of collective resistance that would be striking even for much larger communities. The Davids confronting the Goliaths are seldom numerous in any society, but the Soviet Union had its share of remarkable men and women over more than seven decades who risked much to voice objections to official policy. One ethnic minority, perhaps above all others in that country, has for nearly forty years stood out for its persistent and often vociferous challenge to conditions affecting it particularly if not uniquely. That minority is the Crimean Tatars.

Ethnically and linguistically related to the Turkic family of peoples broadly dispersed across the Eurasian continent from the Mediterranean to the Pacific, the Crimean Tatars entered the historical record as 'Tatars' in the aftermath of the Mongol conquest of the Crimean Peninsula and surrounding territory in the mid-thirteenth century. For the next two hundred years these Tatars lived among and assimilated with other immigrant Turkic peoples, and were governed by representatives of the Khans of the Golden Horde residing in Sarai, on the lower course of the Volga River, all the while shaping the socioeconomic, cultural and political features of an independent polity. By the 1440s, they had succeeded in establishing their first state, the Crimean Khanate, under the leadership of Haci Giray, scion of one of the major clans providing the military/political élite of the territory. The dynasty that Haci Giray created would rule the Khanate until its collapse under Russian assault in 1783. A regional power until the mid-eighteenth century, the Khanate drew legitimacy and strength from proclaimed links to the steppe heritage of Chinggis Khan and from alliance with the Ottoman Empire.

The combination of internal decline and shifts in the balance of power in the greater eastern European/steppe region by the beginning of the eighteenth century undermined the Khanate's pivotal role internationally and lessened its capacity to defend against external threats. The most dangerous challenge came increasingly from a reformed and expansive Russia looking to resolve a long-standing problem along its southern frontier. Four invasions of the Crimean peninsula by Russian troops between 1771 and 1782 led to the Khanate's demise and its territory's annexation.

Under the tsars, Crimea's experience was chequered. As a consequence of several extraordinary waves of out-migration punctuating the century following annexation, the Tatar presence in the peninsula declined by at least half and its percentage of the total population fell to 35.1 according to the census of 1897. Overall the promised benefits of colonialism remained mostly unfulfilled, while the negative consequences – economic exploitation, social discrimination and cultural imperialism – weighed heavily on the local native population that stayed behind.

During the final decades of the *ancien régime*, many Crimean Tatars participated in the liberalising and revolutionary events overtaking the Russian empire as a whole, with some joining all-Union political and social organisations and others forging more limited but highly nationalist (Crimean Tatar) associations. But also, as Muslims, they were caught up in the web of dilemmas and tensions resulting from the challenges of modernism. These, in many ways, had been crucial in generating a cultural and intellectual revival from the 1880s onwards, spearheaded by and most identified with Ismail Bey Gasprinskii (1851–1914). A Crimean Tatar, Gasprinskii nevertheless proclaimed a reform programme (jadidism) that spoke to all the empire's Turco-Muslim peoples, seeking their full integration into modern life through educational, linguistic, and economic reform rooted in a fundamental shift in world-view. If aspects of his programme met with sometimes fierce resistance from imperial agents and more conservative elements within his own cultural milieu, or were eventually treated with disdain by more radical advocates of change, the dynamic spirit of Crimean society and the existence of a modern-thinking intelligentsia by the fateful year 1917 owed much to his efforts. In the long run, the failure to maintain this process – or rather its disruption by the political evolution of the Soviet state – proved a tragic loss for the Crimean Tatars.

## THE CRIMEAN TATARS DURING THE SOVIET PERIOD

By the approach of 1917, anti-tsarist opinion had spread widely among Crimean Tatars, as had the feeling that Russian influence – whether political, economic or cultural – emanating from central institutions was a major obstacle to fulfilment of Tatar national aspirations. During that tumultuous year in the destiny of the Russian empire, those aspirations turned increasingly radical as the definition of 'nationalist' moved from demands for cultural autonomy emphasising freedom, equality, brotherhood and justice to claims for territorial autonomy within a federalist system, and finally to insistence on independence.

The evolution of Tatar sentiment, however, was bound to conflict fundamentally with centrist assumptions that guided virtually every contemporary Russian political ideology, especially, as it turns out, Bolshevism. Ambivalent at best regarding self-determination and national autonomy when those matters were first treated comprehensively in 1913, Bolshevism gradually revealed itself to be antithetical to Tatar hopes through a succession of statements – some public, others confidential – delivered largely by Stalin between 1917 and 1921. Even as the Bolsheviks proclaimed the virtues of self-determination abroad as an antidote to other imperialisms, they were busy fabricating enough caveats to deny such proclamations any effective play domestically. And when Bolshevik troops occupied Crimea for the third time in October 1920, bringing a certain end to the Civil War for that territory and its people, the possibility of real Tatar independence was foreclosed. The Cheka arrived immediately, led by Bela Kun who turned that already notorious instrument of Bolshevik power to the task of eliminating all local opposition to the new regime. How many native inhabitants – both Tatars and others – perished within the next half year may never be known, but their number must be counted in tens of thousands.

Still, sharpened by the inflexible policies of local Bolsheviks who showed every sign of insensitivity to the Tatar population, opposition continued. Troubled by the failure to pacify Crimea fully, Moscow sent the Volga Tatar, Mir Said Sultan Galiev, on an inspection tour early in 1921. Sultan Galiev would soon make a name for himself – and an enemy of Stalin – by enunciating a theory of 'national communism' that if implemented would have shifted the balance of power and socialist development from the Russian centre of the new Soviet society to the non-Russian borderlands. From the report he submitted based on his Crimean observations, which was highly critical of local Bolshevik practice, one can see early evidence of the direction of his thinking. For Crimea the impact was immediate: a shift in Bolshevik tactics (if not long-term goals) whereby the cooperation rather than antagonism of the Tatars was sought. The most important consequence of the new tactic, and one that continued to haunt the relationship between the Crimean Tatars and the Soviet system, was the decree of 18 October 1921 that created the Crimean Autonomous Soviet Socialist Republic (Crimean ASSR) within the jurisdiction of the RSFSR.

The period from 1921 to 1928 is commonly viewed by Crimean Tatars as a 'golden age' within their Soviet experience, in part because of easy positive comparisons with later decades that brought extraordinary Stalinist repression, but also because the heart of the 1920s witnessed genuine efforts to build within the autonomous administrative framework a new Soviet society in Crimea while enhancing and ensuring its Tatar character. There have been tantalising suggestions that in order to win over the Tatars the Bolsheviks went especially far in conceding autonomy in cultural, economic, and even political affairs, but these have proved impossible to corroborate. In any event, it is by now clear that the nationalist interests of the Tatars stood in such sharp contrast to the centralising thrust of the Bolsheviks that, Stalinism aside, the independence of Crimea could not but be narrowly circumscribed over the longer haul. For a while, however, the exigencies of state development and economic recovery following years of war, revolution and civil strife, as well as the uncertainty and confusion engendered by the ideological and experimental nature of Soviet development, provided the conditions within which *korenizatsiya* (nativisation) could briefly thrive and local national/communist leaders, like Veli Ibrahimov, could restrain the demands of the centre.

In Crimea, *korenizatsiya* meant Tatarisation, despite the decided numerical inferiority of Tatars (179,094) to other ethnic groups inhabiting the peninsula (706,757), according to the 1926 census. Until the spring of 1928, Tatar leaders were allowed to encourage not merely the preservation but the enhancement of Tatar culture, and to assert Tatar identity. This was accomplished through the recognition of Tatar as the official language of the republic along with Russian; the inclusion of Tatars in all levels of republican government; the reestablishment and expansion of republican schools in which the language of instruction was Tatar; the creation of cultural institutions (museums, theatres, libraries, reading rooms) and centres for scholarship (including the Oriental Institute, for the study of Tatar language and literature, added in 1925 to Tavrida University); and the publication of books, newspapers, and journals that provided vehicles not only for discussion of current cultural issues but also for examination of the full range of historical themes.

For a brief period, then, CPSU policy coincided with Tatar ethnic aspirations to give substance to the claim of local autonomy. By the end of the 1920s, however, Stalin's rise to preeminence had the consequence of generating a relentless and often deadly campaign against 'nationalist deviations' among minorities throughout the country. Indigenous leaders, only recently the shapers of local policy, now found themselves the objects of criticism and condemnation, and most became victims of the purging process for which the Stalinist era is infamous. Thus, Veli Ibrahimov, who served as chairman of the Crimean Central

Committee and of the Crimean Council of People's Commissars, was accused of an assortment of nationalist crimes as well as subversion of the collectivisation drive, and fell from grace along with a host of other Tatars now suspect in their loyalty to Moscow. In the push for political and economic centralisation, *korenizatsiya* became an inevitable casualty, associated fatally with the worst features of localism imaginable. The 'golden age' of the Crimean ASSR not only was over, but also was smeared as a time of *veliibrahimovshchina* (the 'Veli Ibrahimov years').

With an end to the policy of *korenizatsiya*, Tatar culture began to suffer blows through all the remaining years of peace before the outbreak of the Second World War. Sovietisation, often little more than a code word for Russification, became the goal for a new era that would produce new Soviet men and women immune to nationalism's seductions. Achieving that goal required not only purging Tatar society of 'wrong-thinking' members but also eradicating, or at least severely curtailing, the institutions and practices that might continue to produce such people. Almost all mosques and clerically-controlled schools were closed, the Cyrillic alphabet was 'adopted' for the Tatar language after it had been Latinised in 1928, the number of journals and newspapers in Tatar was reduced, the faculty of the Oriental Institute at Tavrida University was thoroughly 'weeded,' and virtually the gamut of pre-revolutionary Tatar literature was proscribed. And the past began to be rewritten in appropriate fashion, a process epitomised, perhaps, by the condemnation of Ismail Bey Gasprinskii as a 'bourgeois nationalist' that appeared at length in a path-defining study produced by Liutsian Klimovich, a specialist in anti-Islamic polemics, in 1936.[1]

The intervention of the Second World War in Soviet life is well documented in all its horrors and costs. Between September and 30 November 1941, only three months after the initial German invasion of the USSR, divisions under General Manstein captured the entire Crimean Peninsula. For the next two and a half years, the Nazis occupied the territory and ran an administration that to some degree took advantage of strong Tatar resentments toward the Soviet system while for all practical purposes keeping tight control over the local population and evincing the typical ideological disdain for the indigenous peoples as *Untermenschen*. The Tatar response to the German presence was as varied and contradictory as elsewhere in the occupied Soviet Union, and included resistance through regular army and partisan units as well as collaboration for nationalist and other reasons.

What proved unusual, although utterly consistent with the spirit of Stalinism, was the policy pursued by Soviet authorities on reoccupation of Crimea. During the night of 17–18 May 1944, units of the NKVD systematically rounded up virtually the entire Crimean Tatar population, herded it into cattle trucks and train cars, and transported it with almost no humane provision to a primarily Central Asian exile. Charges of collaboration and treason were levelled as justification. The deportation was devastating: Tatar sources, long as *samizdat* but more recently in open publications, have always insisted that nearly half of those making this fateful journey (about 195,000 out of more than 423,000 living in Crimea following the German occupation), died before reaching their destination. Those who survived would be joined later by others demobilised from the Red Army at the war's end. All would be faced with a 'special settlement' (*spetsposelenie*) regime that would remain in place until the mid-1950s. Its primary features, all punitive, were: (1) denial of the right to move about freely – no further than five kilometres – even in the republic of habitation; (2) restrictions on the right to live in major cities; (3) prohibition of involvement in agricultural activity, the traditional livelihood for most Tatars; (4) requirement of reporting personally to the local NKVD office every other week; and (5) exclusion from active military service.

Even more critical, perhaps, was the series of measures designed to eradicate Crimean Tatar identity. All historical, cultural, and linguistic traces of a Tatar presence in the peninsular homeland were removed, even to the point of razing villages and levelling cemeteries. Another reassessment of Tatar history was undertaken, resulting in extraordinary silence about most of the past prior to the late nineteenth century, save for tendentious paeans on the progressive significance of Crimea's annexation to the Russian Empire in 1783. For the twentieth century, the focus was inevitably on the blessings of the October Revolution and the alleged treachery of the Tatars not only during the dark hours of the Great Patriotic War but even before, during the early decades of Sovietisation. As if to seal the drive to make of the Tatars a non-people, the Crimean ASSR was abolished on 30 June 1945 (although the act was not announced until 28 June 1946), and its territory transformed into the Crimean oblast' of the RSFSR (later transferred to the Ukrainian SSR on 19 February 1954). Moreover, the name Tatar, without its Crimean attributive, would serve henceforth as the only identifier recognised officially. In consequence, no 'Crimean' Tatars existed any longer in the USSR, no 'Crimean' Tatar language needed to be studied, taught, or published in, and no 'Crimean' Tatar culture in general required public sustenance. Since numbers always tell some tale, 'Crimean' Tatar ceased to be a statistical category, above all in national censuses.

For nearly a decade, the exiled Tatars suffered under the special settlement restrictions, living initially in primitive conditions before barracks were constructed and bearing the many burdens of discrimination encouraged by official propaganda. A few of the restrictions were lifted in 1954 for those who could prove that they were loyal during the war by service in the Red Army or with partisan units. This concession, never explained publicly, is consistent with numerous

417

measures whose adoption in the first years after Stalin's death in January 1953 were surely designed to bolster national support for an uncertain and anxious new leadership and to minimise any outbursts of popular discontent. What had been applied to a few initially was extended by decree to all Crimean Tatars on 28 April 1956. Since this document was never published, however, the right to move freely about the USSR that it restored – Tatars were reissued internal passports – was largely ineffective, given the nationwide perception of the Tatars and their 'crimes'. Moreover, the decree insisted anew that 'the property of the Crimean Tatars confiscated at the time of their deportation will not be returned, and they do not have the right to return to Crimea'.[2] Together these two restrictions would become the increasing focus of Tatar grievance, especially once some among them decided to make a public issue of their collective plight.

The window of opportunity was cracked by the unfolding process of de-Stalinisation that, even if he was not its sole author, Khrushchev made the palpable theme of his regime. In a speech at a closed session of the Twentieth Congress of the CPSU in February 1956, the Party chairman noted that 'mass deportations from their native places of whole nations, together with all Communists and Komsomol members . . . are rude violations of the basic Leninist principles of the nationality policy of the Soviet state'. Ironically but shrewdly, this appeal to 'Leninist principles' would be seized on by Tatar activists and made a unifying thread for their long struggle against the injustices meted to their people.

But the immediate inspiration for the emergence of a Crimean Tatar movement was similar remarks by A. F. Gorkin, Secretary of the Presidium of the Supreme Soviet, published in *Izvestiya* on 12 February 1957, and a law of the same month that, while exculpating most of the peoples deported during the Second World War, failed to exculpate the Tatars and the Volga Germans.[3] Dismayed yet convinced that the authorities had erred, the Tatars embarked on a potentially dangerous campaign of public relations involving two tactics that became hallmarks of their efforts: mass petitioning and group lobbying of officials and their offices in Moscow. The first such petition, with over 6,000 signatures, was addressed to the Supreme Soviet in June 1957; it would be followed during the next several years by others, culminating in the delivery of one to the Twenty-second Party Congress in October 1961, with over 25,000 names affixed. Full rehabilitation and the right to return to Crimea were constant themes. What the Tatars received, however, were cultural tokens: a newspaper (*Lenin Bayragh'y*) in their native tongue, appearing thrice weekly since 1 May 1957 under the auspices and supervision of Uzbek party and state authorities;[4] an ensemble (named *Kaytarma*) to perform traditional Tatar music and dance; and optional classes in the Crimean Tatar language available to children in a small number of primary schools throughout the Uzbek SSR. The Tatars were not appeased.

While the authorities responded slowly to the Tatars' expanding public activity, when they did it was to use intimidation and the judicial process as means to shatter the movement's cohesion and isolate its leadership. Thus, the immediate crushing in 1962 of the first quasi-formal group spawned by the movement – the League of Crimean Tatar Youth, in Tashkent – as well as the arrest and trial of activists such as Shevket Abduramanov, Enver Seferov and Mustafa Jemilev. Despite this reaction, persistent and systematic lobbying and the formation of initiative groups throughout Tatar society produced important developments during the second half of the 1960s and into the 1970s. On the one hand, the authorities grudgingly agreed to several meetings between Tatar representatives and high-ranking party and state leaders, including one held in June 1967 with the then KGB head, Yuri Andropov. At the latter meeting, Andropov is said to have promised that an announcement would be forthcoming rehabilitating the Tatars and setting the stage for measures to facilitate their return to Crimea. In fact, on 5 September the Presidium of the Supreme Soviet issued two decrees. The first officially exculpated the Tatars of any collective crimes, but said nothing about a return to the homeland, arguably wishful thinking since the Tatars continued to be denied their Crimean identity. The second, however, confirmed the Tatars' right to 'live in any territory of the Soviet Union, in compliance with labour legislation and the passport regime.' On the basis of these decrees, over the next several years, upwards of 100,000 Tatars sought to move to Crimea, only to be prevented from resettling in their homeland by bureaucratic resistance and arbitrariness, as well as police harassment and brutality. As one Tatar source declared, the second of the 1967 edicts was nothing more than a 'veiled instrument for the eviction from Crimea of Crimean Tatars who had returned to the homeland'.[5]

At the same time, initial steps were taken to link the particular grievances of the Tatars with the more universal ones of the Soviet human rights movement. Instrumental in furthering this tactic was an appeal to Moscow members of the Writers' Union in 1966 that drew the support of Aleksei Kosterin, an old writer, and through him, Petr Grigorenko, a retired general; equally significant was the work of Mustafa Jemilev in 1969 as a founding member of the Initiative Group for the Defence of Civil Rights in the USSR. From these developments the Tatars were encouraged to broaden their appeal not only within their own country but, more importantly, abroad, particularly to the United Nations and other international organisations.

From the late 1960s to the early 1980s the Tatars continued their struggle, particularly in trying to register for resettlement in Crimea, which now was presumably their right. Soviet authorities, however, persisted in obstructing their manoeuvres at every turn, utilising as far as possible low-visibility tactics that bore the aura of legalism. Thus, in order to prevent an anticipated large influx of Tatars into Crimea, residence permits, never required previously, were hastily provided to all current inhabitants; unseen pressure was placed on the managers of enterprises in Crimea not to hire Tatars; notary publics were instructed not to approve the purchase of property or homes if the purchaser was a Tatar; and workers were ordered not to provide electrical or water services to dwellings of unregistered Tatars. Complex rules for official recruitment were enacted in the spring of 1968 that made the process of obtaining permission to resettle arduous and so limiting as to render the results insignificant. Ten years later, a resolution of the Council of Ministers ('On Additional Measures for Strengthening Passport Regulations in Crimea') attacked the problem from a different angle by making it easier for state officials to evict and deport passport violators; and an Uzbek republican edict that same year required emigrants to obtain a certificate from the local militia attesting that work and housing were available in the area to which they wished to move. Although figures are not precise, by 1980 perhaps four to five thousand families had arrived in Crimea by way of the organisational levy (*orgnabor*), while only a few hundred families had managed to obtain residence permits otherwise.[6] Fewer than a hundred unregistered Tatars remained.

In early March 1984, barely a year before Mikhail S. Gorbachev's selection as Party Secretary, a document identified as 'Declaration – 1984' was sent with two hundred and forty signatures to the Politburo of the Central Committee of the CPSU by members of the Crimean Tatar community in Krasnodar krai. It summed up in carefully worded and effective fashion the history of the 'Crimean Tatar problem', the 'incredible torments and losses', the 'daily humiliation and insults from . . . local agencies', and the 'self-sacrifice' of this small people as a result of the failure of the Soviet authorities to honour the constitutional guarantees and the earlier Leninist instructions regarding the rights of national minorities. 'The party must boldly correct the errors that have been committed', its authors admonished. Nothing less than 'genuine rehabilitation . . . restoration of the good name and national dignity of our people . . . [and] its right to live in its homeland – in Crimea' would suffice.[7] Would a new leadership offer realistic hope that these long-fought for goals would be achieved? Would the finally recognised general crisis in the Soviet system provide a new kind of opportunity for even a small minority such as the Crimean Tatars?

## THE CRIMEAN TATARS DURING THE GORBACHEV ERA

On 20 March 1988, three years into the Gorbachev era, various wire services reported the following events.

1   Some 2000 Crimean Tatars marched through the city of Simferopol as part of a three-hour rally. Shouting slogans, the demonstrators demanded a return to their historic homeland and a restoration of their national autonomy.

2   About 1000 Crimean Tatars attended two separate meetings held for nearly four hours each in the Uzbek town of Bekabad. Banners were raised declaring 'Crimea – Homeland of the Crimean Tatars, Not Only a Resort', and 'Democracy and *Glasnost*', Even for Crimean Tatars'.

3   Outside the Lenin Library in Moscow, eighteen Crimean Tatars demonstrated in favour of the right to return to their homeland. Carrying portraits of Lenin and Gorbachev, they unfurled a banner recalling the former's decree creating an autonomous Tatar Republic in Crimea in 1921.

By the standards Crimean Tatars had established over the previous twenty-five years, these public demonstrations would not rank among the more dramatic or substantial. Yet, in that single day's actions the observer should be struck by the array of references – some undisguised, some symbolic – to what is most important to many members of this ethnic minority. The locations of these particular public events are a useful case in point. Simferopol, once known by its Tatar name Ak Mesjit, has been second only to Bakhchisarai in the homeland as a site of historic significance to the Crimean Tatars. Yet at the time one would have been hard-pressed to discover there much evidence of that significance, let alone many Tatar inhabitants. Symbolic of the entire Crimean Peninsula, with few of its native people in residence, Simferopol was a city to which its people wished the right of return.

Bekabad has been a place for Tatars by edict since 1944, a settlement for displaced persons whom the managers of Soviet nationalities policy under Stalin uprooted for reasons still veiled. Crimean Tatars still live in Bekabad, as in other Uzbek, Kazakh, and Tajik places, but, congenial as it may be, the city is not a Tatar abode, not part of *ana yurt* (the homeland) steeped in ancestral memory. It always remained a *caravansarai* on the long road home, a temporary residence where one lived and struggled both for survival and for a different future.

Moscow is the cradle of Russian (in the ethnic sense) culture, incubator of much Soviet history, and fortress of national authority. If the city served as capital and symbol of the socialist Motherland, it did so ambivalently for Crimean Tatars. From that imperial seat, since the birth of the Soviet state, had emanated insistent Communist Party voices, all too frequently redolent of Great Russian chauvinism and always dictating not only what the Tatars should do but also what they should be. To that imperious seat, since the first post-Stalin thaw in the mid-1950s, had trekked uncounted heralds of popular protest, bearing petitions signed at times by tens of thousands, setting up camp outside Party and government offices, and speaking as one small but cohesive, vigorous and persistent voice for justice and cultural autonomy.

As a local official in Tashkent once insisted, however, many in the Soviet Union continued to believe and act as if 'small minorities do not have the right to strike or demonstrate'.[8] Leaving aside the question of whether large minorities had this right, it remains true that despite *glasnost'* and *perestroika*, under which the world witnessed truly remarkable public expressions of ethnic aspirations by Soviet standards, what was permissible remained officially limited, with constraints set not by social consensus openly reached but by authority that typically relinquished little of its presumed right to control others except when compelled to do so by the pressure of circumstance or people. Herein rested, of course, one of the fundamental features of the Soviet experience, and one that the Crimean Tatars long understood and sought to turn against the system that had denied them so much. In fairness to the new party leadership, the liberalisation of Soviet society that it wrought, for purposes that are still arguable, made an extraordinary difference by dissipating a good deal of the residual Stalinist mentality that once permeated the USSR and crippled public discourse. One obvious consequence, of which there was often dramatic daily evidence, was the more broadly-based spirit of public challenge continually stretching the bounds of the permissible and, to a significant degree, forcing the regime to adjust its own policies and goals. But what did this mean for the Crimean Tatars?

Heartened by the emergence of Gorbachev and his campaigns for *glasnost'*, *perestroika* and the democratisation of Soviet society, they continued to pursue the traditional tactics of organised petition and demonstration that, despite setbacks, disappointments, and official retribution, had worked remarkably well for them for two and a half decades. Increasingly, it seemed, Gorbachev became the last best hope for the final resolution of their grievances, as several petitions addressed to him personally and numerous other documents, particularly since early 1987, reveal clearly. The overall tenor of the Gorbachev experiment was understandably encouraging, as was the leniency accorded Mustafa Jemilev (in the manner shown earlier to Andrei Sakharov) in January of that year on his release from Magadan at the completion of his sixth term in prison. By the end of May one could discern a renewed upsurge of Tatar activism that included at least one new aspect: appeal for redress of Tatar religious grievances, accompanied by open acknowledgment of Tatar identification with Islam and the linkage of return to the homeland with restoring and safeguarding confessional rights.[9]

A significant juncture was reached towards the end of June when, at a meeting with Petr Demichev, a non-voting member of the Politburo, Tatar spokespersons were promised resolution of their problems in a month's time! Having learned that official promises were seldom what they seemed, the Tatars refused to wait passively. On 6 July, about thirty people demonstrated in Red Square, and were handled with surprising indulgence. After carrying out their protest near Lenin's mausoleum for about forty-five minutes, five of their number again met Demichev, who reiterated his promise and claimed that an entire section (*otdel*) of the Central Committee of the party was working on the matter. In fact, three days later, although the act was not officially announced until 23 July, a special nine-man commission chaired by Andrei Gromyko and including five Politburo members would be created, the first official body we know of specifically created to investigate minority complaints. Within several months, official working commissions were constituted in Uzbekistan, Tajikistan, the RSFSR and Ukraine to support the work of Gromyko's group and involve the republics within which most of the Tatars dwelled.

Attempting to hold Demichev to his word, the Tatars proclaimed 26 July as a deadline and organised demonstrations in numerous locations, including Moscow, throughout the month. On 25 July, in the midst of a three-day sit-in near the Kremlin, activists announced a major demonstration for the following day. What ensued was an unprecedented, tension-filled, twenty-three-hour gathering in Red Square that broke up only when Gromyko agreed to meet with demonstrators and discuss their grievances. Though reluctant to deal with a man so clearly associated with decades of repressive policies, a delegation spoke with Gromyko for two and a half hours the next day. From the Tatar perspective the results were dissatisfying, as Gromyko adopted an 'elder brother' and patronising tone.

In the months that followed, Gromyko's commission went through a 'fact-finding' phase that included on-the-spot investigations by a working group dispatched to Uzbekistan from 29 July to 5 August. Headed by V. I. Bessarabov, member of the CPSU Central Committee, the group visited Tatars living in five districts of the republic. Radio Tashkent, to the surprise of few, reported that all those spoken with declared that they had everything they needed 'for productively working, resting, participating in public life, and fulfilling their constitutional rights'.[10] Despite *glasnost'*, this kind of reporting – denial of the problem even as words and actions belied such denial – remained all too common in defence of official opinion. Insistence that Tatar activism was detrimental to the fulfilment of group aspirations, charges that activists spoke only for a small extremist element among the Tatars and were guilty of breaching the public order, of slander, provocation, parasitism, egotism, hooliganism, and worse, of having Fascist or neo-Fascist links, constituted a perennial tactic to discredit the movement in the eyes of the population at large and avoid accommodating the real wishes of the Tatars themselves.

Other tactics, however, informed the state's approach to dealing with Tatar demands, and they were revealed in numerous pronouncements and acts, especially the three reports issued by the Gromyko Commission on 15 October and 4 February 1987 and 9 June 1988. In the cumulative documentation, three issues dominated: (1) discrimination against Crimean Tatars in housing, employment, and education; (2) promotion of Tatar culture; and (3) regulation of residence in Crimea and other health resort areas of the country. For the first, if we ignore opinion that such discrimination never existed, the official position was that national and local authorities '[had] lifted all restrictions on the rights of Crimean Tatars in various ways and guaranteed their complete equality with other Soviet citizens in all matters, including the choice of place of residence, work, and study'.[11] As if to justify the discrimination that did (not) exist in the past, the public was reminded that at least some Tatars (but members of no other ethnic group?), collaborated with the Nazis and that the Tatars had historically been troublesome to the Slavic peoples as far back as the Mongol era. Besides, as one Muscovite put it, 'what is done is done' and ought to be forgotten.[12]

For the second, one witnessed a general loosening of cultural restrictions, as occurred for most Soviet ethnic groups, as well as an official commitment to broadening state support to rectify particular Tatar problems. The following should suffice to characterise the sorts of changes that were taking place during the final stage of Soviet history. First, courses teaching the Tatar language were instituted in additional schools in Uzbekistan and Ukraine, including Crimea itself.[13] Given the dearth of qualified instructors, these projects were supported by expansion of teacher-training programmes that included the establishment of a Crimean Tatar faculty at Simferopol State University.[14] Moreover, several new textbooks (textbooks were at that time virtually non-existent save for those produced before the Second World War and long out of print) were compiled in Tashkent and, more significantly, Kiev.[15] The Tatars themselves had long fought to preserve their native tongue and had used their newspaper (*Lenin Bayragh'y*) and literary journal (*Yyldyz*) toward this end in many ways, one of which had been to serialise a Tatar–Russian dictionary and introduce a new column in *Lenin Bayragh'y* entitled 'Students' Page' (*Talebeler Saifesi*).[16] Second, radio and television programmes in Crimean Tatar were expanded in number and content in Uzbekistan and introduced in Tadzhikistan.[17] Third, a new newspaper in Crimean Tatar (*Dostluk*) began appearing as a weekly supplement to *Krymskaya pravda*, and at least one non-Tatar newspaper (*Zarya kommunizma*, appearing in the Dzhankoy region of Crimea) began to publish untranslated excerpts from *Lenin Bayragh'y*.[18] Fourth, treatment of the Crimean Tatar past by Tatars increasingly included previously 'blank' periods (e.g. the late imperial decades and the 1920s), new themes (e.g. the richness of Tatar culture, including music and art as well as literature), and persons formerly anathematised by CPSU fiat. The list of rehabilitated Tatar cultural figures continued to lengthen, but the most significant entry was that for the great nineteenth-century reformer, Ismail Bey Gasprinskii. Fifth, 'Crimean Tatar' became a recognised ethnic identifier for the first time since 1946 with its insertion into the list of nationalities for the census conducted in the period 12–19 January 1989, and its inclusion as a separate entry in *Sovetskaya entsiklopediya* published the same year.[19]

As important as these developments were, the Tatars recognised that cultural concessions not only failed to resolve the deeper issues confronting them but also allowed the authorities to 'look good' in the face of Tatar pressure and buy time, hoping that public support for the Tatars would remain minimal and the passage of time would weaken Tatar resolve. In May 1988 the hurried publication in large numbers (50,000 copies) of a collectively produced little book entitled *Krym: proshloe i nastoyashchee* revealed as well as anything else the extent to which piecemeal concessions possessed a tactical dimension. For one thing, none of the contributors was a Crimean Tatar; for another, the critical period from 1860 to the October Revolution continued to be glossed over. Moreover, the purpose of this book was clearly to support the current official line, with its emphasis on the place (Crimea) and not its dominant native population (the Tatars), its insistence over and again on the multiethnic character of the territory since ancient times, and its equation of Tatar nationalism with Fascist collaboration during the war.[20]

This brings us to the third and, by all accounts, most intractable point of dispute between Soviet authorities and the Crimean Tatars: the latter's right to return to Crimea *en masse* and their demand for restoration of autonomous status for their homeland. These had become of almost primal concern for the Tatars, hardening rather than diminishing with the passage of time and generations, yet the official response remained virtually unyielding on both issues. As spokesman for the Special Commission established to deal with Tatar affairs, Gromyko was true to his sobriquet 'Mr Nyet'. The call for national autonomy, rejected time and again over the previous thirty years, was once more dismissed as unreasonable and impossible to grant. (In the word of the Commission's third report, the present territorial boundaries are 'sealed' in the Soviet Constitution.)[21] The demographic character of the peninsula, never favourable to the Tatars in this century (only 19.4 per cent at the time of deportation), was startlingly less so at the end of the 1980s (0.8 per cent), a fact that was at the centre of justifications for the state's position.[22] Moreover, property rights, jobs, housing and all the other considerations of daily life, it was argued, defied just redistribution to accommodate a massive return of Tatars.

Faced with unrelenting Tatar pressure and defiance of regulations by tens of thousands of their number seeking to resettle in the homeland, in part given new impetus by the calls for *glasnost'*, *perestroika* and democratisation, the state had to address the question of resettlement or risk jeopardising some of the key features of the Gorbachev era.

Fearful that acceding to these ultimate Tatar demands would produce undesirable effects in other ethnically contested areas, as well as causing problems within Crimea itself with the population currently ensconced there, the regime clearly wished to tread cautiously along a narrow ridge between choices. Keeping disruption to a minimum, retaining control over all important processes at work within Soviet society, setting the tone and direction for social behaviour from the top: these were agenda that the new leadership, still influenced by the experiences and mentality of the old, found ever essential, even if attenuated by its interests in openness and reform.

Thus, with regard to the matter of resettlement, the authorities gingerly formulated and implemented a policy at the end of the 1980s that sought to defuse the issue by establishing a mechanism for permitting some Tatars to return to Crimea. On 4 August 1987, the chief editor of Novosti News Agency, Valentin Felin, was quoted as saying that 'perhaps 5,000 Tatars would be permitted to resettle' as a test of the concept's feasibility.[23] The first report of the Gromyko Commission, however, was less encouraging, limiting its response to a call for 'more precisely defin[ing]' the existing regulations on residence in Crimea and other health resort areas of the country.[24] This was followed by an unpublished decision of the USSR Council of Ministers (24 December) that 'temporarily' halted the granting of residence permits for fourteen regions and cities in Crimea and for eleven in Krasnodar, effectively excluding new settlement of Tatars from half the peninsula and, from the Tatar perspective, its two most meaningful urban centres: Bakhchisarai and Simferopol.[25]

On 4 February 1988, the second Gromyko report, apparently in keeping with the decision of the Council of Ministers, announced without detail that the procedures for residence registration in all resort areas, including Crimea, were now 'more clearly defined'. Simultaneously it called for the removal of 'unjustified obstacles to their [the Tatars'] change of residence'.[26] *Pravda vostoka* reported on 6 March that Gromyko's commission decided to allow approved Tatars to return to Crimea. Permission would be mainly granted to those who had a good work record and recommendations from official institutions. Resettlement, 'as conditions are created', would be primarily in the northern steppe region, not in resort areas along the Black Sea coast.[27] Incredibly, the first announced group to be permitted resettlement under the new procedure comprised only nine men and their families, although three hundred families were projected to be involved by the end of 1988.[28] Talk was that a ten-year programme for Tatar repatriation was likely.

These insignificant numbers did little to augment the Tatar population in their homeland, which according to a mid-1989 estimate was only about 41,500.[29] In effect, a stalemate obtained between the Tatars wanting to repatriate and the authorities intent on maintaining restrictive policies. Especially telling was the conclusion, more in the form of a warning, of the Gromyko Commission's final report, where it was asserted that this was the extent of its and the authorities' compromise. In the last years of the 1980s, however, the refusal of the Tatars to rest content with the concessions granted was readily apparent. Demonstrations and petitions remained central to their strategy; in response to the brutal treatment of about 5,000 demonstrators in Tashkent on 26 June 1988, the staff of *Lenin Bayragh'y* (twenty-two of its twenty-five members) undertook an immediate political strike; Mustafa Jemilev announced the creation of the Organisation of the Crimean Tatar National Movement (OKND) on 2 May 1989, while information about the establishment of at least nine associations in Crimea and Krasnodar filtered abroad;[30] and reflecting the recent public assertion of Islam's central position among the Tatars, pressure was building for the establishment of an official Muslim Religious Board for Crimea and a religious teaching institution in Simferopol.

## THE TATARS AND POST-SOVIET DEVELOPMENTS

The failed coup of August 1991 and the precipitous demise of the USSR that followed eased for a while the stalemate between Tatars and various authorities by altering the circumstances and rules of their encounter. The disintegration of the Soviet Union solidified the growing tendency on all sides, incorrect though it may have been, to view the Tatar question as a Ukrainian and Crimean one, although Russian interests, temporarily distracted, would gradually reemerge to complicate matters again. It also somewhat quieted what had been a growing incidence of violence directed against returned Tatars in 'tent cities' by Soviet authorities frequently employing the notorious OMON, a local special force. Yet use of strong-arm tactics was a habit not easily abandoned. One shocking instance of authority instigating popular mayhem against the Tatars, appropriately described at the time as a pogrom, occurred on 1 October 1991 when police and about 600 members of the Krasnyi Rai sovkhov invaded a large Tatar encampment, levelled temporary shelters, injured twenty settlers, and arrested 26 more.[31] If the overall climate has softened slightly, to this day violence is waiting to erupt under even slight provocation.

To understand the fate of the Tatars in the post-Soviet context, we might begin with a survey of Crimean politics and the debates that have raged over definition of the region, its relationship to Ukraine and Russia, the political legitimacy of various peninsular institutions, and the conflicting ethnic claims to regional titular status. Thanks to the 'gift' of Crimea to the Ukrainian SSR in 1954, Kiev insists that the peninsula cannot be separated from the independent state that Ukraine has become since the overwhelming popular approval of a referendum on 1 December 1991. The issue, however, is much more complicated. Even accounting for further in-migration of Tatars from the near abroad that is expected to raise the local community to 350,000 within a couple of years, and for a higher fertility rate among Tatars than among other ethnic groups, Crimea will probably enter the 21st century with ethnic Russians still comfortably the majority of the region's population. Moreover, responses to a question in the 1989 census about first language show that 81.4 per cent of Crimea's inhabitants claimed Russian, and evidence from referenda and opinion polls as well as plenty of anecdotal evidence shows the extent of local opposition to Ukrainian influence, whether political or cultural. In 1995, the Ukrainian minority still has few cultural facilities, and schooling in its own language remains non-existent. Finally, pressure from Russia over the disposition of the Black Sea Fleet as well as 'ownership' of Crimea itself, despite Boris Yeltsin's agreement with Kiev on its basic claim to the region, brings an additional factor to bear on what Crimea is to be. In sum, a 'foreign' challenge to Ukraine's preeminence over Crimea looms increasingly large, especially in the aftermath of Yurii Meshkov's victory in the regional presidential election held on 30 January 1994. Meshkov ran on a platform that unabashedly made Crimea's rejoining Russia a primary goal.

The Tatars, meanwhile, have staked much on the definition of Crimea. For them the region is *their* homeland and they believe that *they alone* have the historic, legal, and moral right to determine its destiny. Still comprising less than 10 per cent of the peninsula's population, however, their numbers remain too small to affect consistently the legislation that will make a difference: their voice is loud and persistent, but their votes few. As of the beginning of 1994, for example, the Crimean parliament still had only one Tatar deputy in a body totalling 196, although discussions were under way for some time before the recent presidential election to establish a higher quota for them and other 'deported' groups. Meshkov's very poor relationship with the Tatars suggests that he will not be, as was the former chairman of the Crimean Supreme Soviet, Mykola Bahrov, a supporter of this example of affirmative action.

The Tatars' generally pragmatic leaders have realised the weakness that their community's numbers pose and have tried to compensate in a variety of ways. First and foremost they have been unrelenting in their efforts to repatriate as many of their brethren as possible. Approximately 260,000 had returned as of early 1994, leaving about an equal number in the 'near abroad' (portions of the former Soviet Union). Insufficient funds to move those left behind, inadequate housing and employment opportunities in Crimea, and perennial bureaucratic obstruction from Kiev and Simferopol conspired to slow repatriation significantly in 1993–94. Repatriation is further complicated by two additional factors: the desire of Tatars, the clear majority of whom are urbanites, to settle in Crimean cities, and their wish to settle everywhere in the peninsula, including along the attractive southern coast. Most have been unable to find residence in cities, thereby contributing to their high levels of unemployment and underemployment, and they have been effectively excluded from Crimea's 'Riviera' because of its economic value. Data from mid-1993 reveal that 61 per cent of Tatars in Crimea live in the northern steppe zone and only 5.69 per cent in the coastal region stretching from Sevastopol to Sudak.[32]

If the configuration of power is not likely to shift as a result of demographic trends, the Tatars have balanced a concern for repatriation with a strategy of resolute political manoeuvring. On the one hand, they have consistently sided with Ukraine's interests against Russia's despite Kiev's sometimes tepid and ambiguous support, believing that some bedfellows are better than others for the foreseeable future. On the other hand, they have established a political order in their own name that mimics, yet frequently and perhaps inevitably contradicts, the regular Crimean government. This parallel system comprises a Kurultay (popular assembly that convenes once a year in normal circumstances), a Mejlis (national parliament that meets in frequent session throughout the year), an expanding number of local assemblies of self-governance (mini-Mejlises), and a party (the OKND, or Organisation of the Crimean Tatar National Movement). Together these seek to raise a unified Tatar voice that not only works to protect communal interests but presumes that those interests, under current circumstances at least, can be protected only by the Tatars themselves.

The Kurultay holds a hallowed institutional place in Tatar lore, having roots in Turkic tribal practice and being linked in this century with Crimean Tatar nationalism. The first modern Kurultay was held in 1918; the second met on 26–30 June 1991 in Simferopol, during which it issued a declaration on national sovereignty, created the Mejlis and elected its thirty-one members, adopted a design for the Tatar national flag and a national anthem. The Mejlis held its initial session on 6 July 1991, led by Mustafa Jemilev as chairman and Refat Chubarov as deputy chairman. As the highest representative organ of the Tatar people, the Mejlis quickly became in practice a shadow government that draws its legitimacy not from the Crimean civil authorities or the region's population as a whole but from the Tatar people speaking ultimately through its Kurultay. As such it claims exclusive sovereignty over the whole of Crimea and rejects offers from Kiev of limited self-government in restricted territories, or what would be a kind of Tatar reservation. Moreover, as if to make the point even sharper, its leaders have refused since the Mejlis's inception to recognise the authority of its 'legal' counterpart, the Crimean Supreme Soviet, to register the Mejlis as either a political party or a public organisation, or, more recently, to affirm either the legality of the 1994 presidential election or the legitimacy of its victor, Meshkov. For its part, the Crimean Supreme Soviet at a stormy session on 29 July 1991 revealed a hostile majority viewpoint redolent of extreme chauvinism that produced resolutions refusing to recognise the Mejlis. Prominent among the anti-Tatar deputies was, interestingly, Yurii Meshkov, who branded the Mejlis illegal, called for an investigation of its activities, and demanded 'a thorough registration of all Crimean Tatars to determine the legality and validity of their resettlements'.

Not much information is available on the workings of the mini-Mejlises that have been formed in Tatar communities across Crimea, but they appear to be functioning as important intermediaries between the Tatar 'national government' and its constituency, the people, providing input from below as well as participatory experience in an evolving democratic environment. As for the OKND, its membership overlaps considerably with the Mejlis, and its programme, formulated during the second session of the Second Kurultay (27–31 July 1993), is the same. The obvious unity of purpose that has been such a hallmark of the Tatar national movement continues to serve this minority community well, but it has generated some disaffection over the years, as in relations with the group surrounding Yurii Osmanov (NDKT, or National Movement of the Crimean Tatars), which has been more willing to work with the regional authorities;[33] or with more radical figures such as Il'my Umerov, who announced in July 1993 that he was going to establish a new party, Milli Firka, with a platform calling for an independent, ethnic Tatar state within Crimea, in which Tatar would be the sole national language. That such centrifugal forces exist within the Tatar movement should not be surprising; neither, however, should be their marginality so long as Mustafa Jemilev remains on the scene as the movement's icon.

Internal politics may one day prove more disruptive of Tatar affairs, but for now other issues demand much more of the community's attention. Leading the way will be the ongoing struggle to determine Crimea's fate as a whole and the place within it for the Tatars. We can only speculate as to how the wrestling between Ukraine and Russia will turn out, but in the absence of any startling changes in either country (which is not guaranteed, in view of the recent elections in both) we can be reasonably sure that the Tatar leadership will continue to lean towards Ukraine, however reluctantly. Immediately following the January 1994 presidential election, Mustafa Jemilev summed up the Tatar dilemma on this score when he told a press conference that the Tatars were 'alarmed' by Meshkov's victory and would not recognise him as president if he continued to adhere to views that Tatars considered to be 'chauvinistic and anti-Tatar.' At the same time he criticised Kiev's policy toward Crimea, adding that the Tatars have a right to expect the Ukrainian authorities to adopt a 'firmer' position as regards developments in the peninsula.[34]

On the heels of these political concerns are two other issues whose importance is revealed not only through the various media but also through even minimal direct contact with the Tatar community: the unfinished business of repatriation and restitution, and the dearth of cultural facilities. As mentioned above, in 1993–94 a variety of factors diminished the flow of Tatars from the near abroad to their homeland, leaving approximately a quarter million to wait their turn. The process of repatriation has long been linked to demands for restitution of property confiscated by the authorities in 1944, but restitution has been complicated by an unforeseen development accelerated by post-Soviet conditions: the move to privatisation. What is greeted widely, including in the Tatar community, as a necessary concomitant of the transition to a market economy is equally seen by the Tatars as fraught with a grave danger: if privatisation proceeds before satisfactory restitution, that restitution, especially in the form most desired (land), will be severely jeopardised.

Mustafa Jemilev, speaking for the Presidium of the Mejlis, outlined the problem in an article published in early 1993. He complained that during all the discussions about privatisation in both Ukraine and Crimea, the rights of the Tatars have been completely ignored, their representatives have been excluded, and international norms concerning human rights have been contravened. He further accused the authorities of using their positions to 'squander and appropriate a basic part of the national wealth of Crimea by extralegal means, with the result that the natural wealth and productive potential of the region are passing to private hands and organisations, some of which have no ties to Crimea'. At the same time, 'taking advantage of all sorts of formal tricks,' they are excluding even the Tatars who have already returned. As a result, privatisation, which is 'in and of itself progressive and necessary for the construction of a modern and effective economy, is being turned into another form of colonial suppression and enslavement of the Crimean Tatar people'. Based on this analysis the Mejlis insists on the following: (1) return to Tatars of all property lost as a result of deportation, as well as compensation in full for losses; (2) exclusion from privatisation of all religious and historical monuments, buildings, vakuf, whether or not currently in use; (3) creation of a reserve fund to ensure the rights of Tatars; (4) guarantees to Tatars of equal opportunities with others in the process of privatisation, including availability of credit; and (5) establishment of norms and principles in questions of privatisation.[35]

Crimea has vast potential, particularly with a revitalised and refurbished tourist infrastructure. To generate economic value from tourism at the level many see as possible will, however, require vast sums of investment capital, and privatisation is one means by which to raise these. Jemilev is correct in noting both the corruption factor and the foreign interests that are beginning to flock to the region; each has the influence that comes from having money to prod the authorities to push privatisation without much regard for the Tatars who have little capital with which to argue their case. The Mejlis's position is ultimately a moral one demanding justice; where justice fits into the equation of Crimea's economic and political development has never been clear.

In many ways the cultural questions facing the Tatar community are in the end also about restitution and justice, about giving back to this people their history and their rights, for example, to normal education and religious practice. As with historiography generally under the Soviet system, the Tatar past has suffered from extensive mistreatment; unfortunately, it occasionally still does at the hands of those working in official capacities. A long review of this problem has been provided by Yurii Gorbunov, who examined new textbooks on Crimean history for classroom use at grades eight to eleven. What he found was perpetuation of all the disturbing conventions of Soviet historiography, from careful exclusion of key events and figures in Tatar history to 'reminders' of Tatar perfidy as the cause of their own and others' problems.[36] In these texts Crimea remains a place not for Tatars except, perhaps, as guests.

Education is further affected negatively by the shortage of textbooks for instruction in the Tatar language. Ironically, in Crimea more instruction is now available for Tatar children in their native language than for Ukrainian children in theirs, although the status of both instructional milieu remains abysmal. The small Tatar language and cultural programme at Simferopol State University is valiantly attempting to train people who can then go out into the primary and secondary schools, but its resources are extraordinarily meagre. The head of the programme, the linguist Ayder Memetov, pointed out to me that the library for the programme was the books filling a few shelves in the dormitory room he called home, while he waited for better accommodation to which to bring the family he had had to leave behind in Tashkent.

Meanwhile, the question of the written language has been resolved, at least in theory. The deputies to the first session of the Second Kurultay voted in June 1992 to support the transition of Tatar from Cyrillic to Latin script. A subsequent conference brought together Turkologists and other linguists from around the world to discuss various aspects of this process, from which a sub-committee emerged with the task of devising a variant of the new script. Finally, the second session of the Second Kurultay agreed on 31 July 1993 to accept the sub-committee's recommendation and to begin working out the measures for implementation of an alphabet essentially the same as the one Turkey has used since 1928.[37] If little was accomplished through the first half of 1994, owing largely to more pressing events and issues, the decisive step had at least been taken.

Finally, religious practice has blossomed with the selection of a Mufti to lead the Tatar community and the restoration of mosques in various parts of Crimea, including the main mosque, Kebir Cami, in Simferopol next to the Mufti's current headquarters. Funds to carry on restoration projects, like funds for other purposes, remain slight, and even when they are available the amount is usually insufficient to do a proper job. A major goal of the community has been to reacquire the property on which sits the structure of the Zincirli medresse, one of the main Tatar institutions of higher religious studies prior to 1917. With the school in terrible ruin and its graveyard desecrated, the site of the medresse is currently serving as a mental hospital. Efforts to have the hospital and its patients moved have so far been unsuccessful.

If anything, the keys to Tatar success in the past – the remarkable cohesion, steadfastness and resilience of their community, the flexibility of its tactics, and adherence to simply principles of action that prize struggle within the parameters of domestic and international law and eschewal of all forms of violence – are more likely to reap desired results under the current post-Soviet conditions than under former ones. Whether cultural concessions granted piecemeal will assuage Tatar appetites remains to be seen; they will not, I suspect, prove a substitute for the one demand that has always been at the heart of the movement: return to the homeland for all who desire it and return of the homeland to those who have the longest claim. 'Let no one think', wrote a Tatar poet in 1987, 'that the Crimean Tatar people is a flock of sheep which cares not where it grazes so long as it has its fill'.[38]

# NOTES

1. L. Klimovich *Islam v tsarskoi Rossii* (Moscow 1936), chap. VII.
2. Ann Sheehy *The Crimean Tatars and Volga Germans: Soviet Treatment of Two National Minorities* (London 1971), p. 12.
3. Necip Abdülhamitoglu *Türksüz Kirim: Yüzbinlerin Sürgünü* (Istanbul 1974), pp. 135–36.
4. The name of this newspaper was changed to *Yangy Dyunya* in 1990.
5. 'Declaration – 1984' in Edward Allworth (ed.) *Tatars of the Crimea: Their Struggle for Survival* (Durham, NC, Duke University Press 1988), p. 225.
6. Ibid., p. 226.
7. Ibid., pp. 226, 228.
8. Comrade Terekin, Tashkent city prosecutor, June 1988, as reported by the Centre for Democracy in the USSR, 5 July 1988.
9. See the letter from Server Seutov, identified as the 'official religious representative of the Muslim believers of the Crimean Tatar nation', in *The Central Asian Newsletter* (5–6), December 1988, p. 4.
10. CMD from Munich, 6 August 1987.

11. Reuters in English from Moscow, 9 June 1988; 'Soobshchenie gosudar-stvennoi komissii' *Izvestiya* 10 June 1988.
12. *Izvestiya* 1 August 1987, cited in *The Central Asian Newsletter* VI (6), December 1987, p. 4.
13. See the following: TASS in English from Kiev, 25 August 1988; 'Milletleraga Münasebet ve Milliy Til' *Lenin Bayragh'y* 49, 27 April 1989, p. 4; 'V TsK Kompartii Ukrainy' *Pravda Ukrainy* 5 January 1989, p. 1, reporting a resolution of the Central Committee of the Ukrainian CP on interethnic relations in the republic.
14. On the problems of teacher training, see M. Medzhitov 'K'rymtatar Tilinin yak'yn Keledzhegi' *Lenin Bayragh'y* 147, 17 December 1988, p. 4.
15. The most valuable texts are *Ana Tili* (treating phonetics and morphology), *Ana Tilinde* (a reader drawing on classical and contemporary Tatar writers), and *K'rymtatardzha-Ruscha Lug'at* (a Crimean Tatar–Russian dictionary), all appearing in Kiev in 1988.
16. Portions of the dictionary appeared irregularly for several years through the mid-1980s; the column commenced on 1 May 1989.
17. For Uzbekistan, see the expanded programming as listed in *Lenin Bayragh'y*; for Tajikistan, see TASS in Russian from Dushanbe, 11 January 1989, and TASS in Russian from Kulyab (Tajikistan), 18 February 1989.
18. O. Pronina 'Dostluk – znachit druzhba' *Pravda Ukrainy* 19 April 1989, p. 4; Iu. Kandimov 'K'rimda Ana Tilimizde Gazeta Chik'ip Bashladi' *Lenin Bayragh'y*, 81, 13 July 1989, p. 4.
19. 'Tatar or Crimean Tatar?' *The Crimean Review* 4, (1), June 1989, p. 12; *Sovetskaya entsiklopediya* (Moscow, Narody mira 1989).
20. For critical reviews, see I.I. Krupnik in *Sovetskaya etnografiya* (5), September–October 1988, pp. 157–60 (reprinted in *Lenin Bayragh'y* 146, 15 December 1988, p. 4; and E. Umerov and E. Amit 'Rekord pospeshnosti' *Literaturnaya gazeta* 9 November 1988.
21. 'Soobshchenie gosudarstvennoi komissii' *Izvestiya* 10 June 1988.
22. Novosti Press Agency, 24 May 1988.
23. AP from Frankfurt, 4 August 1987.
24. TASS in English from Moscow, 15 October 1987; 'Zasedanie gosudar-stvennoi komissii' *Pravda* 16 October 1987.
25. AFP from Moscow, 7 February 1988.
26. AP from Moscow, 4 February 1988.
27. AP from Moscow, 12 March 1988.
28. 'V goskomtrude Uzbekskoi SSR i respublikanskoi rabochei komissii predstavitelei Krymskikh tatar' *Pravda vostoka* 30 April 1988.
29. TASS from Moscow, 16 May 1989.
30. The strike was reported by the Centre for Democracy in the USSR, 5 July 1988; the new national organisation was announced in 'Mustafa Dzhemilev's Latest Message,' *The Crimean Review* IV (1), June 1989, p. 8; on the associations, see *Central Asia and Caucasus Chronicle* VIII (2), May 1989, pp. 9–10.
31. Two months earlier, on 2 August, a similar experience befell Tatar squatters in the village of Molodezhnoe, near Simferopol.
32. The figures are for June 1993 and appeared in *Yangy Dyunya* No. 36, 29 June 1993, p. 3.

33. On 8 November 1993, Osmanov was found murdered on a street in Simferopol. News reports say that the authorities suspect robbery, but political motives were also being considered.
34. *RFE/FL Daily Report* No. 21, 1 February 1994.
35. Mustafa Jemilev 'Prezhde chem privatizirovat', nada vernut' otobrannoe!' *Qyrym Dostluk* 6, 6 February 1993, p. 1.
36. Yurii Gorbunov 'Stalinskoe posobie po istorii Kryma' *Avdet* 14, 15 July 1993, p. 3, discussing *Nash Krym. Uchebnoe posobie po istorii* (Two vols.; Simferopol, 1991–92).
37. The new alphabet was published in *Avdet* 16–17, 9 August 1993, p. 1.
38. Reuters from Bakhchisarai, 24 August 1987, quoting the poet Yazydzhiev.

# CHAPTER TWENTY-TWO

# The Jews

## Yoram Gorlizki

Twenty years after the Bolshevik Revolution, anyone wishing to vindicate Lenin's prophecies of 'national assimilation' would have turned to the example of the Jews.[1] By the late 1930s, the Jews were educationally the most mobile, geographically the most urban and linguistically one of the most Russified of the non-Russian nationalities. It seemed, as Lenin had predicted, that once the artificial and discriminatory caste status imposed by the tsars had been erased the Jews would be carried by their vaunted 'internationalism' towards inevitable assimilation. However, the very achievements of Jews under the new order were to arouse a significant measure of social and official resentment. In time the Jews were forced to contend with a new, peculiarly Soviet, mix of governmental restrictions. After the Second World War, these state-imposed impediments were complemented by a stirring of national self-awareness among the Jews brought about by the Holocaust and by the declaration of the State of Israel.

At no time, however, has the failure of Lenin's vision of ethnic integration been more apparent than it is now, as Jewish cultural claims become more assertive, as local strands of anti-Semitism become more overt, and as Jews leave the territories of the former Soviet Union in their tens of thousands. The changes of the past decade have been far-reaching and have revealed most clearly the superficiality of some of the state-imposed identities of the Soviet period. In some respects the present climate of political instability bears close parallels with the pre-revolutionary period when, as now, Jews fled a tottering empire in large numbers. Comparisons with Imperial Russia can, however, be misleading. As we shall see, the roots of the 'defection' of Soviet Jews from ethnic integration are, in part, of the Soviets' own making. Moreover, aside from the present uncertainty, the Jews of the successor states are enjoying freedoms completely unknown to their forebears. To appreciate the radical novelties of the present situation, we shall have to take stock of continuities and parallels with the Soviet and pre-Soviet past. Let us therefore begin with a brief survey of the condition of Russian Jewry on the eve of the October Revolution.

## BACKGROUND

Imperial Russia acquired the vast majority of its Jews in the course of the Partitions of Poland in the last third of the 18th century. The years of tsarist rule that followed saw many reforms and reactions, but two trends in particular stand out. The first of these was the marked deterioration of the Jewish economy. Jewish industry, drastically undercapitalised and largely focused on consumer goods (clothing and textiles) was fettered by the slow and uneven growth of the internal market and undercut by the rise of large-scale non-Jewish manufacturing. Moreover, the many Jews who had formerly worked as independent commercial intermediaries, creditors and tax collectors were marginalised by the introduction of trade barriers and by the expansion of modern financial institutions. From barely over one million at the beginning of the 19th century, the Jewish population had leapt to over five million by 1897. Numerous official reports recount that a large proportion of the Jews had been proletarianised or reduced to petty hawking and peddling, and thrown into a poverty and destitution only partly alleviated by the extensive network of relief.[2]

The second feature of note was the troubled relation between the Jews and the tsarist state. Imperial Russia never fully partook of the emancipation of Jewry that had occurred across the rest of Europe from the 1780s onwards. The reasons for this remain contentious. Traditional interpretations ascribed the failure of emancipation in Russia to virulent anti-Semitism in the higher reaches of the state. But more recent accounts have turned, first, to the *uniqueness* of Russia's 'Jewish problem' (i.e. integrating the largest Jewish community in the world into an agrarian society); and, second, to the congenitally bureaucratic response of the Russian state to *any* threat of social unrest, as the key explanatory factors.[3] Whatever the reasons, the Empire retained a system of civil disabilities that cumulatively subjected the Jews to over 1400 specific legal provisions and thousands of lesser rules.[4] The central pillar of this edifice of 'bureaucratic Judeophobia' was the establishment of the Pale of Settlement, which by law confined the residence and movement of the overwhelming majority of Jews to the western borders of the Empire. But there were other significant restrictions too, and the social and spatial separations they entailed combined to bar the Jews from full admission to citizenship.[5]

It was in response to the especially severe 'May Laws' of 1882, and to the outbreak of anti-Jewish pogroms that had led up to them, that the Jews began to take their fate into their own hands. By the First

World War nearly a third had emigrated, mostly to the United States. Others, meanwhile, were drawn into domestic and Zionist politics, with a particularly high incidence of Jews in the socialist and liberal movements. In reaction to the growing partisan pressures around them, some of the exclusively Jewish groups began to display increasingly nationalist leanings. After 1903, the platform of the most important Jewish party, the Bund, was to depart significantly from that of its one-time allies who had recently come to be known as the Bolshevik wing of the All-Russian Social Democratic Labour Party. The Bund began to insist not only on the equal civil freedoms that the Jews had been denied as individuals, but also on collective national rights, such as cultural and linguistic autonomy for the Jews. But Lenin's retort, that the preservation of national culture would merely service the caste status that had so far separated the Jews from their host environment, was to prove decisive.[6]

## THE JEWS AS PART OF SOVIET LIFE

In April 1917 the Provisional Government legislated to free the Jews from their caste coordinates, thus opening up new lines of employment as well as opportunities for travel and internal migration.[7] True to his word, Lenin did not go back on these newly won freedoms when the Bolsheviks swept to power in October. The price exacted, however, for these personal freedoms was a coordinated crackdown on independent Jewish *national institutions* of virtually any description. The Bund and the Jewish communal councils (the *kahals*) were disbanded, while the Zionist parties and the religious institutions, which proved the most resistant to change, were targeted in a series of intensive campaigns.[8] In this task the regime was assisted, even prompted, by the new Jewish sections of the Party, the *Evsektsii*.[9] But however much the Party may have turned to its Jewish sections to carry out the campaigns of the 1920s, its need for them was strictly provisional. Owing to their lack of a compact historical territory, the Jews did not qualify as a nation in the eyes of the regime.[10] The vain attempts to settle the Jews in common areas, such as the Jewish Autonomous Province first set up in Birobidzhan in 1928, ended in failure. Thus the Jewish sections sowed the seeds of their own destruction by helping to create the conditions under which they were no longer needed. As they did not belong to the class of territorial institutions that had become the only legitimate form of national–Communist organisation, the Jewish sections were dispensed with in January 1930.[11]

These cultural and political upheavals were accompanied by shifts in the occupational structure of the Jews. War, Communism and the pogroms of 1919–1921 had seen the undoing of the Jewish economy in the old Pale of Settlement.[12] The number of Jewish merchants, owners of enterprises (including artisans) and 'persons without a defined occupation' fell dramatically as Jewish workers were rapidly drawn into the nationalised economy. With the majority entering the state's new industrial plants, the proportion of labourers among Jews doubled between 1926 and 1939 (from 15.1 per cent to 30.5 per cent). Moreover, their cultural emphasis on learning fitted the Jews well to the requirements of the flourishing administrative and technical arms of the state. Consequently, the percentage of white-collar workers in the Jewish population swelled from 10 per cent in 1897 to 29 per cent in 1926 and 40 per cent in 1939.[13]

There were spatial corollaries of the conscription of the Jews into the Soviet modernisation programme. First, the already high percentage of urbanised Jews climbed even higher. Second, Jews began to migrate from the traditional small market towns (the *shtetlakh*) to the larger cities.[14] Third, after the abrogation of the Pale there was a sizeable drift of Jews eastwards, with some 400,000 having moved towards the interior by 1939.[15]

These demographic and spatial trends were enhanced by the Second World War and its after-effects. Centres of traditional Jewish life to the West were the worst hit by the ravages of the Holocaust. The Jewish population of the areas gained by the USSR under the Molotov–Ribbentrop pact was cut from 1.8 million to 220,000. In the 'old' Ukraine losses amounted to nearly half the pre-war population.[16] By contrast, the Jews of the interior, who were generally more assimilated, were spared the worst excesses of the war and their proportion consequently grew. Thus the social balance of Soviet Jewry swung further away from the so-called 'westerners' (*zapadniki*), who were relatively prone to ethnic particularism, and towards the more integrated and sovietised 'heartlanders'. By the late 1970s the latter accounted for nearly three-quarters of Soviet Jewry.[17] This process was geographically reflected in the further nationwide dispersal of the Jews. By 1979 just over one-third lived in the Ukraine, nearly two-fifths in the Russian Republic, 12 per cent in the southern republics, 7 per cent in Belarusia and 4 per cent in Moldavia.[18] By this stage the Jews could also be described as the first fully urban Soviet ethnic group.[19] What migration there was had become intra-urban rather than rural–urban, as the Jews came further to be concentrated in the largest cities, republican capitals and centres of higher education.[20]

These trends towards assimilation were, however, significantly offset by the upsurge of Jewish national consciousness after the Second World War. This was caused in part by the ripples sent off by the newly established State of Israel in 1948 and, in part, by the effects of the movement eastwards of the war-wearied and more traditional Jews from the West. However, there were other reasons for the growth of ethnic consciousness, the most significant being the treatment of the Jews by the Soviet state.

First there was the trauma of the 'Black Years' of 1948–1953. In the aftermath of the Second World War the specifically Jewish tragedies of the war[21] had produced a profound sense of shock among many Jews. This prompted a new literary introversion among certain Soviet Jewish writers, in sharp contrast to the official silence on the Holocaust in the mainstream media. However, the new direction in Jewish writing was soon pegged by the regime onto the hook of 'bourgeois nationalism'. As the pitch of the attacks increased, many Jewish writers and cultural activists were arrested and the institutions of Jewish cultural production that had survived the first wave of sovietisation were eliminated. This campaign to neutralise Jewish national feeling was then superseded by a separate offensive against 'rootless cosmopolitanism' which peaked early in 1949. Whereas the campaign against 'bourgeois nationalism' had targeted nationalist writings, the new campaign was aimed at the assimilated Jewish intelligentsia and decried instead its lack of 'Soviet' sentiments.[22] The Jews, it seemed, 'were to be damned for remaining separate and damned for not'.[23] The press was heavy with accusations of anti-patriotism, obsequiousness to the West and 'alienation from Russian culture'. Over 80 per cent of those attacked more than three times in the press were Jews.[24] Four years later the exposure of the 'Doctors' Plot' was apparently designed to lead to a show trial and, possibly, to the mass deportation of Jews.[25] There was reportedly mass panic among Jews in Moscow at the time. Although they were reprieved by Stalin's sudden death, these experiences were to damage irrevocably the image cultivated by the regime of unhindered Jewish assimilation.

The second factor that contributed to a renewed Jewish self-awareness was the appearance of anti-Semitism in the print media from the early 1970s. Located on the fringes of the anti-Zionism campaign that followed the Six Day War, these attacks often fused with popular misconceptions of a Jewish 'conspiracy' to cause great unease among many Soviet Jews. While the ostensible purpose of the campaign was to insulate the loyal and compliant corpus of Soviet Jewry from 'Zionist' elements at home and abroad, the effect was often the reverse. Certain writers and publicists trawled a wider net, using Zionism and Jewishness interchangeably, to the point where it was difficult to distinguish one from the other.[26] Whatever the intentions, official anti-Zionism exacerbated popular conceptions of Jews as a separate and inferior social category.

Growing discriminatory pressures in education and employment were the third and possibly the major factor behind the emerging estrangement of Soviet Jewry. From the late 1930s, Jewish repre-sentation in positions of high visibility such as politics and in the foreign and security services had been slashed. This tended to drive the Jews further in the direction of the relatively secluded backwaters of academic research and the professions. In 1959, the proportion of Jews who had completed at least half a programme of higher education was over four times that of the rest of the urban population.[27] But the Khrushchev educational boom aroused professional career expectations that his successors were hard put to satisfy, thus increasing the competition for jobs traditionally held by Jews. With quotas tacitly organised along national lines, the Jews suffered from the lack of a representative apparatus to safeguard their interests. When combined with the effects of local discrimination, this meant that the marked relative and absolute fall in Jewish students in the 1970s far exceeded the comparative decline of Jews in the age cohort from which students are chosen.[28] With nearly three-fifths of Soviet Jews loosely defined as 'a professional work force',[29] and the Jews over-represented among scientists, doctors, lawyers, journalists and the literary intelligentsia by factors of between five and ten,[30] this squeeze generated an escalation of middle-class ethnic consciousness among the Jews.

With varying degrees of influence and immediacy these three factors helped set the foundation for the demands that, seen in another light, were perhaps the most extreme form of 'exit' from the post-Stalin 'social contract' – namely the demands to leave the USSR, to emigrate.[31] The appeal of winning international trading concessions and of ridding itself of unassimilable traditional and frustrated professional elements meant that these demands unexpectedly met with official Soviet approval in the early 1970s. Over the next ten years, until the final demise of *détente*, a quarter of a million Jews left the Soviet Union, the bulk heading for Israel but a growing portion 'opting out' for the USA.

When taken in conjunction with the effects of war and of the emigration of the 1970s, the various 'modern' demographic patterns exhibited by the Jews – such as low fertility and high rates of mixed marriage – caused a dramatic fall in the Soviet Union's Jewish population: from a high of 5.2 million at the turn of the century to a frayed and ageing 1.45 million in 1989. Moreover, emigration markedly depleted the nationalist section of the community. At the other end of the spectrum stood a Jewish sub-group that continued to strive for maximum integration and to attain the means of prestige still available to the cultural and intellectual élites. In the late 1970s, Jews still had the highest per capita membership of the Communist Party and, after the Russians, they accounted for a higher absolute number of 'scientific workers' than any other national group.[32] Between the nationalist wing and the still successful portion of super-assimilated Jewry stood the so-called 'silent majority' who lowered their sights and adapted to conditions as best they could.

# GORBACHEV AND THE JEWS

In the course of the 1970s the rebirth of a Jewish national movement and the associated phenomena of Jewish dissidence and emigration had attracted much media attention in the West. Under Gorbachev, this focus of overseas concern was soon overshadowed by wider developments. By September 1987 all the veteran Prisoners of Zion, Anatolyi Sharanskii and Iosif Begun among them, had been released, and most had soon left for Israel. The upsurge of national feeling in the Trans-Caucasus, the Baltic republics and elsewhere gradually eclipsed the Jewish issue from the view of mainstream international politics. Domestically, the Jews did not command a high priority on the official political agenda. Indeed, it was difficult to speak with confidence of a specific government policy towards the Jews.

Nevertheless, Soviet Jewry continued to capture attention disproportionate to their numbers. This was, first, because emigration and cultural rights remained a live issue for international Jewry. Although less adversarial than before, Jewish and human rights lobbies abroad continued to bring pressure to bear either on their own governments or directly on the Soviet regime.[33] The other reason for the continued attention bestowed on Soviet Jewry was the exceptionally high cultural and socio-economic profile of the Jews within the USSR. Despite the discrimination of the 1970s, the Jews were still very strongly represented in professional and intelligentsia positions. This was especially so in Leningrad and Moscow where, after the Russians, they constituted the largest nationality.[34] Furthermore, as it had in other periods of transition and uncertainty in Russia, anti-Semitism re-emerged under Gorbachev as an issue of great political resonance in wider internal debates.[35]

## Glasnost' and anti-Semitism

The restoration of a Jewish presence in the media can be regarded as one of the major achievements of glasnost'. After years of submitting to the exclusive dogma of assimilationism, whereby Jewishness was depicted as incidental and Jewish achievements and history were belittled, there was a notable growth in the press of Jewish themes and – where Russian-sounding pseudonyms had been used before – of Jewish names. Following five decades of silence or distortion, the 'Jewish Question' resurfaced as an issue of importance in Soviet public affairs.[36]

Although the emergence of the 'Jewish question' was undoubtedly connected with the general opening of the public sphere, it was also prompted by two more specific political currents. The first of these related to the growth of the anti-Semitic informal associations. The most noteworthy of these groups, Pamyat', was thrown into prominence in December 1985 after the reading at a Pamyat' meeting of the classic anti-Semitic text, 'The Protocols of the Elders of Zion'. Openly priding itself in affinities with various anti-Jewish movements of the turn of the century, Pamyat' peddled stories of a 'Jewish world conspiracy' and proceeded to focus on a 'Zionist–Masonic plot' as the single cause of the Soviet Union's most pressing difficulties.[37] Despite various ructions, in the spring of 1987 the radical wing of the organisation was found sufficiently disturbing to arouse criticism in the official press.[38] At first rather muted, the attacks were stepped up after the publicity given Pamyat' through the meeting of its leaders with Boris Yeltsin on 6 May 1987. For over two months a flurry of leading newspaper articles condemned the organisation and its links with anti-Semitism in terms unseen in the Soviet Union for decades.[39] The severity of this reaction to Pamyat' was prompted by the spread of its message through branch and sister organisations in other cities, and by an anxiety that these ideas might strike a vein of 'social anti-Semitism' previously nourished by the official anti-Zionist campaigns of the 1970s.[40] These campaigns, promoted in high-circulation books and journals, had stressed the conspiratorial form and global intention of international Zionism in a way that now appeared uncomfortably familiar.[41] In order to discredit this line a number of authoritative articles strove, from early 1987, to reassert the orthodox critique of Zionism as a form of bourgeois Jewish nationalism and to return to the classical position that Zionism was a junior and not a senior partner in international imperialism.[42]

Pamyat's extreme anti-Semitism had a complex relationship with a second specific factor that helped thrust anti-Semitism into the limelight: the surrogate role played by anti-Semitism in mainstream debates over politics and history.[43] Initially triggered by a literary controversy in 1986, the anti-Semitic aspects of the debate became increasingly widespread.[44] The most controversial example was the publication of Nina Andreyeva's infamous letter-cum-article in *Sovetskaya Rossiya* on 13 March 1988. Widely considered a manifesto for the conservative opposition to *perestroika*, the article simmered with anti-Semitic innuendo.[45] It surreptitiously tied Soviet Jewish writers to overseas allegiances, scathingly linked 'refusenikism' with 'cosmopolitanism', and adopted plainly Stalinist categories such as the 'counter-revolutionary nations' with barely concealed anti-Jewish intent.[46] Although foiled by the comprehensive retort in Pravda three weeks later, the anti-Semitic leanings of the Andreeva 'counter-offensive' continued to find echoes in the conservative press.[47] A favoured tactic was to divert opprobrium away from Stalin and the economic and political structures shaped under him, and onto Jewish figures, whose original names were on occasion 'unmasked'.[48]

Andreeva's reference to the 'cosmopolitan tendency' and, implicitly, to the attacks of the late Stalin period on the assimilated Jewish intelligentsia, ran counter to the official exoneration of this group that was simultaneously taking place. In particular, Gorbachev's confirmation in November 1987 that the 'Doctors' plot' had been a fabrication gave the most authoritative of signals to a number of personal recollections of the case that appeared the following year.[49] Equally, after many years of petitioning, a front page announcement in *Pravda* on 27 January 1989 finally publicised both the rehabilitation of the Jewish Anti-Fascist Committee (which had been dissolved in the 'Black Years') and the posthumous restoration of eight of their number to Communist Party membership.[50]

These officially sanctioned openings led to initiatives in culture and the arts which extended well beyond what might be conceived of as 'expedient' to the state. Vassily Grossman's long suppressed novel *Zhizn' i Sud'ba*, which was serialised in *Oktyabr'* in early 1988, used anti-Semitism as a thread that ran through the war and post-war periods and through which the Soviet and Nazi systems were implicitly compared.[51] Other direct accounts of the Jewish Holocaust and of anti-Semitism and anti-Jewish discrimination within the Soviet framework followed suit.[52]

The breakdown of Soviet ideology and the relaxation of political controls that occurred from 1989 onwards had two effects on the role of anti-Semitism in public affairs. First, the attempts to contain discussions of Zionism and anti-Semitism within the framework of Marxism-Leninism ceased to have any force. The Aesopian terms in which earlier debates had been conducted were cast aside and, as the traditional system of censorship disintegrated, both attackers and defenders of Soviet Jewry were allowed to become progressively more candid.[53] Second, as the need to couch the debate over anti-Semitism in literary and historical terms declined, the debate was allowed to open up in the newly expanding sphere of electoral politics. The campaign surrounding the elections to the Russian Congress in March 1990, for example, provided an opportunity for various 'patriotic' groupings to voice their demands under a single Russian nationalist banner. The electoral coalition provided a vehicle for a range of anti-Semitic elements in the nationalist camp to air their views. On 18 February a large rally in Moscow called to criticise Gorbachev's leadership attracted a number of anti-Jewish speeches. Two weeks later, on the eve of the elections, a letter signed by 74 leading Russian writers and supporters of the patriotic bloc denounced the 'thoughtless idealisation of Zionism' that, in their view, was pervading official circles.[54] In fact, the patriotic platform fared poorly at the elections. Nor was it the case that all, or even a majority of, its adherents were anti-Semites. Nevertheless, the bloc and the Russian Communist Party formed that summer were now providing political structures through which 'unofficial' anti-Semitism could express itself with an appeal much wider than ever commanded by Pamyat'. Thus the decline of official anti-Semitism was soon overtaken by unofficial variants. With the politicisation of Soviet society its Jewish population became, for the first time in many years, less apprehensive about how it was treated by the state than about how it was viewed by society.[55]

### Jewish issues and organisations

The elevation of the the 'Jewish question' in public affairs should be separated from the various demands that arose from the Jewish community itself. The articulation and, increasingly, the realisation of these demands under Gorbachev indicated that Jews were becoming better able to define their culture in relative autonomy from the state. It was also a reflection of the heterogeneity of Soviet Jewry that these demands could often be diverse and sometimes even contradictory.

One issue under Gorbachev that won broad support within the Jewish movement as a whole was remembrance of the Jewish past. Originally conducted in private appartments, meetings organised to this end gradually moved out into the open. On 26 April 1987 the two largest gatherings of Jews in many years were held in Leningrad and Moscow in commemoration of Jewish resistance during the war.[56] A similar meeting the following year was the first to gain official permission, and from then on a steady stream of demonstrations and commemorative meetings were held, museums opened, study courses introduced and campaigns to erect Jewish national monuments mounted.[57]

The removal of restrictions on the practice of Judaism – the Jewish religion – was a second issue on which Jewish groups campaigned with some success under Gorbachev. Early triumphs included the establishment of a Jewish seminary in Leningrad and the transfer of 10,000 Jewish religious texts to the Soviet Union in the summer of 1988. The following September food supplies were shipped in from abroad for the Holy Days and limited kosher facilities were opened in Moscow.[58] Although most estimates put the number of religious believers at less than five per cent of the Jewish population, the Holy Days reportedly saw increasing throngs at the synagogues.[59] The self-organisation of religious life was further facilitated with the adoption of a new all-Union law on religion in October 1990. This afforded religious organisations the freedom to worship outside prescribed locations, the right to own property and the liberty to receive, produce and disseminate religious articles and literature.[60]

A third issue was that of language. More than the first two, this issue from the very beginning aroused tensions within the Jewish community itself. Early steps endorsed by the regime had included the opening of Yiddish theatres, the expansion of teaching in Yiddish and the relaxation of controls over the Yiddish press institutions.[61] This pleased the older traditional section of Soviet Jewry in which Yiddish was still widely spoken. However, while such developments may have amended the long-term relative underproduction of materials in Yiddish, the stress on Yiddish was challenged by some of the nationalist and Zionist groups, who tended to associate Yiddish with the antiquated culture of the 19th century and to posit Hebrew instead as the linguistic basis of the Jewish renaissance.[62] It was a measure of the linguistic acculturation of the Jews that there was also a third strand, of those who preferred that resources be funnelled into the Russian language, since Russian had become the mother tongue of the vast majority of Soviet Jews.[63]

The reappraisal at the 19th Party Conference in June 1988 of cultural policy towards the non-indigenous nationalities provided an important spur to Jewish cultural demands.[64] One significant step was the approval bestowed on 'seats of national culture' for the non-indigenous nationalities. This gave legitimacy to the Jewish clubs and societies that had already formed in Moscow, Minsk, Tashkent, Lvov, Kiev and the Baltic capitals.[65] Following the Conference the showpiece Solomon Mikhoels Centre was opened in Moscow in February 1989, while other societies were inaugurated as far afield as Tbilisi and Krasnoiarsk.[66] By the autumn of 1989 there were over two hundred Jewish clubs and societies in the USSR. A second important measure of the subsequent growth of Jewish cultural life was the appearance of over fifty Jewish periodical publications across the USSR by the summer of 1990.[67]

The need to organise and represent the active element of Soviet Jewry soon gave rise to attempts to establish republican and all-Union structures. In early December 1989 the Ukrainian Cultural Fund set up a republic-wide Society for Jewish Culture to coordinate the activities of the Jewish organisations that had appeared in 25 Ukrainian towns over the previous year.[68] Later that month on 18–21 December, the Founding Congress of Jewish Organisations and Committees in the USSR was held at the Cinema Centre in Moscow. Attended by 414 delegates from 198 Jewish organisations, the Congress claimed to span the active element of Soviet Jewry.[69] For the first time, the Congress afforded provincial Jewish organisations a national and international audience. Furthermore, the Congress voted in a committee (*vaad*) which it was hoped might be able to represent the needs and wishes of nationally minded Jews, thus overshadowing the puppet committees operated by the state and the numerous international organisations that had earlier stood on behalf of Soviet Jewry. Nevertheless, representatives at the Congress of some of the Jewish organisations from the non-Russian republics distanced themselves from too close an identification with an organisation that was still constituted on a Soviet territorial basis. Other, Zionist groups, which had attended the opening ceremony, later walked out in protest at the illusion, as they saw it, maintained by the Congress that the prospect of a normal Jewish life in the Soviet Union was still possible.[70]

## Emigration

The most controversial and internationally the best known of the issues for which Soviet Jews campaigned was that of emigration. After reaching a high point of 51,000 in 1979, the number of Jews leaving the USSR slumped as dramatically as it had grown ten years earlier, falling to one to two thousand per annum in the mid-1980s. It seemed as if the maverick phenomenon had come to an end. Four years into the Gorbachev administration, however, in an improved international climate, the pace of Jewish emigration picked up again, soaring from 914 in 1986 to 8,155 in 1987, 18,961 in 1988 and 72,500 in 1989.[71] The choice of destination of the migrants seemed to point to the prime motivation behind the exodus. Whereas in the 1970s two-thirds had ended up in Israel, the new wave of the late 1980s was characterised by a marked preference for the United States. Of the 1989 total, 57,800, or 80 per cent, preferred the USA over Israel.[72] It seemed as if the central considerations at play were not cultural or religious but economic. Emigration provided an outlet for a mass of educated urban middle class Jews who, with the weight of past Soviet discrimination in mind, feared above all for their careers and for those of their children.

On 1 October 1989 the US administration introduced new rules for processing visas and set a ceiling of 50,000 on the number of Soviet refugees it was willing to admit in a year. As a result of the complex new procedures the number of Jewish immigrants to the USA fell well below the ceiling, from 57,800 in 1989 to 6,500 in 1990. But the increasingly grim background of political instability, economic upheaval and ethnic strife continued to produce a strong impetus for many Jews to leave. Jewish fears were not eased by the precedent of civil interethnic violence in Baku in January 1990 and by reports in May of a pogrom against Armenians and Jews in Andizhan, Uzbekistan.[73] Despite the drop in numbers leaving for the USA, the rate of overall emigration continued to grow, with 201,300 Jews leaving the USSR in 1990, the overwhelming majority – 181,800 – now heading for Israel.[74] That Jews continued to leave on such a large scale suggested that their chief motive was now, in the words of one commentator, less 'to go to the USA' than 'to get out of the USSR'.[75]

A geographical analysis of emigration between 1989 and 1991 suggests that the republics with the highest proportional rate of Jewish emigration were also those, such as Azerbaijan, Uzbekistan and Moldavia, that were in greatest danger of ethnic violence. The heartland Jewish populations of Russia and Ukraine were less affected. While these two republics accounted for nearly 72 per cent of the Soviet

Jewish population in the 1989 census, they provided only 57 per cent of Jewish emigration over the following two years. While the Jewish population of Tashkent had fallen by a quarter, that of Kishinev by nearly a third and that of Baku by almost a half by the beginning of 1991, the Jewish population of Moscow had declined by less than a tenth.[76]

## JEWS IN THE SUCCESSOR STATES

Since the dissolution of the Soviet Union, emigration has continued to be the most pressing issue affecting the Jews. Yet the rise in emigration that was expected with the collapse of the Soviet state has not occurred. From a peak of over 30,000 a month at the beginning of 1991, the volume of emigrants dropped to an average of 5,000 a month a year later and has remained at that level since. Accordingly, the annual rate of emigration to Israel from the successor states fell from 148,000 in 1991 to 64,000 in 1992 and 63,500 in 1993.[77] The most important reason for this decline has been the lower attractiveness of Israel as a possible destination, a development brought about by the Gulf War and by the poor housing provisions and low job prospects in Israel.[78] The fall in numbers leaving for Israel has been partly compensated for by an increase in movement to other destinations. As it became clearer how to operate the new immigration procedures, the number of immigrants to the USA grew from a low of 5,000 in 1990 to 47,000 from October 1991 to October 1992; similarly, the number of Jews entering Germany quadrupled between 1991 and 1992.[79]

This stabilisation in the total levels of emigration masked an increasing diversity between the successor states as the geopolitical structures that had unified them began to crumble. The exodus of Jews from the major zones of instability now began to coincide with a general outflow of Russians and other non-titular nationals. In central Asia the areas worst affected by violent religious conflict, such as Tajikistan, and those suffering increasing ethnic discrimination, such as Uzbekistan, have lost up to 80 per cent of their Jews since the late 1980s.[80] In the Caucasus, the conflict with Armenia and the resurgence of Islam has driven out almost half of Azerbaijan's Jews since 1988.[81] Another war-ravaged area in the Caucasus, Georgia, lost over a quarter of its Jewish population in the space of the first nine months of 1993.[82] Further, the long-standing community of mountain Jews of the North Caucasus, whose customs and traditions have been preserved by the harsh climate and topography since the destruction of the first temple in 722 BC, is finally caving in. Over half of the estimated 50,000 Jews have left for Israel and the exodus is continuing at a rate of 700 a month.[83] As local conflicts intensified, the stream of Jewish emigration from the Caucasus and central Asia quadrupled between 1992 and 1993. Although less than a sixth of the Jewish population of the former Soviet Union lived in these areas, over half of the migrants from the successor states have come from them.[84]

The breakdown of all-Union structures has also produced other contrasting effects, in some cases inverting patterns from the *perestroika* period. Nowhere has this been more evident than in the Baltic states. Under Gorbachev, the flowering of a Jewish movement in the Baltic republics had occurred simultaneously with the growth of the Baltic popular fronts. The Baltic fronts alleged that anti-Semitism was propagated from Moscow and vowed support for their Jewish communities.[85] Yet relations between the re-emergent Baltic states and their Jewish inhabitants have come under increasing strain since the collapse of the Union. One reason is that in the recovery of their past, the part of the Baltic peoples in the wartime destruction of local Jewry has gradually been revealed. Any attempts to expose complicity in anti-Jewish atrocities have run into incomprehension, while the destruction of local Jewry has received scant attention in new school textbooks.[86] This historical amnesia has been complemented by some instances of active anti-Semitism in contemporary Baltic public life.[87]

The Jews in the Baltics have also suffered as an indirect result of the Baltic governments' discriminatory policies towards their Russian minorities (see chapters nine and twenty-five). The Nazi liquidation of Jews in these territories was so comprehensive that the majority of the present Jewish population in the Baltic states consists of migrants brought in by Stalin and his successors from the Soviet heartlands in order to ensure Soviet hegemony over the new areas. Given the circumstances under which they arrived in these areas – after the Second World War, under the auspices of a Soviet transfer programme – these Jews are now being treated by the Baltic states as alien 'Russians'. Under the new citizenship laws, they have been denied basic rights of citizenship. Thus most of Estonia's 5,000 Jews and two-thirds of Latvia's 17,000 Jews could not vote in the national elections of 1992. In the face of such discrimination, more and more Jews in these areas are apparently considering emigration.[88]

Post-Soviet developments in Ukraine have taken a very different course from those in the Baltic states. Despite, and in some respects because of, a past history of Jewish-Ukrainian animosity, Ukrainian leaders have gone out of their way to encourage mutual understanding between the two peoples. At its constitutive congress in 1990 the Ukrainian People's Front (*Rukh*) adopted a document 'Against Anti-Semitism' and shortly afterwards organised a rally in Kiev on the same theme.[89] Since the declaration of Ukrainian independence Ukrainian officials have put diplomatic relations with Israel on a strong footing by co-sponsoring Israel's petition to the UN to revoke the resolution equating Zionism with racism. Ukrainian writers have also faced Ukrainian anti-Semitism head-on with works on Semen Petliura and the civil war pogroms. The fiftieth anniversary of the Babi-Yar massacre in October 1991 was widely commemorated in the press and the Ukrainian president, Leonid Kravchuk, attending the ceremony, spoke of 'asking forgiveness from the Jewish people in relation to whom so much injustice was perpetrated in our history'.[90] Similarly, new writings in Ukrainian journals have given expression to what unites the Jewish and Ukrainian peoples, such as their joint struggles against the Poles, and have shed light on repressed Ukrainian Jewish political and cultural figures. For the first time, Ukrainian readers have been acquainted with Jewish literature and with the contribution of Jews to Ukrainian culture.[91] Yiddish language programmes have been broadcast on television and there has been a renewal of Jewish theatre.[92] On the educational and religious fronts a Jewish school with 520 students and two synagogues are now operating in Kiev, and a synagogue has been reopened in Lvov after 27 years of closure.[93] By the autumn of 1992 over 120 Jewish religious, secular, cultural and youth organisations were functioning in the country.[94] According to two commentators, the conditions for 'the development of Jewish national–cultural activity in Ukraine ... are perhaps the most favourable since Jews first came to live in the Ukraine'.[95] A new organisational aspect of the renaissance of Jewish life in the country was marked by the First Jewish Congress of the Ukraine, held in October 1992. The congress was addressed by leading Jewish and Ukrainian figures and drew representatives from over seventy towns.[96]

None the less, a community as large and dynamic as Ukrainian Jewry inevitably has its share of conflicts and divisions. These were certainly present at the Congress.[97] Moreover, despite encouraging noises from the Ukrainian state it has had great difficulty in fulfilling pledges of economic assistance to ethnic groups such as the Jews. Because of the dire economic situation in Ukraine, Jewish groups have indeed been loath to press the state for financial assistance.

Yet notwithstanding the internal divisions, the poverty of public institutions and the fact that almost a quarter of a million Jews have left Ukraine since 1988, Jewish culture and Jewish institutions in Ukraine have proved sufficiently robust to support the Jewish community. Emigration has fallen steadily since reaching a peak in the middle of 1992.[98] Despite its lack of resources, Ukrainian state has so far adopted a non-national definition of citizenship. At present the state remains keen to ensure that all citizens of Ukraine should enjoy full rights, regardless of ethnic origin, religion or race. The Jews of Ukraine are thus favourably placed in comparison with those of the Baltic states.

In Russia too, home to almost two-fifths of the CIS's Jews, the state has taken relatively enlightened steps in easing discrimination and prejudice. Thus a number of government-endorsed TV programmes have continued to counter the massive popular ignorance of Jewish and Israeli history, while the Russian government has paid teachers' salaries, bought textbooks and issued standard student subsidies in support of teaching of the core curriculum at new Jewish schools in Moscow.[99] There is now greater cooperation, too, between the state and Jewish organisations in settling internal conflicts. For example the Russian Jewish Council, the *vaad*, intervened on behalf of a Jewish community in the North Caucasus when the local authorities refused to return a synagogue to them. With help from Vice-president Rutskoi, control of the synagogue was eventually restored. Equally, a conflict between a group of orthodox Jews and the Lenin Library over possession of a collection of manuscripts was mediated with the help of the *vaad*.[100]

As the state's role in shaping cultural and educational institutions has subsided, a greater part of the burden of organising Jewish interests has fallen on independent Jewish groups. Jewish press institutions have, with overseas aid, modernised and expanded their geographical distribution and are playing a key role in providing the Jewish community with elementary knowledge on Judaism and Israel. The *Jewish Herald*, Russia's largest Jewish paper, now serves 188 communities with a total circulation of 100,000.[101] As the state's subsidies to virtually all cultural institutions have been drastically reduced or withdrawn, established Jewish enterprises from the Soviet era have had to compete on the open market for consumer support. Some, such as *Sovietish Heymland*, have been unable to meet mounting costs and have been forced to close.[102] Now that the first rush of cultural freedom has lost its novelty value there is a need, in the words of one Jewish communal leader, 'to organize not just events, but quality events; not just to open schools, but to have professionally trained teachers'.[103] With the growth of local autonomous bodies there is also greater competition for funds from Western Jewish organisations, some of which have offices across the CIS.[104]

The conditions that have promoted greater Jewish cultural autonomy in Russia, such as less state interference in public life and the freer flow of information, have also opened up the way for more visible and hostile forms of anti-Semitism. As of mid-1992 there were an estimated 120 anti-Semitic organisations and 56 journals and papers printing anti-Jewish material in Russia.[105] To many Russians who feel betrayed and used by the West, and to others for whom the loss of the Union was a national disaster, nationalism has provided an attractive set of concepts to fill the ideological vaccuum left by the collapse of communism. This environment has provided fertile soil for the new brand of 'grassroots anti-Semitism' which has gradually come to replace the official variants of earlier periods. Some of the uglier manifestations of this phenomenon are the rows of stalls outside the Lenin Museum in Moscow and the Gostinyi Dvor in St Petersburg manned by black-uniformed youths: earlier cries of the Gorbachev period such as 'Down with persons of Zionist nationality!' have reportedly given way to yells of 'Death to the Jews!'. One of the local anti-Semitic papers, *Narodnoe Delo*, has reprinted articles by the Nazi ideologist Alfred Rozenberg and commented: 'So long as the majority of people in our leadership are Jews the gentiles will continue to starve, to fight among themselves, to take to drink and to die out'.[106] At the May Day demonstrations in 1993, which saw the most violent disturbances in the capital since the coup, many of the banners and placards linked current problems to 'Jewish infidels'. Following the event Moscow's only *matso*-making factory suffered extensive damage in a blaze. Soon after, windows were broken and swastikas daubed in broad daylight on Moscow's central synagogue on Arkhipov street.[107] After the dissolution of parliament in September posters in the vicinity depicted Yeltsin as a pig driven by a Jew wielding a whip, and government officials were referred to as 'Zhidy' (Yids).[108]

A further distressing development has been the involvement of the Russian Orthodox church in anti-Semitic incidents. Two Orthodox clerics took part in an attack by Pamyat' supporters on the offices of the liberal newspaper *Moskovskii Komsomolets*;[109] and Metropolitan Johan of St Petersburg, the second most senior clergyman in the Russian Orthodox Church, suggested in the nationalist paper *Sovetskaia Rossiia* that the notorious forgery 'The Protocols of the Elders of Zion' was authentic, and coupled excerpts from the 'protocols' with a description of the serious economic situation in Russia.[110]

But to say that anti-Semitism has become more open in Russia is not necessarily to imply that it has become stronger. For one thing, the forces ranged against anti-Semitism are more powerful than they were under Gorbachev. The two church officials who participated in the Pamyat' attack were severely reprimanded by their superiors, and Metropolitan Johan of St Petersburg was dismissed from his post and replaced by Metropolitan Kyrill, described by the Chief Rabbi of Moscow as a 'friend to the Jews'.[111] Furthermore, for the first time the state machinery has been used to combat the more inflammatory materials that have come out in print. A landmark libel case against the patriotic journal *Nash Sovremmenik* has been followed by 13 criminal cases against racist literature.[112] There have been arrests of Neo-Nazis charged with possessing arms and inciting racial hatred.[113] Official bodies such as the Moscow City Soviet have convened special sessions to discuss ways of tackling anti-Semitism, and Yeltsin himself has gone public with open denunciations of the phenomenon.[114] The mainstream press has continued to print sober analyses of modern Russian anti-Semitism as well as detailed historical accounts of anti-Jewish persecution earlier this century.

In St Petersburg, *Bar'er*, the first specialist anti-fascist journal in the country has been launched.[115]

It is difficult to estimate with confidence the scale of popular support behind the anti-Semitic groups. However, two polls conducted in ten of the successor states in 1990 and 1992 suggest lower levels of intolerance towards the Jews than many had feared. Only a small minority were aggressively hostile towards the Jews. Less than a tenth of those polled blamed the Jews for present difficulties, believed in Jewish 'conspiracies' or felt that their country would be better off without Jews. Most respondents expressed praise for the Jews as workers and a healthy majority opposed discrimination against Jews at the workplace or at centres of higher education.[116]

Indeed, there are some signs that nationalist leaders have recognised the limited mileage to be gained from the Jewish question. In October 1992 the patriotic paper *Sovetsaia Rossiia* called for a truce between 'Russians' and 'Jews' and publicised an appeal from the arch-nationalist Viktor Anpilov for fellow demonstrators to cease carrying anti-Semitic slogans. Anpilov's actions indicated a general concern that anti-Semitism was detrimental to the conservative cause.[117] Even Vladimir Zhirinovsky, whose Liberal Democratic Party fared so well in the December 1993 elections to the state Duma, has on more than one occasion expressed sympathy for the Jews' 'historical tragedy'.[118] Indeed, it has been suggested that one of the reasons for Zhirinovsky's success was that, in contrast to previous patriotic electoral campaigns, he managed successfully to marginalise the 'Jewish question'.[119] The evidence from polls seems to bear out the opinion of some Russian Jewish communal leaders that most Russians are indifferent to the Jews and to Jewish issues.[120] Indeed, despite the existence of fanatical anti-Semitic groups, in the largest Russian cities the main recent problems of racism have been towards the so-called *chernye* (the 'blacks' – Azeris, Chechens, Gypsies, Georgians and Armenians) who are accused of running the mafia, fuelling inflation and causing the Russian refugee problem.

## CONCLUSION

Since 1988 over half a million Jews have left the territories of the former Soviet Union. This latest emigration has taken with it many of the youngest and most vital elements of the Jewish community. Further, it has underlined the limits of Jewish 'integration' in Russia and the other successor states. The much-vaunted 'assimilation' the Soviet regime claimed to have achieved in the 1930s was largely the work of state-coerced processes and state-imposed roles and identities. When the state that supported these structures collapsed a condition of flux, best exemplified by the migrations, took over. As with their early twentieth century forbears, for many Jews of the successor states the prime existential question has become a geographical one: whether to stay put or to leave, be it for Israel, for the United States, for Germany, or even from the war-torn peripheral states for Russia.

If the earlier generation of migrants in the 1970s had been inspired primarily by political, religious or cultural motives, this later wave has been moved more by a mix of economic self-interest and panic. The areas worst affected have been those ravaged by ethnic conflict and violence. But even in the heartland, collective family memories of pogroms, anti-cosmopolitan campaigns and discrimination have not been easily laid to rest. Many parents have chosen to meet the hardships of emigration in exchange for brighter prospects for their children.[121]

In Russia at least, the combination of economic upheaval and the loss of national prestige (brought about by the collapse of empire) that has traditionally fostered anti-Semitism is again present. Now that the state-sponsored forms of anti-Semitism have vanished, they have come to be replaced by a new brand of grassroots or social anti-Semitism. For some nationally minded Russians, Jewish emigration represents the collective betrayal of Russia – abandoning the country at the time of greatest need. On the part of the Jews, the fear of anti-Jewish violence and the lack of faith that the state could protect them in times of trouble has left many with a deep sense of foreboding.

The Jewish communities of some of the peripheral states are now in a condition of advanced decay, and some may well be on the road to extinction. Nevertheless, when taken together the Jewish populations of the three central Slavic states – Russia, Belarus and Ukraine – still form the third-largest Jewish community in the world. Traditional estimates of the Jewish population of these areas have focused on the declared nationality of individuals in official statistics. But as state definitions of nationality carry less weight and official discrimination declines, the need of individual Jews to conceal their Jewish origins diminishes. Estimates of the Jewish populations of the central Slavic areas have, consequently, been revised upwards. According to some estimates, the 'enlarged' Jewish population of these areas – inclusive of persons of mixed parentage – may still be in excess of two million.[122] Although efforts to establish Jewish communal structures on a Soviet territorial basis were delivered a severe blow with the death of the USSR, there are now autonomous Jewish cultural, religious and political bodies to service the nationally minded sections of the population who wish to remain. In the core Slavic states the sheer size of the Jewish population and the extent of existing national–cultural bodies are still arguably, beyond the critical mass necessary to sustain a national future for the Jews. Within the new environment, the Jews who wish to stay are better able to define their culture and to develop new occupations and lines of work. For these Jews at least, there are tentative foundations for speaking of the emergence of an autonomous Jewish cultural life.

## ACKNOWLEDGEMENTS

I would like to thank Yaacov Ro'i for his useful comments on an earlier draft of this chapter, and Howard Spier and the staff at the Institute of Jewish Affairs in London for their assistance in researching it. Inna Berger of the Radio Liberty Institute in Munich provided invaluable help in revising the text for the second edition. The author is solely responsible for the views expressed.

## NOTES

1.  For more on Lenin's predictions of ethnic integration, see Walker Connor, *The Marxist Question in Leninist Theory and Strategy* (Princeton, NJ: Princeton University Press, 1984), pp. 37, 42.
2.  L. Greenberg, *The Jews in Russia*, (New Haven, CT: Yale University Press, 1965), 1, chapter 12; Z. Y. Gitelman, *Jewish Nationality and Soviet Politics* (Princeton, NJ: Princeton University Press, 1972), pp. 19–22.
3.  For an excellent discussion of this question, see H. Rogger, *Jewish Policies and Right-Wing Politics in Imperial Russia* (London: Macmillan, 1986), esp. chapters 1, 2 and 4.
4.  Ibid., pp. 25. 106.
5.  For selected translations of these provisions, see P. R. Mendes-Flohr and J. Reinharz, *The Jew in the Modern World* (Oxford: Oxford University Press, 1980), pp. 303–309.
6.  For the text of the Bund's all-important resolutions at its fourth convention, and of Lenin's response to them, refer to Ibid, pp. 340–1, 344–6.
7.  Text in Ibid., p. 349.
8.  Z. Y. Gitelman, *op. cit.*, chapters 4 and 5; and L. Kochan, ed., *The Jews in Soviet Russia since 1917*, 3rd edn (Oxford: Oxford University Press, 1978), esp. chapters 6 and 8.
9.  Gitelman, *op. cit.*, chapters 3ff.
10. See e.g. J. V. Stalin, 'Marxism and the National Question', in Stalin, *Works*, vol. 2 (1907–1913) (London: Lawrence and Wishart, 1953), pp. 307, 312–313, 344–345.
11. Gitelman, *op. cit.*, pp. 472–475.
12. A. Nove and J. A. Newth, 'The Jewish Population: Demographic Trends and Occupational Patterns', in L. Kochan, *op. cit.*, p. 138.
13. M. Altshuler, *Soviet Jewry Since the Second World War* (Westport: Greenwood Press, 1987), pp. 9–11.
14. Altshuler, *op. cit.*, pp. 5–6 and Gitelman, *op. cit.*, p. 17.

15. At a rate of an estimated 20,000 per annum from 1923 to 1926, and 30,000 per annum between 1926 and 1939. See A. Nove and J. A. Newth, *op. cit.*, pp. 139 and 143. By 1939, 37 per cent of Soviet Jewry lived outside the former Pale (Altshuler, *op. cit.*, p. 5).

16. Ibid., pp. 147–149.

17. See T. Friedgut, 'Soviet Jewry: the Silent Majority', *Soviet Jewish Affairs* (henceforth *SJA*), 10, No. 2 (Summer 1980), p. 5.

18. Altshuler, *op. cit.*, p. 62. This is to be compared with the figures for 1939: 50.8 per cent in the Ukraine, 31.4 per cent in the RSFSR, 5 per cent in the southern republics, and 12.4 per cent in Belorussia (B. Pinkus, *The Soviet Government and the Jews 1948–1967* (Cambridge: Cambridge University Press, 1984), pp. 26–27.

19. Altshuler, *op. cit.*, p. 229. According to the censuses, 87 per cent of Jews were urban dwellers in 1939, 95.3 per cent in 1959, 97.9 per cent in 1970 and 98.5 per cent in 1979 (Ibid., p. 65; and Pinkus, *op. cit.*, p. 28).

20. Ibid., pp. 66, 71 and 230.

21. While the tragedies of the Second World War were far from confined to the Jews, the particularity and purpose with which the Jews were singled out by the Nazis is reflected in the fact that in Soviet territories captured by the Nazis the proportionate losses inflicted on Jews were four times greater than those suffered by the rest of the population (Nove and Newth, *op. cit.*, p. 149).

22. Pinkus, *op. cit.*, chapter 4, esp. pp. 152 and 163.

23. Ibid., p. 5.

24. Ibid., p. 159.

25. Y. Rapoport, 'Vospominaniya o "Dele Vrachei"', *Druzhba Narodov*, No. 4 (1988), p. 225; V. Grossman, 'Vse Techet', *Oktyabr'*, No. 6 *(1989), p. 38 (translated into English as Forever Flowing* (London: Collins Harvill, 1988)); and B. Pinkus, *The Jews of the Soviet Union* (Cambridge: Cambridge University Press, 1988), p. 180.

26. V. Zaslavsky and R. J. Brym, *Soviet Jewish Emigration and Soviet Nationality Policy* (London: Macmillan 1983) pp. 20.

27. Altshuler, *op. cit.*, pp. 108 and 232.

28. Ibid., pp. 112, 118–119 and 127. See also *Human Rights and the Helsinki Accords* (London: Institute of Jewish Affairs, 1985), pp. 23–26.

29. That is, in receipt of an incomplete higher or a secondary vocational education. This is critical since, unlike full university education, the West, state education in the Soviet Union virtually guaranteed later employment in a similar field. (Altshuler, *op. cit.*, pp. 143, 152 and 233.)

30. L. Hirszowicz, 'Gorbachev's *perestroika* and the Jews', *IJA Research Report*, No. 1 (May 1987), p. 3.

31. G. Lapidus, 'State and Society: Toward the emergence of civil Society in the Soviet Union', in S. Bialer, ed., *Inside Gorbachev's Russia*, (Boulder, CO: Westview Press, 1989), pp. 127, 129.

32. Altshuler, *op. cit.*, pp. 163, 210.

33. Witness, for example, the audience granted to representatives of the World Jewish Congress by senior Soviet officials such as Foreign Minister Shevardnadze and the then Central Committee Secretaries Yakovlev and Dobrynin. (*New York Times*, 31 March 1987, p. 14;

and *BBC Summary of World Broadcasts* (henceforth *SWB*), SU/0385(i), 15 February 1989). Also see E. Litvinoff, *Insight: Soviet Jews*, July 1988, p. 8; *Concluding Document of the Vienna Meeting of the CSCE Participating States*, 17 January 1989, pp. 36–41 and *Izvestiya*, 26 January 1989, p. 4.)

34.  *Argumenty i Fakty*, No. 23, 4–10 June 1988, p. 6; *SJA* 18, No. 1, p. 15. In 1970, in Moscow, one in eight *Kandidaty* were Jews, as were one in five *Doktory Nauk* (Doctors of Science) (Altshuler, *op. cit.*, pp. 88 and 167).

35.  See e.g. S. Rogov and V. Nosenko, 'Zachem "Korrektirovat'" Lenina', *Sovetskaya Kul'tura*, 31 May 1989, p. 3.

36.  J. Wishnevsky, 'Some good news for Soviet Jews', *Radio Liberty Research Bulletin* (henceforth *RLRB*), 121/87, 23 March 1987; and 'A little more *Glasnost*', for Soviet Jews', *RLRB*, 100/88, 16 March 1988.

37.  H. Spier, Anti-Semitism Unchained, *Research Report no. 3* (London: Institute of Jewish Affairs, 1987), p. 5. See also *Sovetskaya Rossiya*, 17 July 1987, p. 3; and *Ogonek*, 23, 4–11 June 1988, pp. 6–7.

38.  A. Cherkizov, 'Demokratiya – Ne Raspushchennost', *Sovetskaya Kul'tura* 31 March 1987, p.3.

39.  See esp. articles by E. Lesoto, *Komsomolskaya Pravda*, 22 May 1987, p. 3, and A. Cherkizov, *Sovetskaya Kul'tura*, 18 June 1987, p. 3. See also the pieces in *Ogonek* (No. 21, 23–30 May 1987), *Izvestiya* (3 June 1987) and *Vechernaya Moskva* (15 June 1987). Articles on popular anti-Semitism then became a regular feature of media coverage of domestic affairs. See e.g. *Sovetskaya Kul'tura*, 3 October 1987, p. 6; *Komsomolskaya Pravda*, 19 December 1987, p. 3; and *Izvestiya*, 27 February 1988, p. 5. For two articles that attempted to present a positive, less extreme, side to Pamyat' see *Sovetskaya Rossiya*, 31 January 1988, p. 4; and *Pravda*, 1 February 1988, p. 4.

40.  For example, Pamyat' and 'Patriot' in Leningrad, 'Otechestvo' in Sverdlovsk, 'Soboryanie' in Irkutsk, and a sizeable branch of Pamyat' in Novosibirsk (see *Sovetskaya Kul'tura*, 18 April, pp. 3–4, and 18 June 1987, p. 32; Ogonek, No. 9, 26 February–5 March 1989, pp. 28–31; *Literaturnaya Gazeta*, 5 July 1989, p. 11). Although some publications tried to emphasise the *pre*-Soviet roots of Pamyat' (e.g. *Izvestiya*, 3 June 1987, p. 3 and *Komsomolskaya Pravda*, 19 December 1987, p. 3) there was also an increasing willingness to concede the recent *Soviet* sources of contemporary anti-Semitism (e.g. *Sovetskaya Kul'tura*, 9 February 1989, p. 6; and see the interview with V. I. Tumarkin of the Central Committee apparatus in *Jews and Jewish Topics in Soviet and East European Publications*, Centre for Research and Documentation of East European Jewry at the Hebrew University, 7 (Summer 1988), p. 71).

41.  Much of this material was published under the auspices of the Molodaya Gvardiya publishing house in Moscow. Its authors included Yuri Ivanov (1969), Lev Korneev (1982), Vladimir Begun (1974, 1977 and 1979), Valery Emelyanov (1977) and Evgeni Evseev (1978). The most renowned of the journals were *Molodaya Gvardiya*, *Moskvá* and Safronov's *Ogonek* before its volte-face under the new editorship of Vitalyi Korotich in 1986.

42. For example Dadiani *et al.*, 'O Nekotorykh Voprosakh . . .', *Voprosy Istorii KPSS*, No. 1 (January 1987), pp. 74–77.

43. The strict separation of Pamyat' from the nationalist writers proposed by some commentators (e.g. *Pravda*, 1 February 1988, p. 4) was contested by others (e.g. *Izvestiya*, 27 February 1988, p. 5; and see V. Rasputin, *Nash Sovremennik*, No. 1 (1988), pp. 169–172).

44. See V. Astaf'ev, 'Pechal'nyi Detektiv', *Oktyabr'* No. 1 (1986) and V. Belov, 'Vse Vperedi', *Nash Govremennik*, Nos. 6–7 (1986). For the responses, see V. Lakshin, *Izvestiya*, 4 December 1986, p. 3, and N. Eidelman in *samizdat* (reprinted in *Jews and Jewish topics* . . . No. 5 (Summer 1987), pp. 32–50; and the counter in V. Gorbachev, *Molodaya Gvardiya*, No. 3 (1987), esp. p. 171. For the increasing politicisation of the debate refer to Ligachev's speech at the *Sovestskaya Kul'tura* offices (*Sovestskaya Kul'tura*, 7 July 1987, p. 2).

45. S. Bialer, 'The Changing Soviet Political System', in S. Bialer, ed., *Inside Gorbachev's Russia* (Boulder, CO; Westview Press, 1989), pp. 203–208.

46. One version of the original 'letter', discovered by the Italian paper *L'Unita*, contained the chilling remark that 'on careful scrutiny . . . the majority of [Soviet Jews] display Zionist teeth. The Jews of our country have become a nationality apart.' See K. Devlin, *RLRB*, RL 215/88, 1 June 1988.

47. For example in the journals *Nash Sovremennik, Molodaya Gvardiya* and *Moskva*, and in the regional newspaper *Vologodskii Komsomolets*.

48. N. Gul'binskii, *Ogenek*, No. 23, 3–10 June 1989, pp. 23–24. For specific examples, see V. Kozhinov, *Druzhba Narodov*, 1, 1988, p. 181; I. Sein, *Molodya Gvardiya*, 4, 1988, p. 278; V. Belov, *Pravda*, 15 April 1988, p. 3; and V. Pikul;, *Nash Sovremennik*, 2, 1989, p. 189. Conversely, for a dual denunciation of the Soviet system and its association with Jewish personalities, see A. Kuz'min, *Nash Sovremennik*, 3, 1988, pp. 155 and 157–8. Also see *SJA*, Vol. 19, No. 3, pp.æ5, 9.

49. Y. Rapoport, *Druzhba Narodov*, No. 5 (1988), pp. 222–245; D. Gai, *Moscow News*, No. 4, 7 February 1988, p. 16; N. Rapoport, *Yunost'* No. 4 (1988), pp. 76–81.

50. See also K. Simonov, *Znamya*, No. 4 (1988), esp. pp. 83–95; and M. Geizer, *Literaturnaya Gazeta*, No. 6 (1989), p. 8.

51. *Oktyabr'*, Nos 1–4 (1988) and the addendum in No. 9 (1988), pp. 205–207. Also, see *Ogonek*, No. 40, 3–10 October 1987, pp. 19–23; *Izvestiya*, 25 June 1988, p. 3; *Pravda*, 4 July 1988, p. 4; *Literaturnaya Gazeta*, 34 (1988), p. 5. The book's main character, the vilified Jewish physicist Viktor Shtrum, was partly based on the real figure Lev Davidovitch Landau. See *Ogonek*, No. 3, 16–23 January 1988, pp. 13–15; and *Moscow News*, No. 5, 31 January 1988, p. 10.

52. See for example the pioneering article by S. Rogov and V. Nosenko, 'Chto skazal "A" i chto skazal "B"', *Sovetskaya Kul'tura*, 9 February 1989, p. 6 (translation in *SJA*, 18, 3, pp. 46–55); *Izvestiya*, 19 April 1988, p. 5; and *Literaturnaya Gazeta*, No. 41 (1988), p. 15.

53. See for example the open criticism of Jewry at the November 1989 plenum of the Russian Writers' Union. *SJA*, Vol. 19, No. 3, pp. 3, 6, 14–15; and Vol. 21, No. 1, p. 93.

54. Zvi Gitelman, 'The Decline of Leninism and the Jews of the USSR', *SJA*

Vol. 21, No. 1, p. 106; and see Yoram Gorlizki 'Jewish in Moscow', *London Review of Books*, Vol. 12 No. 3, (1990), p. 14.

56. 400 Jews in Leningrad and 250 at the *Vostryakovo* in Moscow (*Daily Telegraph*, 27 April 1987, p. 26, and *Jews in the USSR*, 16, No. 6, 30 April 1987).

57. See *SJA*, 18, No. 3 (Winter 1988), p. 97. A demonstration of 300 people in Vilnius on 8 July 1988 called for the erection of a memorial to the ghetto; a meeting of 500 people at the Vostryakovo in Moscow on 25 September commemorated Babi Yar; a further 500 in Leningrad marked the fiftieth anniversary of *Kristallnacht*; and on 30 April 1989 1000 people in Moscow collectively mourned the Holocaust (*SJA*, 19, No. 1 (Spring 1989), pp. 93–95; *Jews in the USSR*, 18, No. 9, 4 May 1989, p. 1). A private library and a museum were opened in Moscow in September 1987 and January 1988 respectively; and plans for a Lithuanian museum of Jewish culture and for a memorial to the victims of the Holocaust were announced on 2 December 1987 (See *Jerusalem Post Magazine*, 16 September 1988, pp. 9–11; *SJA*, 18, No. 2, p. 96; and 18, No. 3, pp. 33, 97).

58. *Jewish Press* (New York), 24 June 1988; *Jewish Chronicle* (henceforth *JC*), 10 March 1989, p. 5; *SJA* 18, No. 1, pp. 98–99 and 101; and 20, No. 1, p. 93.

59. See for example *Jews in the USSR*, 17, No. 36, 29 September 1988 and 17, No. 38, 13 October 1988. For reference to the reopening of the synagogue in Lvov, see *SJA*, 20, No. 1, p. 96.

60. *SJA*, 20 Nos 2–3, pp. 30–33.

61. That is, the journal *Sovetish Heymland* and the newspaper *Birobidzhaner Shtern*. See L. Hirszowicz, 'Breaking the mould: The Changing Face of Jewish Culture under Gorbachev', *SJA*, 18, No. 3 (Winter 1988), pp. 36 and 39–40. Also, see *SJA* 21 No. 1, p. 111; *JC*, 24 March 1989, p. 3; and *SJA*, 19, No. 1, pp. 94–95.

62. For example, the first convention of the Union of Hebrew Teachers on 18 September 1988. See *Focus Soviet Jewry* (Tel-Aviv), 2, No. 10, p. 2.

63. According to the 1979 census, less than 20 per cent of Jews declared Yiddish as their second or native tongue, as opposed to the 97 per cent who declared Russian (Altshuler, *op. cit.*, pp. 182, 185).

64. 'O Mezhnatsional'nikh Otnosheniyakh', *Pravda*, 5 July 1988, p. 3. Following the Conference, a Jewish Academy was set up in Moscow and supplied with premises, a grant from the Academy of Sciences, and accommodation for some of its forty full-time and 100 part-time students; a Soviet Committee for the Preservation of Jewish Historical Monuments and Documents was established; and several experimental Jewish newspapers and broadsheets were produced in Russian. See *SJA*, 19, No. 1, p. 96 and 19; *Forward* (New York) 13 January 1989; *SWB*, SU/0358, 14 January 1989; *JC*, 24 February 1989, p. 3; *Jews in the USSR*, 18, No. 5, 2 March 1989, pp. 1–2 and 18, No. 10, 18 May 1989, p. 4; *From Soviet Sources* (London: Institute of Jewish Affairs, July 1989), p. 3. The Conference resolution also added momentum to the many established and fledgling Jewish ensembles and theatre companies in the USSR: theatres in Moscow, Vilnius and Kaunas and ensembles in Kiev,

Chernovtsy, Kherson and Kishinev (interview with Gennadi Eistrakh of *Sovetish Heymland* on 18 July 1988; and L. Hirszowicz, 'Breaking the mould: the Changing Face of Jewish culture under Gorbachev', *SJA*, 18, No. 3 (Winter 1988), pp. 37–38.

65. Hirszowicz, *op. cit.*, p. 38.
66. *Jewish Herald International* (London), 10 February 1988, p. 1; *Jews in the USSR*, 18, No. 4, 16 February 1988; *JC*, 31 March 1989, p. 28; *SJA*, 20 (1) p. 93; 20 (2–3) pp. 48–9.
67. *SJA*, 21 (2), p. 23.
68. *SJA*, 20 (1), p. 96.
69. The main absentees were Aaron Vergelis, editor of *Sovietish Heymland*, and Adolf Shaevich, Rabbi of the Moscow Choral Synagogue, who set up two rival institutions, the All-Union Society of Soviet Jewish Culture and the All-Union Jewish Religious Association, in October 1989 and January 1990 respectively. *SJA*, 19 (3), p. 62.
70. Yoram Gorlizki, 'Jewish in Moscow', *SJA*, 19 (3), pp. 61–4.
71. *SJA*, 17, No. 2, p. 94; 18, No. 2, p. 96; 20 (1) p. 29; 20 (2–3) p. 127.
72. *SJA*, 20 (1), pp. 24–5; 21 (2), p. 15.
73. *SJA*, 20 (2–3), p. 129.
74. *SJA*, 20 (1), p. 94; 21 (2), pp. 3, 13, 15.
75. *SJA*, 21 (1), p. 112.
76. *SJA*, 21 (2), pp. 8–10.
77. *SJA*, 21 (1), (Summer 1991), p. 20; *Jews and Jewish Topics*, No. 19 (Winter 1992), p. 5; *JC*, 3 January 1992, p. 1; 14 February 1992, p. 1; 20 March 1992, p. 3, 25 June 1993, p. 2; *New York Times*, 5 October 1993.
78. It has been estimated that over 20 per cent of new immigrants in Israel are out of work, while many others have found only temporary or highly unsuitable jobs. See *JC*, 17 January 1992, p. 40; 14 February 1992, p. 1; 7 May 1993, p. 1.
79. *JC*, 16 October 1992, p. 3, 5 March 1993, p. 1.
80. *Washington Post*, 28 June 1993; *New York Times*, 19 September 1993; 5 October 1993.
81. *JC*, 16 April 1993, p. 3.
82. *New York Times*, 5 October 1993.
83. *Washington Post*, 28 June 1993.
84. *JC*, 23 April 1993, p. 1; *Washington Post*, 28 June 1993.
85. *SJA*, 21 (2) (Winter 1991), pp. 24–5; *JC*, 24 April 1992, p. 16.
86. *Komsomolskaia Pravda*, 16 January 1993 and 22 April 1993, p. 2.
87. *Rossiiskaia Gazeta*, 4 March 1993, p. 2; *Izvestiia*, 4 August 1992, p. 2.
88. *JC*, 9 October 1992, p. 2; 6 November 1992, p. 6; 11 June 1993, p. 2; *Komsomolskaia Pravda*, 23 April 1993, p. 2.
89. *SJA*, 20 (1) p. 93; 20 (2/3), p. 127; 21 (2) p. 71.
90. *Jews and Jewish Topics*, No. 19, pp. 54, 56, 57, 59.
91. Ibid., pp. 52–55.
92. *JC*, 1 May 1992, p. 2.
93. *Nezavisimost'*, 5 September 1992; *JC*, 11 December 1992, p. 3.
94. *Nezavisimost'*, 17 October 1992, p. 3.
95. Evgenii Golovakha and Natalia Panina, 'Jewish Cultural Activity in the Ukraine' *Jews and Jewish Topics*, No. 18 (Summer 1992), p. 7.

96. *Pravda Ukrainy*, 28 October 1992, p. 2; *Literaturnaia Gazeta*, 4 November 1992, p. 2.
97. *Nezavisimost'*, 17 October 1992, p. 3.
98. *Izvestiia*, 20 January 1993.
99. Programmes on Israel, which have been promoted by the Israeli embassy, include, 'Pillars of Fire', 'Travels in Israel', 'Dreams of Israel', and 'Heritage: Civilization and the Jews'. *JC*, 27 March 1992, p. 2; 7 August 1992, p. 2; 23 April 1993, p. 3.
100. *JC*, 17 January 1992, p. 2; 21 February 1992, p. 40.
101. *JC*, 3 July 1992, p. 8; *Jews and Jewish Topics*, 19, p. 62. See also *JC*, 21 February 1992, p. 5.
102. *JC*, 31 July 1992, p. 3.
103. *JC*, 31 January 1992, p. 18.
104. *JC*, 22 May 1992, p. 2.
105. *JC*, 29 May 1992, p. 2; 9 October 1992, p. 2.
106. Ibid.
107. *JC*, 7 May 1993, p. 1; 18 June 1993, p. 40.
108. Personal observation.
109. *Literaturnaia Gazeta*, 18 November 1992, p. 9.
110. *JC*, 16 April 1993, p. 3.
111. *JC*, 16 April 1993, p. 3; *Literaturnaia Gazeta*, 18 November 1992, p. 9.
112. *Rossiiskaia Gazeta*, 3 June 1993, p. 3; and *JC*, 9 October 1992, p. 3; 17 July 1992, p. 3.
113. *JC*, 2 October 1992, p. 5.
114. *JC*, 4 December 1992, p. 2; 19 March 1993, p. 1.
115. *Literaturnaia Gazeta*, 11 November 1992, p. 3; *Novoe Vremia*, No. 44, (October 1992), pp. 62–63; and see *Izvestiia*, 13 August 1992, p. 7; 12 October 1992, p. 3; *Literaturnaia Gazeta*, 26 August 1992, p. 2; *Argumenty i Fakty*, 1992, No. 2, p. 6.
116. Ibid.; *Megalopolis Express*, 26, 1992, p. 22; *JC*, 26 June 1992, p. 3.
117. *JC*, 9 October 1992, p. 2; see also *Sovetskaia Rossiia*, 21 July 1992; 25 August 1992, p. 2; and *Moskovskii Komsomolets*, 24 June 1992, p. 2.
118. For example *Megalopolis Express*, 26, 1992, p. 22.
119. See Anatole Lieven, *The Times*, 16 December 1993.
120. For example Adolf Shaevich, the Russian Chief Rabbi, and Vladimir Shapiro, the president of the Jewish Research Centre in Moscow. See *JC*, 2 October 1992, p. 5; *Delovoi Mir*, 11 July 1992, p. 12.
121. *Inostranets*, No. 20, 27 October 1993, p. 19.
122. *JC*, 9 October 1992, p. 2; *Delovoi Mir*, 11 July 1992, p. 12; *New York Times*, 19 September 1993.

# CHAPTER TWENTY-THREE

# Volga Germans

Anthony Hyman

## BACKGROUND

'Volga Germans' is the generic name given to the largest group of Soviet Germans. They are descendants of migrants drawn mainly from the southwestern German states, invited to settle in Russia under Catherine the Great from 1762, in a drive to develop the steppe lands of the lower Volga conquered from the Tatars. The Volga Germans were the largest group of many foreigners besides the Russians and Ukrainians in the Volga lands, tempted by offers of land and encouraged to migrate because it was hoped they would spread knowledge of efficient, modern farming techniques. Already by 1767, as many as 27,000 German peasant farmers had settled there in agricultural colonies.[1]

Their striking success in farming was due to efficiency and hard work, but also to the fact that they enjoyed special incentives, being free peasants in a land of serfs. Apart from land, among the privileges granted were religious liberty and freedom from military service. Settled in often thriving agricultural communities in the lower Volga, the Germans were mostly Lutheran Protestants, with a Catholic minority accounting for between 15 and 20 per cent of the total. In addition, there were some small Protestant sects, notably Mennonites, members of a pacific sect akin to Quakers, which migrated from Prussia, the Rhineland and the Netherlands. Together, these disparate sects and groups formed the Volga German community.

Under the Tsars, Volga Germans were not officially classified separately from other ethnic Germans. The Black Sea or Ukrainian Germans were another large group of emigrants, formed from Germans who had settled on lands along the Black Sea. A third group were Baltic Germans, a privileged, educated minority who in the nineteenth century often occupied higher posts in the Russian civil service and army. Further steady German migration to Russia before the 1917 Revolution came from the German states, Austria-Hungary and

Switzerland, in the form of technical specialists, private tutors and artisans.

The sobriety, efficiency and greater productivity of Volga German farmers won praise from many contemporary Western visitors. According to an English traveller in the 1820s to the German farming areas of the lower Volga, the Mennonites in particular 'planted extensive orchards, and laid out great gardens, possessing the finest breeds of cows in the country, and growing a great abundance of corn'.[2]

By the 1890s, though, declining prosperity among the Germans of Russia led to the migration of many thousands of families to North and South America. According to the 1897 official census (the first comprehensive attempt to record the population), Germans constituted the largest diaspora nationality of Tsarist Russia, with 1,790,400, or 1.43 per cent of the total population. Their numbers had risen to nearly two and a half million by 1914.

The Germans of the Russian empire were the smallest of three large German-speaking communities settled outside the *Kaiserreich* itself, the others being in Austria-Hungary and Switzerland. The troubled relations between Russia and Germany did much to determine their fate during the Soviet era.

## THE GERMAN DIASPORA DURING THE SOVIET PERIOD

Of the scores of peoples recognised as nations in the Soviet Union, the two million-odd Germans ranked fifteenth in size (see Table 23.1). This was in itself one good reason why autonomy status was granted in the form of the Volga-German ASSR, established in 1924. The fact that Lenin's mother, Maria Alexandrovna Ulyanova, was a Volga German

Table 23.1  The geographical distribution of Germans in the USSR

| Republic | 1959 | (%) | 1970 | (%) | 1979 | (%) |
|---|---|---|---|---|---|---|
| Russian republic | 320,091 | 50.6 | 761,888 | 41.4 | 790,762 | 40.9 |
| Kazakh SSR | 658,698 | 40.7 | 858,077 | 46.5 | 900,207 | 46.5 |
| Kyrghyz SSR | 39,915 | 2.0 | 89,834 | 4.9 | 101,057 | 5.2 |
| Tadhzik SSR | 32,588 | 2.0 | 37,712 | 2.0 | 38,853 | 2.0 |
| Uzbek SSR | 18,000 | 1.1 | – | – | – | – |
| Other republics* | 50,363 | 3.1 | 98,806 | 5.3 | 105,335 | 5.4 |
| West of Urals | | | 165,237 | 8.9 | | |
| East of Urals | | | 1,681,080 | 91.1 | | |
| Total Germans | 1,619,655 | 100 | 1,846,317 | 100 | 1,936,214 | 100 |

*Source*: S. Heitman 1993, based on official census reports.
*Some confusion has arisen in the figures reported of the Volga German population in Uzbekistan, many of whom were included in the total for 'other republics'.

of the Lutheran rite, and that Simbirsk in the Volga region was his home town, may also have counted. Lower in status and privileges than the 15 Union Republics, the ASSR nevertheless provided a focus for German cultural activity in the Volga region. There were also small autonomous districts of Volga German settlement outside the republic proper, with certain cultural privileges.

In addition, the Volga German republic served as a kind of showpiece for Western visitors to the USSR. It seemed to demonstrate obvious benefits from the application of Lenin's nationality policy. Small though it was, the German republic did have a flourishing cultural life, even though the nation it represented was on a miniature scale and scattered.

A remarkable 21 German language newspapers were published, besides some other periodicals. There was a German-language publishing house in the small capital, Engels, where a theatre was also established. At first, Volga Germans were permitted a considerable degree of religious liberty, with no hindrance to church attendance, and hundreds of church-administered schools. Pastors and priests remained influential leaders in this traditionally-minded, mainly rural community.

The vast spaces of Siberia had also attracted German settlement for decades. By 1926, 135,800 Germans were settled in Siberia and Asiatic Russia. They had settled there voluntarily, but the numbers of Germans in Siberia were soon to be swollen by forced deportation to camps. Early victims came from the Mennonite sect of Germans. When the option of conscientious objection to military conscription was abolished in the 1930s, the Mennonites suffered immediately. Many of the males were sent to prison camps in Siberia.

One aspect of the cultural freedoms given the Germans under the Volga German Republic had undoubtedly been the intention to improve the USSR's relations with the Weimar Republic. But the Volga German community suffered disproportionately in the decade from 1929 through the policy of forced collectivisation. Because of the prosperity of many German farmers, many families were arrested as part of the so-called *kulak* class and punished with expropriation, arrest, death or deportation.

The fate of the Volga Germans was publicised by some refugees who managed to flee to Weimar Germany, and attempts were made to capitalise on sympathy and obtain help for the Volga Germans. A stream of reports, novels and harrowing eyewitness accounts published in Weimar Germany created indignation and resentment at communist persecution.[3]

German awareness of the plight of Volga Germans grew stronger following the change of regime after the 1933 capture of power by Adolf Hitler. New books on the suffering of the Volga Germans published in Nazi Germany included notably Hans Harder's *Das*

*Dorf an der Wolga* (Village on the Volga) and Georg Loedsack's *Einsam kaempft das Wolgaland* (The Volgaland fights alone).

The mass-deportation of Volga Germans from September 1941 was largely due to Stalin's paranoia against foreign spies and agents.[4] It can also be seen as a precaution against their potential collaboration with Nazi Germany after the invasion and conquest of Russia. Hitler's plans for *Lebensraum* were to annex the Volga German lands along with the Baltic states, Galicia, the Crimea, the oil-rich Baku area and the Kola peninsula. None but Germans would be allowed to bear arms.[5]

Germans were the largest of eight smaller nations punished by deportation to remote regions of the USSR over 1000 miles to the north-east. The entire community of Volga Germans was rounded up, and the German ASSR itself abolished by decree. Scores of thousands of men, women and children lost their lives in the brutal process of transportation by cattle truck and forced resettlement to remote, ill-prepared camps in Siberia and rural communities of Kazakhstan, in grim conditions of wartime privation.

The impact of the deportation has been assessed in very different terms by various historians. In the judgment of one analyst, Peter Nettl, the Volga Germans 'henceforward ceased to exist as a distinct ethnic group'.[6] Instead, according to this view, they evolved into a wider, non-territorial community, as ethnic Germans of the USSR as a whole. However, there is a mass of evidence that goes in the opposite direction. A more persuasive interpretation of events is that Volga Germans not only survived persecution, but gradually recovered, actually enhancing their position as the main German diaspora group in the USSR by gradually assimilating some members of the less culturally persistent Black Sea German community.[7]

Little reliable information existed in Germany or the West about the fate of the Volga Germans until after Stalin's death in 1953. Estimates of losses suffered by Soviet Germans as a whole during the Second World War go as high as 500,000, the majority being men. They were kept confined in remote camps until 1955, when Chancellor Konrad Adenauer of West Germany persuaded the Soviet government to issue an amnesty at last. It was only from 1955 that the Volga Germans finally left their wretched camps for new lives in various regions east of the Urals, in south-west Siberia and Kazakhstan, and gradually smaller German communities became established in three other republics of Central Asia – Kyrghyzstan, Uzbekistan and Tajikistan.

Many Germans found jobs in industrial centres or as farmers in collective farms in northern Kazakhstan. As 'special settlers', Germans were obliged to register each week with the commandant of the area. Their freedom of movement was restricted to just three miles out of their communes or rural settlements. The Volga Germans played a major role in opening up the 'virgin lands' in the big Party-led campaign to bring under cultivation millions of hectares of virgin and fallow land in northern Kazakhstan and southern Siberia. The large new exile city of Karaganda in Kazakhstan became a centre for many Germans as well as other exiles. Other centres include Kostroma, Kemerovo, Novosibirsk, Chelyabinsk, Yakutsk, Krasnoyarsk, Balkhash, Temir Tau and Kustanai.

The Germans' relative freedom of expression of religious faith inevitably suffered, partly because so many of their clergy – traditional leaders of the community – had died. For the Mennonites, according to a contemporary investigation, 'no religious life had been possible for the community for more than twenty years, until 1954, and they were no longer taught in their own language'.[8]

It was only in 1958 that the publication of German language newspapers in the USSR restarted, with *Neues Leben* (New Life) from Moscow, which was to remain the main newspaper, and *Arbeit* (Work) from Barnaul in Altai. Yet the Germans remained something of a community apart, preserving some of their traditions, if not always their language. As a rather scornful article in *Neues Leben* later declared, it was simple enough to see where the German section was in a Kazakh village. 'The German streets are neat and tidy, with smart fences, no holes in the roads, no rubbish lying around. In the Russian streets things get sloppier, and as for the Kazakh streets – well, this is the Orient.'[9]

The entire nation had been denounced as public enemies and traitors. Public rehabilitation of the Volga Germans had to wait until 29 August 1964, two decades after the end of the Second World War, and seven years after rehabilitation of the deported peoples of the Caucasus. Yet even then, the Volga Germans (like the Crimean Tatars) were denied permission to return to their homeland, while their pre-1941 republic status was also denied.[10]

When in 1965 leaders among the Volga Germans presented to the authorities requests for restoration of the autonomy status enjoyed by Germans, they were turned down summarily. Next, activists organised a petition with 8,000 signatures, asking for a new German autonomous area to be created. But no hope was given of a future change of policy or of cultural concessions. These rejections made some Volga Germans despair of their future in the Soviet Union, and turn to emigration to West Germany as the sole way to preserve their cultural heritage.

Thus in 1972 there was a split in the German activist group, with the emergence of the 'Union of Soviet German Voluntary Emigrants'. This consisted of 45 representatives from Soviet German communities in Alma Ata, Karaganda, Aktjubinsk, Frunze, Dushanbe, Tallinn and Riga. Their primary goal was restoration of the Volga republic, but they stated that if this proved impossible at the time, Germans eager to migrate should be resettled in the Kaliningrad area, while waiting for exit visas and permission to resettle in either West or East Germany.

Failing either of these options a third alternative was raised, that of free emigration. The members of the Union were quickly made aware of the authorities' anger over their initiative.[11]

However justified the German demand for restoration of their lands and pre-1941 autonomy status for the Volga German republic, it was unwelcome or perhaps even unpractical in the circumstances. The premium on good land and scarce housing in Russia was such that fierce opposition by those with vested interests could be expected. Here Volga Germans and Crimean Tatars faced a similar dilemma: what their community leaders regarded as their lands by right were now occupied by others brought in by the state since 1941.

The allure of the Volga ASSR territory remained strong, but more pragmatic schemes were also aired in the 1960s. The main one was a plea that a German autonomous region should be established in Kazakhstan's Tselinnyy Kray (New Lands Region), where hundreds of thousands of Volga Germans now lived. This had unpredictable consequences, when the mere rumour in 1967 that Moscow was planning to declare a Volga German ASSR in Kazakhstan gave rise to mass protests among Kazakhs. The government was obliged to make a swift public declaration that it was not going to declare a German autonomous region – if, indeed, it had ever intended to do so. This showed that such proposals, with territorial concessions to alien ethnic groups, never take place in a political vacuum.

Few Germans originally from the Volga region had legitimate claims to 'family reunification', the sole ground recognised by the USSR for emigration. Because of the difficulties placed in the way of ethnic Germans, the flow of emigration has been remarkably uneven. In the decade 1971–80, 64,000 Germans, nearly all Volga Germans, left the USSR for the West Germany. A further 1,000 went to the DDR. Although modest, the total was ten times that of the previous decade.

From 1980, though, there was a sharp reduction in numbers emigrating to West Germany, due to poor East–West relations rather than any lack of potential migrants. Probably as an indirect result, more Germans went to the DDR. Statistics show that some 11,000 emigrated to the DDR, compared to 72,500 to West Germany in the fifteen-year period 1971–1986.[12]

## THE GERMAN DIASPORA DURING *PERESTROIKA*

Over two million Soviet Germans remained in the USSR in 1989, mostly settled in Kazakhstan or other republics of Central Asia and Siberia. They were now neither persecuted nor in physical danger; indeed, many were relatively prosperous. However, there is an overwhelming trend among members of this ethnic group to migrate to Germany, a land they identify with but have never seen, from which their ancestors came centuries ago.

Emigration grew sharply after *perestroika*, with greatly liberalised laws. 52,000 Germans left the USSR in 1988, and in 1989 a total of 98,134 went to West Germany alone. Able now to exercise their 'blood-right' to resettle in Germany, 500,000 more Soviet Germans, many from Kazakhstan, put in applications to emigrate by 1990. Many of the earlier wave of emigrants had been from Ukraine or North Caucasus. These figures stand in stark contrast to the total of 74,000 who had emigrated in the twenty years from 1964 to 1984. The emigration total of Germans leaving the USSR for the forty years from 1948 to 1988 was 168,000.

In the context of this striking growth in emigration, it was hardly surprising that renewed demands for autonomy came from German leaders concerned that the community would wither away if no concessions were made. A public call for the restoration of the pre-1941 Volga republic was made in April 1989 by a newly-formed all-union society of Germans. 'An autonomous republic is the only solution to our problems; it is the only way to preserve our culture within the Soviet Union. If an autonomous republic is rejected, it will lead to a new wave of emigration,' warned Hugo Wormsbecher, co-president of the new society.[13]

This unofficial society was Wiedergeburt (Rebirth), formed in March 1989 with the specific goal of re-establishing a German republic on the Volga. Its full name was Union Society for Soviet German 'Rebirth' for Politics, Culture and Education, and it was founded by 135 Germans, mainly from the intelligentsia. Within one year it claimed 50,000 members. Other new German organisations that emerged were *Zwischenstaatlichen Rates der Russland-deutschen, Nationalrats der Deutschen Russlands* (whose chairman was Heinrich Groht), and 'Rates der Deutschen Kasachstans', chaired by Alexander Dederet.

The Volga German resurgence sparked off almost at once a strong reaction from local CP leaders and Russian settlers in control of the lands that used to be farmed by Germans. The actual territory of the Volga republic had been shared out between two Russian provinces. Vladimir Kalashnikov, Party leader of Volgograd, made a vigorous protest at apparent backing for the idea of restoring the Volga republic at the CP Central Committee Plenum in Moscow in April 1989, complaining, 'why are we not asked or consulted?'.

Nevertheless, in November 1989 the Nationalities Council of the USSR went ahead and recommended restoration of the Volga republic, naturally raising hopes that this would be followed by action. The recommendation provoked a Russian delegation from the disputed Volga area to come to Moscow and demonstrate outside the Kremlin a month later. Just days later, another demonstration took place demanding the right to return to their homelands of three 'deported

Peoples' (Crimean Tatars, Germans and Meskhetian Turks). Mounted outside Hotel Rossiya, close to the Kremlim, for three days from 19 December 1989, it attracted much-desired international media publicity. It was organised and led by the far bolder Crimean Tatar activists: Germans numbered only 12 to 15 of the 150 demonstrators in Moscow.

Wiedergeburt held its second all-Union conference in Moscow in January 1990. The mood of resignation or fatalism about gaining autonomy status among its delegates was palpable. They did agree, though, to continue the low-key campaign, and passed resolutions to send a statement on their hopes for a revived Volga German republic to the USSR Council of Ministers and an appeal to the UN Secretary General Perez de Cuellar for the intervention of the UN. Hardly surprisingly, these steps made no substantial difference to the impasse.

When Wiedergeburt deputies met again in Moscow in March 1990, the autonomy question was no longer on the agenda. An outburst typical of the bleak mood of delegates was the following: 'The last hope is finished, there will never again be an Autonomy granted for Russian Germans. We are left with only one alternative – to Germany! Here they don't need us.' Though their mood may have seemed akin to despair, it was probably exaggerated. Many of the German leaders allowed themselves to be guided by their emotions rather than their intelligence.[14]

To many of the German leaders, if not the rank and file, it was already clear that vested interests in the lower Volga region opposing restitution of lands to the displaced Germans were too strong for the mere recommendation of the Nationalities Council to become effective. Latent anti-German prejudices were being mobilised, and among the emotive slogans raised in the disputed Volga area were: 'No Third German Reich', 'No Soviet German Autonomy' and 'No German Republic in Mother Russia's Heart'.[15]

However, a renewed offer of a revived but smaller autonomous Volga German republic was made by President Boris Yeltsin at the end of 1991 during the Russian President's official visit to Germany. The proposed Volgograd area actually forms part of the original German republic abolished under Stalin in 1941. Yeltsin outlined a scheme for a 6,000 square kilometre area stretching from the city of Volgograd to be allotted, in a plan that had long been anticipated by ethnic Germans of the USSR, as well as requested by the German government itself.

The key element in the proposal was German funding to ensure the putative republic's economic viability. Chancellor Kohl pledged on behalf of Germany 50 million DM as initial aid in 1992 for building infrastructure to help attract and house ethnic Germans wishing to settle in the Volga. The aim was to create better living conditions for the USSR's ethnic Germans, as well as to foster a sense of belonging, so as to encourage some 800,000 of them to resettle in the Volga region instead of emigrating, sooner or later, to Germany.

Germany's economic might obviously gives it room for manoeuvre with regard to an extremely weakened Russia. The prospect of generous funding by Germany, rather than mere humanitarian considerations, spurred Anatoly Sobchak, Mayor of St Petersburg, to make an offer to settle ethnic Germans in an area near the city. Three other schemes cannot be totally excluded from future consideration, even if the Volga homeland demand is finally accepted.

The first is in Kaliningrad (formerly Konigsberg), the Russian enclave in what used to be East Prussia, lying on the Baltic coast between Poland and Lithuania. Its future as a Russian naval base and enclave could be in doubt in a rapidly evolving Europe. Since 1992, some 20,000 ethnic Germans, mainly farmers, have been attracted there, by the declaration of a 'free economic zone'. They have joined the one million Russians already settled there.[16] Some local community leaders even recommended that Kaliningrad *oblast* should be resettled *en masse* by Soviet Germans, and its name altered to Kantgrad, in honour of the German philosopher Immanuel Kant, who was born there.

Two further schemes remain in the air, for German mini-homelands to be established far from the Volga region, in areas of Central Asia and Siberia where substantial colonies of Germans currently live. 'We were on the verge of disappearing a decade ago', claimed Viktor Diesendorf, vice-president of the German association of Siberia, an economist trained at Leningrad University who lives in the Kuzbass industrial region of Siberia. Yet, he insisted, the Russians are not the problem, it is rather the Soviet government, which makes promises but only rarely keeps them. According to Diesendorf, 'the Central Asians have always behaved well, better than the Russians in fact', and they appreciated the special skills of Volga Germans.[17]

The dilemma of the Germans is one aspect of the failure of the Soviet nationalities policy. The USSR's scattered German community had long lacked a cultural focus. The two newspapers produced in German, *Deutsche Allgemeine* (formerly titled *Freundschaft* – Friendship) and the weekly *Neues Lebens* (New Life), used to be filled with generally bland, innocuous articles. *Neues Lebens* (with a one time subscription of 86,000 and total readership several times higher) became an important platform for the Wiedergeburt movement. Both became identified with Wiedergeburt, speaking for Germans who were at least partly integrated into Soviet society. By some reckonings these were only a small minority of around 200,000, barely more than ten per cent of the total community.[18]

The columns of these newspapers have printed many letters from Germans from every corner of the Soviet diaspora. One common theme revealed by these, according to a recent study, is overwhelming self-pity along with an almost complete introspection or absorption in the problems of their own community, to the exclusion of general Russian and Soviet problems. 'In the entire history of Mankind there is no other example of the terrible fate of Soviet Germans', reads one characteristic letter.[19]

One major factor in the community's alienation, according to its leaders, has been the poverty of cultural resources available in the German language. 'Those people are leaving who have lost faith in the Soviet government. But the rest of us do not want to leave. This is our home, and we hope the government will listen to us', stated Jakob Fischer, the director of a German language theatre in Temirtau, Kazakhstan in a press interview in 1989.[20]

## THE GERMAN DIASPORA IN THE POST-SOVIET STATES

The sudden disintegration of the USSR came as a great shock to the Germans, as to other Soviet citizens. Though it is difficult to prove, there is much anecdotal evidence, at least, to show that the majority of the Germans living in Almaty, Tashkent, Dushanbe and other Central Asian towns shared the negative attitudes of local Russians and Ukrainians towards independence and the linked greater assertiveness on the part of Asian Muslims.[21]

For many in the Central Asian republics, independence increased their sense of alienation because of the new stress placed on learning Kazakh, Uzbek or other Turkic languages. Along with independence for the Republics came new language laws, giving for the first time formal equality to Uzbek and other Turkic languages with Russian. This worried the Germans as much as the Russians living in Central Asia. Very few of them knew any of the Turkic languages, knowledge of which was now formally required in most of the republics for entrance to higher education or access to many state-sector jobs.

Even more worrying was the economic outlook. As the economy sank into crisis, the numbers of jobless, hungry and angry ordinary people rose. There was a prospect that the Germans, always outsiders in their respective republics, would become convenient scapegoats for peoples' hardships and difficulties, as have the Jews in Uzbekistan, in spite of the presence of long-established Jewish communities in Tashkent and Bukhara. Germans feared that they too might be blamed for shortages of food and goods, however irrationally.

A record 195,000 ethnic Germans left the former USSR for Germany in 1992. Many were from Kazakhstan, where around one million Germans still lived in 1993. There are naturally keen differences of views within the German community about the need to emigrate and the benefits of emigrating. Among the older generation, which has seen and experienced so many terrible things, the wish to emigrate is more general. Many of the younger generation reportedly have no great desire to resettle in Germany, according to many observers. But even if quite a few younger Germans prefer to remain where they were brought up, family pressure may well persuade them to join in a family application to emigrate.

Their speech patterns differ greatly from modern standard German, being based on traditional dialects of the various states of Germany. Actual knowledge of German in the younger generation is generally very weak or non-existent, and most younger ethnic Germans can express themselves efficiently only in Russian, even if they can understand the dialect of their parents. For those who emigrate, standard German usually has to be learned as a foreign language.

In spite of known practical difficulties, such as unemployment in Germany, probably the majority of Soviet Germans desired to leave by 1993. It was simplistic to assume that they were really economic migrants, poor people simply looking for a better standard of living. Most would also face psychological problems in adjustment to life in the West.

There was growing prejudice in Germany against the ethnic German immigrants as well as against Turks and other darker-skinned foreigners. Soviet Germans come out of a different culture. 'While West Germans have established themselves and have pushed away the shadows of history, ethnic Germans seems to have come straight out of history, reminding everyone of what had simply been repressed', claims Klaus Bade.[22]

Political passivity or habitual obedience was part of their culture, for which there were arugably good historical reasons. Soviet Germans had suffered enough for their *Deutschtum*. Explanations for the culture shock commonly experienced by Soviet Germans (along with other ethnic German immigrants) once settled in West Germany include: 'political immaturity and habitual acceptance of a leadership responsible for everything; lack of initiative and of experience with pluralistic thinking and different opinions; fear to ask critical questions and a general bewilderment by the possibilities for freedom and development, and of the risks presented by democracy and a market economy'.[23]

There is no uniform attitude within the administrations of the various republics of the CIS as to policy on the Germans. There appears to be no great eagerness on the part of the government of Kazakhstan to persuade the Germans to stay. 'They were deported here by force under Stalin in the 1940s, and they can freely leave', is reported to be a common stance within the Kazakh-dominated administration in Almaty.[24]

Efforts made by Germany in Kazakhstan to help mount a cultural initiative to sustain a sense of community among Volga Germans are quite impressive, on paper at least. These include arranging air time (albeit very limited) for radio broadcasts in German in

Kazakhstan, and computers and equipment provided by Germany for German-medium schools in various areas of Kazakhstan. Nevertheless, pessimism pervades official circles about the realistic chances of convincing the Volga Germans that they have a bright, attractive future as a community there rather than in Germany.

Applications made for visas to Germany could be seen as ambiguous. It was claimed by some observers that many of the Volga Germans wanted these visas as some form of insurance policy, to be used in case the situation worsened in their present places of residence. But by 1993 it was apparent that hundreds of thousands, and quite possibly the great majority of Volga Germans, intended to use visas to settle in Germany as soon as was feasible. The numbers of visa applications rose steadily. One reliable estimate was that one thousand visas per day were being processed by the end of 1993 in Germany's consulate in Almaty.

Some of the best-educated Germans had already departed by 1992, depriving the community of its natural leaders as well as capable organisers of various cultural initiatives mounted in Central Asia. Migration to Germany is compared to a process of nature by one German based in Almaty. 'It works like an avalanche. When five families leave, others are certain to follow soon after. And then more.'

In the absence of state-funded German schools, it is natural for the government in Bonn to do whatever it can to promote German culture and economic well-being among Kazakhstan's large German population. However, though Germany's cash subsidies are of course welcomed in Almaty, the government of Kazakhstan cannot for political reasons permit these benefits to go exclusively to its German population. Given Kazakhstan's uniquely sensitive demographic balance (between Kazakhs and Russians, Muslims and Christians), no government could contemplate seriously granting autonomous status to Germans in particular areas of German settlement.[25]

Russia and Kazakhstan between them are receiving most of the German state aid aimed at improving cultural and economic conditions for Soviet Germans. More than half of 400 million DM allocated for projects benefiting ethnic Germans in eastern Europe as a whole and the CIS from 1990 to 1993 has been paid to the two republics.

Some 900,000 ethnic Germans lived in Russia as a whole according to the 1989 census. Various bureaucratic concessions have been made to satisfy German cultural needs. In July 1991, Halbstadt in the west Siberian region of Altai was re-designated a German national *rayon*. Soon a second German rural district was designated. In the Omsk region as a whole there are over 500,000 Germans, concentrated in Halbstadt and Asowo. Because of the significant German presence in Omsk, there is said to be growing interest in emigrating there from Germans currently living in the Central Asian republics.

A further bilateral initiative between Bonn and Kiev raised the possibility of settling some 400,000 Germans in south-west Ukraine in rural areas of Odessa, where before the Second World War the same number of Soviet (or 'Black Sea') Germans were settled. Some thousands of Germans had returned to Ukraine by unofficial means during the previous decade. Negotiations with Ukraine began with a visit to Bonn by President Leonid Kravchuk in February 1992. A 'Ukrainian–German Foundation' was begun later the same year.

A substantial minority of almost 100,000 Germans lives in Kyrgyzstan, many of them in its capital Bichkek. President Askar Akayev has shown concern that they should remain in the republic, no doubt because many have special skills. A special 'Congress of the Germans of Kyrgyzstan' was held in January 1992, and Akayev went on to approve the setting up of two German cultural centres near Bichkek.

In Uzbekistan the German community is smaller, estimated at between 30,000 and 40,000. A considerable number of Germans settled in towns of the Fergana valley region left after serious riots or pogroms in 1989. The existence of this community plays a significant part in calculations by the Karimov government that it may succeed in attracting investment and the desired advanced technology from Germany, as seen in publicity given to the official visit by President Karimov to Germany in May 1993.

The contemporary exodus of the Germans is, of course, paralleled by that of Jews of Central Asia and Russia to Israel and the USA, and the case of another deported people, the Pontic (or Black Sea) Greeks who are migrating to Greece. There is a further parallel between ethnic Germans, Jews and Greeks – of the younger generation, at least – in that the great majority of them do not speak the languages of their proposed countries of adoption. Greece, like Germany and Israel, accepts the principle that nationality is in the blood (by *jus sanguinis*), recognising the right of ethnic Greeks to 'return' to their motherland from their various diaspora communities.[26]

The dilemma of Volga German identity can be seen to be part of the unfinished business of the 1940s. It was a common judgement that the post-Second World War expulsions of German minorities from central and eastern Europe, under Section XII of the Potsdam Protocol, had eliminated the problem of German minorities in Europe as a whole. 'The German minority problem had been reduced to an item of minor importance in European politics', wrote Inis Claude. He went on, 'the corollary of the elimination of German minorities from non-German states was the crowding of some nine and a half or ten million refugees into a Germany shorn of one-fourth of its pre-war area.'[27]

The Soviet German 'homecoming' may be the last episode in this saga. The *Deutschtum* ('Germanness') that Germans had preserved in the USSR no longer provides a common identity with Germans in the new/old homeland. The ambiguities of ethnic German identity can be clearly seen in the difficulties experienced by the *Aussiedler*, returnees from the Soviet Union and eastern Europe, once they have 'returned' to

Germany. Germany, the land of their hopes and unrealistic dreams, is an unfamiliar, alien fatherland where Volga Germans are – the ultimate irony – often considered to be Russians, 'because of their inadequate knowledge of the language, their strong accents or "foreign" ways of life'.[28]

There are growing doubts that the mass migration to Germany can now be stemmed, in spite of efforts to improve living standards by large-scale economic aid from Bonn, and a methodical attempt at 'nation-building' (or rather nation-rebuilding) by deliberate fostering of ethnic pride in belonging to this small diaspora German community. If some form of autonomy status is not granted to one or more small areas of German settlement in the post-Soviet states, for those of the two million Germans who choose to remain the realistic prospect appears to be cultural assimilation into the much larger Russian community, whether in Russia itself or in the other republics where they are settled.

## ACKNOWLEDGEMENTS

The author wishes to thank the Social Science Research Council of New York for a SSRC - MacArthur Foundation Fellowship in International Peace and Security which enabled him to research Post-Soviet Central Asia.

## NOTES

1. Andreas Kappler, *Russland als Vielvolkerreich: Enstehung, Geschichte, Zerfall* (Munchen, 1992), p. 52 and tables on p. 325; and see Ingeborg Fleischhauer, *Die Deutschen im Zarenreich. Zwei Jahrunderte deutsch-russische Kulturgemeinschaft* (Stuttgart, 1986).

2. M. Holderness, *New Russia: A Journey from Riga to the Crimea* (London, 1823), pp. 160–161.

3. Walter Laqueur, *Russia and Germany. A Century of Conflict* (London, 1965) chapter 7.

4. See for background Robert Conquest, *The Nation Killers* (London, 1970); *Soviet Minorities, a Minority Rights Group Update* (London, 1991); I. Fleischhauer, B. Pinkus and E. R. Frankel, *The Soviet Germans, Past and Present* (London, 1986).

5. See further Norman Rich, *Hitler's War Aims*, Vol. II (London, 1974), chapter 11.

6. J. P. Nettl, *The Soviet Achievement* (London, 1967), p. 163.

7. Sidney Heitman, The Soviet Germans, *Central Asian Survey*, 1993, p. 77.

8. R. Conquest, *op. cit.* p. 182.

9. Quoted from an article by Angus Roxburgh in *The Sunday Times*, 7 May 1989.

10. For background see Sidney Heitman, Soviet Emigration Policies toward Germans and Armenians, in *Soviet Nationality Policies*, ed. Henry

Huttenbach (London, 1990); Valerii Tishkov, *Glasnost* and the Nationalities within the Soviet Union, *Third World Quarterly*, Vol. 11, No. 4, 1989.

11. See Jorgen Kuhl, *Die nationale Renaissance und die Autonomiediskussion bei den Deutschen in der Sowjetunion* (Munchen, 1990), p. 3.
12. S. Heitman, *op. cit.*, p. 241.
13. Quoted from a Reuters report (Moscow) in *The Independent*, April 1989.
14. J. Kuhl, *op. cit.*, p. 27.
15. J. Kuhl, *op. cit.*, p. 25.
16. Post-Soviet Press Group, University of London, 26 May 1993.
17. Details from an unpublished interview with Viktor Diesendorf in Siberia by Dr Tamara Dragadze of London University.
18. J. Kuhl, *op. cit.*, p. 28.
19. Quoted in J. Kuhl, *op. cit.*, p. 29.
20. *The Independent*, April 1989 (Reuters report).
21. See Ronald Wixman, Ethnic Attitudes and Relations in Modern Uzbek Cities, in *Soviet Central Asia. The Failed Transformation*, ed. W. Fierman (Boulder, CO, 1991).
22. Klaus Bade, Re-Migration to their Father's Land? in *Refugee Participation Network 14*, January 1993, p. 6, Refugee Studies Programme, Queen Elizabeth House, University of Oxford.
23. Quoted by K. Bade, *op. cit.*, p. 5.
24. Interviews by the author in Almaty, April 1993.
25. See Gregory Andrusz, Kazakhstan – Political Perspectives and Military Prospects, *Jane's Intelligence Review*, April 1993.
26. See Effie Voutira, 'Pontic Greeks Today', in The Odyssey of the Pontic Greeks, *Journal of Refugee Studies*, Vol. 4, No. 4, 1991.
27. Quoted by Inis Claude, *National Minorities, An International Problem* (Harvard University Press, Cambridge, MA) 1955, chapter 1, pp. 116–119.
28. K. Bade, *op cit.*, p. 5.

# CHAPTER TWENTY-FOUR

# Russians Outside Russia: the New Russian Diaspora

Aadne Aasland

As a result of the demise of the Soviet Union approximately 25 million ethnic Russians found themselves in the diaspora, most of them without any feeling of ever having emigrated. These Russians, living in states that were formerly Soviet republics outside the Russian Federation,[1] were sometimes referred to in Russia as 'Russians in the near abroad'. The concept of the 'near abroad' (*blizhnee zarubezh'e*) was, however, met with much scepticism in the newly independent states. It was thought that by grading foreign countries into a 'near' and a 'far' abroad, Russia had not really abandoned its imperial policies and intended to retain influence over developments in these new states. Whether they liked it or not, Russians in the new states had to realise that at least for the time being they had been separated from the 'great land' and that they were now simply national minorities in polities where the indigenous populations tended to regard themselves as entitled to cultural and political dominance. This could prove a painful process for an ethnic group that, as a rule, had identified with the Soviet Union and whose presence in the non-Russian territories was to a large extent a legacy of tsarist rule and, later, of the Soviet empire.

## BACKGROUND

The migration of Russians from the core of the empire into its peripheral areas started several centuries ago. The Russian conquest of two Tatar princedoms in the Volga basin in the middle of the 16th century was the start of a territorial expansion during which many Russians settled in the absorbed territories.[2] In the 18th and 19th centuries large-scale migration of Russians took place into 'Novorossiya' (territories to the north of the Black Sea), Belarus, the right bank of the river Dnepr in Eastern Ukraine and certain parts of the

Caucasus, Kazakhstan and Central Asia, of which Russia gradually took possession.[3] The Russian population in the new territories consisted of soldiers and officers, civil servants and other representatives of the empire, traders and constructors. Russians were also engaged in agriculture in some of these regions, such as in northern Kazakhstan and parts of Central Asia.[4] Moreover, some were Russian religious dissenters who had either sought refuge in or been banished to traditionally non-Russian areas.

Only from the 1880s did the tsarist empire directly encourage migration, and it was made somewhat easier for peasants to change their place of residence. Russians accordingly played a prominent role in the industrialisation process of some of the empire's peripheries in this period. At the time of the first all-Russian census in 1897, 8.4 per cent of all Russians lived outside the territory that today is the Russian Federation.[5] More than 40 per cent of these Russians lived in Belarus and Lithuania, 30 per cent lived in Ukraine and 13 per cent in Central Asia and Kazakhstan (1.1 per cent of the total Russian population). By 1916–17 the Russians living in Central Asia and Kazakhstan had increased to 2.0 per cent, and in the same period their proportion of the population in these regions increased from less than 8 to more than 14 per cent. There was also a significant increase of Russians in Belarus and Lithuania, both in absolute and relative terms. In other regions the Russian share of the population increased only slightly or, as in the Ukraine, decreased somewhat. However, the actual number of Russians there continued to increase.[6]

The social upheavals brought about by the Revolution and the Civil War had profound demographic implications for the Russian population. However, the proportion of ethnic Russians living outside the territories of the Russian republic (RSFSR) remained comparatively stable until the end of the 1920s. Industrialisation and urbanisation starting in the 1930s radically altered this state of affairs. A large-scale migration, part of which was involuntary, of Russian specialists and workers took place in the 1930s, so that the proportion of Russians living outside the RSFSR increased from 8.6 per cent in 1926 to 14.9 per cent in 1939.[7] The national composition of the non-Russian republics changed significantly in this period. The changes were particularly extensive in Kazakhstan, where in 1939 just over one-third of the population remained Kazakh while Russians had become the largest ethnic group in the republic.[8]

The migration of Russians into Central Asia and Kazakhstan continued after the Second World War as a consequence of this region's industrial development, combined with the reluctance of the native population to move to the cities. Many Russians were also recruited to work in agriculture, which had developed during the 1950s and 1960s as a result of the virgin lands campaign under Khrushchev.

Large-scale migration to the western parts of the Soviet Union did not start until after the Second World War. Russians were attracted by the high degree of economic development in the western republics. Deportations and a low level of natural increase among the indigenous populations made these republics incapable of supplying the growing industries with labour, and there was a need to import workers. This was particularly the case with the Baltic republics of Estonia and Latvia, where the share of Russians by 1989 had reached 30 and 34 per cent respectively. Lithuania had, for a long time, a higher birth-rate than the two other Baltic republics, and could therefore supply the growing industries with labour from its own reserves.[9] Also, the Communist Party of Lithuania was more successful than the other two Baltic republics in limiting the Russian influx.[10]

Whereas the number of Russians in the western republics continued to increase until the late 1980s, a net out-migration of Russians started from Georgia in the 1960s and from Azerbaijan in the 1970s. By the 1980s the absolute number of Russians in Armenia and most of the Central Asian republics (excluding Kyrgyzstan) had decreased. The rate of increase in the number of Russians in Kazakhstan had decreased (the proportion of Russians in the population started to decrease even earlier). The birthrate among the indigenous populations in these republics was very high, and this led to a surplus population in rural areas which had to move to the cities in order to find work. Competition for jobs increased, resulting in an escalation of ethnic tensions and a rise in the ethnic consciousness among the indigenous populations, who would no longer accept Russian political and economic dominance.[11] Moreover, the Russian population itself increased at a lower rate than previously, and particularly slowly compared with the indigenous populations. There were thus fewer Russians who could be sent to the republics, and the Russians living in these republics reproduced themselves at a much lower rate than did the indigenous populations.

The overall majority of Russians in the non-Russian republics lived in urban areas. However, there was significant variation from one republic to another. Kyrgyzstan and Kazakhstan had the least urban Russian population, with 70 and 77 per cent respectively of Russians living in urban areas, while Uzbekistan, Tajikistan and Turkmenistan had the highest proportions (94–97 per cent).[12] Russians were usually confined to the largest cities, making up over 20 per cent of the population in all the republican capitals, except those in the Transcaucasian republics (see Table 24.1 and Fig. 8).[13]

Table 24.1   The Russian population in the USSR

| Republic | 1959 total (1000s) | 1959 as share of total Russian population in the USSR (%) | 1959 as share of total population of republic (%) | 1970 total (1000s) | 1970 as share of total Russian population in the USSR (%) | 1970 as share of total population of republic (%) |
|---|---|---|---|---|---|---|
| RSFSR | 97,864 | 85.8 | 83.3 | 107,748 | 83.5 | 82.8 |
| Ukraine | 7091 | 6.2 | 16.9 | 9126 | 7.1 | 19.4 |
| Belarusia | 659 | 0.6 | 8.2 | 938 | 0.7 | 10.4 |
| Uzbekistan | 1091 | 1.0 | 13.5 | 1473 | 1.1 | 12.5 |
| Kazakhstan | 3974 | 3.5 | 42.7 | 5522 | 4.3 | 42.4 |
| Georgia | 408 | 0.4 | 10.1 | 397 | 0.3 | 8.5 |
| Azerbaijan | 501 | 0.4 | 13.6 | 510 | 0.4 | 10.0 |
| Lithuania | 231 | 0.2 | 8.5 | 268 | 0.2 | 8.6 |
| Moldova | 293 | 0.3 | 10.2 | 414 | 0.3 | 11.6 |
| Latvia | 556 | 0.5 | 26.6 | 705 | 0.5 | 29.8 |
| Kyrgyzstan | 654 | 0.6 | 31.6 | 856 | 0.7 | 29.2 |
| Tajikistan | 263 | 0.2 | 13.3 | 344 | 0.3 | 11.9 |
| Armenia | 56 | 0.1 | 3.2 | 66 | 0.1 | 2.7 |
| Turkmenistan | 263 | 0.2 | 17.3 | 313 | 0.2 | 14.5 |
| Estonia | 240 | 0.2 | 20.1 | 335 | 0.3 | 24.7 |
| Total | 114,114 | | | 129,015 | | |

| Republic | 1979 total (1000s) | 1979 as share of total Russian population in the USSR (%) | 1979 as share of total population of republic (%) | 1989 total (1000s) | 1989 as share of total Russian population in the USSR (%) | 1989 as share of total population of republic (%) |
|---|---|---|---|---|---|---|
| RSFSR | 113,522 | 82.6 | 82.6 | 119,866 | 82.6 | 81.5 |
| Ukraine | 10,472 | 7.6 | 21.1 | 11,356 | 7.8 | 22.1 |
| Belarusia | 1134 | 0.8 | 11.9 | 1342 | 0.9 | 13.2 |
| Uzbekistan | 1666 | 1.2 | 10.8 | 1653 | 1.1 | 8.3 |
| Kazakhstan | 5991 | 4.4 | 40.8 | 6228 | 4.3 | 37.8 |
| Georgia | 372 | 0.3 | 7.4 | 341 | 0.2 | 6.3 |
| Azerbaijan | 475 | 0.3 | 7.9 | 392 | 0.3 | 5.6 |
| Lithuania | 303 | 0.2 | 8.9 | 344 | 0.2 | 9.4 |
| Moldova | 506 | 0.4 | 12.8 | 562 | 0.4 | 13.0 |
| Latvia | 821 | 0.6 | 32.8 | 906 | 0.6 | 34.0 |
| Kyrgyzstan | 912 | 0.7 | 25.9 | 917 | 0.6 | 21.5 |
| Tajikistan | 395 | 0.3 | 10.4 | 388 | 0.3 | 7.6 |
| Armenia | 70 | 0.1 | 2.3 | 52 | 0.0 | 1.6 |
| Turkmenistan | 349 | 0.3 | 12.6 | 334 | 0.2 | 9.5 |
| Estonia | 409 | 0.3 | 27.9 | 475 | 0.3 | 30.3 |
| Total | 137,397 | | | 145,155 | | |

Source: Soviet census data.

Figure 8 :

# RUSSIAN DIASPORA IN RUSSIA'S NEIGHBOURING STATES

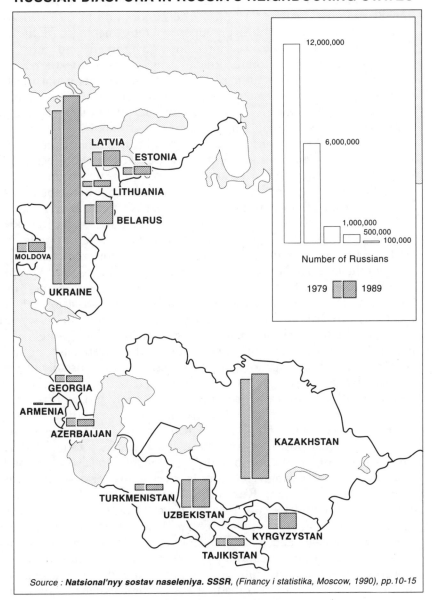

Source : **Natsional'nyy sostav naseleniya. SSSR**, (Financy i statistika, Moscow, 1990), pp.10-15

481

## THE SOVIET PERIOD

The first years of Soviet power were not characterised by a privileged status for Russians in the non-Russian republics. The Soviet leadership declared that Russian chauvinism was the main problem in nationality relations and initiated a programme of developing the cultures of the non-Russian nationalities. A policy of élite cooption or 'indigenisation' (*korenizatsiya*) was put into practice, whereby members of the non-Russian nationalities were recruited into government and party positions. the main aim of these policies was to coopt the non-Russian nationalities in the formation of Soviet élites. Schools using the local languages were set up and the use of these languages was promoted in most spheres of society. Thus, the number of newspapers, journals and books in non-Russian languages increased rapidly.

However, as Stalin consolidated his power, the role of the Russians in the non-Russian republics gradually changed. By the early 1930s ideological uniformity started to be imposed on all national cultures (including Russian). Sovietisation of the union republics depended to a large extent on the increasing number of Russian cadres arriving there in this period. While national élites were arrested and often killed, leading positions in all spheres of society were now normally taken by Russians, or Russian-speaking Slavs, sent in from the centre.

From the mid-1930s Stalin started praising the Russian people openly for its past and present virtues, and its role as an 'elder brother' in the 'Soviet family of nations' was expressed on several occasions.[14] From the 1930s onwards the Russians living in non-Russian union republics were in a better position than other nationalities living outside their national territories, and in some respects they were also privileged compared to the indigenous nationalities. Russians usually came to an established Russian or Russian-speaking environment, where they met with other Russians in their neighbourhood and workplace. The Russian language soon gained a prominent role all over the Soviet Union. A very good knowledge of Russian became a prerequisite for occupying higher positions, and there was a tendency to make Russian the language of instruction not only in higher but also in secondary education. Russian-language schools were more or less identical all over the Soviet Union. Russians migrating to another part of the Soviet Union could be sure that they would find a Russian-speaking environment in their new place of residence. They tended to expect that *their* language, and not the local one, would be used as the means of interethnic communication. A large number of Russian-language newspapers, periodicals and programmes on radio and television in all the union republics also made it easier for Russians living there to manage without knowledge of the local language.

According to 1989 census data, while more than 62 per cent of non-Russians in the Soviet Union were fluent in Russian, only 19 per cent of the Russians living outside the Russian republic were fluent in the language of the titular nationality.[15] There was, however, much variation among the republics in terms of level of language fluency. The cultural and linguistic proximity between Russians and the non-Russian nationality was one important factor in determining this level; the size of the Russian population and the compactness of its settlement another. Moreover, the status the local population enjoyed in the eyes of Russians as well as the history of Russian settlement in the region also seemed to affect the level of language fluency. In 1989 more than one-third of Russians in Ukraine and one-fourth in Belarus were fluent in the local languages. Also, Russians in Lithuania and Armenia had a relatively good knowledge of the titular languages. Russians in the Central Asian republics and Kazakhstan were the least likely to be fluent in the languages of the titular nationality; census date from 1989 indicated fluency rates in these republics ranging from only 0.9 per cent (in Kazakhstan) to 4.5 per cent (in Uzbekistan).

Despite policies of indigenisation of national élites, the Russians were better represented than other non-titular nationalities in the republican hierarchies. Other nationalities (with some exceptions regarding Ukrainians and Belarusians) would normally be confined to their own national territory. Top positions in the union republics were usually filled by Slavs sent in from the centre, and the Soviet authorities had a tendency to avoid drawing on the Russian settler communities.[16]

There is evidence to suggest that the authorities in Moscow encouraged migration, particularly of Russians, as a subtle way of exerting influence over the development of nationality relations. Since Russians and other Slavs were thought to be more loyal to the regime than the other nationalities, many officials seemed to believe that a considerable number of Russians in the union republics would have a stabilising effect on the local populations. The need to obtain a *propiska* (residence permit) for settlement in a certain area was a means by which migration could be directed to areas approved by the authorities. On the other hand, the Soviet leaders do not seem to have utilised this policy very effectively.[17] It could be concluded that Russian and Slavic migration was a natural process solely determined by socio-economic developments, without any monitoring from above. However, the localisation of industry in areas where there was a need to import raw materials, energy and labour in order to produce goods which then would be transported to markets a long distance from the place of production is at least an indication of a different agenda.[18]

The Russian migrant population tended to display a high level of geographical mobility. Many did not move to another republic on a permanent basis, but were searching all the time for other places to move to where there would be better material and social conditions. This made them less inclined to develop roots in any republic they moved to, and the local culture, history and traditions often did not affect or even interest them. Republican borders were seen as symbolic, and only to a minor degree did they affect considerations about where to move. With the exception of a few closed cities, the whole territory of the Soviet Union represented a single labour market.[19]

There was thus an institutional framework that made it possible for Russians to maintain their ethnic identity. Only rarely did Russians assimilate to other nationalities, and when this happened it was mainly to children of mixed marriages between a Russian and a representative of the indigenous population, who at the age of 16 indicated the indigenous nationality in their passports.[20] It was, however, not uncommon for representatives of other nationalities who had left their national territories to assimilate gradually to Russian; they would usually use the Russian language, send their children to Russian-language schools and tend to socialise mostly with other Russian-speakers.

Even though Russians in the union republics were able to maintain their ethnic identity, there are signs that the content of this identity changed considerably. Modernisation and, particularly, urbanisation detached many Russians from their traditional homelands, and thereby from any continuity with the past. Such a group of people was likely to be more receptive to the continued ideological emphasis by the Soviet authorities on the supposed unity of the 'Soviet people'. Instead of focusing on distinctly Russian concerns and problems, it was implicitly understood that Russians should ensure the stability and welfare of the entire multiethnic state. The limits within which they could maintain their separate group identity were restricted.[21] Russians were given a social role as 'first among equals', and in return they were expected to keep their union-wide sense of identity.

The social role of Russians in the non-Russian republics was not limited to representing All-Union statehood. In some regions in recent years, notably in Central Asia and Kazakhstan, Russians were important agents of modernisation, and were often seen as representatives of a more developed culture in backward and traditionalist regions.[22] The social role of Russians in this region was naturally very different from, for example, their role in the Baltic republics, where modernisation had taken place at a much earlier stage and where Russians tended to regard the local cultures as more developed than their own. The actual living conditions of Russians also varied significantly from one republic to another.

The fact that relatively few Russians outside Russia were fluent in the local language, and that they tended to integrate socially mostly with fellow Russians or other Slavs, does not imply that they had not been influenced by the local nationalities and their way of living. On the contrary, there is evidence to show that Russians in the republics often adopted values and norms of nationalities living in their local environment, which distinguished them from Russians of the core group. For example, Russians living in Central Asia and the Caucasus not only had a stronger tendency than Russians in the European part of the Soviet Union to condemn divorce and having children outside marriage,[23] but they also had on average fewer divorces, higher birthrates, lower rates of alcohol consumption and, usually, more respect for their parents and elderly people than Russians in the RSFSR.[24]

There is an abundance of anecdotal evidence of Russians from the republics moving or travelling to the Russian Federation and feeling complete strangers there. At the same time, the local populations in the republics have usually been more positive towards Russians who have lived there for a long time and adopted local customs, traditions and culture than towards Russians who have arrived more recently. In 1978 Matthews Pavlovich suggested that the Russian diaspora was in the process of acquiring an identity of its own, different from the Russian core group in Russia.[25] However, although Russians lost contact 'not only with their former social milieu, but also with the traditional mores of Russian society', this does not seem to have been enough to create a sense of common identity among Russians in, for example, Estonia and Kazakhstan, as opposed to the identity of Russians in Russia itself. If Russians adopted a different identity, it was more likely to be as 'Russians in Moldova' or 'Russians in Kyrgyzstan' than as a Russian diaspora or 'Russians outside Russia'.


## THE *PERESTROIKA* PERIOD

Towards the end of the 1980s, differences between the Russian core group, living in traditionally Russian areas of the RSFSR, and Russians living in other union republics became more evident. Their reactions to the political changes and the many manifestations of ethnic sentiments among the non-Russian nationalities tended to take diverging forms. As a result of increasing ethnocentrism in the union republics, the ethnic awareness among both groups of Russians increased as well. However, to Russians in the republics such an awareness was more often linked to the status of being non-indigenous or 'Russian-speaking' than to a sense of belonging to a more narrowly defined Russian ethnos. Russians in Russia tended to focus mostly on internal Russian problems and were more concerned with the deteriorating state of Russia and with how to improve it, whether inside or outside a Soviet framework. There was, thus, often deep discontent among core-group Russians with the empire in its present form. They tended to think that Russia had wasted too many resources on the material support of the Soviet peripheries, with the result that living conditions in the republics had become considerably better than in Russia itself.[26] Russians living in the RSFSR were therefore inclined to take the position that Russia could no longer afford to subsidise the union republics economically. This opinion was intensified by what Russians believed to be a lack of gratitude among people living in the republics for the support they had received from Russia and a tendency to blame Russia and Russians for all the misfortunes that had taken place during the Soviet period.

There can be no doubt that the preservation of the Soviet Union was regarded as an important issue also by a large proportion of Russians living in the RSFSR. They were often proud of belonging to an empire which inspired a sense of greatness through being a world superpower. However, this question was usually not of the same overriding importance to them as it was to the majority of Russians living in the republics. Russians in the republics tended to see their well-being as dependent on the continued existence of the Soviet state and the symbolic character of the borders between the republics. They were therefore more inclined than their coethnics in Russia to take an 'internationalist' position. Moreover, Russians often depended on all-union structures as their source of income, and many were afraid that their future physical and material security would be threatened were their republic to become independent.

Russians in the republics also tended to see the Soviet state as a protection against increasing ethnocentrism in the union republics. In the Baltic States, Moldova and some other republics a considerable number of Russians joined so-called 'International Fronts'; movements that actively fought for the indivisibility of the Soviet state and, often explicitly, for the interests of the Russian-speaking population in the republics. They organised demonstrations and strikes in all-union enterprises with the aim of halting the drive for independence. These organisations soon formed alliances with the orthodox wing of the Communist Party, and with the Soviet military, and were thus often associated with communist ideology and the Soviet system. This discredited them not only in the eyes of the local populations, but in the eyes of many Russians as well.[27]

Although the International Fronts were the most visible and active spokesmen for the 'Russian cause' on the political arena in many of the union republics, far from all Russians outside Russia were in favour of a preservation of the *status quo*. Many Russians actively supported demands in the republics for more autonomy, and sometimes even for political independence. Several factors seem to be important in explaining such political attitudes. In some cases, such as in the Baltic States, there was a recognition among many Russians of a historic injustice that they thought should be rectified. Moreover, Soviet military interventions in Tbilisi, Baku, Vilnius and Riga in the period from 1989 to 1991 brought the credibility of the whole *perestroika* process into question and made many Russians inclined to interpret the relations between the centre and the republics as those between a dictatorship and aspiring democracies. Finally, and no less importantly, many Russians thought that their economic prospects would be better in small, manageable, autonomous republics than in a vast and chaotic, perhaps unreformable, Soviet economy.

Political disorientation and confusion were, however, more common among the Russian population in the republics than was active participation in political life. Russians often found it very hard to decide which political groups to support, and many of them had stopped believing that politics and politicians could solve their present problems. Although there was usually no lack of organisations claiming to represent the interests of the Russian-speaking population, there was no agreement among Russians about what their actual interests were. Several spokesmen for the Russophone population furthermore saw no need for Russians to unite simply because of their ethnic identity; in their view this could be interpreted as recognising the ethnic principle of political organisation, a principle these spokesmen thought completely unacceptable.[28]

New language laws in the republics introduced from 1989 onwards granting the titular languages a much more prominent role than Russian in office work, science and education affected the interests of most Russians who, as pointed out above, were not as a rule fluent in the local languages. Russians often feared that insufficient language knowledge would be used as a means by which Russians could be excluded from the more influential positions in government and economic structures. There was also general concern about the possibilities of their children obtaining secondary and higher education in their native language.

The inter-ethnic climate in many of the Soviet republics deteriorated during the first years of *perestroika*. The psychological stress this inflicted on the Russians was felt to be particularly strong in certain parts of Central Asia and Transcaucasia. Although Russians themselves were usually not directly involved in the increasing number of incidents of ethnically motivated violence in these regions, such incidents seriously alarmed the Russian population. This, combined with the fears of an Islamisation of some of the republics, induced many Russians to leave. It is therefore no coincidence that the only really large Russian-dominated organisation in these republics, *Migratsiya* in Tajikistan, was involved mostly with providing assistance to Russians emigrating to Russia, while there were no larger organisations aiming at improving the conditions of Russians who wanted to remain in their present place of residence.[29]

In the Baltic republics of Estonia and Latvia the idea that republican citizenship would be granted automatically only to those who were citizens of the interwar republics of Estonia and Latvia and their direct descendants gradually gained ascendancy, and seriously alarmed the Russian population. A majority of them had arrived in these republics after the Second World War, and they would therefore not qualify for citizenship automatically. They could obtain citizenship only after a naturalisation period, during which there would be stiff requirements in terms of length of residence, language knowledge and loyalty to the state. However, although there were signs that ethnic relations in the Baltic deteriorated during the years leading up to restored independent statehood, there were remarkably few incidents of inter-ethnic violence.[30]

There were also regions where relations between Russians and the titular nationality remained relatively stable and good during the years of *perestroika*, for example, eastern and southern parts of Ukraine.[31] There is a long tradition of Russian settlement in these regions, and Russians there are well integrated socially, linguistically and culturally with the Ukrainians. This, however, cannot be the only reason why inter-ethnic relations did not deteriorate. There are many examples of seemingly integrated nationalities who turn against each other when a situation develops where people are forced to choose between loyalties. When inter-ethnic relations remained stable in these parts of Ukraine, an important part of the explanation seems to have been that the Ukrainian political leadership succeeded in presenting the struggle for more autonomy as a national cause in a territorial, and not based on an ethnic, understanding of the term. In western parts of Ukraine, however, where the Russian population is more sparse and consists mainly of migrant workers, the situation was closer to that in the Baltic republics, where the ethnic aspects of the independence struggle were much more pronounced.

## THE RUSSIAN DIASPORA IN THE POST-SOVIET STATES

As has been demonstrated, the Russian diaspora is not a homogeneous group of people; it consists of individuals with varying degrees of affiliation to their present states of residence and to their ethnic homeland, Russia. While some Russians have a strong sense of belonging to a Russian ethnos, there are also many who rarely think of themselves as Russians, and who continue to regard themselves first of all as Soviet, or former Soviet, citizens. Others again are already in the process of becoming assimilated to the dominant ethnos in the place where they live. The problems facing the Russian diaspora also tend to vary significantly from one state or region to another. While certain problems are completely absent in some areas, they may figure among the main concerns of the Russian population in others.

In all the post-Soviet states, the average material standard of living has deteriorated over the past few years, even though economic conditions vary significantly from one state to another. Concern with falling real wages, threats of unemployment and uncertain economic prospects characterises the life of millions of diaspora Russians. Although economic hardship affects all nationalities living in the post-Soviet polities, and as such cannot be regarded as a typical nationality issue, there are situations in which economic issues and nationality issues become more closely interlinked.

A person's nationality and his/her type of occupation have a tendency to correlate, and the effect of economic changes and reforms will therefore often be different for different nationalities. In the Baltic States, for example, where Russians have been overrepresented in industries formerly controlled by all-union ministries, they are disproportionately vulnerable to unemployment as many of these enterprises are expected to close down. The political leaderships are often blamed for problems that affect one nationality more than others, and they may be accused of pursuing policies that favour the indigenous population. In certain Central Asian states, on the other hand, the authorities are sometimes accused by nationalist or fundamentalist forces of giving too many concessions to the Russians, whose technical skills are still required for the economy not to collapse.

Many Russians see the disruption of economic ties between the former Soviet republics as one of the main reasons for present economic problems. Most Russians are therefore in favour of closer economic and political links with Russia and with other CIS states. Some have already been affected personally by increased prices for energy and other inputs from Russia, as the enterprises they work in cannot maintain production at former levels and have to cut real wages or dismiss part of their workforce.[32]

Disruption of previous links between the former Soviet republics have other serious implications for the Russians. Customs barriers, visa requirements and new currencies have made it more problematic to move freely between the post-Soviet states. The widening gap in value between Ukrainian and Russian currencies has, for example, made it much more expensive for Ukrainian Russians to visit their relatives or friends in Russia. Newspapers and journals from Russia are now harder to obtain in most of the former Soviet republics. It has become too expensive to make frequent telephone calls to other post-Soviet states, and to move from one state to another has in most cases become a very costly and troublesome experience. While in some cases these problems are an inevitable consequence of the formation of new states, they are also to a large degree caused or aggravated by tensions in the bilateral relations between the new states, and especially in relations with Russia.

In some of the new states Russians have found themselves in the centre of an armed conflict that seriously affects the quality of their lives. This has been the case in Azerbaijan and Georgia (Abkhazia), in Moldova (Trans-Dniester) and in some of the Central Asian states, notably Tajikistan. Although the local Russians do not usually take part in the actual warfare (the most important exception is the Trans-Dniester conflict), their mere presence in the conflict areas has forced them to become involved. The result has been a stream of Russian refugees (or 'forced migrants') from these republics into Russia.[33] They are often forced to leave most of their possessions behind and normally face great difficulties in finding a new place to settle down in and beginning a new life in Russia.

It is not only threats of armed conflict that alarm Russians: many are also worried about the social transformations taking place in their state of residence. Russians in Central Asia, for example, are often sceptical about the Islamicisation the societies there are undergoing. They tend not to be familiar with the new set of social *moeurs*, while many of the old values characteristic of the Soviet period are gradually disappearing.[34] Thus, although the largest number of Russians leaving these republics come from turbulent Tajikistan, there are also many actual or potential 'voluntary migrants' from Central Asia. However, present conditions in Russia induce many of those who have a choice to think twice before they make the final decision about leaving.

The rate of departure from Central Asia has increased tenfold since the late 1980s, and more recently the rate of departure has increased rapidly also in Southern Kazakhstan.[35] There are significant differences between the republics, however, and Turkmenistan, for example, has not seen the same net departure of Russians as the other republics.[36] In Northern Kazakhstan, where Russians make up a majority and do not perceive the same loss of cultural dominance, there is less Russian discontent, which is likely to be one of the main reasons why fewer Russians are leaving the region.

In most of the other post-Soviet states there is also a net outmigration of Russians, although the figures there are less dramatic than those in Central Asia. There are exceptions to the rule. In Belarus, for example, better living conditions (despite Chernobyl) than in most parts of Russia, combined with a relatively stable political atmosphere and reasonably good inter-ethnic relations, have meant that relatively few Russians leave the country. At the same time a significant number of Russians are continuing to move to Belarus, so that that country, at least for a long time, did not have the net out-migration of Russians that was taking place in most of the other post-Soviet states.[37]

Some Russians in the new post-Soviet polities do not recognise the present state borders as legitimate. It is quite common for them to seek autonomy in (or political independence from) their present state and sometimes even a reunification with Russia. This has been the case, for example, with Russians on the Crimean peninsula, where the 1.6 million ethnic Russian population makes up about two-thirds of the total population.[38] The question of the status of Crimea has not led to serious incidents of violence so far. In the Trans-Dniester conflict in Moldova, however, there has been outright war between the conflicting parties over a disputed area. The battles over the Trans-Dniester territories and the proclamation of an autonomous republic on the left bank of the river Dniester has shown the potentially explosive force of the 'Russian question' in the post-Soviet states.[39]

Most Russians in the former Soviet republics have been granted the right to become citizens of their present state of residence through relatively liberal citizenship laws. However, Russians in many of the new states have shown little interest in obtaining citizenship of the state where they live. In a public opinion poll in December 1991, for example, only between 20 and 25 per cent of Russians in the Transcaucasian republics expressed a wish to obtain the citizenship of their state of residence, while in Kyrgyzstan and Tajikistan the percentage was even lower.[40] According to the citizenship legislation of the Russian Federation, former Soviet citizens can also apply for Russian citizenship, even when they do not intend to move to Russia.[41]

In some of the post-Soviet states Russians have pressed for the option of dual citizenship (of their present state of residence and of the Russian Federation) which, it is argued, would give them more security and better opportunities to maintain links with their ethnic homeland. Many Russians further believe that if they had dual citizenship (or citizenship of Russia alone) they could expect Russia to defend their rights in the state they live in. Dual citizenship has not, however, yet been granted on a large scale, and only a few of the new states allow for this possibility in their legislation.[42] The granting of dual citizenship is unlikely to become a common practice unless there are formal bilateral or multilateral arrangements on the issue between Russia and other post-Soviet states.[43]

The citizenship issue has, however, mainly been focused on the treatment of the non-indigenous minorities in the Baltic states of Estonia and Latvia. The main argument used to justify the rather strict policies on the issue, whereby large segments of the population in these two states are not granted the status of citizens, is that since the Baltic republics were incorporated into the Soviet Union illegally, these states cannot take responsibility for Soviet citizens who arrived in the republics during Soviet rule. Because of the demographic imbalance, former Soviet citizens must at least, it is argued, show that they are willing to integrate into Latvian or Estonian society. Language and other requirements for naturalisation of new citizens have therefore been introduced.

Most Russian immigrants, however, see the division between citizens and non-citizens as artificial and discriminatory, as they arrived in the republic – many were even invited to work there – in accordance with Soviet law, and they now feel they are being deprived of a citizenship they have already earned. Language tests and oaths of loyalty are therefore often thought to be humiliating. Many Russians in these two states are also worried that the gap between non-citizens and citizens will broaden in the future. There are already signs pointing in this direction. While it was long argued that only the political rights of non-citizens would be restricted, there are now laws and resolutions whereby non-citizens in Latvia will not enjoy, for example, the right to own land, the right freely to return to their state of residence, freely to choose a place of residence in any area of that state, etc.[44] Similar restrictions can be found in Estonian legislation. It is not clear whether citizens and non-citizens will receive the same social benefits in these two countries.

Some politicians openly play on anti-Russian sentiments in the population in order to gain popularity among the titular nationality and to maintain political power. Not uncommonly they are the same politicians who occupied leading positions during the Soviet period, and who need to use the nationality question in order to distract attention from their own political past or from a poor economic performance. Russians are, sometimes with a certain degree of relevance, referred to as potential fifth columnists and accused of running errands for Moscow. However, in emphasising and upholding the large gulf between Russians and the titular nationality they also prevent the integration of Russians from taking place; this again makes Russians insecure and easier to manipulate. Policies of confrontation are also easy to exploit by forces of the far right (or left; the distinction is often hard to draw) both in Russia and among Russians in the new states themselves.

Economic problems in the new states are another reason why local authorities do not and cannot fulfil their promises about financial support for the cultural development of Russians and other national minorities. However, in this respect Russians are usually in a better position than many of the other national minorities. The Russian language still enjoys a prominent position in most of the post-Soviet states, and Russians can usually still find schools teaching in Russian for their children. Moreover, it is usually not a great problem to obtain Russian literature, and Russians normally have access to Russian television which, combined with the size and density of the Russian population in certain localities, makes it relatively easy to maintain a Russian identity. It is also worth stressing that Russians tend to be more active in defending their economic interests than in the struggle for greater financial support for their cultural needs.[45]

This phenomenon is likely to be related to the fact that Russians in the republics have not attributed the same degree of significance to their ethnic origin as have other nationalities in the former Soviet Union. The future of the Russian diaspora will, however, be determined to a large degree by their ethnic identification. In other words, the degree to which Russians will identify with the Soviet past, their present state of residence, or Russia itself is likely to play an important role in defining their future position in the new states. Individual Russians have a degree of free choice as to which type of identification they assume, but their choice will usually be influenced by the way in which other Russians choose to identify. The treatment Russians receive from the local nationalities and the political leadership in the new states is also likely to play an important role in this process.

It may become easier to break free from the past Soviet identity now that the Soviet Union has been formally dissolved, but there can be no doubt that the Soviet Union continues to exist in the consciousness of a great number of former Soviet citizens, and especially among many of those who live outside their ethnic homelands. The important distinction between a cultural or ethnic identity, on the one hand, and political loyalty towards a state, on the other, must also be emphasised.[46] It seems reasonable to suggest that, among Russians who decide to remain in their present state of residence, those who already possess or develop an identification with this new state are more likely to adapt themselves to the new conditions. This does not imply that they necessarily need to adopt the cultural or ethnic identity of the dominant nationality of the state. However, such assimilation should not always be considered an evil, especially not if it takes place in the course of a natural process, for example through intermarriage.

While much will depend on the Russian diaspora itself and on how Russians are treated by the political leadership in the post-Soviet states in which they live, a third actor will be crucial in determining the future of the Russian population living outside Russia. The attitude taken by the Russian government, and its degree and form of involvement in the Russian diaspora question, will be of great importance in shaping the attitudes and actions of the two other main groups of actors. There is no reason to doubt that many Russian politicians have a genuine concern for Russians and other former Soviet citizens who suddenly find themselves in the diaspora, and often perceive it as a duty to protect their interests. At the same time there are also forces that are more inclined to use the Russian population in the post-Soviet states as a political card and as a means by which Russia can retain influence in the post-Soviet polities. Responsible politicans are subject to constant pressure from forces on the far right (or left) to take tougher measures in order to support Russians in the post-Soviet states who, it is argued, are subject to discrimination and wide-scale violation of their rights. Recently Boris Yeltsin and his government made the question of a troop withdrawal from Estonia and Latvia conditional on an improvement in the treatment of Russians, or ethnic *rossiyane*,[47] in the two countries.

The Russian diaspora question will thus be an important element in determining future relations between Russia and the new post-Soviet states and, thereby, the prospects for regional stability. The size alone of the Russian diaspora makes it a force that should not be underestimated by the political leadership in the Soviet successor states.[48] Although there is a danger that the Russian question could be exploited and manipulated in a high-level political game, there is reason to hope that all three groups of actors involved will realise that without a willingness to find compromises and mutually acceptable solutions to existing conflicts and tensions, the economic, political and social costs to all of them could be immense.

## ACKNOWLEDGEMENTS

I would like to thank Pål Kolstø, Martin Dewhirst and Åse Berit Grødeland for their help in preparing this chapter.

## NOTES

1. According to my definition of the Russian diaspora, I do not include the more than 8 million Russians living in autonomous territories within the Russian Federation. Similarly, military personnel in the Russian Army located outside the Russian borders are not here regarded as belonging to the Russian diaspora.
2. P. Kolstø, *The New Russian Diaspora* (London: Hurst, 1994).
3. See S. I. Bruk and V. M. Kabuzan, Dinamika chislennosti i rasselenie russkogo etnosa (1678–1917), *Sovetskaya etnografiya*, no. 4, 1982, pp. 9–25.
4. W. H. Parker, *A Historical Geography of Russia*, (London: University of London Press, 1968), no. 293.
5. G. Simon, *Nationalism and Policy Toward the Nationalities in the Soviet Union* (Boulder, CO: Westview Press, 1991), p. 119. One should, however, treat these figures with some caution, as the 1897 census did not ask about the ethnicity of the respondents but about their religion and mother tongue.
6. See Bruk and Kabuzan, op. cit.
7. Simon, op. cit., p. 119.
8. See S. I. Bruk and V. M. Kabuzan, Dinamika chislennosti i rasselenie russkikh posle Velikoi Oktyabr'skoi sotsialisticheskoi revolyutsii, *Sovetskaya etnografiya*, no. 5, 1982, pp. 3–21.
9. R. J. Misiunas and R. Taagepera, *The Baltic States: Years of Dependence 1940–1980* (London: Hurst, 1983) p. 186.
10. However, after the death of the Lithuanian First Party Secretary Snieckus in 1974 the rate of immigration increased also in Lithuania, which was

also caused by the fact that industrial expansion continued after rural labour reserves had been exhausted. See Lieven, A., *The Baltic Revolution – Estonia, Latvia, Lithuania and the Path to Independence* (New Haven, CT and London. Yale University Press, 1993), pp. 183–84.

11. See L. Gudkov, The Disintegration of the USSR and Russians in the Republics, *Journal of Communist Studies*, Vol. 9, March 1993, No. 1, pp. 76–77.

12. Arutyunyan *et al.* (ed.), *Russkie – Etnosotsiologicheskie ocherki* (Moscow: Nauka, 1992), p. 25.

13. Ibid., pp. 46–47. It is noteworthy that Russians in the cities of Alma-Ata (Kazakhstan) and Bishkek (Kyrgyzstan) made up between 55 and 60 per cent of the population.

14. See for example F. C. Barghoorn, *Soviet Russian Nationalism* (New York: Oxford University Press, 1956).

15. Since census data on language fluency are based on the subjective evaluation of each respondent, they should be treated with great caution. It is worth noting that the censuses asked about fluency (*svobodnoe vladenie*) in a second Soviet language, and census data therefore do not give an estimate of the proportion of the population with language knowledge at a conversational level.

16. J. H. Miller, Cadres Policy in Nationality Areas, *Soviet Studies*, Vol. XXIX, no. 1, January 1977, pp. 3–36 (see p. 35).

17. W. Connor, *The National Question in Marxist-Leninist Theory and Practice* (Princeton, NJ: Princeton University Press, 1984), p. 319.

18. It could, however, also be argued that Soviet politicians, who did not operate according to signals from the market, had completely different intentions when they took decisions about where to locate new industries.

19. P. Kolstø, Unionsopplosning og det russiske diaspora-spørsmål: Et stabilitetsperspektiv, *Internasional Politikk* (Oslo), nos 1–2, 1992, pp. 95–122 (see p. 102).

20. See R. Karklins, *Ethnic Relations in the USSR* (Boston, MA: Unwin Hyman, 1986) p. 39.

21. R. O. Rasiak, 'The Soviet People': Multiethnic Alternative or Ruse, in E. Allworth (ed.), *Ethnic Russia in the USSR. The Dilemma of Dominance* (New York: Pergamon, 1980), p. 160.

22. See for example L. Gudkov, Attitudes Towards Russians in the Union Republics, *Sociological Research* (Moscow), 31:6, November–December 1992, pp. 11–29.

23. Y. V. Arutyunyan and L. M. Drobyzheva, Russkie v raspadayushchemsya soyuze, *Otechestvennaya Istoriya*, no. 3, 1992, pp. 3–15.

24. E. Starikov, Rossiya i 'drugie russkie', *Znamya* (Moscow), no. 2, 1993, p. 186.

25. M. Pavlovich, Ethnic impact of Russian Dispersion in and beyond the RSFSR, *Ethnic Russia in the USSR. The Dilemma of Dominance* (New York: Pergamon, 1980), pp. 294–305. See also P. Kolstø, The Russian Diaspora – an Identity of Its Own, presented at a conference on 'The New Russian Diaspora', Riga, 10–12 November 1992.

26. Starikov, op. cit., p. 187.

27. P. Kolstø, The New Russian Diaspora: Minority Protection in the Soviet Successor States, *Journal of Peace Research*, 30:2, May 1993, p. 200.

28. See for example B. Tsilevich, Na iskhode tret'ego goda, *SM-segodnya*, 24 March 1993, p. 2. Tsilevich himself is not a Russian by nationality, and considers himself a 'cosmopolitan'.

29. I. Rotar', Slavyane v Srednei Azii – adaptatsiya ili begstvo?, *Nezavisimaya gazeta*, 29 April 1993, p. 3.

30. Smith, Aasland and Mole, The New States, Ethnic Relations and Citizenship, in G. Smith (ed.), *The Baltic States. The National Self-Determination of Estonia, Latvia and Lithuania* (London: Macmillan, 1994).

31. While a majority of the Russophone populace of Western Ukraine (according to a survey from 1991) believed that the attitude to Russians in that area had worsened over the past two to three years, the same was true of only one in ten respondents in Eastern Ukraine. J. B. Dunlop, Will a Large-Scale Migration of Russians to the Russian Republic Take Place in the Near Future?, presented at a conference on The New Russian Diaspora, Jurmala, Latvia, 10–12 November 1992.

32. One example is the Donbas coal miners (mostly ethnic Russians) in South-Eastern Ukraine who went on strike in June 1993 as a reaction against increasing prices and deteriorating living conditions. It appeared that one of the reasons for the problems was that Russia no longer supplied the mining industry with required inputs at reduced prices. See A. Wilson, The Growing Challenge to Kiev from the Donbas, *RFL/RL Research Report*, Vol. 2, No. 33, 20 August 1993, pp. 8–13.

33. According to Russian legislation, a 'refugee' is a person without Russian citizenship, while 'involuntary' or 'forced migrants' are those who qualify under the 1992 citizenship law as citizens of the Russian Federation. The laws on refugees and forced migrants were published in *Rossiiskie vesti*, 30 March 1993.

34. There is, for example, concern that female labour could be specifically affected by the growing Islamicisation of labour traditions, and that Russian women could be pushed out from certain technical fields of occupation. See V. Tishkov, The Russians are Leaving, presented to the North South Roundtable of Policy-Makers on the Population Movements in the 1990s, Geneva, December 1991.

35. *Rossiiskaya Gazeta*, 27 August 1993, p. 7.

36. *Trud*, 14 April 1993, p. 2.

37. See *Svobodnaya mysl'*, no. 12, 1992, p. 5.

38. See I. Bremmer, Ethnic Issues in Crimea, *RFL/RL Research Report*, Vol. 2, No. 18, 30 April 1993.

39. Although only approximately 25 per cent of the population in the Trans-Dniester republic are Russians (40 per cent are Moldovans and 28 per cent Ukrainians), the Russians dominate industry, political structures, the army and police, while the Moldovans live in rural areas without significant political representation. For more on this conflict, see P. Kolstø and A. Yedemskii, The Dniester Conflict: Between Irredentism and Separatism, *Europe–Asia Studies*, vol. 45, no. 6, 1993, pp. 973–1000.

40. L. Gudkov, The Disintegration of the USSR and Russians in the Republics, *Journal of Communist Studies*, Vol. 9, March 1993, No. 1, p. 81.

41. They must, however, have made up their minds by February 1995 in order to be granted citizenship.
42. This is, for example, the case in Ukraine, where it was included at a later stage. See S. Stewart, Ukraine's Policy toward its Ethnic Minorities, *RFL/RL Research Report*, Vol. 2, No. 36, 10 September 1993, p. 56.
43. The law on citizenship of the Russian Federation (the text of the law can be found in *Rossiiskaya gazeta*, 6 February 1992) stipulates formal bilateral agreements as a requirement in order for Russia to allow for dual citizenship.
44. B. Tsilevich, Citizenship Issues and Language Legislation in Today's Latvia, presented at a conference on Citizenship and Language Laws of the Newly Independent States of Europe, Copenhagen, 9–10 January 1993.
45. Although Russians have been quite active in defending the right to secondary and higher education in Russia, this should not be seen mainly as a cultural demand, since it is also to a large extent motivated by a wish not to see their children lose out in the competition for higher education. On the other hand, some Russians believe that in order to help their children to upward mobility, it is better to send them to schools with instruction in the local language.
46. See P. Kolstø, The Russian Diaspora – an Identity of Its Own, *op. cit.*
47. *Rossiyane* is the term used to denote citizens of the Russian Federation, regardless of their nationality. Ethnic *rossiyane* are, thus, people who belong to the Russian ethnos or to other ethnic groups with their ethnic homeland inside the Russian Federation. For a critical view on the concept of 'ethnic *rossiyane*' and its implementation in Russian legislation, see Kudryavtsev, Strategiia zashchity, *Nezavisimaya gazeta*, 3 September 1993, p. 6.
48. This includes the Baltic states, although in strictly legal terms they are not successor states of the Soviet Union.

Appendix 1 : **ETHNIC AND TERRITORIAL CLAIMS OF THE POST-SOVIET STATES**

## TRANSCAUCASIA AND SOUTHERN RUSSIA

Demands for creation of separate nationality-based administrative units in Karachay-Cherkessia, Kabardino-Balkar, Chechnya and Ingushetia

Demands for merger of North Ossetia and South Ossetia

Demand from Abkhazia for elevation to republican status

(K) Kurdish communities demanding creation of nationality-based administrative units in Southern Caucasus

(P) Polish communities demanding the creation of nationality-based administrative units in Belarus and Lithuania

(G) Demands from Gagauz communities for the creation of an Autonomous region in Southern Moldova

CASPIAN SEA

DAGESTAN

CHECHNYA
INGUSHETIA
NORTH OSSETIA
KABARDINO-BALKAR
SOUTH OSSETIA
KARACHAY-CHERKESSIA
ADZHARIA

RUSSIA

GEORGIA

ARMENIA

AZERBAIJAN

NAGORNO-KARABAKH

NACHICEVAN

(K)

IRAN

TURKEY

BLACK SEA

0    200
kilometres

Secessionist movements

Contested territory

claimant

Agay-Buryatia

BURYATIA

TUVA

Gorno-Altay
Altay

RUSSIA

KAZAKHSTAN

KYRGYZSTAN

TAJIKISTAN

UZBEKISTAN

TURKMENISTAN

KARAKALPAKSTAN

KALMYKIA

BASHKORTOSTAN

TATARSTAN

KARELIA

ESTONIA

LATVIA

LITHUANIA

(P)

KALININGRAD

BELARUS

UKRAINE

MOLDOVA

(G)

CRIMEA

DONBAS

GEORGIA

ARMENIA

AZERBAIJAN

SEE INSET

0    1000
kilometres

# Comparative Tables for the Major Nationalities in the Post-Soviet States

Table no.

Table 1   Populations of the republics/post-soviet states, total and urban, 1979 and 1989

|  | 1979 Total (000s) | 1979 Urban (000s) | % urban | 1989 Total (000s) | 1989 Urban (000s) | % urban |
|---|---|---|---|---|---|---|
| Russia | 137,551 | 95,374 | 69 | 147,386 | 108,419 | 74 |
| Estonia | 1,466 | 1,022 | 70 | 1,573 | 1,127 | 71 |
| Latvia | 2,521 | 1,726 | 68 | 2,681 | 1,907 | 71 |
| Lithuania | 3,398 | 2,062 | 61 | 3,690 | 2,509 | 68 |
| Ukraine | 49,755 | 30,512 | 61 | 51,704 | 34,591 | 67 |
| Belarus | 9,560 | 5,263 | 55 | 10,200 | 6,676 | 65 |
| Moldova | 3,947 | 1,551 | 39 | 4,341 | 2,037 | 47 |
| Armenia | 3,031 | 1,993 | 66 | 3,283 | 2,225 | 68 |
| Azerbaijan | 6,028 | 3,200 | 53 | 7,029 | 3,785 | 54 |
| Georgia | 5,015 | 2,601 | 52 | 5,499 | 3,033 | 56 |
| Kazakhstan | 14,685 | 7,920 | 54 | 16,538 | 9,465 | 57 |
| Uzbekistan | 15,391 | 6,348 | 41 | 19,906 | 8,106 | 41 |
| Turkmenistan | 2,759 | 1,323 | 48 | 3,534 | 1,603 | 45 |
| Tajikistan | 3,801 | 1,325 | 35 | 5,112 | 1,667 | 33 |
| Kyrgyzstan | 3,529 | 1,366 | 39 | 4,291 | 1,641 | 38 |

*Sources*: Tsentral'noe Statisticheskoe Upravlenie SSSR, *Naselenie SSSR, Po Vsesoyuznoi Perepisi Naseleniya 1979 goda* (Moscow, Izdatel'stvo Politicheskoi Literatury 1980), pp. 4–11; *Izvestiya* 28 April 1989; Pravda 29 April 1989.

Table 2  Nationality composition of the union republics/post-soviet states, 1959–1989

| | 1959 | | | | 1979 | | | | 1989 | | | |
|---|---|---|---|---|---|---|---|---|---|---|---|---|
| | Total (000s) | Percentage Indigenous | Russian | Other | Total (000s) | Percentage Indigenous | Russian | Other | Total (000s) | Percentage Indigenous | Russian | Other |
| Russia | 117,534 | 83.3 | 83.3 | 16.7 | 130,079 | 82.8 | 82.8 | 17.2 | 148,041 | 81.5 | – | 18.5 |
| Estonia | 1,197 | 74.6 | 20.1 | 5.3 | 1,464 | 64.7 | 27.9 | 7.4 | 1,583 | 61.5 | 30.3 | 8.2 |
| Latvia | 2,093 | 62.0 | 26.6 | 11.4 | 2,503 | 53.7 | 32.8 | 13.5 | 2,687 | 52.0 | 34.0 | 14.0 |
| Lithuania | 2,711 | 79.3 | 8.5 | 12.2 | 3,391 | 80.0 | 8.9 | 11.1 | 3,723 | 79.6 | 9.4 | 11.0 |
| Ukraine | 41,869 | 76.8 | 16.9 | 6.3 | 49,609 | 73.6 | 21.1 | 5.3 | 51,839 | 72.7 | 22.1 | 5.2 |
| Belarus | 8,056 | 81.1 | 8.2 | 10.7 | 9,532 | 79.4 | 11.9 | 8.7 | 10,259 | 77.9 | 13.2 | 8.9 |
| Moldova | 2,885 | 65.4 | 10.1 | 24.4 | 3,950 | 63.9 | 12.8 | 23.3 | 4,362 | 64.5 | 13.0 | 22.5 |
| Armenia | 1,763 | 88.0 | 3.2 | 8.8 | 3,037 | 89.7 | 2.3 | 8.0 | 3,293 | 93.3 | 1.6 | 5.1 |
| Azerbaijan | 3,698 | 67.5 | 13.6 | 18.9 | 6,027 | 78.1 | 7.9 | 14.0 | 7,131 | 82.7 | 5.6 | 11.7 |
| Georgia | 4,044 | 64.3 | 10.1 | 25.6 | 5,015 | 68.8 | 7.4 | 23.8 | 5,456 | 70.1 | 6.3 | 23.6 |
| Kazakhstan | 9,295 | 30.0 | 42.7 | 27.3 | 14,684 | 36.0 | 40.8 | 23.2 | 16,691 | 39.7 | 37.8 | 22.5 |
| Uzbekistan | 8,119 | 62.1 | 13.5 | 24.4 | 15,789 | 68.7 | 10.8 | 20.5 | 20,322 | 71.4 | 8.3 | 21.3 |
| Turkmenistan | 1,516 | 60.9 | 17.3 | 21.8 | 2,765 | 68.4 | 12.6 | 19.0 | 3,622 | 72.0 | 9.5 | 19.5 |
| Tajikistan | 1,981 | 53.1 | 13.3 | 33.6 | 3,806 | 58.8 | 10.4 | 30.8 | 5,248 | 62.3 | 7.6 | 31.1 |
| Kyrgyzstan | 3,523 | 47.9 | 25.9 | 26.2 | 3,523 | 47.9 | 25.9 | 26.2 | 4,367 | 52.4 | 21.5 | 26.1 |

Sources: Tsentral'noe Statisticheskoe Upravlenie pri Sovete Ministrov SSSR Itogi Vsesoyuznoi Perepisi Naseleniya 1970 goda (Moscow, Statistika, 1973) vol. IV, p. 144; Tsentral'noe Statisticheskoe Upravlenie SSSR, Naselenie SSSR. Po Vsesoyuznoi Perepisi Naseleniya 1979 goda (Moscow, Izdatel'stvo Politicheskoi Literatury 1980) pp. 27–30; Natsionalnyi Sostav Nasekniya SSSR (Moscow, 1990).

Table 3   Proportion of the major Northern Eurasian nationalities declaring their nationality language as their native tongue, 1959, 1979 and 1989

| | 1959 | | | | 1979 | | | | 1989 |
| --- | --- | --- | --- | --- | --- | --- | --- | --- | --- |
| | Total | Urban | Residing in own nationality homeland | Residing outside nationality homeland | Total | Urban | Residing in own nationality homeland | Residing outside nationality homeland | Total |
| Russians | 99.8 | 99.9 | 100.0 | 99.3 | 99.8 | 99.4 | 100.0 | 99.9 | 99.8 |
| Estonians | 95.2 | 93.1 | 99.3 | 56.6 | 95.3 | 93.4 | 99.0 | 33.3 | 95.5 |
| Latvians | 95.1 | 93.1 | 98.4 | 53.2 | 95.0 | 93.3 | 97.8 | 55.3 | 94.8 |
| Lithuanians | 97.8 | 96.6 | 99.2 | 80.3 | 97.9 | 97.4 | 97.9 | 63.9 | 97.7 |
| Ukrainians | 87.7 | 77.2 | 93.5 | 51.2 | 82.8 | 73.7 | 89.1 | 43.8 | 81.1 |
| Belarusians | 84.2 | 63.5 | 93.2 | 41.9 | 74.2 | 59.1 | 83.5 | 36.8 | 70.9 |
| Moldovans | 95.2 | 78.4 | 98.2 | 77.7 | 93.2 | 81.3 | 96.5 | 74.3 | 91.6 |
| Armenians | 89.9 | 84.4 | 99.2 | 78.1 | 90.7 | 87.6 | 99.4 | 73.9 | 91.6 |
| Azerbaijanis | 97.5 | 96.4 | 98.1 | 95.1 | 97.9 | 96.2 | 98.7 | 92.7 | 97.6 |
| Georgians | 98.6 | 96.8 | 99.5 | 73.4 | 98.3 | 96.9 | 99.4 | 67.3 | 98.2 |
| Kazakhs | 98.4 | 96.7 | 99.2 | 95.6 | 97.5 | 97.1 | 98.6 | 92.8 | 97.0 |
| Uzbeks | 98.4 | 96.7 | 98.6 | 97.4 | 98.5 | 96.1 | 98.8 | 96.9 | 98.3 |
| Turkmens | 98.9 | 97.3 | 99.5 | 92.0 | 98.7 | 97.0 | 99.2 | 90.4 | 98.5 |
| Tajiks | 98.1 | 96.4 | 99.3 | 94.6 | 97.8 | 95.9 | 99.3 | 92.8 | 97.7 |
| Kyrgyz | 98.7 | 97.4 | 99.7 | 92.3 | 97.9 | 97.3 | 99.6 | 84.8 | 97.8 |

Table 3—Contd.

| | Total | Urban | 1959 Residing in own nationality homeland | Residing outside nationality homeland | total | Urban | 1979 Residing in own nationality homeland | Residing outside nationality homeland | 1989 Total |
|---|---|---|---|---|---|---|---|---|---|
| Tatars | 92.0 | 87.5 | 98.9 | 89.3 | 85.9 | 81.0 | 97.9 | 81.8 | 83.2 |
| Chuvash | 90.8 | 71.2 | 97.5 | 83.2 | 81.7 | 64.7 | 89.8 | 73.4 | 76.5 |
| Bashkirs | 61.9 | 73.3 | 57.6 | 75.1 | 67.0 | 72.8 | 64.4 | 72.6 | 72.3 |
| Mordovians | 78.1 | 52.2 | 97.3 | 70.9 | 72.6 | 55.1 | 94.3 | 63.9 | 67.0 |
| Chechens | 98.8 | 97.0 | 99.7 | 97.8 | 98.6 | 96.3 | 99.7 | 94.0 | 98.0 |
| Udmurts | 89.1 | 69.7 | 93.2 | 75.9 | 76.5 | 60.6 | 82.3 | 64.4 | 69.6 |
| Mari | 95.1 | 75.8 | 97.8 | 91.6 | 86.7 | 72.3 | 83.7 | 79.9 | 80.8 |
| Ossetians | 89.1 | 82.0 | 98.0 | 73.1 | 88.2 | 84.2 | 92.3 | 75.8 | 87.0 |
| Buryats | 94.9 | 81.5 | 97.3 | 84.9 | 90.2 | 78.8 | 93.1 | 86.0 | 86.3 |
| Yakut | 97.5 | 90.7 | 98.2 | 82.8 | 95.3 | 86.1 | 96.4 | 72.3 | 93.8 |
| Germans | 75.0 | 66.3 | – | – | 57.0 | 48.5 | – | – | 48.7 |
| Jews | 21.5 | 21.0 | – | – | 14.2 | 12.3 | – | – | 11.1 |
| Poles | 45.2 | 38.6 | – | – | 29.1 | 27.8 | – | – | 30.4 |
| Crimean Tatars | – | – | – | – | – | – | – | – | 92.5 |

*Sources:* Tsentral'noe Statisticheskoe Upravlenie pri Sovete Ministrov SSSR *Itogi Vsesoyuznoi Perepisi Naseleniya 1970 goda* (Moscow, Statistika 1973) vol. IV, p. 144; Tsentral'noe Statisticheskoe Upravlenie SSSR *Naselenie SSSR. Po Vsesoyuznoi Perepisi Naseleniya 1979 goda* (Moscow, Izdatel'stvo Politicheskoi Literatury 1980); Gosudarstvennyi Komitet SSSR Po Statistike Soobshchaet, *Natsional'nyi Sostav Naseleniya* (Moscow, 1990), Vol. 11, pp. 3–5.

Table 4   Proportion of the major Northern Eurasian nationalities declaring a knowledge of Russian as a second language, 1970, 1979 and 1989 (percentages)

|  | *1970* | *1979* | *1989* |
|---|---|---|---|
| Russians | 0.1 | 0.1 | 0.1 |
| Estonians | 29.0 | 24.2 | 33.8 |
| Latvians | 45.2 | 56.7 | 64.4 |
| Lithuanians | 35.9 | 52.1 | 37.9 |
| Ukrainians | 36.3 | 49.8 | 56.2 |
| Belarusians | 49.0 | 57.0 | 54.7 |
| Moldovans | 36.1 | 47.4 | 53.8 |
| Armenians | 30.1 | 38.6 | 47.1 |
| Azerbaijanis | 16.6 | 29.5 | 34.4 |
| Georgians | 21.3 | 26.7 | 33.1 |
| Kazakhs | 41.8 | 52.3 | 60.4 |
| Uzbeks | 14.5 | 49.3 | 23.8 |
| Turkmens | 15.4 | 25.4 | 27.8 |
| Tajiks | 15.4 | 29.6 | 27.7 |
| Kyrgyz | 19.1 | 29.4 | 35.2 |
| Tatars | 62.5 | 68.9 | 70.8 |
| Chuvash | 58.4 | 64.8 | 65.1 |
| Bashkirs | 53.3 | 64.9 | 71.8 |
| Mordovians | 65.7 | 65.5 | 62.5 |
| Chechens | 66.7 | 76.0 | 74.0 |
| Udmurts | 63.3 | 64.4 | 61.3 |
| Mari | 62.4 | 69.9 | 68.8 |
| Ossetians | 58.6 | 64.9 | 68.9 |
| Buryats | 66.7 | 71.9 | 72.0 |
| Yakut | 41.7 | 55.6 | 64.9 |
| Germans | 59.6 | 51.7 | 45.0 |
| Jews | 16.3 | 13.7 | 10.1 |
| Poles | 37.0 | 44.7 | 43.9 |
| Crimean Tatars | – | – | 76.0 |

*Sources*: Tsentral'noe Statisticheskoe Upravlenie SSSR, *Naselenie SSSR, Po Vsesoyuznoi Perepisi Naseleniya 1979 goda* (Moscow, Izdatel'stvo Politicheskoi Literatury 1980), pp. 23–6; Gosudarstvennyi Komitet SSSR Po Statistike Soobshchaet, *Natsional'nyi Sostav Naseleniya* (Moscow, 1990), Vol. 11, pp. 3–5.

Table 5 The Ethnic Composition of the Russian Federation's republics

| | Population ('000s) | % Titular | % Russian |
|---|---|---|---|
| **Central Russia** | | | |
| Bashkortostan | 3.9 | 22 | 39 |
| Chuvashia | 1.3 | 68 | 27 |
| Karelia | 0.8 | 10 | 74 |
| Komi | 1.3 | 23 | 58 |
| Marii-El | 0.8 | 43 | 47 |
| Mordovia | 0.6 | 32 | 61 |
| Tatarstan | 3.6 | 49 | 43 |
| Udmurtia | 1.6 | 31 | 59 |
| **North Caucasus** | | | |
| Adygeya | 0.4 | 22 | 68 |
| Chechnya Ingushetia | 1.3 | 58 | 23 |
| Dagestan | 1.8 | 80 | 9 |
| Kabardino-Balkaria | 0.8 | 53 | 39 |
| Kalmykia | 0.3 | 45 | 38 |
| Karachi-Cherkesia | 0.4 | 31 (Karachis) 10 (Cherkess) | 42 |
| North Ossetia | 0.6 | 53 | 30 |
| **Siberia** | | | |
| Buryatia | 1.0 | 24 | 70 |
| Gorny-Attai | 0.2 | 31 | 60 |
| Khakassia | 0.6 | 11 | 79 |
| Sakha | 1.1 | 33 | 50 |
| Tuva | 0.3 | 64 | 32 |

*Source*: Based on data from the 1989 All-Union Soviet Census. *Natsional'nyi sostav naseleniya SSSR (Moscow: Finansy i Statistika, 1991)*

# Select Bibliographic Guide to Further Reading in the English Language

## GENERAL

Bremmer, I. and Taras, R. eds *Nations and Politics in the Soviet Successor States* (Cambridge, Cambridge University Press 1993).

Connor, W. *The National Question in Marxist-Leninist Theory and Strategy* (Princeton, NJ, Princeton University Press 1984).

Dawisha, K. and Parrot, B. *Russia and the New State of Eurasia. The Politics of Upheaval*, (Cambridge, Cambridge University Press, 1994).

Gellner, E. 'Ethnicity and Faith in Eastern Europe' *Daedalus* vol. 119 (1), 1990, pp. 279–94.

Gleason, G. *Federalism and Nationalism. The Struggle for Republic Rights in the USSR* (Boulder, CO, Westview Press 1990).

Hajda, I. and Beissinger, M. eds *The Nationalities Factor in Soviet Politics and Society* (Boulder, CO, Westview Press, 1990).

Hosking, G., Aves, J. and Duncan, P. *The Road to Post-Communism: Independent Political Movements in the Soviet Union, 1985–1991* (London, Pinter 1992).

Huttenbach, H. ed. *Soviet Nationality Policies, Ruling Ethnic Groups in the USSR* (London, Mansell Press 1990).

Kaiser, R. *The Geography of Nationalism in Russia and the USSR* (Princeton, NJ, Princeton University Press 1994).

Lapidus, G., Zaslavsky, V. and Goldman, P. eds *From Union to Commonwealth: Nationalism and Separatism in the Soviet Republics* (Cambridge, Cambridge University Press 1992).

McAuley, A. ed. *Soviet Federalism. Nationalism and Economic Decentralisation* (Leicester University Press, Leicester 1991).

Motyl, A. *Will the Non-Russians Rebel? State, Ethnicity and Stability in the USSR* (Ithica, NY and London, Cornell University Press 1987).

Motyl, A. ed. *Thinking Theoretically about Soviet Nationalities. History and Comparisons in the Study of the USSR* (New York, Columbia University Press 1992).

Nahaylo, B. and Swoboda, V. *Soviet Disunion: A History of the Nationalities Problem in the USSR* (London, Hamish Hamilton 1990).

Smith, G. 'Gorbachev's Greatest Challenge: Perestroika and the National Question' *Political Geography Quarterly* vol. 8(1), 1989, pp. 409–24.

Smith, G. The State, Nationalism and the Soviet Republics. In C. Merridale and C. Ward eds *Perestroika in Historical Perspective* (London, Edward Arnold 1991), pp. 202–16.

Smith, G. Federation, refederation, defederation. From the Soviet Union to Russian Statehood. In G. Smith ed., *Federalism: The Multiethnic Challenge* (London, Longman 1995).

Szporluk, R. (ed) *National Identity and Ethnicity in Russia and the New States of Eurasia* (New York and London, M.E. Sharpe, 1994).

Zaslavsky, V. *The Neo-Stalinist State. Class, Ethnicity and Consensus in Soviet Society* (New York, M E Sharpe 1982).

# RUSSIA, THE RUSSIANS AND THE NON-RUSSIANS

Bawden, C. *Shamans, Lamas and Evangelicals* (London, Routledge and Kegan Paul 1985).

Blum, D. ed. *Russia's Future. Consolidation or Disintegration?* (Boulder, CO, Westview Press 1994).

Dunlop, J. *The Rise of Russia and the Fall of the Soviet Empire* (Princeton, NJ, Princeton University Press 1993).

Carter, S. *Russian Nationalism: Yesterday, Today and Tomorrow* (London, Pinter 1990).

Emerson, C. 'The Shape of Russian Cultural Criticism in the Post-Communist Period' *Canadian Slavonic Papers*, vol 34 (4), 1992.

Hosking, G. The Russian Myth: Empire and People, in P. Duncan and M. Rady eds, *Towards a New Community: Culture and Politics in Post-Totalitarian Europe* (Hamburg and Münster, LIT Verlag).

Humphrey, C. *Karl Marx Collective: Economy, Society and Religion in a Siberian Collective Farm* (Cambridge, Cambridge University Press 1983).

McKean, R. ed. *New Perspectives in Modern Russian History* (London, Macmillan 1992).

Rorlich, A. A. *The Volga Tatars: The Profile of a People in National Resilience* (Stanford, CA, Hoover Institution Press, Stanford University 1986).

Smith, G. The Ethnopolitics of Federation without Federation. In D. Lane (ed) *Russia in Transition*, (London, Longman, 1995).

Szporluk, R. 'Dilemmas of Russian Nationalism' *Problems of Communism* 38 (4), 1989, pp. 15–35.

White, S. *et al.* 'Religion and Politics in Post-Communist Russia' *Religion, State, and Society* vol. 22 (1), 1994.

Wood, A. and French, A. eds *The Development of Siberia: People and Resources* (London, Macmillan 1989).

Yanov A. *The Russian Challenge* (Oxford, Basil Blackwell 1987).

## BALTIC STATES

Hiden, J. and Salmon, P. *The Baltic Nations and Europe. Estonia, Latvia and Lithuania in the Twentieth Century* (London, Longman 1991).

Karklins, R. *Ethnopolitics and Transition to Democracy. The Collapse of the USSR and Latvia* (Baltimore, MD and London, Johns Hopkins University Press 1994).

Lieven, A. *The Baltic Revolution. Estonia, Latvia, Lithuania and the Path to Independence* (New Haven, CT and London, Yale University Press 1993).

Misiunas, R. and Taagepera, R. *The Baltic States: Years of Dependence, 1940–1980* (Berkeley, CA, University of California Press 1983).

Park, A. 'Ethnicity and Independence: The Case of Estonia in Comparative Perspective' *Europe-Asia Studies*, vol 46 (10), 1994, pp. 69–87.

Rauch, Georg von *The Baltic States. The Years of Independence 1917–1940* (London, C. Hurst and Co. 1974).

Senn, A. E. *Lithuania Awakening* (Berkeley, CA, University of California Press 1990).

Smith, G. ed. *The Baltic States. The National Self-Determination of Estonia, Latvia and Lithuania* (London, Macmillan 1994).

Smith, G. 'The Nationalities Problem in the Soviet Baltic republics of Estonia, Latvia and Lithuania' *Acta Baltica* vol. 21 (1982), pp. 147–77.

Taagepera, R. *Estonia. Return to Independence* (Boulder, CO, Westview Press 1993).

Vardys, V. S. *The Catholic Church, Dissent and Nationality in Soviet Lithuania* (Boulder, CO and New York, Columbia University Press 1978).

## THE SOUTH-WESTERN BORDERLANDS

Bilinsky, Y. *Ukraine: From Nationality to Nation* (Boulder, CO, Westview Press, 1995).

Bremmer, I. 'The Politics of Ethnicity: Russians in the New Ukraine' *Europe-Asia Studies*, vol 46(2), 1994.

Crowther, W. 'The Politics of Mobilisation: Nationalism and Reform in Soviet Moldavia' *Russian Review* vol 50, no. 2, April 1991.

Dima, N. *From Moldavia to Moldova: The Soviet–Romanian Territorial Dispute* (Boulder, CO, Westview Press, 1991).

Dima, N. Moldavians or Romanians? In R. Clem ed. *The Soviet West* (New York, Praeger 1975).

Gow, J. 'Independent Ukraine: The Politics of Security' *International Affairs*, vol XI (3), 1992.

Kuzio, T. and Wilson, A. *Ukraine: Perestroika to Independence* (London, Macmillan 1994).

Morrison, J. 'Pereyaslav and After: The Russian–Ukrainian Relationship' *International Affairs*, vol. 69 (4), 1993.

Motyl, A. *Dilemmas of Independence: Ukraine After Totalitarianism* (New York, Council on Foreign Relations 1993).

Nahaylo, B. *The New Ukraine* (London, Royal Institute of International Affairs 1992).

Saunders, D. 'What Makes a Nation a Nation? Ukraine Since 1600' *Ethnic Studies* vol. 10, 1993.

Solchanyk, R. *Ukraine: From Chernobyl to Sovereignty* (Basingstoke, Macmillan 1992).

Solchanyk R. 'Russia, Ukraine and the Imperial Legacy' *Post-Soviet Affairs* vol. 9(4), 1993.

Solchanyk, R. 'The Politics of State-Building: Centre–Periphery Relations in Post-Soviet Ukraine' *Europe-Asia Studies*, vol. 46(1), 1994.

Zaprudnik, J. 'Belarus Awakening' *Problems of Communism*, vol. 38(4), 1989.

Zaprudnik, J. *Belarus: At A Crossroads in History* (Boulder, CO, Westview Press 1993).

## TRANSCAUCASIA

Bournoutian, G. *A History of the Armenian People*, vol. 1, Pre-History to 1500 AD (CA, Mazda Publishers, 1993).

Dragadze, T. 'The Armenian-Azerbaijhani Conflict: Structure and Sentiment' *Third World Quarterly* vol. 11 (1), 1989.

Goldenberg, S. *The Caucasus and Post Soviet Disorder* (London, Zed Books 1995).

Jones, S. 'The Establishment of Soviet Power in Transcaucasia: the case of Georgia, 1921–1928' *Soviet Studies*, vol. 40 (4), December 1988.

Libaridian, G. ed., *Armenia at the Cross-roads: Democracy and Nationhood in the Post-Soviet Era: Essays, Interviews and Speeches by the Leaders of the National Democratic Movement in Armenia* (Watertown, MA, Zoryan Institute 1991).

Parsons, R. 'National Integration in Soviet Georgia' *Soviet Studies*, vol. 34 (4), October 1982.

Suny, R. *Armenia in the Twentieth Century* (Chico, CA, Scolar's Press 1983).

Sunny, R. *The Making of the Modern Georgian Nation* (London, Tauris 1989).

Suny, R. *Looking Toward Ararat, Armenia in Modern History* (Bloomington and Indianapolis, IN, Indiana University Press 1993).

Walker, C. ed. *Armenia and Karabagh. The Struggle for Unity* (London, Minority Rights Publications 1991).

Walker, C. *Armenia: The Survival of a Nation* (London, Routledge 1990).

## MUSLIM CENTRAL ASIA

Akiner, S. *Central Asia: A New Arc of Crisis?* (London, Royal United Services Institute 1993).

Akiner, S. ed. *Cultural Change and Continuity in Central Asia* (London, Kegan Paul 1991).

Atkin, M. Tajikistan: ancient heritage, new politics. In R. Bremmer and I. Tauras eds *Politics and Nations in the Soviet Successor States* (Cambridge, Cambridge University Press 1993), pp. 361–83.

Benningsen, A. and Wimbush, A. *Muslims of the Soviet Empire: a Guide* (London, C. Hurst and Co. 1986).

Benson, L. and Svanberg, I. *The Kazaks of China. Essays on an Ethnic Minority* (Uppsala, Almquvist and Wiksell International 1988).

Critchlow, J. *Nationalism in Uzbekistan: A Soviet Republic's Road to Sovereignty* (Boulder CO, Westview Press 1991).

Glazebrrok, P. *Journey to Khiva* (London, Harvill 1992).

Lewis, R. ed. *Geographic Perspectives on Soviet Central Asia* (New York, Columbia University Press 1992).

Naumkin, V. ed. *State, Religion and Society in Central Asia. A Post-Soviet Critique* (Reading, Ithica Press 1993).

Olcott, M. *The Kazakhs* (Stanford, CA, Hoover Institution Press 1987).

Rumer, B. *Central Asia: A Tragic Experiment* (Unwin Hyman, London 1989).

Rywkin, M. *Moscow's Muslim Challenge: Soviet Central Asia* (New York and London, Hurst 1982).

Taheri, *A Crescent in a Red Sky* (London, Hutchinson 1989).

# THE DIASPORA NATIONALITIES

Allworth, E. ed. *Tatars of the Crimea: Their Struggle for Survival* (Durham, NC, Duke University Press 1988).

Fisher, A. *The Crimean Tatars* (Stanford, CA, Hoover Institution Press 1978).

Freedman, I. ed. *Soviet Jewry in the 1980s* (Durham, NC, Duke University Press 1989).

Koch, F. *The Volga Germans in Russia and the Americas from 1763 to the Present* (PA, Pennsylvania University Press 1977).

Kochan, L. ed. *The Jews in Soviet Russia since 1917* (Oxford, Oxford University Press 1978).

Kriendler, I. 'The Soviet Deported Nationalities: A Summary and an Update' *Soviet Studies*, vol. 38 (3), 1986, pp. 387–405.

Pinkus, B. *The Soviet Government and the Jews, 1948–1967* (Cambridge, Cambridge University Press 1984).

Pinkus, B. *The Jews of the Soviet Union. The History of a National Minority* (Cambridge, Cambridge University Press 1988).

Gitelman, Z. *A Century of Ambivalence* (New York, Schocken Books 1988).

Kolstø, P. *The New Russian Diaspora* (London, Hurst 1994).

Kolstø, P. 'The New Russian Diaspora: Minority Protection in the Soviet Successor States' *Journal of Peace Research*, vol. 30 (2), 1993, pp. 197–217.

Solchanyk, R. 'The Politics of State-building: Centre–Periphery Relations in Post-Soviet Ukraine' *Europe-Asia Studies*, No. 1 (1994), pp. 47–68.

Shlapentokh, V., Sendich, M. and Payin, E. (eds) *The New Russian Diaspora. Russian Minorities in the Former Soviet Republics* (New York and London, M.E. Sharpe, 1994).

Wilson, A. *The Crimean Tatars* (London, International Alert 1994).

# Index